Fodor's 2000

W9-BJC-680

Florida

Fodor's Travel Publications, Inc. • New York, Toronto, London, Sydney, Auckland
www.fodors.com/florida

CONTENTS

MAPS

Circled letters in text correspond to letters on the photographs. For more information on the sights pictured, turn to the indicated page number Ⓐ on each photograph.

DESTINATION FLORIDA

The beaches in Florida are legendary. Long, straight, and surf-pounded on the east coast, they're powder-soft, pure white, and gently washed by the Gulf to the west. Resorts come in all shapes and sizes, and theme parks and minigolf courses thrive: Fun in the sun is high art in Florida. But stray a few miles from your air-conditioned hotel room and you might glimpse the land that welcomed sponge divers from Greece, cigar makers from Cuba, and boat people from Haiti. Cattle ranches and horse farms extend long, empty miles from the border of Walt Disney World. And as glittering, high-energy Miami anchors the south, rockets tower over the east coast and red-soil hills and sleepy Southern villages crowd the Georgia border to the north. Every corner of Florida richly rewards those who take the time to know it better.

MIAMI AND MIAMI BEACH

Ⓐ 56

To get the most out of Miami and its neighbor, Miami Beach, it helps to be a bit of a hedonist. By day, many local pleasures revolve around water and sunshine, as at the Ⓐ **Venetian Pool,** perhaps the most whimsical municipal swimming hole anywhere, complete with gondola moorings and Italian architecture. You can also learn to enjoy life with a Latin rhythm. Practical seminars are on view daily at Ⓒ**Little Havana's Domino Park,** on Southwest 15th Avenue, where Cuban-American retirees spend long afternoons indulging their passion. Forget about joining them, even if you

Ⓒ 51

Ⓑ 100

D > 91

think of yourself as a pretty fair domino player—these guys will clean your clock. Instead, watch and wait for the subtropical sunset to turn up the tempo: After nightfall, Miami is playland for party animals. Street musicians rule on

E > 51

Ⓔ **Calle Ocho** (Southwest 8th Street), not far from Domino Park. The area around the Ⓑ**Bayside Marketplace** offers live music and cuisines of the world until late, as well as till-you-drop shopping until 11 on weekends. The pastels that brighten Miami's days give way to hot neon hues at bars like Ⓓ**The Clevelander.** Spend an hour strolling in super-hip Ⓕ**South Beach,** home to hundreds of historic Art Deco buildings, where even the lifeguard stations have a retro look. If you know how to have fun, Miami is for you. If you're not sure how, well, *practice.* You've come to the right place.

F > 39

To visit the Everglades is to see South Florida as it has been for millennia, since long before the coastal swamps were drained and long before Miami rose a short heron's flight to the east. This wilderness of almost otherworldly beauty stands in perfect, fragile counterpoint to Miami's throbbing Latin energy, offering refuge not only to hundreds of species of plants and animals but also to humans in need of communion with the natural world.

THE EVERGLADES

On guided day trips, by walkway or boat, you'll see things of ineffable beauty, like snowy egrets feeding among the mangrove trees, in zones where no discernible boundary exists between the sea and the land. You're likely to come upon alligators, too, key players in the delicate Everglades ecosystem—strikingly on display at attractions such as the ©**Everglades Gator Park.** (The vast majority of a gator's facial muscles are devoted to snapping its jaws shut. The remaining muscles, which open the jaws, are few and weak. In theory—mind you, in *theory*—a headlock applied to an alligator's jaws can keep them from opening. If a gator comes at you with jaws wide open, run.) To properly see the River of Grass preserved by the ⒹEverglades National Park, rent a canoe for a multi-

Ⓐ〉130

Ⓑ〉130

© 122

day paddle. Or climb into an airboat for a ride through similar terrain nearby. (Mosquito repellent is mandatory.) Or drive on down to Ⓔ**Smallwood's Store** in Chokoloskee Bay near Everglades City, built as a trading post in 1906 by an undauntable Everglades pioneer. When the din of the cicadas palls, try snorkeling among the reefs or canoeing through the mangroves that edge the shore of ⒶⒷ**Biscayne National Park.** The northern extremity of Florida's living reef, with 180,000 acres of coral and cays in Biscayne Bay, this, too, is Florida at its wild, gorgeous best, and its beauty puts description to shame.

Ⓓ 119

Ⓔ 126

AROUND
FORT LAUDERDALE

It didn't always look this pretty. A decade ago, Fort Lauderdale was an undistinguished resort town with a beachfront dominated by T-shirt emporiums and fast-fooderies. Few thought of it as a hot vacation destination, except perhaps the 350,000 students who descended during spring break to party hearty (often heartier than necessary). Growing weary of busted-up hotel rooms and the abuse of their splendid beaches, the city fathers put the squeeze on the scholarly revelers. Now family fun can be had all 52 weeks of the year, and more and more families are having it, drawn by massive renovation that has transformed Fort Lauderdale. In fact, the ⒷⒸ**Fort Lauderdale beachfront** is looking better than ever. Yachts are spiffily tied up in the heart of

Ⓐ▷151

Ⓕ▷146

© 146

① 166

town alongside humbler craft at Ⓐ**Pier Sixty-Six.** If you're yachtless, not to worry: You can tour the city's 300 miles of navigable waterways by water taxi. Downtown has also become a good-time venue. Ritzy shops have long done business there, but the area used to shut down at dusk. Now, along Las Olas Boulevard, musicians and crowds of strollers bring the night alive. Foodies love the Las Olas scene; culinary invention makes headlines at dozens of new restaurants. If you're feeling lucky, head south of town to wager on the ponies at Hollywood's Gulfstream Park or on the humans at the Ⓓ**Dania Jai-Alai Palace.** The pelota has been clocked at speeds exceeding 150 miles per hour—worth knowing in case you're thinking of taking up the sport yourself. Better to take it easy on Fort Lauderdale's renovated Ⓔ**Riverwalk,** where cafés and gazebos line the pretty promenade along the New River. And if you're a student, come on down! Just don't reenact *Animal House.*

Ⓔ 145

Ⓐ 196

AROUND
PALM BEACH

Ⓑ 204

To see how the other half of one percent lives, a visit to Palm Beach is a must. This is a town unabashedly built by—and exclusively *for*—the very rich, who, as F. Scott Fitzgerald reminded us, "are different from you and me." If the dearth of public parking is any evidence, Fitzgerald might have added that they *like* it that way. The quest for a parking space does have its payoff, though, when it brings you to ©**Worth Avenue,** where even the window-shoppers are dressed up. The tone of the city was set by second homes like Whitehall, now the Ⓓ**Henry Morrison Flagler Museum,** named after the plutocrat who lived in the mansion and who made all this possible. Flagler's railroad brought the super-rich to Florida for winter warmth 100 years ago, and Palm Beach is just one of the results. Through tireless promotion and development, Flagler "invented" Florida as a resort destination, and the rest is

Ⓒ 179

ⓓ〉176

history. Above and below Palm Beach other affluent towns, ideal for gawking in, dot the coast. In elegant Boca Raton, where anyone with a polo pony can find a pickup game, the Ⓐ**Gumbo Limbo Nature Center** is a great place to get back to basics; nighttime turtle walks are on every nature lover's agenda in spring and early summer. Other good places to decompress from conspicuous consumption are the lovely town of Ⓑ**Stuart,** Ⓕ**Hutchinson Island,** and the Ⓔ**Jupiter Inlet Lighthouse,** which sits near Burt Reynolds Park, named for a local boy who made good and who still lives nearby. Who can blame him? It's beautiful here.

Ⓕ〉206

Ⓔ〉202

No other place in America, much less Florida, resembles the Keys. For starters, the largest portion of the continental United States' only living coral reef is here. Protecting the reef and the fragile

THE FLORIDA KEYS

Ⓐ 233

ecosystems it supports is a matter of critical concern. Appreciate the reef when you drive the Overseas Highway; it may not be with us forever. The beauty of the Keys would be reason enough to visit. A bonus is the Keys lifestyle. This is where America goes Caribbean. Your wristwatch starts to chafe, and napping at midday feels obligatory (though not much else does). Welcome to the Land That Stress Forgot. As you roll westward, leave the highway now and again to marvel at sun and sea or lay your head in places like Ⓐ**The Moorings** on Islamorada, as charming a lodging as you'll find, or the Ⓑ**Hawk's Cay Resort,** with its own movie-set appeal. The end of the road, literally, is Key West, a capital of High Quirk and, regrettably to admirers, no longer

Ⓑ 238

Ⓒ 250

off the beaten track. No matter. If the crowds that gather daily at ©**Key West's Mallory Square** to watch the sunsets are bigger than ever, well, that just makes for a better street party afterward (and a party it is). Following your own sun worship, repair to ⑩**Duval Street** for pure living theater. There is *nothing* you might not see here. On the way back to America proper, stop at ⑤**John Pennekamp Coral Reef State Park** on Key Largo. As you snorkel or scuba dive among the vivid coral reefs swarming with bewitchingly bright fish, time stands still, which might just make your vacation feel a little longer.

Ⓓ250

Ⓔ225

Orlando's main industry and chief attraction is *fantasy*. If Florida is Escape Country, then this is Escape Central, where

Ⓐ▷302

visitors may think they've landed on another, far happier planet. A local icon is the Ⓑ**Cinderella Castle in Walt Disney World's Magic Kingdom,** one of four major theme parks in this world-famous 330,000-acre vacation development (the others are Epcot, Disney–MGM Studios, and Disney's Animal King-

DISNEY WORLD AND ORLANDO

Ⓑ▷282

dom). You could easily spend an entire week exploring its resorts, water parks, and other attractions, but you would still see only a fraction. Wonderful as it all is, however, the experiences that stand out most in your mind when you get back may well be those in the burgeoning entertainment megaplex known as Universal Studios Escape: © **Terminator 2 3-D** in Universal Studios Florida and © **The Amazing Adventures of Spider-Man** ride in the new Islands of Adventure theme park. Or you may well fall for intimate, lovable Ⓐ **SeaWorld Orlando,** where marine creatures large and small charm visiting humans and inspire commitments

Ⓓ 346

to conservation. For dinner, catch the spectacular horsemanship at Kissimmee's Ⓓ **Arabian Nights Dinner Theater,** near Disney's main gate. Need a reality check? Head for Harry P. Leu Gardens or Winter Park's Mead Gardens, or study the splendid Tiffany stained-glass collection at the Charles Hosmer Morse Museum of American Art.

Ⓔ 309

Ⓐ▷ 382

Ⓑ 358

Other parts of Florida draw bigger crowds. But in the Tampa Bay area the sand splashed by the gentle gulf surf is deliciously soft and white, and a coterie of devotees comes back year after year to lovely resorts such as the Ⓒ**Colony Beach and Tennis Resort** on Longboat Key, a barrier island sheltering Sarasota Bay. Circus magnate John Ringling noticed the beauty of

TAMPA BAY AREA

the area a century ago and decreed that his performers would spend their winters in Sarasota. While they lived in bungalows, the boss lived in a Venetian-style palace. It is now part of Sarasota's Ⓐ**Ringling Museums,** where you can view both circus memorabilia and great masterworks of Renaissance art and begin to catch the flavor of the

rich cultural life that sets Sarasota apart from other Florida cities. North of Sarasota in dynamic, fast-evolving Ⓑ**Tampa,** you'll get the Floridian take on urban bustle, complete with skyline. While business folk yak on their cell phones downtown, vacationers head for Busch Gardens, an animal kingdom in its own right with its more than 3,000 beasts. Killer coasters like Kumba and Montu, skyrocketing above and between savanna and rain-forest habitats, let you prove to yourself that Newton was right about gravity. So do awesome water slides like Busch's Ⓓ**Tampa Typhoon** at Adventure Island, one of the best water parks in a state where water parks are serious business. Farther north, in Greek-American Tarpon Springs, have an Aegean-style lunch. And beyond that, stop at Ⓔ**Weeki Wachee Spring** to catch the "mermaids." They've been doing underwater shows for decades, expertly taking unobtrusive hits on conveniently placed oxygen hoses. Wherever you go, enjoy the scenery and the balmy breezes. That's what the area was made for.

ⓒ➙384

ⓓ➙361

ⓔ➙375

Drive south from Tampa, past Sarasota, and you enter what many consider the best of all Floridian worlds, with a natural beauty that is rare even by Florida standards. Lettuce Lake in Ⓕ**Corkscrew Swamp Sanctuary** near Bonita Springs is just one case in point. Another is Sanibel Island's ⒶⒷ**J. N. "Ding" Darling National Wildlife Refuge.** Bird-watchers happily fill their notebooks while shell-gatherers on the soft white sand beaches here and on ⒸⒹ**Captiva Island,** a tiny causeway away from Sanibel, crouch into the celebrated "Sanibel stoop" in search of some of the prettiest seashells in the world. Shelling is espe-

THE SOUTHWEST

cially good after big winter storms. Farther south, the pier at Ⓔ**Naples** offers wall-to-wall sunsets, minus Key West crowds. Here, sunsets are low-key—they just happen and quietly fill the souls of all who happen to see them. If you are moved to lighten your wallet, you have plenty of

options in Naples, in some of the country's most elegant hotels and in shops often reminiscent of those in Palm Beach. All around you see sprawl and growth and golf courses (four dozen, to be exact), yet the place retains a core of real charm in a classic small-town way. If Miami is an electric party town and Orlando a hub of high-tech fantasy, the southwest is a place where you can simply sit down amid great beauty and become serene.

You can spend a lot of time in much of Florida and hardly notice that you're in the South. Not so in the Panhandle, where the accents, the historic architecture (antebellum), and the vegetation (heavy on the live oaks and the Spanish moss) constantly remind you that a bagel will not be an easy find. What will be an easy find, and what has made the area prime vacation territory for southerners, is pure recreational fun

THE PANHANDLE

A 436

B 432

in the sun, at prices often a few notches lower than elsewhere in the state—although, remember, the season here doesn't really get going until May. The Panhandle is about deep-sea fishing for billfish off a chartered boat out of ⑧**Destin** (more billfish are hauled in here than from any other port on the Gulf coast). It's about the sports like parasailing on ④**Panama City Beach,** whose sands shine gleaming white in the lee of shoulder-to-shoulder condos. It's about beaches, beaches, and more beaches—hundreds of miles of pristine beaches with gentle surf perfect for toddlers—at places like ©**St. Andrews State Recreation Area,** whose strands stand out even by Florida standards. Families with kids are everywhere. Don't let the area's nickname—the Redneck Riv-

© 437

iera—put you off. The lovely new town of ⒟**Seaside** is the picture of gentility. To promote geniality among residents, the town's architect-planner gave the development a 19th-century look and put downtown within easy distance of all, encouraging people to walk. Bring an extra roll of film: you'll use it capturing Kodak moments among the sparkling white verandas and gingerbread details. Walking the nature trails in ⒠**Apalachicola National Forest,** without a palm tree in sight, reminds you just how far north you've come from the rest of Florida (yet how much more in the South you are).

Ⓔ 445

Ⓓ 435

THE
NORTHEAST

The Northeast is known for its wide, long, rock-hard beaches and their vigorous Atlantic surf. But the area is also Florida's transition zone. As you approach from the south, drawls get thicker and plantations dot the landscape. Perhaps the most telling sign that Dixie is near comes at Ⓐ**Daytona Beach,** where motor sports, especially stock-car racing, are a passion. They used to run the Daytona 500—the most prestigious stock-car race in the world—right here on the hard-packed sand, in the days before big TV money and corporate sponsorship. Tooling along the beach in a vehicle is still a local pastime, so look both ways before you walk down to the water's edge. Daytona, the city where college kids now unwind every year during spring break, also welcomes black-leather-jacketed bikers by the

Ⓐ 470

Ⓑ 462

Ⓒ 460

thousands in March, for Bike Week. Sometimes, down at the ⒟**Daytona International Speedway,** cars give way to racing bikes. But basically, if you love the internal combustion engine, you will love this town. On the other hand, if you love history, you will love the Ⓑ**St. Augustine Historic District**—the city was founded in 1565 and a huge section of the old city is preserved—and the Civil War reenactments at Ⓒ**Fort Clinch**

State Park on Amelia Island. Whether or not you're interested in the Space Age, make a beeline for the ⒠**Kennedy Space Center** on Cape Canaveral to see the rockets that took American heroes into space and, if timing is with you, to see a real launch. If your good luck was at Hialeah or Gulfstream (or a track nearer home), find out which Thoroughbred stables near ⒡**Ocala** open their gates to pilgrims, and stop in the lush green horse country, all immaculately maintained fences and gleaming horseflesh, to pay your respects to your colt's dam or sire.

GREAT ITINERARIES

Highlights of Florida
9 to 13 days

Florida is far more diverse than you might realize. Sure there are the world-class theme parks, with the biggest, most sparkling rides on the globe. And if you're the average tourist, that's one of the things you come for. But if you've got time to stop and smell the orange blossoms, there's a lot more here. The state is full of natural wonders and cultural experiences from Latin-American rhythms to

hip, movie-star chic. If you have at least a week, plan on flying to Orlando—an ideal gateway because of its central location (which is why Walt Disney chose it) and its abundance of direct flights.

ORLANDO

3 or 4 days. Unless you've been here in the last 60 days, Orlando will have changed significantly since your previous visit. Returnees will probably want to budget two days for new Disney offerings, including Disney's Animal Kingdom. If you've got youngsters, a day at the Magic Kingdom, including a character breakfast, is a must. Universal essentially doubled in size in 1999 by adding its own new park—Universal Studios Islands of Adventure (worth at least a day)—to its movie-theme

Universal Studios Florida. The charming, water-based SeaWorld Orlando and dozens of other, smaller amusements could easily take up a week, but to glimpse a whole different Florida, pick the attractions most interesting to you and then hit the road.
☞ *Disney Theme Parks* and *Theme Parks Beyond Disney* in Chapter 6.

TAMPA AND ST. PETE

1 day. There are two must-dos when you visit these Gulf Coast cities on a 5-mi-wide bay: Get a taste of Latin culture in Tampa's Ybor City (originally a Cuban cigar-manufacturing district and now a neighborhood abounding in culinary spots and hot nightclubs), and watch a classic Florida sunset at St. Petersburg Beach.
☞ *Tampa* and *St. Petersburg* in Chapter 7.

SANIBEL AND CAPTIVA

1 day. Lee County has wonderful barrier islands, including charming Sanibel, home of the J. N. "Ding" Darling National Wildlife Refuge, where you can canoe through a rich mangrove swamp. The beaches of Sanibel and its neighbor, Captiva, have exceptional shelling, and you may see loggerhead turtles and other extraordinary wildlife.
☞ *The Barrier Islands* in Chapter 8.

NAPLES AND MARCO ISLAND

1 day. Naples, a sophisticated town 40 minutes south of Sanibel, backs up to the western Everglades. If you don't have time to access the Glades from the east, you may want to take a swamp buggy or airboat tour from Naples or Marco Island. Marco, which has great beaches and beachfront hotels, makes a good overnight stop because of a "shortcut" to Key West—a three-hour ferry as opposed to a six-hour drive.
☞ *Naples Area* in Chapter 8.

THE FLORIDA KEYS

1 or 2 days. ⓐ Key West, 100 mi by boat or bridge-laden highway from the mainland, has a classic island feel, with a laid-back culture and a quaint downtown dotted with famous watering holes. Clear waters make a snorkel or dive trip a must. It's also great fun to tour the island by moped, which you can rent at numerous spots downtown.
☞ *Key West* in Chapter 5.

MIAMI AND MIAMI BEACH

1 or 2 days. Miami is the only city in Florida big and urbane enough to rival the L.A.s and Chicagos of the world. But Miami has its own spin on the urban experience, a cultural confluence of Latin vibes and subtropical hedonism mixed with an economic vibrancy based on its status as the U.S. gateway to Latin America. Miami is considered hot by most anyone in this hemisphere who is chic or wants to be. In Miami Beach's South Beach you're as likely to see Madonna or Elton John as you would in Hollywood. Because it's a big port, Miami's a great departure point for a Caribbean or Bahamas cruise. You can envelop yourself in Latin culture in the Calle Ocho district, and Everglades National Park is only 45 mi southwest.
☞ *Exploring Miami and Miami Beach* in Chapter 1 and *Everglades National Park* in Chapter 2.

PALM BEACH

1 or 2 days. If you feel at home at a polo match and don't shop at anyplace less upscale than Neiman-Marcus, Palm Beach is for you. It's the richest town, per capita, in Florida and one of the world's playgrounds for the extremely wealthy. And the rich don't choose shabby places. The sun-drenched beaches here are as impressive as the shopping and dining along Worth Avenue and the luxurious hotels, including the famous Breakers.
☞ *Palm Beach* in Chapter 4.

Natural Wonders

5 to 8 days

Having no appreciable winter has done more for Florida than make it a good place for theme parks and golf courses. The constant spring-summer seasonal mix that has prevailed for 100 millennia or so has created beautiful forests and wetlands. Anyone with a map, a car, and several days can see a side of nature here you won't see elsewhere.

BISCAYNE NATIONAL PARK AND KEY LARGO

1 or 2 days. At Biscayne National Park, 30 minutes south of Miami, you can see living coral reefs by snorkeling, scuba diving, or taking a glass-bottom boat. Perhaps the best snorkeling and scuba diving, however, is another hour south at magnificent John Pennekamp Coral Reef State Park, near Key Largo, the northernmost of the Florida Keys.
☞ *Biscayne National Park* in Chapter 2 and *The Upper Keys* in Chapter 5.

THE EVERGLADES

1 or 2 days. For nature lovers, going to Florida and not seeing the Everglades would be like going to Arizona and not seeing the Grand Canyon. Miami is a great gateway to America's biggest protected wetland, and you can try anything from self-guided canoe tours (probably not a good idea for first-timers) to swamp buggy, airboat, and even airplane tours, offered by several parks and commercial operators on U.S. 41 west of Miami.
☞ *Everglades National Park* in Chapter 2.

ORLANDO AREA

1 or 2 days. Wekiva Springs State Park is 45 minutes from Disney but may as well be on another planet. Here you'll find the still unspoiled, undeveloped, and un-neoned Florida, the way it was before the civilized world laid a hand on it. While you're around Orlando, check out a less wild side of nature, plus some expensive waterfront homes, on Winter Park's Scenic Boat Tour, near downtown Winter Park.
☞ *Away from the Theme Parks* and *Walt Disney World and the Orlando Area A to Z* in Chapter 6.

The map at the top shows the region with locations: Florida Caverns S.P., Marianna, GEORGIA, Falling Waters SRA, Pensacola, Grayton Beach SRA, Panama City, Tallahassee, Wakulla Springs SP, Gulf of Mexico, with distances (15 mi, 60 mi, 270 mi, 250 mi, 25 mi, 36 mi, 47 mi) and highways (10, 331, 231, 98, 319).

TALLAHASSEE AREA

2 days. Within an hour of Florida's capital you'll find a variety of natural treasures. Florida Caverns State Park, near Marianna, offers guided tours of a huge underground cave, where you can see Carlsbad-like formations, including stalactites and stalagmites, along with thousands of critters that live in the dark. A short drive west, near Chipley, Falling Waters State Recreation Area contains Florida's largest, and perhaps only, waterfall. The falls alone wouldn't warrant a trip to the Panhandle, but they make a nice side trip from Florida Caverns. Wakulla Springs State Park, 15 mi south of Tallahassee, offers glass-bottom boat tours of impressive junglelike waterways. You'll see incredible wildlife, including the ubiquitous and much-loved alligator.
☞ *Lower Alabama* and *Tallahassee* in Chapter 9.

Great Beaches

6 to 10 days

With more than 1,200 mi of coastline, it's obvious that Florida has many beaches. However, if you're a beach connoisseur, someone who spends as much on sunblock as, say, auto insurance or utility bills, you probably also know that Florida has some of North America's *best* beaches. The variety of beaches—secluded beaches, people-watcher beaches, family beaches—is equaled by the variety of reasons to visit them. You can marvel at amazing sand or fabulous sunsets, undertake countless waterborne activities, or reenergize after more tiring pursuits, since many Florida beaches are close to other popular attractions.

Ⓑ 462

MIAMI AREA

1 or 2 days. Beaches in the Miami area are not unlike some Los Angeles–area beaches, with lots of male and female model would-be's rollerblading along walkways adjacent to the strand. In Miami Beach's South Beach, a vibrant café and nightclub district faces the beach. Ten miles north at Haulover Beach you'll find Florida's only legal nude beach. (Signs mark the area.) Or try the sands at Key Biscayne's Bill Baggs Cape Florida State Recreation Area, a lovely park with a lighthouse and a great view of the Miami skyline. Along with their particular "scene," Miami's beaches offer surprisingly clear aqua water.
☞ *South Beach/Miami Beach* and *Virginia Key and Key Biscayne* in Chapter 1.

DAYTONA BEACH AND THE SPACE COAST

1 or 2 days. A sand pail's throw from one another sit one of America's most famous beaches, Daytona Beach, and one of its least spoiled, Canaveral National Seashore. Daytona is one of the few places in the nation where you can drive on the sand, which backs up right on a hotel and nightlife strip that keeps hopping after sundown. Canaveral closes after dark, but by day you can gaze at windswept dunes and the blue Atlantic along 24 mi of beachfront and then visit the adjacent Kennedy Space Center or Merritt Island National Wildlife Refuge.
☞ *Along the Coast* in Chapter 10.

ST. AUGUSTINE AND AMELIA ISLAND

2 days. Heading north you can relax on Ⓑ St. Augustine Beach or Vilano Beach on Anastasia Island, near historic St. Augustine. North of Jacksonville, Amelia Island has great beaches and the historic town of Fernandina Beach, which is loaded with B&Bs. From Jacksonville you can also pick up I–10, which heads west to the Florida Panhandle.
☞ *St. Augustine* and *Jacksonville to Amelia Island* in Chapter 10.

THE PANHANDLE

1 or 2 days. The beaches of northwest Florida are justifiably renowned, routinely making the annual best-beaches list of the University of Maryland's Laboratory for Coastal Research. In fact Grayton Beach State Recreation Area, one of Florida's prettiest beaches, made the list so consistently that it has essentially been retired from contention. Halfway between Panama City and Pensacola, Grayton Beach has sugar-white sands and aqua waters as clear as you'd find in the Keys or the Bahamas. And that's just one of many fine Panhandle beaches. If you like hotels, nightclubs, and arcades near your beach blanket, visit Ⓒ Panama City Beach, which actively courts spring-break revelers.
☞ *Around Pensacola Bay* and *The Gulf Coast* in Chapter 9.

Ⓒ 436

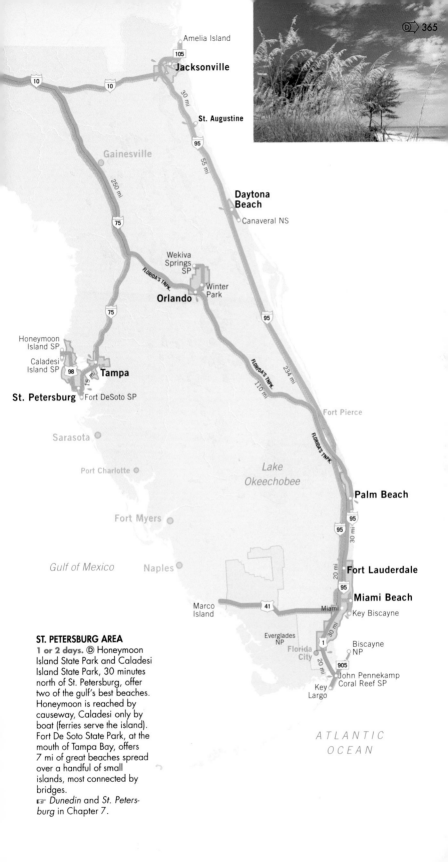

Amelia Island

105

Jacksonville

I-10 · 10

30 mi

St. Augustine

95

Gainesville

55 mi

Daytona
Beach

Canaveral NS

250 mi

75

Wekiva
Springs
SP

FLORIDA'S TNPK.

Winter
Park

Orlando

75

95

Honeymoon
Island SP

Caladesi
Island SP   98

15 mi

Tampa

St. Petersburg   Fort DeSoto SP

Sarasota

FLORIDA'S TNPK.

234 mi

110 mi

Fort Pierce

Port Charlotte

Lake
Okeechobee

FLORIDA'S TNPK.

Palm Beach

Fort Myers

95

95

30 mi

Gulf of Mexico

Naples

20 mi

Fort Lauderdale

95

Marco
Island

41

Miami

Miami Beach

Key Biscayne

Everglades
NP

30 mi

Biscayne
NP

Florida
City

1

20 mi

905

John Pennekamp
Coral Reef SP

Key
Largo

ATLANTIC
OCEAN

ST. PETERSBURG AREA

1 or 2 days. Ⓓ Honeymoon
Island State Park and Caladesi
Island State Park, 30 minutes
north of St. Petersburg, offer
two of the gulf's best beaches.
Honeymoon is reached by
causeway, Caladesi only by
boat (ferries serve the island).
Fort De Soto State Park, at the
mouth of Tampa Bay, offers
7 mi of great beaches spread
over a handful of small
islands, most connected by
bridges.
☞ *Dunedin* and *St. Petersburg* in Chapter 7.

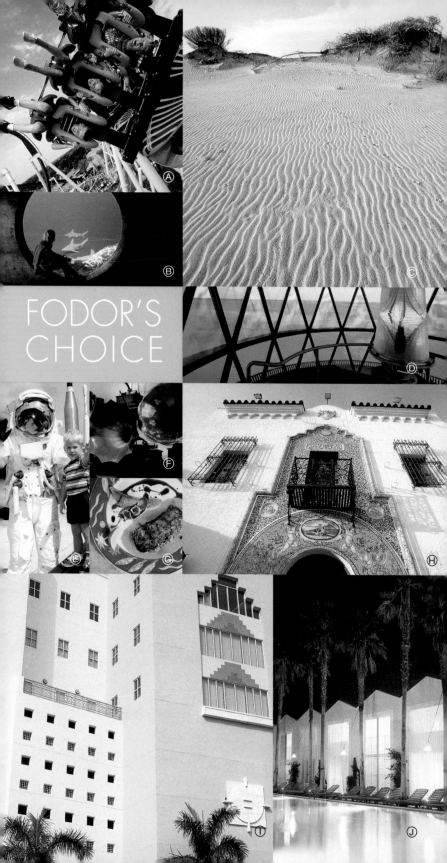

FODOR'S
CHOICE

Even with so many special places in Florida, Fodor's writers and editors have their favorites. Here are a few that stand out.

BEACHES

Ⓓ Bill Baggs Cape Florida State Recreation Area. Consistently voted one of South Florida's best beaches, this 414-acre park in Key Biscayne has a plethora of facilities, a historic lighthouse, and great views of the Miami skyline. ☞ p. 60

Canaveral National Seashore. With its 24 mi of undeveloped coastline backed by windswept dunes stretching from New Smyrna Beach to Titusville, this 57,000-acre park is remarkable. ☞ p. 477

Fort Clinch State Park, Amelia Island. A beach runs the entire length of Amelia Island's east coast. Its northernmost section is an almost empty expanse of white sand, part of a park with a well-preserved brick fort. ☞ p. 460

Ⓒ Grayton Beach. Blue-green waters, white-sand beaches, and salt marshes make it one of the most scenic spots along the Gulf Coast. There's also camping and snorkeling. ☞ p. 434

St. Andrews State Recreation Area. This much-visited park at the eastern tip of Panama City Beach has an artificial reef that creates a calm, shallow area perfect for young children. ☞ p. 437

THEME PARKS AND ATTRACTIONS

Ⓐ Busch Gardens, Tampa. Two of the world's largest roller coasters, good shows, and live animals are loosely brought together under a turn-of-the-century Africa theme on 335 acres. ☞ p. 360

Ⓑ Florida Aquarium, Tampa. Follow the path of a drop of water through springs and wetlands, bay and barrier beach, a coral reef, and the Gulf Stream. ☞ p. 358

Ⓔ Kennedy Space Center Visitor Complex, Cocoa Beach. The home of the real *Apollo 13* illuminates the romance of the early space program. One of Florida's best bargains. ☞ p. 477

SeaWorld Orlando. Weaving learning and laughter, this water-centered mega-zoo lets you get up close to all sorts of ocean life. ☞ p. 302

Universal Studios Escape, Orlando. The saucy, sassy, and hip movie-theme Universal Studios Florida has been joined by the fabulous new Universal Studios Islands of Adventure in a Universal empire. ☞ p. 304

Walt Disney World, Orlando. It's everything it's cracked up to be—and there's more of it every year. ☞ p. 277

LODGING

The Breakers, Palm Beach. The building, an opulent Italian Renaissance palace, is amazing as is the resort's ability to balance old-world luxury with modern conveniences. $$$$ ☞ p. 181

Ⓙ Delano Hotel, Miami Beach. An air of surrealism hangs about this much-talked-about SoBe hotel, *the* hot spot for celebrities and other well-to-do visitors. $$$$ ☞ p. 82

Little Palm Island. On its own palm-fringed island 3 mi off the shores of Little Torch Key, this dazzling resort of thatch-roof villas on stilts provides a secluded, one-of-a-kind experience you could only have in the Keys. $$$$ ☞ p. 247

Ritz-Carlton Amelia Island. Ritz-Carltons are known for stylish elegance, superb comfort, and excellent service. This one also comes with a pristine beach, its own golf course, and the outstanding and unusual Grill restaurant. $$$$ ☞ p. 460

New World Inn, Pensacola. Exquisite furnishings reflect different periods and influences in Pensacola history. $–$$ ☞ p. 427

DINING

Ⓖ Norman's, Coral Gables. Chef Norman Van Aken turns out artful masterpieces of New World cuisine, combining bold tastes from Latin, American, Caribbean, and Asian traditions. $$$$ ☞ p. 65

Cafe des Artistes, Key West. Chef Andrew Berman's brilliant tropical version of French cuisine is served in a series of intimate dining rooms filled with tropical art and on an outdoor patio. $$$–$$$$ ☞ p. 257

Armadillo Cafe, Davie. The atmosphere is as creative and fun as the award-winning southwestern-style South Florida seafood. $$ ☞ p. 166

Ⓗ Columbia, Tampa. Flamenco dancing and paella set the scene at this Ybor City institution. $$ ☞ p. 362

Le Coq au Vin, Orlando. The traditional French cuisine is expertly prepared, and the setting is delightfully unstuffy. $$ ☞ p. 325

VIEWS

Everglades National Park from the tower on Shark Valley Loop. This 50-ft observation tower yields a splendid panorama of the River of Grass. ☞ p. 123

Inland Waterway, Sanibel. Scattered here are dozens and dozens of tiny mangrove islets, a lovely sight. ☞ p. 403

Ⓘ Ocean Drive in the Art Deco District, Miami Beach. This palm-lined beachfront is hopping around the clock. ☞ p. 39

Shuttle launch, Cocoa Beach area. By day you see a thick ropy curl of white smoke; by night it's a brilliant orange burst of fire. ☞ p. 477

Sunshine Skyway across Tampa Bay. One of the world's great monumental sculptures carries six lanes of traffic soaring across the mouth of Florida's largest estuary. ☞ p. 366

HISTORIC SITES

Castillo de San Marcos National Monument, St. Augustine. The 300-year-old fort comes with moat, turrets, and 16-ft-thick walls. ☞ p. 463

Ⓕ Edison's winter home and museum, Fort Myers. Everything is just as the inventor left it, and you can imagine him tinkering with the first phonograph. ☞ p. 394

Henry Morrison Flagler Museum, Palm Beach. Whitehall, Flagler's mansion, is the backdrop for art and railway memorabilia. ☞ p. 176

Morikami Museum and Japanese Gardens, Delray Beach. The leading U.S. center for Japanese and American cultural exchange is housed in a model of a Japanese imperial villa. ☞ p. 193

Vizcaya Museum and Gardens, Coconut Grove. The Italian Renaissance–style villa anchoring the estate of industrialist James Deering contains Renaissance, Baroque, Rococo, and Neoclassical art and furniture. ☞ p. 59

1 MIAMI AND MIAMI BEACH

Miami is arguably the most exotic city that Americans can visit without a passport. On a typical evening in South Beach, you'll witness the energy and passion of Rio, Monte Carlo, Havana, and Hemingway's Paris. Other neighborhoods also bring the world into clearer focus through diverse architecture, dining, and customs, sparking a renaissance for Miami and its sultry sister, Miami Beach, that's reminiscent of the cities' glory days in the 1920s.

Updated by
Gary
McKechnie

MIAMI IS DIFFERENT from any other city in America—or any city in Latin America for that matter, though it has a distinctly Latin flavor. Both logically and geologically, Miami shouldn't even be here. Resting on a paved swamp between the Everglades and the Atlantic Ocean, the city is subject to periodic flooding, riots, hurricanes, and the onslaught of swallow-size mosquitoes. Despite the downsides, however, Miami is a vibrant city that works and plays with vigor.

The Tequesta Indians called this area home long before Spain's gold-laden treasure ships sailed along the Gulf Stream a few miles offshore. Foreshadowing 20th-century corporations, they traded with mainland neighbors to the north and island brethren to the south. Today their descendants are the 150-plus U.S. and multinational companies whose Latin American headquarters are based in Greater Miami. For fans of international business and random statistics, Greater Miami is home to more than 40 foreign bank agencies, 11 Edge Act banks, 23 foreign trade offices, 31 binational chambers of commerce, and 53 foreign consulates.

For tourists, far more intriguing is Miami's developing profile as a cruise-ship port. Miami's six cruise lines and 21 cruise ships wisely avoid those pesky icebergs by carrying more than 3 million passengers a year to the sunny Caribbean and on over to Mexico. And if you've ever dreamed of traveling aboard a tramp steamer, head to the docks, and you'll also find a flood of cargo freighters. It's no surprise that more than 40% of all U.S. exports to South America, Central America, and the Caribbean travel through the Miami Customs District. Miami is the U.S. gateway to the southern hemisphere.

The city has seen a decade of big changes. In the late 1980s Miami Beach was an ocean-side geriatric ward. Today's South Beach residents have the kind of hip that doesn't break. The average age dropped from the mid-sixties in 1980 to a youthful early forties today. Toned young men outnumber svelte young women 2 to 1, and hormones are as plentiful as pierced tongues. At night the revitalized Lincoln Road Mall is in full swing with cafés and galleries and theaters, but it is also suffering vacancies due to rapidly rising rents. The bloom may not be off the rose, but cash-crazy entrepreneurs hoping to strike it rich on Miami's popularity are finding the pie isn't large enough to feed their financial fantasies. Those who have seen how high rents can crush a dream are heading to North Beach and the southern neighborhoods of South Beach, whose derelict buildings are a flashback to the pre-renaissance days of the 1980s. Perhaps this is where the next revival will take place (file this under insider information).

As you plan your trip, know that winter *is* the best time to visit, but if money is an issue, come in the off-season—after Easter and before October. You'll find plenty to do, and room rates are considerably lower. Summer brings many European and Latin American vacationers, who find Miami congenial despite the heat, humidity, and intense afternoon thunderstorms.

Regardless of when you arrive, once you're here, you'll suspect that you've entered Cuban air space. No matter where you spin your radio dial, virtually every announcer punctuates each sentence with an emphatic "COO-BAH!" Look around, and you'll see Spanish on billboards, hear it on elevators, and pick it up on the streets. But Miami sways to more than just a Latin beat. *Newsweek* called the city "America's

Casablanca," and it may be right. In addition to populations from Brazil, Colombia, El Salvador, Haiti, Jamaica, Nicaragua, Panama, Puerto Rico, Venezuela, and of course Cuba, there are also representatives from China, Germany, Greece, Iran, Israel, Italy, Lebanon, Malaysia, Russia, and Sweden—all speaking a veritable babel of tongues. Miami has accepted its montage of nationalities, and it now celebrates this cultural diversity through languages, festivals, world-beat music, and a wealth of exotic restaurants.

If you're concerned about Miami crime, you'll be glad to know that criminals are off the street—and seem to be running for public office. Forget about D.C. If you want weird politics, spread out a blanket and enjoy the show. Mayor Xavier Suarez was removed from office in March 1998 after a judge threw out absentee ballots that included votes from dead people. The Miami City Commission chairman was also removed following a voter fraud conviction, and a state senator was re-elected despite being under indictment for pocketing profits from sham home-health-care companies.

Corrupt politicians aside, Miami has its share of the same crimes that plague any major city. However, you'll be happy to know that the widely publicized crimes against tourists of the early '90s led to stepped-up and effective visitor-safety programs. Highway direction signs with red-sunburst logos are installed at ¼-mi intervals on major roads and lead directly to such tourist hot spots as Coconut Grove, Coral Gables, South Beach, and the Port of Miami. Patrol cars bearing the sunburst logo are driven by TOP (Tourist Oriented Police) Cops, who cruise heavily touristed areas and add a sense of safety. Identification that made rental cars conspicuous to would-be criminals has been removed, and multilingual pamphlets on avoiding crime are widely distributed. The precautions have had a positive impact. From 1992 to 1998 the number of tourist robberies in Greater Miami decreased more than 80%.

What *is* on the increase is Miami's film profile. In recent years Arnold Schwarzenegger and Jamie Lee Curtis filmed *True Lies* here, Al Pacino and Johnny Depp dropped by to shoot scenes for *Donnie Brasco,* Jim Carrey rose to stardom through the Miami-based *Ace Ventura: Pet Detective,* Robin Williams and Nathan Lane used two Deco buildings on Ocean Drive as their nightclub in *The Birdcage,* and Cameron Diaz discovered a new brand of hair gel in *There's Something About Mary.* All in all, it's a far cry from when Esther Williams used to perform water ballet in Coral Gables' Venetian Pool. Add to this mix daily fashion-magazine and TV shoots, and you'll see that Miami is made for the media.

It may be this synergy that prompted a slew of international celebrities to move or purchase homes here. Although Madonna and Sylvester Stallone are selling their houses, Al Pacino, Michael Caine, and Whitney Houston are here now. Three major-league sports franchises call Miami home, along with the Doral-Ryder Open Tournament, the Lipton Championships, and the culture-contributing Miami City Ballet and Florida Grand Opera. Miami played host to the Summit of the Americas in 1994 and to the Super Bowl in 1999. Nearly 10 million tourists arrive annually to see what's shaking in Miami-Dade County and discover a multicultural metropolis that invites the world to celebrate its diversity.

New and Noteworthy

There's so much construction going on in Miami, you'd suspect they're trying to tear down the town and put up a city. Tool belts are nearly as prevalent as bikinis, and building sounds echo everywhere.

One of the most noteworthy arrivals is the new **American Airlines Arena,** which sits downtown on Biscayne Bay near the entrance to the Port of Miami. Scheduled to open on December 31, 1999, this will be the new home of the NBA's Miami Heat. Up Biscayne Boulevard, the **Freedom Tower,** one of downtown's most prominent landmarks, is being restored by the Cuban American National Foundation to house its museum. **Parrot Jungle** is destined to give up its South Miami location for digs near Watson Island by the Port of Miami. The move is scheduled for mid-2000, although the date has changed several times.

The **Royal Palm Crowne Plaza Resort** is being promoted as the first African-American majority–owned four-star convention hotel in the United States. Planned for the spring of 2000, the 422-room, two-tower Collins Avenue hotel (near the new Loews) was designed by Arquitectonica, an internationally known Miami architectural firm. Over in the financial district, on Brickell Avenue, the new 21-story, $60 million **J. W. Marriott Hotel** is supposed to open in fall 1999, although early 2000 seems more likely. A new **Ritz-Carlton** may arrive in Coconut Grove by the end of 2000. Their next project is in SoBe, where $95 million will be poured into the less-than-impressive DiLido to bring it up to Ritz standards.

The **Dolphin Mall,** west of the Miami airport, expects to be open by fall 2000. If you're wondering what $250 million buys these days, it's 1.4 million square ft of retail outlets, theme restaurants, cafés, nightclubs, a 30-screen theater, and an amusement park. In South Miami the **Shops at Sunset Place** opened in the spring of 1999. Mighty impressive entryways, winding paths, and a variety of retailers make this the Main Street of the 21st century.

Pleasures and Pastimes

Beaches

Greater Miami has numerous free beaches to fit every style. A sandy, 300-ft-wide beach with several distinct sections extends for 10 mi from the foot of Miami Beach north to Haulover Beach Park. Amazingly, it's all man-made. Seriously eroded during the mid-1970s, the beach was restored in a $51.5 million project between 1977 and 1981 and remains an ongoing project for environmental engineers, who spiff up the sands every few years. Between 23rd and 44th streets, Miami Beach built boardwalks and protective walkways atop a dune landscaped with sea oats, sea grape, and other native plants whose roots keep the sand from blowing away. Farther north there's even a nude beach, and Key Biscayne adds more great strands to Miami's collection. Even if the Deco District didn't exist, the area's beaches would be enough to satisfy tourists.

Boating

It's not uncommon for traffic to jam at boat ramps, especially on weekend mornings, but the waters are worth the wait. If you have the opportunity to sail, do so. Blue skies, calm seas, and a view of the city skyline make for a pleasurable outing—especially at twilight, when the fabled "moon over Miami" casts a soft glow on the water. Key Biscayne's calm waves and strong breezes are perfect for sailing and windsurfing, and though Dinner Key and the Coconut Grove waterfront remain the center of sailing in Greater Miami, sailboat moorings and rentals sit along other parts of the bay and up the Miami River.

Miami's idle rich prefer attacking the water in sleek, fast, and nicotine-free cigarette boats, but there's plenty of less powerful powerboating to enjoy as well. Greater Miami has numerous marinas, and dockmasters can provide information on any marine services you may need. Ask for *Teall's Tides and Guides, Miami-Dade County,* and other nautical publications.

Dining

Miami cuisine is what mouths were made for. The city serves up a veritable United Nations of dining experiences, including dishes native to Spain, Cuba, and Nicaragua as well as China, India, Thailand, Vietnam, and other Asian cultures. Chefs from the tropics combine fresh, natural foods—especially seafood—with classic island-style dishes, creating a new American cuisine that is sometimes called Floribbean. Another style finding its way around U.S. restaurants is the Miami-born New World cuisine. The title comes from chefs who realized their latest creations were based on ingredients found along the trade routes discovered by early explorers of the "New World."

Nightlife

Miami has more clubs than a deck of cards, but the ones that command the most attention are those where people pose with less expression than Mona Lisa and where mirrored balls salvaged from the set of *Saturday Night Fever* spin as fast as the techno-pop CDs.

The heaviest concentration of these nightspots is in South Beach along Ocean Drive, Washington Avenue, and Lincoln Road Mall. Other nightlife centers on Little Havana, Coconut Grove, and the fringes of downtown Miami. Clubs offer jazz, reggae, salsa, various forms of rock, disco, and Top 40 sounds on different nights of the week—most played at a body-thumping, ear-throbbing volume. If you prefer to hear what people are saying, look for small lobby bars in Art Deco hotels. Throughout Greater Miami, bars and cocktail lounges in larger hotels operate nightly discos with live weekend entertainment. Many hotels extend their bars into open-air courtyards, where patrons dine and dance under the stars throughout the year. Some clubs refuse entrance to anyone under 21, others to those under 25, so if that is a concern, call ahead. It's also a good idea to ask in advance about cover charges; policies change frequently. And be warned: Even the most popular club can fall out of favor quickly. Ask your hotel's concierge, check Friday's *Miami Herald,* or grab a copy of *New Times,* an entertainment tabloid that includes listings of alternative clubs and live bands. With this and some insider info from locals, you should be able to tell what's hot and what's just a dying ember.

Spectator Sports

Greater Miami has franchises in basketball, football, and baseball. Thanks to Dan Marino's record-breaking accomplishments, fans still turn out en masse for the Dolphins, as they do for basketball's Heat and the 1997 World Series champion Marlins. Miami also hosts top-rated events in boat racing, jai alai, and tennis. Generally you can find daily listings of local events in the sports section of the *Miami Herald,* while Friday's "Weekend" section carries more detailed schedules and coverage.

Activities of the annual Orange Bowl and Junior Orange Bowl Festival take place from early November until well into the new year. Best known for its King Orange Jamboree Parade and the Federal Express/Orange Bowl Football Classic, the festival also includes two tennis tournaments. The Junior Orange Bowl Festival is the world's largest youth festival, with more than 20 events between November and January, including sports, cultural, and performing arts activities held throughout Miami-Dade County.

EXPLORING MIAMI AND MIAMI BEACH

If you had arrived here 40 years ago with Fodor's guide in hand, chances are you'd be thumbing through listings looking for alligator wrestlers and u-pick citrus groves. Well, things have changed. While Disney sidetracked families in Orlando, Miami was developing a grown-up attitude courtesy of *Miami Vice,* European fashion photographers, and historic preservationists. Nowadays the wildest ride is the city itself.

Climb aboard and check out the different sides of Greater Miami. Miami, on the mainland, is South Florida's commercial hub, while its sultry sister, Miami Beach (America's Riviera), encompasses 17 islands in Biscayne Bay. Seducing winter refugees with its warm sunshine, sandy beaches, shady palms, and ever-rocking nightlife, this is what most people envision when planning a trip to a trip to what they think of as Miami. These same visitors fail to realize that there's more to Miami Beach than the bustle of South Beach and its Deco District. Indeed there are quieter areas to the north, with names like Sunny Isles, Surfside, Bal Harbour, and—you guessed it—North Beach.

During the day downtown Miami has become the lively hub of the mainland city, now more accessible thanks to the Metromover extension (☞ Getting Around by Train *in* Miami and Miami Beach A to Z, *below*). Other major attractions include Coconut Grove, Coral Gables, Little Havana, and, of course, the South Beach/Art Deco District, but since these areas are spread out beyond the reach of public transportation, you'll have to drive. Rent a convertible if you can. There's nothing quite like wearing cool shades and feeling the wind in your hair as you drive across one of the causeways en route to Miami Beach. Take precautions if you wear a rug.

You're in luck: Finding your way around Greater Miami is easy if you know how the numbering system works—just as quantum mechanics is easy for physicists. Miami is laid out on a grid with four quadrants—northeast, northwest, southeast, and southwest—which meet at Miami Avenue and Flagler Street. Miami Avenue separates east from west, and Flagler Street separates north from south. Avenues and courts run north–south; streets, terraces, and ways run east–west. Roads run diagonally, northwest–southeast. But other districts—Miami Beach, Coral Gables, and Hialeah—may or may not follow this system, and along the curve of Biscayne Bay, the symmetrical grid may shift diagonally. It's best to buy a detailed map, stick to the major roads, and ask directions early and often. However, make sure you're in a safe neighborhood or public place when you seek guidance; cabbies and cops are good resources.

Numbers in the text correspond to numbers in the margin and on the Miami Beach; Downtown Miami; Miami, Coral Gables, Coconut Grove, and Key Biscayne; and South Dade maps.

Great Itineraries

IF YOU HAVE 3 DAYS

To recuperate from your journey, grab your lotion and head to the ocean, more specifically Ocean Drive on South Beach, where you can catch some rays while relaxing on the white sands. Afterward, take a guided or self-guided tour of the Art Deco District to see what all the fuss is about. Keep the evening free to socialize with the oh-so-trendy people who gather at Ocean Drive cafés. The following day drive through Little Havana to witness the heartbeat of Miami's Cuban culture (and snag a stogie) on your way south to Coconut Grove's Vizcaya. Wrap up the evening a few blocks away in Coconut Grove, enjoying its partylike atmosphere and many nightspots. On the last day head over to Coral Gables to take in the eye-popping display of 1920s Mediterranean Revival architecture in the neighborhoods surrounding the city center and the majestic Biltmore Hotel; then take a dip in the fantastic thematic Venetian Pool. That night indulge in an evening of fine dining at your choice of gourmet restaurants in Coral Gables.

IF YOU HAVE 5 DAYS

Follow the suggested three-day itinerary, and on day 4 add a visit to the beaches of Virginia Key and Key Biscayne, where you can take a diving trip or fishing excursion, learn to windsurf, or do absolutely nothing but watch the water. On day 5 step back to the 1950s with a cruise up Collins Avenue to some of the monolithic hotels, such as the Fontainebleau Hilton and Eden Roc; continue north to the swank shops of Bal Harbour; and return to South Beach for an evening of shopping, drinking, and outdoor dining at Lincoln Road Mall.

IF YOU HAVE 7 DAYS

A week gives you just enough time to experience fully the multicultural, cosmopolitan, tropical mélange that is Greater Miami and its beaches. On day 6 see where it all began. Use the Miami Metromover to ride above downtown Miami before touring the streets (if possible, on a tour with historian Dr. Paul George). Take time to visit the Miami-Dade Cultural Center, home of art and history museums. In the evening check out the shops and clubs at Bayside Marketplace. The final day can be used to visit South Miami, site of Parrot Jungle (for now), Fairchild Tropical Garden, and the new, commercial Shops at Sunset Place. Keep the evening free to revisit your favorite nightspots and get jiggy with your new pals, Madonna and Will Smith.

South Beach/Miami Beach

The hub of Miami Beach is South Beach (SoBe, to the truly hip), and the hub of South Beach is the 1-square-mi Art Deco District, fronted on the east by Ocean Drive and on the west by Alton Road. The story of South Beach has become the story of Miami. In the early 1980s South Beach's vintage hotels were badly run down, catering mostly to infirm retirees. But a group of visionaries led by Barbara Baer Capitman, a spirited New York transplant, saw this collection of buildings as an architectural treasure to be salvaged from a sea of mindless urban renewal. It was, and is, a peerless grouping of Art Deco architecture from the 1920s to 1950s, whose forms and decorative details are drawn from nature, the streamlined shapes of modern transportation and industrial machinery, and human extravagance.

Investors started fixing up the interiors of these hotels and repainting their exteriors with a vibrant pastel palette—a look made famous by *Miami Vice*. International bistro operators sensed the potential for a new café society. Fashion photographers and the media took note, and celebrities like singer Gloria Estefan; the late designer Gianni Versace, whose fashions captured the feel of the awakening city; and record executive Chris Blackwell bought a piece of the action.

As a result, South Beach now holds the distinction of being the nation's first 20th-century district on the National Register of Historic Places, with more than 800 significant buildings making the roll. But it hasn't all been smooth. Miami officials seem to lack the gene enabling them to appreciate residents who help the city. Barbara Capitman was well into her sixties when she stepped in front of bulldozers ready to tear down the Senator, a Deco hotel. Her reward for helping to save the

Deco District and laying the groundwork for a multibillion-dollar tourist trade is a side street named in her honor.

More recently, SoBe hoteliers were similarly rewarded for successfully renovating old or abandoned buildings by having their taxes quadrupled—an attempt by the local government to make up for the lack of tax revenues generated in other areas of Miami-Dade County. Nevertheless, SoBe continues to roll 24 hours a day. Photographers pose beautiful models for shoots, tanned skaters zip past palm trees, and tourists flock to see the action.

Yet Miami Beach is more than just SoBe. (The northern edge of South Beach is generally considered to be around 24th–28th streets, while Miami Beach itself extends well north.) It also consists of a collection of quiet neighborhoods where Little Leaguers play ball, senior citizens stand at bus stops, and locals do their shopping away from the prying eyes of visitors. Surprisingly, Miami Beach is a great walking town in the middle of a great city.

Several things are plentiful in SoBe: pierced body parts, cell phones, and meter maids. Tickets are given freely when meters expire, and towing charges are high. Check the meter to see when parking fees are required; times vary by district. From mid-morning on, parking is scarce along Ocean Drive. You'll do better on Collins or Washington avenues, the next two streets to the west. Fortunately, there are several surface parking lots south and west of the Jackie Gleason Theater, on 17th Street, and parking garages on Collins Avenue at 7th and 13th streets, on Washington Avenue at 12th Street, and west of Washington at 17th Street. Keep these sites in mind, especially at night, when cruising traffic makes it best to park your car and see SoBe on foot.

A Good Walk

The stretch of Ocean Drive from 1st to 23rd streets—primarily the 10-block stretch from 5th to 15th streets—has become the most talked-about beachfront in America. A bevy of Art Deco jewels hug the drive, while across the street lies palm-fringed **Lummus Park** ①, whose south end is a good starting point for a walk. Beginning early (at 8) gives you the pleasure of watching the awakening city without distraction. Sanitation men hose down dirty streets, merchants prepare window displays, bakers bake, and construction workers change the skyline one brick at a time. Cross to the west side of Ocean Drive, where there are many sidewalk cafés, and walk north, taking note of the Park Central Hotel, built in 1937 by Deco architect Henry Hohauser.

At 10th Street recross Ocean Drive to the beach side and visit the **Art Deco District Welcome Center** ② in the 1950s-era Oceanfront Auditorium. Here you can rent tapes or hire a guide for a Deco District tour.

Look back across Ocean Drive and take a look at the wonderful flying-saucer architecture of the Clevelander, at No. 1020. On the next block you'll see the late Gianni Versace's Spanish Mediterranean **Amsterdam Palace** ③. Graceful fluted columns stand guard at the Leslie (No. 1244) and **The Carlyle** ④. A few doors down, at No. 1300, is the Cardozo (☞ Lodging, *below*), which was recently brought up to super snuff by Miami icon/hotelier Gloria Estefan and her man, Emilio.

Walk two blocks west (away from the ocean) on 13th Street to Washington Avenue, where a mix of chic restaurants, avant-garde shops, delicatessens, produce markets, and nightclubs have spiced up a once-derelict neighborhood. Turn left on Washington and walk 2½ blocks south to the **Wolfsonian–FIU Foundation Gallery** ⑤, which showcases artistic movements from 1885 to 1945.

Provided you haven't spent too long in the museum, return north on Washington Avenue past 14th Street, and turn left on **Espanola Way** ⑥, a narrow street of Mediterranean Revival buildings, eclectic shops, and a weekend market. Continue west to Meridian Avenue and turn right. Three blocks north of Espanola Way is the redesigned **Lincoln Road Mall** ⑦, which is often paired with Ocean Drive as part of must-see South Beach.

The next main street north of Lincoln Road is 17th Street, and to the east is the Miami Beach Convention Center. Walk behind the massive building to the corner of Meridian Avenue and 19th Street to see the chilling **Holocaust Memorial** ⑧, a monumental record honoring the 6 million Jewish victims of the Holocaust.

Head east and return to Ocean Drive in time to pull up a chair at an outdoor café, order an espresso, and settle down for an evening of people-watching, SoBe's most popular pastime. If you've seen enough people, grab some late rays at one of the area's beaches, which offer different sands for different tans. You can go back to Lummus Park (*the* beach) or head north, where there's a boardwalk for walking but no allowance for skates and bicycles.

TIMING

To see only the Art Deco buildings on Ocean Drive, allow one hour minimum. Depending on your interests, schedule at least five hours and include a drink or meal at a café and browsing time in the shops on Ocean Drive, along Espanola Way, and at Lincoln Road Mall.

Start your walking tour as early in the day as possible. In winter the street becomes crowded as the day wears on, and in summer, afternoon heat and humidity can be unbearable, wilting even the hardiest soul. Finishing by mid-afternoon also enables you to hit the beach and cool your heels in the warm sand.

Sights to See

❸ **Amsterdam Palace.** In the early 1980s, before South Beach became the hotbed of chicness, the late Italian designer Gianni Versace purchased this run-down Spanish Mediterranean residence, built before the arrival of Deco. Today the home is an ornate three-story palazzo with a guest house and a copper-dome rooftop observatory and pool that were added at the expense of a 1950s hotel, the Revere. Its loss and the razing of the fabled Deco Senator became a rallying point for preservationists, who like to point out that although they lost a few, they saved 40. In July 1997 Versace was tragically shot and killed in front of his home. Like a tropical Ford's Theatre, this now attracts picture-taking tourists. Eerie. ⊠ *1114 Ocean Dr.*

❷ **Art Deco District Welcome Center.** Run by the Miami Design Preservation League, this clearinghouse in the Oceanfront Auditorium provides information about the buildings in the Art Deco District. A well-stocked gift shop sells 1930s–1950s Art Deco memorabilia, posters, and books on Miami's history. Several tours—covering Lincoln Road, Espanola Way, North Beach, the entire Art Deco District, and more—start here. You can choose to rent audiotapes for a self-guided tour, join the regular Saturday-morning or Thursday-evening walking tour, or take a bicycle tour, all providing detailed histories of the Deco hotels. ⊠ *1001 Ocean Dr., at Barbara Capitman Way,* ☎ *305/531-3484.* ☞ *Free.* ⊙ *Daily 11–6, open later Thurs.–Mon. in season.*

Bal Harbour. This tony community, known for its upscale shops (also known as "shoppes"), has a stretch of prime beach real estate, where wealthy condominium owners cluster during the winter. Look close,

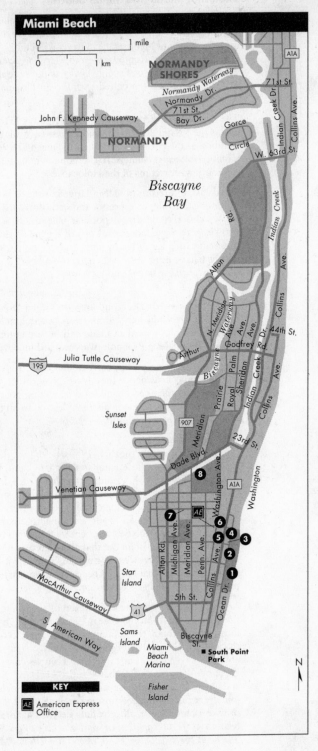

and you may spy·Bob Dole sunning himself outside his condo. ⊠ *Collins Ave. between 96th and 103rd Sts.*

Bass Museum of Art. A diverse collection of European art is the focus of this fortresslike museum made of keystone, a short drive north of SoBe's key sights. Works on display include *The Holy Family,* a painting by Peter Paul Rubens; *The Tournament,* one of several 16th-century Flemish tapestries; and works by Albrecht Dürer and Henri de Toulouse-Lautrec. An $8 million, three-phase expansion, expected to be completed shortly after 2000, will add a new wing, cafeteria, and theater, doubling the museum's size to nearly 40,000 square ft. ⊠ *2121 Park Ave.,* ☎ *305/673–7530.* ☞ *$5.* ☺ *Tues.–Sat. 10–5, except 1–9 the 2nd and 4th Wed. of each month; Sun. 1–5.*

❹ **The Carlyle.** Built in 1941, this empty Deco building no longer functions as a hotel, but it's still popular as a movie location. Fans will recognize it and its neighbor, the Leslie, as the nightclub from *The Birdcage,* starring Robin Williams and Nathan Lane. ⊠ *1250 Ocean Dr.*

★ ❻ **Espanola Way.** The Mediterranean Revival buildings along this road were constructed in 1925 and frequented through the years by artists and writers. In the 1930s future bandleader Desi Arnaz strapped on a conga drum and started beating out a rumba rhythm at a nightclub that is now the Clay Hotel, a youth hostel. Since high rents have pushed some merchants out and vacant storefronts have resulted, try to visit this quaint avenue on a Sunday afternoon, when itinerant dealers and craftspeople set up shop to sell everything from garage-sale items to handcrafted bongo drums. Between Washington and Drexel avenues, the road has been narrowed to a single lane, and Miami Beach's trademark pink sidewalks have been widened to accommodate sidewalk cafés and shops selling imaginative clothing, jewelry, and art.

★ **Fontainebleau Hilton Resort and Towers.** For a sense of what Miami was like during the Fabulous '50s, take a drive north to see the finest example of SoBe's grandiose architecture. By the 1950s smaller Deco-era hotels were passé, and architects like Morris Lapidus got busy designing free-flowing hotels that affirmed the American attitude of "bigger is better." Even if you're not a guest, wander through the lobby and pool area just to feel the energy generated by an army of bellhops, clerks, concierges, and travelers. ⊠ *4441 Collins Ave.,* ☎ *305/ 538–2000.*

Haulover Beach Park. At this county park, far from the action of SoBe, you can see the Miami of 30 years ago. Pack a picnic, use the barbecue grills, or grab a snack at the concession stand. If you're into fitness, you may like the tennis and volleyball courts or paths designed for exercise, walking, and bicycling. If you're into cleanliness, take advantage of the shower facilities. The beach is nice for those who want water without long marches across hot sand, and Florida's only authorized clothing-optional beach lures people who want to tan every nook and cranny. Other offerings are kite rentals, kayak rentals, charter fishing excursions, and a par-3, nine-hole golf course. ⊠ *10800 Collins Ave., Sunny Isles,* ☎ *305/947–3525.* ☞ *$3.50 per vehicle.* ☺ *Daily sunrise–sunset.*

❽ **Holocaust Memorial.** The focus of the memorial is a 42-ft-high bronze arm rising from the ground, with sculptured people climbing the arm seeking escape. Don't stare from the street. Enter the courtyard to see the chilling memorial wall and hear the eerie songs that seem to give voice to the victims. ⊠ *1933–1945 Meridian Ave.,* ☎ *305/538–1663.* ☞ *Donation welcome.* ☺ *Daily 9–9.*

ART DECO HOTELS: MIAMI NICE

WITH APOLOGIES TO the flamingo, Miami's most recognizable icons are now the Art Deco hotels of South Beach. Their story begins in the 1920s, when Miami Beach was a winter playground of the rich, and grand themed hotels ruled. By the late '20s, however, shipping problems and a hurricane turned the boom to bust, and another approach to attract vacationers was needed.

In the early 1930s it was the turn of the middle class, which was drawn south by a more affordable version of paradise. New hotels were needed, and the architectural motif of choice became what we call Deco (for purists, Moderne), based on a sleek and cheerful look with geometric designs and creative colors. It was introduced in Paris in the '20s and later crossed the Atlantic.

In South Beach, architects added other shapes brought to America by industrial designers: streamlined, aerodynamic forms based on trains, ocean liners, and automobiles. Using a steel-and-concrete box as a foundation, architects dipped into this new grab bag of styles to accessorize their hotels. Pylons, spheres, cylinders, and cubes thrust out from facades and roofs. "Eyebrows," small ledges topping window frames, popped out of buildings like concrete caps. To soften sharp edges, designers added wraparound windows and curved corners, many ornamented with racing stripes. To reflect the beach locale, nautical elements were added: Portholes appeared in sets of three. Small etchings of seaweed, starfish, and rolling waves were plastered, painted, or etched on walls. Buildings looked ready to go to sea. Also taking advantage of the environment, sunlight, an abundant commodity, was brought indoors through glass blocks. But because there was no air-conditioning, coolness was achieved by planting shady palms and laying terrazzo tile.

Of course, everything has a life span, and the Deco hotels were no exception. Eventually, bold colors and creative accents became cliché, and ensuing decades saw owners hide their hotels beneath coats of plain white or beige paint. Deco still had its proponents, inspiring later architects, most notably Morris Lapidus, to create larger-than-life 1950s Deco hotels, such as the Fontainebleau and Eden Roc. But the days of small Deco hotels had passed. By the 1970s they were no longer welcoming tourists. . . or welcoming to look at. Most had matured into flophouses or dirt-cheap homes for retirees. Various plans ranging from leveling the buildings to legalizing gambling were proposed—and defeated.

THEN IN THE 1980s, an unusual confluence of people and events proved the area's salvation. The hyperactive cop show *Miami Vice,* set against the newly painted pastel facades of Ocean Drive, portrayed an exotic tropical appeal. European fashion photographers, restaurateurs, and entrepreneurs started using the area as a backdrop for models, cafés, and resurrected hotels. Above all, there was Barbara Baer Capitman, a senior citizen who reviewed South Beach's buildings and proposed it for the National Register of Historic Places. Thanks to her efforts and the ongoing drive of others to rescue, maintain, and improve these historic jewels, a new generation (yourself included) can experience the same tropical pleasures enjoyed by travelers of the 1930s.

NEED A
BREAK?

If your feet are still holding up, head to the **Delano Hotel** (✉ 1685 Collins Ave., ☎ 305/674–6400) for a drink. This surrealistic hotel, like a Calvin Klein ad come to life, continues to generate a buzz among SoBe's fashion models and hepcats.

★ ❼ **Lincoln Road Mall.** A playful redesign of this grande dame of Miami Beach overran its original $16 million budget, but the results were worth the extra bucks. The renovation spruced up the futuristic 1950s vision of Fontainebleau designer Morris Lapidus and added a grove of 20 towering date palms and five linear pools. Indicative of the road's resurgence is the restoration of dozens of buildings, including a former Jehovah's Witness hall that actor Michael Caine transformed into a restaurant. The best times to hit the road are during Sunday-morning farmers' markets and on weekend evenings, when cafés are bustling; art galleries, like Romero Britto's Britto Central, schedule openings; street performers take the stage; and bookstores, import shops, and clothing stores are open for late-night purchases. If things are slower when you arrive, credit SoBe's omnipresent high rents, which have forced many merchants out.

In the classical four-story Deco gem with friezes at 541–545 Lincoln Road, the **New World Symphony,** a national advanced-training orchestra led by Michael Tilson Thomas, rehearses and performs. To the west, the street is lined with chic food markets, cafés, and boutiques. Even farther west is the **South Florida Art Center,** home to one of the first arts groups to help resurrect the area. Still farther west (actually just a few blocks) is a black-and-white Deco movie house with a Mediterranean barrel-tile roof, which is now the **Colony Theater.** ✉ *Lincoln Rd. between Collins Ave. and Alton Rd.*

☝ ❶ **Lummus Park.** Once part of a turn-of-the-century plantation owned by brothers John and James Lummus, this palm-shaded oasis on the beach side of Ocean Drive attracts beach-going families with its children's play area. Senior citizens predominate early in the day. Volleyball, in-line skating along the wide and winding sidewalk, and a lot of posing go on here, and officials don't enforce the law against topless female bathers, as long as everyone behaves with decorum. Gays like the beach between 11th and 13th streets. The lush foliage is a pleasing, natural counterpoint to the ultrachic atmosphere just across the street, where endless sidewalk cafés make it easy to come ashore for everything from burgers to quiche. Like New York's Central Park, this is a natural venue for big-name public concerts by such performers as Luciano Pavarotti and past Art Deco Weekend stars Cab Calloway and Lionel Hampton. ✉ *East of Ocean Dr. between 5th and 15th Sts.*

North Beach. Families and those who like things quiet prefer this section of beach. Metered parking is ample right behind the dune and a block behind Collins Avenue along a pleasant, old shopping street. With high prices discouraging developers from SoBe, this area will no doubt see some redevelopment in years to come. However, without the cafés or 300-ft-wide beach to lure tourists, it may never match SoBe's appeal. ✉ *Ocean Terr. between 73rd and 75th Sts.*

OFF THE
BEATEN PATH

OLETA RIVER STATE RECREATION AREA – At more than 1,000 acres, this is the largest urban park in Florida. It's backed by lush tropical growth rather than hotels and offers interpretive talks, group and youth camping, 14 log cabins, kayak and canoe rentals, bicycle trails, and a fishing pier. Popular with outdoors enthusiasts, it also attracts dolphins, ospreys, and manatees, who arrive for the winter. ✉ *3400 N.E. 163rd St., North Miami,* ☎ *305/919–1846.* ☑ *$3.25 per vehicle with up to 8 people, $1 for pedestrians.* ☺ *Daily 8–sunset.*

SANFORD L. ZIFF JEWISH MUSEUM OF FLORIDA. This museum chronicles 230 years of the Jewish experience in Florida through lectures, films, storytelling, walking tours, and special events. If you've never seen a crate of kosher citrus, drop in. From the photo of a party girl in a seashell dress to ark ornaments from a Florida synagogue to a snapshot of Miss Florida 1885 (Mena Williams), exhibits reflect all things Jewish. Even the building is the former Congregation Beth Jacob Synagogue. ⊠ *301 Washington Ave.,* ☎ *305/672–5044.* ✑ *$5.* ⊙ *Tues.–Sun. 10–5.*

South Pointe Park. From the 50-yard Sunshine Pier, which adjoins the 1-mi-long jetty at the mouth of Government Cut, you can fish while watching huge ships pass. No bait or tackle is available in the park. Facilities include two observation towers, rest rooms, and volleyball courts. ⊠ *1 Washington Ave.*

Surfside. *Parlez-vous français?* If you do, you'll feel quite comfortable in and around this community, a French Canadian enclave. Many folks have spent their winters along this stretch of beach (and elsewhere down to 72nd Street) for years. ⊠ *Collins Ave. between 88th and 96th Sts.*

❺ Wolfsonian–FIU Foundation Gallery. An elegantly renovated 1927 storage facility is now both a research center and home to the 70,000-plus-item collection of modern design and "propaganda arts" amassed by Miami native Mitchell Wolfson, Jr., a world traveler and connoisseur. Included in the museum's eclectic holdings, representing Art Moderne, Art Nouveau, Arts and Crafts, and other artistic movements, is a 1930s braille edition of Hitler's *Mein Kampf.* Exhibitions such as World's Fair designs and the architectural heritage of S. H. Kress add to the appeal. ⊠ *1001 Washington Ave.,* ☎ *305/531–1001.* ✑ *$5, free Thurs. 6–9.* ⊙ *Mon.–Tues. and Fri.–Sat. 11–6, Thurs. 11–9, Sun. noon–5.*

Downtown Miami

Although steel-and-glass buildings have sprung up around downtown, the heart of the city hasn't changed much since the 1960s—except that it's a little seedier. Not surprising for a city that, though one of the country's greatest, has its share of political corruption, cronyism, nepotism, shortsightedness, and insensitivity. In 1997 a proposal to disband the city actually reached voters, but they voted overwhelmingly to keep it, flaws and all.

Nevertheless, by day there's plenty of activity downtown, as office workers and motorists crowd the area. Staid, suited lawyers and bankers share the sidewalks with Latino merchants wearing open-neck, intricately embroidered shirts called guayaberas. Fruit merchants sell their wares from pushcarts, young European travelers with backpacks stroll the streets, and foreign businesspeople haggle over prices in import-export shops, including more electronics and camera shops than you'd see in Tokyo. You hear Arabic, Chinese, Creole, French, German, Hebrew, Hindi, Japanese, Portuguese, Spanish, Swedish, Yiddish, and even a little English now and then. But what's best in the heart of downtown Miami is its Latinization and the sheer energy of Latino shoppers.

At night, however, downtown is sorely neglected. Except for Bayside Marketplace, the old Miami Arena, and the new American Airlines Arena, the area is deserted, and arena patrons rarely linger. Visitors spend little time here since most tourist attractions are in other neighborhoods, but there is a movement afoot to bring a renaissance to downtown. A new performing arts center and a CocoWalk-style pedestrian mall are expected in 2000.

Thanks to the Metromover (☞ Getting Around by Train *in* Miami and Miami Beach A to Z, *below*), which has inner and outer loops through downtown plus north and south extensions, this is an excellent tour to take by rail, and it's only 25¢ to boot. Attractions are conveniently located within about two blocks of the nearest station. Parking downtown is no less convenient or more expensive than in any other city, but the best idea is to park near Bayside Marketplace or leave your car at an outlying Metrorail station and take the train downtown.

A Good Tour

A smart place to start is at the Bayfront Park Metromover stop. There's plenty of parking in lots in the median of Biscayne Boulevard and slightly more expensive covered parking at the Bayfront Marketplace. If you want, you can wait until you return to walk through the **Mildred and Claude Pepper Bayfront Park** ⑨, but look south of the park, and you'll see the Hotel Inter-Continental Miami, which displays *The Spindle,* a huge sculpture by Henry Moore, in its lobby. West of Bayfront Park Station stands the tallest building in Florida, the **First Union Financial Center** ⑩.

Now it's time to board the Metromover northbound and take in the fine view of Bayfront Park's greenery, the bay beyond, the Port of Miami in the bay, and Miami Beach across the water. The next stop, College/Bayside, serves the downtown campus of **Miami-Dade Community College** ⑪, which has two fine galleries.

As the Metromover rounds the curve after the College/Bayside station, look northeast for a view of the vacant **Freedom Tower** ⑫, an important milepost in the history of Cuban immigration. You'll also catch a view of the *Miami Herald* building, home to columnists/authors Dave Barry and Carl Hiaasen.

Survey the city as the train works its way toward Government Center station. Look off to your right (north) as you round the northwest corner of the loop to see the round, windowless, pink **Miami Arena** ⑬.

Now it's time to see the city on foot. Get off at Government Center, a large station with small shops, restaurants, and a hair salon, in case you're looking shaggy. It's also where the 21-mi elevated Metrorail commuter system connects with the Metromover, so this is a good place to start your tour if you're coming downtown by train. Walk out the east doors to Northwest 1st Street, and head a block south to the **Miami-Dade Cultural Center** ⑭, which contains the city's main art museum, historical museum, and library and made an appearance in the movie *There's Something About Mary.*

After sopping up some culture, hoof it east down Flagler Street. On the corner is the **Dade County Courthouse** ⑮, whose pinnacle is accented by circling vultures. Now you're in the heart of downtown, where the smells range from pleasant (hot dog carts) to rancid (hot dog carts). If you cleaned up the streets and put a shine on the city, you'd see Miami circa 1950. Still thriving today, the downtown area is a far cry from what it was in 1896, when it was being carved out of pine woods and palmetto scrub to make room for Flagler's railroad. If you're in the market for jewelry, avoid the street peddlers and duck into the Seybold Building, at 36 Northeast 1st Street; it comprises 10 stories with 250 jewelers hawking watches, rings, bracelets, etc.

Just a few blocks from your starting point at the Bayfront Park Metromover station, duck into the **Gusman Center for the Performing Arts** ⑯, a stunningly beautiful movie palace that now serves as downtown Miami's concert hall. If there's a show on—even a bad one—get tickets. It's worth it just to sit in here.

When you get back to your car and the entrance to the Bayfront Marketplace, you can opt to hit the road, go shopping, or grab a brew at a bay-front bar.

TIMING

To walk and ride to the various points of interest, allow two hours. If you want to spend additional time eating and shopping at Bayside, allow at least four hours. To include museum visits, allow six hours.

Sights to See

American Police Hall of Fame and Museum. This museum exhibits more than 11,000 law enforcement–related items, including weapons, a jail cell, and an electric chair, as well as a 400-ton marble memorial listing the names of more than 6,000 police officers killed in the line of duty since 1960. ⊠ *3801 Biscayne Blvd.,* ☎ *305/573–0070.* ☑ *$6.* ☉ *Daily 10–5:30.*

⑮ **Dade County Courthouse.** Built in 1928, this was once the tallest building south of Washington, D.C. Unlike Capistrano, turkey vultures—not swallows—return to roost here in winter. ⊠ *73 W. Flagler St.*

⑩ **First Union Financial Center.** The tallest building in Florida is this 55-story structure. Unfortunately, there's no observation deck, but a 1-acre plaza graced by towering palms can be a nice place to rest your feet. ⊠ *200 S. Biscayne Blvd.*

⑫ **Freedom Tower.** In the 1960s this imposing Spanish Baroque structure was used by the Cuban Refugee Center to process more than 500,000 Cubans who entered the United States after fleeing Fidel Castro's regime. Built in 1925 for the *Miami Daily News,* it was inspired by the Giralda, an 800-year-old bell tower in Seville, Spain. Preservationists were pleased to see the tower restored to its original grandeur in 1988, but the building remains vacant awaiting the arrival of a proposed Cuban museum. ⊠ *600 Biscayne Blvd.*

★ ⑯ **Gusman Center for the Performing Arts.** Carry an extra pair of socks when you come here; the beauty of this former movie palace will knock yours clean off. Restored as a concert hall, it resembles a Moorish courtyard on the inside, with twinkling stars in the sky. You can catch performances by the Florida Philharmonic and movies of the Miami Film Festival. If the hall is closed, call the office and they may let you in. ⊠ *174 E. Flagler St.,* ☎ *305/374–2444 administration, 305/372–0925 box office.*

⑬ **Miami Arena.** Currently the home of the NBA's Miami Heat (at least until the new American Airlines Arena opens by the bay), the arena also hosts a variety of other sports and entertainment events. ⊠ *701 Arena Blvd.,* ☎ *305/530–4444.*

⑪ **Miami-Dade Community College.** The campus houses two fine galleries: The larger, third-floor **Centre Gallery** hosts various photography, painting, and sculpture exhibitions, and the fifth-floor **Frances Wolfson Art Gallery** houses smaller photo exhibits. ⊠ *300 N.E. 2nd Ave.,* ☎ *305/237–3278.* ☑ *Free.* ☉ *Mon.–Thurs. 9–4:30.*

★ ♨ ⑭ **Miami-Dade Cultural Center.** Containing three important cultural resources, this 3-acre complex is one of the focal points of downtown. From books to paintings to history, you'll find it all right here. The **Miami Art Museum** (☎ 305/375–3000) displays a permanent collection as well as putting on major touring exhibitions of work by inter-

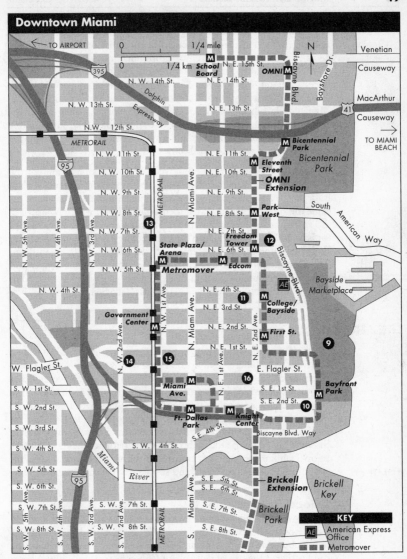

Downtown Miami

Dade County
Courthouse, **15**

First Union
Financial Center, **10**

Freedom Tower, **12**

Gusman Center for
the Performing
Arts, **16**

Miami Arena, **13**

Miami-Dade
Community
College, **11**

Miami-Dade Cultural
Center, **14**

Mildred and Claude
Pepper Bayfront
Park, **9**

national artists, focusing on work completed since 1945. Open Tuesday–Friday 10–5 and weekends noon–5, the museum charges $5 admission. At the **Historical Museum of Southern Florida** (☎ 305/375–1492), visitors are treated to pure Floridiana, including an old Miami streetcar, cigar labels, and a railroad exhibit as well as a display on prehistoric Miami. Admission is $5, and hours are Monday–Wednesday and Friday–Saturday 10–5, Thursday 10–9, and Sunday noon–5. The **Main Public Library** (☎ 305/375–2665), which is open Monday–Wednesday and Friday–Saturday 9–6, Thursday 9–9, and Sunday 1–5, contains nearly 4 million holdings and offers art exhibits in the auditorium and second-floor lobby. ⊠ *101 W. Flagler St.*

❾ Mildred and Claude Pepper Bayfront Park. This oasis among the skyscrapers borders the Bayfront Marketplace, making it a natural place for a pre- or post-shopping walk. An urban landfill in the 1920s, it became the site of a World War II memorial in 1943, which was revised in 1980 to include the names of victims of later wars. Japanese sculptor Isamu Noguchi redesigned the park before his death in 1989 to include two amphitheaters, a memorial to the *Challenger* astronauts, and a fountain honoring the late Florida congressman Claude Pepper and his wife. At the park's north end, the Friendship Torch was erected to honor JFK during his presidency and was dedicated in 1964. ⊠ *Biscayne Blvd. between 2nd and 3rd Sts.*

Little Havana

Nearly 40 years ago the tidal wave of Cubans fleeing the Castro regime flooded into an older neighborhood west of downtown Miami. Don't expect a sparkling and lively reflection of 1950s Havana, however. What you will find are ramshackle motels and cluttered storefronts. With a million Cubans and other Latinos—making up more than half the metropolitan population—dispersed throughout Greater Miami, Little Havana and neighboring East Little Havana remain magnets for Hispanics and Anglos alike, who come to experience the flavor of traditional Cuban culture. That culture, of course, functions in Spanish. Many Little Havana residents and shopkeepers speak little or no English.

A Good Tour

From downtown go west on Flagler Street across the Miami River to Teddy Roosevelt Avenue (Southwest 17th Avenue) and pause at **Plaza de la Cubanidad** ⑰, on the southwest corner. The plaza's monument is indicative of the prominent role of Cuban history and culture here.

Turn left at Douglas Road (Southwest 37th Avenue), drive south to **Calle Ocho** ⑱ (Southwest 8th Street), and turn left again. You are now on the main commercial thoroughfare of Little Havana. After you cross Unity Boulevard (Southwest 27th Avenue), Calle Ocho becomes a one-way street eastbound through the heart of Little Havana.

At Avenida Luis Muñoz Marín (Southwest 15th Avenue), stop at **Domino Park** ⑲, where elderly Cuban men pass the day with their black-and-white play tiles. The **Brigade 2506 Memorial** ⑳, commemorating the victims of the unsuccessful 1961 Bay of Pigs invasion, stands at Memorial Boulevard (Southwest 13th Avenue). A block south are several other monuments relevant to Cuban history, including a bas-relief of and quotations by José Martí.

TIMING
If the history hidden in the monuments is your only interest, set aside one hour. Allow more time to stop along Calle Ocho for a strong cup

of Cuban coffee or to shop for a cigar made of Honduran tobacco hand-rolled in the United States by Cubans.

Sights to See

⑳ **Brigade 2506 Memorial.** To honor those who died in the Bay of Pigs invasion, an eternal flame burns atop a simple stone monument with the inscription CUBA—A LOS MARTIRES DE LA BRIGADA DE ASALTO ABRIL 17 DE 1961. The monument also bears a shield with the Brigade 2506 emblem, a Cuban flag superimposed on a cross. ⊠ *S.W. 8th St. and S.W. 13th Ave.*

⑱ **Calle Ocho.** In Little Havana's commercial heart, experience such Cuban customs as hand-rolled cigars or sandwiches piled with meats and cheeses. Though it all deserves exploring, if time is limited, try the stretch from Southwest 14th to 11th avenues. ⊠ *S.W. 8th St.*

⑲ **Domino Park.** Officially known as Maximo Gomez Park, this is a major gathering place for elderly, guayabera-clad Cuban males, who, after 40 years, still pass the day playing dominoes while arguing anti-Castro politics. ⊠ *S.W. 8th St. and S.W. 15th Ave.* ☉ *Daily 9–6.*

⑰ **Plaza de la Cubanidad.** Redbrick sidewalks surround a fountain and monument with the words of José Martí, a leader in Cuba's struggle for independence from Spain and a hero to Cuban refugees and immigrants in Miami. The quotation, LAS PALMAS SON NOVIAS QUE ESPERAN (The palm trees are girlfriends who will wait), counsels hope and fortitude to the Cubans. ⊠ *W. Flagler St. and S.W. 17th Ave.*

Coral Gables

If not for George E. Merrick, Coral Gables would be just another suburb. Merrick envisioned an American Venice, with canals and gracious homes spreading across the community. In 1911 his minister father died, and Merrick inherited 1,600 acres of citrus and avocado groves; by 1921 he had upped that to 3,000 acres. Using this as a foundation, Merrick began designing a city based on centuries-old prototypes from Mediterranean countries. He began planning lush landscaping, magnificent entrances, and broad boulevards named for Spanish explorers, cities, and provinces. His uncle, Denman Fink, helped Merrick crystallize his artistic vision, and he hired architects trained abroad to create themed neighborhood villages, such as Florida pioneer, Chinese, French city, Dutch South African, and French Normandy. The result was a planned community with Spanish Mediterranean architecture that justifiably calls itself the City Beautiful—a moniker it acquired by following the Garden City method of urban planning in the 1920s.

That's the good news. The bad news is that, unfortunately for Merrick, the devastating no-name hurricane of 1926 and the Great Depression prevented him from fulfilling many of his plans. He died at 54, working for the post office. His city languished until after World War II but then grew rapidly. Today Coral Gables has a population of about 41,000. In its bustling downtown, more than 140 multinational companies maintain headquarters or regional offices, and the University of Miami campus in the southern part of Coral Gables brings a youthful vibrancy: The median age of residents is 36.

Like much of Miami, Coral Gables has realized the aesthetic and economic importance of historic preservation and has passed a Mediterranean design ordinance, rewarding businesses for maintaining their building's architectural style. Even the street signs (ground-level markers that are hard to see in daylight, impossible at night) are preserved

Miami, Coral Gables, Coconut Grove, and Key Biscayne

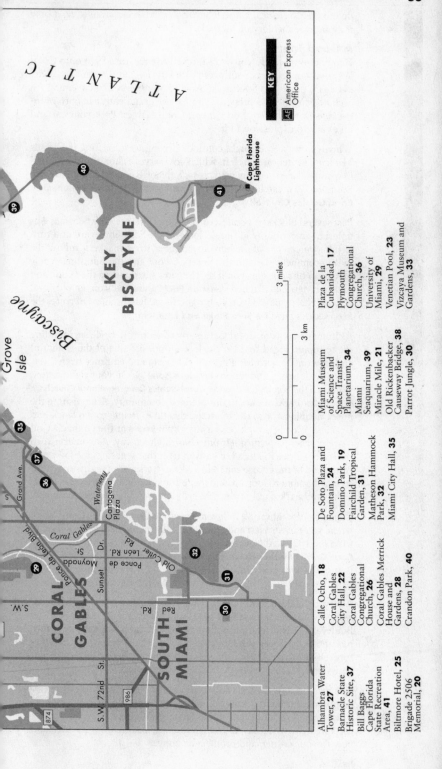

due to their historical value. They're worth the inconvenience, if only to honor the memory of Merrick.

A Good Tour

Heading south on downtown's Brickell Avenue, turn right onto Coral Way—also marked as Southwest 13th Street—and stay on Coral Way even as it turns into Southwest 3rd and Southwest 22nd avenues. An arch of banyan trees prepares you for the grand entrance onto **Miracle Mile** ㉑, the heart of downtown Coral Gables. Park your car and take time to explore on foot.

When you've seen enough, continue driving west, passing the 1930s Miracle Theater on your left, which now serves as home of the Actors' Playhouse. Keep heading west, cross LeJeune Road, and bear left onto Biltmore Way, catching an eyeful of the ornate Spanish Renaissance **Coral Gables City Hall** ㉒.

Past several blocks of nondescript condos, Biltmore Way becomes Andalusia, whereupon you should look for De Soto Boulevard and turn left. If you can't read the hard-to-decipher street markers, follow the more prominent signs to the Venetian Pool and the Biltmore. A few blocks up on your left, you'll see the gates surrounding the exotic and unusual Merrick-designed **Venetian Pool** ㉓, created from an old coral quarry. There's parking on your right. Immediately ahead of you is the Merrick-designed **De Soto Plaza and Fountain** ㉔.

As in many areas of Coral Gables, there's a traffic circle surrounding the fountain. Head to 12 o'clock (the opposite side of the fountain) and stay on De Soto for a magnificent vista and entrance to the, yes, Merrick-designed and reborn **Biltmore Hotel** ㉕. On your right, before you reach the hotel, you'll see the **Coral Gables Congregational Church** ㉖, one of the first churches in this planned community. After visiting the hotel, double back to the fountain, this time circling to 9 o'clock and Granada Way. Several blocks away you'll arrive at the Granada Golf Course, where you turn left onto North Greenway. As you cruise up the street, notice the stand of banyan trees that separates the fairways. At the end of the course the road makes a horseshoe bend, but instead cross Alhambra to loop around the restored **Alhambra Water Tower** ㉗, a city landmark dating from 1924. By the way, it's Merrick designed.

Return to Alhambra and follow it straight to the next light (Coral Way), where you can turn left and ogle beautifully maintained Spanish homes from the 1920s. Although there's only a small sign to announce it, the **Coral Gables Merrick House and Gardens** ㉘, Merrick's boyhood home, is at Coral Way and Toledo Street. If you love planned development, stop in to pay your respects. Parking is behind the house.

Afterward, take a right on Coral Way, followed by a left on Granada, which winds south past Bird Road and eventually to Ponce de León Boulevard. Turn right and follow it to the entrance of the main campus of the **University of Miami** ㉙. Turn right at the first stoplight (Stanford Drive) to enter the campus, and park in the lot on your right designated for visitors to the Lowe Art Museum.

You may have noticed that this tour contains some backtracking. Unfortunately, no matter how you navigate Coral Gables, directions get confusing. This tour takes in the highlights first and lets you fill out the balance of your day as you see fit. Now bow to your partner, and bow to your corner, and promenade home.

TIMING

Strolling Miracle Mile should take slightly more than an hour—about 63 minutes—unless you plan to shop (and you should). In that case, allow four hours. Save time for a refreshing dip at the Venetian Pool, and plan to spend at least an hour getting acquainted with the Biltmore—longer if you'd like to order a drink and linger poolside. If you can pull yourself away from the lap of luxury, allow an hour to visit the University of Miami campus (if you're into college campuses).

Sights to See

㉗ Alhambra Water Tower. In 1924 this city landmark stored water and was clad in a decorative Moresque, lighthouselike exterior. After more than 50 years of disuse and neglect, the windmill-like tower was completely restored in 1993 with a copper-rib dome and multicolored frescoes. Pretty impressive when you consider its peers are merely steel containers. ⊠ *Alhambra Circle, Greenway Ct., and Ferdinand St.*

㉕ Biltmore Hotel. Bouncing back from dark days as an army hospital, this hotel has become the jewel of Coral Gables. After extensive renovations it reopened in 1992 and hosted the Summit of the Americas in 1994. Its 16-story tower, like the Freedom Tower in downtown Miami, is a replica of Seville's Giralda Tower. To the west is the Biltmore Country Club, a richly ornamented Beaux Arts–style structure with a superb colonnade and courtyard; it was reincorporated into the hotel in 1989. Free tours are offered. ⊠ *1200 Anastasia Ave.,* ☎ *305/445-1926.* ☉ *Tours Sun. 1:30, 2:30, and 3:30.*

㉒ Coral Gables City Hall. Far more attractive than today's modular city halls, this 1928 building has a three-tier tower topped with a clock and a 500-pound bell. A mural by Denman Fink (George Merrick's uncle and artistic adviser), inside the dome ceiling on the second floor, depicts the four seasons. (Although not as well known as Maxfield Parrish, Fink demonstrated a similar utopian vision.) Also on display are paintings, photos, and ads touting 1920s Coral Gables. ⊠ *405 Biltmore Way,* ☎ *305/446-6800.* ☉ *Weekdays 8-5.*

NEED A
BREAK?

Whether you want to relax or grab an on-the-go snack, you can't miss with **Wrapido** (⊠ 2334 Ponce de León Blvd., ☎ 305/443-1884), Florida's first wrapper restaurant. The funky, upbeat atmosphere shows signs of SoHo, and the healthy wraps, soups, and smoothies are made from scratch. Strawberry Fields, the restaurant's best-selling smoothie, is prepared with fresh bananas, strawberries, apple juice, and low-fat yogurt.

㉖ Coral Gables Congregational Church. The parish was organized in 1923, and with George Merrick as a charter member (and donor of the land), this small church became the first in the city. Rumor has it Merrick built it in honor of his father, a Congregational minister. The original interiors are still in magnificent condition. ⊠ *3010 De Soto Blvd.,* ☎ *305/448-7421.* ☉ *Weekdays 8:30-4:30, services Sun. 9:15 and 10:45.*

㉘ Coral Gables Merrick House and Gardens. In 1976 the city of Coral Gables acquired George Merrick's boyhood home. Restored to its 1920s appearance, it contains Merrick family furnishings and artwork. The lush and lazy tropical atmosphere suggests the inspiration for George's masterpiece: Coral Gables. ⊠ *907 Coral Way,* ☎ *305/460-5361.* ☒ *House $2, grounds free.* ☉ *House Wed. and Sun. 1-4, grounds daily 8-sunset, also by appointment.*

㉔ De Soto Plaza and Fountain. Water flows from the mouths of four sculpted faces on a classical column on a pedestal in this Denman Fink–designed fountain from the early 1920s. The closed eyes of the face looking west symbolize the day's end. ⊠ *Granada Blvd. and Sevilla Ave.*

㉑ Miracle Mile. This upscale yet neighborly stretch of retail stores is actually only ½ mi long. Appealing to residents who predated Miami's resurgence, it has managed to maintain its 1960s premall existence. Cafeterias mingle with high-tone jewelers, and independent bookstores share customers with major book chains. The street appears to have the world's greatest concentration of bridal shops, and for support, florists fill in many of the neighboring storefronts. ⊠ *Coral Way between S.W. 37th Ave. (Douglas Rd.) and S.W. 42nd Ave. (LeJeune Rd.).*

㉙ University of Miami. With almost 14,000 full-time, part-time, and noncredit students, UM is the largest private research university in the southeast. Walk around campus and visit the **Lowe Art Museum,** which has a permanent collection of 8,000 works that include Renaissance and Baroque art, American paintings, Latin American art, and Navajo and Pueblo Indian textiles and baskets. The museum also hosts traveling exhibitions. ⊠ *1301 Stanford Dr.,* ☎ *305/284–3535 or 305/284–3536.* ☞ *$5.* ☾ *Tues.–Wed. and Fri.–Sat. 10–5, Thurs. noon–7, Sun. noon–5.*

★ ☙ **㉓ Venetian Pool.** Sculpted from a rock quarry in 1923 and fed by artesian wells, this 825,000-gallon municipal pool remains quite popular due to its themed architecture—a fantasized version of a waterfront Italian village—created by Denman Fink. The pool has earned a place on the National Register of Historic Places and showcases a nice collection of vintage photos depicting 1920s beauty pageants and swank soirees held long ago. Paul Whiteman played here, Johnny Weissmuller and Esther Williams swam here, and you should, too. A snack bar, lockers, and showers make this must-see user-friendly as well. ⊠ *2701 De Soto Blvd.,* ☎ *305/460–5356.* ☞ *$5, free parking across De Soto Blvd.* ☾ *Weekends 10–4:30; plus June–Aug., weekdays 11–7:30; Sept.–Oct. and Apr.–May, Tues.–Fri. 11–5:30; and Nov.–Mar., Tues.–Fri. 10–4:30.*

South Miami

South of Miami and Coral Gables is a city called South Miami, which is not to be confused with the region known as South Dade. A pioneer farm community, it grew into a suburb but retains its small-town charm. Fine old homes and stately trees line Sunset Drive, a city-designated Historic and Scenic Road to and through the town. A local chamber of commerce provides a free map listing u-pick farms where your fresh fruit can be blended in with a creamy milk shake. All this could change slightly, however, with the arrival of the Shops at Sunset Place, a retail complex larger than Coconut Grove's CocoWalk—big digs for a quiet town.

A Good Tour

Drive south from Sunset Drive on Red Road (watching for the plentiful orchid merchants), and turn right just before Killian Drive (Southwest 112th Street) into the 13-acre grounds of **Parrot Jungle** ㉚, one of Greater Miami's oldest and most popular commercial tourist attractions.

From Parrot Jungle follow Red Road ⅓ mi south and turn left on scenic Old Cutler Road, which curves north along the uplands of southern Florida's coastal ridge toward the 83-acre **Fairchild Tropical Garden** ㉛. Just north of the gardens, Old Cutler Road traverses Dade County's lovely **Matheson Hammock Park** ㉜. From here you can follow the road back to U.S. 1, heading north to Miami.

TIMING

Most people should allow at least half a day to see these three natural attractions, but dedicated ornithologists and botanists will want to leave a full day. Driving from SoBe should take only 25 minutes—longer during afternoon rush hour.

Sights to See

㉛ **Fairchild Tropical Garden.** Comprising 83 acres, this is the largest tropical botanical garden in the continental United States. Eleven lakes, a rain forest, and lots of flowers, including orchids, mountain roses, bellflowers, coral trees, bougainvillea, and fire trees, make it a garden for the senses—and there's special assistance for deaf guests. As covering the whole garden would make for a very long walk, take the free guided tram tour, which leaves on the hour. Spicing up the social calendar are garden sales, theatrical performances, moonlight strolls, and symphony concerts. A combination bookstore–gift shop is a popular source for books on gardening and horticulture, ordered by botanists the world over. ⊠ *10901 Old Cutler Rd.,* ☎ *305/667–1651.* ☞ *$8.* ☉ *Daily 9:30–4:30.*

㉜ **Matheson Hammock Park.** In the 1930s the Civilian Conservation Corps developed this 100-acre tract of upland and mangrove swamp on land donated by a local pioneer, Commodore J. W. Matheson. The park, Miami-Dade County's oldest and most scenic, features a bathing beach and changing facilities. In 1997 the marina was expanded to include 243 slips, 71 dry-storage spaces, a bait-and-tackle shop, and a restaurant. Noticeably absent are fishing and diving charters, although there is a sailing school. ⊠ *9610 Old Cutler Rd., Coral Gables,* ☎ *305/ 665–5475.* ☞ *Parking for beach and marina $3.50 per car, $8 per car with trailer, $6 per bus and RV; limited free upland parking.* ☉ *Daily 6–sunset; pool lifeguards winter, daily 8:30–5; summer, weekends 8:30–6.*

㉚ **Parrot Jungle.** One of South Florida's original tourist attractions, Parrot Jungle opened in 1936 and is now home to more than 1,100 exotic birds, who look for handouts from visitors. The tone is kitschy (in the tradition of Florida favorites Silver Springs and Cypress Gardens) but oddly peaceful and exotic after you've experienced the urban jungle. Once you've photographed the postcard-perfect Caribbean flamingos and watched a trained-bird show, stroll among orchids and other flowering plants nestled in ferns, bald cypress, and massive live oaks. An imminent move (sometime in mid-2000) will take the birds to a new home on Watson Island, across from the Port of Miami, but this park will be preserved as some type of wildlife sanctuary. ⊠ *11000 S.W. 57th Ave.,* ☎ *305/666–7834.* ☞ *$13.95.* ☉ *Daily 9:30–6, last admission 5; café daily 8–5.*

Coconut Grove

South Florida's oldest settlement, the Grove was inhabited as early as 1834 and established by 1873, two decades before Miami. Its early settlers included Bahamian blacks, "Conchs" (white Key Westers, many originally from the Bahamas), and New England intellectuals. They built a community that attracted artists, writers, and scientists to establish winter homes. By the end of World War I more people listed in *Who's Who* gave addresses in Coconut Grove than any other place in the country.

To this day Coconut Grove reflects its pioneers' eclectic origins. Posh estates mingle with rustic cottages, modest frame homes, and stark modern dwellings, often on the same block. To keep Coconut Grove a village in a jungle, residents lavish affection on exotic plantings while battling to protect remaining native vegetation.

The historic center of the Village of Coconut Grove went through a hippie period in the 1960s, a laid-back funkiness in the 1970s, and a teenybopper invasion in the early 1980s. Today the tone is upscale and urban, with a mix of galleries, boutiques, restaurants, bars, and sidewalk cafés. On weekends the Grove is jam-packed with both locals and tourists shopping at the Streets of Mayfair, CocoWalk, and small boutiques. Parking can be a problem, especially on weekend evenings, when police direct traffic and prohibit turns at some intersections to prevent gridlock. Be prepared to walk several blocks from the periphery into the heart of the Grove.

A Good Tour

From downtown Miami take Brickell Avenue south and follow the signs pointing to Vizcaya and Coconut Grove. If you're interested, keep your eyes peeled to see where Madonna lived, at 3029 Brickell, and Sylvester Stallone's old estate, the faux-finished yellow house with blue trim and huge gates a few doors south on the corner of Brickell and Southwest 32nd. Turn right on Southwest 32nd and then left at the next street.

Although the road is called South Miami Avenue here, it soon turns into South Bayshore Drive. With either name, it's the easiest route into the village. Continue south and watch on your left for the entrance to the don't-miss **Vizcaya Museum and Gardens** ㉝, an estate with an Italian Renaissance–style villa. Less than 100 yards down the road on your right is the **Miami Museum of Science and Space Transit Planetarium** ㉞, a participatory museum with animated displays for all ages.

The road switches from four lanes to two and back again as you approach the village. If you're interested in the history of air travel, take a quick detour down Pan American Drive to see the 1930s Art Deco Pan Am terminal, which has been horribly renovated inside to become **Miami City Hall** ㉟. You'll also see the Coconut Grove Convention Center, where antiques, boat, and home shows are held, and Dinner Key Marina, where seabirds soar and sailboats ride at anchor.

With 28 waterfront acres of Australian pine, lush lawns, and walking and jogging paths, the bayside David T. Kennedy Park makes one more pleasant stop before it's time to hit the village. South Bayshore Drive heads directly into McFarlane Road, which takes a sharp right into the center of the action. If you can forsake instant gratification, turn left on Main Highway and drive less than ½ mi to Devon Road and the interesting **Plymouth Congregational Church** ㊱ and its gardens.

Return to Main Highway and travel northeast toward the historic Village of Coconut Grove. As you reenter the village center, note on your left the Coconut Grove Playhouse. On your right, beyond the benches and shelter, is the entrance to the **Barnacle State Historic Site** ㊲, a pioneer residence built by Commodore Ralph Munroe in 1891. After getting your fill of history, relax and spend the evening mingling with Coconut Grove's artists and intellectuals.

TIMING

Plan on devoting from six to eight hours to enjoy Vizcaya, other bayfront sights, and the village's shops, restaurants, and nightlife.

Sights to See

③⑦ Barnacle State Historic Site. The oldest Miami home still on its original foundation rests in the middle of 5 acres of native hardwood and landscaped lawns surrounded by flashy Coconut Grove. Built by Florida's first snowbird—New Yorker Commodore Ralph Munroe—the home features many original furnishings, a broad sloping roof, and deeply recessed verandas that channel sea breezes into the house. If your timing is right, you may catch one of the monthly Moonlight Concerts. ✉ *3485 Main Hwy.,* ☎ *305/448–9445.* ✎ *$1, concerts $5.* ☉ *Fri.– Sun. 9–4; tours 10, 11:30, 1, and 2:30, but call ahead; group tours (10 or more) Mon.–Thurs. by reservation; concerts on day near full moon 6 PM–9 PM, but call ahead.*

NEED A BREAK? Although **Joffrey's Coffee Co.** (✉ 3434A Main Hwy., ☎ 305/448–0848) is a chain, it's still a nice place to drop by for a cappuccino, espresso, tea, or chilled coffee from morning to midnight. Tables at the sidewalk café enable you to critique the trendies that inhabit the neighborhood. Muffins, bagels, and cakes bring the bill to about $5.

③⑤ Miami City Hall. Built in 1934 as the terminal for the Pan American Airways seaplane base at Dinner Key, the building retains its nautical-style Art Deco trim. Sadly, the interior is generic government, but a 1938 Pan Am menu on display (with filet mignon, *petit pois au beurre,* and Jenny Lind pudding) lets you know Miami officials appreciate from whence they came. ✉ *3500 Pan American Dr.,* ☎ *305/250–5400.* ☉ *Weekdays 8–5.*

③④ Miami Museum of Science and Space Transit Planetarium. This museum is chock-full of hands-on sound, gravity, and electricity displays for children and adults alike. A wildlife center houses native Florida snakes, turtles, tortoises, and birds of prey. Outstanding traveling exhibits appear throughout the year, and virtual reality, life-science demonstrations, and Internet technology are on hand every day. The spinning 1933 Pan Am globe—once the focal point of the airline's terminal—is now the focal point of the museum's lobby. ✉ *3280 S. Miami Ave.,* ☎ *305/854–4247 museum; 305/854–2222 planetarium information hotline.* ✎ *Museum, planetarium, and wildlife center $9; laser-light rock-and-roll concert $6.* ☉ *Daily 10–6.*

③⑥ Plymouth Congregational Church. Opened in 1917, this handsome coral-rock structure resembles a Mexican mission church. The front door, made of hand-carved walnut and oak with original wrought-iron fittings, came from an early 17th-century monastery in the Pyrenees. Also on the 11-acre grounds are the first schoolhouse in Miami-Dade County (one room), which was moved to this property, and the site of the original Coconut Grove waterworks and electric works. ✉ *3400 Devon Rd.,* ☎ *305/444–6521.* ☉ *Weekdays 9–4:30, Sun. service 10 AM.*

★ ③③ Vizcaya Museum and Gardens. Of the 10,000 people living in Miami between 1912 and 1916, about 1,000 of them were gainfully employed by Chicago industrialist James Deering to build this $20 million neoclassical winter residence. Once comprising 180 acres, the grounds now cover a still-substantial 30-acre tract, including a native hammock and more than 10 acres of formal gardens and fountains overlooking Biscayne Bay. The house, open to the public, contains 70 rooms, 34 of which are filled with paintings, sculpture, antique furniture, and other decorative arts dating from the 15th through the 19th centuries and representing the Renaissance, Baroque, rococo, and neoclassical styles. So unusual and impressive is Vizcaya, its guest list has included Ronald Reagan, Pope John Paul II, Queen Elizabeth II, Bill Clinton, and Boris Yeltsin. It's a shame the guided tour can be far less impressive and interesting than the home's guest list and surroundings. ✉ *3251 S. Miami Ave.,* ☎ *305/250–9133.* ✆ *$10.* ⊙ *House and ticket booth daily 9:30–4:30, garden daily 9:30–5:30.*

Virginia Key and Key Biscayne

Government Cut and the Port of Miami separate the city's dense urban fabric from two of its playground islands, Virginia Key and Key Biscayne. Parks occupy much of both keys, providing facilities for golf, tennis, softball, picnicking, and sunbathing, plus uninviting but ecologically valuable stretches of dense mangrove swamp. Key Biscayne's long and winding roads are great for rollerblading and bicycling, and its lush, lazy setting provides a respite from the buzz-saw tempo of SoBe.

A Good Tour

To reach Virginia Key and Key Biscayne take the Rickenbacker Causeway ($1 per car) across Biscayne Bay from the mainland at Brickell Avenue and Southwest 26th Road, about 2 mi south of downtown Miami. The causeway links several islands in the bay.

The William M. Powell Bridge rises 75 ft above the water to eliminate the need for a draw span. The panoramic view from the top encompasses the bay, keys, port, and downtown skyscrapers, with Miami Beach and the Atlantic Ocean in the distance. Just south of the Powell Bridge, a stub of the **Old Rickenbacker Causeway Bridge** ㉜, built in 1947, is now a fishing pier with a nice view.

Immediately after crossing the Rickenbacker Causeway onto Virginia Key, you'll see a long strip of bay front popular with windsurfers and jet skiers. Nearby rest rooms and a great view of the curving shoreline make this an ideal place to park and have your own tailgate party. Look for the gold dome of the **Miami Seaquarium** ㉝, one of the country's first marine attractions. Opposite the causeway from the Seaquarium, a road leads north to Virginia Key Beach and the adjacent Virginia Key Critical Wildlife Area, which is often closed to the public to protect nesting birds.

From Virginia Key the causeway crosses Bear Cut to the north end of Key Biscayne and becomes Crandon Boulevard. The boulevard bisects 1,211-acre **Crandon Park** ㊵, which has a popular Atlantic Ocean beach and nature center. On your right are entrances to the Crandon Park Golf Course and the Tennis Center at Crandon Park, home of the Lipton Championships. Keep your eyes open for pure Miami icons: coconut palms and iguana-crossing signs.

From the traffic circle at the south end of Crandon Park, Crandon Boulevard continues to the **Bill Baggs Cape Florida State Recreation Area** ㊶, a 460-acre park containing, among other things, the brick Cape Florida Lighthouse and light keeper's cottage.

Follow Crandon Boulevard back to Crandon Park through Key Biscayne's downtown village, where shops and a 10-acre village green cater mainly to local residents. On your way back to the mainland, pause as you approach the Powell Bridge to admire the Miami skyline. At night the brightly lighted NationsBank Tower looks like a clipper ship running under full sail before the breeze.

TIMING

Set aside the better part of a day for this tour, double that if you're into beaches, fishing, and water sports.

Sights to See

★ ❹ **Bill Baggs Cape Florida State Recreation Area.** Thanks to great beaches, blue-green waters, amenities, sunsets, and a lighthouse, this park at Key Biscayne's southern tip is worth the drive. Since Hurricane Andrew, it has returned better than ever, with new boardwalks, 18 picnic shelters, and a café that serves beer, wine, and meals ranging from hot dogs to lobster. An additional 54 acres of wetlands were acquired in 1997, and a marina is on the drawing board. A stroll or ride along walking and bicycle paths and boardwalks provides wonderful views of Miami's dramatic skyline. Also on site are bicycle and skate rentals, a playground, fishing piers, and kayak rental. Guided tours of the cultural complex and the ☺ **Cape Florida Lighthouse,** South Florida's oldest structure, are offered, but call for availability. The lighthouse was erected in 1845 to replace an earlier one destroyed in an 1836 Seminole attack, in which the keeper's helper was killed. Climb 118 steps to visit a replica of the keeper's house. ⊠ *1200 S. Crandon Blvd.,* ☎ *305/361–5811 or 305/361–8779.* ⊡ *$4 per vehicle with up to 8 people; $1 per person on bicycle, bus, motorcycle, or foot.* ☉ *Daily 8–sunset, tours Thurs.–Mon. 10 and 1.*

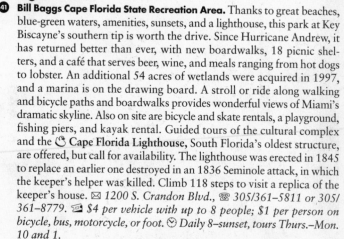

❹ **Crandon Park.** This laid-back park in northern Key Biscayne is popular with families, and many educated beach enthusiasts rate the 3½-mi county beach here among the top 10 beaches in North America. The sand is soft, there's a great view of the Atlantic, and parking is both inexpensive and plentiful. So large is this park that it includes a marina, golf course, tennis center, and ball fields. At the north end of the beach is the free **Marjory Stoneman Douglas Biscayne Nature Center** (☎ 305/642–9600). Explore a variety of natural habitats by taking a tour that includes dragging nets through sea-grass beds to catch, study, and release such marine creatures as sea cucumbers, seahorses, crabs, and shrimp. Nature center hours vary, so call ahead. ⊠ *4000 Crandon Blvd.,* ☎ *305/361–5421.* ⊡ *$3.50 per vehicle.* ☉ *Daily 8–sunset.*

☺ ❸ **Miami Seaquarium.** This old-fashioned attraction has six daily shows featuring sea lions, dolphins, and Lolita, a killer whale. (Lolita's tank is small for seaquariums—just three times her length—and so some wildlife advocates are trying to get her back to sea.) Exhibits include a shark pool, a 235,000-gallon tropical-reef aquarium, and manatees. Glass-bottom boats take tours of Biscayne Bay. Want to get your feet (and everything else) wet? The Water and Dolphin Exploration program (WADE) enables you to swim with dolphins during a two-hour session. Reservations are required. ⊠ *4400 Rickenbacker Causeway,* ☎ *305/361–5705.* ⊡ *$20.95, WADE $125, parking $3.* ☉ *Daily 9:30–6, last admission 4:30; WADE Wed.–Sun. 8:30 and noon.*

❸ **Old Rickenbacker Causeway Bridge.** Here you can watch boat traffic pass through the channel, pelicans and other seabirds soar and dive, and dolphins cavort in the bay. Park at its entrance, about a mile from the tollgate, and walk past anglers tending their lines to the gap where the center draw span across the Intracoastal Waterway was removed. ⊠ *South of Powell Bridge.*

DINING

By Kendall Hamersly

So successful have Miami's better restaurants been that the local dining scene has attracted worldwide attention. The city is a cradle of culinary imagination, where international and indigenous flavors collide in delicious inspiration. Dining in Miami is also an essential part of nightlife, whether in the Cuban restaurants on Calle Ocho or in the

ATLANTIC OCEAN

KEY

AE American Express Office

N

MIAMI BEACH

Collins Ave.

Broad Causeway

Biscayne Blvd.

JFK Causeway

Julia Tuttle Causeway

Biscayne Blvd.

N.E. 2nd Ave.

N. Miami Ave.

NORTH MIAMI BEACH

NORTH MIAMI

N. Miami Beach Blvd.

Miami Gdns. Dr.

N. Miami Ave.

N.E. 6th Ave.

N.E. 35th St.

N.E. 103rd St.

N.E. 95th St.

Gratigny Rd.

7th Ave.

Florida's Turnpike

Palmetto Expwy

Miami Gdns. Dr.

N.W. 135th St.

N.W. 8th Ave.

N.W. 27th Ave.

N.W. 103rd St.

N.W. 95th St.

N.W. 79th St.

N.W. 62nd St.

N.W. 54th St.

Robert Frost Expwy.

N.W. 36th St.

N.W. 20th St.

E. 25th St.

Hialeah Dr.

Miami River

Red Rd.

W. 4th Ave.

E. 49th St.

W. 49th St.

N.W. 72nd Ave.

W. 72nd Ave.

N.W. 58th St.

N.W. 39th St.

N.W. 87th Ave.

Dairy Rd.

Okeechobee Rd.

Palmetto Expwy

Miami International

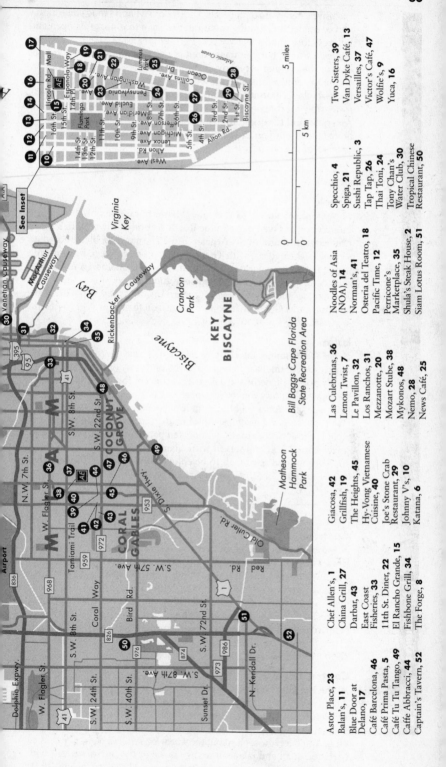

See Inset

Astor Place, 23
Balan's, 11
Blue Door at Delano, 21
Café Barcelona, 46
Café Prima Pasta, 5
Café Tu Tu Tango, 49
Caffe Abbracci, 44
Captain's Tavern, 52

Chef Allen's, 1
China Grill, 27
Darbar, 43
East Coast Fisheries, 33
11th St. Diner, 22
El Rancho Grande, 15
Fishbone Grill, 34
The Forge, 8

Giacosa, 42
Grillfish, 19
The Heights, 45
Hy-Vong Vietnamese Cuisine, 40
Joe's Stone Crab Restaurant, 29
Johnny V's, 10
Katana, 6

Las Culebrinas, 36
Lemon Twist, 7
Le Pavillon, 32
Los Ranchos, 31
Mezzanotte, 20
Mozart Stube, 38
Mykonos, 48
Nemo, 28
News Café, 25

Noodles of Asia (NOA), 14
Norman's, 41
Osteria del Teatro, 18
Pacific Time, 12
Perricone's Marketplace, 35
Shula's Steak House, 2
Siam Lotus Room, 51

Specchio, 4
Spiga, 21
Sushi Republic, 3
Tap Tap, 26
Thai Toni, 24
Tony Chan's Water Club, 30
Tropical Chinese Restaurant, 50

Two Sisters, 39
Van Dyke Café, 13
Versailles, 37
Victor's Café, 47
Wolfie's, 9
Yuca, 16

exclusive eateries of South Beach. The sizzle in Miami's food scene means fierce competition among restaurateurs, such that hopefuls open and failures close almost every week. Restaurants listed here have passed the test of time, but you might double-check by phone before you set out for the evening. At many of the hottest spots, you'll need a reservation to avoid a long wait for a table. And when you get your check, note whether a gratuity is already included; most restaurants add 15% (ostensibly for the convenience of and protection from the many Latin-American and European tourists who are used to this practice in their homelands), but you can reduce or supplement it depending on your opinion of the service.

Coconut Grove

Greek

$–$$$ ✕ **Mykonos.** Since 1973 this busy Miami fixture has brightened the intersection at Five Points (in the Roads section of town) with a beautiful exterior mural of the Aegean. Inside, a sparkling blue-and-white setting is dressed up with Greek travel posters. Specialties include gyros, moussaka, marinated lamb and chicken, calamari and octopus sautéed in wine and onions, and sumptuous Greek salads thick with feta cheese and briny olives. Vegetarian moussaka, eggplant roll, lasagna, and a Greek-style omelet are also on the menu. ✉ *1201 Coral Way,* ☎ *305/856–3140. AE, DC, MC, V. No lunch Sun.*

Latin

$–$$ ✕ **Café Tu Tu Tango.** Local artists set up their easels in the rococo-modern arcades of this café-lounge on the second story of Coconut Grove's highly popular CocoWalk. The artistic concept follows through to the menu, which allows you to pick appetizers as if you were selecting paints from a palette. A never boring parade of people passes by outside, while inside, guests graze on chips, dips, breads, and spreads. House specials include frittatas, crab cakes, *picadillo* empanadas (pastries stuffed with spicy ground beef and served with cilantro sour cream), and chicken and shrimp orzo paella, all to be enjoyed with some of the best sangria in the city. ✉ *3015 Grand Ave. (CocoWalk),* ☎ *305/529–2222. AE, MC, V.*

Coral Gables

Austrian

$$–$$$ ✕ **Mozart Stube.** It's Oktoberfest year-round at this Austrian *schnitzelhaus.* The Bitburger flows early and often as you peruse a menu loaded down with heavy but scrumptious food. Start with a light garlic soup or maybe some snails in a lagoon of butter and garlic. A terrific side of German potato salad, homemade slaw, and more precedes ultrameaty entrées like veal shank, roast duckling, medallions of filet mignon in peppercorn-mushroom sauce, and of course wurst and schnitzel. The Black Forest cake is legendary. ✉ *325 Alcazar Ave.,* ☎ *305/446–1600. AE, D, DC, MC, V.*

Contemporary

$$$–$$$$ ✕ **The Heights.** Food as design is the rule at this stylish Gables spot,
★   but there's integrity, too. Pan-seared Sonoma Valley foie gras with clove-spiked caramelized pear, chile-spiced corn cake, toasted walnuts with port, and red chile drizzlers seems almost too much to take until you eat it. You'll feel the same about the wheat-berry salad with chile-crusted barbecue quail and jalapeño-orange sauce or the organic greens with apple cider vinaigrette, sweet roast garlic, and toasted *pepitas* (little pumpkin seeds). Tuna gets a crust of New Mexican chile, served with

cactus tempura and Japanese-style soy-ponzu sauce, and sea bass is glazed with *achiote* (a yellow-orange Mexican spice) and served with jicama, asparagus, and a citrus beurre blanc. And there's more—pumpkin pie with pink-peppercorn ice cream—making for heady Heights indeed. ⊠ *2530 Ponce de León Blvd.,* ☎ *305/461–1774. AE, D, DC, MC, V.*

Eclectic

$$$$ ✕ **Norman's.** This elegantly casual restaurant, which has won as many
★ awards as it has customers, turns out gourmet cuisine with an edge. Nationally acclaimed chef Norman Van Aken has created a buzz by perfecting the art of New World cuisine—a combination rooted in Latin, North American, Caribbean, and Asian influences. Bold tastes are delivered in every dish, whether it's a simple black-and-white bean soup with sour cream, chorizo, and tortillas or a rum-and-pepper-painted grouper on a mango-*habanero mojo* sauce. From the comfortable decor to the staff that never seems harried even when all seats are filled (usually every minute between opening and closing), Norman's has captured the essence of Miami dining. ⊠ *21 Almeria Ave.,* ☎ *305/446–6767. AE, DC, MC, V. Closed Sun. No lunch Sat.*

$$–$$$ ✕ **Two Sisters.** Competition among Coral Gables restaurants means the food here has to be better than fantastic. This restaurant, on the ground floor of the Hyatt Regency, approaches nirvana. Though the mood is understated, the Pacific Rim–inspired dishes have definite pizzazz. Entrées such as wok-cooked tangled shrimp with jungle curry, rice ribbons, and coconut glaze or the jerk marinated snapper with red onion confit and ginger butter might make you consider a vacation in the South Pacific. But stay in South Florida with your attentive servers and experience incredibly delicious desserts. ⊠ *50 Alhambra Plaza,* ☎ *305/441–1234. AE, MC, V.*

Indian

$–$$ ✕ **Darbar.** Owner Bobby Nangia's impeccably arranged Darbar (Royal Court, in English) is the leader among Miami's Indian restaurants. Surrounded by portraits of turbaned maharajas, witness flavors rise as if in a dance from the *bangan bharta* (eggplant mashed with onions, tomatoes, herbs, and spices and baked in a tandoori oven). The menu focuses on northern Indian, or frontier, cuisine—various kebabs, tandoori platters, and *tikkas* (chicken or lamb marinated in yogurt and spices and cooked tandoori style)—although there are also curries from different regions and *biryani* specialties prepared with basmati rice and garnished with boiled egg, tomato, nuts, and raisins. Everything, including the delectable Indian breads, is cooked to order. ⊠ *276 Alhambra Circle,* ☎ *305/448–9691. AE, DC, MC, V. No lunch Sun.*

Italian

$$$–$$$$ ✕ **Giacosa.** Named for one of Puccini's librettists, Giacosa is both superbly evocative and just plain superb. The thickly carpeted room resembles a smart Venetian salon, courtesy of fresh flowers and chair cushions with designs inspired by tapestries. From the moment they place your napkin in your lap to the moment they discreetly present your check, the smooth staff is the standard of competence. While you contemplate your choices, a server whisks a tower of airy pita bread with a carafe of olive oil to your table. A salad *tricolore* imparts the bitter kiss of arugula; pastas, veal, and fresh seafood are all prepared for peak taste. Whenever you request it, Parmesan is freshly grated on the plate. ⊠ *394 Giralda Ave.,* ☎ *305/445–5858. AE, DC, MC, V. No lunch weekends.*

$$–$$$ ✕ **Caffe Abbracci.** Although the kitchen closes at midnight, the last wave of weekend customers—usually Brazilians—is still partying to flamenco or salsa music at 2 AM. The graciously Deco setting overflows with flowers, and the light above each table operates on an individual dimmer. After the cold and hot antipasti—various carpaccios, porcini mushrooms, calamari, grilled goat cheese, shrimps, mussels—come festive entrées. Most pasta is made fresh, so consider sampling two or three, maybe with pesto sauce, Gorgonzola, and fresh tomatoes. Room for dessert? Napoleons and tiramisu are made here daily, and there's always a choice of fresh fruit tarts. ⊠ *318 Aragon Ave.,* ☎ *305/441–0700. Reservations essential. AE, DC, MC, V. No lunch weekends.*

Spanish

$ ✕ **Café Barcelona.** In a room with high ceilings and coral walls, gilt-framed art and slender ceiling lamps with tiny, green fluted shades impart a rich glow. The result is an ambience that's part art gallery and part private home. Exceptional food matches the exceptional mood, and in a city where fresh fish has gotten priced off the deep end, entrées here range a good $5 below comparable dishes at the top restaurants. The chef does a sea bass in sea salt for two, a traditional codfish with garlic confit, and a grouper in a clay pot with seafood sauce, as well as lamb, duck, and several affordable rice dishes, including three types of paella. The *crema Catalana,* a version of flan, is not to be missed. ⊠ *160 Giralda Ave.,* ☎ *305/448–0912. AE, D, DC, MC, V.*

Downtown Miami

Chinese

$$–$$$$ ✕ **Tony Chan's Water Club.** One of a pair of outstanding Chinese restaurants, this beautiful dining room just off the lobby of the high-rise DoubleTree Grand Hotel looks onto a bay-side marina. Filled with art and detailed with chrome, the long room is modern rather than stereotypically Chinese. On the menu of more than 200 appetizers and entrées are minced quail tossed with bamboo shoots and mushrooms wrapped in lettuce leaves. Indulge in a seafood spectacular of shrimp, conch, scallops, fish cakes, and crabmeat tossed with broccoli in a bird's nest, or go for pork chops sprinkled with green pepper in a black bean–garlic sauce. A lighter favorite is steamed sea bass with ginger and garlic. ⊠ *1717 N. Bayshore Dr.,* ☎ *305/374–8888. AE, D, DC, MC, V.*

Contemporary

$$$ ✕ **Le Pavillon.** The mahogany, jade marble, and leather appointments of the dining room in the Hotel Inter-Continental evoke the conservative air of an English private club. Beautiful floral displays enhance the mood as the attentive staff serves regional American fare from a limited but frequently changing menu, including items low in calories, cholesterol, and sodium. Specialties are char-grilled bluefin tuna fillet, poached yellowtail snapper, panfried corn-fed squab, roasted free-range chicken, spring lamb, and roasted fillet of milk-fed veal. For a light dessert try red-berry soup with vanilla ice cream. The wine list is extensive. ⊠ *100 Chopin Plaza,* ☎ *305/577–1000, ext. 4494; 305/577–1000, ext. 4494 or 4462. AE, DC, MC, V. Closed Sun. No dinner.*

Italian

$$–$$$ ✕ **Perricone's Marketplace.** The emerging neighborhood along Brickell Avenue south of the Miami River seems to be swelling with Italian restaurants. This one, housed in a 120-year-old barn brought down from Vermont by the owner, is the biggest and most popular among them. The recipes are ancient, too, handed down grandmother to mother to daughter, and the cooking is simple and good. Next door, a deli carries a selection of wine that you can bring to the table for a small corkage fee. Enjoy a glass with homemade minestrone; a generous antipasto; linguine with a sauté of jumbo shrimp, fresh asparagus, and chopped tomatoes; or gnocchi with four cheeses. The homemade

tiramisu and fruit tart are top-notch. ⊠ *15 S.E. 10th St.,* ☎ *305/374–9449. AE, MC, V. Beer and wine only. Closed Sun. No lunch Sat.*

Latin

$–$$$ ✕ **Los Ranchos.** Owner Carlos Somoza, nephew of Nicaragua's late president Anastasio Somoza, sustains the tradition of Managua's original Los Ranchos by serving Argentine-style beef—lean, grass-fed tenderloin with chimichurri. Nicaragua's own sauces are a tomato-based marinara and the fiery *cebollitas encurtidas,* with jalapeño and pickled onion. Specialties include chorizo and *cuajada con maduro* (skim cheese with fried bananas). Don't look for veggies or brewed decaf, but there is live entertainment. ⊠ *Bayside Marketplace, 401 Biscayne Blvd.,* ☎ *305/375–8188 or 305/375–0666;* ⊠ *2728 Ponce de León Blvd., Coral Gables,* ☎ *305/446–0050;* ⊠ *Kendall Town & Country, 8505 Mills Dr., Kendall (South Miami),* ☎ *305/596–5353;* ⊠ *The Falls, 8888 S.W. 136th St., Suite 303, South Miami,* ☎ *305/238–6867;* ⊠ *125 S.W. 107th Ave., Little Managua (West Dade),* ☎ *305/221–9367. AE, DC, MC, V.*

Seafood

$$–$$$$ ✕ **East Coast Fisheries.** This friendly family-owned restaurant and retail fish market on the Miami River offers fresh Florida seafood caught by its own 38-boat fleet in the Keys. From tables along the second-floor balcony, watch the cooks prepare your dinner in the open kitchen below. Specialties include a complimentary fish-pâté appetizer, blackened pompano with owner Peter Swartz's personal herb-and-spice recipe, lightly breaded fried grouper, and a homemade key lime pie. ⊠ *360 W. Flagler St.,* ☎ *305/372–1300. AE, MC, V. Beer and wine only.*

$–$$ ✕ **Fishbone Grill.** The artsy humor of this place is evident in the menus, each of which bears a different magazine cover, but the fish here is no-nonsense and impeccably fresh. Start with hearty, cheesy, cakelike jalapeño corn bread, served alongside a small salad with your entrée. Smoked salmon mousse with French bread is tasty, too, as is gazpacho. Order your fresh fish from a blackboard, and have it grilled, blackened, sauteed, baked, Française-style, or Oriental. Pizzas are available, too, as is a mean cioppino, the San Francisco–style fish stew in a tomato base. ⊠ *650 S. Miami Ave.,* ☎ *305/530–1915. AE, MC, V. Beer and wine only. No dinner Sun.*

Little Havana

Cuban

$$–$$$ ✕ **Victor's Café.** The look of this popular restaurant was inspired by
★ *casonas,* the great houses of colonial Cuba. The mood is old Havana, with Cuban art and antiques and a glass-covered fountain courtyard; come on Friday afternoon, when the tapas bar is packed and lunch often lasts until dusk, in Cuban fashion. A Cuban immigrant, owner Victor del Corral runs the place with his daughter, Sonia Zaldivar, and her son Luis. Hot appetizers, such as a puff pastry filled with aromatically herbed lump crabmeat or savory cassava turnover filled with Florida lobster, can be enough for a meal. Truly jumbo shrimp come with yam quenelles in a creamy champagne sauce sprinkled with salmon roe. Entrées come with rice and black beans, and romantic music plays nightly. ⊠ *2340 S.W. 32nd Ave.,* ☎ *305/445–1313. AE, MC, V.*

$–$$ ✕ **Versailles.** Cubans meet to dine on Calle Ocho in what is quite possibly the most garish budget restaurant you'll ever see. It's all mirrors and candelabras and hairdos and tuxedoed waiters, with hundreds of seats and a tremendous din. The food is terrific, especially classics like *ropa vieja* (Cuban-style shredded beef), arroz con pollo, *palomilla* steak, *sopa de platanos* (plantain soup), ham shank, and roast pork. To achieve a total experience, have the town's strongest Cuban coffee and a terrific flan or sweet *tres leches* to finish. ⊠ *3555 S.W. 8th St.,* ☎ *305/444–0240. AE, D, DC, MC, V.*

Spanish

$–$$ ✕ **Las Culebrinas.** A Spanish *tapaceria* ("house of little plates") is a place to live each meal as if it were your last, with much wine, much fun, much noise, and much food. Tapas are not small at all; some are entrée size, such as a succulent mix of garbanzos with ham, sausage, red peppers, and oil, or the Spanish tortilla, a giant Frisbee-shape omelet. Entrée-wise, indulge in tender fillet of crocodile, fresh fish, grilled pork, and more. For dessert, there's a bit of a show—crema Catalana, a puffy cream caramelized at the table with, you guessed it, a blowtorch. ⊠ *4700 W. Flagler St.,* ☎ *305/445–2337. AE, MC, V. Beer and wine only.*

Vietnamese

$–$$ ✕ **Hy-Vong Vietnamese Cuisine.** Beer-savvy proprietor Kathy Manning
★   serves a half-dozen top brews (Double Grimbergen, Moretti, and Spaten, among them) at this plain little restaurant, and magic pours forth from the tiny kitchen. Come before 7 to avoid a wait. Favorites include spring rolls of ground pork, cellophane noodles, and black mushrooms wrapped in homemade rice paper; whole fish panfried with *nuoc mam,* a garlic-lime fish sauce; and thinly sliced pork barbecued with sesame seeds and fish sauce and served with bean sprouts, rice noodles, and slivers of carrots, almonds, and peanuts. ⊠ *3458 S.W. 8th St.,* ☎ *305/446–3674. No credit cards. Closed Mon. and 2 wks in Aug. No lunch.*

Miami Beach North of South Beach

Continental

$$$–$$$$ ✕ **The Forge.** Often compared to a museum, this landmark restaurant, which bills itself as "the Versailles of steak," stands behind a facade like that of a 19th-century Parisian mansion. Each intimate dining salon has its own historical artifacts, including a chandelier that hung in James Madison's White House. The wine cellar contains 380,000 bottles—including more than 500 dating from 1822 (and costing as much as $35,000) and recorked in 1989 by experts from Domaines Barons de Rothschild. In addition to steak, specialties include Norwegian salmon served over fresh garden vegetables with spinach vinaigrette and free-range Wisconsin duck roasted with black currants. For dessert try the blacksmith pie. This place is a hot party spot on Wednesday night, and the adjoining club, Jimmy'z at the Forge, is very popular with the rich and famous. ⊠ *432 Arthur Godfrey Rd.,* ☎ *305/538–8533. AE, DC, MC, V. No lunch.*

Italian

$–$$ ✕ **Café Prima Pasta.** As many Italian restaurants in Miami are run by
★   Argentines as by Italians. One of the best is this cozy spot in the emerging North Beach neighborhood. Consistently intense flavors, high-quality ingredients, and just plain good cooking are the key. Service can be disjointed and erratic, but you forget it all upon delivery of fresh-made bread with a dipping oil of garlic, parsley, virgin olive oil, and crushed red pepper. Also good are carpaccio, antipasto, pasta *e fagioli* (a soup with pasta and beans), and a gigantic platter of pasta with seafood. Have a legendary tiramisu to finish. ⊠ *414 71st St.,* ☎ *305/ 867–0106. No credit cards.*

$–$$ ✗ **Specchio.** Homemade pastas and sauces, rich soups, and luscious meats draw a sophisticated before- and after-theater crowd to this brightly lit, fun dining room. You can buy art right off the wall, but it's better to devote most of your attention to the brilliant food. Chomp on crusty bread with chopped tomato, garlic, and basil as you select from a broad menu. Grilled vegetables are a light starter, as are cream-free pureed vegetable soups and an arugula salad with crabmeat and avocado. Beef gets real-food treatment with *tagliata di manzo al rosmarino* (sliced sirloin steak with rosemary and arugula), or try black-ink linguine with shrimp and fresh tomato. ⊠ *9485 Harding Ave., Surfside,* ☎ *305/865–5653. MC, V.*

Japanese

$–$$ ✗ **Sushi Republic.** This tiny spot lies on the main drag of Surfside, a resort area that straddles an Annette Funicello–style past and a Euro-tourist future. Here you'll find one of the freshest and tastiest sushi spreads in town, along with cooked items that excel. Try *shumai* (soft shrimp dumplings with ponzu sauce), whole fried softshell crab, and succulent salmon teriyaki. Among rolls, the Tiger Woods roll—tuna rolled with cream cheese and topped with avocado and salmon—is a hole in one. Cool nights call for a steaming noodle soup like *nabeyaki udon,* a broth laden with udon noodles, eggs, mushrooms, and big pieces of shrimp tempura. ⊠ *9583 Harding Ave., Surfside,* ☎ *305/867–8036. AE, D, DC, MC, V. Closed Mon. No lunch Sun.*

$ ✗ **Katana.** Here's a sushi spot where you not only eat the fish, you catch it. An oval moat is the centerpiece of the tiny (only 30 seats) bar. It's filled with little wooden boats that circle the moat and deliver bits of sushi on color-coded plates. Pluck the plates that appeal to you and pay by the plate at the end. What could be more fun? Gimmicks aside, this is tasty sushi and a real value for a quick, quick bite. Best are rainbow rolls (California rolls with thin-sliced tuna, salmon, and avocado arrayed on top); *futomaki* (pickled Japanese vegetables rolled with rice and seaweed) with spinach, crab, and egg; and simple, fresh sashimi of tuna or salmon. But go early: Katana is packed every night. ⊠ *920 71st St.,* ☎ *305/864–0037. AE, MC, V. Closed Mon. No lunch.*

Mediterranean

$–$$ ✗ **Lemon Twist.** From the start—a complimentary bowl of green and black olives with virgin olive oil, garlic, lemon, cayenne pepper, lavender, and thyme—you know you're in for South Beach style in a quiet North Beach setting. The model-pretty crowd makes the pilgrimage north to visit this French-Mediterranean spot. Try an excellent gazpacho with condiments you add at the table, a nosh of roasted vegetables with lemony cream, and meaty entrées including a beautiful pounded chicken breast with lemon and butter. One luscious side dish to look for is baked potato casserole au gratin; also keep an eye out for lasagna with salmon in lobster-tomato bisque. ⊠ *908 71st St.,* ☎ *305/868–2075. AE, MC, V. No lunch.*

North Miami Beach and North Dade

Contemporary

$$$–$$$$ ✗ **Chef Allen's.** In this Art Deco world of glass block, art, neon trim,
★ and fresh flowers, your gaze remains riveted on the kitchen. Chef Allen Susser designed it with a picture window 25 ft wide, so you can watch him create contemporary American masterpieces from a menu that changes nightly. After a salad of baby greens and warm wild mushrooms or a rock-shrimp hash with roasted corn, consider *orecchiette* pasta with sun-dried tomatoes, goat cheese, spinach, and toasted pine nuts; swordfish with conch-citrus couscous, macadamia nuts,

and lemon; or grilled lamb chops with eggplant timbale and a three-nut salsa. A favorite dessert is the double-chocolate soufflé with lots of nuts. New is Chef Allen's Gourmet to Go, a takeout place with excellent food at grocery store–deli prices. Take home a bottle of Chef Allen's mango ketchup as a tasty souvenir. ⊠ *19088 N.E. 29th Ave., Aventura,* ☎ *305/935–2900. AE, DC, MC, V.*

Steak

$$–$$$$ ✕ **Shula's Steak House.** Prime rib, fish (including dolphin), and award-winning steaks are almost an afterthought to the icons in this shrine for the NFL-obsessed, located at the club part of Don Shula's Hotel & Golf Club (☞ Lodging, *below*). Dine in a woody setting with a fireplace, surrounded by memorabilia of retired coach Don Shula's perfect 1972 season with the Miami Dolphins, including game footballs, assistant coach Howard Schnellenberger's pipe, and a playbook autographed by President Richard Nixon. Polish off the 48-ounce porterhouse steak and achieve a sort of immortality—your name on a plaque and an autographed picture of Shula. Also for fans, there's shula's steak 2 (lowercase borrowed from espn2), a sports celebrity hangout in the resort's hotel section, as well as a branch at the Alexander Hotel (☞ Lodging, *below*), in Miami Beach. ⊠ *7601 N.W. 154th St., Miami Lakes,* ☎ *305/820–8102. AE, DC, MC, V.*

South Beach

American

$–$$ ✕ **11th Street Diner.** Come here to relive the sights, sounds, and smells of the '50s, without the artificial ambience of James Dean cutouts and poodle skirts. Since serving its first plate of meat loaf in 1992, the diner has become a low-priced, unpretentious hangout for locals. The best time to visit is weekend mornings, when the stragglers from the night before and early birds with their morning papers converge for conversation. At this busy, bustling eatery in a 1948 Deco-style dining car, you can grab a corner booth and order a cherry cola, a blue-plate special, or a milk shake and pretend you've traveled back in time. ⊠ *11th St. and Washington Ave.,* ☎ *305/534–6373. AE, MC, V.*

Café

$–$$ ✕ **News Café.** An Ocean Drive landmark, this 24-hour café attracts
★   a big crowd around the clock with snacks, light meals, drinks, and the sidewalk people parade. There's a bar with 12 stools in back, but most diners prefer sitting outside, where they can feel the salt breeze and gawk at the human scenery. Offering a little of this and a little of that—bagels, pâtés, chocolate fondue, sandwiches, and a terrific wine list—this joint has something for everyone. In 1997 the café spawned a new location— twice as large—in Coconut Grove; by 2000 the owners hope to open another, on Biscayne Boulevard. ⊠ *800 Ocean Dr.,* ☎ *305/538–6397;* ⊠ *2901 Florida Ave., Coconut Grove,* ☎ *305/774–6397. AE, DC, MC, V.*

Caribbean

$–$$ ✕ **Tap Tap.** South Beach style is in full flower at this Haitian bar/restaurant on the northern fringe of SoFi, the part of South Beach south of 5th Street. It's an art gallery and concert venue as well as the Beach's only spot to try spicy, fascinating Haitian cuisine. Luxuriate in a bowl of pumpkin chowder, with *calabaza* (a Caribbean pumpkin), chayote, and yam, plus the ever-present scotch bonnet pepper. Conch fritters come with *malanga* fritters and a cooling watercress sauce. Goat is simmered in a sauce made of tomato and chayote; shrimp are creole and tender; and fish is whole and served with a spicy fruit salsa. To finish, dip into the delectable coconut custard with almonds and cream. ⊠ *819 5th St.,* ☎ *305/672–2898. AE, DC, MC, V. No lunch.*

Contemporary

$–$$ ✕ **Johnny V's.** "Cowboy chef" Johnny Vinzencz, ringleader at Astor Place (☞ *below*), has a casual place here. Diner design belies gourmet aspirations, and some menu items are even duplicated from the swanky Astor at a much lower price. Southwestern flavors, such as barbecue, chilies, smoked meats, and roasted corn, predominate—each one a revelation. Homemade soups change daily. Mango inspires coleslaw, and handmade potato chips are spicy. If you're hungry, dig into the Miami Thanksgiving—herb-roasted turkey with plantain stuffing and mango-cranberry chutney. The fainter of heart won't find relief with the smoked turkey sandwich, which is nearly unfinishable, but after the main course the bold will be tempted by the Double Mac Daddy Brownie, as big and caloric as it sounds. Walk out the door with a jar of pickles, salsa, sauce, chutney, oil, stock, or ketchup to go. ⊠ *1671 Alton Rd.,* ☎ *305/534–2433. AE, MC, V.*

$–$$ ✕ **Van Dyke Café.** Just as its parent, News Café, draws the fashion crowd, this offshoot attracts the artsy crowd. Of course, tourists like it, too. In the restored 1924 Van Dyke Hotel, this place seems even livelier than its Ocean Drive counterpart, with pedestrians passing by on the Lincoln Road Mall and live jazz playing upstairs every evening. The kitchen serves three meals daily, featuring dishes from mammoth omelets with home fries to soups and grilled dolphin sandwiches to basil-grilled lamb and pasta dishes. There's an impressive list of wines and desserts. ⊠ *846 Lincoln Rd.,* ☎ *305/534–3600. AE, DC, MC, V.*

Cuban

$$–$$$$ ✕ **Yuca.** Top-flight Cuban dining can be had at this bistro-chic restau-
★ rant on Lincoln Road. Yuca, the potatolike staple of Cuban kitchens, also stands for the kind of Young Urban Cuban-Americans who frequent the place. The food rises to high standards: traditional corn tamales filled with conch and a spicy jalapeño and creole cheese pesto, the namesake yuca stuffed with *mamacita's picadillo* and dressed in wild mushrooms on a bed of sautéed spinach, and plantain-coated dolphin with a tamarind tartar sauce. Featured desserts include classic Cuban rice pudding in an almond basket and coconut pudding in its shell. Friday- and Saturday-evening entertainment is provided by Albita, a popular Cuban chanteuse. ⊠ *501 Lincoln Rd.,* ☎ *305/532–9822. AE, DC, MC, V.*

Delicatessen

$ ✕ **Wolfie's.** If there's one place in Miami that screams New York, this is it. A bakery featuring giga-caloric desserts, steaming bowls of matzo ball soup, and sandwiches stacked high with pastrami make you feel like you're eating in Brooklyn. If you want to see what Miami looked like 40 years ago, sidle up to the counter or share a round booth in Celebrity Corner. Open 24 hours, this is a perfect place to soak up some local color or satisfy a late-night craving for corned beef. ⊠ *2038 Collins Ave.,* ☎ *305/538–6626. D, DC, MC, V.*

Eclectic

$$$$ ✕ **Blue Door at Delano.** In a hotel where style reigns supreme, service
★ and meals at its restaurant are in fact quite good. Acclaimed chef Claude Troisgros combines the flavors of classic French cuisine with South American influences to create dishes like the Big Raviole, filled with taro-root mousseline and white-truffle oil, and *boeuf au manioc* (a beef tenderloin in a cabernet sauce and yuca biscuit). The dessert menu showcases such selections as a Brazilian coffee and sweet chocolate mousse as well as banana puff pastry with strawberries and cin-

namon. Equally pleasing is dining with the crème de la crème of Miami (and New York and Paris) society. *Bon appétit!* ⊠ *1685 Collins Ave.,* ☎ *305/674–6400. Reservations essential. AE, D, DC, MC, V.*

$$$–$$$$ ✕ **Astor Place.** The Hotel Astor had already earned a reputation for
★ exceptional service, so it was only natural that its basement-turned-bright-and-airy-restaurant followed suit. Chef Johnny Vinzencz wows diners with his "New Floridian Barbecue," centered on grilled meats, tropical fruits, and such Floridian ingredients as *boniato* (a big, white, potatolike tuber) and stone crab. He puts creative spins on appetizers like yellowtail snapper soft tacos and entrées that include ancho-cinnamon pork tenderloin and skillet-steamed sea bass. Critics nationwide have admired the signature short stack of wild-mushroom pancakes drizzled with balsamic syrup. The lunch menu is just as interesting as dinner's. ⊠ *956 Washington Ave.,* ☎ *305/672–7217. AE, DC, MC, V.*

$$$–$$$$ ✕ **China Grill.** This crowded, noisy place has no view, but that doesn't
★ detract from its popularity or that of the original China Grill in New York. Jack Nicholson, Joe Pesci, and other celebs are regulars—perhaps hoping to live the dream of finishing the Grill's 38-ounce porterhouse steak. Contrary to what you might think, chef Ephraim Kadish turns out not Chinese food but rather "world cuisine," in portions large and meant for sharing. Crispy duck with caramelized black vinegar sauce and scallion pancakes is a nice surprise, as is pork and beans with green apple and balsamic mojo. Don't miss the broccoli rabe dumpling starter, the wild-mushroom pasta entrée, or the flash-fried crispy spinach that shatters when eaten. ⊠ *404 Washington Ave.,* ☎ *305/ 534–2211. AE, DC, MC, V. No lunch Sat.*

$$$–$$$$ ✕ **Nemo.** Back in 1994, chef Michael Schwartz took a chance open-
★ ing this restaurant in the struggling south end of SoBe. Today, however, Nemo is receiving raves from gourmands, and the neighborhood—fueled by luxury condominium and hotel projects—is emerging as SoBe's next hot spot. So get here while you can still find a table. The open-air atmosphere, bright colors, copper fixtures, and tree-shaded courtyard lend casual comfort, and a menu that blends Caribbean, Japanese, and Southeast Asian influences promises an explosion of cultures in each bite. Popular appetizers include garlic-cured salmon rolls with *tabiko* caviar and wasabi mayo and crispy prawns with spicy salsa *cruda*. Favorite entrées? Try the wok-charred salmon or the grilled Indian-spiced pork chop—and there's more where those came from. Nemo also serves up a terrific Sunday brunch. ⊠ *100 Collins Ave.,* ☎ *305/532–4550. AE, MC, V.*

$$$–$$$$ ✕ **Pacific Time.** Packed nearly every night, this superb eatery owned
★ by chef Jonathan Eismann has a high blue ceiling and banquettes, accents of mahogany and brass, plank floors, and an open-window kitchen. The brilliant American-Asian cuisine includes such entrées as cedar-roasted salmon, rosemary-roasted chicken, and dry-aged Colorado beef grilled with shiitake mushrooms. The cuttlefish appetizer and the Florida pompano entrée are masterpieces. Rice dishes, potatoes, and vegetables are à la carte; however, a pretheater prix-fixe dinner ($20), served 6–7, comes with a noodle dish, Szechuan mixed grill, and grilled ginger chicken. Desserts (around $7) include a fresh pear-pecan spring roll. There's an extensive California wine list. Pacific Time/Next Door, a casual satellite restaurant a door to the west, has the same excellent food and service for a bit less. ⊠ *915 Lincoln Rd.,* ☎ *305/534–5979. AE, DC, MC, V.*

$–$$ ✕ **Balan's.** The British are coming, all right—to Lincoln Road and this low-priced, stylish spot. However, aside from breakfast and desserts, this outpost of an English chain bears scant stamp of the mother country. Instead, a fusion of Mediterranean, Middle Eastern, and Thai delights the fashionable crowd here. Try deep-fried goat cheese and mushrooms in a beer and caraway bread crust; Moroccan chicken with a spicy, spicy sauce; sea bass over oven-roasted Italian tomatoes and sautéed potato slices; or sirloin steak with balsamic glaze and black lentils. The place is especially busy at breakfast. ⊠ *1022 Lincoln Rd.,* ☎ *305/534–9191. AE, D, MC, V.*

Italian

$$–$$$ ✕ **Mezzanotte.** Sometime between 6 and 10, this big square room with a square bar transforms from an empty catering hall to a New Year's Eve party. Many weekend nights you'll see guests—and staff—dancing on tabletops. Trendoids call for cappellini with fresh tomato and basil; calamari in clam juice, garlic, and red wine; or scallopini with mushroom, pepper, and white wine. In the off-season lobster specials are a great deal. Top off your meal with a *dolci* such as a fresh napoleon, chocolate mousse, or tiramisu. Chic and intimate, Mezzanotte is known for fine food at moderate prices. ⊠ *1200 Washington Ave.,* ☎ *305/673–4343;* ⊠ *3390 Mary St., Coconut Grove,* ☎ *305/ 448–7677. AE, D, DC, MC, V. No lunch in Miami Beach.*

$$–$$$ ✕ **Osteria del Teatro.** Thanks to word of mouth, this northern Italian
★ restaurant is constantly full. Orchids grace the tables in the intimate gray-on-gray room with a low laced-canvas ceiling, Deco lamps, and the most refined clink and clatter along Washington Avenue's remarkable restaurant row. You'll start with large hunks of homemade bread lightly toasted. Then try an appetizer such as grilled Portobello mushrooms topped with fontina cheese and served over a bed of arugula with a green peppercorn–brandy sauce. For the main course, one standout is the linguine sautéed with chunks of jumbo shrimp, roasted peppers, capers, black olives, fresh diced tomato, and herbs in a tangy garlic–olive oil sauce. ⊠ *1443 Washington Ave.,* ☎ *305/538– 7850. AE, DC, MC, V. Closed Tues. No lunch.*

$$–$$$ ✕ **Spiga.** When you need a break from Miami's abundant exotic fare, savor the modestly priced Italian standards that are served with flair in this small, pretty place. Homemade is the hallmark here, and pastas and breads are fresh daily. Carpaccio *di salmone* (thinly sliced salmon with mixed greens) is a typical appetizer, and the *zuppa di pesce* (fish soup) is unparalleled. Entrées include ravioli *di vitello ai funghi shitaki,* homemade ravioli stuffed with veal and sautéed with shiitake mushrooms. The cozy restaurant has become a neighborhood favorite where customers sometimes bring in CDs for their personal enjoyment. ⊠ *1228 Collins Ave.,* ☎ *305/534–0079. AE, D, DC, MC, V.*

Mexican

$–$$ ✕ **El Rancho Grande.** The location (just off Lincoln Road) and the menu (mainstream Mexican) have made this neighborhood restaurant popular with locals and earned it a slew of "best" awards in area dining polls. Prices are reasonable, and service is casual and laid-back. Beef *flautas,* chicken enchiladas, *taquitas,* and more are served in a cantina-style setting. This is a good option for a quick and inexpensive meal. ⊠ *1626 Pennsylvania Ave.,* ☎ *305/673–0480. AE, MC, V.*

Pan-Asian

$$ ✕ **Noodles of Asia (NOA).** This inexpensive house of noodles once again proves that South Beach takes style seriously. Green-glass etchings, stained wood ceilings, gleaming metal stairwell walls, brushed metal stairs, and burlap-covered booths all contribute to a modern-art-museum look. Food is similarly artistic, but portions can be scant. All entrées feature some sort of noodle, representing a pan-Asian array from Malaysia, China, Thailand, Vietnam, Japan, and other countries. Most dishes are rather spicy, and some are fantastic: smoky pork dumplings, Vietnamese-style grape leaves with beef and lemongrass, Thai beef salad. Various sorbets are the best choices for dessert. ⊠ *801 Lincoln Rd.,* ☎ *305/925–0050. AE, MC, V.*

Seafood

$$$–$$$$ ✕ **Joe's Stone Crab Restaurant.** "Before SoBe, Joe Be," touts this fourth-generation family restaurant with a chest-puffing facade at the base of Washington Avenue. Joe's attracts phenomenal crowds despite stubbornly refusing reservations, so go prepared to wait—up to an hour to register for a table, perhaps another *three* to sit down. Depending on the crowd, the wait can be convivial or contentious. The centerpiece of the menu is, of course, stone crab: About a ton of claws are served daily with drawn butter, lemon wedges, and piquant mustard sauce. Save room for dessert—key lime pie or apple pie with a crumbpecan topping. If you can't stand loitering hungrily while self-important patrons try to grease the maître d's palm, go next door for Joe's takeout. ⊠ *227 Biscayne St.,* ☎ *305/673–0365; 305/673–4611 for takeout; 800/780–2722 for overnight shipping. Reservations not accepted. AE, D, DC, MC, V. Closed Sept. 1–Oct. 15. No lunch Sun.–Mon.*

$–$$$ ✕ **Grillfish.** An eclectic crowd of over-it locals and Bermuda-shorted tourists get along happily at this dramatically Deco-style spot in the heart of South Beach. They watch as delicacies emerge from a busy, open, stainless-steel kitchen. Delicious takes on grilled fish grace the tables—perhaps simple grilled tuna, seared outside, rosy pink inside, and just how you like it. Or get the seafood quesadilla if it's available. Some of the world's best fried calamari, with marinara, shows up, and squid over pasta with marinara is a tasty bargain. ⊠ *1444 Collins Ave.,* ☎ *305/538–9908. AE, DC, MC, V.*

Thai

$$ ✕ **Thai Toni.** Enjoy upscale dining in an exceptional restaurant with bamboo floors and teakwood tables that bring to mind Laos, Vietnam, and other Southeast Asian countries. Mellow Thai Singha beer complements the spicy jumping squid appetizer with chili paste and hot pepper or the hot, hot pork. Choose from a large variety of inexpensive noodle, fried-rice, and vegetarian dishes or such traditional entrées as beef and broccoli, basil duck, or hot-and-spicy deep-fried whole snapper with basil leaves and mixed vegetables. Fresh whole fish fillets are specialties. The homemade lemonade is distinctly tart. ⊠ *890 Washington Ave.,* ☎ *305/538–8424. AE, MC, V. No lunch.*

South Miami

Seafood

$$–$$$$ ✕ **Captain's Tavern.** This family fish house has an unusually interesting menu fortified with Caribbean and South American influences. The decor may be hokey, with paneled walls and witty sayings on plaques hung here and there, but the food can fascinate. Beyond good versions of the typical fare—conch chowder and conch fritters—you'll find a Portuguese fish stew, fish with various tropical fruits, a delightful black-bean soup, and oysters in cream sauce with fresh rosemary, not to mention decadent desserts. ⊠ *7495 S.E. 98th St.,* ☎ *305/661–4237. AE, MC, V.*

Thai

$–$$ ✕ **Siam Lotus Room.** This aqua-color piece of motel architecture isn't much to look at, but it's great eating; in fact, it's one of South Florida's best Thai restaurants. Jump at the chance to eat spicy jumping squid and savory, coconut-silky *tom kar pla,* a fish soup. Spicy bamboo shoots with shrimp, beef, chicken, and pork is fantastic, as is a bubbly yellow curry. All the other basics are here, from basil, garlic, and red-curry treatments for various meats to whole fried snapper. For dessert the Thai donut makes a light-sweet finish. Try it with thick, creamy Thai iced coffee. ⊠ *6388 S. Dixie Hwy.,* ☎ *305/666–8134. AE, MC, V.*

West Miami

Chinese

$–$$ ✕ **Tropical Chinese Restaurant.** This big, lacquer-free room feels as open and busy as a railway station. You'll find unfamiliar items on the menu—early spring leaves of snow pea pods, for example, which are sublimely tender and flavorful. The extensive menu is filled with tofu combinations, poultry, beef, and pork, as well as tender seafood. A dim sum lunch is served from great carts. In the big, open kitchen 10 chefs prepare everything as if for dignitaries. ⊠ *7991 S.W. 40th St.,* ☎ *305/ 262–7576 or 305/262–1552. AE, DC, MC, V.*

LODGING

Few urban areas can match Greater Miami's diversity of accommodations. South Beach alone had more than 2,000 rooms, even before the 1998 arrival of the Loews Miami Beach Hotel boosted that number by another 800. Miami offers hundreds of hotels, motels, resorts, spas, and B&Bs, with prices ranging from $12 a night in a dormitory-style hostel to $2,000 a night in a luxurious presidential suite (if you can swing it, take the suite). Although some hotels (especially on the mainland) have adopted steady year-round rates, many adjust their rates to reflect seasonal demand. The peak occurs in winter, with a dip in summer (prices are often more negotiable than rate cards let on).

You'll find the best values between Easter and Memorial Day (which is actually a delightful time in Miami but a difficult time for many people to travel) and in September and October (the height of hurricane season). Keep in mind that Miami hoteliers collect roughly 12.5%—ouch—for city and resort taxes; parking fees can run up to $16 per evening; and tips for bellhops, valet parkers, concierges, and housekeepers add to the expense. Some hotels actually tack on an automatic 15% gratuity. All told, you can easily spend 25% more than your room rate to sleep in Miami.

Coconut Grove

$$$$ ★ 🏨 **Grand Bay Hotel.** Combining the classical elegance of Greece, a stepped facade that looks vaguely Aztec, a hint of the South, and a brush of the tropical, this hotel is like no other in South Florida. Guest rooms are filled with superb touches, such as antique sideboards that hold house phones and matched woods variously inlaid and fluted. Whoopi, Schwarzenegger, and Willis have all stayed here, perhaps enjoying the easterly views that look over the bay. Afternoon tea is served. ⊠ *2669 S. Bayshore Dr., 33133,* ☎ *305/858–9600 or 800/327–2788,* FAX *305/ 859–2026. 132 rooms, 49 suites. Restaurant, 2 bars, pool, beauty salon, hot tub, massage, saunas, health club, concierge. AE, DC, MC, V.*

$$$$ 🏨 **Mayfair House.** This European-style luxury hotel sits within the Streets of Mayfair, an exclusive open-air shopping mall just steps from the heart of the Grove. A cross between a business hotel and romantic getaway, it has public areas done in Art Nouveau instead of Art Deco. Soft, flowing lines are reflected in Tiffany windows, polished mahogany, marble, imported ceramics and crystal, and an impressive glassed-in elevator. The individually furnished suites have outdoor terraces fac-

Miami Area Lodging

KEY

AE American Express Office

N

ATLANTIC OCEAN

MIAMI BEACH

NORTH MIAMI BEACH

NORTH MIAMI

Miami Gdns. Dr.
Miami Gdns. Dr.

N. Miami Beach Blvd.
Biscayne Blvd.
Broad Causeway
Collins Ave.
Collins Ave.

JFK Causeway
Julia Tuttle Causeway

Florida's Turnpike
Palmetto Expwy.
Palmetto Expwy.
Robert Frost Expwy.
Okeechobee Rd.
Gratigny Rd.
Red Rd.
Hialeah Dr.
Dairy Rd.

N.E. 6th Ave.
N.E. 2nd Ave.
N. Miami Ave.
N.W. 7th Ave.
N.W. 27th Ave.
N.W. 135th St.
N.W. 8th Ave.
W. 4th Ave.
W. 49th St.
N.W. 72nd Ave.
N.W. 39th St.
N.W. 58th St.
N.W. 87th Ave.

135th St.
N.E. 103d St.
N.E. 95th St.
N.W. 103d St.
N.W. 95th St.
N.W. 79th St.
N.W. 62nd St.
N.W. 54th St.
N.W. 36th St.
N.W. 20th St.
E. 25th St.
E. 49th St.

Miami River
Miami International

826
856
441
860
826
817
75
441
909
915
A1A
195
27
27
27
9
944
932

The Albion, **18**
Alexander Hotel, **7**
Banana Bungalow, **12**
Bay Harbor Inn, **6**
Bayliss, **20**
Biltmore Hotel, **36**
Cadet Hotel, **12**
Cardozo, **23**

Casa Grande, **30**
Cavalier, **22**
Days Inn Convention Center, **13**
Delano Hotel, **16**
Don Shula's Hotel & Golf Club, **5**
Doral Golf Resort and Spa, **32**

Eden Roc, **9**
Essex House, **28**
Fontainebleau Hilton Resort and Towers, **11**
Grand Bay Hotel, **38**
Hotel Astor, **29**
Hotel Impala, **24**

Hotel Place St. Michel, **35**
Hyatt Regency Miami, **33**
Indian Creek Hotel, **10**
Kenmore, **27**
Loews Miami Beach Hotel, **19**

Mayfair House, **37**
Nassau Suite Hotel, **21**
National Hotel, **17**
Newport Beachside Resort, **4**
Ocean Front Hotel, **25**
Pelican, **31**

Raleigh Hotel, **14**
Sheraton Biscayne Bay, **34**
Sonesta Beach Resort Key Biscayne, **39**
Suez Oceanfront Resort, **3**
Thunderbird, **2**

The Tides, **26**
Turnberry Isle Resort & Club, **1**
Wyndham Miami Beach Resort, **8**

ing the street, screened by vegetation and wood latticework. Each has a relatively small Japanese hot tub on the balcony or a Roman tub inside, and 10 have antique pianos. A rooftop recreation area is peaceful (although the miniature lap pool is odd for such a large hotel), and the quiet Orchid Bar, a ground-floor lounge, attracts a trendy clientele. If you can't sleep, go downstairs and chat with the 24-hour concierge. ⊠ *3000 Florida Ave., 33133,* ☎ *305/441–0000 or 800/433–4555,* 𝔽𝔸𝕏 *305/447–9173. 179 suites. Restaurant, bar, snack bar, pool, hot tubs, sauna, concierge. AE, D, DC, MC, V.*

Coral Gables

$$$$ 🖬 **Biltmore Hotel.** Miami's grand boom-time hotel has undergone two
★   renovations since 1986 but still manages to recapture a bygone era. Now owned by the city of Coral Gables and operated by Westin, the 1926 Biltmore rises like a sienna-color wedding cake in the heart of a residential district. The vaulted lobby has hand-painted rafters on a twinkling sky-blue background. Large guest rooms are done in a restrained Moorish style, and for slightly more than the average rate ($2,550) you can book the Everglades (a.k.a. Al Capone) Suite—President Clinton's room when he's in town. Each month a visiting French chef drops by to surprise diners and teach Biltmore chefs something new, and the Cellar Club offers fine wines and premium cigars. ⊠ *1200 Anastasia Ave., 33134,* ☎ *305/445–1926 or 800/727–1926,* 𝔽𝔸𝕏 *305/913–3159. 237 rooms, 38 suites. Restaurant, bar, café, pool, sauna, spa, 18-hole golf course, 10 lighted tennis courts, health club, concierge, meeting rooms. AE, DC, MC, V.*

$$–$$$ 🖬 **Hotel Place St. Michel.** Art Nouveau chandeliers suspended from
★   vaulted ceilings grace the public areas of this intimate boutique hotel in the heart of downtown. Built in 1926, the historic low-rise was restored between 1981 and 1986 and yet again after a 1995 fire. Within easy walking distance of the Miracle Mile, the charming inn is filled with the scent of fresh flowers, circulated by paddle fans. Its fine restaurant is an undeniable asset. Each room has its own dimensions, personality, and antiques imported from England, Scotland, and France, although plusher beds would be a more welcome accent. A complimentary Continental breakfast is served. ⊠ *162 Alcazar Ave., 33134,* ☎ *305/444–1666 or 800/848–4683,* 𝔽𝔸𝕏 *305/529–0074. 24 rooms, 3 suites. Restaurant, bar. AE, DC, MC, V.*

Downtown Miami

$$$–$$$$ 🖬 **Sheraton Biscayne Bay.** When you arrive at the entrance, you'll have a hard time believing that this waterfront establishment is on busy Brickell Avenue. A short drive through a grove of oak trees will calm you down. As at most large hotels, the lobby is designed for business (as is the conference center) and features a bar, restaurant, and gift shop, but the back patio and green space softens the experience. Rooms have all the accoutrements you'd expect: irons, hair dryers, voice mail. Thank management for providing self-parking for those who want it (valets are standing by), although you will pay a fee. ⊠ *495 Brickell Ave., 33131,* ☎ *305/373–6000 or 800/284–2000,* 𝔽𝔸𝕏 *305/374–2279. 598 rooms, 14 suites. Restaurant, bar, pool, exercise room, meeting rooms, parking (fee). AE, DC, MC, V.*

$$–$$$$ 🖬 **Hyatt Regency Miami.** The blend of leisure and business has positioned the Hyatt well for the downtown renaissance that began with the opening of the new Miami Avenue Bridge in 1996 and continues with the upsurge in business at the Port of Miami and the arrival of the American Airlines Arena. If your vacation is based on boats, basketball, or business, you can't do much better. The distinctive public spaces are more colorful than businesslike, and guest rooms are done in an unusual combination of avocado, beige, and blond. Rooms yield views of the river or port, and not surprisingly the best ones occupy the upper floors. The James L. Knight International Center is accessible without stepping outside, as is the downtown Metromover and its Metrorail connection. ⊠ *400 S.E. 2nd Ave., 33131,* ☎ *305/358–1234,* FAX *305/358–0529. 615 rooms, 25 suites. Restaurant, bar, pool. AE, D, DC, MC, V.*

Key Biscayne

$$$$ 🏨 **Sonesta Beach Resort Key Biscayne.** This excellent resort with a great
★ seaside setting is now more tropical than ever, offering stunning sea views from east-facing units. Rooms are done in a sand tone with fabrics in emerald, purple, gold, and ruby. Villas are actually three-bedroom homes with full kitchen and screened pool. The property's size, Olympic pool, activities, and Just Us Kids program (9 AM–10 PM) make it a good family getaway. Don't miss the museum-quality modern art, especially Andy Warhol's drawings of rock star Mick Jagger in the hotel's disco bar, Desires. The 750-ft beach, one of Florida's best, has a wide variety of recreational opportunities, including catamarans and sailing lessons. ⊠ *350 Ocean Dr., 33149,* ☎ *305/361–2021 or 800/766–3782,* FAX *305/361–3096. 284 rooms, 15 suites, 3 villas. 3 restaurants, 3 bars, snack bar, pool, massage, steam rooms, 9 tennis courts (3 lighted), aerobics, health club, beach, windsurfing, parasailing, children's program. AE, D, DC, MC, V.*

Miami Beach North of South Beach

$$$$ 🏨 **Alexander Hotel.** Amid the high-rises of the mid-Beach district, this
★ 16-story hotel exemplifies the elegance of Miami Beach. It has immense suites furnished with antiques and reproductions, each with a terrace yielding ocean or bay views and each with a living and dining room, kitchen, and two baths. The beachside Aqua Sports Center provides wave runners, catamarans, paddleboats, and volleyball courts. With the addition of the Aveda salon and an outpost of Shula's Steak House, you can pamper your body and your appetite without leaving the property. Beware of mandatory gratuities attached to everything from valet parking to bellhop and maid service to deliveries. ⊠ *5225 Collins Ave., 33140,* ☎ *305/865–6500 or 800/327–6121,* FAX *305/341–6553. 150 1- and 2-bedroom suites. Restaurant, coffee shop, 2 pools, beauty salon, exercise room, volleyball, beach, dock, boating, jet skiing. AE, D, DC, MC, V.*

$$$$ 🏨 **Eden Roc.** Who knows why this grand 1950s hotel designed by Morris Lapidus is overshadowed by the larger, more prominent Fontainebleau (☞ *below*)? From the moment you enter, the free-flowing lines of its nautical Deco architecture make you feel casual and comfortable. In the late '90s a major renovation added three new ballrooms and meeting facilities, as well as an indoor basketball court and a rock-climbing wall for fitness and motivation. The resort's yacht is available for oceangoing meetings. The 55,000-square-ft Spa of Eden usually runs full tilt, while Dolphins coach Jimmy Johnson's beachside sports bar caters to those who prefer lifting weights 16 ounces at a time. Rooms blend a touch of the '50s with informal '90s elegance. ⊠ *4525 Collins Ave., 33140,* ☎ *305/531–0000 or 800/327–8337,* FAX *305/674–5555. 346 rooms. 2 restaurants, sports bar, pool, massage, spa, basketball, exercise room, racquetball, meeting rooms. AE, MC, V.*

$$$$ 🏨 **Fontainebleau Hilton Resort and Towers.** This big, busy, and ornate grand dame is scheduled to wrap up a complete overhaul by 2000. Corridors, guest rooms, suites, pools, recreation areas, and the building's

exterior have been spiffed up with new carpet, wall coverings, lighting, and furnishings. Tower rooms, already luxurious, are now even more exclusive, with upgraded linens, multiline phones, fax, minibars, a personal concierge, and Italian marble baths. Room decor varies throughout the property, from the 1950s to contemporary—very contemporary. Even the smallest room is large by Miami standards, as are the convention facilities, which rank second only to the city-owned convention center. A 40,000-square-ft beachside spa is ideal for self-indulgence. Guests enjoy complimentary admission to the hotel's *Club Tropigala*, a Vegas-style floor show with a Latin twist. ⊠ *4441 Collins Ave., 33140,* ☎ *305/538–2000 or 800/548–8886,* ⅢⅨ *305/531–9274. 1,146 rooms, 60 suites. 12 restaurants, 3 bars, 2 pools, saunas, spa, 7 lighted tennis courts, health club, volleyball, beach, windsurfing, boating, parasailing, children's programs, convention center. AE, D, DC, MC, V.*

$$$$ 🏨 **Wyndham Miami Beach Resort.** Of the great Miami Beach hotels,
★   this 18-story glass tower remains a standout. A renovation completed in 1998 upgraded the lobby, pool, facade, sleeping rooms, meeting rooms, and landscaping. Warm-tone guest rooms are filled with nice details: mini-refrigerator; three layers of drapes, including blackout curtains; big closets; and bathrooms with high-quality toiletries and a magnifying mirror. Two presidential suites were designed in consultation with the Secret Service, and a rooftop meeting room offers views of bay and ocean. Free transportation to Doral Golf Resort and Spa is provided. ⊠ *4833 Collins Ave., 33140,* ☎ *305/532–3600 or 800/203–8368,* ⅢⅨ *305/534–7409. 378 rooms, 46 suites. 2 restaurants, 2 bars, pool, tennis court, exercise room, beach, helipad, meeting rooms. AE, D, DC, MC, V.*

$$–$$$$ 🏨 **Indian Creek Hotel.** Not as grand as the North Beach behemoths or as hectic as the Ocean Drive offerings, this 1936 Pueblo Deco jewel may just be Miami's most charming and sincere lodge—and it gets nicer every year. Owner Marc Levin rescued the inn by adding a cozy dining room with an eclectic and appetizing menu, relandscaping a lush pool and garden, and restoring rooms using Deco furniture, much of it discovered in the basement. Items were cleaned, reupholstered, and put on display, helping the hotel win the Miami Design Preservation League's award for outstanding restoration. Suites have refrigerators, cable TV, VCR/CD players, and modem capabilities; safe-deposit boxes are available. The hotel restaurant now flows outside to a secluded poolside dining area—yet another comforting touch. Stay a while, and manager Zammy Migdal and his staff will have you feeling like family. ⊠ *2727 Indian Creek Dr., 33140,* ☎ *305/531–2727,* ⅢⅨ *305/531–5651. 61 rooms. Restaurant, pool, concierge. AE, D, DC, MC, V.*

North Miami, North Miami Beach, and North Dade

$$$$ 🏨 **Turnberry Isle Resort & Club.** Finest of the grand resorts, Turnberry
★   is a tapestry of islands and waterways on 300 superbly landscaped acres by the bay. Choose from the Yacht Club, on the Intracoastal Waterway; the intimate Marina Hotel; a beautiful three-wing Mediterranean-style annex; and the Addison Mizner–style Country Club Hotel. Oversize rooms have light woods and earth tones, large curving terraces, Jacuzzis, honor bars, and safes. The marina has moorings for 117 boats up to 150 ft long, there's a free shuttle to the beach club and the Aventura Mall, and Robert Trent Jones stopped by to design two tropical golf courses. A new seven-story building, adding 128 rooms, offices, and a terrace restaurant, opens in 1999. ⊠ *19999 W. Country Club Dr., Aventura 33180,* ☎ *305/936–2929 or 800/223-6800,* ⅢⅨ *305/933–6560. 300 rooms, 40 suites. 7 restaurants, 5 bars, 4 pools,*

saunas, spa, steam rooms, driving range, 2 18-hole golf courses, 24 tennis courts (18 lighted), health club, jogging, racquetball, beach, dive shop, docks, windsurfing, boating, helipad. AE, D, DC, MC, V.

$$$–$$$$ 🏨 **Bay Harbor Inn.** Although the inn's not on the ocean, the tranquil Indian Creek flowing outside is sure to soothe. Rooms with queen- and king-size beds are quite pleasant, baths are large, and you receive a complimentary breakfast each morning. One of the nicest features is your own front porch, where you can sit with a book or drink or both and view the village of Bal Harbour, just a five-minute walk away. The restaurant here (Islands) is very nice, but it's also pleasant to walk around the corner to a small Italian restaurant (Da Vinci's) or over the bridge to Surfside for a wider selection of neighborhood bars and eateries. One caveat: The hotel staff is largely composed of students from Johnson & Wales University, so service is enthusiastic but not flawlessly professional. ⊠ *9601 E. Bayshore Dr., Bal Harbour 33154,* ☎ *305/868–4141,* FAX *305/867–9094. 22 rooms, 23 suites. Restaurant, bar, pool. AE, DC, MC, V.*

$$$–$$$$ 🏨 **Newport Beachside Resort.** The nicest place to stay in Sunny Isles,
★ and more upscale than most, is this combination time share/hotel. While mom or dad is in Miami on business, the family can enjoy the beach and the plentiful activities. Check out the fishing pier, the kids' center (with diversions from painting to videos), or the midday calypso entertainment. The pool area is perfectly suited for enjoying the sun, and the large, bright lobby is brightened further by colorful macaws. The tropical rooms feature king-size beds, mini-refrigerators, and microwaves; one- and two-bedroom suites are similar but are much larger and include a marble bath. The resort even has a travel agency, though once you check in you'll never have to leave. ⊠ *16701 Collins Ave., Sunny Isles 33160,* ☎ *305/949–1300 or 800 327–5476,* FAX *305/947–5873. 300 rooms, 20 suites. Restaurant, sports bar, pool, wading pool, exercise room, beach, dive shop, jet skiing, fishing, nightclub, concierge, meeting rooms, travel services. AE, DC, MC, V.*

$$$ 🏨 **Don Shula's Hotel & Golf Club.** This low-rise resort is part of Miami Lakes, a planned town about 14 mi northwest of downtown. Opened in 1962, the golf club includes a championship course, a lighted executive course, and a golf school. All club rooms have balconies, and the theme is English traditional, rich in leather and wood. The hotel, on the other hand, has a typical Florida-tropics look—light pastels and furniture of wicker and light wood. In both locations the best rooms are near the lobby for convenient access; ask for a room away from the elevators. Sixteen executive two-bedroom suites (geared for extended stays) were opened in early 1999. ⊠ *6840 Main St., Miami Lakes 33014,* ☎ *305/821–1150 or 800/247–4852,* FAX *305/820–8190. 269 rooms, 32 suites. 5 restaurants, 2 bars, 2 pools, saunas, steam rooms, driving range, 2 golf courses, 9 lighted tennis courts, aerobics, basketball, health club, racquetball, volleyball. AE, DC, MC, V.*

$$–$$$ 🏨 **Thunderbird.** One of the nicest finds in North Beach, this hotel is well priced for such a clean and neat place. Right off the bat the lobby—warmer than Deco and with an attractive chandelier and staircase—puts you at ease. The good vibes continue in the rooms, done in a typical Miami tropical floral style but particularly bright, especially those that open to the courtyard. Accommodating four people at no extra charge, rooms include a mini-refrigerator; a few efficiencies are also available. Outdoors is even more appealing. The tropical courtyard, tennis courts, and an Olympic-size pool create a miniature oasis, and the tiki bar is a perfect place to watch the waves. A supermarket across the street is an added convenience. ⊠ *18401 Collins Ave., North Miami Beach 33139,* ☎ *305/931–7700 or 800/327–2044,* FAX *305/932–7521. 180 rooms. Restaurant, 2 bars, 2 pools, beauty salon,*

2 *tennis courts, exercise room, coin laundry, dry cleaning. AE, D, DC, MC, V.*

$$ ☒ **Suez Oceanfront Resort.** Several miles north of Miami Beach, along what's known as Motel Row, the carousel-striped, family-run Suez stands out from the area's pricier but nondescript motels. Look beyond the tacky sphinx statuary to the quiet, gardenlike lounge and the landscaped palm courtyard. Rooms have Chinese-style furniture and dazzling color, offsetting generally small spaces. Those in the north wing, with parking-lot views, are the smallest and least expensive. Modified American Plan availability, refrigerators in all rooms, kitchens in some, free laundry service, and special kids' rates make this an especially good value, popular with Europeans. ☒ *18215 Collins Ave., Sunny Isles 33160,* ☎ *305/932–0661 or 800/327–5278; 800/432–3661 in FL;* ℻ *305/937–0058. 196 rooms. Restaurant, bar, freshwater and saltwater pools, wading pool, lighted tennis court, shuffleboard, volleyball, beach, playground, laundry service. AE, DC, MC, V.*

South Beach

$$$$ ☒ **The Albion.** The owners of this resurrected hotel just off Lincoln Road brought it back in style, hiring Carlos Zapata to update the 1939 nautical Art Deco building by Igor Polevitzky. The focal point is a two-story lobby, which sweeps into a secluded courtyard and is framed by a flowing indoor waterfall. A prosperous young and young-at-heart crowd of hip but friendly types makes up the clientele; they like to gather at the mezzanine-level pool, which is unusual for its depth (9 ft), its artificial beach (Florida's first), and portholes that allow courtyard strollers an underwater view of swimmers. The blond-wood Fallabella Bar recalls the styling of Heywood-Wakefield, and the Pantry offers breakfast and sandwiches overlooking the pool or lobby. Guest rooms are minimalist in design though filled with what travelers expect: data ports, two-line phones, minibars, and stereos. The owners of the chic Cuban restaurant Yuca (☞ Dining, *above*) also run Maya, the restaurant here. ☒ *1650 James Ave., Miami Beach 33139,* ☎ *305/913–1000 or 888/665–0008,* ℻ *305/674–0507. 85 rooms, 9 suites. 2 restaurants, bar, pool, exercise room. AE, D, DC, MC, V.*

$$$$ ☒ **Casa Grande.** The first of SoBe's new top-flight hotels, this is still
★ one of the best, with the level of quality characteristic of Chris Blackwell's other five Island Outpost hotels in Miami: the Tides and the Cavalier (☞ *below*), the Leslie, the Marlin, and the Kent. The lobby's teak, tile, and recessed lighting create a warm and relaxing look. Luxurious suites capture the fashionable air of Ocean Drive yet reflect fine taste. Done in Balinese-inspired teak and mahogany, units have dhurrie rugs, beautiful Indonesian fabrics and artifacts, two-poster beds with ziggurat turns, full kitchens with fine European utensils, and large baths—practically unheard of in the Deco District—adorned with green decorator tiles. Goodies range from a daily newspaper and in-room coffee to fresh flowers and evening turndown with Italian chocolates. Insulated windows keep the noise from Ocean Drive revelers at bay. Book early for peak periods. ☒ *834 Ocean Dr., Miami Beach 33139,* ☎ *305/672–7003 or 800/688–7678,* ℻ *305/673–3669. 34 suites. Café, laundry service and dry cleaning, concierge. AE, D, DC, MC, V.*

$$$$ ☒ **Delano Hotel.** If Calvin Klein had teamed with Salvador Dalí to build
★ a hotel, this weird—really weird—wonderful, and slightly snooty property would be it. Tourists marvel at the lobby hung with massive, white billowing drapes and try to act casual while watching for U2, Elvis Costello, George Clooney, Michael Keaton, and Spike Lee (an actual week's roster of celebrity guests). Fashion models and men of in-

dependent means gather beneath cabanas, pose by the pool, and sniff fragrances wafting in from the orchard. Business travelers are offered comprehensive executive services, guests can access 1,500 videos, and men and women have the run of a rooftop bathhouse and solarium on alternating schedules. Although the standard rooms are of average size, their stark whiteness makes them appear larger. The gift shop carries magazines you wouldn't want your parents to see. The real appeal here is the surrealism. ⊠ *1685 Collins Ave., Miami Beach 33139,* ☎ *305/672–2000 or 800/555–5001,* ℻ *305/532–0099. 184 rooms, 24 suites. Restaurant, bar, pool, spa, health club, business services. AE, D, DC, MC, V.*

$$$$ 🏨 **Loews Miami Beach Hotel.** Miami has been waiting for a major new beachfront luxury hotel for 30 years. Although others have been renovated, this 18-story, 800-room gem was built from the blueprints up. Not only did Loews manage to snag 99 ft of oceanfront, it took over the vacant St. Moritz next door and restored it to its original 1939 Art Deco splendor, adding another 100 rooms to the complex. The resort features kids' programs (SoBe Kids Camp), a health spa, and 85,000 square ft of meeting space with a 28,000-square-ft ocean-view grand ballroom. Dining, too, is a pleasure, courtesy of the Argentinian-inspired Gaucho Room, Preston's SoBe Coffee Bar, and Hemisphere Lounge. But won't someone please do something about those garish uniforms? ⊠ *1601 Collins Ave., Miami Beach 33139,* ☎ *305/604–1601,* ℻ *305/531–8677. 743 rooms, 57 suites. 4 restaurants, 2 bars, lobby lounge, pool, spa, beach, children's programs, meeting rooms. AE, D, DC, MC, V.*

$$$$ 🏨 **National Hotel.** This resurrected 1939 shorefront hotel reopened in 1997 and took a few years to work out the kinks. Miami Beach's longest (205 ft) tropical pool sparkles at night with illuminated messages and logos, and its presence makes a perfect backdrop for the film crews who work here almost daily. With curtains closed, poolside rooms could be generic Holiday Inn, displaying little of the flair of other recent arrivals. Rooms in the main building are far more appealing, however, and the interiors approach a higher level of creativity. Applause is in order for preserved pieces, such as the original dining-room chandelier and furniture, as well as such modern in-room amenities as ironing boards, safes, data ports, and robes. Another notable is the intimate 1930s-style Press Room cigar bar and meeting room. Unfair, however, is the $16-per-day parking fee. ⊠ *1677 Collins Ave., Miami Beach 33139,* ☎ *305/532–2311 or 800/327–8370,* ℻ *305/534–1426. 115 rooms, 39 suites. Restaurant, bar, pool, beach, concierge, meeting rooms, parking (fee). AE, DC, MC, V.*

$$$$ 🏨 **The Tides.** Miami hotels like white, and this one is no exception.
★ The nice twist here is the added features that owner Chris Blackwell introduced with a flawless renovation. Some touches are small—spyglasses in each room (fitting since they all face the ocean), a blackboard for messages to maids. Others are large—every room has a king-size bed, capacious closets, and generous post-Moderne baths, the result of turning 115 rooms into 45 suites. Elvis would have liked the blackout curtains and private VIP entrance. The downstairs lobby is large and austere (and white), and facilities include a reading room, hypercool terrace dining, and a mezzanine pool where women can go topless (total nudity is "undesirable"). Wondering what's happening in the outside world? Request a newspaper, which you can read beside Ocean Drive's only Olympic-size pool. If you're bored with the pool, the entire Atlantic Ocean is a short walk away. This hotel is generating a buzz, so check it out, hipsters. ⊠ *1220 Ocean Dr., Miami Beach 33139,* ☎ *305/604–5000 or 800/688–7678,* ℻ *305/604–5180. 45 suites. Restaurant, café, pool, exercise room. AE, D, DC, MC, V.*

$$$-$$$$ 🏨 **Cardozo.** Perhaps it's because this hotel is owned by Gloria and Emilio Estefan that there's such lively and loud music in the lobby. (Unfortunately, on weekend nights loud music from the disco can still be heard in the otherwise quiet and comfortable rooms.) The Estefans completed the hotel's makeover in 1998, deciding—wisely—to forsake cold tile floors for the warmth of the building's original hardwood. Leopard-print blankets and large baths with mosaic-tile sinks give rooms a warm African tint, but the terra-cotta walls cool things off. Whether you opt for a standard room or suite, you'll have room to spread out. Units feature minibar and TV/VCR/CD, and views from oceanfront rooms are impressive (especially from Number 202). The staff is just as pleasant as the hotel's design. ✉ *1300 Ocean Dr., Miami Beach 33139,* ☎ *305/535–6500,* FAX *305/673–8609. 44 rooms, 7 suites. Restaurant, bar. AE, DC, MC, V.*

$$$-$$$$ 🏨 **Essex House.** Already adequate before renovation, the hotel annexed the building next door and prettied it up with 20 large suites, putting the Essex House well above average. All the work put into the suites, which are reached by crossing a tropical courtyard, has paid off: Each includes a wet bar, king-size bed, pullout sofa, 100-square-ft bathroom, refrigerator, and hot tub. Rooms are no slouches, either. Club chairs, custom carpet and lighting, mahogany entertainment units and matching desks, marble tubs, two phone lines, computer data ports, and voice mail make them like the home office you wish you had built. Although the hotel is in the heart of the city, sound-absorbing windows keep things quiet, just as the free Continental breakfast keeps your stomach quiet, too. ✉ *1001 Collins Ave., Miami Beach 33139,* ☎ *305/534–2700 or 800/553–7739,* FAX *305/532–3827. 59 rooms, 20 suites. Bar, pool. AE, D, DC, MC, V.*

$$$-$$$$ 🏨 **Hotel Astor.** How does yet another Art Deco hotel stand out from ★ the crowd? This one does it by double-insulating walls against noise and offering such luxuries as ambient low-voltage lighting, thick towels, down pillows, paddle fans, and a seductive pool. The renovation also included expansion of guest rooms and baths and the addition of custom-milled French furniture, blackout Roman shades, and sleek sound and video systems. A tasteful, muted color scheme and the most comfortable king-size beds imaginable make for eminently restful rooms, and excellent service eliminates any worries about practical matters. The Astor Place restaurant (☞ Dining, *above*) is exceptional. Those in the know come to be pampered at this lavishly understated hotel two blocks from the frenzy of Ocean Drive. ✉ *956 Washington Ave., Miami Beach 33139,* ☎ *305/531–8081 or 800/270–4981,* FAX *305/531–3193. 40 rooms. Restaurant, bar, pool, massage. AE, MC, V.*

$$$-$$$$ 🏨 **Hotel Impala.** One of the nicest inns in the area, this former store-★ front for drug dealers was reborn in a stunning tropical Mediterranean Revival style that distinguishes it from the Art Deco pack. Iron, mahogany, and stone on the inside are in synch with the sporty white-trim ocher exterior and quiet courtyard. Rooms, among the cleanest in SoBe, are elegant, comfortable, and complete, with a TV/VCR/stereo and a stock of CDs and videos. It's all very European, from mineral water and orchids to the Mediterranean-style armoires, Italian fixtures, heavy ornamental drapery rods, and Spanish surrealist art above white-on-white, triple-sheeted modified Eastlake sleigh beds. Everything from wastebaskets to towels to toilet paper is of extraordinary quality. This place definitely has great *feng shui*. ✉ *1228 Collins Ave., Miami Beach 33139,* ☎ *305/673–2021 or 800/646–7252,* FAX *305/673–5984. 17 rooms, 3 suites. Restaurant, bar. AE, DC, MC, V.*

$$$–$$$$ ⊞ **Ocean Front Hotel.** If the street signs didn't read Ocean Drive, you might suspect you were whiling away the day on the Riviera. The tropical French feel is evident when you enter the shaded, bougainvillea-draped courtyard and see diners enjoying a complimentary casual breakfast in the hotel's brasserie. Two buildings connected by this courtyard contain many pleasant surprises. The comfortable rooms (which average 425 square ft each) are highlighted by soft beds, authentic 1930s Art Deco pieces, large foldout couches, and clean, spacious baths. Add to this wet bars with refrigerators, TV/VCR/CD players, and two phone lines with data-port access. If you spring for the penthouse suite, be sure to settle on the balcony and grab an eyeful of ocean. Blessedly, rooms have soundproofed windows. ⊠ *1230–38 Ocean Dr., Miami Beach 33139,* ☎ *305/672–2579,* FAX *305/672–7665. 4 rooms, 23 suites. Restaurant, bar, concierge. AE, D, DC, MC, V.*

$$$–$$$$ ⊞ **Raleigh Hotel.** Hidden behind a thick veil of tropical foliage is one of SoBe's nicest oceanfront hotels. Among the first Art Deco District hotels to be renovated, it added Victorian accents (hallway chandeliers and in-room oil paintings) to soften the hard Deco edges. The hotel has been a consistent favorite of fashion photogs and production crews, who appreciate state-of-the-art rooms with three phones and two lines. Even standard rooms are spacious, and suites are more so. Each unit offers a VCR, radio/CD/cassette player, safe, and refrigerator stocked to your taste. The gorgeous fleur-de-lis pool is the focal point year-round, but especially on December 31, when synchronized swimmers dive in at the stroke of midnight. If you prefer salt with your water, sample the 300-ft beach. Other pluses are the lobby coffee bar, a romantic restaurant (Tiger Oak Room), and the 1940s-style Martini Bar. ⊠ *1775 Collins Ave., Miami Beach 33139,* ☎ *305/534–6300 or 800/848–1775,* FAX *305/538–8140. 107 rooms, 1176 suites. Restaurant, bar, pool, beach, laundry service. AE, DC, MC, V.*

$$$ ⊞ **Pelican.** Dazzling, brilliant spaces with Art Deco–inspired frivolity result from the transformation from another tired Ocean Drive home for the elderly into pop-eyed digs for the gay, hip, and adventurous. Rooms, with names like Leafforest, Best Whorehouse, People from the 1950s, and Cubarrean, are all different, but all have small sleeping chambers and triple-size bathrooms with outrageous industrial piping. Best Whorehouse envelops you in black silk and thoroughly red-flocked wallpaper flecked with gold. Ornaments are bordello extravagant: a heart-shape red-velvet chair, hideously aqua night tables, whorish art, and griffins with voluptuous mammaries. Each room comes with its own cylindrical entertainment center. Room for room, Pelican outweirds even the Delano. Guests have included JFK Jr. and Yoko Ono. ⊠ *826 Ocean Dr., Miami Beach 33139,* ☎ *305/673–3373 or 800/773–5422,* FAX *305/673–3255. 22 rooms, 5 suites. Restaurant, café, concierge. AE, DC, MC, V.*

$$–$$$$ ⊞ **Cavalier.** Chris Blackwell is consistent. In any of his Island Outpost hotels (☞ Casa Grande *and* the Tides, *above*), you can count on a clean room, good service, and creative surroundings. In most cases you can expect to pay dearly for the privilege, but not here if you get a standard room. Rooms start at a Miami-modest $125 and include TV/VCR, CD, safe, minibar, queen-size bed, and access to the pool at the Tides. Batik fabrics, the requisite Deco furniture, and vintage B&W photos set the mood. Suites get an ocean view and king-size bed. And talk about location: You're right across the street from that great big Atlantic. ⊠ *1320 Ocean Dr., Miami Beach 33139,* ☎ *305/604–5064 or 800/688–7678,* FAX *305/531–5543. 43 rooms, 4 suites. Concierge, meeting rooms. AE, DC, MC, V.*

$$–$$$ ☒ **Nassau Suite Hotel.** The sister property of the Bayliss (☞ *below*), this relative bargain offers huge studio suites at a third of the price demanded by Ocean Drive properties. The original 1937 floor plan of 50 rooms gave way to 22 spacious and smart-looking suites. King-size beds, fully equipped kitchens, hardwood floors, white wood blinds, voice mail, data ports, plush sofas, free local calls, mini-refrigerators. . . why they don't charge more is a mystery, though there's no 24-hour staff. The hotel is in the heart of the action yet quiet enough to give travelers the rest they need. Note: This three-floor hotel has no elevator and no bellhop. ✉ *1414 Collins Ave., Miami Beach 33139,* ☎ *305/531–3755 or 888/305–4683,* ℻ *305/673–8609. 22 suites. Concierge. AE, D, DC, MC, V.*

$$ ☒ **Cadet Hotel.** Clark Gable stayed in Room 225 when he came to Miami for Army Air Corps training in the 1940s. Although this Lincoln Road district lodging doesn't have the glamour to attract stars today, it's still a clean, friendly, and perfectly placed little hotel. Just a few minutes' walk from the Theater of the Performing Arts and the convention center and five minutes from the ocean, it's about half the cost of an Ocean Drive hotel. The other big difference is a staff that doesn't act like it's doing you a favor by letting you stay here. Bright without glitz, the Cadet features soft pastels in the lobby, blues and creams in rooms. Ordinary furniture is mixed but not necessarily matched—nor is it crummy. Tiled baths have tubs, and a complimentary breakfast is served in the lobby or on the terrace. ✉ *1701 James Ave., Miami Beach 33139,* ☎ *305/672–6688 or 800/432–2338,* ℻ *305/532–1676. 44 rooms. AE, D, DC, MC, V.*

$$ ☒ **Days Inn Convention Center.** Nothing flashy and nothing trashy, this link in a chain is a fairly pleasant one. The lobby is bright and floral, with a fountain and a gift shop that remind you that this is one of many, not one of a kind. Standard hotel rooms include in-room safes and cable TV; deluxe rooms throw in impressive views of the ocean. If you're more concerned about your wallet than your image, this can be a good bet. Though you can find lodgings at the same rates with more character, here you will find everything you'd expect at a franchise (including a pool)—all literally seconds from the beach, the boardwalk, and the Bass Museum. ✉ *100 21st St., Miami Beach 33139,* ☎ *305/ 538–6631 or 800/451–3345,* ℻ *305/674–0954. 172 rooms. Restaurant, pool, beach, laundry service. AE, D, DC, MC, V.*

$$ ☒ **Kenmore.** Understated comfort is the hallmark of this hotel, part of an entire block of accommodations known collectively as the Park Washington Resort. Although other Art Deco hostelries accessorize to achieve a 1930s feel, this place seems to have captured the essence of the period on its own. The lobby's glass-block facade, the courtyard bar, and inviting patio furniture complement rooms that are clean but not overly spacious. Tropical-theme rooms have twin- or king-size beds and a refrigerator. On a very active street the Kenmore has a privacy that's surprising. A quiet pool hidden behind a low wall allows you to tan in an Adirondack chair without being subject to voyeurs. It's only a short walk to the clubs and shops of SoBe, and you get a free breakfast, to boot. ✉ *1020–1050 Washington Ave., Miami Beach 33139,* ☎ *305/532–1930 or 888/424–1930,* ℻ *305/972–4666. 60 rooms. Restaurant, bar, pool. AE, DC, MC, V.*

$–$$ ☒ **Bayliss.** Paul Crowley is Chris Blackwell on a budget. With no recording empire to support him, he reinvests his hotel profits to make his guests as comfortable as possible. At his properties (☞ Nassau Suite Hotel, *above*), the clean and bright rooms are abnormally large and surprisingly inexpensive—you may even think you've rented a house when you check into an efficiency or apartment here. And not only are the bedrooms large; so, too, are the kitchens (not in standard rooms), sitting rooms, and baths. An easy three blocks west of the ocean, the Bayliss is in a residential neighborhood that's comfortably close to—but far enough away from—the din of the Art Deco District. You can't do much better than this, if you don't mind carrying your own bags. ⊠ *500 14th St., Miami Beach 33139,* ☎ *305/531–3755 or 888/ 305–4683,* FAX *305/673–8609. 12 rooms, 7 suites. Coin laundry. AE, DC, MC, V.*

$ 🏨 **Banana Bungalow.** This may seem like a university dormitory—indeed, some rooms have dorm-style bunk beds for about $14 a night—but the cleanliness, friendliness, and abundance of activities make this lodge worth checking into, especially for hard-core student travelers. A large pool, the bungalow's social center, is surrounded by a patio bar, Ping-Pong table, game room, outdoor grills, a café, and an activity board announcing kayak rentals, scenic flights, and beach volleyball games held across the street. Some may be put off by the smell of the brackish canal nearby and the recently increased prices, but for others it's a small price to pay for a small price to stay. ⊠ *2360 Collins Ave., Miami Beach 33139,* ☎ *305/538–1951 or 800/746–7835,* FAX *305/531– 3217. 40 private rooms, 20 dorm-style rooms, all with bath. Bar, café, pool, Ping-Pong, billiards, recreation room, video games. MC, V.*

West Dade

$$$$ 🏨 **Doral Golf Resort and Spa.** This 650-acre golf-and-tennis resort has made major renovations, adding a lighter tone to the eight separate three- and four-story lodges nestled beside golf courses. At the world-renowned spa, a 148,000-square-ft paradise, massages from head to foot, European facials, aroma scrubs and wraps, stress reduction, hypnotherapy, and several dozen other indulgences rejuvenate the mind, body, and soul. Dining ranges from a sports bar to an informal trattoria to an elegant restaurant, Windows on the Green. The famed Blue Monster course has been redesigned, and the other four 18-hole courses were increased in size and difficulty, which makes things tougher on guests as well as the pros who compete in the annual $2 million Doral-Ryder Open Tournament. In 1999 Blue Lagoon, an extravagant water play area, opened at the resort. ⊠ *4400 N.W. 87th Ave., 33178-2192,* ☎ *305/592–2000 or 800/713–6725,* FAX *305/594– 4682. 694 rooms, 48 suites. 4 restaurants, 3 bars, 4 pools, spa, driving range, 99 holes of golf, 10 tennis courts (4 lighted), health club, jogging, fishing, pro shop. AE, D, DC, MC, V.*

NIGHTLIFE AND THE ARTS

For information on what's happening around town, Greater Miami's English-language daily newspaper, the **Miami Herald,** publishes reliable reviews and comprehensive listings in its "Weekend" section on Friday and in the "Lively Arts" section on Sunday. Call ahead to confirm details. *El Nuevo Herald* is the paper's Spanish version.

If you read Spanish, check **Diario Las Américas,** the area's largest independent Spanish-language paper, for information on the Spanish theater and a smattering of general performing arts news.

A good source of information on the performing arts and nightspots is the calendar in **Miami Today,** a free weekly newspaper available each Thursday in downtown Miami, Coconut Grove, and Coral Gables. The best, most complete source is the **New Times,** a free weekly distributed throughout Miami-Dade County each Thursday. Various tabloids reporting on Deco District entertainment and the Miami social scene come and go. **Ocean Drive** outglosses everything else. **Wire** reports on the gay community.

The free **Greater Miami Calendar of Events** is published twice a year by the Miami-Dade County Cultural Affairs Council (⊠ 111 N.W. 1st St., Suite 625, 33128, ☎ 305/375–4634).

Real Talk/WTMI (93.1 FM, ☎ 305/856–9393) provides classical concert information in on-air reports three times daily at 7:30, 12:50, and 6:30. Call the station if you miss the report.

You can find out about activities from Miami's **Arts & Entertainment Hotline** (☎ 305/557–5600), but it takes a while to reach a human. The **Greater Miami Convention & Visitors Bureau** (☎ 305/539–3000 or 800/283–2707) publishes a comprehensive list of dance venues, theaters, and museums as well as a seasonal guide to cultural events.

The Arts

Miami's performing arts aficionados will tell you they survive quite nicely, thank you, despite the area's historic inability to support a county-based professional symphony orchestra. But in recent years this community has begun to write a new chapter in its performing arts history.

In addition to established music groups, several churches and synagogues run classical-music series with international performers. In theater, Miami offers English-speaking audiences an assortment of professional, collegiate, and amateur productions of musicals, comedy, and drama. Spanish theater also is active.

The not-for-profit **Concert Association of Florida** (⊠ 555 17th St., Miami Beach 33139, ☎ 305/532–3491), led by Judith Drucker, presents classical arts, music, and dance in venues throughout Miami-Dade and Broward counties. It boasts of presenting the world's greatest music and dance—Itzhak Perlman, Isaac Stern, Baryshnikov, Pavarotti, and the Russian National Ballet.

To order tickets for performing arts events by telephone, call **Ticketmaster** (☎ 305/358–5885). **Ticket Madness** (☎ 305/460–3188) promises half-price tickets for same-day performances.

Arts Venues

What was once a 1920s movie theater has become the 465-seat **Colony Theater** (⊠ 1040 Lincoln Rd., Miami Beach 33139, ☎ 305/674–1026). The city-owned performing arts center features dance, drama, music, and experimental cinema.

If you have the opportunity to attend a concert, ballet, or touring stage production at the **Gusman Center for the Performing Arts** (⊠ 174 E. Flagler St., Miami 33131, ☎ 305/374–2444 for administration; 305/372–0925 for box office), do so. Originally a movie palace, this 1,700-plus-seat theater is as far from a mall multiplex as you can get. The stunningly beautiful hall resembles a Moorish courtyard, with twinkling stars and rolling clouds skirting across the ceiling and Roman statues guarding the wings.

Not to be confused with the ornate Gusman theater, **Gusman Concert Hall** (⊠ 1314 Miller Dr., Coral Gables 33146, ☎ 305/284–2438) is a 600-seat facility on the University of Miami campus. Presenting primarily recitals and concerts by students, it has good acoustics and plenty of room, but parking is a problem when school is in session.

Acoustics and visibility are perfect for all 2,700 seats in the **Jackie Glea-son Theater of the Performing Arts** (TOPA, ⊠ 1700 Washington Ave., Miami Beach 33139, ☎ 305/673–7300). A pleasant walk from the heart of SoBe, TOPA hosts the Broadway Series, with five or six major productions annually; guest artists, such as David Copperfield, Stomp, and Shirley MacLaine; and classical-music concerts.

Midway between Coral Gables and downtown Miami, the **Miami-Dade County Auditorium** (⊠ 2901 W. Flagler St., Miami 33135, ☎ 305/545–3395) satisfies patrons with nearly 2,500 comfortable seats, good sight lines, and acceptable acoustics. Opera, concerts, and touring musicals are usually on the schedule, and past performers have included David Helfgott and Celia Cruz.

Dance
The **Miami City Ballet** (⊠ 905 Lincoln Rd., Miami Beach 33139, ☎ 305/532–7713 or 305/532–4880) has risen rapidly to international prominence since its arrival in 1985. Under the direction of Edward Villella (a principal dancer with the New York City Ballet under George Balanchine), Florida's first major, fully professional resident ballet company has become a world-class ensemble. The company re-creates the Balanchine repertoire and introduces works of its own during its September–March season. Performances are held at the Jackie Gleason Theater of the Performing Arts; the Broward Center for the Performing Arts; Bailey Concert Hall, also in Broward County; the Raymond F. Kravis Center for the Performing Arts; and the Naples Philharmonic Center for the Arts.

Film
Alliance Film/Video Project (⊠ Sterling Building, Suite 119, 927 Lincoln Rd. Mall, Miami Beach 33139, ☎ 305/531–8504) presents cutting-edge international cinema and art films, with special midnight shows. Movies—or should we say *films*—are $6, less at matinees.

Screenings of new films from all over the world—including some made here—are held as part of the **Miami Film Festival** (⊠ 444 Brickell Ave., Suite 229, Miami 33131, ☎ 305/377–3456). Each year more than 45,000 people descend on the eye-popping Gusman Center for the Performing Arts to watch about 25 movies over 10 days in late January and early February.

Music
From October to May **Friends of Chamber Music** (⊠ 44 W. Flagler St., Suite 1725, Miami 33130, ☎ 305/372–2975) presents a series of chamber concerts by internationally known guest ensembles, such as the Emerson and Guarneri quartets. Concerts are held at the Gusman Concert Hall at the University of Miami, with tickets averaging about $20.

Because Greater Miami has no resident symphony orchestra, the **New World Symphony** (⊠ 541 Lincoln Rd., Miami Beach 33139, ☎ 305/673–3331 or 305/673–3330), a unique advanced-training orchestra conducted by Michael Tilson Thomas, helps fill the void. Since 1986 musicians ages 22–30 who have finished their academic studies have performed here before moving on to other orchestras. With luck, you may arrive while one of the 60–75 coaches is here to help students. Past "coaches" (and guest conductors) have included Leonard Bernstein and Georg Solti.

Opera
South Florida's leading company, the **Florida Grand Opera** (⊠ 1200 Coral Way, Miami 33145, ☎ 305/854–1643) presents five operas

each year in the Miami-Dade County Auditorium, featuring the Florida Philharmonic Orchestra (Stewart Robinson, musical director). The series brings such luminaries as Placido Domingo and Luciano Pavarotti (Pavarotti made his American debut with the company in 1965 in *Lucia di Lammermoor*). Operas are sung in the original language, with English subtitles projected above the stage.

Theater

Actors' Playhouse (✉ 280 Miracle Mile, Coral Gables 33134, ☎ 305/444–9293), a year-round professional Equity company, presents family fare—musicals, comedies, and dramas—that's mostly good quality, in the very cool 600-seat Miracle Theater. The 1940s-era movie house received a $6 million renovation in the late '90s. Productions of musical theater for younger audiences began in the 300-seat Children's Balcony Theatre in 1997.

Built in 1926 as a movie theater, the **Coconut Grove Playhouse** (✉ 3500 Main Hwy., Coconut Grove 33133, ☎ 305/442–4000 or 305/442–2662) became a legitimate theater in 1956 and is now owned by the state of Florida. The Spanish rococo Grove fixture stages tried-and-true Broadway plays and musicals as well as experimental productions in its main theater and cabaret-style/black box Encore Room. Although onetime Coconut Grove coffee bar singer Jimmy Buffett premiered his play *Don't Stop the Carnival* at the playhouse, its most popular event occurred in 1996, when David Letterman hosted an on-the-road *Late Show* here. Parking is $4 during the day, $5 in the evening.

The **GableStage** (✉ 1200 Anastasia Ave., Coral Gables 33134, ☎ 305/446–1116) presents classic and contemporary theater in a beautiful 154-seat hall at the Biltmore Hotel.

The **Gold Coast Theatre Company** (✉ 345 W. 37th St., Miami Beach 33140, ☎ 305/538–5500), in Miami since 1989, performs a combination of physical theater, mime, and vaudeville comedy. The touring company performs year-round; call to find its current venue.

The **New Theatre** (✉ 65 Almeria Ave., Coral Gables 33134, ☎ 305/443–5909) is a year-round showcase for contemporary and classical plays. Packed houses and critical acclaim are a testament to the skill of Havana-born artistic director Rafael de Acha.

On the campus of the University of Miami, **Ring Theater** (✉ 1380 Miller Dr., Coral Gables 33124, ☎ 305/284–3355) is the 311-seat hall of UM's Department of Theatre Arts. Six plays a year are performed.

SPANISH THEATER

Spanish theater prospers, although many companies have short lives. About 20 Spanish companies perform light comedy, puppetry, vaudeville, and political satire. To locate them, read the Spanish newspapers. When you call, be prepared for a conversation in Spanish—few box-office personnel speak English.

The 255-seat **Teatro de Bellas Artes** (✉ 2173 S.W. 8th St., Miami 33135, ☎ 305/325–0515), on Calle Ocho, presents eight Spanish plays and musicals year-round. Midnight musical follies and female impersonators round out the showbiz lineup.

Nightlife

Bars and Lounges

COCONUT GROVE

CocoWalk presents three different but all potentially decadent drinking establishments. Drinking cold beer and gorilla-size margaritas in the middle of the Grove is part of the fun at **Fat Tuesday** (⊠ 3015 Grand Ave., ☎ 305/441–2992). With more flavors than in a roll of Life Savers, the bar offers up drinks called 190 Octane (190-proof alcohol), Swampwater (also 190 proof), and Grapeshot (a meager 151-proof rum and bourbon concoction). Can you say, "designated driver"? **Hooters** (⊠ 3015 Grand Ave., ☎ 305/442–6004) and its well-known distractions will take you back to high school, but now you have credit cards to keep the party going. A few drinks can lower the inhibitions of even the most reserved and tone-deaf person. This explains the magic of **Howl at the Moon Saloon** (⊠ 3015 Grand Ave., ☎ 305/441–4411), where dueling pianists get the crowd worked up with sing-alongs. Imagine Ferrante and Teicher on pep pills, and you can picture this place.

The **Hungry Sailor** (⊠ 3064½ Grand Ave., ☎ 305/444–9359) serves up Jamaican-English food, British beer, rock on Monday and Tuesday, and reggae from Thursday through Sunday. Hit it on Thursday night and order a round of 1¢ beers. Yes, they're a penny a pop. Bring a quarter and buy a case. The **Taurus Steak House** (⊠ 3540 Main Hwy., ☎ 305/448–0633) is an unchanging oasis in the trendy Grove. The bar, built of native cypress in 1919, draws an over-30 singles crowd nightly. A band plays from Tuesday through Saturday.

CORAL GABLES

Two Irishmen missed the Emerald Isle so they opened **John Martin's Restaurant and Irish Pub** (⊠ 253 Miracle Mile, ☎ 305/445–3777). It serves up fish-and-chips, bangers and mash, shepherd's pie, and all the accoutrements of a Dublin pub—plus the requisite pints of Guinness, Harp, Bass, and other ales. In a building that dates from 1926, **Stuart's Bar-Lounge** (⊠ 162 Alcazar Ave., ☎ 305/444–1666), inside the charming Hotel Place St. Michel, was named one of the best new bars of 1987 by *Esquire,* and it's still favored by locals. The style is fostered by beveled mirrors, mahogany paneling, French posters, pictures of old Coral Gables, and Art Nouveau lighting. Stuart's is closed Sunday.

MIAMI

Tobacco Road (⊠ 626 S. Miami Ave., ☎ 305/374–1198), opened in 1912, holds Miami's oldest liquor license: Number 0001! Upstairs, in space occupied by a speakeasy during Prohibition, blues bands perform nightly, accompanied by single-malt scotch and bourbon.

MIAMI BEACH

Blue Steel (⊠ 2895 Collins Ave., ☎ 305/672–1227) is a cool but unpretentious hangout with pool tables, darts, live music, comfy old sofas, and beer paraphernalia. Open-mike night is Friday, and there's a jam on Monday. German *Vogue* liked it so much they named it the "hippest and hottest" club in SoBe. At **The Clevelander** (⊠ 1020 Ocean Dr., ☎ 305/531–3485), a giant pool-bar area attracts revelers for happy hour drink specials and live music. *Ach du lieber!* Here since 1926, **Mac's Club Deuce** (⊠ 222 14th St., ☎ 305/673–9537) must be doing something right. This is a South Beach gem where top international models pop in to have a drink, listen to the jukebox, and shoot some pool (surprising, considering the working-class atmosphere). All you get late at night are minipizzas, but the pizzazz lasts long. In a nondescript motel row with nudie bars, baby stores, and bait-and-tackle shops, **Molly Malone's** (⊠ 166 Sunny Isles Blvd., ☎ 305/948–9143) is the only cool, down-to-earth spot that thrives in this neighborhood. The Irish pub, a big local fave, has a traditional European look, with oak paneling, live Irish music on Friday, and acoustic sounds Saturday. **Rose's Music Bar & Lounge** (⊠ 754 Washington Ave., ☎ 305/532–0228) is a casual neighborhood bar with Monday-night football and Friday-night blues. An ATM and 5 PM–5 AM hours mean you can muscle up to the bar *and* save money on a hotel room. **Zeke's Road House** (⊠ 625 Lincoln Rd., ☎ 305/532–0087) arrived just before Lincoln Road got its spit and polish (when it was just spit). A neighborhood bar that transcends trends, it's hidden amid revitalized buildings but keeps it simple with sandwiches and draft beers such as Chester, Harp, and Ybor Gold.

Dance Clubs

KEY BISCAYNE

Stefano's of Key Biscayne (⊠ 24 Crandon Blvd., ☎ 305/361–7007) is a northern Italian restaurant with a disco that changes formats nightly: Thursday, Latin; Friday, ladies' night; Saturday, standard disco; and Sunday, oldies. There's a cover charge Friday and Saturday.

MIAMI BEACH

South Beach is headquarters for nightclubs that start late and stay open until the early morning. The clientele is largely a mix of freak-show rejects, sullen male models, and sultry women.

Amnesia (⊠ 136 Collins Ave., ☎ 305/531–5535), open Thursday–Sunday, specializes in mega-events, but be warned: Tea dances here are nothing like those in Mayberry. Formats range from Friday's Reggae Island Dance to Saturday's techno music and Sunday's gay night. The indoor/outdoor venue is like a luxurious amphitheater in the tropics, complete with rain forest, what used to be called go-go dancers, and frenzied dancing in the rain when showers pass over the open-air ground-level club. Here since 1993, this is one of the old-timers—but still a fave. One look at the padded walls of another venue, and you'll think you've entered an asylum; but rest assured: You're only at **Bash** (⊠ 655 Washington Ave., ☎ 305/538–2274). With two DJs spinning dance music—sometimes reggae, sometimes Latin, plenty of loud disco, and world-beat sounds—the party is always going full tilt. You can catch some fresh air by heading to the patio, which is overshadowed by a towering parking garage and a chicken-wire ceiling. The scene is just as lively, but it's strangely calming to be outside. As in other clubs, the posing doesn't stop. If you're anxious to enter one of the three VIP rooms, strike a pose and try joining the chic crowd. The **Bermuda Bar & Grille** (⊠ 3509 N.E. 163rd St., ☎ 305/945–0196) is way north of SoBe but worth the drive if you want to hang with the locals. Rock radio stations do remote broadcasts, and hard liquor and bottled beer are favored over silly drinks with umbrellas. The music is as loud as the setting is large—two floors and seven bars—and hours run 4 PM–6 AM. Male bartenders wear knee-length kilts, while female bartenders are in matching minis. The atmosphere and crowd, though, are stylish, and there's a big tropical-forest scene, booths you can hide in, and pool tables to dive into. The joint is closed from Sunday through Tuesday.

Chaos (⊠ 743 Washington Ave., ☎ 305/674–7350) presents themed evenings from Wednesday's LoveSexy and Thursday's World Tour to Fashion Friday and Saturday evening's Total Chaos. It must be hot: One night it hosts Playboy models, and the next George Foreman's here celebrating his birthday. If Desi Arnaz were still around, he wouldn't recognize **Club Lua** (⊠ 409 Espanola Way, ☎ 305/534–0061), one of the places where he played in the '30s. Dark as night, the tomblike club changes formats from retro to gothic to hip-hop depending on the night. The still hot, still happenin' **Groove Jet** (⊠ 323 23rd St., ☎ 305/532–2002) breaks new ground by featuring DJs from the worldwide musical underground. (If you're not in tune with the subtle nuances of techno pop, however, it'll all sound the same.) Since the club's open 11 PM–5 AM, you'll have plenty of time to break your eardrums with hypnotic dance music played in three rooms. Just remember to say, "I'll be home late, Mom!" To avoid a cover, hit this one on Thursday night. **Liquid** (⌧ 1437–39 Washington Ave., ☎ 305/532–9154), open 10 PM–5 AM, is a high-energy dance club with themed evenings. Thursday's NFA is hip-hop, Friday brings the Kingdom, Saturday welcomes top New York DJs, Sunday is Manwich Night (for gays), and Monday throbs to funk and soul during Fat Black Pussycat. Weekdays' staid conventioneers give way to the chic crowd on weekends.

Designed like a sultan's palace, the very classy and elegant **Living Room at the Strand** (⌧ 671 Washington Ave., ☎ 305/532–2340) draws A-list celebs and sheiks who drop $1,000 tips. If your bankroll hasn't risen to that level, just shoot a game of pool or have dinner before the club crowd arrives. After dinner the club hops with techno pop. There's great service all around, and the comfortable couches are a welcome addition. A truly frightening evening can be spent at the **Shadow Lounge** (⌧ 1532 Washington Ave., ☎ 305/531–9411), where the club kids look like mannequins come to life. By mixing Berlin of the '30s with Havana of the '50s and New York of the '70s, it creates a weird atmosphere that attracts Miami's crème de la creepy. If you can't take it and are afraid you'll whimper like a beaten puppy, stay home and watch *The Twilight Zone* instead. SoBe's warhorse, **Warsaw Ballroom** (⌧ 1450 Collins Ave.) has outlasted most other clubs, becoming an institution. Once Gianni Versace's party central, it boasts a guest list that's included Madonna, Sean Penn, Jack Nicholson, and Dennis Rodman. The 9:30 PM–5 AM hours (Wednesday–Saturday only) turn a traditional work schedule on its head. Though most nights are becoming gay, there's still an occasional straight night with hip-hop and disco. Beware of cover charges ranging from $7 on up to $40 to cover the occasional $12,000-a-night DJ.

Jazz

MIAMI BEACH

Jazid (⌧ 1342 Washington Ave., ☎ 305/604–9798) is the place for blues and jazz from swing to traditional jazz. Performers change nightly, but the intimate candlelit atmosphere and no-cover policy remain constant. More restaurant than jazz club, **Van Dyke Café** (⌧ 846 Lincoln Rd., ☎ 305/534–3600) serves music on the second floor seven nights a week. Its location on the Lincoln Road Mall makes it a great spot to take a break during an evening shopping excursion.

Nightclub

MIAMI BEACH

You can dine as you watch the show at the Fontainebleau Hilton's **Club Tropigala** (⌧ 4441 Collins Ave., ☎ 305/672–7469), which tries to blend modern Vegas with 1950s Havana. The four-tier round room is decorated with orchids, banana leaves, and philodendrons to create an indoor tropical jungle. The performances themselves can be less satisfying, sometimes consisting of disappointing writing, choreography, and acting. Hotel guests are comped, but others pay a $20 cover. Reservations are suggested, and men should wear jackets.

OUTDOOR ACTIVITIES AND SPORTS

In addition to contacting the addresses below directly, you can get tickets to major events from **Ticketmaster** (☎ 305/358–5885).

Auto Racing

Hialeah Speedway, the area's only independent raceway, holds stock-car races on a ⅓-mi asphalt oval in a 5,000-seat stadium. Don't be fooled: The enthusiasm of the local drivers makes this as exciting as Winston

Cup races. Five divisions of cars run weekly. The Marion Edwards, Jr., Memorial Race, for late-model cars, is held in November. The speedway is on U.S. 27, ¼ mi east of the Palmetto Expressway (Route 826). ⊠ *3300 W. Okeechobee Rd., Hialeah,* ☎ *305/821–6644.* ⛬ *$10, special events $15.* ۞ *Late Jan.–early Dec., Sat.; gates open at 5, racing 7–11.*

Baseball

Although the **Florida Marlins** (⊠ 2267 N.W. 199th St., Miami 33056, ☎ 305/626–7400) team that won the 1997 World Series was split up soon afterward, games are still as exciting as baseball can be. Home games are played at Pro Player Stadium, which is 16 mi northwest of downtown. On game days the Metro-Dade Transit Agency runs buses to the stadium.

Basketball

The NBA's **Miami Heat** (⊠ 1 S.E. 3rd Ave., Miami 33131, ☎ 305/577–4328) were Atlantic Division champs for the 1996–97 and 1997–98 seasons. Their reward, it would seem, is the new 20,000-seat, waterfront American Airlines Arena (scheduled to open December 31, 1999), which features a scoreboard with special effects and indoor fireworks. Home games are held November–April.

Biking

Perfect weather and flat terrain make Miami-Dade County a popular place for cyclists. A free color-coded map highlighting the cyclability of local roads as well as bike shops, parks, safety tips, and the routes of bike rack–equipped buses make it even better. The map is available from area bike shops and from the **Miami-Dade County Bicycle Coordinator** (⊠ Metropolitan Planning Organization, 111 N.W. 1st St., Suite 910, Miami 33128, ☎ 305/375–4507, ext. 1735), whose purpose in life is to share with you the glories of Miami's bicycle-friendly roads. For information on dozens of monthly group rides, contact the **Everglades Bicycle Club** (⊠ Box 430282, South Miami 33243-0282, ☎ 305/598–3998). For bike rentals check out the **Miami Beach Bicycle Center** (MBBC; ⊠ 601 5th St., Miami Beach, ☎ 305/674–0150), in business since 1975. MBBC's proximity to Ocean Drive and the ocean itself make it worth the $20 per day (or $5 per hour), which includes a helmet, lock, and basket on a mountain bike or cruiser. Tours of the Deco District are offered twice a month.

Boating

The popular full-service **Crandon Park Marina** is a one-stop shop for all things ocean-y. You can embark on deep-sea fishing or scuba-diving excursions, dine at a marina restaurant, or rent powerboats through **Club Nautico** (⊠ 5420 Crandon Blvd., Key Biscayne, ☎ 305/361–9217; also ⊠ 2560 Bayshore Dr., Coconut Grove, ☎ 305/858–6258), a national powerboat rental company. Half- to full-day rentals range from $109 to $419, or you can buy a membership, which costs a bundle at first but saves around 60% on future rentals. ⊠ *4000 Crandon Blvd., Key Biscayne,* ☎ *305/361–1281.* ۞ *Office daily 8–6.*

Named for an island where early settlers had picnics, **Dinner Key Marina** is Greater Miami's largest, with nearly 600 moorings at nine piers. There is space for transients and a boat ramp. ⊠ *3400 Pan American Dr., Coconut Grove,* ☎ *305/579–6980.* ۞ *Daily 7 AM–11 PM.*

Haulover Marine Center is low on glamour but high on service. It offers a bait-and-tackle shop, marine gas station, and boat launch. ⊠ *15000 Collins Ave., Miami Beach,* ☎ *305/945–3934.* ۞ *Bait shop and gas station open 24 hours.*

Although **Matheson Hammock Park** has no charter services, it does have 243 slips and boat ramps. It also has **Castle Harbor** (☎ 305/665–4994), a sailing school that relocated here from Coconut Grove in 1998. In operation since 1949, it offers sailboat rentals for those with U.S. Sailing certification as well as classes held in outdoor—and very warm—Seminole Indian–style chickees. When you're ready to rent, take your pick of boats ranging from 23 ft to 41 ft. ✉ *9610 Old Cutler Rd., Coral Gables,* ☎ *305/665–5475.* ☼ *Daily 6–sunset.*

A happening waterfront mecca, **Miami Beach Marina** is the nearest marina to the Deco District, about a 15-minute walk away. It has restaurants, charters, boat and vehicle rentals, a complete marine hardware store, dive shop and excursions, large grocery store, fuel dock, concierge services, and 400 slips accommodating vessels up to 190 ft. Facilities include air-conditioned rest rooms, washers and dryers, U.S. Customs clearing, and a heated pool. One charter outfit here is family-owned **Florida Yacht Charters** (☎ 305/532–8600 or 800/537–0050). After completing a checkout cruise and paperwork, slap down a deposit and take off for the Keys or Bahamas on a catamaran, sailboat, or motor yacht. Charts, lessons, and captains are available if needed. Call for a comprehensive info kit. ✉ *300 Alton Rd., Miami Beach,* ☎ *305/673–6000 for marina.* ☼ *Daily 7–6.*

Dog Racing

In the middle of Little Havana, **Flagler Greyhound Track** has dog racing during its June–November season and a poker room that's open when the track is running. Closed-circuit TV brings harness-racing action here as well. The track is five minutes east of Miami International Airport, off Dolphin Expressway (Route 836) and Douglas Road (Northwest 37th Avenue). ✉ *401 N.W. 38th Ct., Miami,* ☎ *305/649–3000.* ✑ *$1, clubhouse $3, parking 50¢–$2.* ☼ *Racing daily 7:30, plus Tues.–Wed. and Sat. 12:30.*

Fishing

Before there was fashion, there was fishing. Deep-sea fishing is still a major draw, and anglers drop a line for sailfish, kingfish, dolphin, snapper, wahoo, grouper, and tuna. Smaller charter boats can cost $350–$400 for a half day and provide everything but food and drinks. If you're on a budget, you might be better off paying around $25 for passage on a larger fishing boat. Rarely are they filled to capacity. Most charters have a 50-50 plan, which allows you to take (or sell) half your catch while they do the same. Nearby general stores sell such essentials as fuel, tackle, sunglasses, and beer. Don't let them sell you a fishing license, however; a blanket license should cover all passengers.

Crandon Park Marina (✉ 4000 Crandon Blvd., Key Biscayne, ☎ 305/361–1281) has earned an international reputation for knowledgeable captains and good catches. Heading out to the edge of the Gulf Stream (about 3 to 4 mi), you're sure to wind up with something on your line—although sailfish is one fish that's catch and release. Many ocean-fishing charters sail out of **Haulover Park** (✉ 10800 Collins Ave., Miami Beach), including **Blue Waters Sportfishing Charters** (☎ 305/944–4531), four boats in the **Kelley Fleet** (☎ 305/945–3801), *Therapy IV* (☎ 305/945–1578), and about 10 additional charter services. Among the charter services at the **Miami Beach Marina** (✉ 300 Alton Rd., MacArthur Causeway, Miami Beach) is **Reward Fleet** (☎ 305/372–9470). It operates two boats at moderate prices: $28 per person including bait, rod, reel, and tackle, less for kids.

Football

Despite the resignation of legendary coach Don Shula in 1995, fans keep coming to watch the NFL's **Miami Dolphins**—probably still waiting for a repeat of the 17–0 record of 1972 (a record that still stands). The team plays at the former Joe Robbie Stadium, renamed Pro Player Stadium in honor of a sports apparel company and a $20 million check. The state-of-the-art stadium, which has 75,000 seats and a grass playing surface, is on a 160-acre site 16 mi northwest of downtown Miami, 1 mi south of the Miami-Dade–Broward County line and accessible from I–95 and Florida's Turnpike. On game days the Metro-Dade Transit Agency runs buses to the stadium. ⊠ *2269 N.W. 199th St., Miami 33056,* ☎ *305/620–2578.* ☉ *Box office weekdays 8:30–6, also Sat. during season.*

After calling the venerable Orange Bowl home for many years, the **University of Miami Hurricanes** (⊠ 1 Hurricane Dr., Coral Gables 33146, ☎ 305/284–2263), once contenders for the top collegiate ranking, are playing their home games at Pro Player Stadium (☞ *above*) from September to November.

Golf

Greater Miami has more than 30 private and public courses. Fees at most courses are higher on weekends and in season, but you can save money by playing weekdays and after 1 PM or 3 PM (call to find out when afternoon or twilight rates go into effect). That said, costs are reasonable to play in such an appealing setting as Miami.

To get the **"Golfer's Guide for South Florida,"** which includes information on most courses in Miami and surrounding areas, call ☎ 800/864–6101. The cost is $3.

The 18-hole championship **Biltmore Golf Course** (⊠ 1210 Anastasia Ave., Coral Gables, ☎ 305/460–5364), known for its scenic layout, has been restored to its original Donald Ross design, circa 1925. Greens fees range from $39 to $59 in season, and the gorgeous hotel makes a scenic backdrop. The **California Golf Club** (⊠ 20898 San Simeon Way, North Miami Beach, ☎ 305/651–3590) has an 18-hole course made challenging by a tight front nine and three of the area's toughest finishing holes. Eighteen holes will set you back between $40 and $50. Overlooking the bay, the **Crandon Park Golf Course** (⊠ 6700 Crandon Blvd., Key Biscayne, ☎ 305/361–9129), formerly the Links at Key Biscayne, is a top-rated public course in a beautiful tropical setting. Expect to pay around $90 for a round. **Don Shula's Hotel & Golf Club** (⊠ 7601 Miami Lakes Dr., Miami Lakes, ☎ 305/820–8106) has one of the longest championship courses in Miami (7,055 yards), a lighted par-3 course, a golf school, and more than 100 tournaments a year. Weekdays you can play for about $65, $90 on weekends. With four championship courses and one executive course, the **Doral Golf Resort and Spa** (⊠ 4400 N.W. 87th Ave., Doral, ☎ 305/592–2000 or 800/713–6725) is known for the Blue Monster course and the annual Doral-Ryder Open Tournament, with $2 million in prize money. If you're ready for the challenge, you'll pay fees of $110 to $240—less after 3.

Now operated by the city of Coral Gables, the **Granada Golf Course** (⊠ 2001 Granada Blvd., Coral Gables, ☎ 305/460–5367) is the oldest nine-hole course in Florida and costs only $16.25 with cart, $11 walking. If you aren't quite in Tiger Woods's league, you may enjoy the large fairways, minimal bunkers, and lack of water hazards. Then again, the par-36 layout is a respectable 3,001 yards. **Normandy Shores Golf Course** (⊠ 2401 Biarritz Dr., Miami Beach, ☎ 305/868–6502) is good for seniors, with some modest slopes and average distances. The

Turnberry Isle Resort & Club (⊠ 19999 W. Country Club Dr., Aventura, ☎ 305/933–6929) has 36 holes designed by Robert Trent Jones. The South Course's 18th hole is a killer, and the course is very expensive, but since it's private, you won't be able to play unless you're a hotel guest.

Horse Racing

The **Calder Race Course,** opened in 1971, is Florida's largest glass-enclosed, air-conditioned sports facility. It often has an unusually extended season, from late May to early January, though it's a good idea to call the track for specific starting and wrap-up dates, since Calder, Hialeah Park, and Gulfstream Park rotate their race dates. Each year between November and early January, Calder holds the Tropical Park Derby for three-year-olds. The track is on the Miami-Dade–Broward County line near I–95 and the Hallandale Beach Boulevard exit, ¾ mi from Pro Player Stadium. ⊠ *21001 N.W. 27th Ave., Miami,* ☎ *305/625–1311.* ⊠ *$2, clubhouse $4, parking $1–$4.* ☉ *Gates open at 11, racing 12:30–5.*

A superb setting for Thoroughbred racing, **Hialeah Park** has 228 acres of meticulously landscaped grounds surrounding paddocks and a clubhouse built in a classic French-Mediterranean style. Since it opened in 1925, Hialeah Park has survived hurricanes and now seems likely to survive even changing demographics, as the racetrack crowd has steadily moved north and east. Although Hialeah tends to get the less prestigious racing dates from March to May, it still draws crowds. The park is open year-round for free sightseeing, during which you can explore the gardens and admire the park's breeding flock of Cuban flamingos. Metrorail's Hialeah Station is on the grounds. ⊠ *2200 E. 4th Ave., Hialeah,* ☎ *305/885–8000.* ⊠ *Weekdays, grandstand $1, clubhouse $2; weekends, grandstand $4, clubhouse $4; parking $1–$4.* ☉ *Gates open at 10:30, racing 1–5:30.*

Jai Alai

Built in 1926, the **Miami Jai-Alai Fronton,** a mile east of the airport, is America's oldest fronton. It presents 13 games—14 on Friday and Saturday—some singles, some doubles. This game, invented in the Basque region of northern Spain, is the world's fastest. Jai-alai balls, called pelotas, have been clocked at speeds exceeding 170 mph. Players ducking from the pelotas have been clocked at 175 mph. The game is played in a 176-ft-long court, and players literally climb the walls to catch the ball in a cesta—a woven basket—with an attached glove. You can bet on a team to win or on the order in which teams will finish. Dinner is available. ⊠ *3500 N.W. 37th Ave., Miami,* ☎ *305/633–6400.* ⊠ *$1, reserved seats $2, Courtview Club $5.* ☉ *Mon., Wed., and Fri.– Sat. noon–5 and 7–midnight, Thurs. 7–midnight, Sun. 1–6.*

Jogging

There are numerous places to run in Miami, but these recommended jogging routes are considered among the most scenic and the safest: in Coconut Grove, along the pedestrian-bicycle path on South Bayshore Drive, cutting over the causeway to Key Biscayne for a longer run; from the south shore of the Miami River, downtown, south along the sidewalks of Brickell Avenue to Bayshore Drive, where you can run alongside the bay; in Miami Beach, along Bay Road (parallel to Alton Road) or on the sidewalk skirting the Atlantic Ocean, opposite the cafés of Ocean Drive; and in Coral Gables, around the Riviera Country Club golf course, just south of the Biltmore Country Club. A good source of running information is the **Miami Runners Club** (⊠ 7920 S.W. 40th St., Miami, ☎ 305/227–1500), although the volunteer group often has an answering machine on. An even better source may be **Foot Works**

(✉ 5724 Sunset Dr., South Miami, ☎ 305/667–9322), a running-shoe store that's open every day. Since 1971 it has hosted races and marathon training.

Scuba Diving and Snorkeling

Though winter storms can cause dive boats to vary their schedules, summer diving conditions in Greater Miami have been compared to those in the Caribbean. Chances are excellent you'll come face to face with a flood of tropical fish. One option is to find real reefs, such as Fowey, Triumph, Long, and Emerald, in 10- to 15-ft dives that are perfect for snorkelers and beginning divers. On the edge of the continental shelf a little more than 3 mi out, these reefs are ¼ mi from depths greater than 100 ft. Another option is to paddle around the tangled prop roots of the mangrove trees that line the coast, peering at the fish, crabs, and other creatures hiding there.

Perhaps the most unusual option, however, is to dive on one of the local artificial reefs. In 1981 Dade County's Department of Environmental Resources Management (DERM) started sinking tons of limestone boulders and more than 65 tankers, trawlers, tugs, a water tower, two M-60 tanks, and a 727 jet to create a "wreckreational" habitat where divers can swim with yellow tang, barracudas, nurse sharks, snappers, eels, and groupers. Most dive shops sell a book listing the location of these wrecks.

Information on wreck diving can be obtained from the Miami Beach Chamber of Commerce's **WaterSports Marketing Council** (✉ 1920 Meridian Ave., Miami Beach, ☎ 305/672–1270 or 888/728–2262), composed of hotels and dive shops involved in finding big stuff to sink.

Bubbles Dive Center (✉ 2671 S.W. 27th Ave., Miami, ☎ 305/856–0565), an all-purpose dive shop with PADI affiliation, runs night and wreck dives. Its boat, *Divers Dream*, is kept on Watson Island on MacArthur Causeway. **Divers Paradise of Key Biscayne** (✉ 4000 Crandon Blvd., Key Biscayne, ☎ 305/361–3483) has a complete dive shop and diving-charter service inside a trailer next to the Crandon Park Marina. On offer are equipment rental and PADI-affiliated scuba instruction. A 3½-day accelerated course ($399) is available for beginners. The PADI-affiliated **Diving Locker** (✉ 223 Sunny Isles Blvd., North Miami Beach, ☎ 305/947–6025) offers full sales, service, and repairs, plus three-day and three-week international certification courses as well as more advanced certifications. Wreck and reef sites are reached aboard fast and comfortable six-passenger dive boats.

Spa

Housed in a small coral building in SoBe, **White** bills itself as a salon, spa, and café, so you can walk in dirty, tired, and hungry and walk out completely satisfied. A destination for wealthy retirees and hot young models, it offers everything from body wraps and massages to cuts, makeovers, and pedicures. An Hour of Power will set you back $240. ✉ *900 Collins Ave., Miami Beach,* ☎ *305/538–0604.* ☉ *Tues. 11–8, Wed. 11–7, Thurs.–Fri. 11–9, Sat.–Mon. 11–6.*

Tennis

Greater Miami has more than a dozen tennis centers open to the public, and countywide nearly 500 public courts are open to visitors. Nonresidents are charged an hourly fee. If you're on a tight schedule, try calling in advance, as some courts take reservations on weekdays.

Biltmore Tennis Center has 10 hard courts and the added bonus of being located at the beautiful Biltmore Hotel (☞ Lodging, *above*). ✉ *1150 Anastasia Ave., Coral Gables,* ☎ *305/460–5360.* ▣ *Day rate $4.30,* *night rate $5 per person per hour.* ⊙ *Weekdays 8* AM–10 PM, *weekends 8–8.*

Very popular with locals, **Flamingo Tennis Center** has 19 clay courts smack dab in the middle of Miami Beach. ✉ *1000 12th St., Miami Beach,* ☎ *305/673–7761.* 🎾 *Day rate $2.67, night rate $3.20 per person per hr.* ⊙ *Weekdays 8* AM–9 PM, *weekends 8–8.*

North Shore Tennis Center, within the North Shore Park, has six clay and five hard courts. ✉ *350 73rd St., Miami Beach,* ☎ *305/993–2022.* 🎾 *Day rate $2.66, night rate $3.20 per person per hr.* ⊙ *Weekdays 8* AM–9 PM, *weekends 8–7.*

The $18 million, 30-acre **Tennis Center at Crandon Park** is one of America's best. Included are 2 grass, 8 clay, and 17 hard courts. Reservations are required for night play. The only time courts are closed to the public is during the **Lipton Championships** (☎ 305/442–3367), held for 11 days each spring. The tournament is one of the best attended in the world, and with prize money nearing $5 million, it has the cash clout to attract players like Michael Chang, Pete Sampras, Venus Williams, and Martina Hingis. It's played in a 14,000-seat stadium. ✉ *7300 Crandon Blvd., Key Biscayne,* ☎ *305/365–2300.* 🎾 *Laykold courts day rate $3, night rate $5 per person per hr; clay courts $6 per person per hour.* ⊙ *Daily 8* AM–9 PM.

Windsurfing

New lightweight boards and smaller sails make learning windsurfing easier. The safest and most popular windsurfing area in city waters is south of town at Windsurfer Beach, just beyond the Rickenbacker Causeway on your way to Key Biscayne. Miami Beach's best windsurfing is at 1st Street just north of the Government Cut jetty and at 21st Street. You can also windsurf from Lummus Park at 10th Street and around 3rd, 14th, and 21st streets.

Sailboards Miami, just past the tollbooth for the Rickenbacker Causeway, claims to be the largest windsurfing school in the United States. It rents equipment, offers year-round lessons, and promises to teach anyone within two hours. ✉ *Key Biscayne,* ☎ *305/361–7245.* 🎾 *1 hr $20, 10 hrs $150, 2-hr lesson $49.* ⊙ *Daily 10–5:30.*

SHOPPING

Visitors to Greater Miami are never more than 15 minutes from a major shopping area and the familiar *ca-ching* of a cash register. Miami-Dade County has more than a dozen major malls, an international free-trade zone, and hundreds of miles of commercial streets lined with stores and small shopping centers. Latin neighborhoods contain a wealth of Latin merchants and merchandise, including children's *vestidos de fiesta* (party dresses) and men's guayaberas (a pleated, embroidered tropical shirt), conveying the feel of a South American *mercado* (market).

Malls

Aventura Mall (✉ 19501 Biscayne Blvd., Aventura) has more than 250 shops anchored by Macy's, Lord & Taylor, JCPenney, Sears, and Bloomingdale's. Who else is there? Guess. And a Disney Store and Banana Republic and . . . and . . . A recent expansion, which nearly doubled the mall's size, now accommodates a 24-screen theater, a Cheesecake Factory, Rainforest Café, China Grill, Burdines, and—surprise—a Starbucks. In a tropical garden setting, **Bal Harbour Shops** (✉ 9700 Collins Ave., Bal Harbour) is a swank collection of 100 shops, boutiques, and department stores, such as Chanel, Gucci, Cartier, Fendi, Bruno Magli, Neiman Marcus, and Florida's largest Saks Fifth Avenue.

It was named by fashionable *Elle* magazine as one of the top five shopping collections in the United States. **Bayside Marketplace** (⊠ 401 Biscayne Blvd., Miami), the 16-acre shopping complex on Biscayne Bay, has more than 150 specialty shops, entertainment, tour-boat docks, and a food court. It's open late (10 during the week, 11 on Friday and Saturday), but its restaurants stay open even later. It's a nice place for a bayside drink, and the cafés and bars will only get more popular when the neighboring arena opens for basketball.

A complex of clapboard, coral-rock, and stucco buildings, **Cauley Square** (⊠ 22400 Old Dixie Hwy., Goulds) was erected in 1907–20 as housing for railroad workers who built and maintained the line to Key West. Crafts, clothing, and antiques shops are well represented. The heartbeat of Coconut Grove, **CocoWalk** (⊠ 3015 Grand Ave., Coconut Grove) has three floors of nearly 40 specialty shops (Victoria's Secret, the Gap, Banana Republic, among others) that stay open almost as late as the popular restaurants and clubs. Kiosks with cigars, beads, incense, herbs, and other small items are scattered around the ground level, while the restaurants and nightlife (e.g., Hooters, Fat Tuesday, an AMC theater) are upstairs. If you're ready for an evening of people-watching, this is the place.

The oldest retail mall in the county, **Dadeland** (⊠ 7535 N. Kendall Dr., Miami) is always upgrading. It sits at the south side of town close to the Dadeland North and Dadeland South Metrorail stations. Retailers include Saks Fifth Avenue, JCPenney, Lord & Taylor, more than 175 specialty stores, 17 restaurants, and the largest Burdines, Limited, and Limited Express in Florida. When it opens in fall 2000, the $250 million **Dolphin Mall** (⊠ Rte. 836 and Florida's Turnpike, Miami), 5 mi west of the airport, will offer plenty of less-expensive shopping, including Marshall's, Oshman's Super Sports, and Saks off Fifth, plus a Regal Cinema. The **Falls** (⊠ 8888 S.W. 136th St., at U.S. 1, Miami), which derives its name from the several waterfalls inside, is the most upscale mall on the south side of the city. It contains a Macy's and Bloomingdale's as well as another 50 specialty stores, restaurants, and a 12-theater multiplex.

The downtown **Omni International Mall** (⊠ 1601 Biscayne Blvd., Miami) rises vertically alongside the atrium of the Crowne Plaza Miami, whose eye-popping feature is an old-fashioned carousel. Among its 75 shops are a JCPenney, many restaurants, and 10 movie screens. You'll find **Paseos** (⊠ 3301 Coral Way, Coral Gables) as you roll into Coral Gables on Coral Way. The plain but imposing exterior hides a collection of shops, cafés, and movie theaters. To compete with trendy Coconut Grove, the **Shops at Sunset Place** (⊠ U.S. 1 and Red Rd. [S.W. 57th Ave.], South Miami) is larger than CocoWalk. The three-story, 519,000-square-ft, family-oriented center upped the ante for entertainment complexes with a 24-screen multiplex, IMAX theater, Barnes & Noble, Virgin Megastore, F.A.O. Schwarz, NikeTown, and Game-Works (a Spielberg-movie-inspired virtual-reality attraction wrapped into a restaurant). **Streets of Mayfair** (⊠ 2911 Grand Ave., Coconut Grove) is an active, bustling group of shops both day and night. Thanks to its Grove setting, along with the News Café, Planet Hollywood, the Limited, Borders, and a few dozen other shops and restaurants, this is a safe bet. Entertainment is provided by an improv comedy club, a 10-screen theater, and the Iguana Cantina, a nightclub, martini bar, and pool room.

Outdoor Markets

Coconut Grove Farmers Market (⊠ Grand Ave., 1 block west of Mac-Donald Ave. [S.W. 32nd Ave.], Coconut Grove), open Saturday 8–2, originated in 1977 and was the first in the Miami area. The **Espanola Way Market** (⊠ Espanola Way, Miami Beach), Sunday noon–9, has been a city favorite since its debut in 1995. Scattered among the hand-crafted items and flea market merchandise, musicians beat out Latin rhythms on bongos, conga drums, steel drums, and guitars. Food vendors sell inexpensive Latin snacks and drinks. Each Saturday morning from mid-January to late March, some 25 produce and plant vendors sell herbs, fruits, fresh-squeezed juices, chutneys, cakes, and muffins at the **Farmers Market at Merrick Park** (⊠ LeJeune Rd. [S.W. 42nd Ave.] and Biltmore Way, Coral Gables). Regular features include gardening workshops, children's activities, and cooking demonstrations offered by Coral Gables' master chefs. More than 500 vendors sell a variety of goods at the **Flagler Dog Track** (⊠ 401 N.W. 38th Ct., Miami), every weekend 9–4. The **Lincoln Road Farmers Market** (⊠ Lincoln Rd. between Meridian and Euclid Aves., Miami Beach), open Sunday November–March, brings about 15 local produce vendors coupled with plant workshops and children's activities. With 1,200 dealers, **Opa-Locka/Hialeah Flea Market** (⊠ 12705 N.W. 47th Ave., Miami) is one of the largest in South Florida. Though it's open seven days, weekends are best. From 10 to 5 on the second and fourth Sundays of each month, locals set up the **Outdoor Antique and Collectibles Market** (⊠ Lincoln and Alton Rds., Miami Beach). The eclectic goods should satisfy post-Impressionists, Deco-holics, Edwardians, Bauhausers, and Gothic, atomic, and '50s junkies.

Shopping Districts

The shopping is great on a two-block stretch of **Collins Avenue** (⊠ Between 6th and 8th Aves., Miami Beach). Vidal Sassoon, Nicole Miller, Nike, Kenneth Cole, Guess, and Banana Republic are among the high-profile tenants, and a parking garage is just a block away. The busy **Lincoln Road Mall** is just a few blocks from the beach and convention center, making it popular with locals and tourists. Despite some empty storefronts caused by escalating rents, there's still an energy to shopping here. Creative merchandise, galleries, and a Sunday-morning antiques market can be found among the theaters and cool cafés.

There are 500 garment manufacturers in Miami and Hialeah, and many sell their clothing locally in the **Miami Fashion District** (⊠ 5th Ave. east of I–95, between 25th and 29th Sts., Miami), making Greater Miami the fashion marketplace for the southeastern United States, the Caribbean, and Latin America. Most of the more than 30 factory outlets and discount fashion stores are open Monday–Saturday 9–5. The **Miami International Arts and Design District** (⊠ Between N.E. 38th and N.E. 42nd Sts. and between Federal Hwy. and N. Miami Ave., Miami), also known as 40th Street, contains some 225 wholesale stores, showrooms, and galleries specializing in interior furnishings, decorative arts, and a rich mix of exclusive and unusual merchandise. Don't expect to find a flood of shoppers here; the surrounding neighborhood keeps many tourists away. **Miracle Mile** (⊠ Coral Way between 37th and 42nd Aves., Coral Gables) consists of some 160 shops along a wide, tree-lined boulevard. Shops range from posh boutiques to bargain basements, from beauty salons to chain restaurants. As you go west, the quality increases.

Specialty Stores

ANTIQUES

A&J Unique Deco (⊠ 2000 Biscayne Blvd., Miami, ☎ 305/576–5170) is constantly rotating its inventory of Deco furniture, collected from Europe and the United States. In a world of reproductions, this is the real thing: 5,000 square ft of cool armoires, dressers, beds, and bars.

Alhambra Antiques Center (⊠ 3640 Coral Way, Miami, ☎ 305/446–1688) is a collection of four antiques dealers that sell high-quality decorative pieces from Europe. **Architectural Antiques** (⊠ 2500 S.W. 28th La., Coconut Grove, ☎ 305/285–1330) carries large and eclectic items—railroad crossing signs, statues, English roadsters—in a setting so cluttered that shopping here becomes an adventure promising hidden treasures for the determined.

BOOKS

Like others in the superstore chain, **Barnes & Noble** (⊠ 152 Miracle Mile, Coral Gables, ☎ 305/446–4152) manages to preserve the essence of a neighborhood bookstore by encouraging customers to pick a book off the shelf and lounge on a couch without being hassled. A well-stocked magazine and national/international news rack and an espresso bar–café complete the effect. Greater Miami's best English-language bookstore, **Books & Books, Inc.** (⊠ 296 Aragon Ave., Coral Gables, ☎ 305/442–4408; ⊠ Sterling Bldg., 933 Lincoln Rd., Miami Beach, ☎ 305/532–3222) specializes in books on the arts, architecture, Florida, and contemporary and classical literature. At the Coral Gables location, a true old-fashioned bookstore, collectors enjoy browsing through the rare-book room upstairs, which doubles as a photography gallery. There are frequent poetry readings and book signings. The Lincoln Road shop always has a desk filled with intriguing discounted tomes. If being in the Grove prompts you to don a beret, grow a goatee, and sift through a volume of Kerouac, head to **Borders** (⊠ Grand Ave. and Mary St., Coconut Grove, ☎ 305/447–1655) at the Streets of Mayfair. Its 100,000 book titles, 70,000 CDs, 10,000 video titles, and more than 2,000 periodicals and newspapers in 10 languages from 15 countries make it seem like the southern branch of the Library of Congress.

CHILDREN'S BOOKS AND TOYS

F.A.O. Schwarz (⊠ 9700 Collins Ave., Bal Harbour Shops, Bal Harbour, ☎ 305/865–2361; ⊠ 19501 Biscayne Blvd., Aventura Mall, Aventura, ☎ 305/692–9200; ⊠ 5701 Sunset Dr., Shops at Sunset Place, South Miami, ☎ 305/668–2300) has three area stores. **A Likely Story** (⊠ 5740 Sunset Dr., South Miami, ☎ 305/667–3730) has been helping Miamians choose books and educational toys appropriate to children's interests and stages of development since 1978.

CIGARS

Although Tampa is Florida's true cigar capital, Miami's Latin population is giving it a run for its money. Smoking anything even remotely affiliated with a legendary Cuban has boosted the popularity of Miami cigar stores and the small shops where you can buy cigars straight from the press.

The **Cigar Connection** (⊠ 534 Lincoln Road Mall, Miami Beach, ☎ 305/531–7373) is hoping to capture the trendy tastes of pedestrians strolling on Lincoln Road. Carrying such premium cigars as the Arturo Fuente Opus X and Paul Garmirians, the shop also serves coffees and cappuccino. With soft terra-cotta and ochre tones suggestive of an Italian villa, **Condal & Peñamil** (⊠ 741 Lincoln Road Mall, Miami Beach, ☎ 305/604–9690) is Miami's most beautiful cigar bar. In addition to carrying the traditional ashtrays, cutters, and humidors, C&P has a "cigar cave" with a private salon, enabling you to complement your smoke with a coffee or cocktail. In the heart of Little Havana, **El Credito** (⊠ 1106 S.W. 8th St., Miami, ☎ 305/858–4162 or 800/726–9481) seems to have been transported from the Cuban capital lock, stock, and stogie. Rows of workers at wooden benches rip through giant tobacco leaves, cut them with rounded blades, wrap them tightly, and press them in vises. Dedicated smokers like Robert De Niro, Gregory Hines, and George Hamilton have found their way here to pick up a $90 bundle or peruse the *gigantes, supremos,* panatelas, and Churchills available in natural or maduro wrappers.

It's the only cigar shop on Miracle Mile, but that's not the sole reason to drop by **Giorgio's Cigars** (✉ 210 Miracle Mile, Coral Gables, ☎ 305/448–2992 or 888/833–8819). The standard lineup (Espinosa, Arturo Fuente, Macanudo, Partagas, et al.) is complemented by a large humidor, coffee bar, nice leather sofas, and a cheesy nude painting. There's added applause for the friendly staff. **Havana Ray's** (✉ 3111 Grand Ave., Coconut Grove, ☎ 305/446–4003 or 800/732–4427) continues a cigar-making dynasty that began in 1920s Cuba. The Quirantes family's devotion to cigars has resulted in this cozy Streets of Mayfair shop, where you can buy cigars and related accouterments. **Smokers' Notch** (✉ 425 Washington Ave., Miami Beach, ☎ 305/534–4090) has a terrific location (across from the China Grill), which means celebs (Nicholson) and regular folks (you) can drop in for an after-dinner smoke or stock up on pipe tobacco, cutters, humidors, cigar mags, and more than 100 cigar brands, including Sweet Millionaires (flavored cigars). **South Beach Cigar Cafe** (✉ 710 Washington Ave., No. 9, Miami Beach, ☎ 305/673–3002) has expanded beyond simple cigars to carry imported wines and beers, gourmet espresso and coffee, sandwiches, and croissants. But the real draw is cigars made on the premises or imported from the Dominican Republic, Nicaragua, and Honduras.

COLLECTIBLES

CJ's Animation Art Gallery (✉ 279 Miracle Mile, Coral Gables, ☎ 305/529–1700) carries animation and cel art from Warner Brothers, Disney, and Marvel artists. Prices range from $20 to thousands of dollars, with some pieces on consignment. **Gotta Have It! Collectibles** (✉ 504 Biltmore Way, Coral Gables, ☎ 305/446–5757) will make fans of any kind break out in a cold sweat. Autographed sports jerseys, canceled checks from the estate of Marilyn Monroe, fabulously framed album jackets signed by all four Beatles, and an elaborate autographed montage of all the *Wizard of Oz* stars are among this intriguing shop's museum-quality collectibles. Looking for an Einstein autograph? A Jack Nicklaus–signed scorecard? Look no farther. And if they don't have the autograph you desire, fear not—they'll track one down.

DECORATIVE AND GIFT ITEMS

American Details (✉ 3107 Grand Ave., Coconut Grove, ☎ 305/448–6163) sells colorful, trendy arts and crafts handmade by American artists. Jewelry and handblown glass are popular sellers. The **Indies Company** (✉ 101 W. Flagler St., Miami, ☎ 305/375–1492), the Historical Museum of Southern Florida's gift shop, offers interesting artifacts reflecting Miami's history, including some inexpensive reproductions. The collection of books on Miami and South Florida is impressive.

ESSENTIALS

Wall-to-wall merchandise is found at the **Compass Market** (✉ 860 Ocean Dr., Miami Beach, ☎ 305/673–2906), a cute and cozy basement shop that carries all the staples you'll need, especially if you're staying in an efficiency. The market stocks sandals, souvenirs, cigars, deli items, umbrellas, newspapers, and produce. If the heat of Miami gets you hot and bothered, try **Condom USA** (✉ 3066 Grand Ave., Coconut Grove, ☎ 305/445–7729) on for size. Sexually oriented games and condoms are sold by the gross. If you're easily offended, stay away. If you're easily aroused, stay the night.

JEWELRY

Easily overlooked in the quick pace of downtown, the 10-story **Seybold Building** (⊠ 36 N.E. 1st St., Miami, ☎ 305/374–7922) is filled from bottom to top with more than 250 independent jewelry companies. Diamonds, bracelets, necklaces, and rings are sold in a crowded, lively setting. Word is that competition makes prices flexible, but it's closed Sunday. **Stones of Venice** (⊠ 550 Biltmore Way, Coral Gables, ☎ 305/444–4474), operated by a three-time winner of the DeBeers Diamond Award for jewelry, sells affordable creations. Customers have included Elliott Gould, Pope John Paul II, and film director Barbet Schroeder.

LIGHTING

If you thought designers just keep coming up with the same old stuff, check out **Lunatika** (⊠ 900 Lincoln Rd., Miami Beach, ☎ 305/534–8585). It lights up SoBe with funky, creative lighting from chandeliers to wall sconces to floor lamps. Prices range from a $35 desk clock to a dizzying color-changing clock for $3,000. One look and you'll say, "Yowsa!"

SIDE TRIP

South Dade

Although the population of these suburbs southwest of Dade County's urban core was largely dislocated by Hurricane Andrew in 1992, little damage is evident today. Indeed, FEMA grants and major replanting have made the area better than ever. All attractions—many of which are especially interesting for kids—have reopened, and a complete exploration of them would probably take two days. Keep an eye open for hand-painted signs announcing agricultural attractions, such as orchid farms, fruit stands, u-pick farms, and horseback riding.

✥ ❷ Aviation enthusiasts touch down at **Weeks Air Museum** to view some 15 planes of World War II vintage. Sadly, Hurricane Andrew destroyed the World War I aircraft, and those from World War II suffered damage as well. What you will find are extensive videos, a 707 cockpit you can peer into, and a nose section of a B-29 Superfortress. The museum is inside Tamiami Airport. ⊠ 14710 S.W. 128th St., ☎ 305/233–5197. ☜ $7.95. ☉ Daily 10–5.

✥ ❸ One of the only zoos in the United States in a subtropical environment, the first-class, 290-acre **Metrozoo** is state of the art. Inside the cageless zoo, some 800 animals roam on islands surrounded by moats. Major attractions include the Tiger Temple, where white tigers roam, and the African Plains exhibit, where giraffes, ostriches, and zebras graze in a simulated habitat. There are also koalas, Komodo dragons, and other animals whose names begin with a K. Paws, a petting zoo for children, features three shows daily; during the Wildlife Show, trained animals demonstrate natural behavior on cue. Kids can touch Florida animals such as alligators and possums at the Ecology Theater. ⊠ 12400 Coral Reef Dr. (S.W. 152nd St.), ☎ 305/251–0401. ☜ $8, 45-min tram tour $2. ☉ Daily 9:30–5:30, last admission 4.

✥ ❹ Historic railroad cars on display at the **Gold Coast Railroad Museum** include a 1949 *Silver Crescent* dome car and the *Ferdinand Magellan,* the only Pullman car constructed specifically for U.S. presidents. It was used by Franklin Delano Roosevelt, Harry Truman, Dwight Eisenhower, and Ronald Reagan. On weekends, a train ride is included in the price of admission to the museum, which is next to the zoo. ⊠ 12450 Coral

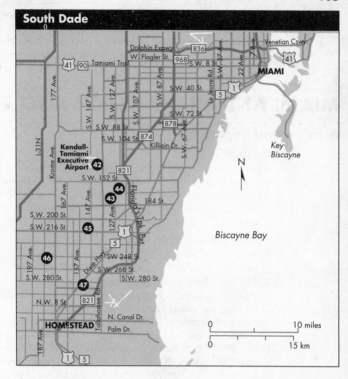

Reef Dr. (S.W. 152nd St.), ☎ 305/253–0063. ☒ $5. ☉ Weekdays 11–3, weekends 11–4.

☝ ⑮ Still a kitschy attraction for adults, **Monkey Jungle** claims to be home to more than 300 monkeys representing 25 species—including orangutans from Borneo and Sumatra and golden lion tamarins from Brazil. Unfortunately, it's showing its age with empty cages, sad-looking monkeys, and shows performed without showmanship. Perhaps the most fun is feeding monkeys who scurry across the fences overhead, hauling up peanuts you place in a metal cup. ☒ *14805 Hainlin Mill Dr. (S.W. 216th St.), ☎ 305/235–1611. ☒ $13.50. ☉ Daily 9:30–5, last admission 4.*

⑯ The 35-acre **Redland Fruit & Spice Park** has been a Dade County treasure since 1944, when it was opened as a 20-acre showcase of tropical fruits and vegetables. Two of the park's three historic buildings were ruined by Hurricane Andrew, as well as about half its trees and plants, but it's now back in full swing. Plants are now grouped by country of origin and include more than 500 economically important varieties of exotic fruits, herbs, spices, nuts, and poisonous plants from around the world. A sampling reveals 80 types of bananas, 30 varieties of grapes, and 100 kinds of citrus fruits. The park store offers many varieties of tropical-fruit products, jellies, seeds, aromatic teas, and reference books. ☒ *24801 Redland Rd. (S.W. 187th Ave.), ☎ 305/247–5727. ☒ $3.50. ☉ Daily 10–5, tours daily 1 and 3.*

☝ ⑰ **Coral Castle of Florida** was born when 26-year-old Edward Leedskalnin, a Latvian immigrant, was left at the altar by his 16-year-old fiancée. She went on with her life, while he went off the deep end and began carving a castle out of coral rock. It's hard to believe that Eddie, only 5 ft tall and 100 pounds, could maneuver tons of coral rock single-handedly. Built between 1920 and 1940, the 3-acre castle is one of

South Florida's original tourist attractions. There is a 9-ton gate a child could open, an accurate working sundial, and a telescope of coral rock aimed at the North Star. This weird, wonderful place is the inspiration for Billy Idol's *Sweet Sixteen*. ⊠ *28655 S. Dixie Hwy.,* ☎ *305/248–6344 or 305/248–6345.* ⊑ *$7.75.* ☉ *Sun.–Thurs. 9–7, Fri.–Sat. 9–8.*

MIAMI AND MIAMI BEACH A TO Z

Arriving and Departing

By Boat

If you enter the United States in a private vessel along the Atlantic Coast south of Sebastian Inlet, you must call the **U.S. Customs Service** (☎ 800/432–1216 near Miami; 305/536–5263 otherwise). Customs clears most boats of less than 5 tons by phone, but you may be directed to a marina for inspection.

The **Port of Miami** (⊠ 1015 North American Way, Miami, ☎ 305/347–4860 or 305/371–7678) bills itself as the "cruise capital of the world," appropriate since its 21 cruise ships (with several more due by 2001) and six cruise lines accommodate more than 3 million passengers a year—representing one out of every three North American cruise passengers. Containing car rental agencies and a limousine service, the port connects passengers to the Bahamas, Mexico, Jamaica, Europe, and around the world. Cruise lines operating out of the port are **Carnival Cruise Lines** (☎ 305/599–2600), **Cunard Line, Ltd.** (☎ 305/463–3000), **Discovery Cruise Lines** (☎ 800/937–4477), **Norwegian Cruise Lines** (☎ 305/436–4000 or 800/327–7030), **Premier Cruise Lines** (☎ 305/358–5122), and **Royal Caribbean Cruise Lines** (☎ 305/539–6000 or 800/255–4373).

By Bus

Greyhound (☎ 800/231–2222) buses stop at four terminals in Greater Miami (⊠ 700 Biscayne Blvd., Miami; ⊠ 4111 N.W. 27th St., Miami; ⊠ 16560 N.E. 6th Ave., North Miami; ⊠ 20505 S. Dixie Highway, South Miami) and at Miami International Airport.

By Car

The main highways into Greater Miami from the north are Florida's Turnpike (a toll road) and I–95. From the northwest take I–75 or U.S. 27 into town. From the Everglades, to the west, use the Tamiami Trail (U.S. 41), and from the south use U.S. 1 and the Homestead Extension of Florida's Turnpike.

By Plane

Miami International Airport (MIA, ☎ 305/876–7000), 6 mi west of downtown Miami, is the only airport in Greater Miami that provides scheduled service. With a daily average of 1,400 flights, it handled more than 35 million passengers in 1997, nearly half of them international travelers. MIA is also the nation's busiest airport for international freight. Altogether more than 120 airlines serve 200 cities and five continents with nonstop or one-stop service. MIA has 102 aircraft gates and eight concourses.

Anticipating continued growth, the airport has begun a more than $4 billion expansion program that is expected to be completed by 2005. Passengers will mainly notice rebuilt and expanded gate and public areas, which should reduce congestion.

A greatly underused convenience for passengers who have to get from one concourse to another in this long, horseshoe-shape terminal is the amazingly convenient moving walkway, on the skywalk level (third floor), with access points at every concourse. Also available on site is the 259-room **Miami International Airport Hotel** (✉ Concourse E, upper level, ☎ 305/871–4100), which has the Top of the Port restaurant on the seventh floor and the Port Lounge on the eighth. MIA, the first to offer duty-free shops, now boasts 18, carrying liquors, perfumes, electronics, and various designer goods.

Heightened security at MIA has meant that it's suggested you check in 90 minutes before departure for a domestic flight, two hours for an international flight. Services for international travelers include 24-hour multilingual information and paging phones and currency conversion booths throughout the terminal. There is an information booth with a multilingual staff across from the 24-hour currency exchange at the entrance of Concourse E on the upper level. Other tourist information centers are at the customs exit, Concourse E, lower level (daily 5 AM–11 PM); customs exit, Concourse B, second level (daily 11–11); Concourse G, lower level (daily 11–7); Concourse D, lower level (daily 11–11); and Satellite Terminal (daily 11–7).

Airlines that fly into MIA include **Aeroflot** (☎ 888/340–6400), **Aerolineas Argentinas** (☎ 800/333–0276), **AeroMexico** (☎ 800/237–6639), **AeroPeru** (☎ 800/777–7717), **Air Aruba** (☎ 800/882–7822), **Air Canada** (☎ 800/776–3000), **Air France** (☎ 800/237–2747), **Air Jamaica** (☎ 800/523–5585), **Alitalia** (☎ 800/223–5730), **American/American Eagle** (☎ 800/433–7300), **American TransAir** (☎ 800/225–2995), **Avensa** (☎ 800/428–3672), **Avianca** (☎ 800/284–2622), **Aviateca** (☎ 800/327–9832), **Bahamasair** (☎ 800/222–4262), **British Airways** (☎ 800/247–9297), **BWIA** (☎ 305/371–2942), **Cayman Airways** (☎ 800/422–9626), **Comair** (☎ 800/354–9822), **Continental** (☎ 800/525–0280), **Delta** (☎ 800/221–1212), **El Al** (☎ 800/223–6700), **Finnair** (☎ 800/950–5000), **Gulfstream International** (☎ 800/992–8532), **Guyana Airways** (☎ 800/242–4210), **Iberia** (☎ 800/772–4642), **LAB** (☎ 800/327–7407), **Lacsa** (☎ 800/225–2272), **Lan Chile** (☎ 800/735–5526), **Lauda Air** (☎ 800/588–8399), **LTU** (☎ 800/888–0200), **Lufthansa** (☎ 800/645–3880), **Martinair Holland** (☎ 800/366–4655), **Mexicana** (☎ 800/531–7921), **Northwest** (☎ 800/225–2525), **Paradise Island** (☎ 800/786–7202), **Saeta** (☎ 800/827–2382), **Servivensa** (☎ 800/428–3672), **South African Airways** (☎ 800/722–9675), **Taca** (☎ 800/535–8780), **Tower Air** (☎ 800/348–6937), **Transbrasil** (☎ 800/872–3153), **TWA** (☎ 800/221–2000), **United** (☎ 800/241–6522), **US Airways/US Airways Express** (☎ 800/428–4322), **Varig** (☎ 800/468–2744), and **Virgin Atlantic** (☎ 800/862–8621).

Pan Am Air Bridge (✉ 1000 MacArthur Causeway, Miami, ☎ 305/373–1120 or 800/424–2557) is starting over where the original Pan Am began—with seaplane flights. Departing from Watson Island, the 30- to 60-minute rides to Bimini, Paradise Island, and Walkers Cay in the Bahamas are exciting, anachronistic, and somewhat cramped. Still, if you've got an extra $200–$250, a round-trip could be quite fun.

BETWEEN THE AIRPORT AND CENTER CITY

By Bus: The county's **Metrobus** (☎ 305/770–3131) still costs $1.25, though equipment has improved. From Concourse E on the ground level, you can take Bus 7 to downtown (weekdays 5:30 AM–9 PM every 40 minutes; weekends 6:30 AM–7:30 PM every 40 minutes), Bus 37 south to Coral Gables and South Miami (6 AM–10 PM every 30 minutes) or north to Hialeah (5:30 AM–11:30 PM every 30 minutes), Bus J south to Coral Gables (6 AM–12:30 AM every 30 minutes) or east to Miami Beach (4:30 AM–11:30 PM every 30 minutes), and Bus 42 to Coconut Grove (5:30 AM–7:20 PM hourly). Some routes change to 60-minute schedules after 7 PM and on weekends, so be prepared to wait or call the information line for exact times.

By Limousine: Miami has more than 100 limousine services, though they're frequently in and out of business. If you rely on the Yellow Pages, look for a company with a street address, not just a phone. Offering 24-hour service, **Club Limousine Service** (⊠ 12050 N.E. 14th Ave., Miami 33161, ☎ 305/893–9850; 800/824–4820; 800/325–9834 in FL) has shuttle vans and minibuses as well as limos. One of the oldest companies in town is **Vintage Rolls Royce Limousines of Coral Gables** (⊠ 4501 Monserrate St., Coral Gables 33146, ☎ 305/444–7657 or 800/888–7657), which operates a 24-hour reservation service and provides chauffeurs for privately owned, collectible Rolls-Royces from the 1940s.

By Taxi: Except for the flat-fare trips described below, cabs cost $3.25 for the first mile, $2 a mile after that, plus a $1 toll for trips originating at MIA or the Port of Miami. Approximate fares from MIA include $17 to Coral Gables or downtown Miami, $31 to Key Biscayne. In addition, Miami's regulatory commission has established flat rates for five zones of the city, four of which are listed here: $24 to between 63rd Street and the foot of Miami Beach (including South Beach); $41 to Golden Beach and Sunny Isles, north of Haulover Beach Park; $34 to between Surfside and Haulover Beach Park; and $29 to between 63rd and 87th streets. These fares are per trip, not per passenger, and include tolls and $1 airport surcharge but not tip. The approximate fare between MIA and the Port of Miami is $18.

For taxi service to destinations in the immediate vicinity, ask a uniformed county taxi dispatcher to call an **ARTS** (Airport Region Taxi Service) cab for you. These special blue cabs offer a short-haul flat fare in two zones. An inner-zone ride is $7; the outer-zone fare is $10. The area of service is north to 36th Street, west to the Palmetto Expressway (77th Avenue), south to Northwest 7th Street, and east to Douglas Road (37th Avenue). Maps are posted in cab windows on both sides.

By Van: SuperShuttle (☎ 305/871–2000 from MIA; 954/764–1700 from Broward [Fort Lauderdale]; 800/874–8885 from elsewhere) vans transport passengers between MIA and local hotels, the Port of Miami, and even individual residences on a 24-hour basis. At MIA the vans pick up at the ground level of each concourse (look for clerks with yellow shirts, who will flag one down). The company's service area extends from Palm Beach to Monroe County (including the Lower Keys). Drivers provide narration en route. Service from MIA is available around the clock on demand; for the return it's best to make reservations 24 hours in advance, although the firm will try to arrange pickups within Miami-Dade County on as little as four hours' notice. The cost from MIA to downtown hotels runs $9–$10; to the beaches it can be $11–$16 per passenger, depending on how far north you go. Additional members of a party pay a lower rate for many destinations, and children under three ride free with their parents. There's a pet transport fee of $10 for animals in kennels.

By Train

Amtrak (☎ 800/872–7245) runs three trains daily between New York City and Miami (⊠ 8303 N.W. 37th Ave., ☎ 305/835–1223 for recorded arrival and departure information; 800/368–8725 for shipping); the trains make several stops along the way.

Tri-Rail (⊠ 1 River Plaza, 305 S. Andrews Ave., Suite 200, Fort Lauderdale, ☎ 800/874–7245) is Florida's only commuter train system. Daily runs connect Miami with Broward and Palm Beach, stopping at 18 stations along the 70-mi route. Fares are established by zones, with prices ranging from $2 to a high of $9.25 round-trip. Tri-Rail connects with Miami's Metrorail, so you may not have to drive at all.

Getting Around

Greater Miami resembles Los Angeles in its urban sprawl and traffic. You'll need a car to visit many attractions and points of interest. Some are accessible via the public transportation system, run by a department of the county government—the **Metro-Dade Transit Agency,** which consists of 650 Metrobuses on 70 routes, the 21-mi Metrorail elevated rapid-transit system, and the Metromover, an elevated light-rail system. Free maps and schedules are available. ⊠ *Government Center Station, 111 N.W. 1st St., Miami 33128,* ☎ *305/654–6586 for Maps by Mail; 305/770–3131 for route information weekdays 6 AM–10 PM and weekends 9–5.*

By Bus

Metrobus stops are marked by blue-and-green signs with a bus logo and route information. The frequency of service varies widely, so call in advance to obtain specific schedules. The fare is $1.25 (exact change), transfers 25¢; 60¢ with 10¢ transfers for people with disabilities, senior citizens (65 and older), and students. Some express routes carry surcharges of $1.50. Reduced-fare tokens, sold 10 for $10, are available from Metropass outlets. Lift-equipped buses for people with disabilities are available on 16 routes, including one from the airport that links up with many routes in Miami Beach as well as Coconut Grove, Coral Gables, Hialeah, and Kendall. All but four of these routes connect with Metrorail. Those unable to use regular transit service should call **Special Transportation Services** (☎ 305/263–5400) for information on such services as curb-to-curb van pickup.

By Car

In general, Miami traffic is the same as in any other big city, with the same rush hours and the same likelihood that parking garages will be full at peak times. Many drivers who aren't locals and don't know their way around might turn and stop suddenly, or drop off passengers where they shouldn't. Some drivers are short-tempered and will assault those who cut them off or honk their horn.

Motorists need to be careful, even when their driving behavior is beyond censure, however, especially in rental cars. Despite the removal of identifying marks, cars piled with luggage or otherwise showing signs that a tourist is at the wheel remain prime targets for thieves. Your best bet is to "follow the sun"; major (and safer) travel routes are marked by huge sunburst logos, which connect to tourist hot spots like the Deco District. Stick with these, and you should get where you need to go fairly easily and quickly. The city has also initiated a TOP (Tourist Oriented Police) Cops program to assist tourists with directions and safety. For more safety advice on driving in Miami, *see* Driving *in* Smart Travel Tips A to Z.

By Taxi

One cab "company" stands out immeasurably above the rest. It's actually a consortium of drivers who have banded together to provide good service, in marked contrast to some Miami cabbies, who are rude, unhelpful, unfamiliar with the city, or dishonest, taking advantage of visitors who don't know the area. To plug into this consortium—they don't have a name, simply a number—call the **dispatch service** (☎ 305/888–4444)—although they can be hard to understand over the phone. If you have to use another company, try to be familiar with your route and destination. For information call the **Metro-Dade Passenger Transportation Regulatory Service** (☎ 305/375–2460), also known as the Hack Bureau. It takes complaints and monitors all for-hire vehicles.

Starting in 1998, fares were set at $3.25 per first mile and $2 every mile after, with no additional charge for up to five passengers, luggage, and tolls. Taxis can be hailed on the street, although you may not always find one when you need one—it's better to call for a dispatch taxi or have a hotel doorman hail one for you. Some companies with dispatch service are **Central Taxicab Service** (☎ 305/532–5555), **Diamond Cab Company** (☎ 305/545–5555), **Metro Taxicab Company** (☎ 305/888–8888), **Miami-Dade Yellow Cab** (☎ 305/633–0503), **Society Cab Company** (☎ 305/757–5523), **Super Yellow Cab Company** (☎ 305/888–7777), **Tropical Taxicab Company** (☎ 305/945–1025), and **Yellow Cab Company** (☎ 305/444–4444). Many now accept credit cards; inquire when you call.

By Train
Elevated **Metrorail** (☎ 305/770–3131) trains run from downtown Miami north to Hialeah and south along U.S. 1 to Dadeland, daily 5:30 AM–midnight. Trains run every five minutes in peak hours, every 15 minutes at other times. The fare is $1.25. Transfers, which cost 25¢, must be bought at the first station entered. Parking at train stations costs $2.

Metromover (☎ 305/770–3131) has two loops that circle downtown Miami, linking major hotels, office buildings, and shopping areas. The system spans 4½ mi, including the 1½-mi Omni Extension, with six stations to the north, and the 1-mi Brickell Extension, with six stations to the south. Quite convenient and amazingly cheap, it beats walking all around downtown. Service runs daily every 90 seconds, 6 AM–midnight. The fare is 25¢. Transfers to Metrorail are $1.

By Trolley
The best thing to arrive in Miami Beach since sand, the **Electro-Wave** (☎ 305/843–9283) is a fleet of *free* electric trolleys running every few minutes up and down Washington Avenue between 5th and 17th streets. New service continues south of 5th Street, west to Alton Road, and over by the Miami Beach Marina. Considering the great lengths between SoBe attractions, it'll save a lot of shoe leather. Trolleys operate Monday–Wednesday 8 AM–2 AM, Thursday–Saturday 8 AM–4 AM, and Sunday and holidays 10 AM–2 AM.

By Water Taxi
A **water taxi service** (☎ 954/467–6677), inaugurated in 1988 in Fort Lauderdale, began Miami area operations in 1993. Canopied boats, 28 ft and longer, run between Miami Beach and the Bayside Marketplace. Routes cover downtown restaurants and the Watson Island airboat station. Taxi hours vary by season, with average fares from Bayside Marketplace of $3.50 one-way and $6 round-trip to waterfront stops in Miami and $7 one-way and $13 round-trip to Miami Beach. An all-day pass is $15.

Contacts and Resources

Emergencies
Dial **911** for police or ambulance. You can dial free from pay phones.

AMBULANCE

Randle Eastern Ambulance Service Inc. (✉ 7255 N.W. 19th St., Suite C, Miami 33126, ☎ 305/718–6400) operates at all hours, although in an emergency they'll direct you to call 911.

DENTISTS

East Coast District Dental Society (⊠ 420 S. Dixie Hwy., Suite 2E, Coral Gables, ☎ 305/667–3647) is open weekdays 9–4:30 for dental referral. After hours stay on the line and a recording will direct you to a dentist. Services include general dentistry, endodontics, periodontics, and oral surgery.

DOCTORS

Dade County Medical Association (⊠ 1501 N.W. North River Dr., Miami, ☎ 305/324–8717) is open weekdays 9–5 for medical referral.

HOSPITALS

Miami has 32 hospitals and more than 34,000 health-care professionals. The following hospitals have 24-hour emergency rooms.

In Miami Beach: **Miami Heart Institute** (⊠ 4701 N. Meridian Ave., Miami Beach, ☎ 305/672–1111; 888/432–7848 physician referral), **Mt. Sinai Medical Center** (⊠ Off Julia Tuttle Causeway, I–195 at 4300 Alton Rd., Miami Beach, ☎ 305/674–2121; 305/674–2200 emergency; 305/674–2273 physician referral), and **South Shore Hospital & Medical Center** (⊠ 630 Alton Rd., Miami Beach, ☎ 305/672–2100).

In the north: **Parkway Regional Hospital** (⊠ 160 N.W. 170th St., North Miami Beach, ☎ 305/651–1100; 800/833–8005 physician referral).

In central Miami: **Coral Gables Hospital** (⊠ 3100 Douglas Rd., Coral Gables, ☎ 305/445–8461; 305/444–2100 physician referral), **Jackson Memorial Hospital** (⊠ 1611 N.W. 12th Ave., near Dolphin Expressway, Miami, ☎ 305/585–1111; 305/585–6901 emergency; 305/243–5757 physician referral), **Mercy Hospital** (⊠ 3663 S. Miami Ave., Coconut Grove, ☎ 305/854–4400; 305/285–2171 emergency; 305/285–2929 physician referral), and **Pan American Hospital** (⊠ 5959 N.W. 7th St., Miami, ☎ 305/264–1000, ext. 6125 emergency; 305/264–5118 physician referral).

In the south: **Baptist Hospital of Miami** (⊠ 8900 N. Kendall Dr., Miami, ☎ 305/596–1960; 305/596–6556 emergency; 305/596–6557 physician referral) and **South Miami Hospital** (⊠ 6200 S.W. 73rd St., South Miami, ☎ 305/661–4611; 305/662–8181 emergency; 305/596–6557 physician referral).

LATE-NIGHT PHARMACIES

Eckerd Drug (⊠ 1825 Miami Gardens Dr. NE, at 185th St., North Miami Beach, ☎ 305/932–5740) is open until midnight. **Eckerd Drug** (⊠ 200 Lincoln Rd., Miami Beach, ☎ 305/532–6978) has a pharmacy open until 8 PM weekdays, 6 PM Saturday. Also in South Beach, **Walgreen** (⊠ 524 Jefferson Ave., Miami Beach, ☎ 305/531–7688) has a pharmacy open until 10 PM weekdays, 6 PM weekends. The following are open 24 hours: **Eckerd Drug** (⊠ 9031 S.W. 107th Ave., Miami, ☎ 305/274–6776) and **Walgreens** (⊠ 500-B W. 49th St., Palm Springs Mall, Hialeah, ☎ 305/557–5468; ⊠ 2750 W. 68th St., Hialeah, ☎ 305/828–0268; ⊠ 12295 Biscayne Blvd., North Miami, ☎ 305/893–6860; ⊠ 5731 Bird Rd., Miami, ☎ 305/666–0757; ⊠ 1845 Alton Rd., Miami Beach, ☎ 305/531–8868; ⊠ 791 N.E. 167th St., North Miami Beach, ☎ 305/652–7332).

Car Rentals

The following agencies have booths near the baggage-claim area on MIA's lower level: **Alamo** (☎ 800/468–2583), **Avis** (☎ 800/331–1212), **Budget** (☎ 800/527–0700), **Dollar** (☎ 800/800–4000), **Hertz** (☎ 800/654–3131), and **National** (☎ 800/227–7368). Avis and Budget have offices at the Port of Miami.

If money is no object, check out **Excellence Luxury Car Rental** (☎ 305/ 526–0000). As the name implies, you can rent some wheels (a Ferrari, perhaps?) to cruise SoBe and pretend you're Don Johnson. If you can't find the excellent car you want, you can rent a Dodge Viper, BMW, Hummer, Jag, Porsche, or Rolls from **Exotic Cars** (☎ 888/541–1789). Airport pickup is provided.

Guided Tours

BOAT TOURS

Bay Ex.Cape (✉ 401 Biscayne Blvd., ☎ 305/373–7001) cruises in air-conditioned comfort past Millionaires' Row and the Venetian Islands during bilingual excursions that depart from the Bayside Marketplace at 11, 1, 3, 5, and 7.

Heritage of Miami II (✉ 401 Biscayne Blvd., ☎ 305/442–9697) offers sightseeing cruises on board a two-masted, 85-ft topsail schooner. Tours start and end at Bayside Marketplace. One-hour sails cost $10 per person, and two-hour sails are $15. Tours loop through lower Biscayne Bay, with views of the Vizcaya Museum and Gardens; the homes of Madonna, Sly, Luciano, and Whitney; the Port of Miami; and several residential islands. It's a little money for a lot of fun.

Island Queen, Island Lady,* and *Pink Lady (✉ 401 Biscayne Blvd., ☎ 305/379–5119) are 150-passenger double-decker tour boats docked at Bayside Marketplace. They go on daily 90-minute narrated tours of the Port of Miami and Millionaires' Row, costing $12. Refreshments are available.

Casino gambling is illegal in Florida, which explains the popularity of ***SeaKruz*** (✉ 300 Alton Rd., Miami Beach, ☎ 305/538–8300). For $15 you can travel into international waters and drop cash into craps, roulette, blackjack, and even pai gow—whatever floats your boat! If you're annoyed by mediocre food, cigarette smoke, and the hell's bells of slots, it'll be a loooong trip. Cruises depart from the Miami Beach Marina.

HISTORICAL TOURS

Art Deco District Tour (✉ 1001 Ocean Dr., Bin L, Miami Beach 33139, ☎ 305/672–2014), operated by the Miami Design Preservation League, is a 90-minute guided walking tour ($6) departing from the league's welcome center at the Oceanfront Auditorium at 10:30 AM Saturday and 6:30 PM Thursday. Private group tours can be arranged with advance notice. You can go at your own pace with a self-guided $5 audio tour, which takes roughly an hour. The league also sells the *Art Deco District Guide,* a book of six detailed walking or driving tours of the Art Deco District, for $10. A two-hour bike tour leaves from the **Miami Beach Bicycle Center** (✉ 601 5th St., Miami Beach, ☎ 305/ 674–0150) at 10:30 on the first and third Sundays of the month. Led by a guide from the Miami Design Preservation League, this tour costs $15 including a rental bike, $6 with your own bike.

Deco Tours Miami Beach (✉ 420 Lincoln Rd., Suite 412, Miami Beach, ☎ 305/531–4465) offers walking tours of the Art Deco District, with 24-hour notice for reservations preferred. These 90-minute tours, which cost $15, depart from the National Hotel, on Collins Avenue. Tours of the city are conducted in vans and buses.

Professor Paul George (✉ 1345 S.W. 14th St., Miami, ☎ 305/858–6021), a history professor at Miami-Dade Community College and past president of the Florida Historical Society, leads a variety of walking tours as well as boat tours and tours that make use of the Metrorail and Metromover. Pick from tours covering downtown, historic neighborhoods, cemeteries, Coconut Grove, and the Miami River. They start Saturday at 10 and Sunday at 11 at various locations, depending on the tour, and generally last about 2½ hours. Call for each weekend's schedule and for additional tours by appointment. The fee is $15.

RICKSHAW TOURS

Coconut Grove Rickshaw centers its operations at CocoWalk. Two-person rickshaws scurry along Main Highway in Coconut Grove's Village Center, nightly 7 PM–midnight. You can take a 10-minute ride through Coconut Grove or a 20-minute lovers' moonlight ride to Biscayne Bay; prices start at $5 per person.

Motorcycle Rentals

American Road Collection (⊠ 3970 N.W. 25th St., Miami, ☎ 305/871–1040 or 888/736–8433) rents new Harleys for half days, full days, or longer.

Services for People with Hearing Impairments

Fire, police, medical, rescue (☎ 305/595–4749 TDD; 305/595–6263 voice; 911 voice).

Operator and directory assistance (☎ 800/855–1155 TDD).

Deaf Services of Miami (⊠ 9100 S. Dadeland Blvd., Suite 104, Miami 33156; ☎ 305/668–3323 TDD; 305/668–4407 voice; 305/668–4693 24-hour hot line; 305/806–6090 24-hour emergency numerical pager for interpreters).

Florida Relay Service (☎ 800/955–8771 TDD; 800/955–8770 voice).

Visitor Information

Greater Miami Convention & Visitors Bureau (⊠ 701 Brickell Ave., Suite 2700, Miami 33131, ☎ 305/539–3063 or 800/283–2707). Satellite tourist information centers are at **Bayside Marketplace** (⊠ 401 Biscayne Blvd., Miami 33132, ☎ 305/539–2980) and **South Dade Visitor Information Center** (⊠ 160 U.S. 1, Florida City 33034, ☎ 305/245–9180 or 800/388–9669, FAX 305/247–4335).

Coconut Grove Chamber of Commerce (⊠ 2820 McFarlane Rd., Coconut Grove 33133, ☎ 305/444–7270, FAX 305/444–2498). **Coral Gables Chamber of Commerce** (⊠ 50 Aragon Ave., Coral Gables 33134, ☎ 305/446–1657, FAX 305/446–9900). **Florida Gold Coast Chamber of Commerce** (⊠ 1100 Kane Concourse, Suite 210, Bay Harbor Islands 33154, ☎ 305/866–6020) serves the beach communities of Bal Harbour, Bay Harbor Islands, Golden Beach, North Bay Village, Sunny Isles, and Surfside. **Greater Miami Chamber of Commerce** (⊠ 1601 Biscayne Blvd., Miami 33132, ☎ 305/350–7700, FAX 305/374–6902). **Greater North Miami Chamber of Commerce** (⊠ 13100 W. Dixie Hwy., North Miami 33181, ☎ 305/891–7811, FAX 305/893–8522). **Greater South Dade/South Miami Chamber of Commerce** (⊠ 6410 S.W. 80th St., South Miami 33143-4602, ☎ 305/661–1621, FAX 305/666–0508). **Key Biscayne Chamber of Commerce** (⊠ Key Biscayne Bank Bldg., 95 W. McIntyre St., Key Biscayne 33149, ☎ 305/361–5207). **Miami Beach Chamber of Commerce** (⊠ 1920 Meridian Ave., Miami Beach 33139, ☎ 305/672–1270, FAX 305/538–4336). **Surfside Tourist Board** (⊠ 9301 Collins Ave., Surfside 33154, ☎ 305/864–0722 or 800/327–4557, FAX 305/861–1302).

2 THE EVERGLADES

South Florida's wide, slow-moving "River of Grass"—the largest roadless expanse in the United States—is home to Everglades National Park and spectacular plant and animal life found no place else in the country. Nearby Biscayne National Park protects living coral reefs, mangroves, undeveloped islands, a shallow bay, and all the wild things that come with them. Both areas, within minutes of Miami's metropolis, maintain a fragile balance between humans and nature.

Updated by
Diane P.
Marshall

THE ONLY METROPOLITAN AREA in the United States with two national parks in its backyard is Miami. Everglades National Park, created in 1947, was meant to preserve the slow-moving "River of Grass"—a freshwater river 50 mi wide but only 6 inches deep, flowing from Lake Okeechobee through marshy grassland into Florida Bay. Along the Tamiami Trail (U.S. 41), marshes of cattails extend as far as the eye can see, interspersed only with hammocks or tree islands of bald cypress and mahogany, while overhead southern bald eagles make circles in the sky. A wide variety of trees and flowers, including ferns, orchids, and bromeliads, share the brackish waters with otters, turtles, marsh rabbits, and occasionally that gentle giant, the West Indian manatee. Not so gentle, though, is the saw grass. Deceptively graceful, these tall, willowy sedges have small sharp teeth on the edges of their leaves.

Biscayne National Park, established as a national monument in 1968 and 12 years later expanded and designated a national park, is the nation's largest marine park and the largest national park within the continental United States with living coral reefs. A small portion of the park's almost 274 square mi consists of mainland coast and outlying islands, but 96% is under water, much of it in Biscayne Bay. The islands contain lush, heavily wooded forests with an abundance of ferns and native palm trees. Of particular interest are the mangroves and their tangled masses of stiltlike roots and stems that thicken the shorelines. These "walking trees," as locals sometimes call them, have striking curved prop roots, which arch down from the trunk, while aerial roots drop from branches. These trees draw freshwater from saltwater and create a coastal nursery capable of sustaining all types of marine life.

Unfortunately, Miami's backyard is threatened by suburban sprawl and agriculture. What results is competition among environmental, agricultural, and developmental interests. The biggest issue is water. Originally, alternating floods and dry periods maintained wildlife habitat and regulated the water flowing into Florida Bay. The brackish seasonal flux sustained a remarkably vigorous bay, including the most productive shrimp beds in American waters, with thriving mangrove thickets and coral reefs at its Atlantic edge. The system nurtured sea life and attracted anglers and divers. Starting in the 1930s, however, a giant flood-control system began diverting water to canals running to the gulf and the ocean. As you travel Florida's north–south routes, you cross this network of canals symbolized by a smiling alligator representing the South Florida Water Management District, ironically known as "Protector of the Everglades."

The unfortunate side effect of flood control has been devastation of the wilderness. Park visitors decry diminished bird counts (a 90% reduction over 50 years); the black bear has been eliminated; and the Florida panther is nearing extinction. In 1997 the nonprofit group American Rivers again ranked the Everglades among the most threatened rivers of North America. Meanwhile, the loss of freshwater has made Florida Bay more salty, devastating breeding grounds and creating dead zones where pea green algae has replaced sea grasses and sponges.

Even as the ecosystem fades, new policies, still largely on paper, hold promise. Some 40% of what is commonly called Big Cypress Swamp was established as Big Cypress National Preserve in 1974 to protect the watershed of Everglades National Park. Some 22 government agencies and a host of conservation groups and industries are working on restoration plans. Some of the 40,000 acres of filtration marshes that will remove harmful agricultural nutrients before they enter the protected wetlands have been constructed as part of the Everglades Forever Act. Within the next decade farming must sharply reduce its phosphorus runoff, and the U.S. Army Corps of Engineers, which maintains Florida's flood-control system, proposes restoring a more natural flow of water into the Everglades and its related systems. Although the future of the natural system hangs uncertainly as engineers and ecologists battle over what to do and when to do it, there are promising signs.

New and Noteworthy

In Florida City, a new **aquarium** should be open by the year 2000.

Guests wanting to stay in the heart of the Everglades started checking into the **Miccosukee Resort & Convention Center** in June 1999.

Pleasures and Pastimes

Biking and Hiking

In the Everglades there are several nice places to ride and hike. The Shark Valley Loop Road (15 mi round-trip) makes a good bike trip. "Foot and Canoe Trails of the Flamingo Area," a leaflet, lists others. Inquire about insect conditions before you go and plan accordingly, stocking up on insect repellent, sunscreen, and water, as necessary.

Boating and Canoeing

One of the best ways to experience the Everglades is by boat, and almost all of Biscayne National Park is accessible only by water. Boat rentals are available in both parks. Rentals are generally for half day (four hours) and full day (eight hours).

In the Everglades the 99-mi inland Wilderness Trail between Flamingo and Everglades City is open to motorboats as well as canoes, although powerboats may have trouble navigating the route above Whitewater Bay. Flat-water canoeing is best in winter, when temperatures are moderate, rainfall is minimal, and mosquitoes are tolerable. You don't need a permit for day trips, but tell someone where you're going and when you expect to return. Getting lost is easy, and spending the night without proper gear can be unpleasant, if not dangerous.

On the Gulf Coast you can explore the nooks, crannies, and mangrove islands of Chokoloskee Bay, as well as many rivers near Everglades City. The Turner River Trail, a good day trip, passes through mangrove, dwarf cypress, coastal prairie, and freshwater slough ecosystems of Everglades National Park and Big Cypress National Preserve.

Dining

With a few exceptions, dining centers on low-key mom-and-pop places that serve hearty home-style food and small eateries specializing in local fare: seafood, conch, alligator, turtle, and frogs' legs. Native American restaurants add another dimension, serving local favorites as well as catfish, Indian fry bread (a flour-and-water dough), pumpkin bread, Indian burgers (ground beef browned, rolled in fry-bread dough, and deep-fried), and tacos (fry bread with chili, lettuce, tomato, and shredded cheddar cheese on top). Restaurants in Everglades City appear to operate with a "captive audience" philosophy: Prices run high, service is mediocre, and food preparation is uninspired. The closest good restaurants are in Naples, 35 mi northwest.

Although both Everglades and Biscayne national parks are wilderness areas, there are restaurants within a short drive. Most are between Miami and Shark Valley along the Tamiami Trail (U.S. 41), in the Homestead–

Florida City area, in Everglades City, and in the Florida Keys along the Overseas Highway (U.S. 1). The only food service in either park is at Flamingo, in the Everglades, but many independent restaurants will pack picnics. (You can also find fast-food establishments on the Tamiami Trail east of Krome Avenue and along U.S. 1 in Homestead–Florida City.)

Fishing

Largemouth bass are plentiful in freshwater ponds, while snapper, redfish, and sea trout are caught in Florida Bay. The mangrove shallows of the Ten Thousand Islands, along the gulf, yield tarpon and snook. Whitewater Bay is also a favorite spot. Note: The state has issued health advisories for sea bass, largemouth bass, and other freshwater fish, especially those caught in the canals along the Tamiami Trail, due to their high mercury content. Signs are posted throughout the park, and consumption should be limited.

Exploring the Everglades

The southern tip of the Florida peninsula is largely taken up by Everglades National Park, but land access to it is primarily by two roads: The main park road traverses the southern Everglades from the gateway towns of Homestead and Florida City to the outpost of Flamingo, on Florida Bay. In the northern Everglades you can take the Tamiami Trail (U.S. 41) from the Greater Miami area in the east to the western park entrance in Everglades City. In far southeastern Florida, Biscayne National Park lies almost completely offshore. As a result, most sports and recreational opportunities in both national parks are based on water, the study of nature, or both, so even on land, be prepared to get a bit damp on the region's marshy trails.

Though relatively compact, as compared with the national parks of the West, these parks still require a bit of time to see. The narrow, two-lane roads through the Everglades make for long travel, whereas it's the necessity of sightseeing by boat that takes time at Biscayne.

Numbers in the text correspond to numbers in the margin and on the Everglades and Biscayne National Parks map.

Great Itineraries

IF YOU HAVE 1 DAY

You'll have to make a choice—the Everglades or Biscayne. If you want quiet and nature, go with the Everglades. If you're interested in boating or underwater flora and fauna, Biscayne is your best bet. Either way, you'll experience a little of what's left of the "real" Florida.

For a day in Everglades National Park, begin in **Florida City** ⑭, gateway to the park and site of a museum on Florida pioneer life. Head to the **Ernest F. Coe Visitor Center** ① for an overview of the park and its ecosystems and continue to the **Royal Palm Visitor Center** ② for a look at several unique plant systems. Then go to **Flamingo** ③, where you can rent a boat or take a tour of Florida Bay.

If Biscayne is your preference, begin at **Convoy Point** ⑮ for an orientation before forsaking dry land. Sign up for a snorkel or dive trip or an outing on a glass-bottom boat, or explore an island.

IF YOU HAVE 3 DAYS

With three days you can explore both the northern and southern Everglades as well as Biscayne National Park. Start in the north by driving west along the Tamiami Trail, stopping at **Everglades Safari Park** ④ for an airboat ride; at **Shark Valley** ⑥ for a tram tour, walk, or bicycle trip; at the **Miccosukee Indian Village** ⑦ for lunch; at the **Big Cy-**

press Gallery ⑧ to see Clyde Butcher's photographs; and then at the **Ochopee post office** ⑩, before ending in ⊞ **Everglades City** ⑫, home of the Gulf Coast Visitor Center. From here you can visit historic Smallwood's Store on Chokoloskee Island and watch the sunset. Day two is for exploring the south. Return east on the Tamiami Trail to **Homestead** ⑬, pausing at Everglades Air Tours to take a sightseeing trip before following the one-day Everglades itinerary above and overnighting in ⊞ **Florida City** ⑭. Biscayne National Park is the subject of day three. If you plan to scuba or take the glass-bottom boat, get an early start. You can explore the visitor center at **Convoy Point** ⑮ when you return and finish your day checking out sights in Florida City and Homestead. Snorkel trips leave later, giving you time to see Florida City and Homestead, have lunch, and learn about the park's ecosystem at the visitor center first. Be warned that though you can fly and then scuba dive, you can't dive and then fly within 24 hours. So if you're flying out, reverse the days' sequence accordingly.

IF YOU HAVE 5 DAYS

Follow day one above, spending the night in ⊞ **Everglades City** ⑫. Begin the second day with a canoe, kayak, or boat tour of the Ten Thousand Islands. In the late afternoon take a walk on the boardwalk at **Faka-hatchee Strand State Preserve** ⑪ to see rare epiphytic orchids or on a 2½-mi trail at the Big Cypress National Preserve. Drive east to Coopertown and take a nighttime ride with Ray Cramer's Everglades Airboat Tours. Spend the night in ⊞ **Florida City** ⑭. Day three is spent at Biscayne National Park, then sightseeing in **Homestead** ⑬ and **Florida City** ⑭ as suggested above. Begin day four at Everglades Air Tours in Homestead; then browse the antiques shops along Krome Avenue before picking up a picnic lunch and seeing some of South Dade's other nearby attractions. On day five, augment your picnic lunch with goodies from the remarkable fruit stand Robert Is Here, before heading to the southern portion of Everglades National Park, as described above.

When to Tour the Everglades

Winter is the best time to visit Everglades National Park. Temperatures and mosquito activity are low to moderate, low water levels concentrate the resident wildlife around sloughs that retain water all year, and migratory birds swell the avian population. Winter is also the busiest time in the park. Make reservations and expect crowds at Flamingo, the main visitor center (known officially as the Ernest F. Coe Visitor Center), and Royal Palm.

In spring the weather turns hot and rainy, and tours and facilities are less crowded. Migratory birds depart, and you must look harder to see wildlife. Be careful with campfires and matches; this is when the wildfire-prone saw grass prairies and pinelands are most vulnerable.

Summer brings intense sun and billowing clouds unleashing torrents of rain almost every afternoon. Start your outdoor activities early to avoid the rain and the sun's strongest rays, and use sunscreen. Water levels rise and wildlife disperses. Mosquitoes hatch, swarm, and descend on you in voracious clouds. (Carrying mosquito repellent is a good idea at any time of year, but it's a necessity in summer.) Europeans constitute 80% of the summer visitors.

Even if you're not lodging in Everglades National Park, try to stay until dusk, when dozens of bird species feed around the ponds and trails. While shining a flashlight over the water in marshy areas, look for two yellowish-red reflections above the surface—telltale alligator signs.

EVERGLADES NATIONAL PARK

11 mi southwest of Homestead, 45 mi southwest of Miami International Airport.

The best way to experience the real Everglades is to get your feet wet, like paddling a canoe into the River of Grass to stay in a backcountry campsite. Most visitors won't do that, however. Luckily, there are several ways to see the wonders of the park with dry feet. Take a boat tour in Everglades City or Flamingo, ride the tram at Shark Valley, or walk the boardwalks along the main park road. And there's more to see than natural beauty. Miccosukee Indians operate a range of attractions and restaurants worthy of a stop.

Admission to Everglades National Park is valid at all entrances for seven days. Coverage below begins in the southern Everglades, followed by the northern Everglades, starting in the east and ending in Everglades City.

The Main Park Road

The main park road (Route 9336) travels from the main visitor center to Flamingo, across a section of the park's eight distinct ecosystems: hardwood hammock, freshwater prairie, pineland, freshwater slough, cypress, coastal prairie, mangrove, and marine-estuarine. Highlights of the trip include a dwarf cypress forest, the ecotone (transition zone) between saw grass and mangrove forest, and a wealth of wading birds at Mrazek and Coot Bay ponds. Boardwalks, looped trails, several short spurs, and observation platforms allow you to stay dry.

❶ The **Ernest F. Coe Visitor Center,** at park headquarters, houses numerous interactive exhibits and films. Stand in a simulated blind and peer through a spyglass to watch birds in the wild; though it's actually a film, the quality is so good you'll think you're outside. Move on to a bank of telephones to hear differing viewpoints on the Great Water Debate. There's a 15-minute film on the park, two movies on hurricanes, and a 45-minute wildlife film for children. Computer monitors present a schedule of daily ranger-led activities park-wide as well as information on canoe rentals and boat tours. In the Everglades Discovery Shop you can browse through lots of neat nature, science, and kids' stuff and pick up the insect repellent you forgot. The center provides information on the entire park. ⊠ *11 mi southwest of Homestead on Rte. 9336,* ☎ *305/242–7700.* ⊡ *Park $10 per car, $5 per pedestrian or bicyclist, $5 per motorcycle.* ☉ *Daily 8–5.*

❷ The **Royal Palm Visitor Center** is a must for anyone who wants to experience the real Everglades. You can stroll along the Anhinga Trail boardwalk or follow the Gumbo Limbo Trail through a hardwood hammock. The visitor center has an interpretive display, a bookstore, and vending machines. ⊠ *4 mi west of Ernest F. Coe Visitor Center on Rte. 9336,* ☎ *305/242–7700.* ☉ *Daily 8–5.*

Flamingo

❸ *38 mi southwest of Ernest F. Coe Visitor Center.*

Here at the far end of the main road you'll find a cluster of buildings containing a visitor center, lodge, restaurant and lounge, gift shop, marina, and bicycle rentals, plus an adjacent campground. Tour boats narrated by interpretive guides, fishing expeditions of Florida Bay, and canoe and kayak trips all leave from here. Nearby is Eco Pond, one of the most popular wildlife observation areas.

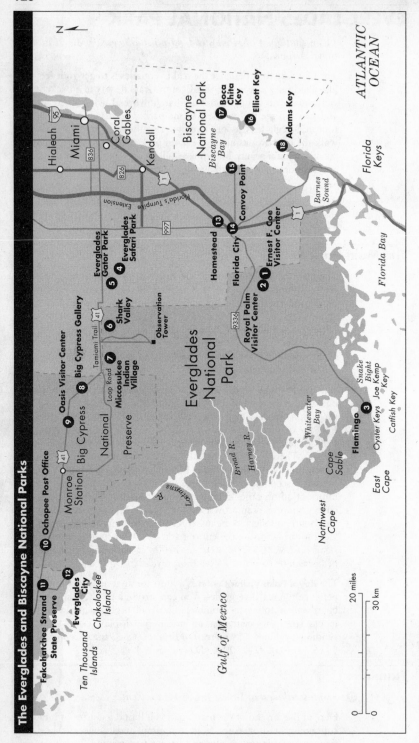

The Everglades and Biscayne National Parks

N

ATLANTIC OCEAN

Hialeah

Miami

Coral Gables

Kendall

95

836

826

Biscayne National Park

Biscayne Bay

17 Boca Chita Key

16 Elliott Key

18 Adams Key

Florida's Turnpike Extension

15 Convoy Point

Barnes Sound

1

997

13 Homestead

14 Florida City

Ernest F. Coe Visitor Center

2 1

Florida Keys

Florida Bay

Everglades Gator Park

4 Everglades Safari Park

5

6 Shark Valley

Observation Tower

Tamiami Trail 41

Big Cypress Gallery

7 Miccosukee Indian Village

8

Oasis Visitor Center

Loop Road

9

Big Cypress National Preserve

9336

Royal Palm Visitor Center

Everglades National Park

Whitewater Bay

Snake Bight

Joe Kemp Key

3 Flamingo

Oyster Keys

Catfish Key

Monroe Station

10 Ochopee Post Office

41

Broad R.

Harney R.

Cape Sable

East Cape

Lostmans R.

Northwest Cape

Fakahatchee Strand State Preserve 11

12

Everglades City

Chokoloskee Island

Ten Thousand Islands

Gulf of Mexico

20 miles

30 km

0

0

The **Flamingo Visitor Center** provides an interactive display and has natural history exhibits in the Florida Bay Museum. Check the schedule for ranger-led activities, such as naturalist discussions, evening programs in the campground amphitheater, and hikes along area trails. ☎ *305/242–7700.* ◷ *Daily 8–5.*

Dining and Lodging

$–$$ ✕ **Flamingo Restaurant.** The grand view, convivial lounge, and casual style are great. Big picture windows on the visitor center's second floor overlook Florida Bay, revealing soaring eagles, gulls, pelicans, terns, and vultures. Dine at low tide to see birds flock to the sandbar just offshore. Though the restaurant, which serves palatable seafood, pasta, and grills, is only open in high season, the marina store is open all year for pizza, sandwiches, and salads. ⊠ *Flamingo Lodge, 1 Flamingo Lodge Hwy.,* ☎ *941/695–3101. AE, D, DC, MC, V. Closed May–Oct.*

$$ ▥ **Flamingo Lodge, Marina & Outpost Resort.** This simple low-rise motel is the only lodging inside the park. Accommodations are basic but well kept, and an amiable staff helps you adjust to bellowing alligators, roaming raccoons, and ibis grazing on the lawn. Rooms have contemporary furniture, floral bedspreads, and art prints of bird life. Though they face Florida Bay, they don't necessarily look out over it. Bathrooms are small. Cottages, in a wooded area on the margin of a coastal prairie, have kitchenettes and accommodate up to six people. Reservations are essential in winter; Continental breakfast is included from May to October. Some facilities, like the restaurant, are seasonal. ⊠ *1 Flamingo Lodge Hwy., 33034,* ☎ *941/695–3101 or 800/600–3813,* Ⓕ𝔸𝕏 *941/695–3921. 103 rooms, 24 cottages, 1 suite. Restaurant, bar, snack bar, pool, coin laundry. AE, D, DC, MC, V.*

$ ⚠ **Everglades National Park.** Three developed campgrounds and group campsites have drinking water, sewage dump station, and rest rooms. Some also have picnic tables, grills, cold-water showers, and tent and trailer pads. Long Pine Key has 108 drive-up sites; Flamingo has 234 drive-up sites, 64 walk-in sites, and cold showers; and Chekika has 20 sites, warm showers, and a sulfur spring where you can swim. Pets are allowed. From late November through April sites at Long Pine Key and Flamingo are available through a reservation system, but the rest of the year all sites are first-come, first served. In addition, deep in the park are 48 backcountry sites, many inland with some on the beach. Three are accessible by land, the others by canoe; 16 have *chickees* (raised wooden platforms with thatched roofs). Most have chemical toilets. Several are within an easy day's canoeing of Flamingo; five are near Everglades City. You'll need to carry your food, water, and supplies in; carry out all trash. You'll also need a site-specific permit, available on a first-come, first-served basis from the Flamingo or Gulf Coast Visitor Center (☞ Contacts and Resources *in* Everglades A to Z, *below,* for both). Developed sites are free June–August and $14 the rest of the year, groups pay $28, and backcountry sites cost $10 or more depending on group size. ☎ *305/242–7700 or 305/251–0371; 800/365–2267 for campsite reservations. 471 sites. Picnic areas. No credit cards.*

Outdoor Activities and Sports

BIKING

Flamingo Lodge, Marina & Outpost Resort (☎ 941/695–3101) rents bikes for $14 a day and $8 per half day.

BOATING

The marina at **Flamingo Lodge, Marina & Outpost Resort** (☎ 941/695–3101) rents power skiffs for $90 per day and $65 per half day, four Carolina skiffs for $155 per day, as well as fully furnished and outfitted houseboats that sleep up to six. Rates (two-day minimum) run $475 without air-conditioning for two days, $575 with air-conditioning for two days. Several private boats are also available for charter. There are two ramps, one for Florida Bay, the other for Whitewater Bay and the backcountry. The hoist across the plug dam separating Florida Bay from the Buttonwood Canal can take boats from 16 ft to 26 ft long. A small store sells food, camping supplies, bait and tackle, propane, and fuel.

CANOEING AND KAYAKING

The Everglades has six well-marked canoe trails in the Flamingo area, including the south end of the 99-mi Wilderness Trail from Everglades City to Flamingo. **Flamingo Lodge, Marina & Outpost Resort** (☎ 941/695–3101) rents canoes in two sizes: small (up to two paddlers) and family size (up to four). Small canoes rent for $32 per day and $22 per half day; family-size run $40 and $30, respectively. Single-person kayaks cost $43 per day and $27 per half day; doubles rent for $54 and $38, respectively.

FISHING

Flamingo Lodge, Marina & Outpost Resort (☎ 941/695–3101) helps arrange charter fishing trips for two to six persons. The cost is $300 a day for up to two people, $25 each additional person.

Tamiami Trail

141 mi from Miami to Fort Myers.

In 1915, when officials decided to build an east–west highway linking Miami to Fort Myers and continuing north to Tampa, someone suggested calling it the Tamiami Trail. In 1928 the road became a reality, cutting through the Everglades and altering the natural flow of water and the lives of the Miccosukee Indians who eked out a living fishing, hunting, and frogging here.

Today the traffic screams through Everglades National Park, Big Cypress National Preserve, and Fakahatchee Strand State Preserve. The landscape is surprisingly varied, changing from hardwood hammocks to pinelands, then abruptly to tall cypress trees dripping with Spanish moss and back to coastal prairie. Those who slow to take in the scenery can see alligators sunning themselves along the banks of roadside canals and in the shallow waters, hundreds of waterbirds, chickee huts, people fishing, Native American villages, and airboats parked at roadside enterprises.

Businesses along the trail give their addresses either based on their distance from Krome Avenue, Florida's Turnpike, and Miami on the east coast or Fort Myers and Naples on the west coast or by mile marker. Between Miami and Fort Myers the road goes by several names, including Tamiami Trail, U.S. 41, and, at the Miami end, Southwest 8th Street.

4 Attractions at **Everglades Safari Park** include a jungle trail, an educational alligator show and wrestling demonstration, a wildlife museum, airboat rides (included in admission), and a restaurant and gift shop. Climb the observation platform and take in the beauty of the Glades. ⊠ *26700 Tamiami Trail, 9 mi west of Krome Ave.,* ☎ *305/226–6923 or 305/223–3804.* ☞ *$15.* ⏰ *Daily 8:30–5.*

5 At **Everglades Gator Park,** you can hold a baby alligator while friends snap a photo, squirm in a "reptilium" of venomous and nonpoisonous native snakes, or learn about Native Americans of the Everglades through a reproduction of a Miccosukee village. The park also features airboat tours, fishing charters, and RV campsites as well as a gift shop and restaurant. ⊠ *24050 Tamiami Trail, 12 mi west of Florida's Turn-*

pike, ☎ *305/559–2255 or 800/559–2205.* ✆ *Free, tours $12.* ◔ *Daily 9–sunset.*

❻ Though **Shark Valley** is the national park's north entrance, no roads here lead to other parts of the park. The only route is a paved 15-mi loop (you can walk, bicycle, or take a tram tour); at the half-way point there's a concrete observation tower built by an oil company in the early 1940s. Climb the ramp that spirals skyward 50 ft. From there everything as far as the eye can see is the vast River of Grass. Expect to see all kinds of waterbirds as well as alligators warming themselves along the banks and on the road (most quickly move out of the way). Just behind the bike rental area, a short boardwalk trail meanders through the saw grass. A small visitor center features rotating exhibits, a bookstore, and park rangers ready to answer questions. ✉ *23.5 mi west of Florida's Turnpike,* ☎ *305/221–8776.* ✆ *Park $8 per car, $4 per pedestrian, bicyclist, or motorcyclist.* ◔ *Visitor center daily 8:30–5:30.*

❼ At the **Miccosukee Indian Village,** Miccosukee families prepare food and make crafts, on sale at the cultural center. Informative alligator-wrestling shows as well as airboat rides and a restaurant are other attractions. The Everglades Music & Craft Festival falls on a July weekend, and the weeklong Indian Arts Festival is in late December. ✉ *Just west of Shark Valley entrance, 25 mi west of Florida's Turnpike,* ☎ *305/223–8380.* ✆ *$5, rides $7.* ◔ *Daily 9–5.*

❽ Clyde Butcher does for the River of Grass what Ansel Adams did for the West, and you can check out his stunning photographs at his **Big Cypress Gallery,** in the Big Cypress National Preserve. Working with large-format black-and-white film, Butcher captures every blade of grass, barb of feather, and flicker of light. Volunteers lead "Muck-About" swamp tours at the gallery's annual Labor Day weekend open house, during which there are also tours of the dark room and slide shows by naturalists and historians. Other events, special exhibits, lectures, tours, photo expeditions, and slide presentations are given throughout the year. ✉ *52388 Tamiami Trail, 37 mi west of Miami, 45 mi east of Naples,* ☎ *941/695–2428.* ✆ *Free, $20 suggested donation for Big Cypress Preserve Boardwalk Fund on Labor Day weekend.* ◔ *Fri.–Mon. 9:30–5.*

❾ Pause at the **Oasis Visitor Center** to learn about the national park's northern neighbor, the Big Cypress National Preserve. Through the 1950s and early 1960s, the world's largest cypress-logging industry prospered in the Big Cypress Swamp. The industry died out in the 1960s, and the government began buying parcels. Today part of the swamp, which encompasses more than 729,000 acres, has become this national preserve. Its variegated pattern of wet prairies, ponds, marshes, sloughs, and strands provides a sanctuary for a variety of wildlife, but because of a politically dictated policy of balanced land use—"use without abuse"—the watery wilderness is devoted to research and recreation as well as preservation. The preserve allows—in limited areas—hunting, off-road vehicle (airboat, swamp buggy) use by permit, and cattle grazing. The 8-mi Turner River Canoe Trail begins here and crosses through Everglades National Park before ending in Chokoloskee Bay, near Everglades City. Hikers can join the Florida National Scenic Trail, which runs north–south through the preserve for 31 mi. The visitor center provides a schedule of myriad seasonal ranger-led and self-guided activities, such as campfire talks, bike hikes, slough slogs, and canoe excursions. Seven primitive campsites are available on a first-come, first-served basis. ✉ *50 mi west of Miami, 20 mi west of Shark Valley,* ☎ *941/695–4111.* ✆ *Free.* ◔ *Daily 8:30–4:30.*

⑩ The tiny **Ochopee post office** is the smallest post office in North America. Buy a picture postcard of the little one-room shack and mail it to a friend, thereby helping to keep this picturesque spot in business. ⊠ *75 mi west of Miami, Ochopee,* ☎ *941/695–4131.* ☉ *Weekdays 9:30–noon and 12:30–4, Sat. 9:30–11:30.*

⑪ The ½-mi boardwalk at the **Fakahatchee Strand State Preserve** affords an opportunity to see rare plants, bald cypress, and North America's largest stand of native royal palms and largest concentration and variety of epiphytic orchids. ⊠ *Rte. 29 and Tamiami Trail; ranger station 3 mi north of Tamiami Trail on Rte. 29, Box 548, Copeland 34137,* ☎ *941/695–4593.* ⌾ *Free.* ☉ *Daily 8–sunset.*

Dining and Lodging

$ ✕ **Coopertown Restaurant.** For more than a half century this rustic eatery just into the Everglades west of Miami has been full of Old Florida style—not to mention alligator skulls, stuffed alligator heads, and gator accessories. House specialties are frogs' legs and alligator tail prepared breaded or deep-fried, and they're available for breakfast, lunch, or dinner. You can also order more conventional selections, such as catfish, shrimp, or sandwiches. ⊠ *22700 S.W. 8th St., Miami,* ☎ *305/226–6048. MC, V. Beer only.*

$ ✕ **Joanie's Blue Crab Cafe.** Movie set designers could not have designed
★ a more quintessential 1950s-style swamp café and country store than this landmark restaurant diagonally across from the Ochopee post office. The decor consists of wood-plank floors, open rafters hung with cobwebs, stuffed owls, postcards from around the globe, and kitschy gator art. Joanie, the chief cook and bottle washer, came here in 1987. Tony, her partner and "crab-ologist," picks the fresh blue crabs—up to 372 pounds in a weekend—that they catch each day to go into sandwiches, soups, and stuffed shrimp. Although the steamed crabs and crab sandwich served on a kaiser roll are the stars, the fresh sautéed vegetables—not always on the menu, but ask anyway—are delicious, too. A new screened deck will house a draft beer and wine bar. ⊠ *50 mi west of Florida's Turnpike, Ochopee,* ☎ *941/695–2682. No credit cards.*

$ ✕ **Miccosukee Restaurant.** Murals depict Native American women cooking and men engaged in a powwow in this Native American restaurant at the Miccosukee Indian Village. Favorites are catfish and frogs' legs breaded and deep-fried, Indian fry bread, pumpkin bread, and Indian burgers and tacos. Breakfast is served daily, but weekends bring a breakfast buffet (8–noon) featuring meats, eggs, breads, and lots more. ⊠ *25 mi west of Florida's Turnpike,* ☎ *305/223–8380 ext. 332. MC, V.*

$ ✕ **Pit Bar-B-Q.** The intense aroma of barbecue and blackjack-oak smoke will overwork your salivary glands. Order at the counter, pick up your food when called, and eat at one of the indoor or outdoor picnic tables. Specialties include barbecued chicken and ribs with a tangy sauce, french fries, coleslaw, and a fried biscuit as well as catfish and frogs' legs deep-fried in vegetable oil. Heed the scribbled message on the blackboard menu not to cross the grass median out front. It's an $85 fine if you're caught. ⊠ *16400 Tamiami Trail, Miami,* ☎ *305/226–2272. AE, MC, V.*

$$–$$$ ⌂ **Miccosukee Resort & Convention Center.** If location is everything, then this new resort at the crossroads of Tamiami Trail and Krome Avenue is a gold mine. Like an oasis, it's the only facility for miles, situated to attract visitors going to the Everglades, driving across the state, or looking for casino action. Most units have a view of Everglades sawgrass and wildlife. However, a pool, 8,500-sq-ft kids' play area, teen video center, gaming complex, tours to Everglades National Park and the Miccosukee Indian Village, shops, live entertainment, places to eat,

and shuttles to area malls are enough to distract guests from staring out the window. ✉ *500 S.W. 177th Ave., Miami 33194,* ☎ *305/221–8623 or 877/242–6464. 256 rooms, 46 suites. 2 restaurants, deli, indoor pool, beauty salon, sauna, spa, exercise room, casino, nightclub, video games, children's programs, convention center, meeting rooms, travel services, airport shuttle. AE, D, DC, MC, V.*

$ ⚠ **Everglades Gator Park.** Popular with the RV set, the park has full hookups for as many as 80 vehicles in addition to airboats, Everglades attractions, and a small store. You can rent a campsite by the night ($25), week ($100), or month ($350) or store your RV in the short-term area. ✉ *24050 S.W. 8th St., Miami,* ☎ *305/559–2255 or 800/559–2205;* ✉ *mailing address: 13800 S.W. 8th St., Box 107, Miami 33184. 80 sites. Restaurant, lake, fishing. D, MC, V.*

Outdoor Activities and Sports

Shark Valley Tram Tours (✉ Shark Valley, ☎ 305/221–8455) rents bikes daily 8:30–4 (last rental at 3) for $3.85 per hour.

Shopping

At the **Miccosukee Indian Village** (✉ Just west of Shark Valley entrance, 25 mi west of Florida's Turnpike, ☎ 305/223–8380), you can buy Native American crafts, including beadwork, moccasins, dolls, pottery, baskets, and patchwork fabric and clothes, as well as kitschy Florida souvenirs.

Everglades City

⑫ *35 mi southeast of Naples, 83 mi west of Miami.*

The western gateway to Everglades National Park, this community, just off the Tamiami Trail, has been around since the late 19th century, when Barron Collier, a wealthy advertising man, bought a lot of land and formed Collier County with the town of Everglades as county seat. Collier built a company town to house workers for his numerous projects, including construction of the Tamiami Trail. The town grew rapidly and prospered until the Depression and World War II, and in 1953 it changed its name to Everglades City. Today the biggest draw is the park, especially the canoeing, fishing, and bird-watching excursions you can take within it. (Airboat tours, though also popular, do not operate within the park.) The annual Seafood Festival, held the first weekend of February, attracts 60,000–75,000 visitors to eat seafood, hear nonstop music, and buy crafts.

The **Gulf Coast Visitor Center,** at the Everglades' western entrance, offers interpretive exhibits about local flora and fauna. Backcountry campers can purchase the required permits, and for those in need of a little more guidance, there are naturalist-led boat trips. The center offers access to the Ten Thousand Islands region along the Gulf of Mexico, but there are no roads from here to other sections of the park. ✉ *Rte. 29,* ☎ *941/695–3311.* 🎫 *Park free.* ☉ *Mid-Nov.–mid-Apr., daily 7:30–5; reduced hrs mid-Apr.–mid.-Nov.*

The new **Museum of the Everglades** chronicles the 2,000-year history of human habitation in the southwestern Everglades. It's housed in the only remaining unaltered structure original to the town of Everglades, where it opened in 1927 as the town's laundry. In addition to artifacts, photographs, and a 1923 model of the town, there are traveling exhibits, lectures, and works by local artists. ✉ *105 W. Broadway,* ☎ *941/695–0008.* 🎫 *$2.* ☉ *Tues.–Sat. 11–4.*

OFF THE
BEATEN PATH

SMALLWOOD'S STORE – Ted Smallwood pioneered this last American frontier in 1906 and built a 3,000-square-ft pine trading post raised on pilings in Chokoloskee Bay. Smallwood's granddaughter Lynn McMillin reopened it in 1989, after it had been closed several years, and installed a small gift shop and museum chock-full of original goods from the store; historic photographs; Indian clothing, furs, and hides; and area memorabilia. In March a festival celebrates the nearly 100-year relationship the store has had with local Native Americans. ✉ 360 *Mamie St., Chokoloskee Island,* ☎ *941/695–2989.* ☎ *$2.50.* ☉ *Dec.–May, daily 10–5; May–Nov., daily 10–4.*

Dining and Lodging

$–$$ ✕ **Everglades Seafood Depot.** This 1928 Spanish-style stucco structure on Lake Placid has had many lives. It began as the old Everglades depot, was part of the University of Miami, appeared in the film *Winds Across the Everglades,* and has housed several restaurants. Today veteran restaurateur Billy Potter serves up well-prepared seafood—from shrimp and grouper to frogs' legs and alligator—any way you like it, and the staff is eager to please. For big appetites there are generously portioned entrées that include soup or salad, potato or rice, and warm, fresh-baked biscuits. If you aren't very hungry, choose the smaller "lunch-able appetites" portion, which includes potato, slaw, and a biscuit. ✉ *102 Collier Ave.,* ☎ *941/695–0075, MC, V.*

$–$$ ✕ **Oar House Restaurant.** With wood paneling, picnic table–style booths, and a mishmash of fishing and Glades decor, the first full-service eatery in town has the ambience of a diner. The menu features a blend of seafood and such local specialties as frogs' legs, turtle, conch, and gator. To its credit, the service is friendly, prices are very reasonable, the food is fried in canola and corn oils, and most dishes can be grilled or broiled, if you prefer. It's open for breakfast, and there is a lounge. ✉ *305 Collier Ave.,* ☎ *941/695–3535. AE, D, MC, V.*

$ ✕ **Ivey House Restaurant.** Home-style meals are served every night at 6 (call for a reservation by 4 if you're not a guest of the hotel). The nightly changing menu features a mix of meat and vegetarian selections. For $10–$15 you can dine on barbecued chicken with potatoes, vegetable, salad, pineapple upside-down cake, and coffee or tea, and on Mexican night the fare is chicken fajitas, tortillas, beans, rice, flan, and coffee or tea. ✉ *107 Camellia St.,* ☎ *941/695–3299. MC, V. Closed May–Oct.*

$$ ▦ **Rod and Gun Club.** With a veranda, dark cypress fixtures, and a nautical theme, this landmark inn is like a time-warp trip back to the '20s, when wealthy hunters, anglers, and yachting parties from all over the world came to Florida for the winter season. The old guest rooms above the restaurant and bar aren't open anymore, but you can stay in comfortable cottages (no phone, however). The food is more than passable. Breakfast, lunch, and dinner are still served in the original dining room or on the wide veranda, and as in olden days, if you catch a "keeper," the chef will prepare it for your dinner. ✉ *200 Riverside Dr., Box 190, 34139,* ☎ *941/695–2101. 17 rooms. Restaurant, bar, pool, 2 tennis courts, fishing. No credit cards.*

$–$$ ▦ **On the Banks of the Everglades.** Built in 1923, this lodging takes its name from the building it occupies, the former Bank of Everglades. Patty Flick Richards and her father, Bob Flick, created minirooms for single travelers ($35–$40), spacious rooms, suites, and efficiencies with queen- or king-size beds and stylish coordinating linens, wall coverings, and draperies. Suites and efficiencies have private baths and kitchens (the staff does the dishes); a few single rooms share a women's or men's bath. Amenities include hair dryers and in-room ironing boards. At night you can snack on popcorn and watch movies in the parlor. A breakfast of baked goods, cereal, fresh fruit, juices, and coffee and tea is served in the bank's vault. There is no smoking. Tennis rackets are provided for use on the public courts next door. ⊠ *201 W. Broadway, Box 455, 34139,* ☎ *941/695–3151 or 888/431–1977,* FAX *941/695–3335. 8 units (3 share baths). Bicycles. AE, D, MC, V.*

$ ⏍ **Ivey House B&B.** This clean, friendly bargain is run by the folks who operate North American Canoe Tours (NACT), David and Sandee Harraden. The shotgun-style cracker house was once a boardinghouse for workers building the Tamiami Trail. Today's guests are well educated, well traveled, and in tune, as shown by the new annex, whose rooms have modem connections so "guests can hook up their laptop computers to stay in touch with their families." In the evening people talk about adventures and do jigsaw puzzles in the living room. Family-style dinners ($10–$15) often end with homemade apple pie. Guests save 10% on NACT canoe, kayak, and powerboat rentals. ⊠ *107 Camellia St., 34139,* ☎ *941/695–3299,* FAX *941/695–4155. 30 rooms, 20 with bath, 1 2-bedroom cottage. Bicycles, recreation room, library. MC, V. Closed May–Oct.*

Outdoor Activities and Sports

BIKING

North American Canoe Tours (⊠ Ivey House, 107 Camellia St., ☎ 941/695–4666) rents bikes for $3 per hour, $15 per day (free for Ivey House guests).

BOATING

North American Canoe Tours (⊠ Ivey House, 107 Camellia St., ☎ 941/695–4666) rents 16-ft Carolina skiffs with a 25-horsepower outboard, cooler, map, anchor, and safety equipment for $70 for a half day, $110 for a full day.

CANOEING AND KAYAKING

Everglades National Park Boat Tours (⊠ Gulf Coast Visitor Center, ☎ 941/695–2591; 800/445–7724 in FL) rents 17-ft Grumman canoes for day and overnight use. Rates are $20 per day. Car shuttle service is provided for canoeists paddling the Wilderness Trail, and travelers with disabilities can be accommodated. **North American Canoe Tours** (⊠ Ivey House, 107 Camellia St., ☎ 941/695–4666) is an established source for canoes, sea kayaks, and guided Everglades trips (November–April). Canoes cost $25 the first day, $20 for each day thereafter, while kayaks are $35–$55 per day. Half-day rentals are available. Car shuttles for canoeists paddling the Wilderness Trail are $135 with NACT canoe rental or $170 if you're using your own, plus the $10 park entrance fee.

GATEWAY TOWNS

The farm towns of Homestead and Florida City, flanked by Everglades National Park on the west and Biscayne National Park to the east, provide the closest visitor facilities to the parks. (The area's better restaurants are in Homestead, but the best lodgings are in Florida City.) The towns date from early in the century, when Henry Flagler extended his railroad to Key West but soon decided that farming would do more for rail revenues than ferrying passengers.

Homestead

⑬ *30 mi southwest of Miami.*

When Hurricane Andrew tore across South Florida with winds approaching 200 mph, it ripped apart lives and the small community of

Homestead. The city rebuilt itself, redefining its role as the "Gateway to the Keys" and attracting hotel chains, a shopping center, sports complex, and residential development. The historic downtown area has become a preservation-driven Main Street city. Krome Avenue (Route 997), which cuts through the city's heart, is lined with restaurants and antiques shops.

West of north–south Krome Avenue, miles of fields grow fresh fruits and vegetables. Some are harvested commercially. Others have U-PICK signs, inviting families to harvest their own. Stands that sell farm-fresh produce abound.

In addition to its agricultural legacy, the town has an eclectic flavor, attributable to its population mix: descendants of pioneer Crackers, Hispanic growers, and farmworkers as well as latter-day northern retirees. Until Hurricane Andrew the military had a huge presence at Homestead Air Force Base. The economy still suffers from its loss.

With a saltwater atoll pool that's flushed by tidal action, **Homestead Bayfront Park,** adjacent to Biscayne National Park, is popular among local families as well as anglers and boaters. Highlights include a playground, ramps for people with disabilities (including a ramp that leads into the swimming area), a picnic pavilion with grills, showers, and rest rooms. ⊠ *9698 S.W. 328th St.,* ☎ *305/230–3034.* ☞ *$3.50 per passenger vehicle, $8 per vehicle with boat, $6 per RV.* ☾ *Sunrise–sunset.*

To find out about more area attractions, *see* the South Dade side trip *in* Chapter 1.

Dining

$　✕ **El Toro Taco.** This family-run area institution features a rustic atmo-
★　sphere, good Mexican food in generous servings, homemade tortilla chips (sometimes a little greasy), and friendly service. Selections range from tasty favorites like beef or chicken fajitas, enchiladas, tamales, burritos, and tacos to more traditional Mexican dishes like *mole de pollo,* which combines cooking chocolate and spices with chicken. Desserts include *tres leches* (a cake soaked in a syrup of three types of milk—evaporated, sweetened condensed, and heavy cream) and flan. You can order spicing from mild to tongue challenging. The restaurant is also open for breakfast. ⊠ *1 S. Krome Ave.,* ☎ *305/245–8182. D, MC, V. BYOB.*

$　✕ **Tiffany's.** What looks like a converted pioneer house with a high-pitched roof and lattice under a big banyan tree is in reality a cluster of shops and this casual restaurant. The decor is frilly nouveau Victorian, with teaberry-color tablecloths and floral place mats, and the atmosphere is quaint but noisy. Featured entrées include hot crabmeat au gratin and asparagus rolled in ham with hollandaise sauce. Among the homemade desserts, choose from a very tall carrot cake, strawberry whipped-cream cake, and a harvest pie with double crust that has layers of apples, cranberries, walnuts, raisins, and a caramel topping. Sunday brunch is served, too. ⊠ *22 N.E. 15th St.,* ☎ *305/246–0022. MC, V. Closed Mon. No dinner.*

Outdoor Activities and Sports

AUTO RACING

The **Miami-Dade Homestead Motorsports Complex** (⊠ 1 Speedway Blvd., 33035, ☎ 305/230–7223) is a state-of-the-art facility with two tracks: a 2.21-mi continuous road course and a 1½-mi oval. There's a schedule of year-round manufacturer and race-team testing, club racing, and other national events.

BOATING

Boaters give high ratings to the facilities at **Homestead Bayfront Park.** The 174-slip marina has a ramp, dock, bait-and-tackle shop, fuel station, ice, dry storage, and boat hoist, which can handle vessels up to 25 ft long with lifting rings. The park also has a tidal swimming area. ⊠ *9698 S.W. 328th St.,* ☎ *305/230–3033.* ⊠ *$3.50 per passenger vehicle, $8 per vehicle with boat, $6 per RV, $10 hoist.* ☉ *Sunrise–sunset.*

Shopping

In addition to Homestead Boulevard (U.S. 1) and Campbell Drive (Southwest 312th Street and Northeast 8th Street), **Krome Avenue** is popular for shopping. In the heart of old Homestead, it has a brick sidewalk and many antiques stores.

Florida City

⑭ *2 mi southwest of Homestead.*

Florida's Turnpike ends in this southernmost town on the peninsula, spilling thousands onto U.S. 1 and eventually west to Everglades National Park, east to Biscayne National Park, or south to the Florida Keys. As the last civilization before 18 mi of mangroves and water, this stretch of U.S. 1 is lined with fast-food eateries, service stations, hotels, bars, dive shops, and restaurants.

Like Homestead, Florida City has roots planted in agriculture, as shown by the hundreds of acres of farmland west of Krome Avenue and a huge farmers' market that processes produce to be shipped around the country. Plans to build a new aquarium and IMAX theater, which will eventually show a film on Everglades and Biscayne national parks, were delayed after the sponsor, Destination Cinema, was purchased by *National Geographic*. But it should open sometime in 2000.

In the **Florida Pioneer Museum,** a former station agent's house, you can pore over a collection of articles from daily life that evokes the area's homestead period on the last frontier of mainland America. Items recall a time when Henry Flagler's railroad vaulted the development of the Florida Keys all the way to Key West, and Homestead and Florida City were briefly the take-charge supply outposts. A caboose outside, which dates from the days of the old Florida East Coast Railway station, is one of a few wooden cars left in the country. It's staffed by volunteers, so call first. ⊠ *826 N. Krome Ave.,* ☎ *305/246–9531.* ⊠ *$1.* ☉ *Daily 1–5.*

Dining and Lodging

$$–$$$ ✕ **Mutineer Restaurant.** Former Sheraton Hotels builder Allan Bennett created this roadside steak and seafood restaurant with an indoor-outdoor fish and duck pond in 1980, back when Florida City was barely on the map. Etched glass divides the bilevel dining rooms, where striped-velvet chairs, stained glass, and a few portholes set the scene; in the lounge are an aquarium and nautical antiques. The big menu offers 18 seafood entrées plus another half-dozen daily seafood specials, as well as game, ribs, and steaks. There's live music Friday and Saturday evenings. ⊠ *11 S.E. 1st Ave. (U.S. 1 and Palm Dr.),* ☎ *305/ 245–3377. AE, D, DC, MC, V.*

$–$$$ ✕ **Richard Accursio's Capri Restaurant and King Richard's Room.** Lo-
★ cals have been dining here—one of the oldest family-run restaurants in Miami-Dade County—since 1958. Outside it's a nondescript building in the middle of a big parking lot. Inside there are dark wood paneling and heavy wooden furniture. The tasty fare ranges from pizza

with light, crunchy crusts and ample toppings to mild, meaty conch chowder. Mussels come in garlic or marinara sauce, and the yellow-tail snapper *française* is a worthy selection. More than a half-dozen early bird entrées are offered 4:30–6:30 for $9.45, including soup or salad and potato or spaghetti. ⊠ *935 N. Krome Ave.,* ☎ *305/247–1544. AE, MC, V.*

$ ✗ **Farmers' Market Restaurant.** Although it's in the farmers' market and serves fresh vegetables, this restaurant's specialty is seafood. A family of fishermen runs the place, so fish and shellfish are only hours from the sea. Catering to the fishing and farming crowd, it opens at 5:30, serving pancakes, jumbo eggs, and fluffy omelets with home fries or grits. The lunch and dinner menus have shrimp, fish, steaks, and conch baskets, as well as burgers, salads, and sandwiches. Normally the fish comes fried, but you can ask for it broiled or grilled. ⊠ *300 N. Krome Ave.,* ☎ *305/242–0008. No credit cards.*

$$ ☷ **Best Western Gateway to the Keys.** This two-story motel sits well back from the highway and contains such amenities as full closets, a heat lamp in the bathroom, and complimentary Continental breakfast. Standard rooms have two queen-size beds or one king-size bed. More expensive rooms come with wet bar, refrigerator, microwave, and cof-feemaker. Otherwise it's a standard modern motel with floral prints and twin reading lamps. ⊠ *1 Strano Blvd., 33034,* ☎ *305/246–5100,* FAX *305/242–0056. 114 units. Pool, coin laundry, dry cleaning. AE, D, DC, MC, V.*

$$ ☷ **Hampton Inn.** This two-story motel just off the highway has good clean rooms (including a post–Hurricane Andrew wing) and public-friendly policies, including free Continental breakfast, local calls, and movie channels. All rooms have at least two upholstered chairs, twin reading lamps, a desk and chair, coffeemaker, and an iron and ironing board. Units are color-coordinated and carpeted. Baths have tub-show-ers. ⊠ *124 E. Palm Dr., 33034,* ☎ *305/247–8833 or 800/426–7866,* FAX *305/247–6456. 123 units. Pool. AE, D, DC, MC, V.*

Shopping

Prime Outlets at Florida City (⊠ 250 E. Palm Dr.) has more than 50 discount stores plus a small food court. **Robert Is Here** (⊠ 19200 Palm Dr. [S.W. 344th St.], ☎ 305/246–1592), a remarkable fruit stand, sells vegetables, fresh-fruit milk shakes, 10 flavors of honey, more than 100 flavors of jams and jellies, fresh juices, salad dressings, and some 40 kinds of tropical fruits, including carambola, litchi, egg fruit, monstera, sapodilla, soursop, sugar apple, and tamarind. The stand started in 1960, when seven-year-old Robert sat at this spot selling his father's bumper crop of cucumbers. Now Robert ships around the world, and every-thing is first quality. Seconds are given to needy area families. The stand opens at 8 and never closes earlier than 7.

BISCAYNE NATIONAL PARK

Occupying 180,000 acres along the southern portion of Biscayne Bay, south of Miami and north of the Florida Keys, this national park is 96% underwater, and its altitude ranges from 4 ft above sea level to 10 fathoms, or 60 ft, below. Contained within it are four distinct zones, which from shore to sea are mangrove forest along the coast, Biscayne Bay, the undeveloped upper Florida Keys, and coral reefs.

Mangroves line the mainland shore much as they do elsewhere in South Florida. Biscayne Bay functions as a lobster sanctuary and a nursery for fish, sponges, and crabs. Manatees and sea turtles frequent its warm, shallow waters. Lamentably, the bay is under assault from forces similar to those in Florida Bay.

To the east, about 8 mi off the coast, lie 44 tiny keys, stretching 18 nautical mi north–south and accessible only by boat. There is no commercial transportation between the mainland and the islands, and only a handful can be visited: Elliott, Boca Chita, Adams, and Sands keys. The rest either are wildlife refuges, are too small, or have rocky shores or waters too shallow for boats. It's best to explore the Keys between December and April, when the mosquito population is relatively quiescent.

Another 3 mi east of the Keys, in the ocean, lies the park's main attraction—the northernmost section of Florida's living tropical coral reefs. Some are the size of a student's desk, others as large as a football field. You can take a glass-bottom boat ride to see this underwater wonderland, but you really have to snorkel or scuba dive to appreciate it fully. A diverse population of colorful fish—angelfish, gobies, grunts, parrot fish, pork fish, wrasses, and many more—flits through the reefs.

More than 170 species of birds have been seen around the park. Though all the Keys offer excellent birding opportunities, Jones Lagoon, south of Adams Key, between Old Rhodes Key and Totten Key, is one of the best. It's approachable only by nonmotorized craft.

Convoy Point

15 *9 mi east of Florida City, 30 mi south of downtown Miami.*

Reminiscent of area pioneer homes, the **Convoy Point Visitor Center** is a wooden building with a metal roof and wide veranda from which you can look out across mangroves and Biscayne Bay and see the Miami skyline. Inside is a museum, where hands-on and historical exhibits and videos explore the park's four ecosystems. Among the facilities are a 50-seat auditorium, the park's canoe and tour concessioner, rest rooms with showers, a ranger information area, and gift shop. A short trail and boardwalk lead to a jetty and launch ramp. This is the only area of the park accessible without a boat. ⊠ *9700 S.W. 328th St., Homestead,* ☎ *305/230–7275.* 🎟 *Free.* ☉ *Daily 8:30–5.*

Outdoor Activities and Sports

CANOEING

Biscayne National Underwater Park, Inc. (⊠ Convoy Point Visitor Center, ☎ 305/230–1100), the park's official concessioner, has half a dozen canoes for rent on a first-come, first-served basis. Prices are $8 an hour, $22 for four hours.

SCUBA DIVING AND SNORKELING

Biscayne National Underwater Park, Inc. (⊠ Convoy Point Visitor Center, Box 1270, Homestead 33090, ☎ 305/230–1100) rents equipment and conducts snorkel and dive trips aboard the 45-ft *Boca Chita.* Snorkel trips ($27.95) leave daily at 1:30 and include mask, fins, snorkel, and vest. Trips include 1¼ hours on reefs and wrecks. Two-tank scuba trips, which leave at 9 on weekdays, 8:30 on weekends, cost $35. Complete gear rental is $37, and instruction is available. Even with a reservation (recommended), you should arrive 45 minutes before departure.

Elliott Key

⑯ *9 mi east of Convoy Point.*

This key, accessible only by boat (on your own or by special arrangement with the concessioner), has a rebuilt boardwalk made from recycled plastic and two nature trails with tropical plant life. Take an informal, ranger-led nature walk or walk its 7-mi length on your own along a rough path through a hammock. Videos shown at the ranger station describe the island. Facilities include rest rooms, fresh water, showers (cold), grills, and a campground. Pets are allowed on the island but not on trails.

A 30-ft-wide sandy beach about a mile north of the harbor on the west (bay) side of the key is the only one in the national park. Boaters like to anchor off it to swim. For day use only, it has picnic areas and a short trail that follows the shore and cuts through the hammock.

Lodging

$ ⚠ **Biscayne National Park.** Elliott Key has 40 primitive campsites, for which there are neither fees nor reservations. Just bring plenty of insect repellent. The park concessioner runs boats to the key periodically to drop off campers ($21 round-trip) because there is no regular ferry service or boat rental. There is a $10-per-night charge for docking private vessels.

Boca Chita Key

⑰ *10 mi northeast of Convoy Point.*

This island was once owned by Mark C. Honeywell, former president of Minneapolis's Honeywell Company. There is no fresh water, but grills, campsites (details similar to those at Elliott Key), and rest rooms are available. Access is by private boat only. No pets are allowed.

Adams Key

⑱ *9 mi southeast of Convoy Point.*

This small key, a stone's throw off the western tip of Elliott Key, is open for day use and has picnic areas, rest rooms, dockage, and a short trail that runs along the shore and through a hardwood hammock. Access is by private boat.

THE EVERGLADES A TO Z

Arriving and Departing

By Boat

If you're entering the United States by pleasure boat, you must phone **U.S. Customs** (☎ 800/432–1216) either from a marine phone or on first arriving ashore.

By Car

From Miami the main highways to the area are U.S. 1, the Homestead Extension of Florida's Turnpike, and Krome Avenue (Route 997 [old U.S. 27]).

By Plane

Miami International Airport (MIA) is 34 mi from Homestead and 83 mi from Flamingo in Everglades National Park.

BETWEEN THE AIRPORT AND TOWNS

Airporter (☎ 800/830–3413) runs shuttle buses three times daily off-season, four times daily in winter, that stop at the Hampton Inn in Florida City on their way between MIA and the Florida Keys. Shuttle service, which takes about an hour, runs 6:10–5:20 from Florida City, 7:30–6 from the airport. Reserve in advance. Pickups can be arranged for all baggage-claim areas. The cost is $20 one-way.

Greyhound Lines (☎ 800/231–2222) buses from MIA to the Keys make a stop in Homestead (⊠ 5 N.E. 3rd Rd., ☎ 305/247–2040) four times a day. Buses leave from Concourse E, lower level, and cost $8 one-way, $16 round-trip.

SuperShuttle (☎ 305/871–2000) operates 11-passenger air-conditioned vans to Homestead. Service from MIA is available around the clock; booths are outside most luggage areas on the lower level. For the return to MIA, reserve 24 hours in advance. The one-way cost is $28 per person for the first person, $12 for each additional person at the same address.

Getting Around

By Boat

Bring aboard the proper *NOAA Nautical Charts* before you cast off to explore park waters. The charts run $15–$15.95 at many marine stores in South Florida, at the Convoy Point Visitor Center in Biscayne National Park, and at Flamingo Marina in the Everglades.

The annual **Waterway Guide** (southern regional edition) is widely used by boaters. Bookstores all over South Florida sell it, or you can order it directly from the publisher (⊠ Intertec Publishing, Book Department, Box 12901, Overland Park, KS 66282-2901, ☎ 800/233–3359) for $36.95 plus $3 shipping and handling.

By Car

To reach Everglades National Park's Ernest F. Coe Visitor Center and Flamingo, head west on Route 9336 in Florida City and follow signs. From Homestead the Ernest F. Coe Visitor Center is 11 mi; Flamingo is 49 mi.

The north entrance of Everglades National Park at Shark Valley is reached by taking the Tamiami Trail about 20 mi west of Krome Avenue.

To reach the west entrance of Everglades National Park at the Gulf Coast Visitor Center in Everglades City, take Route 29 south from the Tamiami Trail.

To reach Biscayne National Park from Homestead, take U.S. 1 or Krome Avenue to Lucy Street (Southeast 8th Street) and turn east. Lucy Street becomes North Canal Drive (Southwest 328th Street). Follow signs for about 8 mi to the park headquarters.

By Taxi

Cab companies servicing the area include **Action Express Taxi** (☎ 305/743–6800) and **South Dade Taxi** (☎ 305/256–4444).

Contacts and Resources

Car Rentals

Agencies in the area include **A&A Auto Rental** (⊠ 30005 S. Dixie Hwy., Homestead 33030, ☎ 305/246–0974), **Budget** (⊠ 29949 S. Dixie Hwy., Homestead 33030, ☎ 305/248–4524 or 800/527–0700), and **Enterprise Rent-a-Car** (⊠ 29130 S. Dixie Hwy., Homestead 33030, ☎ 305/246–2056 or 800/736–8222).

Emergencies

Dial **911** for police, fire, or ambulance. If you are a TTY caller, tap the space bar or use a voice announcer to identify yourself. In the national parks, rangers answer police, fire, and medical emergencies: **Biscayne** (☎ 305/247–7272) or **Everglades** (☎ 305/247–7272). **Florida Marine Patrol** (☎ 305/795–2145), a division of the Florida Department of Natural Resources, maintains a 24-hour telephone service for reporting boating emergencies and natural-resource violations. **Miami Beach Coast Guard Base** (✉ 100 MacArthur Causeway, Miami Beach, ☎ 305/535–4300 or 305/535–4314) responds to local marine emergencies and reports of navigation hazards. The base broadcasts on VHF-FM Channel 16. The **National Weather Service** (☎ 305/229–4522) supplies local forecasts.

HOSPITALS

Hospital emergency line (☎ 305/596–6556). **SMH Homestead Hospital** (✉ 160 N.W. 13th St., Homestead, ☎ 305/248–3232; 305/596–6557 physician referral).

Guided Tours

The National Park Service organizes a variety of free programs, typically focusing on native wildlife, plants, and park history. At Biscayne National Park, for example, rangers give informal tours of Elliott and Boca Chita keys, which you can arrange in advance, depending on ranger availability. Contact the respective visitor centers for details.

AIRBOAT TOURS

In Everglades City, **Captain Doug's Florida Boat Tours** (✉ 200 Rte. 29, ☎ 941/695–4400; 800/282–9194 in FL) runs 30- to 40-minute backcountry tours ($12.95) aboard custom-designed jet airboats. Even more popular, however, are one-hour tours ($30) through mangrove trails on a six-passenger airboat. The smaller boat allows visitors to get up close to wild animals, including birds. **Wooten's Everglades Airboat Tours** (✉ Wooten's Alligator Farm, 1½ mi east of Rte. 29 on Tamiami Trail, ☎ 941/695–2781 or 800/282–2781) runs airboat and swamp-buggy tours ($12.50) through the Everglades. (Swamp buggies are giant tractorlike vehicles with oversize rubber wheels.) Tours last approximately 30 minutes.

Southwest of Florida City near the entrance to Everglades National Park, **Everglades Alligator Farm** (✉ 40351 S.W. 192nd Ave., ☎ 305/247–2628 or 800/644–9711) runs a 4-mi, 30-minute tour of the River of Grass with departures 20 minutes after the hour. The tour ($12.50) includes a free hourly alligator, snake, or wildlife show, or you can take in the show only ($7).

From the Shark Valley area, **Buffalo Tiger's Florida Everglades Airboat Ride** (✉ 12 mi west of Krome Ave., 20 mi west of Miami city limits on Tamiami Trail, ☎ 305/559–5250) is led by a former chairman of the Miccosukee tribe. The 35- to 40-minute trip includes a stop at an old Native American camp. Tours cost $12 and operate daily 10–5. Reservations are not required. **Coopertown Airboat Ride** (✉ 5 mi west of Krome Ave. on Tamiami Trail, ☎ 305/226–6048) operates the oldest airboat rides in the Everglades (since 1945). The 30- to 35-minute tour visits two hammocks and alligator holes. The charge is $10, with a $24 minimum for the boat. **Everglades Gator Park** (✉ 12 mi west of Florida's Turnpike on Tamiami Trail, ☎ 305/559–2255 or 800/559–2205) offers 45-minute narrated airboat tours ($12). **Everglades Safari Park** (✉ 26700 Tamiami Trail, 9 mi west of Krome Ave., ☎ 305/226–6923 or 305/223–3804) runs 40-minute airboat rides for $15. The price includes a show and gator tour. The **Miccosukee Indian Village**

(✉ 25 mi west of Florida's Turnpike on Tamiami Trail, ☎ 305/223–8380) offers 30-minute airboat rides ($7) in addition to its other attractions.

Ray Cramer's Everglades Airboat Tours, Inc. (✉ Coopertown, ☎ 305/852–5339 or 305/221–9888; ✉ mailing address: Box 651711, Miami 33265) conducts airboat trips accommodating from 6 to 12, for $42.60 per person. Ray Cramer recently sold the business to longtime friend Bill Barlow, who has fished, frogged, and hunted in the Everglades with Cramer since 1949. Though daytime trips are offered, a better option is the tour that departs an hour before sundown so you can see birds and fish in daylight and alligators, raccoons, and other nocturnal animals when night falls.

AIR TOURS

Everglades Air Tours (✉ Homestead General Aviation Airport, 28790 S.W. 217th Ave., Homestead, ☎ 305/247–7757) gives bird's-eye tours of the Everglades and Florida Bay that last 30 minutes and cost $45 per person, with a two-passenger minimum.

BOAT TOURS

Tours at Biscayne National Park are run by people-friendly **Biscayne National Underwater Park, Inc.** (✉ Convoy Point, east end of North Canal Dr. [S.W. 328th St.], Box 1270, Homestead 33090, ☎ 305/230–1100). Daily trips (at 10, with a second trip at 1 during high season, according to demand) explore the park's living coral reefs 10 mi offshore on *Reef Rover IV*, a 53-ft glass-bottom boat that carries up to 48 passengers. On days when the weather is unsuitable for reef viewing, an alternative three-hour, ranger-led interpretive tour visits Elliott Key. Reservations are recommended. The cost is $19.95, and you should arrive at least 45 minutes before departure.

Everglades National Park Boat Tours (✉ Gulf Coast Visitor Center, Everglades City, ☎ 941/695–2591; 800/445–7724 in FL) is the official park concession authorized to operate tours ($13) through the Ten Thousand Islands region and mangrove wilderness. Boats can accommodate large numbers and wheelchairs (not electric), and the two biggest boats have drink concessions. Trips that stop on Sandfly Island include a 30-minute ranger-led tour of the island's flora and fauna. **Flamingo Lodge, Marina & Outpost Resort Boat Tours** (✉ 1 Flamingo Lodge Hwy., Flamingo, ☎ 941/695–3101, ext. 286 or 180) is the official concession authorized to operate sightseeing tours through Everglades National Park. The two-hour backcountry cruise ($16) is the most popular. The boat winds under a heavy canopy of mangroves, revealing abundant wildlife—from alligators, crocodiles, and turtles to herons, hawks, and egrets. The 90-minute Florida Bay cruise ($10) ventures into the bay to explore shallow nursery areas and encounter plentiful bird life and often dolphins, sea turtles, and sharks. To get really close to nature, adults can take the *Everglades Queen* cruise ($32), a three-hour, small-group backcountry cruise narrated by the captain.

Majestic Everglades Excursions (✉ Box 241,, Everglades City 34139, ☎ 941/695–2777) are led by exceptionally well-informed guides Frank and Georgia Garrett. The 3½- to 4-hour ecotours, on a 24-ft boat with a covered deck, take in Everglades National Park and the Ten Thousand Islands. Narration focuses on the region's unique flora and fauna and its colorful early residents. Departing from Glades Haven, just shy of a mile south of the circle in Everglades City, tours are limited to six passengers and include brunch or afternoon snacks. The cost is $65.

North American Canoe Tours (✉ Ivey House, 107 Camellia St., Box 5038, Everglades City 34139, ☎ 941/695–3299) leads one-day to five-night Everglades tours November–April. Highlights include bird and gator sightings, mangrove forests, no-man's-land beaches, relics of the hideouts of infamous and just plain reclusive characters, and spectacular sunsets. Included in the cost of extended tours ($250–$800) are canoes or kayaks, all necessary equipment, a guide, meals, and lodging for the first night at the Ivey House B&B. Day trips by kayak, canoe, or powerboat cost $40–$60.

Starting at the Shark Valley visitor center, **Shark Valley Tram Tours** (✉ Box 1739, Tamiami Station, Miami 33144, ☎ 305/221–8455) follows a 15-mi loop road into the interior, stopping at a 50-ft observation tower especially good for viewing gators. Two-hour narrated tours cost $9 and depart hourly 9–4, except May 1–Christmas, when they run every two hours. Reservations are recommended December–April.

Visitor Information

Big Cypress National Preserve (✉ HCR61, Box 11, Ochopee 34141, ☎ 941/695–4111). **Biscayne National Park** Convoy Point Visitor Center (✉ 9700 S.W. 328th St., Box 1369, Homestead 33090-1369, ☎ 305/230–7275). **Everglades City Chamber of Commerce** (✉ Rte. 29 and Tamiami Trail, Box 130, Everglades City 34139, ☎ 941/695–3941). **Everglades National Park** Ernest F. Coe Visitor Center (✉ 40001 Rte. 9336, Homestead 33034-6733, ☎ 305/242–7700). **Flamingo Visitor Center** (✉ 1 Flamingo Lodge Hwy., Flamingo 33034-6798, ☎ 941/695–2945). Gulf Coast Visitor Center (✉ Rte. 29, Everglades City 34139, ☎ 941/695–3311). **Greater Homestead–Florida City Chamber of Commerce** (✉ 43 N. Krome Ave., Homestead 33030, ☎ 305/247–2332 or 888/352–4891). **Tropical Everglades Visitor Association** (✉ 160 U.S. 1, Florida City 33034, ☎ 305/245–9180 or 800/388–9669).

3 FORT LAUDERDALE AND BROWARD COUNTY

From Hollywood north to Fort Lauderdale and beyond, the county's famous beaches are just one of the attractions. Downtowns are being spruced up, and Fort Lauderdale's Arts and Science District draws the culturally minded.

Updated
by Alan
Macher

A COLLEGE STUDENT FROM THE 1960S returning to Fort Lauderdale for a vacation today wouldn't recognize the place. Back then, the Fort Lauderdale beachfront was lined with bars, T-shirt shops, souvenir stores, and fast-food stands, and the downtown area consisted of a single office tower and some government buildings. Now, following an enormous renovation program, the beach is home to upscale shops and restaurants, including the popular Beach Place retail and dining complex, while downtown growth continues at a rapid pace. The long-awaited movie and entertainment complex, Las Olas Riverfront, is complete; several new office towers have been built; and a major airport expansion is finished.

In the years following World War II, sleepy Fort Lauderdale—with miles of inland waterways—promoted itself as the "Venice of America" and the nation's yachting capital. But in 1960 the film *Where the Boys Are* changed everything. The movie described how college students—upward of 20,000—were beginning to swarm to the city for spring break. By 1985 the 20,000 had mushroomed to 350,000. Hotel owners complained of 12 students to a room, the beachfront was littered with tacky bars, and drug trafficking and petty theft were major problems. So city leaders put in place policies and restrictions designed to encourage students to go elsewhere. They did, and no one seems to miss them.

Now the city has been totally transformed into a leading warm-weather vacation destination. This remarkable turnaround has resulted from major investments by both the private and public sectors. Fort Lauderdale has clearly become a city with a mission.

A major beneficiary is Las Olas Boulevard, whose emergence has been credited with creating a whole new identity for Fort Lauderdale. Though it was already famous for its trendy shops, now the sidewalks aren't rolled up when the sun goes down. Nearly two dozen new restaurants have sprung up, and on weekend evenings hundreds of strollers tour the boulevard, taking in the food, the jazz bands, and the scene. On-street parking on weekends has slowed traffic, and the street has a village atmosphere.

Farther west, along New River, is evidence of Fort Lauderdale's cultural renaissance: the arts and entertainment district and its crown jewel, the Broward Center for the Performing Arts. Still farther west the county has entered major-league sports with a new $212 million arena for the National Hockey League's Florida Panthers, in Sunrise.

Of course, what makes Fort Lauderdale and Broward County a major draw for visitors is the beaches. Fort Lauderdale's 2-mi stretch of unobstructed beachfront has been enhanced even further with a sparkling look designed for the pleasure of pedestrians rather than cars.

Tying this all together is a transportation system that is relatively hassle free, unusual in congested South Florida. A new expressway system, including the long-awaited widening of I–95, connects the city and suburbs and even provides a direct route to the airport and Port Everglades. For a slower and more scenic ride to really see this canal-laced city, cruise aboard the water taxi.

None of this was envisioned by Napoleon Bonaparte Broward, Florida's governor from 1905 to 1909, for whom the county was named. His drainage schemes opened much of the marshy Everglades region for farming, ranching, and settling (in retrospect, an environmental disaster). Fort Lauderdale's first-known white settler, Charles Lewis, established a plantation along the New River in 1793. But it was for Major

William Lauderdale, who built a fort at the river's mouth in 1838 during the Seminole Indian wars, that the city was named.

Incorporated in 1911 with just 175 residents, Fort Lauderdale grew rapidly during the Florida boom of the 1920s. Today its population is 160,000, and its suburbs keep growing—1.4 million live in the county. New homes, offices, and shopping centers have filled in the gaps between older communities along the coastal ridge. Now they're marching west along I–75, I–595, and Route 869 (the Sawgrass Expressway). Broward County is blessed with near-ideal weather, with some 3,000 hours of sunshine a year. The average temperature is 66°F–77°F in winter, 84°F in summer. Once a home for retirees, the county today attracts younger, working-age families, many living in such new communities as Weston, southwest of Fort Lauderdale. The area has always been a sane and pleasant place to live. Now it's also becoming one of Florida's most diverse and dynamic places to vacation.

New and Noteworthy

Fort Lauderdale's new **Las Olas Riverfront** offers a variety of shopping, dining, and entertainment choices. Outside are picturesque plazas and sweeping terraces with splashing fountains, making a tranquil spot for relaxing along the New River. Inside is where the action is: 18 restaurants ranging from upscale to casual; the city's first downtown movie complex, with 23 screens and stadium seating; and a two-level spread of video and virtual-reality games.

National Car Rental Center is not where tourists pick up and return rental vehicles. It's Broward County's new 18,000-seat arena and home to the NHL Florida Panthers. The Sunrise facility also gives Broward its first large-capacity indoor venue, drawing big-name performers like Billy Joel and Celine Dion.

Opening its doors in 1999, **World Fishing Center** is an angler's mecca on dry land. The draw is an impressive collection of sportfishing exhibits and demonstrations as well as the World Fishing Hall of Fame.

Pleasures and Pastimes

Beaches

Broward County's beachfront extends for miles without interruption, although the character of the communities behind the beach changes. For example, in Hallandale, the beach is backed by towering condominiums; in Hollywood, by motels and the Broadwalk; and just north of there—blessedly—there's nothing at all.

Dining

Food critics in dining and travel magazines agree that the Greater Fort Lauderdale area offers some of the finest and most varied dining of any U.S. city its size. You can choose from the cuisines of Asia, Europe, or Central and South America—and, of course, good ol' American—and enjoy more than just the food. The ambience, wine, service, and decor can be as varied as the language spoken, and as memorable, too.

Fishing

Four main types of fishing are available in Broward County: bottom or drift-boat fishing from party boats, deep-sea fishing for large sport fish on charters, angling for freshwater game fish, and dropping a line off a pier. For bottom fishing, party boats typically charge between $20 and $22 per person for up to four hours, including rod, reel, and bait. For charters, a half day for as many as six people runs up to $325, six-hour charters up to $495, and full-day charters (eight hours) up to $595.

Skipper and crew plus bait and tackle are included. Split parties can be arranged at a cost of about $85 per person for a full day.

Several Broward towns—Dania, Lauderdale-by-the-Sea, Pompano Beach, and Deerfield Beach—have fishing piers that draw anglers for pompano, amberjack, bluefish, snapper, blue runners, snook, mackerel, and Florida lobster.

Golf

More than 50 courses green the landscape in Greater Fort Lauderdale, including famous championship links. Most area courses are inland, in the suburbs west of the city, and there are some great bargains. Off-season (May–October) greens fees start at $15; peak-season (November–April) charges run from $35 to more than $100. Fees can be trimmed by working through Next Day Golf, a local service, and many hotels offer golf packages.

Scuba Diving

Good diving can be enjoyed within 20 minutes of shore. Among the most popular of the county's 80 dive sites is the 2-mi-wide, 23-mi-long Fort Lauderdale Reef, the product of Florida's most successful artificial reef–building program. More than a dozen houseboats, ships, and oil platforms have been sunk in depths of from 10 to 150 ft to provide a habitat for fish and other marine life, as well as to help stabilize beaches. The most famous sunken ship is the 200-ft German freighter *Mercedes,* which was blown onto Palm Beach socialite Mollie Wilmot's pool terrace in a violent Thanksgiving storm in 1984; the ship is now underwater a mile off Fort Lauderdale beach.

Exploring Fort Lauderdale and Broward County

Though most activity centers on Fort Lauderdale, there's plenty to see in other parts of Broward County, to the north, south, and, increasingly, west.

The metro area is laid out in a basic grid system, and only the hundreds of canals and waterways interrupt the straight-line path of the streets and roads. Nomenclature is important here. Streets, roads, courts, and drives run east–west. Avenues, terraces, and ways run north–south. Boulevards can run any which way. Las Olas Boulevard is one of the most important east–west thoroughfares, whereas Route A1A—referred to as Atlantic Boulevard and Ocean Boulevard along some stretches—runs along the north–south oceanfront. These names can be confusing to visitors, as there are separate streets called Atlantic and Ocean in Hollywood and Pompano Beach.

The boulevards, those that are paved and those made of water, give Fort Lauderdale its distinct character. Honeycombed with more than 260 mi of navigable waterways, the city is home port for about 40,000 privately owned boats. You won't see the gondolas you'd find in Venice, but you will see just about every other type of craft imaginable docked beside the thousands of homes and businesses that each have a little piece of waterfront. Visitors can tour the canals via the city's water-taxi system, made up of small motor launches that provide transportation and quick, narrated tours. Larger, multideck touring vessels and motorboat rentals for self-guided tours are other options. The Intracoastal Waterway, a massive canal that parallels Route A1A, is the nautical equivalent of an interstate highway. It runs north–south through the metro area and provides easy access to neighboring beach communities; Deerfield Beach and Pompano Beach lie to the north and Dania and Hollywood lie to the south. All are within a 15-mi radius of the city center.

Great Itineraries

Since most Broward County sights are relatively close to each other, it's easy to pack a lot into very little time, but you will probably need a car. You can catch a lot of the history, the museums, and the shops and bistros in Fort Lauderdale's downtown area and along Las Olas Boulevard, and then if you feel like hitting the beach, just take a 10-minute drive east to the intersection of Las Olas and A1A and you're there. Many of the neighboring suburbs, with attractions of their own, are just north or south of Fort Lauderdale. As a result, you can hit most of the high points in three days, and with seven to 10 days, you can see virtually all of Broward's mainstream charms.

Numbers in the text correspond to numbers in the margin and on the Broward County and Fort Lauderdale maps.

IF YOU HAVE 3 DAYS

With a bigger concentration of hotels, restaurants, and sights to see than its suburban neighbors, ⊞ **Fort Lauderdale** ①–⑪ makes a logical base of operations for any visit. On your first day there see the downtown area, especially Las Olas Boulevard between Southeast 6th and Southeast 11th avenues. After enjoying lunch at a sidewalk café, head for the nearby Arts and Science District and the downtown **Riverwalk** ⑤, which you can see at a leisurely pace in half a day. On your second day spend at least some time at the beach, shopping when the hot sun drives you off the sand. Tour the canals on the third day, either on a rented boat from one of the various marinas along Route A1A, or via the water taxi or a sightseeing boat, both of which can be boarded all along the Intracoastal Waterway.

IF YOU HAVE 5 DAYS

With additional time you can see more of the beach and the arts district and still work in some outdoor sports—and you'll be more able to rearrange your plans depending on the weather. On the first day visit the Arts and Science District and the downtown **Riverwalk** ⑤. Set aside the next day for an offshore adventure, perhaps a deep-sea fishing charter or a dive trip to the Fort Lauderdale Reef. On the third day shop, dine, and relax along the **Fort Lauderdale beachfront** ⑨, and at the end of the day, sneak a peak at the Hillsboro Light, at **Lighthouse Point** ⑱. Another good day can be spent at the **Hugh Taylor Birch State Recreation Area** ⑩. Enjoy your fifth day in **Hollywood** ⑳, perhaps combining time on the Broadwalk with a visit to the Anne Kolb Nature Center, at West Lake Park.

IF YOU HAVE 7 DAYS

With a full week you have time for a wider variety of attractions, fitting in beach time around other activities. In fact, enjoy any of the county's public beach areas on your first day. The second day can be spent in another favorite pastime—shopping, either at chic shops or one of the malls. On the next day tour the canals on a sightseeing boat or water taxi. Then shop and dine along Las Olas Boulevard. The fourth day might be devoted to the many museums in downtown Fort Lauderdale and the fifth to an airboat ride at **Sawgrass Recreation Park** ⑭, at the edge of the Everglades. Fort Lauderdale offers plenty of facilities for outdoor recreation; spend the sixth day fishing and picnicking on one of the area's many piers or playing a round at a top golf course. Set aside the seventh day for **Hollywood** ⑳, where you can stroll along the scenic Broadwalk or walk through the aviary at Flamingo Gardens, in **Davie** ㉒, before relaxing in peaceful Hollywood North Beach Park.

When to Tour Fort Lauderdale and Broward County

Tourists visit the area all year long, choosing to come in winter or summer depending on interests, hobbies, and the climate where they live. The winter season, about Thanksgiving through March, still sees the biggest influx of visitors and "snowbirds"—seasonal residents who show up when the snow starts to fly up north. Concert, art, and show seasons are at their height then, and restaurants and highways all show the stress of crowds, Americans and Europeans alike.

Summer has its own fans. Waits at even the most popular restaurants are likely to be reasonable or even nonexistent, but though few services close in the summer, some may establish slightly shorter hours than during the peak season. Summer is the rainy season; the tropics-style rain arrives about mid-afternoon and is usually gone in an hour. When downpours hit, however, driving can be treacherous.

For golfers, almost anytime is great for playing. Just like everywhere else, waits for tee times are longer on weekends year-round.

Remember that sun can cause real scorching burns all year long, especially at midday, marking the tourist from the experienced resident or vacationer. You might want to plan your beach time for morning and late afternoon and go sightseeing or shopping in between.

FORT LAUDERDALE

Like some southeast Florida neighbors, Fort Lauderdale has been revitalizing itself for several years. What's unusual in a state where gaudy tourist zones stand aloof from workaday downtowns is that the city exhibits consistency at both ends of the 2-mi Las Olas corridor. The sparkling look results from a decision to thoroughly improve both beachfront and downtown, as opposed to focusing design attention in town and letting the beach fall prey to development solely by T-shirt retailers. Matching the downtown's new arts district, cafés, and boutiques is an equally inventive beach area with its own share of cafés and shops facing an undeveloped shoreline.

Downtown

The jewel of the downtown area along the New River is a new arts and entertainment district. Pricey tickets are available for Broadway shows at the riverfront Broward Center for the Performing Arts. Clustered within a five-minute walk are the Museum of Discovery and Science, the expanding Fort Lauderdale Historical Museum, and the Museum of Art. Restaurants, sidewalk cafés, delis, and blues, folk, jazz, reggae, and rock clubs flourish. The latest gem is Las Olas Riverfront, a multistory entertainment, dining, and retail complex along several blocks once owned by pioneers William and Mary Brickell.

Tying this district together is the Riverwalk, which extends 2 mi along the New River's north and south banks. Tropical gardens with benches and interpretive displays fringe the walk on one side, boat landings on the other. East along Riverwalk is Stranahan House, and a block away Las Olas attractions begin. Tropical landscaping and trees separate the traffic lanes in some blocks, setting off fine shops, restaurants, and popular nightspots. From here it's five minutes by car or 30 minutes by water taxi back to the beach.

A Good Tour

Start on Southeast 6th Avenue at Las Olas Boulevard, where you'll find **Stranahan House** ①, a turn-of-the-century structure that's now a museum. Between Southeast 6th and 11th avenues, Las Olas has Spanish Colonial buildings housing high-fashion boutiques, jewelry shops, and art galleries. If you drive east, you'll cross into the Isles, Fort Lauderdale's most prestigious neighborhood, where homes line canals with large yachts beside the seawalls.

Return west on Las Olas to Andrews Avenue, turn right, and park in one of the municipal garages so you can walk around downtown Fort Lauderdale. First stop is the **Museum of Art** ②, which has a major collection of works from the CoBrA (Copenhagen, Brussels, and Amsterdam) movement. Walk one block north to the **Broward County Main Library** ③ to see works from Broward's Art in Public Places program.

Go west on Southeast 2nd Street to Southwest 2nd Avenue, turn left, and stop at the **Fort Lauderdale Historical Museum** ④, which surveys the city's not-so-recent history. Just to the south is the palm-lined **Riverwalk** ⑤, a good place for a leisurely stroll. Head north toward a cluster of new facilities collectively known as the Arts and Science District. The district contains the outdoor Esplanade, whose exhibits include a hands-on display of the science and history of navigation, and the major science attraction, the **Museum of Discovery and Science** ⑥. The adjacent Broward Center for the Performing Arts, a massive glass-and-concrete structure by the river, opened in 1991.

Finally, go west along Las Olas Boulevard to Southwest 7th Avenue and the entrance to **Sailboat Bend** ⑦. You can return to the start of the tour by traveling east along Las Olas Boulevard.

TIMING
Depending on how long you like to linger in museums and how many hours you want to spend in the quaint shops on Las Olas Boulevard, you can spend anything from half a day to an entire day on this tour.

Sights to See

③ Broward County Main Library. This distinctive building was designed by Marcel Breuer. Works on display from Broward's Art in Public Places program include a painting by Yaacov Agam, a wooden construction by Marc Beauregard, an outdoor aluminum-and-steel sculpture by Dale Eldred, and ceramic tile by Ivan Chermayeff. (Art in Public Places displays more than 200 works—painting, sculpture, photographs, weaving—by nationally renowned and Florida artists. Pieces can be found at 13 major sites, including the main bus terminal and the airport.) A community technology center offers personal computers for public use and assistive/adaptive devices for persons with special learning and physical disabilities. Productions from theater to poetry readings are presented in a 300-seat auditorium. ⊠ *100 S. Andrews Ave.,* ☎ *954/357-7444; 954/357-7457 for self-guided Art in Public Places walking tour brochure.* ⌸ *Free.* ☉ *Mon.–Thurs. 9–9, Fri.–Sat. 9–5, Sun. noon–5:30.*

④ Fort Lauderdale Historical Museum. The museum surveys city history from the Seminole era to World War II. A model in the lobby depicts old Fort Lauderdale. In recent years the museum has expanded into several adjacent historic buildings, including the King-Cromartie House and the New River Inn. ⊠ *219 S.W. 2nd Ave.,* ☎ *954/463-4431.* ⌸ *$2.* ☉ *Tues.–Fri. 10–4.*

★ **② Museum of Art.** Housed in an Edward Larrabee Barnes–designed building that's considered an architectural masterpiece, this museum has Florida's largest art exhibition space. The impressive permanent collection features 20th-century European and American art, including works by Picasso, Calder, Moore, Dalí, Rivers, Warhol, and Stella, as

Broward County

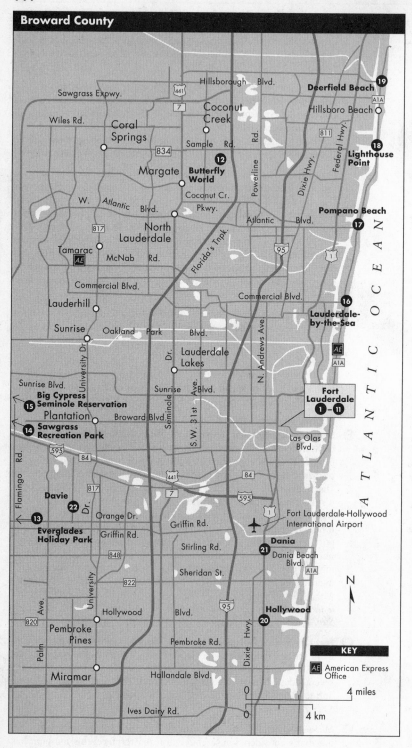

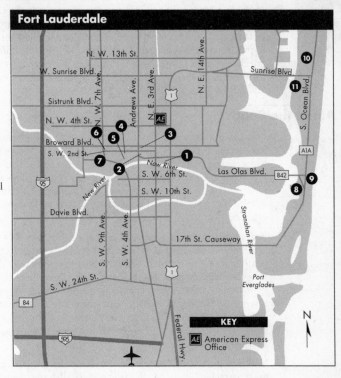

Fort Lauderdale

well as a notable collection of works by celebrated Ashcan School artist William Glackens. Opened in 1986, the museum launched a revitalization of the downtown district and nearby Riverwalk area. ⊠ *1 E. Las Olas Blvd.,* ☎ *954/763–6464.* ◫ *$6.* ⊙ *Tues.–Thurs. and Sat. 10– 5, Fri. 10–8, Sun. noon–5.*

★ ☺ ❻ **Museum of Discovery and Science.** Like other similar museums, the aim here is to show children—*and* adults—the wonders of science in an entertaining fashion. And as soon as visitors see the 52-ft-tall Great Gravity Clock in the courtyard entrance, they know they're in for a cool experience. Inside, exhibits include Choose Health, about making healthy lifestyle choices; Kidscience, which encourages youngsters to explore the world around them; and Gizmo City, a look at how gadgets work. Florida Ecoscapes has a living coral reef and also features live bees, bats, frogs, turtles, and alligators. An IMAX theater, part of the complex, shows changing films (some 3-D) on a five-story screen. More than 700,000 visit the museum annually, making it downtown's most popular attraction. ⊠ *401 S.W. 2nd St.,* ☎ *954/467–6637 for museum; 954/463–4629 for IMAX.* ◫ *Museum $6, IMAX $9, both $12.50.* ⊙ *Mon.–Sat. 10–5, Sun. noon–6.*

★ ❺ **Riverwalk.** This lovely, paved promenade on the north bank of the New River is great for entertainment as well as views. On the first Sunday of every month a jazz brunch attracts visitors. The walk has been extended 2 mi on both sides of the beautiful urban stream, connecting the facilities of the Arts and Science District.

❼ **Sailboat Bend.** Between Las Olas and the river, as well as just across the river, lies a neighborhood with much of the character of Old Town in Key West and historic Coconut Grove in Miami. No shops or services are located here.

❶ Stranahan House. The oldest standing structure in the city was once the home of pioneer businessman Frank Stranahan. Stranahan arrived in 1892 and, with his wife, Ivy, befriended the Seminole Indians, traded with them, and taught them "new ways." In 1901 he built a store and later made it his home. Now it's a museum with many of his original furnishings on display. ⌧ 335 S.E. 6th Ave. (at Las Olas Blvd.), ☎ 954/524–4736. ⌧ $5. ☉ Wed.–Sat. 10–4, Sun. 1–4.

Along the Beach

Fort Lauderdale's beachfront offers the best of all possible worlds, with easy access to restaurants and shops. For 2 mi beginning just north of the welcome center and the Bahia Mar yacht basin, strollers and café goers along Route A1A enjoy clear views, typically across rows of colorful beach umbrellas, to the sea and ships passing in and out of nearby Port Everglades. Those on the beach can look back on an exceptionally graceful promenade.

Pedestrians rank ahead of cars in Fort Lauderdale. Broad walkways line both sides of the beach road, and traffic has been trimmed to two gently curving northbound lanes, where in-line skaters dance alongside slow-moving cars. On the beach side, a low masonry wall, which serves as an extended bench, extends the promenade. At night the wall is wrapped in ribbons of fiber-optic color. The most crowded portion of beach is between Las Olas and Sunrise boulevards. This onetime strip—famous from the *Where the Boys Are* era of spring-break madness—is now but a memory.

North of the redesigned beachfront is another 2 mi of open and natural coastal landscape. Much of the way parallels the Hugh Taylor Birch State Recreation Area, which preserves a patch of primeval Florida.

A Good Tour

Go east on Southeast 17th Street across the Brooks Memorial Causeway over the Intracoastal Waterway and bear left onto Seabreeze Boulevard (Route A1A). You will pass through a neighborhood of older homes set in lush vegetation before emerging at the south end of Fort Lauderdale's beachfront strip. On your left is the Radisson Bahia Mar Beach Resort, where novelist John McDonald's fictional hero, Travis McGee, is honored with a plaque at marina slip F-18, where he docked his houseboat. Three blocks north, visit the **International Swimming Hall of Fame Museum and Aquatic Complex** ⑧, which celebrates its 35th anniversary in 2000. As you approach Las Olas Boulevard, you will see the lyrical styling that has given a distinctly European flavor to the **Fort Lauderdale beachfront** ⑨. Plan to break for lunch and perhaps a bit of shopping at Beach Place, the 100,000-square-ft entertainment, retail, and dining complex just north of Las Olas.

Turn left off Route A1A at Sunrise Boulevard, then right into **Hugh Taylor Birch State Recreation Area** ⑩, where many outdoor activities can be enjoyed amid picturesque flora and fauna. Cross Sunrise Boulevard and visit the **Bonnet House** ⑪ to marvel at both the mansion and the surrounding subtropical 35-acre estate.

TIMING

The beach is all about recreation and leisure. To enjoy it as it's meant to be, allow at least a day to loll about, or rent a fishing boat.

Sights to See

★ ⑪ **Bonnet House.** A 35-acre oasis in the heart of the beach area, this subtropical estate is a tribute to the history of old South Florida. The charming mansion was the winter residence of Frederic and Evelyn Bartlett, artists whose personal touches and small surprises are evident throughout. Whether you're interested in architecture, artwork, or the natural environment, this is a special place. ✉ *900 N. Birch Rd.,* ☎ *954/563–5393.* ✍ *$9.* ☉ *Wed.–Fri. 10–1:30, weekends noon–2:30.*

★ **⑨** **Fort Lauderdale beachfront.** A wave theme unifies the setting—from the low, white wave wall between the beach and widened beachfront promenade to the widened and bricked inner promenade in front of shops, restaurants, and hotels. Alone among Florida's major beachfront communities, Fort Lauderdale's beach remains open and uncluttered. More than ever, the boulevard is worth promenading.

⑩ **Hugh Taylor Birch State Recreation Area.** Amid the tropical greenery of this 180-acre park you can stroll along a nature trail, visit the Birch House Museum, picnic, play volleyball, pitch horseshoes, and paddle a rented canoe. Since parking is limited on A1A, beachgoers can park here and take a walkway underpass to the beach (between 9 and 5). ✉ *3109 E. Sunrise Blvd.,* ☎ *954/564–4521.* ✍ *$3.25 per vehicle with up to 8 people.* ☉ *Daily 8–sunset; ranger-guided nature walks Fri. at 10:30.*

★ **⑧** **International Swimming Hall of Fame Museum and Aquatic Complex.** This monument to underwater accomplishments has two 10-lane, 50-meter pools and an exhibition building featuring photos, medals, and other souvenirs from major swimming events around the world, as well as a theater that shows films of onetime swimming stars Johnny Weissmuller and Esther Williams. ✉ *1 Hall of Fame Dr.,* ☎ *954/462–6536 for museum; 954/468–1580 for pool.* ✍ *$3 museum, $3 pool.* ☉ *Museum and pro shop daily 9–7; pool weekdays 8–4 and 6–8, weekends 8–4; closed late Dec.–mid-Jan.*

Dining

American

$$–$$$ ✕ **Burt & Jack's.** At the far end and most scenic lookout of Port Everglades, this local favorite has been operated by veteran restaurateur Jack Jackson and actor Burt Reynolds since 1984. Behind the heavy mission doors and bougainvillea, guests are presented with Maine lobster, steaks, and chops, and the waitstaff displays the main ingredients in the raw before orders are taken. The two-story gallery of hacienda-like dining rooms surrounded by glass has views of both Port Everglades and John U. Lloyd Beach State Recreation Area. Come for cocktails in early evening on Saturday or Sunday and watch the cruise ships steam out. ✉ *Berth 23, Port Everglades,* ☎ *954/522–2878 or 954/525–5225. Jacket required. AE, D, DC, MC, V. No lunch.*

$$–$$$ ✕ **Shula's on the Beach.** With all the sports figures attaching their names to restaurants, it's only fitting that Don Shula, a legendary coach in the rough and tough world of pro football, should have a steak house. The good news for steak—and sports—fans is that the staff here turns out winners. The meat is cut thick, grilled over a superhot fire (for quick charring), and served from rare to well done. This is a pure steak house, so don't look for many other menu choices. Appetizers are adequate though unexciting; you'll probably want to go straight to the porterhouse. An outside table gives you a delightful view of sand and ocean. Inside, a spacious bar is decorated with sports memorabilia and large-screen TVs so you can watch your favorite game. ✉ *Sheraton Yankee Trader, 321 N. Atlantic Blvd.,* ☎ *954/355–4000. AE, D, DC, MC, V.*

Cajun/Creole

$$–$$$ ✕ **Evangeline.** Set inside and out on the ocean drive just south of its sister restaurant Mistral (☞ *below*), Evangeline celebrates Acadian Louisiana in decor and food. The mood is created by paneled wainscoting and plank floors—a tankard and tavern look—highlighted by verse from Longfellow's legendary poem inscribed along the turn of the ceiling. Traditional favorites include smoked rabbit gumbo with andouille sausage, a crawfish Caesar salad, jambalaya (clams, mussels, shrimp, and chicken andouille with a creole sauce), sautéed alligator in a meunière sauce topped with flash-fried oysters, and duckling with poached plums and prunelle brandy. There's music nightly, and a Dixieland band plays weekends, including Sunday afternoon. ⊠ *211 S. Atlantic Blvd. (Rte. A1A)*, ☎ *954/522–7001. AE, MC, V.*

Contemporary

$$–$$$ ✕ **Mark's Las Olas.** Mark Militello, a star among South Florida chefs,
★ is in command at this popular restaurant, where metallic finishes bounce the hubbub around the room. Militello's loyal following is enchanted with his Florida-style cuisine, which blends flavors from Caribbean, southwestern, and Mediterranean traditions. Entrées change daily, but typical choices include gulf shrimp, dolphinfish, yellowtail snapper, grouper, swordfish, Florida lobster, and callaloo (a West Indian spinach), chayote, ginger, jicama, and plantain, all brilliantly presented and combined in sauces that tend to be low fat. Pastas and full-size dinner pizzas are thoughtful offerings. ⊠ *1032 E. Las Olas Blvd.*, ☎ *954/463–1000. AE, DC, MC, V. No lunch weekends.*

$$ ✕ **Mistral.** This dining room, surrounded by tropical art and pottery,
★ rates high in both taste and looks. The kitchen staff turns out hearty pastas, such as a *primavera* redolent with garlic and herbs and *tagliolini* (an angel-hair pasta) with prosciutto, pine nuts, and tomatoes. Other favorites are grilled shrimp and black-bean cakes as well as panseared dolphin. Pizzas, big salads, and a strong selection of affordable wines, available by the bottle and by the glass, are also served. ⊠ *201 S. Atlantic Blvd. (Rte. A1A)*, ☎ *954/463–4900. AE, MC, V.*

French

$$ ✕ **French Quarter.** This 1920 building, formerly a Red Cross headquarters, sits on a quiet street, just off bustling Las Olas Boulevard. The French-style architecture has a touch of New Orleans style, and the food captures both creole and traditional French elements. Interior rooms are small and intimate, watched over by the friendly, excellent waitstaff. Among the favorites are shrimp *maison* (large shrimp sautéed with carrots and mushrooms in beurre blanc), bouillabaisse, crab cakes, and escargot appetizers. French baking is done on site, and fresh bread and all pastry desserts are made daily. A fixed-price three-course pretheater dinner ($18.95) is served until 6:30. ⊠ *215 S.E. 8th Ave.*, ☎ *954/463–8000. AE, MC, V. Closed Sun. No lunch Sat.*

$$ ✕ **La Coquille.** Although this French restaurant sits at the edge of busy Sunrise Boulevard, it seems worlds away thanks to a new art deco look, along with paintings of the sea and a tropical garden. The friendly and helpful service comes with a delightful French accent, and the cuisine is equally authentic: Dubonnet and vermouth cassis aperitifs are a prelude to seared sea scallops with spring vegetables, honey-glazed duckling with lingonberry sauce and wild rice, sweetbreads in a morel and truffle sauce, or veal with shallots and sweet bell peppers. There's always a soufflé among the desserts as well as a multicourse dinner special most nights. Chef/owner Jean Bert has been serving up award-winning dishes for 18 years, so he must be doing something right. ⊠ *1619 E. Sunrise Blvd.*, ☎ *954/467–3030. AE, MC, V. Closed Mon. No lunch Sat.–Thurs.*

$$ ✕ **Studio One French Bistro.** More like an art gallery—intimate, black-
★ and-white, mirrored—this restaurant serves up bountiful portions at low prices. About 30 choices are offered as part of the $20 fixed-price dinner. Food is thoughtfully presented, from high-gluten breads through

a dozen or so appetizers, dinner-size salads, and entrées that include a grilled salmon in puff pastry with lobster sauce, Camembert-stuffed chicken breast with French cranberry sauce, and roasted duckling with vanilla sauce. Chef Bernard Asendorf has charge of the kitchen, and his wife, Roberta, carries on the tradition of greeting by name the locals who return time and again. ⊠ *2447 E. Sunrise Blvd.,* ☎ *954/565–2052. AE, DC, MC, V. Closed Mon. mid-May–mid-Dec. No lunch.*

Italian

$$–$$$ ✗ **Primavera.** Northern Italian food is the specialty at this lovely find in the middle of an ordinary shopping plaza. Elegant floral arrangements enhance the fine dining experience. In addition to interesting pasta and risotto entrées, there is a wide variety of creative fish, poultry, veal, and beef dinners. One of chef/owner Giacomo Dresseno's favorites is veal chop Boscaiola (with shallots, wild mushrooms, and bordelaise sauce). Primavera is renowned for its spectacular assortment of both appetizers and desserts. ⊠ *830 E. Oakland Park Blvd.,* ☎ *954/564–6363. AE, D, DC, MC, V. No lunch.*

Mexican

$$ ✗ **Eduardo de San Angel.** Forget tacos and burritos, which aren't even available here, and try the classic dishes served in true Mexican style. Authentic chilies, spices, and herbs enhance an array of seafood, meat, and poultry dishes. Typical specialties are beef tenderloin tips sautéed with Portobello mushrooms and onions with a chipotle chili sauce, and a marvelous mesquite-grilled red snapper flavored with jalapeños and mango salsa. The gourmet dishes are matched by a sophisticated setting. ⊠ *2822 E. Commercial Blvd.,* ☎ *954/772–4731. AE, MC, V. Closed Sun. No lunch.*

Seafood

$$ ✗ **Blue Moon Fish Company.** The setting, on the Intracoastal Water-
★   way, is superb; virtually every table has a lovely water view. But the real magic is in the kitchen, where chefs Baron Skorish and Bryce Statham create some of the region's best seafood dishes. Favorites include pan-seared snapper with asparagus, sea bass fillet crusted with macadamia nuts, and rare-charred tuna. The appetizer selection features choices from the raw bar, including a sushi sampler, plus tasty crab and crawfish cakes and charred portobello mushrooms. On Saturday night, a blues band performs. This is a stunning addition to the waterfront dining scene. ⊠ *4405 W. Tradewinds Ave.,* ☎ *954/267–9888. AE, MC, V.*

$–$$ ✗ **Rustic Inn Crabhouse.** Wayne McDonald started with a cozy one-room roadhouse in 1955, when this was a remote service road just west of the little airport. Now, the plain, rustic place is huge. Steamed crabs seasoned with garlic and herbs, spices, and oil are eaten with mallets on tables covered with newspapers; peel-and-eat shrimp are served either with garlic and butter or spiced and steamed with Old Bay seasoning. The big menu includes other seafood items as well. Pies and cheesecakes are offered for dessert. ⊠ *4331 Ravenswood Rd.,* ☎ *954/584–1637. AE, D, DC, MC, V.*

$–$$ ✗ **Shirttail Charlie's.** Diners look out on the New River from the outdoor deck or upstairs dining room of this restaurant, named for a yesteryear Seminole Indian who wore his shirttails out. A free 30- to 40-minute after-dinner cruise on *Shirttail Charlie's Express* chugs upriver past an alleged Al Capone speakeasy or across the river to and from the Broward Center for the Performing Arts. Charlie's is built to look old, with a 1920s tile floor that leans toward the water. Florida-style seafood includes conch served four ways, crab balls, blackened tuna with Dijon mustard sauce, crunchy coconut shrimp with a not-too-sweet piña colada sauce, and three fresh catches nightly. A children's menu is available. ✉ *400 S.W. 3rd Ave.,* ☎ *954/463–3474. AE, MC, V. Closed Mon. June–Sept.*

Southwestern

$–$$ ✕ **Canyon.** Adventurous southwestern cuisine helps you escape the ordinary at this small but very popular spot. Take, for example, the ostrich skewers, smoked salmon tostada, brie and wild-mushroom quesadilla, and marvelous Chilean sea bass. Free-range chicken and brook trout are served with a tempting crabmeat salsa. Many guests like to start off with Canyon's famous prickly pear margaritas, or choose from a well-rounded wine list or selection of beers, including many microbrews. ✉ *1818 E. Sunrise Blvd.,* ☎ *954/765–1950. AE, MC, V. No lunch.*

Lodging

On the Beach

$$$$ ☷ **Marriott's Harbor Beach Resort.** If you look down from the upper stories (14 in all) at night, this 16-acre property south of the big public beach shimmers like a jewel. Spacious guest rooms are done in tropical colors, lively floral prints, rattan, wicker, and wood. Each has a balcony facing the ocean or the Intracoastal Waterway, and there are in-room minibars. Sheffield's (Dining, *above*) is one of the city's top restaurants. No other hotel gives you so many options. ✉ *3030 Holiday Dr., 33316,* ☎ *954/525–4000 or 800/222–6543,* FAX *954/766–6152. 588 rooms, 36 suites. 5 restaurants, 3 bars, pool, massage, saunas, 5 tennis courts, health club, beach, windsurfing, boating, parasailing, children's program (ages 5–12). AE, DC, MC, V.*

$$$–$$$$ ☷ **Lago Mar Resort Hotel & Club.** The sprawling Lago Mar has been owned by the Banks family since the early 1950s. In 1999 they added 42 new guest accommodations at a cost of $5 million. The lobby is still luxurious, with fanlight surrounds, a coquina-rock fireplace, and an eye-popping saltwater aquarium behind the registration desk. Allamanda trellises and bougainvillea plantings edge the swimming lagoon, and guests have use of the broadest beach in the city. Lago Mar is less a big resort than a small town—and, in its way, a slice of Old Florida. If price is no object, try one of the two new oceanfront penthouse suites. For $600 a night you get 1,800 square ft of luxury. ✉ *1700 S. Ocean La., 33316,* ☎ *954/523–6511 or 800/524–6627,* FAX *954/524–6627. 52 rooms, 143 1-bedroom suites, 17 2-bedroom suites. 4 restaurants, 2 pools, miniature golf, 2 tennis courts, shuffleboard, volleyball. AE, DC, MC, V.*

$$–$$$ ☷ **Bahia Cabana Beach Resort.** *Boating Magazine* ranks the waterfront bar and restaurant here among the world's 10 best, but it's far enough from guest rooms so that nightly entertainment is not disturbing. A video bar yields a sweeping view of the marina. Rooms are spread among five buildings furnished in tropical-casual style. Those in the 500 building are more motel-like and overlook the parking lot, but rates here are lowest. ✉ *3001 Harbor Dr., 33316,* ☎ *954/524–1555; 800/922–3008; 800/232–2437 in FL;* FAX *954/764–5951. 52 rooms, 10 suites, 37 efficiencies. Restaurant, 2 bars, café, 3 pools, hot tub, saunas, shuffleboard. AE, D, DC, MC, V.*

$$ ☷ **La Casa Del Mar.** This is a Florida rarity: a true bed-and-breakfast inn located at the beach. Co-owners Larry Ataniso and Lee Prellwitz took the plunge three years ago, and guests have been delighted ever since. Rooms have names like Stolen Kiss, Monet, and Southwest. The full American breakfast might consist of orange-flavored French toast, buttermilk pancakes, poached eggs, and mushroom-sausage casserole, among other treats, and guests can indulge again in the late afternoon at the poolside wine and cheese party. ⊠ *3003 Granada St., 33304,* ☎ *954/467–2037,* FAX *954/467–7439. 10 units. Pool. AE, MC, V.*

$–$$ 🖫 **Nina Lee Imperial House.** Recently the Nina Lee acquired the adjacent Imperial House. Both now operate as one property, having been extensively refurbished with new carpeting, TVs, furniture, and drapes. The Nina Lee is typical of the modest, affordable 1950s-style lodgings that can be found within a block or two of the ocean along Fort Lauderdale beach. Rooms are homey and clean, but not tiny. Efficiencies have gas kitchens, large closets, and tub-showers. The pool is set in a garden, and the entire property is just removed enough from the beach causeway to be quiet. The Imperial House has apartment-style accommodations consisting of living room, kitchen, and bedroom. Guests may use the facilities at the nearby beachfront Sheraton Yankee Clipper hotel. ⊠ *3048 Harbor Dr., 33316,* ☎ *954/524–1568. 26 units. 2 pools. MC, V.*

Downtown and Beach Causeways

$$$$ 🖫 **Hyatt Regency Pier Sixty-Six.** The trademark of this high-rise re-
★ sort on the Intracoastal Waterway is its rooftop Pier Top Lounge. Overlooking the resort's marina, it revolves every 66 minutes and is reached by an exterior elevator. The 17-story tower dominates a 22-acre spread that includes the Spa LXVI. Tower and lanai lodgings are tops from the ground up. (In 1999 the resort completed an $8.8 million improvement program, which upgraded all guest rooms and put more lavish touches on the spa.) In the early evening guests try to perch at the Pelican Bar; at 6:06 a cannon is fired, and anybody around the bar gets a drink on the house. When you want to swim in the ocean, hail the water taxi at the resort's dock for a three-minute trip to the beach. ⊠ *2301 S. 17th St., 33316,* ☎ *954/525–6666 or 800/327–3796,* FAX *954/728–3541. 380 rooms, 8 suites. 3 restaurants, 3 bars, pool, hot tub, spa, 2 tennis courts, dock, snorkeling, boating, parasailing, waterskiing, fishing. AE, D, MC, V.*

$$$–$$$$ 🖫 **Riverside Hotel.** This six-story hotel was built in 1936 and has been steadily upgraded. A sidewalk café fronts Bob Jenny's tropical murals, one of which is a New Orleans–style work that stretches across 725 square ft of the hotel's facade. Old Fort Lauderdale photos grace the hallways, and rooms are outfitted distinctively, with antique oak furnishings, framed French prints, and European-style baths. The poolside bar in back offers a great view of the New River, as do the best guest rooms; the least desirable are the 36 series, from which you can hear the elevator. No-smoking rooms are available. An attentive staff includes many who have been with the hotel for two decades or more. ⊠ *620 E. Las Olas Blvd., 33301,* ☎ *954/467–0671 or 800/325–3280,* FAX *954/462–2148. 109 rooms, 7 suites. 2 restaurants, bar, pool, dock. AE, DC, MC, V.*

$$–$$$ 🖫 **Banyan Marina Apartments.** These outstanding waterfront apart-
★ ments, on a residential island just off Las Olas Boulevard, are set amid imaginative landscaping that includes a walkway through the upper branches of a banyan tree. Featuring leather sofas, springy carpets, real potted plants, sheer curtains, custom drapes, high-quality art, French doors, and jalousies for sweeping the breeze in, the luxurious units are as comfortable as any first-class hotel—but for half the price. Also included are a full kitchen, dining area, beautiful gardens, dockage for eight yachts, and exemplary housekeeping. Recent upgrades include a new phone system and a remodeling of all bathrooms. ⊠ *111 Isle of Venice, 33301,* ☎ *954/524–4430,* FAX *954/764–4870. 10 rooms, 1 efficiency, 4 1-bedroom apartments, 2 2-bedroom apartments. Dining room, pool, dock. MC, V.*

Nightlife and the Arts

For the most complete weekly listing of events, read the **"Showtime!"** entertainment insert and events calendar in the Friday *Fort Lauderdale News/Sun Sentinel.* **"Weekend,"** in the Friday edition of the *Herald,* the Broward edition of the *Miami Herald,* carries listings of area happenings. The weekly **City Link** is principally an entertainment and dining paper with a relic "underground" look. A 24-hour **Arts & Entertainment Hotline** (☎ 954/357–5700) provides updates on art, attractions, children's events, dance, festivals, films, literature, museums, music, opera, and theater.

Tickets are sold at individual box offices and through **Ticketmaster** (☎ 954/523–3309); there is a service charge.

The Arts

Broward Center for the Performing Arts (✉ 201 S.W. 5th Ave., ☎ 954/462–0222) is the waterfront centerpiece of Fort Lauderdale's cultural arts district. More than 500 events a year are scheduled at the 2,700-seat architectural masterpiece, including Broadway musicals, plays, dance, symphony and opera, rock, film, lectures, comedy, and children's theater.

Nightlife

BARS AND LOUNGES

Baja Beach Club (✉ 3339 N. Federal Hwy., ☎ 954/563–7889), now at a new location, offers the same trendy entertainment: karaoke, lip synching, virtual reality, performing bartenders, temporary tattoos—plus a 40-ft free buffet. At Beach Place, **Cafe Iguana** (✉ 17 S. Atlantic Blvd., ☎ 954/763–7222) has a nightly DJ to keep the dance floor hopping. **Cheers** (✉ 941 E. Cypress Creek Rd., ☎ 954/771–6337) is an action-filled nightspot with a wide variety of rock bands, two bars, and a dance floor. **Chili Pepper** (✉ 200 W. Broward Blvd., ☎ 954/525–0094) brings hot current rock bands to the stage. **O'Hara's Pub & Sidewalk Cafe** (✉ 722 E. Las Olas Blvd., ☎ 954/524–1764) features live jazz and blues nightly. It's packed for TGIF, though usually by the end of each day the trendy crowd spills onto this prettiest of downtown streets. The **Parrot Lounge** (✉ 911 Sunrise La., ☎ 954/563–1493) is a loony feast for the eyes, with a casual, friendly local crowd. Fifteen TVs and frequent sing-alongs add to the fun. A jukebox jams all night. **Squeeze** (✉ 3045 N. Federal Hwy., ☎ 954/564–1074), a favorite of alternative-music fans, continues in a new location at the Culture Room.

COUNTRY AND WESTERN

Desperado (✉ 2520 S. Miami Rd., ☎ 954/463–2855) offers a mechanical bull and free line-dance lessons. The club is open from Wednesday through Sunday.

Outdoor Activities and Sports

Baseball

From mid-February to March the **Baltimore Orioles** (✉ Fort Lauderdale Stadium, N.W. 12th Ave., ☎ 954/776–1921) are in spring training.

Biking

Some of the most popular routes are Route A1A and Bayview Drive, especially early in the morning before traffic builds, and a 7-mi bike path that parallels Route 84 and the New River and leads to Markham Park, which has mountain-bike trails. Most area bike shops also have cycling maps.

Fishing

If you're interested in a saltwater charter, check out the **Radisson Bahia Mar Beach Resort** (✉ 801 Seabreeze Blvd., ☎ 954/627–6357). Both sportfishing and drift fishing bookings can be arranged.

Scuba Diving and Snorkeling

Lauderdale Diver (✉ 1334 S.E. 17th St. Causeway, ☎ 954/467–2822 or 800/654–2073), which is PADI affiliated, arranges dive charters throughout the county. Dive trips typically last four hours. Nonpackage reef trips are open to divers for $40; scuba gear is extra.

Pro Dive (✉ Radisson Bahia Mar Beach Resort, 801 Seabreeze Blvd., ☎ 954/761–3413 or 800/772–3483), a PADI five-star facility, is the area's oldest diving operation and offers packages with Radisson Bahia Mar Beach Resort, from where its 60-ft boat departs. Snorkelers can go out for $24 on a two-hour snorkeling trip, which includes equipment. Scuba divers pay $39 using their own gear or $89 with all rentals included.

Soccer

Major-league soccer has returned to South Florida in the form of the **Fusion** (✉ 5301 N.W. 12th Ave., ☎ 954/717–2200). Their season, which begins in March, includes 20 home games at 20,000-seat Lockhart Stadium.

Tennis

With 21 courts, 18 of them lighted clay courts, the **Jimmy Evert Tennis Center at Holiday Park** is Fort Lauderdale's largest public tennis facility. Chris Evert, one of the game's greatest players, learned the sport here under the watchful eye of her father, Jimmy, who retired after 37 years as the tennis professional here. ✉ *701 N.E. 12th Ave.,* ☎ *954/761–5378.* 🎟 *$4.50 per person per hr.* ☉ *Weekdays 8 AM–9:15 PM, weekends 8–7.*

Shopping

Malls

Just north of Las Olas Boulevard on Route A1A is the happening **Beach Place** (✉ 17 S. Atlantic Blvd.). Here you can browse through such shops as the Gap, Bath & Body Works, and Banana Republic; have lunch or dinner at an array of restaurants, from casual Caribbean to elegant American; or carouse at a selection of nightspots—all open late. By and large, eateries on the lower level are more upscale, whereas on the upper level, the prices are lower and the ocean view is better.

With a convenient in-town location just west of the Intracoastal Waterway, the split-level **Galleria Mall** (✉ 2414 E. Sunrise Blvd.) contains more than 1 million square ft of space. It's anchored by Neiman-Marcus, Lord & Taylor, Dillards, and Saks Fifth Avenue and features 150 world-class specialty stores with an emphasis on fashion and sporting goods.

Shopping Districts

When you're downtown, check out the new **Las Olas Riverfront** (✉ 1 block west of Andrews Ave. on the New River) shopping, dining, and entertainment complex. If only for a stroll and some window-shopping, don't miss the **Shops of Las Olas** (✉ 1 block off New River east of U.S. 1). The city's best boutiques plus top restaurants (many affordable) and art galleries line a beautifully landscaped street.

Side Trips

The Western Suburbs and Beyond

West of Fort Lauderdale is an ever-growing mass of suburbs flowing one into the other. They're home to most of the city's golf courses as well as some attractions and large malls. As you head farther west, the terrain becomes more Everglades-like, and you'll occasionally see an alligator sunning itself on a canal bank. No matter how dedicated developers are to building over this natural resource, the Everglades keeps trying to assert itself. Waterbirds, fish, and other creatures are found in canals and lakes, even man-made ones, throughout the western areas.

Thousands of caterpillars representing as many as 150 species pupate and emerge as butterflies in the walk-through laboratory that is **Butterfly World,** on 3 acres inside Tradewinds Park. A screened aviary called North American Butterflies is reserved for native species. The Tropical Rain Forest is a 30-ft-high construction, with observation decks, waterfalls, ponds, and tunnels where colorful butterflies flit and shift about. ⊠ *3600 W. Sample Rd., Coconut Creek,* ☎ *954/977–4400.* ☑ *$11.95.* ⊙ *Mon.–Sat. 9–5, Sun. 1–5.*

The 30-acre **Everglades Holiday Park** provides a good glimpse of the Everglades. Here you can take an airboat tour, look at an 18th-century-style Native American village, or watch an alligator-wrestling show. A souvenir shop, TJ's Grill, a convenience store, and a campground with RV hookups and a tent are all on site. ⊠ *21940 Griffin Rd.,* ☎ *954/434–8111.* ☑ *Free, $12.50 airboat tour.* ⊙ *Daily 9–5.*

To understand and enjoy the Everglades, take an airboat ride at **Sawgrass Recreation Park.** You'll probably see all sorts of plants and wildlife, such as birds, alligators, turtles, snakes, and fish. Included in the entrance fee along with the airboat ride is admission to an Everglades nature exhibit, a native Seminole Indian village, and exhibits about alligators, other reptiles, and birds of prey. A souvenir and gift shop, food service, and an RV park with hookups are also at the park. ⊠ *U.S. 27 north of I–595,* ☎ *954/426–2474.* ☑ *$14.68.* ⊙ *Daily 6–6, airboat rides 8–5.*

Some distance from Fort Lauderdale's tranquil beaches, but worth the one-hour drive, is the **Big Cypress Seminole Reservation** and its two very different attractions. At the **Billie Swamp Safari,** you can experience the majesty of the Everglades firsthand. Daily tours of the wetlands and hammocks, where wildlife abound, yield sightings of deer, water buffalo, bison, wild hogs, hawks, eagles, alligators, and even the rare Florida panther. Tours are provided aboard swamp buggies—customized motor vehicles specially designed to provide visitors with an elevated view of the frontier. ⊠ *Snake Rd., 19 mi north of I–75 Exit 14,* ☎ *941/983–6101 or 800/949–6101.* ☑ *Free, $38 swamp buggy ecotour/alligator and snake education show/airboat ride package.* ⊙ *Daily 8–5.*

Not far away from the Billie Swamp Safari is the **Ah-Tha-Thi-Ki Museum,** whose name means "a place to learn, a place to remember." It is just that. The museum honors the culture and tradition of the Seminoles through artifacts and reenactments of rituals and ceremonies. The site includes a living Seminole village, nature trails, and a boardwalk through a cypress swamp. ⊠ *Snake Rd., 17 mi north of I–75 Exit 14,* ☎ *954/792–0745.* ☑ *$6.* ⊙ *Tues.–Sun. 9–5.*

LODGING

$$$$ 🏨 **Wyndham Resort & Spa Fort Lauderdale.** As its name suggests, this resort offers the luxury, amenities, and facilities of a resort with the health-consciousness of a spa. Spacious guest rooms and suites are done in tropical colors with rattan seating and overlook a lake or golf course. Oversize baths have dressing areas. In the morning complimentary caffeine-free herbal teas are offered; in the afternoon it's fresh fruit. The staff nutritionist follows American Heart Association and American Cancer Society guidelines and can accommodate macrobiotic and vegetarian diets. Also on site and open to the public is a full-service beauty salon. The resort offers combination spa-tennis and spa-golf packages. ⊠ *250 Racquet Club Rd., 33326,* ☎ *954/389–3300 or 800/ 327–8090,* FAX *954/384–0563. 493 units. 4 restaurants, 2 bars, 5 pools, beauty salon, spa, 2 golf courses, 24 tennis courts, bowling, horseback riding, roller-skating rink, shops. AE, D, MC, V.*

NIGHTLIFE AND THE ARTS

Sunrise Musical Theatre (⊠ 5555 N.W. 95th Ave., Sunrise, ☎ 954/741–7300) is a 4,000-seat theater featuring everything from ballet to top-name pop, rock, and country artists.

OUTDOOR ACTIVITIES AND SPORTS

Fishing. The marina at **Everglades Holiday Park** (⊠ 21940 Griffin Rd., ☎ 954/434–8111) caters to freshwater fishing. For $52.50 for five hours, you can rent a 14-ft johnboat (with a 9.9-horsepower Yamaha outboard) that carries up to four people. A rod and reel rent for $9 a day, and bait is extra. For two people, a fishing guide for a half day (four hours) is $140; for a full day (eight hours), $190. A third person adds $35 for a half day, $70 for a full day. You can also buy a freshwater fishing license (mandatory) here; a seven-day nonresident license is $17. Freshwater fishing with a guide out of **Sawgrass Recreation Park** (⊠ U.S. 27 north of I–595, ☎ 954/426–2474) costs $175 for two people for a half day, $225 for a full day. Resident and nonresident fishing licenses and live bait are available.

Golf. Next Day Golf (☎ 954/772–2582) provides access at no extra fee to private courses normally limited to members and arranges bookings up to 12 months in advance—a big advantage for golfers planning trips during the busy winter months. And they also offer last-minute discount tee times (call 12 hours in advance). **Bonaventure Country Club** (⊠ 200 Bonaventure Blvd., ☎ 954/389–2100) has 36 holes. **Broken Woods Country Club** (⊠ 9000 Sample Rd., Coral Springs, ☎ 954/752–2140) has 18 holes. **Colony West Country Club** (⊠ 6800 N.W. 88th Ave., Tamarac, ☎ 954/726–8430) offers play on 36 holes. Just west of Florida's Turnpike, the **Inverrary Country Club** (⊠ 3840 Inverrary Blvd., Lauderhill, ☎ 954/733–7550) has three 18-hole courses. **Jacaranda Golf Club** (⊠ 9200 W. Broward Blvd., Plantation, ☎ 954/ 472–5855) has 18 holes to play. **Sabal Palms Golf Course** (⊠ 5101 W. Commercial Blvd., Tamarac, ☎ 954/731–2600) has 18 holes. **Sunrise Country Club** (⊠ 7400 N.W. 24th Pl., Sunrise, ☎ 954/742–4333) provides 18 holes.

Ice Hockey. National Car Rental Center, Broward's new arena, is the home of the National Hockey League's **Florida Panthers** (⊠ 2555 N.W. 137th Way, Sunrise, ☎ 954/523–3309).

SHOPPING

Broward's shopping extravaganza, **Fashion Mall at Plantation** (⊠ University Dr. north of Broward Blvd., Plantation) is a jewel of a mall. The three-level complex includes such department stores as Macy's, Lord & Taylor, and Burdines; a Sheraton Suites Hotel; and more than 100 specialty shops. In addition to a diverse food court, the Brasserie Max restaurant offers gourmet dining.

Containing more than 270 stores, the huge (2 million square ft) **Sawgrass Mills Mall** (⊠ 12801 W. Sunrise Blvd., at Flamingo Rd., Sunrise),

---

Close-Up

THE MALL

TRAVEL INDUSTRY SURVEYS reveal that shopping is vacationers' number one activity. With 25 million visitors annually, Sawgrass Mills proves the point, ranking as the second-biggest tourist attraction in Florida, behind Disney. This so-called world's largest retail outlet mall is one of the first places visitors ask about. And they come from all over; in 1999, 48% were international, primarily from Latin America, Germany, and the United Kingdom.

Sawgrass Mills: the adventure. This is not your average mall. Tour buses hum near entrances with names like Pink Flamingo, Red Snapper, and White Seahorse. The complex itself is alligator shaped, and walking every nook and cranny is about 2 mi. (If the 800-member Mall Walkers Club—mostly seniors—can do it, so can you.) Mall sections are called halls; for example, the Designer Hall contains women's designer clothing. At the Oasis, a Hard Rock Cafe and 24-screen movieplex are being joined by Wolfgang Puck's first South Florida eatery. And then there are the prices—as much as 80% below retail according to management, but buyers should compare.

Sawgrass Mills: the growth magnet. Western Broward, especially Sunrise, has seen huge growth. In addition to the nearby National Car Rental Center, a number of companies, other retail and restaurant operations, and even residential communities have located nearby, and with the mall has come sprawl.

---

9 mi west of downtown Fort Lauderdale, is a destination in itself. Travelers and locals alike come for shopping, restaurants, food courts, and entertainment, and the place teems on weekends and holidays. Shops, many of them manufacturer's outlets, retail outlets, and name-brand discounters, include Neiman-Marcus, Loehmann's, JCPenney, Ann Taylor, Alfred Angelo Bridal, Levi's, TJ Maxx, Donna Karan, Saks Fifth Avenue, and Kenneth Cole. The mall is also accessible from Miami-Dade and the Palm Beaches via the Sawgrass Expressway.

NORTH ON SCENIC A1A

North of Fort Lauderdale's Birch Recreation Area, Route A1A edges back from the beach through the section known as the Galt Ocean Mile, and a succession of ocean-side communities line up against the sea. Traffic can line up, too, as it passes through a changing pattern of beach-blocking high-rises and modest family vacation towns and back again. Here and there a scenic lighthouse or park punctuates the landscape, while other attractions and recreational opportunities are found inland.

Lauderdale-by-the-Sea

16 *5 mi north of Fort Lauderdale.*

Tucked just north of Fort Lauderdale's northern boundary, this low-rise family resort town bans construction of more than three stories. You can drive along lawn-divided El Mar Drive, lined with garden-style motels a block east of Route A1A. However, you don't actually need a car in Lauderdale-by-the-Sea. Dozens of good restaurants and shops are in close proximity to hotels and the beach.

Where Commercial Boulevard meets the ocean, you can walk out onto **Anglin's Fishing Pier,** stretching 875 ft into the Atlantic. Here you can fish, stop in at any of the popular restaurants clustered around the seafront plaza, or just soak up the scene.

Dining and Lodging

$$ ✕ **Sea Watch.** It's set back from the road and easy to miss, but after 25 years, this nautical-theme restaurant right on Lauderdale-by-the-Sea's beach stays packed during lunch and dinner. Waits can be as long as 30 minutes, but time passes quickly in the sumptuous upstairs lounge with comfy sofas and high-back rattan chairs. The menu has all the right appetizers: oysters Rockefeller, gulf shrimp, clams casino, and Bahamian conch fritters. Typical daily specials might be sautéed yellowtail snapper, oat-crusted with roasted red bell pepper sauce and basil, or a charbroiled dolphin fillet marinated with soy sauce, garlic, black pepper, and lemon juice. Desserts include a cappuccino brownie and strawberries Romanoff. Good early bird specials are offered off-season. ⊠ *6002 N. Ocean Blvd. (Rte. A1A), Fort Lauderdale,* ☎ *954/ 781–2200. AE, MC, V.*

$ ✕ **Aruba Beach Cafe.** This is your best bet at the pier. A big beachside barn of a place—very casual, always crowded, always fun—it serves large portions of Caribbean conch chowder, Cuban black-bean soup, fresh tropical salads, burgers, sandwiches, and seafood. A reggae/jazz band performs Friday and Sunday 2–6. ⊠ *1 E. Commercial Blvd.,* ☎ *954/776–0001. AE, D, DC, MC, V.*

$$–$$$ ⛉ **A Little Inn by the Sea.** French, German, and English are spoken at this inn, which caters to a very international clientele. Innkeeper Uli Brandt and his family maintain tropical charm and bed-and-breakfast style. Since taking over the property in 1994, they have continued to make upgrades, including remodeled kitchens in efficiencies and one- and two-bedroom suites, and new bamboo and rattan furniture throughout. Adding to the flavor are fountains and classical background music at breakfast. The inn is directly on the ocean, and rooms have nice views from private balconies. ⊠ *4546 El Mar Dr., 33308,* ☎ *954/772–2450 or 800/492–0311,* FAX *954/938–9354. 10 rooms, 7 suites, 12 efficiencies. Pool, beach, bicycles. AE, D, DC, MC, V.*

$$ ⛉ **Tropic Seas Resort Inn.** It's only a block off A1A, but it's a million-dollar location—directly on the beach and two blocks from municipal tennis courts. Built in the 1950s, units are plain but clean and comfortable, with tropical rattan furniture and ceiling fans. Managers Sandy and Larry Lynch tend to the largely repeat, family-oriented clientele. The complimentary Sunday brunch and weekly wiener roast and rum swizzle party are good opportunities to mingle with other guests. ⊠ *4616 El Mar Dr., 33308,* ☎ *954/772–2555 or 800/952–9581,* FAX *954/771–5711. 16 rooms, 6 efficiencies, 7 apartments. Pool, beach. AE, D, DC, MC, V.*

$–$$ ⛉ **Blue Seas Courtyard.** Bubbly innkeeper Cristie Furth runs this one- and two-story motel with her husband, Marc, and small as it is, they keep investing their future in it. Lattice fencing and gardens of cactus and impatiens were added in front for more privacy around the brick patio and garden-set pool. Guest quarters feature kitchenettes, terra-cotta tiles, bright Haitian and Peruvian art, and generally Tex-Mex and Danish furnishings, whose woody textures work well together. Hand-made painted shutters and indoor plants add to the look. This remains an excellent buy in a quiet resort area just a block from the beach. ⊠ *4525 El Mar Dr., 33308,* ☎ *954/772–3336 or 877/225–8373,* FAX *954/772–6337. 12 units. Pool, coin laundry. MC, V.*

Outdoor Activities and Sports

Anglin's Fishing Pier (☎ 954/491–9403) is open for fishing 24 hours a day. Fishing costs $3 for adults and $2 for children up to 12, tackle rental is an additional $5 (plus $10 deposit), and bait averages $2.

Pompano Beach

⓱ *3 mi north of Lauderdale-by-the-Sea.*

As Route A1A enters this town directly north of Lauderdale-by-the-Sea, the high-rise procession begins again. Sportfishing is big in Pompano Beach, as its name implies, but there's more to beachside attractions than the popular Fisherman's Wharf. Behind a low coral-rock wall, Alsdorf Park extends north and south of the wharf along the road and beach.

Dining and Lodging

$$$ ✕ **Cafe Maxx.** New-wave epicurean dining had its South Florida start
★   here in the early 1980s, and Cafe Maxx remains popular among regional food lovers. The setting is ordinary, in a little strip of stores, but inside there's a holiday glow year-round. Chef Oliver Saucy demonstrates ritual devotion to the preparation of fine cuisine. The menu changes nightly but always showcases foods from the tropics: jumbo stone-crab claws with honey-lime mustard sauce and black-bean and banana pepper chili with Florida avocado. Appetizer favorites include duck and smoked mozzarella ravioli with brown butter, basil, and sun-dried tomatoes—a pure delight. Desserts also reflect a tropical theme, from praline macadamia mousse over chocolate cake with butterscotch sauce to candied ginger with pears poached in muscatel and sun-dried cherry ice cream. More than 200 wines are offered by the bottle, another 20 by the glass. ⊠ *2601 E. Atlantic Blvd.,* ☎ *954/782–0606. AE, D, DC, MC, V. No lunch.*

$$$–$$$$ 🏨 **Palm-Aire Spa Resort.** This 750-acre health, fitness, and stress-reduction spa offers exercise activities, personal treatments, and calorie-controlled meals. Separate men's and women's pavilions have private sunken Roman baths, Swiss showers, and some of the most experienced hands in the massage business. There are 166 spacious rooms and 18 golf villas with private terraces. All have separate dressing rooms, and some have two baths. You can have use of the spa for $96 for a half day or $220 for the whole day, including lunch, massage, facial, and fitness classes. ⊠ *2601 Palm-Aire Dr. N, 33069,* ☎ *954/972–3300 or 800/272–5624. 184 units. Restaurant, pools, hot tubs, massage, saunas, spa, steam rooms, 94 holes of golf, 37 tennis courts, aerobics, exercise room, racquetball, squash. AE, D, MC, V.*

$$$ 🏨 **Beachcomber.** This Best Western property's beach location is central to most Broward County attractions. Ocean views are everywhere, from the oversize guest room balconies to the dining rooms. Though there are also villas and penthouse suites atop the eight-story structure, standard rooms are spacious. The multilingual staff seems attentive to guest requests. ⊠ *1200 S. Ocean Blvd., 33062,* ☎ *954/941–7830 or 800/231–2423. 134 rooms, 9 villas, 4 suites. Restaurant, bar, 2 pools, beach. AE, D, MC, V.*

Outdoor Activities and Sports

FISHING

Pompano Pier (☎ 954/943–1488) extends 1,080 ft into the Atlantic. The cost is $2.65 for adults, $1.06 for children under 10; rod-and-reel rental is $10.18 (including admission and initial bait).

For drift fishing try **Fish City Pride** (⊠ Fish City Marina, 2621 N. Riverside Dr., ☎ 954/781–1211). Morning, afternoon, and evening trips cost $25 and include fishing gear. You can arrange for a saltwater charter boat through the **Hillsboro Inlet Marina** (⊠ 2629 N. Riverside Dr., ☎ 954/943–8222). The 10-boat fleet offers half-day charters for $325, including gear, for up to six people.

GOLF

Crystal Lake South Course (⊠ 3800 Crystal Lake Dr., ☎ 954/943–2902) has 18 holes. **Palm-Aire Country Club & Resort** (⊠ 3701 Oaks Clubhouse Dr., ☎ 954/978–1737; 954/975–6244 for tee line), part of the Palm-Aire Spa Resort, has 94 holes of golf, including a course with an extra four holes.

HORSE RACING

Pompano Harness Track, Florida's only harness track, features world-class trotters and pacers during its October–August meet. The Top o' the Park restaurant overlooks the finish line. ⊠ 1800 S.W. 3rd St., ☎ 954/972–2000. ⊠ Grandstand free, clubhouse $2. ⊙ Racing Mon., Wed., Fri., and Sat. 7:30.

ICE-SKATING

Visitors from the North who miss ice and cold can skate at the **Gold Coast Ice Arena** during morning, afternoon, or evening sessions. You can also watch the NHL Florida Panthers practice mornings during the hockey season. ⊠ 4601 N. Federal Hwy., ☎ 954/943–1437. ⊠ Sessions $5 ($5.50 weekend evenings), skate rental $2. ⊙ Sun.–Thurs. 8:30–4 plus Tues. 8:15 PM–10 PM, Fri.–Sat. 8:15 AM–11 PM.

Shopping

Bargain hunters head to the **Festival Flea Market** (⊠ 2900 W. Sample Rd.), where more than 600 vendors sell merchandise in a 400,000-square-ft building. There are also a games section for youngsters and an 18-screen cinema. The old Pompano Fashion Square has been reborn as **Pompano Square** (⊠ 2001 N. Federal Hwy.) and now features a tropical motif. This comfortably sized city mall has 60 shops, three department stores, and a few places for food.

Lighthouse Point

18 2 mi north of Pompano Beach.

A big attraction here is the view across Hillsboro Inlet to **Hillsboro Light,** the brightest lighthouse in the Southeast. Mariners have used this landmark for decades. From the ocean you can see the light almost halfway to the Bahamas. Although the lighthouse is on private property and is inaccessible to the public, it's well worth a peek.

Dining

$$–$$$ ✕ **Cafe Arugula.** Chef Dick Cingolani draws upon the culinary tradi-
★ tions of warm climates from Italy to the American Southwest. The decor, too, blends southwestern with Mediterranean looks—a row of mauve-velvet booths beneath steamboat-wheel windows surrounds an entire wall of chili peppers, corn, cactus, and garlic cloves. A frequently changing menu may include succulent fresh hogfish with capers and shaved almonds over fettuccine or a free-range loin of venison with juniper–wild mushroom sauce, quesadilla, and stir-fried vegetables. ⊠ 3110 N. Federal Hwy., ☎ 954/785–7732. AE, D, DC, MC, V. No lunch.

$$ ✕ **Cap's Place.** On an island that was once a bootlegger's haunt, this
★ seafood restaurant is reached by launch and has served such luminaries as Winston Churchill, FDR, and John F. Kennedy. Cap was Captain Theodore Knight, born in 1871, who, with partner-in-crime Al Hasis, floated a derelict barge to the area in the 1920s. Today the rustic restaurant, built on the barge, is run by descendants of Hasis. Baked wahoo steaks are lightly glazed and meaty, the long-cut french fries

arouse gluttony, hot and flaky rolls are baked fresh several times a night, and tangy lime pie is a great finishing touch. Turn east off Federal Highway onto Northeast 24th Street (two blocks north of Pompano Square); follow the double yellow line to the launch. ⊠ *Cap's Dock, 2765 N.E. 28th Ct.,* ☎ *954/941–0418. AE, MC, V. No lunch.*

En Route   To the north, Route A1A traverses the so-called Hillsboro Mile (actually more than 2 mi), a millionaire's row of some of the most beautiful and expensive homes in Broward County. The road runs along a narrow strip of land between the Intracoastal Waterway and the ocean, with bougainvillea and oleanders edging the way and yachts docked along both banks. In winter the traffic often creeps at a snail's pace, as vacationers and retirees gawk at the views.

Deerfield Beach

⑲   *3½ mi north of Lighthouse Point.*

☾   The name **Quiet Waters Park** belies what's in store for kids here. Splash Adventure is a high-tech water-play system with swings, slides, and tunnels, among other activities. There's also cable waterskiing and boating on the park's lake. ⊠ *401 S. Powerline Rd.,* ☎ *954/360–1315.* ☜ *$1 weekends, free weekdays; Splash Adventure $2.* ☾ *Daily 8–6.*

Deerfield Island Park, an 8½-acre island that can only be reached by boat, is a paradise of coastal hammock, or tree islands. Officially designated an urban wilderness area along the Intracoastal Waterway, it contains mangrove swamp that provides critical habitat for gopher tortoises, gray foxes, raccoons, and armadillos. ⊠ *1 Deerfield Island; boat landing at Riverview Restaurant, Riverview Rd.,* ☎ *954/360–1320.* ☜ *Free.* ☾ *Boat shuttles run on the hr Wed. 10–noon and Sun. 10–3; call for special events and tours.*

Dining and Lodging

$$ ✕ **Brooks.** This is one of the city's better restaurants, thanks to a
★   French perfectionist, Bernard Perron. Meals are served in a series of rooms filled with replicas of old masters, cut glass, antiques, and tapestrylike floral wallpapers, though the shedlike dining room still feels very Florida. Fresh ingredients go into distinctly Floridian cuisine. Main courses include red snapper in papillote, broiled fillet of pompano with seasoned root vegetables, and a sweet lemongrass linguine with bok choy and julienned crisp vegetables. ⊠ *500 S. Federal Hwy.,* ☎ *954/427–9302. AE, D, MC, V.*

$ ✕ **Whale's Rib.** If you're looking for a casual, almost funky, nautical
★   setting near the beach, look no farther. For nearly 20 years the Williams family has been serving up excellent seafood and good cheer. Fish specials are offered daily, along with Whale Fries—thinly sliced potatoes that look like hot potato chips. Those with smaller appetites can choose from a good selection of salads and fish sandwiches. Other favorites are specials from the raw bar and a popular fish dip for starters. The place is crowded on weekends, and parking is limited. ⊠ *2031 N.E. 2nd St.,* ☎ *954/421–8880. AE, MC, V.*

$$–$$$$ ▣ **Ocean Terrace Suites.** This four-story motel is in one of the quieter sections of north Broward, just south of the Palm Beach county line, across the narrow shore road from the beach. Large units—efficiencies and one- and three-bedroom apartments—all have big balconies overlooking the sea. Colors vary from shore washed to bright; pink and green pastels tint the bedrooms. The furniture is rattan, and units are clean and neat. Art is throwaway, flowers are artificial, and materials are bargain quality. Still, for size, location, and price this is a good buy. An outdoor barbecue grill is available. ⊠ *2080 E. Hillsboro Blvd., 33441,* ☎ *954/427–8400,* ℻ *954/427–0555. 30 units. Pool. AE, D, DC, MC, V.*

$$–$$$ 🏨 **Royal Flamingo Villas.** This small community of houselike villas, built in the 1970s, reaches from the Intracoastal Waterway to the ocean. The roomy and comfortable one- and two-bedroom villas are all condominium owned, so they're fully furnished the way owners want them. All are so quiet that you hear only the soft click of ceiling fans and kitchen clocks. The development is wisely set back a bit from the beach, which is scheduled to be restored. If you don't need lavish public facilities, this is your upscale choice at a reasonable price. ⊠ *1225 Hillsboro Mile (Rte. A1A), Hillsboro Beach 33062,* ☎ *954/427–0669, 954/427–0660, or 800/241–2477,* ℻ *954/427–6110. 41 villas. Pool, putting green, shuffleboard, beach, dock, boating, coin laundry. D, MC, V.*

$–$$ 🏨 **Carriage House Resort Motel.** This clean and tidy motel sits one block from the ocean. Run by a French-German couple, the white, two-story Colonial-style motel with black shutters is actually two buildings connected by a second-story sundeck. Steady improvements have been made to the facility, including the addition of Bahama beds that feel and look like sofas. Kitchenettes are equipped with good-quality utensils. Rooms are self-contained and quiet and have walk-in closets and room safes. ⊠ *250 S. Ocean Blvd., 33441,* ☎ *954/427–7670,* ℻ *954/428–4790. 6 rooms, 14 efficiencies, 10 apartments. Pool, shuffleboard, coin laundry. AE, MC, V.*

Outdoor Activities and Sports

FISHING

The **Cove Marina** (⊠ Hillsboro Blvd. and the Intracoastal Waterway, ☎ 954/360–9343) is home to a deep-sea charter fleet. During the winter season there are excellent runs of sailfish, kingfish, dolphinfish, and tuna. A half-day charter costs about $325 for six people. Enter the marina through the Cove Shopping Center.

GOLF

Off Hillsboro Boulevard west of I–95, **Deer Creek Golf Club** (⊠ 2801 Country Club Blvd., ☎ 954/421–5550) has 18 holes.

SCUBA DIVING

One of the area's most popular dive boats, the 43-ft *Get Down* (⊠ Cove Marina, Hillsboro Blvd. and the Intracoastal Waterway, ☎ 954/421–2601) goes on morning and afternoon dives, plus evening dives on weekends. Divers can explore the marine life of nearby reefs and shipwrecks. The cost is $39 for a two-tank dive, and riders are welcome for $18.

SOUTH BROWARD

From Hollywood's Broadwalk, a 27-ft-wide thoroughfare paralleling 2 mi of palm-fringed beach, to the western reaches of Old West–flavored Davie, this region has a personality all its own. South Broward's roots are in early Florida settlements. Thus far it has avoided some of the glitz and glamour of its neighbors to the north and south, and folks here like it that way. Still, there's plenty to see and do—excellent restaurants in every price range, world-class pari-mutuels, and a new focus on the arts.

Hollywood

➍ *7 mi south of Fort Lauderdale.*

Hollywood is a city undergoing a revival. New shops, restaurants, and art galleries are opening at a rate that rivals that of Miami's South Beach. The city recently spiffed up its Broadwalk, a wide pedestrian walkway along the beach, where Rollerbladers are as common as visitors from the North. Trendy sidewalk cafés have opened, vying for space with mom-and-pop T-shirt shops. Downtown, along Harrison Street, jazz clubs and still more fashionable restaurants are drawing young professionals to the scene.

In 1921 Joseph W. Young, a California real estate developer, began developing the community of Hollywood from the woody flatlands. It quickly became a major tourist magnet, home to casino gambling and everything else that made Florida hot. Reminders of the glory days of the Young era remain in places like Young Circle (the junction of U.S. 1 and Hollywood Boulevard) and the stately old homes that line east Hollywood streets.

The **Art and Culture Center of Hollywood** is a visual and performing arts center with an art reference library, outdoor sculpture garden, arts school, and museum store. It's just east of Young Circle. ✉ *1650 Harrison St.,* ☎ *954/921–3274.* ✆ *Wed.–Sat. $3, Sun. $8 (including classical or jazz concert); donation welcome Tues.* ☉ *Tues.–Sat. 10–4, Sun. 1–4.*

With the Intracoastal Waterway to its west and the beach and ocean to the east, the 2.2-mi paved promenade known as the **Broadwalk** has been popular with pedestrians and cyclists since 1924. Expect to hear French spoken along this scenic stretch, especially during the winter; Hollywood Beach has been a favorite winter getaway for Québecois ever since Joseph Young hired French-Canadians to work here in the 1920s.

Hollywood North Beach Park is at the north end of the Broadwalk. No high-rises overpower the scene, nothing hip or chic, just a laid-back old-fashioned place for enjoying the sun, sand, and sea. ✉ *Rte. A1A and Sheridan St.,* ☎ *954/926–2444.* ✆ *Free; parking $4 until 2, $2 after.* ☉ *Daily 8–6.*

Comprising 1,500 acres at the Intracoastal Waterway, **West Lake Park** is one of Florida's largest urban nature facilities, providing a wide range of recreational activities. You can rent a canoe, kayak, or boat with an electric motor (no fossil fuels are allowed in the park) or take the 40-minute environmental boat tour. Extensive boardwalks traverse a mangrove community, where endangered and threatened species abound. A 65-ft observation tower allows views of the entire park. More than $1 million in exhibits are on display at the **Anne Kolb Nature Center,** named after the late county commissioner who was a leading environmental advocate. A great place to take youngsters, the center's exhibit hall features 27 interactive displays, an ecology room, and a trilevel aquarium. ✉ *1200 Sheridan St.,* ☎ *954/926–2410.* ✆ *Weekends $1, weekdays free; exhibit hall $3.* ☉ *Daily 8–6.*

At the edge of Hollywood lies **Seminole Native Village,** a reservation where you can pet a cougar, hold a baby alligator, and watch other wildlife demonstrations. The Seminole Indians also sell their arts and crafts. ✉ *3551 N. Rte. 7,* ☎ *954/961–4519.* ✆ *Self-guided tour $5, guided tour including alligator wrestling and snake demonstrations $10.* ☉ *Daily 9–5.*

Across the street from the Seminole Native Village, **Hollywood Seminole Gaming** features high-stakes bingo, low-stakes poker, and more than 500 gaming machines. ✉ *4150 N. Rte. 7,* ☎ *954/961–3220.* ✆ *Free.* ☉ *Daily 24 hrs.*

In addition to displaying a collection of artifacts from the Seminoles and other tribes, Joe Dan and Virginia Osceola sell contemporary Native American arts and crafts at the ☾ **Anhinga Indian Museum and Art Gallery.** It's also across the street from the Seminole Native Village, though that technically puts it over the Fort Lauderdale border. ⊠ *5791 S. Rte. 7, Fort Lauderdale,* ☎ *954/581–0416.* ☼ *Daily 9–5.*

Dining and Lodging

$$$ ✕ **Martha's.** Guests have two choices of dining location, both providing impressive views of the Intracoastal Waterway. Martha's Tropical Grille, on the upper deck, is more informal. Martha's Supper Club, on the lower level, is dressier—tables adorned with orchid buds, fanned napery, etched-glass dividers, brass, rosewood, and an outdoor patio surrounded by a floral mural. Piano music accompanies dinner downstairs, and later a band plays for dancing, setting a supper-club mood. Both floors offer similar menus, however—chiefly Florida seafood: flaky dolphinfish in a court bouillon; shrimp dipped in a piña colada batter, rolled in coconut, and panfried with orange mustard sauce; and snapper prepared 17 ways. For dessert try sorbet and vanilla and chocolate ice cream topped with meringue and hot fudge brandy sauce. Complimentary dock space is provided for those arriving by boat. ⊠ *6024 N. Ocean Dr.,* ☎ *954/923–5444. Reservations essential. AE, D, DC, MC, V.*

$$ ✕ **Las Brisas.** There's a wonderful bistro atmosphere at this small and cozy restaurant with Mexican tiles and blue-and-white-checked tablecloths beneath paddle fans. Right next to the beach, Las Brisas offers eating inside or out, and the food is Argentine with an Italian flair. Antipasto salads are prepared for two; the roasted vegetables are crunchy and flavorful. A small pot sits on each table filled with *chimichurri* (a paste made of oregano, parsley, olive oil, salt, garlic, and crushed pepper), for spreading on steaks. Grilled or deep-fried fish are favorites, as are pork chops, chicken, and pasta entrées. Desserts include a rum cake, a flan like *mamacita* used to make, and a *dulce con leche* (a sweet milk pudding). The wine list is predominantly Argentine. ⊠ *600 N. Surf Rd.,* ☎ *954/923–1500. AE, MC, V. Closed Mon. No lunch.*

$–$$ ✕ **Revolution 2029.** Chef David Sloane and partner William Kassner have created a restaurant that pleases both the eye and the palate. Revolution 2029 takes its name from a combination of the address and its role in revolutionizing (i.e., reviving) the area. The kitchen is topflight, the young staff experienced, and the atmosphere decidedly trendy. On offer is creative Pacific Rim cuisine, including such appetizers as saffron-herb-seared tuna and jumbo lump crab cake. Entrées feature ginger-plum-seared Atlantic salmon, pasta with mesquite chicken, and bourbon-glazed beef tenderloin. ⊠ *2029 Harrison St.,* ☎ *954/920–4748. AE, MC, V. Closed Mon. No lunch weekends.*

$–$$ ✕ **Sushi Blues Cafe.** First-class Japanese food is served up in a cubicle setting that's so jammed you wonder where this hip group goes by day. Japanese chefs prepare conventional and macrobiotic-influenced dishes that range from a variety of sushi and rolls (California, tuna, and the Yozo roll, with snapper, flying-fish eggs, asparagus, and Japanese mayonnaise) to steamed veggies with tofu and steamed snapper with miso sauce. Also available are a few wines by the glass or bottle, a selection of Japanese beers, and some very un-Japanese desserts—fried banana and Swiss chocolate mousse cake. The house band, the Sushi Blues Band, performs on Friday and Saturday; guest musicians often sit in. ⊠ *1836 S. Young Circle,* ☎ *954/929–9560. No credit cards. Closed Sun. No lunch.*

$ ✕ **Istanbul.** The owners of this Turkish delight take pride in preparing everything from scratch: hummus, tabbouleh, *adana* kebab (partially grilled, chopped lamb on skewers on a bed of yogurt-soaked pita squares, oven-finished with hot butter sauce), pizza, salads, soups, and phyllo-pie fingers filled with spinach, chicken, or meat. At lunch blue-suited attorney types dine alongside beachgoers. You should also consider getting takeout. After all, how often can you lounge on the beach with a reasonably priced Turkish picnic? ⊠ *707 N. Broadwalk,* ☎ *954/ 921–1263. No credit cards.*

$ ✕ **Le Tub.** Formerly a Sunoco gas station, this place is now a quirky waterside saloon with a seeming affection for claw-foot bathtubs. Hand-painted tubs are everywhere—under ficus, sea grape, and palm trees. The eatery is highly favored by locals for affordable food: mostly shrimp, burgers, and barbecue. ⊠ *1100 N. Ocean Dr.,* ☎ *954/921– 9425. No credit cards.*

$$–$$$ 🏨 **Greenbriar Beach Club.** In a neighborhood of Hollywood Beach known for its flowered streets, this oceanfront all-suites hotel retains its 1950s style outside, but inside the rooms have been upgraded and feature full kitchens. The staff is multilingual, and the TVs even feature four Spanish and two French channels. Fronting on a 200-ft stretch of beach, the hotel bills itself as "Florida's best-kept secret," and it just could be. ⊠ *1900 S. Surf Rd., 33019,* ☎ *954/922–2606,* ℻ *954/923–0897. 47 suites. Pool, volleyball, beach, coin laundry. AE, MC, V.*

$$ 🏨 **Manta Ray Inn.** Canadians Donna and Dwayne Boucher run this
★ exemplary two-story lodging on the beach and have kept the place immaculate and the rates affordable. Dating from the 1940s, the inn offers the casual, comfortable beachfront for which vacations in Hollywood are famous. Nothing's fussy—white spaces with burgundy trim and rattan furniture—and everything's included. Kitchens are equipped with pots, pans, and mini-appliances that make housekeeping convenient. All apartments have full closets, and all except for two-bedroom units with stalls have tub-showers. Grills are available. ⊠ *1715 S. Surf Rd., 33019,* ☎ *954/921–9666,* ℻ *954/929–8220. 12 units. Beach. No credit cards.*

$–$$ 🏨 **Sea Downs.** This three-story lodging directly on the Broadwalk is a good choice for efficiency or apartment living (one-bedroom apartments can be joined to make two-bedroom units). All but two units have ocean views, and all are comfortably done in chintz, but with blinds, not drapes. Kitchens are fully equipped, and most units have tub-showers and closets. Housekeeping is provided once a week. In between, guests receive fresh towels daily and sheets on request, but they make their own beds. Sea Downs's sister property, Bougainvillea, is a few paces off the beach, so rates are slightly lower. However, Bougainvillea's guests can use the Sea Downs pool, while those at Sea Downs can enjoy Bougainvillea's gardens. ⊠ *2900 N. Surf Rd., 33019-3704,* ☎ *954/923–4968,* ℻ *954/923–8747. 5 efficiencies, 8 1-bedroom apartments. Pool. No credit cards.*

$ 🏨 **Driftwood on the Ocean.** This attractive late-'50s-era resort motel faces the beach at the secluded south end of Surf Road. The setting is what draws guests, but attention to maintenance and frequent refurbishing are what make it a value. Accommodations range from a standard hotel room to a deluxe two-bedroom, two-bath suite. Most units have a kitchen, one-bedroom apartments have a daybed, and standard rooms have a queen-size Murphy bed. All have balconies. ⊠ *2101 S. Surf Rd., 33019,* ☎ *954/923–9528,* ℻ *954/922–1062. 6 rooms, 4 suites, 39 efficiencies. Pool, shuffleboard, beach, bicycles, coin laundry. AE, MC, V.*

Outdoor Activities and Sports

BIKING

The 2-mi **Broadwalk,** which has its own bike path, is popular with cyclists.

DOG RACING

Hollywood Greyhound Track has dog-racing action during its December–May season. There is a clubhouse dining room. ⌧ *831 N. Federal Hwy., Hallandale,* ☏ *954/454–9400.* ☜ *Grandstand $1, clubhouse $3; parking free.* ☉ *Racing Tues., Thurs., and Sat. 12:30 and 7:30; Sun.–Mon., Wed., and Fri. 7:30.*

FISHING

Sea Leg's III (⌧ 5400 N. Ocean Dr., ☏ 954/923–2109) runs drift-fishing trips from 8 to 12:30 and 1:30 to 6 and bottom-fishing trips from 7 PM to midnight. All trips cost $25 and include fishing gear.

GOLF

The **Diplomat Country Club** (⌧ 501 Diplomat Pkwy., Hallandale, ☏ 954/457–2000), with 18 holes, is south of town. The course at **Emerald Hills** (⌧ 4100 Hills Dr., ☏ 954/961–4000) has 18 holes.

HORSE RACING

Gulfstream Park Race Track is the winter home of some of the nation's top Thoroughbreds. The park greatly improved its facilities during the past few years: Admission costs have been lowered, time between races shortened, and the paddock ring elevated for better viewing by fans. The season is capped by the $500,000 Florida Derby, which always features Kentucky Derby hopefuls. Racing is held from January through mid-March. ⌧ *901 S. Federal Hwy., Hallandale,* ☏ *954/454–7000.* ☜ *$3, including parking and program; clubhouse $5 plus $2 for reserved seat or $1.75 for grandstand.* ☉ *Racing Wed.–Mon. 1.*

Dania

㉑ *3 mi north of Hollywood, 4 mi south of Fort Lauderdale.*

This town at the south edge of Fort Lauderdale is probably best known for its antiques dealers, but there are other attractions as well.

The **Graves Museum of Archaeology & Natural History,** a little-known treasure, has the goal of becoming the "Smithsonian of the South." Its wide-ranging collections feature everything from pre-Columbian art and Greco-Roman materials to underwater artifacts from the St. Thomas harbor and a 9,000-square-ft dinosaur hall. Also on display are a 3-ton quartz crystal and dioramas on Tequesta Indian life and jaguar habitat. Monthly lectures, conferences, field trips, and a summer archaeological camp are offered. The museum bookstore is one of the best in Florida. ⌧ *481 S. Federal Hwy.,* ☏ *954/925–7770.* ☜ *$6.* ☉ *Tues.–Sat. 10–6, Sun. 1–5.*

★ The **John U. Lloyd Beach State Recreation Area** is a pleasant plot of land with a pine-shaded beach, a jetty pier where you can fish, a marina, nature trails, and canoeing on Whiskey Creek. This is a great spot to watch cruise ships entering and departing Port Everglades, to the west across the waterway. ⌧ *6503 N. Ocean Dr.,* ☏ *954/923–2833.* ☜ *$4 per vehicle with up to 8 people.* ☉ *Daily 8–sunset.*

The new **World Fishing Center,** which opened in 1999, is a shrine to the sport of fishing. Near the Fort Lauderdale airport, the center is the creation of the International Game Fishing Association, which spent $32 million to develop the campus at 51-acre Sportsman's Park. In addition to checking out the World Fishing Hall of Fame, a marina, and an extensive museum and research library, you can visit seven galleries with virtual-reality fishing and other interactive displays. For example, in the Catch Gallery, you can cast off via virtual reality and try to reel in a marlin, sailfish, or bass. ⌧ *I–95 and Griffin Rd., Fort Lauderdale,* ☏ *954/924–4310.* ☜ *$9.* ☉ *Daily 10–5.*

Outdoor Activities and Sports

FISHING

The 920-ft **Dania Pier** (☎ 954/927–0640) is open around the clock. Fishing is $3 for adults (including parking), tackle rental is $6, bait is about $2, and spectators pay $1.

JAI ALAI

Dania Jai-Alai Palace has one of the fastest games on the planet, scheduled year-round. ⊠ *301 E. Dania Beach Blvd.,* ☎ *954/428–7766.* ☞ *$1.50; reserved seats $2–$7, including parking and program.* ☉ *Games Tues. and Sat. noon and 7:15, Wed.–Fri. 7:15, Sun. 1; closed Wed. in June.*

Shopping

More than 75 **antiques** dealers line Federal Highway (U.S. 1), ½ mi south of the Fort Lauderdale airport and ½ mi north of Hollywood. Take the Stirling Road or Griffin Road East exit off I–95.

Davie

22   *4 mi west of Dania.*

This town's horse farms and estates are the closest thing to the Old West in South Florida. Folks in western wear ride their fine horses through downtown and order up takeout at "ride-through" windows. A weekly rodeo is Davie's most famous activity.

Gators, crocodiles, river otters, and birds of prey can be seen at **Flamingo Gardens,** as can a 23,000-square-ft walk-through aviary, a plant house, and an Everglades museum in the pioneer Wray Home. A half-hour guided tram ride winds through a citrus grove and wetlands area. ⊠ *3750 Flamingo Rd.,* ☎ *954/473–2955.* ☞ *$10, tram ride $2.* ☉ *Daily 9:30–5:30.*

At the **Young at Art Children's Museum,** kids can work in paint, graphics, sculpture, and crafts according to themes that change three times a year. Then they take their masterpieces home with them. ⊠ *11584 Rte. 84, in the Plaza,* ☎ *954/424–0085.* ☞ *$4.* ☉ *Mon.–Sat. 10–5, Sun. noon–5.*

Dining

$$ ✕ **Armadillo Cafe.** Eve Montella and Kevin McCarthy have created a
★   restaurant whose southwestern theme, casual decor, and award-wining food make it worth the drive from anywhere in Broward County. It has been named to best-restaurant lists in local and national publications, and visitors from around the world have feasted on its southwestern-style South Florida seafood. In addition to fish dishes, other specialties include boneless duck and marinated leg of lamb. Though some exotic dishes are prepared, everything is served in a creative and fun atmosphere. ⊠ *4630 S.W. 6th Ave.,* ☎ *954/791–5104. AE, D, DC, MC, V.*

Nightlife and the Arts

THE ARTS

Bailey Concert Hall (⊠ Central Campus of Broward Community College, 3501 S.W. Davie Rd., ☎ 954/475–6884) is a popular place for classical music concerts, dance, drama, and other performing arts activities, especially October–April.

NIGHTLIFE

Uncle Funny's Comedy Club (⊠ 9160 Rte. 84, ☎ 954/474–5653) showcases national and local comics Wednesday–Sunday at 8:30 plus Friday and Saturday at 11.

Outdoor Activities and Sports

BIKING

Bicycle enthusiasts can ride at the **Brian Piccolo Park velodrome** (⊠ Sheridan St. and N.W. 101st Ave., Cooper City), south of Davie.

GOLF

Rolling Hills (⊠ 3501 Rolling Hills Circle, ☎ 954/475–3010) has 18 holes.

RODEO

The local **rodeo** (⊠ 6591 S.W. 45th St., ☎ 954/475–9787) is held every Wednesday night. Special national rodeos come to town some weekends.

FORT LAUDERDALE AND BROWARD COUNTY A TO Z

Arriving and Departing

By Bus

Greyhound Lines (☎ 800/231–2222) buses stop in Fort Lauderdale (⊠ 515 N.E. 3rd St., ☎ 954/764–6551).

By Car

Access to Broward County from north or south is via Florida's Turnpike, I–95, U.S. 1, or U.S. 441. I–75 (Alligator Alley) connects Broward with Florida's west coast and runs parallel to Route 84 within the county.

By Plane

Fort Lauderdale–Hollywood International Airport (☎ 954/359–6100), 4 mi south of downtown Fort Lauderdale and just off U.S. 1, is one of Florida's busiest, serving more than 12 million passengers a year. A major airport expansion added 5,000 parking spaces, and new access roads are due in 2000. Scheduled airlines include **Air Canada** (☎ 800/776–3000), **Air Jamaica** (☎ 800/523–5585), **AirTran** (☎ 800/825–8538), **American** (☎ 800/433–7300), **America West** (☎ 800/235–9282), **Comair** (☎ 800/354–9822), **Continental** (☎ 800/525–0280), **Delta** (☎ 800/221–1212), **Icelandair** (☎ 954/359–2735), **Island Express** (☎ 954/359–0380), **Laker** (☎ 888/525–3724), **Midway** (☎ 800/446–4392), **Northwest** (☎ 800/225–2525), **Southwest** (☎ 800/435–9792), **TWA** (☎ 800/221–2000), **United** (☎ 800/241–6522), and **US Airways** (☎ 800/428–4322).

BETWEEN THE AIRPORT AND CENTER CITY

Broward Transit (☎ 954/357–8400) operates bus route Number 1 between the airport and its main terminal at Broward Boulevard and Northwest 1st Avenue, in the center of Fort Lauderdale. Service from the airport begins daily at 5:30 AM; the last bus from the downtown terminal to the airport leaves at 9:50 PM. The fare is $1 (50¢ for senior citizens). **Airport Express** (☎ 954/561–8886) provides limousine service to all parts of Broward County. Fares to most Fort Lauderdale beach hotels are in the $8–$10 range.

By Train

Amtrak (☎ 800/872–7245) provides daily service to the Fort Lauderdale station (⊠ 200 S.W. 21st Terr., ☎ 954/463–8251) as well as other Broward County stops at Hollywood and Deerfield Beach.

Tri-Rail (☎ 954/728–8445) operates train service daily 5 AM–11 PM (more limited on weekends) through Broward, Miami-Dade, and Palm Beach counties. There are six Broward stations west of I–95: Hillsboro Boulevard in Deerfield Beach, Cypress Creek, Fort Lauderdale, Fort Lauderdale Airport, Sheridan Street in Hollywood, and Hollywood Boulevard.

Getting Around

By Boat

Water Taxi (☏ 954/467–6677) provides service along the Intracoastal Waterway in Fort Lauderdale between the 17th Street Causeway and Commercial Boulevard 10 AM–1 AM. Boats stop at more than 30 restaurants, hotels, shops, and nightclubs; the fare is $7 one-way, $13 round-trip, and $15 for an all-day pass. Children under 12 accompanied by an adult pay half fare.

By Bus

Broward County Mass Transit (☏ 954/357–8400) bus service covers the entire county. The fare is $1 plus 15¢ for a transfer. Service on all beach routes starts before 6 AM and continues past 10 PM except on Sunday. Call for route information. Special seven-day tourist passes, which cost $9, are good for unlimited use on all county buses. These are available at some hotels, at Broward County libraries, and at the main bus terminal (✉ Broward Blvd. at N.W. 1st Ave., Fort Lauderdale).

Fort Lauderdale has replaced its motorized trolley service with expanded, free **TMAX** (☏ 954/761–3543) bus service. Routes cover both the downtown loop and the beach area, with the Las Olas/Beach Line connecting major tourist sites in both places. Buses run every 30 minutes, weekdays 11:15–3:15 and Friday and Saturday nights 7–2.

By Car

Except during rush hour, Broward County is a fairly easy place in which to drive. East–west I–595 runs from westernmost Broward County and links I–75 with I–95 and U.S. 1, providing handy access to the airport. The scenic but slow Route A1A generally parallels the beach. Another road less traveled is the Sawgrass Expressway (Route 869), a toll road that's a handy link to Sawgrass Mills shopping and the new ice-hockey arena, both in Sunrise.

By Taxi

It's difficult to hail a cab on the street. Sometimes you can pick one up at a major hotel. Otherwise, phone ahead. Fares are not cheap; meters run at a rate of $2.45 for the first mile and $1.75 for each additional mile; waiting time is 25¢ per minute. The major company serving the area is **Yellow Cab** (☏ 954/565–5400).

Contacts and Resources

Car Rentals

Agencies in the airport include **Avis** (☏ 954/359–3255), **Budget** (☏ 954/359–4700), **Dollar** (☏ 954/359–7800), **Hertz** (☏ 954/359–5281), and **National** (☏ 954/359–8303). In addition, **Alamo** (☏ 954/525–4713) and **Enterprise** (☏ 954/760–9888) offer shuttle service to nearby rental centers.

Emergencies

Dial **911** for police or ambulance.

Florida Poison Information Center (☏ 800/282–3171).

HOSPITALS

The following hospitals have a 24-hour emergency room: **Broward General Medical Center** (✉ 1600 S. Andrews Ave., Fort Lauderdale, ☏ 954/ 355–4400; 954/355–4888 physician referral), **Columbia Plantation**

General Hospital (✉ 401 N.W. 42nd Ave., Plantation, ☎ 954/797–6470; 954/587–5010 physician referral), **Coral Springs Medical Center** (✉ 3999 Coral Hills Dr., Coral Springs, ☎ 954/344–3000; 954/355–4888 physician referral), **Florida Medical Center** (✉ 5000 W. Oakland Park Blvd., Fort Lauderdale, ☎ 954/735–6000; 954/730–2700 physician referral), **Hollywood Medical Center** (✉ 3600 Washington St., Hollywood, ☎ 954/966–4500; 800/237–8701 physician referral), **Holy Cross Hospital** (✉ 4725 N. Federal Hwy., Fort Lauderdale, ☎ 954/771–8000; 954/771–9082 physician referral), **Imperial Point Medical Center** (✉ 6401 N. Federal Hwy., Fort Lauderdale, ☎ 954/776–8500; 954/355–4888 physician referral), and **North Broward Medical Center** (✉ 201 E. Sample Rd., Pompano Beach, ☎ 954/786–6400; 954/355–4888 physician referral).

LATE-NIGHT PHARMACIES

The following are open 24 hours: **Eckerd Drug** (✉ 1385 S.E. 17th St., Fort Lauderdale, ☎ 954/525–8173; ✉ 1701 E. Commercial Blvd., Fort Lauderdale, ☎ 954/771–0660; ✉ 154 University Dr., Pembroke Pines, ☎ 954/432–5510) and **Walgreens** (✉ 2855 Stirling Rd., Fort Lauderdale, ☎ 954/981–1104; ✉ 5001 N. Dixie Hwy., Oakland Park, ☎ 954/772–4206; ✉ 289 S. Federal Hwy., Deerfield Beach, ☎ 954/481–2993).

Guided Tours

BOAT TOURS

Carrie B. (✉ Riverwalk at S.E. 5th Ave., Fort Lauderdale, ☎ 954/768–9920), a 300-passenger day cruiser, gives 90-minute tours up the New River and Intracoastal Waterway. Cruises depart at 11, 1, and 3 each day and cost $10.50.

Jungle Queen III and IV (✉ Radisson Bahia Mar Beach Resort, 801 Seabreeze Blvd., Fort Lauderdale, ☎ 954/462–5596) are 175-passenger and 527-passenger tour boats that take day and night cruises up the New River through the heart of Fort Lauderdale. The sightseeing cruises at 10 and 2 cost $11.50, while the evening dinner cruise costs $24.50. You can also take a daylong trip to Miami's Bayside Marketplace ($14.95), on Biscayne Bay, for shopping and sightseeing.

Patriot (✉ Cove Shopping Center, Hillsboro Blvd. at Intracoastal Waterway, Deerfield Beach, ☎ 954/428–4026) offers leisurely narrated tours along the Intracoastal Waterway. There are two options: cruise only ($9.50), which departs at 12:30, and a cruise/meal combination ($28.50), which leaves at 10 and features lunch at the dockside Charley's Crab restaurant.

Professional Diving Charters (✉ Radisson Bahia Mar Beach Resort, 801 Seabreeze Blvd., Fort Lauderdale, ☎ 954/761–3413) operates the 60-ft glass-bottom boat *Pro Diver II*. On Tuesday through Saturday mornings and Sunday afternoon, two-hour sightseeing trips take in offshore reefs, and snorkeling can be arranged.

ECOTOURS

National Audubon Society Education Dept. (✉ 444 Brickell Ave., Suite 850, Miami 33131, ☎ 305/371–6399 or 800/498–8129), a not-for-profit organization, conducts dry-land field trips throughout South Florida and one-day, overnight, and longer boat tours as part of its program. Call in advance for availability.

WALKING TOURS

Cosponsored by the Fort Lauderdale Historical Society, **Walking Tours** (✉ 219 S.W. 2nd Ave., Fort Lauderdale, ☎ 954/463–4431) traces the New River by foot during the winter and spring.

Visitor Information

Chamber of Commerce of Greater Fort Lauderdale (⊠ 512 N.E. 3rd Ave., Fort Lauderdale 33301, ☎ 954/462–6000). **Davie/Cooper City Chamber of Commerce** (⊠ 4185 S.W. 64th Ave., Davie 33314, ☎ 954/581–0790). **Greater Deerfield Beach Chamber of Commerce** (⊠ 1601 E. Hillsboro Blvd., Deerfield Beach 33441, ☎ 954/427–1050). **Greater Fort Lauderdale Convention & Visitors Bureau** (⊠ 1850 Eller Dr., Suite 303, Fort Lauderdale 33301, ☎ 954/765–4466). **Hollywood Chamber of Commerce** (⊠ 330 N. Federal Hwy., Hollywood 33019, ☎ 954/923–4000). **Lauderdale-by-the-Sea Chamber of Commerce** (⊠ 4201 N. Ocean Dr., Lauderdale-by-the-Sea 33308, ☎ 954/776–1000). **Pompano Beach Chamber of Commerce** (⊠ 2200 E. Atlantic Blvd., Pompano Beach 33062, ☎ 954/941–2940).

4 PALM BEACH AND THE TREASURE COAST

Long stretches of golden beaches are the unifying theme along this part of the Florida coast. The southern end is anchored by the sophisticated beach towns of Boca Raton and Delray Beach. Just north is wealthy and glitzy Palm Beach, internationally known for power shopping and pricey dining. Then comes the Treasure Coast, a collection of quaint, rustic, and uncrowded beach towns and peaceful nature preserves.

Updated by
Pamela
Acheson

THIS SECTION OF ATLANTIC COAST defies categoriza-
tion. Though it's easy to affix labels—the stretch
from Palm Beach to Boca Raton is considered the
northern reaches of the Gold Coast (which in its entirety extends all
the way to Miami), while north of Palm Beach is called the Treasure
Coast—the individual communities along this section of the Florida
coastline all have their own personalities. Here you'll find the center-
stage glitziness of Palm Beach and the low-key quiet of Hutchinson Island. The unifying attraction is compelling—golden beaches bordered
by luxuriant palms. The arts also flourish here. In town after town you
will find a profusion of museums, galleries, theaters, and groups com-
mitted to historic preservation.

The focus of the region is indisputably Palm Beach. Although tourists
may go to Delray Beach or Jupiter Island or scores of other towns to
catch some rays and feel sand between their toes, most stop in Palm
Beach for a completely different pastime: gawking. The gold on this
stretch of coast is the kind you put in a vault, and for a century now
the island town has been a hotbed of conspicuous consumption. Palm
Beach is the richest city in Florida and would easily compete for honors with places like Monaco and Malibu as the most affluent community
in the world. It has long been the winter address for families with names
such as Rockefeller, Vanderbilt, Kennedy, and Trump.

It all started with Henry Morrison Flagler, cofounder of Standard Oil,
who, in addition to bringing the railroad to Florida in the 1890s,
brought his own view of civilization. The poor and middle-class fishermen and laborers who inhabited the place in the pre-Flagler era
were moved a mile west or so to West Palm Beach. Still a proletarian
cousin, West Palm is home to those who serve Flagler's successors on
the island.

The town of Palm Beach represents only 1% of the land area in Palm
Beach County, however. The rest is given over to sprawling West Palm
Beach, classic Florida beach towns, malls, and to the west, citrus farms,
the Arthur R. Marshall–Loxahatchee National Wildlife Refuge, and
Lake Okeechobee, the largest lake in Florida and one of the country's
hot spots for bass-fishing devotees.

Also worth exploring is the Treasure Coast, which encompasses the
northernmost part of Palm Beach County plus Martin, St. Lucie, and
Indian River counties. Although late to develop, the Treasure Coast
now has its share of malls and beachfront condominiums, and yet much
of its shoreline is laid-back and peaceful. Inland is largely devoted to
citrus and sugar production and cattle ranching in rangelands of pine
and palmetto scrub.

Along the coast the broad tidal lagoon called the Indian River separates the barrier islands from the mainland. In addition to sheltering
boaters on the Intracoastal Waterway and playing nursery for many
saltwater game fish, it's a natural radiator, keeping frost away from
the tender orange and grapefruit trees that grow near its banks. Sea
turtles come ashore at night from late April to September to lay their
eggs on the beaches.

Pleasures and Pastimes

Beaches

Half the towns in the area include the word *beach* in their name, and
for good reason. Here are miles of golden strands—some relatively re-

mote and uncrowded, some buzzing with activity, and all blessed with the kind of blue-green waters you just won't find farther north. Among the least crowded are those at Hobe Sound National Wildlife Refuge and Fort Pierce Inlet State Recreation Area. Boca Raton's three beaches and Delray Beach's broad stretch of sand are among the most popular.

Dining

Not surprisingly, numerous elegant establishments offer Continental and contemporary cuisine that stacks up well among foodies, but the area also has many good, casual waterfront watering holes that serve up a mean fried or blackened grouper. Just an hour west, on Lake Okeechobee, you can dine on panfried catfish a few hundred yards from where it was caught. Most restaurants have early bird menus, a Florida hallmark, which usually offer most or all dinner entrées at a reduced price if ordered during certain hours.

Fishing

Within a 50-mi radius of Palm Beach, you'll find virtually every form of fishing except, of course, ice fishing. If it involves a hook and a line, you can do it here—year-round. Charter a boat for deep-sea fishing out of towns from Boca Raton to Sebastian Inlet. West of Vero Beach, there's tremendous marsh fishing for catfish, bass, and perch. Lake Okeechobee is one of the world's bass-fishing capitals.

Golf

Palm Beach County is to golf what Saudi Arabia is to oil. For openers, there's the Professional Golfing Association (PGA) headquarters at the PGA National Resort & Spa in Palm Beach Gardens (a mere five golf courses). In all, there are approximately 150 public, private, and semiprivate golf courses in Palm Beach County. A Golf-A-Round program, in which more than 100 hotels participate, lets you play at one of 10 courses each day, with no greens fees.

Shopping

Some of the most expensive stores in the United States cluster on Worth Avenue, which is comparable to Rodeo Drive in Beverly Hills as an upscale shopper's nirvana. But there's also plenty of middle-American shopping nearby, including the likes of the Palm Beach Mall and the Manufacturers Outlet Center. You can browse in art galleries and antiques shops in Vero Beach, Delray Beach, and Boca Raton's Mizner Park.

Exploring Palm Beach and the Treasure Coast

The center of most any visit to the area is Palm Beach proper (and it certainly is!). Not only is it within an hour's drive of most of the region, but its Gatsby-era architecture, stunning mansions, and highbrow shopping make it unlike any other place in Florida. From there you can head in any of three directions: south along the Gold Coast toward Boca Raton, back to the mainland and north to the barrier-island treasures of the Treasure Coast, or west for some inland delights.

Great Itineraries

Tucked into an island 12 mi long and about ¼ mi wide, Palm Beach is easy to cover thoroughly in just a day or two. If you have several days, you can take in a lot of varied sights, exploring everything from galleries to subtropical wildlife preserves, and with a week you'll easily be able to see the whole area. Of course you could just do what a lot of visitors prefer—laze around soaking up the rays and the atmosphere.

Numbers in the text correspond to numbers in the margin and on the Gold Coast and Treasure Coast and the Palm Beach and West Palm Beach maps.

IF YOU HAVE 3 DAYS

With a short amount of time, make ☷ **Palm Beach** ①–⑪ your base. On the first day start in the middle of downtown, **Worth Avenue** ⑦, to do some window-shopping and gallery browsing. After you've refreshed yourself with a *très* chic bistro lunch, head for that other must-see on even the shortest itinerary: the **Henry Morrison Flagler Museum** ②. Your second day is for the beach; two good options are Lantana Public Beach, which has great food concessions, and Oceanfront Park, in **Boynton Beach** ㉔. Spend the better part of your last day exploring attractions you wouldn't expect to find in South Florida, such as the Morikami Museum and Japanese Gardens in nearby **Delray Beach** ㉖. Trite as it may sound, it's like a one-day visit to Japan.

IF YOU HAVE 5 DAYS

With five days you can be more contemplative at the galleries and museums, more leisurely at the beaches, and have time for more serendipitous exploring. Stay in ☷ **Palm Beach** ①–⑪ for two nights. The first day visit the **Henry Morrison Flagler Museum** ② and the luxury hotel known as **The Breakers** ④, another Flagler legacy. Then head to **Worth Avenue** ⑦ for a leisurely lunch and an afternoon of window-shopping. On the second day drive over to **West Palm Beach** ⑫–㉑ and the **Norton Museum of Art** ⑬, which has an extensive collection of 19th-century French Impressionists. On day three, choose between making an overnight visit to ☷ **Lake Okeechobee**, the bass-fishing capital of the world, and staying in Palm Beach another night and driving a half hour to explore the Arthur R. Marshall–Loxahatchee National Wildlife Refuge. Head south to ☷ **Boca Raton** ㉗ on the fourth day, and check into a beachfront hotel before spending the rest of the afternoon wandering through Mizner Park's shops. On your fifth day meander through the Boca Raton Museum of Art in the morning and get some sun at South Beach Park after lunch.

IF YOU HAVE 7 DAYS

With an entire week you can see the Gold and Treasure coasts thoroughly, with time left to fit in such recreational pursuits as taking sailboard or croquet lessons, catching a polo match, or going deep-sea fishing or jet skiing. Stay two nights in ☷ **Palm Beach** ①–⑪, spending your first day taking in its best sights, mentioned above. On day two, rent a bicycle and follow the 10-mi path along Lake Worth, providing a great look at the backyards of many of Palm Beach's big mansions. Drive north on day three, going first to the mainland and then across Jerry Thomas Bridge to Singer Island and John D. MacArthur Beach State Park. Spend the third night farther north, on ☷ **Hutchinson Island** ㉝, and relax the next morning on the beach in front of your hotel. On your way back south, explore **Stuart** ㉜ and its tiny but interesting historic downtown area, and pause at the Arthur R. Marshall–Loxahatchee National Wildlife Refuge before ending up in ☷ **Boca Raton** ㉗, for three nights at a beachfront hotel. Split day five between shopping at Mizner Park and beaching it at South Beach Park. Day six is for cultural attractions: the Boca Raton Museum of Art followed by the galleries and interesting Japanese museum in **Delray Beach** ㉖. If you have time on your last day, take in one of Boca Raton's other two beaches, Spanish River and Red Reef parks.

When to Tour Palm Beach and the Treasure Coast

The weather is optimum November–May, but the trade-off is that facilities are more crowded and prices somewhat higher. In summer you'll need a tolerance for heat and humidity if you want to spend time outside; also watch for frequent afternoon downpours. If you're set on watching the sea turtles come ashore to nest, make sure to visit between mid-May and early August, which is when most of the turtles lay their eggs, and remember that nesting occurs at night. No matter when you visit, bring insect repellent if you plan outdoor outings.

PALM BEACH

78 mi north of Miami.

Setting the tone in this incredibly wealthy town is the ornate architecture of developer Addison Mizner, who began building homes, stores, and public buildings here in the 1920s and whose Moorish-Gothic style has influenced virtually all the landmarks of the community. Thanks to Mizner and those influenced by him, Palm Beach looks like a kind of neo-Camelot, the perfect backdrop for a playground of the rich and famous.

Exploring Palm Beach

You can get a taste of what this town is all about when you squeeze into a parking place on Worth Avenue, among the Mercedes and Bentleys, and head to its boutiques to rub Versace-covered shoulders with shoppers whose credit card limits likely exceed the gross national product of Liechtenstein. Away from downtown, along County Road and Ocean Boulevard (the shore road, also designated as Route A1A), are Palm Beach's other defining landmarks: mansions. In some parts they're fronted by thick 20-ft hedgerows and topped by the seemingly de rigueur barrel-tile roofs. The low wall that separates the dune-top shore road from the sea hides a badly eroded beach in many places. Here and there, where the strand deepens a bit, homes are built directly on the beach.

A Good Tour

Start on the north end of the island with a quick look at the sandstone and limestone minicanyon that is the **Canyon of Palm Beach** ①, on Lake Way Road. Drive south, across Royal Poinciana Way, to the **Henry Morrison Flagler Museum** ②, in a 73-room palace that was once Flagler's home. From here backtrack to Royal Poinciana Way, turn right, and follow the road until it ends at North County Road and the Spanish-style **Palm Beach Post Office** ③. Here County Road changes from north to south designations. Take it southbound and look for the long, stately driveway on the left that leads to **The Breakers** ④, a famous hotel built in the style of an Italian Renaissance palace. Continue south on South County Road about ¼ mi farther to **Bethesda-by-the-Sea** ⑤, a Spanish Gothic Episcopal church. Keep driving south on South County Road until you reach Royal Palm Way; turn right, then right again on Cocoanut Row. In just a few blocks you'll see the gardens of the **Society of the Four Arts** ⑥.

Head south on Cocoanut Row until you reach famed **Worth Avenue** ⑦, where you can park and walk around—that is, if the prices in the art galleries and designer shops haven't knocked your socks off. After taking in the sights, drive south on South County Road for a peek at some magnificent estates, including **El Solano** ⑧, built by Addison Mizner, and **Mar-A-Lago** ⑨, now owned by Donald Trump. At this point you might want to get out of the car for some sun and fresh air, so continue south on South County Road until you reach **Phipps Ocean**

Park ⑩ and its stretch of sandy beach, or head back toward town along South Ocean Boulevard to the popular **Mid-Town Beach** ⑪.

TIMING

You'll need half a day minimum to see these sights. A few of the destinations are closed Sunday or Monday, so be sure to do your sightseeing during daytime business hours. In the winter, traffic can be very heavy and usually gets worse as the day wears on. Consider doing your exploring in the morning, when sights are less crowded and roads are less congested.

Sights to See

❺ **Bethesda-by-the-Sea.** This Spanish Gothic Episcopal church was built in 1927 by the first Protestant congregation in southeast Florida. Next to it are the formal, ornamental **Cluett Memorial Gardens.** ⊠ *141 S. County Rd.,* ☎ *561/655–4554.* ☉ *Church and gardens daily 8–5; services Sept.–May, Sun. 8, 9, and 11; June–Aug., Sun. 8 and 10; call for weekday schedule.*

★ ❹ **The Breakers.** Originally built by Henry Flagler in 1895 and rebuilt by his descendants after a fire in 1925, this luxury hotel was one of the starting points of Florida tourism. It resembles an ornate Italian Renaissance palace and was renovated to the tune of $150 million not long ago. Walk into the lobby and take a look at the painted arched ceilings hung with crystal chandeliers, and peek into the ornate Florentine Dining Room with its 15th-century Flemish tapestries. ⊠ *1 S. County Rd.,* ☎ *561/655–6611.*

❶ **Canyon of Palm Beach.** A road cut about 25 ft deep through a ridge of reddish-brown sandstone and oolite limestone gives you a brief feeling of being in the desert Southwest. ⊠ *Lake Way Rd.*

❽ **El Solano.** Perhaps no Palm Beach mansion represents the town's ongoing generations of flashbulb fame better than this one. The Spanish-style home was built by Addison Mizner as his personal residence in 1925. Mizner then sold it to Harold Vanderbilt, and the property made the rounds of socialites, photo shoots, and expansions until it was bought by John Lennon and Yoko Ono 10 months before Lennon's death. Now owned by a banking executive, El Solano is not open to the public. ⊠ *721 S. County Rd.*

★ ❷ **Henry Morrison Flagler Museum.** The opulence of Florida's Gilded Age is still apparent at Whitehall, the palatial 73-room mansion Henry Flagler had built in 1901 for his third wife, Mary Lily Kenan, and that is now home to a museum. Then-famous architects John Carrère and Thomas Hastings were instructed to spare no expense in creating the finest home they could imagine. They did as they were told, and Whitehall rivals some of the fine palaces of Europe. In 1960 Flagler's granddaughter, Jean Flagler Matthews, bought the building and made it a museum. On display are many of the original furnishings, an art collection, a 1,200-pipe organ, and exhibits on the history of the Florida East Coast Railway. Flagler's personal railroad car, the *Rambler,* is parked behind the building. A tour by well-informed guides takes about an hour. ⊠ *1 Whitehall Way,* ☎ *561/655–2833.* ☎ *$7.* ☉ *Tues.–Sat. 10–5, Sun. noon–5.*

❾ **Mar-A-Lago.** Still one of the grandest of homes along Ocean Boulevard, the former estate of breakfast-food heiress Marjorie Meriweather Post has Italianate towers silhouetted against the sky. It's currently owned by real estate magnate Donald Trump, who first turned it into a membership club and is continuing with plans (despite local opposition) to

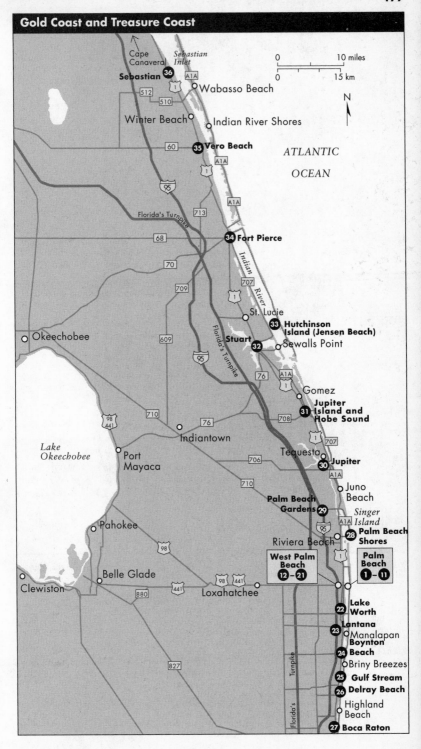

Gold Coast and Treasure Coast

Palm Beach and West Palm Beach

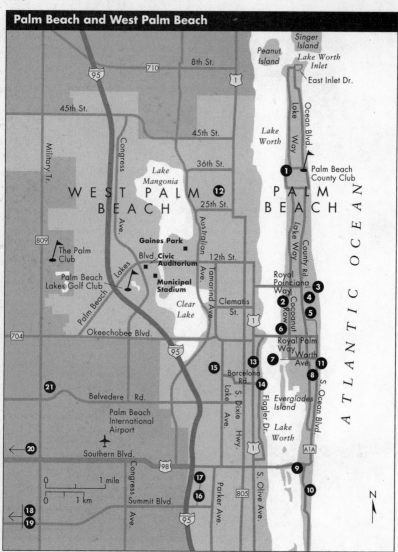

subdivide the property, which curves for ⅓ mi along the road. ⊠ *1100 S. Ocean Blvd.*

⑪ Mid-Town Beach. This small beach directly east of Worth Avenue is especially popular because it's so close to town. But be warned: The only parking meters along Ocean Boulevard—ergo, the only convenient public beach access—are found between Worth Avenue and Royal Palm Way. ⊠ *400 S. Ocean Blvd.,* ☎ *no phone.* ⌐ *Parking 25¢ for 15 mins.* ☉ *Daily 8–8.*

❸ Palm Beach Post Office. Spanish-style architecture defines the exterior, while inside murals depict Seminole Indians in the Everglades and stately royal and coconut palms. ⊠ *95 N. County Rd.,* ☎ *561/832–1867.*

⑩ Phipps Ocean Park. Besides the ubiquitous beautiful beach, some picnic tables, and grills, this park contains a Palm Beach County landmark in the **Little Red Schoolhouse.** Dating from 1886, it was the first schoolhouse in what was then Dade County and is open Monday–Saturday 8–8. ⊠ *2145 S. Ocean Blvd.,* ☎ *no phone.* ⌐ *Parking 25¢ for 20 mins.*

❻ Society of the Four Arts. In addition to presenting cultural events, this privately endowed arts and educational institution incorporates an exhibition hall, library, 13 distinct gardens, and the Philip Hulitar Sculpture Garden. ⊠ *Four Arts Plaza,* ☎ *561/655–7226.* ⌐ *$3.* ☉ *Galleries Dec.–mid-Apr., Mon.–Sat. 10–5, Sun. 2–5; library, children's library, and gardens Nov.–May, weekdays 10–5, Sat. 9–1.*

★ **❼ Worth Avenue.** This ¼-mi-long street is synonymous with posh, pricey shopping. A stroll amid the Moorish architecture of its scores of top-drawer shops—Cartier, Charles Jourdan, and Giorgio Armani, to name a few—gives you a taste of what the good life must be like. ⊠ *Between Cocoanut Row and S. Ocean Blvd.*

Dining and Lodging

$$$–$$$$ ✕ **Café L'Europe.** This is one of the most popular and elegant restau-
★ rants in Palm Beach. Sumptuous oak paneling, dim lighting, and elaborate flower bouquets set the mood. Ladies-who-lunch can enjoy spa cuisine, whereas evening guests dine expensively on specialty pastas such as *orecchiette* with broccoli rapini, Italian sausage, tomato, and ricotta; seafood dishes like sautéed pompano with herbal mustard crust; or a traditional Wiener schnitzel with spinach spaetzle and red cabbage. Veal chops and steaks are on the menu, too. Apple pancake with lingonberries is the signature dessert, and a caviar bar has a wide assortment of the delicacy, with prices to match. ⊠ *331 S. County Rd.,* ☎ *561/655–4020. Reservations essential. Jacket required. AE, DC, MC, V. No lunch Sun.–Mon.*

$$$–$$$$ ✕ **Janeiro.** Versace-designed Rosenthal china and Riedel crystal on black-
★ on-black tablecloths provide the setting for a spectacularly elegant contemporary French dining experience. Wild mushrooms sautéed with garlic, scallopini of goose liver with shredded turnips and port wine, and baked goat cheese with tomatoes in a pastry shell are some of the appetizers. Entrées, brought to the table under silver domes, include Mediterranean bouillabaisse, lemon sole fillets with tomato and black squid and spinach lasagna, boneless rack of lamb stuffed with spinach and wild mushrooms wrapped in puff pastry, and a beef fillet with green peppercorn sauce. Save room for the chocolate soufflé dessert. It's topped with edible 24-carat gold leaf! ⊠ *191 Bradley Pl.,* ☎ *561/659–5223. Reservations essential. Jacket required. AE, DC, MC, V. No lunch.*

$$$ ✕ **Bice Ristorante.** This dining establishment is so thoroughly Italian that it's easy to be disappointed when the parking attendant speaks to you in English. Brilliant flower arrangements and lots of brass accent a dark beige-and-yellow color scheme. Aromas of basil, chives, and oregano fill the air as waiters bring out the divine home-baked focaccia accompanying such house favorites as *Robespierre alla moda della Bice* (sliced steak topped with arugula salad) and *costoletta di vitello impanata alla milanese* (breaded veal cutlet with a tomato salad). The name is short for Beatrice, mother of Roberto Ruggeri, who founded the original in Milan in 1926 and has opened branches here and in other smart places since then. ✉ *313¼ Worth Ave.,* ☎ *561/835–1600. Jacket required. AE, DC, MC, V.*

$$–$$$$ ✕ **Amici.** Night after night a steady stream of six-figure automobiles
★ pulls into the valet parking spot of this trendy eatery. Inside, the lighting is dim, and tables are close together but never empty. The northern Italian menu features such house specialties as antipasti of cold marinated and grilled vegetables, rigatoni with spicy tomato sauce and roasted eggplant, potato gnocchi with grilled chicken and roasted peppers, grilled veal chops, risottos, and a long list of pizzas cooked in the wood-burning oven. There are nightly pasta and fresh-fish specials as well. If you want to avoid the crowds, stop by for a late lunch. ✉ *228 S. County Rd.,* ☎ *561/832–0201. Reservations essential. AE, D, DC, MC, V. No lunch Sun.*

$$–$$$$ ✕ **Chuck & Harold's.** Ivana Trump, Larry Holmes, Brooke Shields, and Michael Bolton are among the celebrities who have eaten at this combination power-lunch bar, sidewalk café, and jazz–big band garden, which is popular day and night, as well as for breakfast. Locals who want to be part of the scenery and tourists hot to people-watch catch a seat and linger in the outdoor café, next to pots of red and white begonias mounted on the sidewalk rail. Specialties include conch chowder, terrific hamburgers, an onion-crunchy gazpacho, grilled steaks, and tangy key lime pie. A big blackboard lists daily specials and celebrity birthdays. ✉ *207 Royal Poinciana Way,* ☎ *561/659–1440. AE, DC, MC, V.*

$$–$$$ ✕ **Ta-boó.** Dressed in gorgeous pinks, greens, and florals, the spaces
★ of this Worth Avenue landmark are divided into discreet salons: One resembles a courtyard, another an elegant living room with a fireplace, and a third a skylighted gazebo. The Tiki Tiki bar makes an elegant salon for the neighborhood crowd. Appetizers range from a very proletarian nachos grande with chili to Beluga caviar; dinners include chicken and arugula from the grill, prime rib, steaks, frogs' legs, and main course salads. White pizza with goat and mozzarella cheeses, pesto, and sweet roasted red peppers is a favorite. Drop in late at night during the season, and you're bound to spot a famous face or two. ✉ *221 Worth Ave.,* ☎ *561/835–3500. AE, MC, V.*

$$ ✕ **Aquaterra.** Chef Charlie Palmer, of New York City's famed Aureole, brings his culinary talents south to this popular 150-seat eatery. Decor is artistic but spare and the atmosphere more electric than romantic, but the cuisine, billed as progressive American, is definitely star quality. Choices abound. There's a long list of hors d'oeuvres, almost as many side dishes, and a dozen entrées from land and sea (Aquaterra—get it?), such as fresh Florida grouper, large gulf shrimp, or filet mignon roasted, grilled, or sautéed. ✉ *230 Sunrise Ave.,* ☎ *561/366–9693. AE, MC, V. Closed Mon. No lunch.*

$ ✕ **TooJay's.** New York deli food served in a bright California-style setting—what could be more Florida? The menu at this spot, one of nine TooJay's in the Sunshine State, includes matzo ball soup, corned beef on rye, and a killer cake made with five kinds of chocolate and topped with whipped cream. A salami-on-rye sandwich layered with onions,

Muenster cheese, coleslaw, and Russian dressing is a house favorite. On the High Holidays look for carrot tzimmes (a sweet vegetable compote), brisket, and roast chicken. Wisecracking waitresses keep the pace fast. ✉ *313 Royal Poinciana Plaza,* ☎ *561/659–7232. AE, DC, MC, V. Beer and wine only.*

$$$$ 🏨 **Brazilian Court.** Spread out over half a block, the yellow-stucco Span-
★ ish-style facade with a red-tile roof reminds you of this hotel's Roaring '20s origins. Rooms and spacious suites are decorated in soft, muted tones, and original art hangs on the walls. Remodeled bathrooms are marble and completely modernized. The closets, however, are still big enough for people who once brought trunks for the entire season (some still do). Outside, stone fountains and private courtyards (one with a wishing well) offer peaceful oases. Not only are pets welcome, there's a pet room-service menu, with items like Chancellor Chow and Chicken Meow Mein. ✉ *301 Australian Ave., 33480,* ☎ *561/655–7740; 800/552–0335; 800/228–6852 in Canada;* FAX *561/655–0801. 63 rooms, 40 suites. Restaurant, bar, pool, beauty salon, exercise room, library. AE, D, DC, MC, V.*

$$$$ 🏨 **The Breakers.** Dating from 1926 and enlarged in 1969, this opu-
★ lent seven-story Italian Renaissance–style resort sprawls over 140 splendidly manicured acres. Cupids frolic in the Florentine fountain at the main entrance, while majestic ceiling vaults and frescoes grace the lobby and the long hallways that lead to restaurants and ballrooms. A recent $100 million renovation included the construction of a fabulous spa and beach club plus a complete modernization of the rooms and bathrooms. Though the resort's elegance has been enhanced, a new relaxed atmosphere has replaced the old-world formality that prevailed for three-quarters of a century. For example, men are no longer *required* to wear jackets and ties everywhere after 7 PM. ✉ *1 S. County Rd., 33480,* ☎ *561/655–6611 or 800/833–3141,* FAX *561/659–8403. 572 rooms, 48 suites. 5 restaurants, 2 bars, 5 pools, saunas, spa, 2 18-hole golf courses, putting green, 14 tennis courts, croquet, health club, jogging, shuffleboard, beach, boating, children's programs. AE, D, DC, MC, V.*

$$$$ 🏨 **The Chesterfield.** Just two blocks north of famous Worth Avenue,
★ you'll find this four-story, white stucco, European-style hotel. Inviting rooms are on the small side but are individually and richly decorated with print bedspreads and draperies, plush upholstered chairs, antique desks, paintings, and marble bathrooms. Service is exceptional. Settle into a leather couch in front of the cozy library's fireplace with the latest newspapers from around the world or with a book selected from the floor-to-ceiling shelves. A quiet courtyard surrounds a large pool. ✉ *363 Cocoanut Row, 33480,* ☎ *561/659–5800 or 800/243–7871,* FAX *561/659–6707. 44 rooms, 11 suites. Restaurant, bar, pool, library. AE, D, DC, MC, V.*

$$$$ 🏨 **The Colony.** What distinguishes this legendary pale, pale yellow Georgian-style hotel only steps from Worth Avenue is its attentive staff; youthful yet experienced, they demonstrate a buzz of competence and a true desire to please. Cool and classical guest rooms have fluted blond cabinetry and matching draperies and bedcovers in deep floral prints. As in many older hotels, bathrooms are small. The "scene" for glitterati after charity balls at the Breakers, this is where Roxanne Pulitzer retreated after her infamous seven-week marriage in 1992. ✉ *155 Hammon Ave., 33480,* ☎ *561/655–5430 or 800/521–5525,* FAX *561/832–7318. 63 rooms, 39 suites and apartments, 7 villas. Restaurant, bar, pool, spa. AE, D, DC, MC, V.*

$$$$ 🏨 **Four Seasons Ocean Grand.** This 6-acre property at the south end
★ of town is coolly elegant but warm in detail. Marble, art, fanlight windows, swagged drapes, chintz, and palms create a serene atmosphere.

Rooms are spacious, with a separate seating area and private balcony, and many have gorgeous ocean views. On weekend evenings year-round, piano music accompanies cocktails in the Living Room lounge. On some weekend nights in season, jazz groups perform, and there are classical recitals on Sunday afternoon. Although its name suggests grandeur, this four-story hotel with a long beach is more like a small jewel. ⊠ *2800 S. Ocean Blvd., 33480, ☎ 561/582–2800 or 800/432–2335, FAX 561/547–1557. 203 rooms, 7 suites. 2 restaurants, bar, pool, saunas, 3 tennis courts, health club, beach. AE, D, DC, MC, V.*

$$$ 🏨 **Plaza Inn.** This three-story hotel, Deco-designed from the 1930s,
★   operates B&B style; a full breakfast is included. The pool, gardens, and piano bar have the intimate charm of a trysting place for the likes of Cary Grant and Katharine Hepburn. Inn owner Ajit Asrani is a retired Indian army officer who raises show horses and polo ponies. The courteous staff and location in the heart of Palm Beach are pluses, and the uncluttered, individually decorated rooms with phone and refrigerator provide a welcome change from other B&Bs. So, too, does the appealing courtyard with waterfalls and a pool. ⊠ *215 Brazilian Ave., 33480, ☎ 561/832–8666 or 800/233–2632, FAX 561/835–8776. 50 rooms and suites. Bar, pool, hot tub. AE, MC, V.*

$$–$$$$ 🏨 **Palm Beach Historic Inn.** Longtime hoteliers Harry and Barbara Kehr manage this delightfully unexpected inn in the heart of downtown. The setting, tucked between Town Hall and a seaside residential block, combines town and vacationland. B&B touches include flowers, wine and fruit, snacks, seasonal turndown, tea and cookies in rooms, and a generous Continental breakfast. Guest rooms tend to the frilly with lots of lace, ribbons, and scalloped edges. Most are furnished with Victorian antiques and reproductions (some out of old mansions, others more secondhand than authentic) and chiffon wall drapings above the bed. A 1944 Coke machine still supplies an 8-ounce bottle for a dime. Bath towels are as thick as parkas. ⊠ *365 S. County Rd., 33480, ☎ 561/832–4009, FAX 561/832–6255. 9 rooms, 4 suites. Library. AE, D, DC, MC, V.*

$$–$$$ 🏨 **Palm Beach Sea Lord Hotel.** If you don't need glamour or brand names, and you're not the B&B type, this garden-style hideaway is for you. Choose from accommodations that overlook Lake Worth, the pool, or the ocean; the reasonably priced café adds to the at-home, comfy feeling and attracts repeat customers. Units are plain but not cheap in season and come with carpet, at least one comfortable chair, small or large refrigerator, and tropical print fabrics. ⊠ *2315 S. Ocean Blvd., 33480, ☎ FAX 561/582–1461. 23 rooms, 11 apartments, 6 efficiencies. Restaurant, pool, beach. D, MC, V.*

Nightlife and the Arts

The Arts

The **Royal Poinciana Playhouse** (⊠ 70 Royal Poinciana Plaza, ☎ 561/659–3310) presents seven productions each year between December and April. **Society of the Four Arts** (⊠ Four Arts Plaza, ☎ 561/655–7226) offers concerts, lectures, and Friday films December–March. Movie tickets can be purchased at time of showing; other tickets may be obtained a week in advance.

Nightlife

Cheek-to-cheek dancers head to the **Colony** (⊠ 155 Hammon Ave., ☎ 561/655–5430) for a spin around the dance floor. A trio plays Thursday, Friday, and Saturday nights. Young professionals gather at **E. R. Bradley's Saloon** (⊠ 111 Bradley Pl., ☎ 561/833–3520) to trade stories of the day and to try their hand at 3-D video golf. As the weekend dinner crowd thins out, late-night party seekers fill up **Ta-boó** (⊠

221 Worth Ave., ☎ 561/835–3500), where a DJ keeps everyone on their feet.

Outdoor Activities and Sports

Biking

Bicycling is an excellent way to get a good look at Palm Beach, which is as small and flat as the top of a billiard table (and just as green). The wonderful 10-mi, palm-fringed **Palm Beach Bicycle Trail** (⊠ Parallel to Lake Way) skirts the backyards of many palatial mansions and the edge of Lake Worth. Just a block from the bike trail, the **Palm Beach Trail Bicycle Shop** (⊠ 223 Sunrise Ave., ☎ 561/659–4583) rents bikes by the hour or day.

Dog Racing

Since 1932 the hounds have been racing year-round at the 4,300-seat **Palm Beach Kennel Club.** There are also simulcasts of jai alai and horse racing, as well as wagering on live and televised sports. ⊠ *1111 N. Congress Ave.,* ☎ *561/683–2222.* ☜ *50¢, terrace level $1, parking free.* ☽ *Racing Mon. 12:30, Wed.–Thurs. and Sat. 12:30 and 7:30, Fri. 7:30, Sun. 1; simulcasts Mon. and Fri. noon, Tues. 12:30.*

Golf

Breakers Hotel Golf Club (⊠ 1 S. County Rd., ☎ 561/655–6611 or 800/833–3141) features 36 holes. The **Palm Beach Par 3** (⊠ 2345 S. Ocean Blvd., ☎ 561/547–0598) has 18 holes, including four on the Atlantic and three on the inland waterway.

Shopping

One of the world's showcases for high-quality shopping, **Worth Avenue** runs ¼-mi east–west across Palm Beach, from the beach to Lake Worth. The street has more than 250 shops, and many upscale stores (Cartier, Gucci, Hermès, Pierre Deux, Saks Fifth Avenue, and Van Cleef & Arpels) are represented, their merchandise appealing to the discerning tastes of Palm Beach clientele. The six blocks of **South County Road** north of Worth Avenue have appealing (and somewhat less expensive) stores. For specialty items (out-of-town newspapers, health foods, and books), try the shops along the north side of **Royal Poinciana Way.**

WEST PALM BEACH

2 mi west of Palm Beach.

Long considered Palm Beach's impoverished cousin, West Palm is now economically vibrant in its own right. Far larger in area than its upper-crust neighbor to the east, it has become the cultural, entertainment, and business center of the county and of the region to the north. Sparkling government buildings like the mammoth $124 million Palm Beach County Judicial Center and Courthouse and the State Administrative Building exemplify the health of the city's corporate life, and facilities such as the $60 million Kravis Center for the Performing Arts attest to the strength of the arts and entertainment community.

Downtown

The heart of revived West Palm Beach is a small but attractive downtown area, which has been spurred on by an active historic preservation movement. Along beautifully landscaped Clematis Street, you'll find boutiques and restaurants in charmingly restored buildings and exuberant nightlife that mimics that of South Beach. Even at the downtown's fringes, you'll encounter sights of cultural interest. There's a free downtown shuttle by day and free on-street parking at night and on weekends.

A Good Tour

From a geographical perspective, the best place to start is at the north end of the city with a walk through the **Old Northwood Historic District** ⑫, on the National Register of Historic Places. Drive south on U.S. 1, take a left onto 12th Street, and then a right onto South Olive Avenue to view the exceptional art collection at the **Norton Museum of Art** ⑬. From here it is just a few blocks farther south to the peaceful **Ann Norton Sculpture Gardens** ⑭. Finally, drive west across Barcelona Road to the **Armory Arts Center** ⑮ and check out the current exhibit.

TIMING

Late morning is a good time to start this tour, so you can walk through the historic neighborhood before having lunch on Clematis Street. In the afternoon you'll need about three hours at the various arts-oriented sights. It's important to take this tour during daytime business hours.

Sights to See

⑭ **Ann Norton Sculpture Gardens.** This monument to the late American sculptor Ann Weaver Norton, second wife of Norton Museum founder Ralph H. Norton, consists of charming 3-acre grounds displaying seven granite figures and six brick megaliths. The plantings were designed by Norton, an environmentalist, to attract native bird life. ⊠ *253 Barcelona Rd.,* ☎ *561/832–5328.* ⊡ *$3.* ☼ *Tues.–Sat. 10–4 (call ahead; schedule is not always observed) or by appointment.*

⑮ **Armory Arts Center.** Built by the WPA in 1939, the facility is now a complete visual arts center. Its gallery hosts rotating exhibitions, and classes are held throughout the year. ⊠ *1703 S. Lake Ave.,* ☎ *561/ 832–1776.* ⊡ *Free.* ☼ *Weekdays 9–5, Sun. 10–2.*

★ ⑬ **Norton Museum of Art.** Constructed in 1941 by steel magnate Ralph H. Norton, this museum boasts an extensive permanent collection of 19th- and 20th-century American and European paintings with special emphasis on 19th-century French Impressionists. There are also Chinese bronze and jade sculptures, a sublime outdoor patio with sculptures on display in a tropical garden, and a library housing more than 3,000 art books and periodicals. Nine galleries showcase traveling exhibits as well as art from the permanent collection. ⊠ *1451 S. Olive Ave.,* ☎ *561/832–5194.* ⊡ *$5.* ☼ *Tues.–Sat. 10–5, Sun. 1–5.*

⑫ **Old Northwood Historic District.** This 1920s-era neighborhood, on the National Register of Historic Places, hosts special events and Sunday walking tours (☞ Guided Tours *in* Palm Beach and the Treasure Coast A to Z, *below*). ⊠ *West of Flagler Dr. between 26th and 35th Sts.*

Away from Downtown

At its outskirts, West Palm Beach sprawls. Flat, straight stretches lined with fast-food outlets and car dealerships may not be pretty to drive past, but it's worth it to reach some of the interesting attractions scattered around the southern and western reaches of the city. Several are especially rewarding for children and other animal- and nature lovers.

A Good Tour

Head south from downtown and turn right on Southern Boulevard, left onto Parker Avenue, and right onto Summit Boulevard to reach the **Dreher Park Zoo** ⑯. In the same area (just turn right onto Dreher

Trail) and also appealing to kids, the **South Florida Science Museum, Planetarium, and Aquarium** ⑰ is full of hands-on exhibits.

Backtrack to Summit Avenue and go west to the 150-acre **Pine Jog Environmental Education Center** ⑱. For more natural adventure, head farther west on Summit until you reach Forest Hills Boulevard, where you turn right to reach the **Okeeheelee Nature Center** ⑲ and its miles of wooded trails.

Now retrace your steps to Summit Boulevard, drive east until you reach Military Trail, and take a left. Drive north to Southern Boulevard and turn west to reach **Lion Country Safari** ⑳, a 500-acre cageless zoo. For the last stop on this tour, backtrack to Military Trail and travel north to the gardens of the **Mounts Horticultural Learning Center** ㉑.

TIMING

You could easily spend most of a day at some of these sights, so you'll want to pick and choose based on your interests, creating your own subtour. During morning and afternoon rush hours and in the winter, be prepared for heavy traffic; sightseeing in the morning (not *too* early) will help somewhat.

Sights to See

⑯ **Dreher Park Zoo.** This wild kingdom is a 22-acre complex with more than 500 animals representing more than 100 species, including Florida panthers, red kangaroos, and Bengal tigers. Also of note are a nature trail, an Australian Outback exhibit, and a children's zoo. ⊠ *1301 Summit Blvd.,* ☎ *561/533–0887 or 561/547–9453.* 🎟 *$6, boat rides $1.* ☉ *Daily 9–5 (until 7 on spring and summer weekends), boat rides every 15 mins.*

⑳ **Lion Country Safari.** Drive (with car windows closed, please) on 8 mi of paved roads through a 500-acre cageless zoo where 1,300 wild animals roam. Lions, elephants, white rhinoceroses, giraffes, zebras, antelopes, chimpanzees, and ostriches are among those in residence. Special exhibits include the Kalahari Bushvelt, designed after a South African plateau and featuring water buffalo and Nilgai (the largest type of Asian antelope), and the Gir Forest, modeled after a game forest in India and showcasing a pride of lions. Stop by the petting zoo, or take a ride on the *Safari Queen* cruise. ⊠ *Southern Blvd. W,* ☎ *561/793–1084.* 🎟 *$15.50, van rental $6 per hr.* ☉ *Daily 9:30–5:30.*

㉑ **Mounts Horticultural Learning Center.** Take advantage of balmy weather by walking among the tropical and subtropical plants here. Free tours are given. ⊠ *531 N. Military Trail,* ☎ *561/233–1749.* 🎟 *Free.* ☉ *Mon.–Sat. 8:30–5, Sun. 1–5; tours Sat. 11, Sun. 2:30.*

⑲ **Okeeheelee Nature Center.** At this popular spot, you can explore 5 mi of trails through 90 acres of native pine flat woods and wetlands. A spacious visitor center/gift shop features hands-on exhibits. ⊠ *7715 Forest Hill Blvd.,* ☎ *561/233–1400.* 🎟 *Free.* ☉ *Visitor center Tues.–Fri. 1–4:45, Sat. 8:15–4:45; trails open daily.*

⑱ **Pine Jog Environmental Education Center.** The draw here is 150 acres of mostly undisturbed Florida pine flat woods with two self-guided ½-mi trails. Formal landscaping around the five one-story buildings features an array of native plants, and dioramas and displays show native ecosystems. Trails are reserved for the classes that are given here during the week but are open to the public on Sunday. ⊠ *6301 Summit Blvd.,* ☎ *561/686–6600.* 🎟 *Free.* ☉ *Sun. 2–5.*

⑰ **South Florida Science Museum, Planetarium, and Aquarium.** Here you'll find hands-on exhibits, aquarium displays with touch tanks, planetarium shows, and a chance to observe the heavens Friday nights through the most powerful telescope in South Florida (weather permitting). ✉ *4801 Dreher Trail N,* ☎ *561/832–1988.* 🎫 *$5, planetarium $2 extra, laser show $4 extra.* ☉ *Sat.–Thurs. 10–5, Fri. 10–10.*

Dining and Lodging

$$–$$$ ✕ **Café Protégé.** The restaurant of the Florida Culinary Institute, this is the place to come to sample superb cuisine at less than astronomical prices. The contemporary Continental menu changes frequently, and patrons can watch students at work slicing, dicing, and sautéing in the unique observation kitchen. ✉ *2400 Metrocentre Blvd.,* ☎ *561/687–2433. AE, MC, V. No lunch weekends; no dinner Sun.–Mon.*

$$ ✕ **Rain Dancer Steak House.** Since 1975 steak lovers have been stopping by this dark and cozy establishment to indulge in thick and juicy filet mignons, giant 24-ounce porterhouse steaks, sizzling sirloins for two, and grilled lean flank steaks. But if beef isn't your entrée of choice, there are lobster, shrimp scampi, baked scallops, stuffed shrimp, and a bountiful salad bar. ✉ *2300 Palm Beach Lakes Blvd.,* ☎ *561/ 684–2811. AE, MC, V. No lunch.*

$–$$ ✕ **Aleyda's Tex-Mex Restaurant.** Since 1981 this casual family-friendly eatery has been showing up as a favorite on local popularity polls. Fajitas, the house specialty, are brought to the table sizzling in the pan, and enchiladas, chili con queso, and quesadillas are just a few more examples of the classic Mexican offerings. The bar claims to make the best margaritas in town. ✉ *1890 Okeechobee Blvd.,* ☎ *561/688–9033. AE, DC, MC, V. No lunch Sun.*

$–$$ ✕ **Pescatore Seafood and Oyster Bar.** When you want to rest your feet after wandering around Clematis Street, slip through the handsome French doors of this trendy spot for a light lunch, an afternoon snack, or a leisurely dinner. Tables are close together, and there's a sophisticated bustle. Naturally, fresh oysters and clams are on the menu, but you'll also find a variety of grilled fish, including mahimahi, tuna, and salmon; steamed Maine lobster; grilled shrimp; assorted pasta dishes; and a grilled Black Angus burger. ✉ *200 Clematis St.,* ☎ *561/837–6633. AE, DC, MC, V.*

$$–$$$ 🏨 **Hibiscus House.** Few Florida B&B hosts work harder at hospital-
★   ity and at looking after their neighborhood than Raleigh Hill and Colin Rayner. As proof, since the inn opened in the late 1980s, 11 sets of guests have bought houses in Old Northwood, which is listed on the National Register of Historic Places thanks to Hill and Rayner's efforts. Their Cape Cod–style B&B is full of the antiques Hill has collected during decades of in-demand interior designing: a 150-year-old four-square piano, a gorgeous green cane planter chair, and Louis XV pieces in the living room. Outstanding, too, is the landscaped, tropical pool-patio area. Both Hill and Rayner are informed about the best—and most affordable—dining in the area. ✉ *501 30th St., 33407,* ☎ *561/863–5633 or 800/203–4927. 8 rooms. Pool. AE, DC, MC, V.*

$–$$ 🏨 **Tropical Bed & Breakfast.** More informal and Key West–like than most of Old Northwood, this tiny cottage-style B&B has a clump of rare paroutis palms out front. The three cozy rooms are individually decorated, but the splashy poolside carriage house and the brightly striped cottage with the fruity fabrics and Peter Max–style posters are where you want to be. ✉ *419 32nd St., 33407,* ☎ *561/848–4064 or 800/ 736–4064,* FAX *561/842–1688. 3 rooms, carriage house, cottage. Pool, bicycles. AE, MC, V.*

Nightlife and the Arts

The Arts

Part of the treasury of arts attractions is the **Raymond F. Kravis Center for the Performing Arts** (⊠ 701 Okeechobee Blvd., ☎ 561/832–7469), a $60 million, 2,200-seat glass, copper, and marble showcase occupying the highest ground in West Palm Beach. Its 250-seat Rinker Playhouse includes a space for children's programming, family productions, and other special events. Some 300 performances of drama, dance, and music—everything from gospel and bluegrass to jazz and classical—are scheduled each year.

Palm Beach Opera (⊠ 415 S. Olive Ave., ☎ 561/833–7888) stages four productions each winter at the Kravis Center. The **Carefree Theatre** (⊠ 2000 S. Dixie Hwy., ☎ 561/833–7305) is Palm Beach County's premier showcase of foreign and art films.

Nightlife

The **Jamestown Cigar Bar** (⊠ 330 Clematis St., ☎ 561/659–7273) not only carries the best selection of cigars in Palm Beach County; it also features live jazz and blues. The **Respectable Street Cafe** (⊠ 518 Clematis St., ☎ 561/832–9999) explodes in high energy like an indoor Woodstock. It's open until 4 AM Tuesday–Saturday (Thursday night features the best in underground alternative sound) and for special concerts on other days. **Underground Coffeeworks** (⊠ 105 S. Narcissus Ave., ☎ 561/835–4792), a retro '60s spot, has "something different going on" (but always live music) Tuesday–Saturday. The cover charge varies, depending on the performers.

Outdoor Activities and Sports

Picturesque **Binks Forest Golf Club** (⊠ 400 Binks Forest Dr., Wellington, ☎ 561/795–0595) has an 18-hole layout. The plush **Emerald Dunes** (⊠ 2100 Emerald Dunes Dr., ☎ 561/684–4653) sports 18 holes of golf. **Palm Beach Polo and Country Club** (⊠ 13198 Forest Hill Blvd., Wellington, ☎ 561/798–7000 or 800/327–4204) features 45 holes with an excellent overall layout. The **West Palm Beach Country Club** (⊠ 7001 Parker Ave., ☎ 561/582–2019) offers 18 holes with no water hazards, unusual for Florida.

Shopping

As good as the malls are, they're sterile compared to the in-the-midst-of-things excitement—the mix of food, art, performance, landscaping, and retailing—that has renewed downtown West Palm around **Clematis Street.** Water-view parks, outdoor performing areas, and attractive plantings and lighting—including fanciful palm tree sculptures—add to the pleasure of browsing, window-shopping, and resting at an outdoor café. For those single-mindedly bent on mall shopping, the **Palm Beach Mall** (⊠ Palm Beach Lakes Blvd. at I–95) has a Burdines, JCPenney, Lord & Taylor, and Sears.

Side Trip

Lake Okeechobee

40 mi west of West Palm Beach.

Rimming the western shore of Palm Beach and Martin counties, this second-largest freshwater lake in the United States is girdled by 120 mi of roads; yet for almost its entire circumference, it remains hidden from sight. The Seminole's Big Water and the heart of the great Everglades watershed, Lake Okeechobee measures 730 square mi—roughly

33 mi north–south and 30 mi east–west—with an average natural depth of only 10 ft (flood control brings the figure up to 12 ft and deeper). Six major lock systems and 32 separate water-control structures manage the water.

Encircling the lake is a 30-ft-high grassy levee, known locally as the "wall," and the Lake Okeechobee Scenic Trail, a coarse track that has been integrated into the Florida National Scenic Trail. Inside the wall, on the big lake itself, fisherfolk come from everywhere for reputedly the best bass fishing in North America.

Small towns dot the lakeshore in an area that's still largely agricultural. To the southeast is Belle Glade, whose motto—"Her soil is her fortune"—results from the town's role as the eastern hub of the 700,000-acre Everglades Agricultural Area, the crescent of farmlands lying south and east of the lake. To the southwest lies Clewiston, the most prosperous lake town. It's known as "the sweetest town in America" thanks to the resident headquarters of the United States Sugar Corporation. At the north end of the lake, around Okeechobee, citrus production has outgrown cattle ranching as the principal economy, while dairying, though still important, is diminishing as the state acquires land in its efforts to reduce water pollution. Somewhat set back from the lake, Indiantown is the western hub of Martin County, noteworthy for citrus production, cattle ranching, and timbering. The town reached its apex in 1927, when the Seaboard Airline Railroad briefly established its southern headquarters and a model town here.

Grouped together in Belle Glade's **Municipal Complex** are the public library and the **Lawrence E. Will Museum**, both with materials on the town's history. On the front lawn is a Ferenc Verga sculpture of a family fleeing the wall of water that rose from the lake during the catastrophic hurricane of 1928. More than 2,000 people lost their lives and 15,000 families were left homeless by the torrential flood. ✉ *530 Main St., Belle Glade,* ☎ *561/996–3453.* ✇ *Free.* ☉ *Mon.–Tues. and Fri. 9–4, Wed. and Sat. 9–1, Thurs. 9–8.*

The **Clewiston Museum** details the history of the city, with stories not only of sugar and of the Herbert Hoover Dike construction, but also of a ramie crop grown here to make rayon, of World War II RAF pilots who trained at the Clewiston airfield, and of a German POW camp. ✉ *112 S. Commercio St., Clewiston,* ☎ *941/983–2870.* ✇ *Free.* ☉ *Tues.–Fri. 10–4.*

The Florida Power and Light Company's Martin Power Plant maintains the **Barley Barber Swamp**, a 400-acre freshwater cypress swamp preserve. A 5,800-ft-long boardwalk enables you to walk through this vestige of what near-coastal Florida was largely like before vast water-control efforts began in the 19th century. Dozens of birds, reptiles, and mammals inhabit these wetlands and lowlands, with an outstanding reserve of bald cypress trees, land and swamp growth, and slow-flowing coffee-color water. Reservations are required at least one week in advance for tours. During certain times of the year there are manatee and turtle walks. Call for schedules. ✉ *Rte. 710, Indiantown,* ☎ *800/ 552–8440.* ✇ *Free.* ☉ *Tours Fri.–Wed. 8:30 and 12:30.*

DINING AND LODGING

$–$$ ✕ **Colonial Dining Room.** The Clewiston Inn's restaurant has ladderback chairs, chandeliers, and fanlight windows, and though the food is good, the attitude's not fancy. Southern regional and Continental dishes—chicken, pork, steak, and the ubiquitous catfish—are served. ✉ *108 Royal Palm Ave., at U.S. 27, Clewiston,* ☎ *941/983–8151. MC, V.*

$–$$ ✕ **Lightsey's.** The pick of the lake, this beautiful lodgelike restaurant at the Okee-Tantie Recreation Area started closer to town as a fish company with four tables in a corner. Now everybody comes out here. You can get most items fried, steamed, broiled, or grilled. The freshest are the catfish, cooter (freshwater turtle), frogs' legs, and gator. ✉ *10430 Rte. 78W, Okeechobee,* ☎ *941/763–4276. MC, V. Beer and wine only.*

$–$$ 🏨 **Seminole Country Inn.** This two-story, Mediterranean Revival inn,
★ once the southern headquarters of the Seaboard Airline Railroad, was restored by longtime Indiantown patriarch the late Holman Wall. It's now being run for the second time (other innkeepers didn't get it right) by his daughter, Jonnie Wall Williams, a fifth-generation native, who is devoted to the inn's restoration. Rooms are done in country ruffles and prints, with full carpeting and comfy beds. There are rocking chairs on the porch, Indiantown memorabilia in the lobby, a sitting area on the second floor, and good local art throughout. ✉ *15885 S.W. Warfield Blvd., Indiantown 34956,* ☎ *561/597–3777. 21 rooms. 2 restaurants, pool. AE, D, MC, V.*

$ 🏨 **Clewiston Inn.** This classic antebellum-style country hotel in the heart of town was built in 1938. Its cypress-panel lobby, wood-burning fireplace, Colonial Dining Room, and Everglades Lounge with a wraparound Everglades mural are standouts. Rooms are pleasant but basic, with reproduction furniture. Still it's worth a stay to soak up the lore and take advantage of the excellent value (full breakfast included). A pool is across the street in the park. ✉ *108 Royal Palm Ave., at U.S. 27, Clewiston 33440,* ☎ *941/983–8151 or 800/749–4466,* 🖷 *941/983–4602. 48 rooms, 5 suites. Restaurant, bar, 6 tennis courts, jogging. AE, MC, V.*

$ 🏨 **Okeechobee Days Inn Pier II.** This modern two-story motel on the
★ rim canal has a five-story observation tower for looking over the levee to the lake. Large, clean, motel-plain rooms are well maintained. Out back there are a 600-ft fishing pier and the Oyster Bar, one of the best hangouts on the lake for shooting a game of pool or watching a game on TV. It attracts a good mix of locals and out-of-towners. ✉ *2200 S.E. U.S. 441, Okeechobee 34974,* ☎ *941/763–8003 or 800/874–3744,* 🖷 *941/763–2245. 89 rooms. Bar, fishing. AE, D, DC, MC, V.*

$ 🏨 **Okeechobee Inn.** Rooms in this simple, two-story L-shape motel, 2 mi west of Belle Glade, are furnished in green floral prints. Large windows let in plenty of light. All rooms have balconies that overlook the pool, and fishing and boat ramps are just a mile away. ✉ *265 N. U.S. 27, South Bay 33493,* ☎ *561/996–6517. 115 rooms. Pool, playground. MC, V.*

$ ⛺ **Belle Glade Marina Campground.** A few miles north of downtown Belle Glade, just offshore in Lake Okeechobee, is Torry Island. Campsites have water and electrical hookups; some have sewer hookups and docking facilities. ✉ *Torry Island 33493,* ☎ *561/996–6322. 350 campsites. Picnic area, horseshoes, shuffleboard, dock, boating, fishing. MC, V.*

$ ⛺ **Okee-Tantie Recreation Area.** In addition to its recreational facilities, the park offers 215 RV sites, 38 tent sites, picnic spots, rest rooms, showers, Lightsey's restaurant, and a shop at which you can buy groceries and sandwiches. ✉ *10430 Rte. 78W, Okeechobee 34974,* ☎ *941/763–2622. Restaurant, grocery, picnic area, dock, boating, fishing, playground. MC, V.*

OUTDOOR ACTIVITIES AND SPORTS

Biking. Okeechobee Cycling & Fitness (✉ 50 S.E. U.S. 441, Okeechobee, ☎ 941/357–0458) is the only source for bicycle rentals and repairs on the lake.

Fishing. In addition to operating the bridge to Torry Island (the last remaining swing bridge in Florida, it is cranked open and closed by hand, swinging at right angles to the road), brothers Charles and Gordon Corbin run **Slim's Fish Camp** (⊠ Torry Island, ☎ 561/996–3844). Here you'll find a complete tackle shop, guides, camping facilities, fully equipped bass boats, and even the name of a good taxidermist to mount your trophy. **J-Mark Fish Camp** (⊠ Torry Island, ☎ 561/996–5357) provides fully equipped bass boats, fishing guides, tackle, bait, and licenses. Since the **Okee-Tantie Recreation Area** (⊠ 10430 Rte. 78W, Okeechobee, ☎ 941/763–2622) has direct access to the lake, it's a popular place for fishing. There are two public boat ramps, fish-cleaning stations, a marina, picnic areas and a restaurant, a playground, rest rooms, showers, and a bait shop (☎ 941/763–9645) that stocks groceries.

Golf. Belle Glade Municipal Country Club (⊠ Torry Island Rd., Belle Glade, ☎ 561/996–6605) features an 18-hole golf course and restaurant open to the public.

SOUTH TO BOCA RATON

Strung together by Route A1A, the towns between Palm Beach and Boca Raton are notable for their variety. Though the glamour of Palm Beach has rubbed off on many towns, there are pockets of modesty and unpretentiousness alongside the well-established high and mighty. In one town you might find a cluster of sophisticated art galleries and fancy eateries, while the very next town could have a few hamburger stands and mom-and-pop "everything" stores.

Lake Worth

㉒ *2 mi south of West Palm Beach.*

Tourists are mainly interested in this mainland town for its inexpensive lodging in close proximity to Palm Beach, which is accessible via a nearby bridge.

Lake Worth Municipal Park, also known as Casino Park, has a beach, Olympic-size swimming pool, fishing pier, picnic areas, shuffleboard, restaurants, and shops. ⊠ *Rte. A1A at end of Lake Worth Bridge,* ☎ *561/533–7367.* ⌑ *Pool $2, parking 25¢ for 15 mins.* ☉ *Daily 9–4:45.*

The Arts
Klein Dance Company (⊠ 3208 2nd Ave. N, No. 10, 33461, ☎ 561/586–1889) is a nationally acclaimed, world-touring professional troupe that also gives local performances.

Dining and Lodging
$ ✕ **John G's.** About the only time the line lets up is when the restaurant closes at 3 PM. The menu is as big as the crowd: big fruit platters, sandwich-board superstars, grilled burgers, seafood, and eggs every which way, including a United Nations of omelets. Breakfast is served until 11. ⊠ *Lake Worth Casino,* ☎ *561/585–9860. No credit cards. No dinner.*

$ ⛏ **New Sun Gate Motel.** Each room is dedicated to a famous movie star of a bygone era—Cary Grant, Rita Hayworth, James Dean—in this simple establishment near downtown. Units are decorated in Art Deco style, and some have microwaves. ⊠ *901 S. Federal Hwy., 33460,* ☎ *561/588–8110,* ℻ *561/588–8041. 31 rooms. Restaurant, pool, coin laundry. AE, MC, V.*

Outdoor Activities and Sports

The **Gulfstream Polo Club,** the oldest club in the Palm Beach area, began in the 1920s and plays medium-goal polo (for teams with handicaps of 8–16 goals). There are six polo fields. ⊠ *4550 Polo Rd.,* ☎ *561/965–2057.* ⊡ *Free.* ⊙ *Games Dec.–Apr.*

Lantana

㉓ *2 mi south of Lake Worth.*

Like Lake Worth, Lantana has inexpensive lodging and a bridge connecting the town to Palm Beach's barrier island. It's just a bit farther away from Palm Beach. A closer island neighbor is **Manalapan,** a tiny residential community with a luxury beach resort.

Lantana Public Beach has one of the best food concessions around. You'll find fresh fish on weekends and breakfast and lunch specials every day outdoors under beach umbrellas. ⊠ *100 N. Ocean Ave.,* ☎ *no phone.* ⊡ *Parking 25¢ for 15 mins.* ⊙ *Daily 9–4:45.*

Dining and Lodging

$$ ✕ **Old House.** Overlooking the Intracoastal Waterway, the 1889 Lyman House has grown in spurts over the years and is now a patchwork of shedlike spaces. Partners Wayne Cordero and Captain Bob Hoddinott have turned it into an informal Old Florida seafood house that serves not only local seafood but also, incongruously, Baltimore steamed crab—the specialty. Although there's air-conditioning, dining is still open-air most evenings and in cooler weather. ⊠ *300 E. Ocean Ave.,* ☎ *561/533–5220. AE, MC, V.*

$$$$ 🏨 **Ritz-Carlton, Palm Beach.** Despite its name, this hotel is actually in
★ Manalapan, halfway between Palm Beach and Delray. The bisque-color, triple-tower landmark may look like the work of Addison Mizner, but in fact it was built in 1991. Dominating the lobby is a huge double-sided marble fireplace, foreshadowing the luxury of the guest rooms' marble tubs and upholstered furniture. Most rooms have ocean views, and oceanfront rooms have balconies. Not to be outdone by the fabulous beaches, a large pool and courtyard area has more than 100 coconut palms. Bikes and scuba and snorkeling equipment can be rented. ⊠ *100 S. Ocean Blvd., Manalapan 33462,* ☎ *561/533–6000 or 800/241–3333,* 🖷 *561/588–4555. 257 rooms, 13 suites. 4 restaurants, 2 bars, pool, beauty salon, massage, sauna, spa, steam room, 7 tennis courts, beach, bicycles. AE, D, DC, MC, V.*

$ 🏨 **Super 8 Motel.** There's nothing special about this sprawling one-story motel except the price—a real bargain, considering the proximity to Palm Beach. Efficiencies and rooms (some with refrigerators) are clean but basically furnished. ⊠ *1255 Hypoluxo Rd., 33462,* ☎ *561/585–3970,* 🖷 *561/586–3028. 129 rooms, 11 efficiencies. Pool, coin laundry. AE, DC, MC, V.*

Outdoor Activities and Sports

B-Love Fleet (⊠ *314 E. Ocean Ave.,* ☎ *561/588–7612*) offers three deep-sea fishing excursions daily: 8–noon, 1–5, and 7–11. No reservations are needed; just show up 30 minutes before the boat is scheduled to leave. The cost is $24 per person.

Boynton Beach

㉔ *3 mi south of Lantana.*

This town is far enough from Palm Beach to have kept its laid-back, low-key atmosphere. Its two parts, on the mainland and the barrier island, are connected by a causeway.

Knollwood Groves dates from the 1930s, when it was planted by the partners of the *Amos & Andy* radio show. You can take a 30-minute, 30-acre tram tour through the orange groves and a processing plant and visit the **Hallpatee Seminole Indian Village**, where there are an alligator exhibit and crafts shop. During the busy season, special guest Martin Twofeather gives a weekly one-hour alligator-handling show. ⊠ *8053 Lawrence Rd.,* ☎ *561/734–4800.* 🖾 *Tour $1, show $5.* ☉ *Daily 8:30–5:30, show Sat. 2.*

☜ The **Puppetry Arts Center** provides shows and educational programs from the home of the Gold Coast Puppet Guild. ⊠ *3633 S. Federal Hwy.,* ☎ *561/687–3280.* 🖾 *Shows $2.50.* ☉ *Call for schedule.*

Oceanfront Park has a beach, boardwalk, concessions, grills, a jogging trail, and playground. Parking is expensive if you're not a Boynton resident. ⊠ *Ocean Ave. at Rte. A1A,* ☎ *no phone.* 🖾 *Parking $10 per day in winter, $5 per day rest of year.* ☉ *Daily 9 AM–midnight.*

OFF THE
BEATEN PATH

ARTHUR R. MARSHALL–LOXAHATCHEE NATIONAL WILDLIFE REFUGE – The most robust part of the Everglades, this 221-square-mi refuge is one of three huge water-retention areas that account for much of the Everglades outside the national park. These areas are managed less to protect natural resources, however, than to prevent flooding to the south. Start from the visitor center, where there are two walking trails: a boardwalk through a dense cypress swamp and a marsh trail to a 20-ft-high observation tower overlooking a pond. There is also a 5½-mi canoe trail, recommended for more experienced canoeists because it's rather overgrown. Wildlife viewing is good year-round, and you can fish for bass and panfish. ⊠ *10119 Lee Rd., off U.S. 441 between Boynton Beach Blvd. (Rte. 804) and Atlantic Ave. (Rte. 806), west of Boynton Beach,* ☎ *561/734–8303.* 🖾 *$5 per vehicle, $1 per pedestrian.* ☉ *Daily 6 AM–sunset; visitor center weekdays 9–4, weekends 9–4:30.*

Dining

$-$$ ✕ **Mama Jennie's.** Tucked at the end of a strip mall, this inviting, casual Italian restaurant attracts families, who come here to share large, traditional pizza pies topped with mozzarella, mushrooms, and anchovies. Spaghetti with meatballs, eggplant parmigiana, and stuffed shells are also fine choices, and all dishes are homemade. ⊠ *706 W. Boynton Beach Blvd.,* ☎ *561/737–2407. AE, MC, V. No lunch.*

Outdoor Activities and Sports

FISHING

You can fish the canal at the **Arthur R. Marshall–Loxahatchee National Wildlife Refuge** (☎ 561/734–8303). There's a boat ramp, and the waters are decently productive, but bring your own equipment.

GOLF

Boynton Beach Municipal Golf Course (⊠ 8020 Jog Rd., ☎ 561/742–6500) offers 27 holes.

Gulf Stream

㉕ *2 mi south of Boynton Beach.*

This beautiful little beachfront community was also touched by Mizner. As you pass the bougainvillea-topped walls of the Gulf Stream Club, a private police officer may stop traffic for a golfer to cross.

Lodging

$ 🏨 **Riviera Palms Motel.** Hans and Herter Grannemann have owned this small two-story motel dating from the 1950s since 1978. It has two primary virtues: It's clean, and it's well located. Across Route A1A from mid-rise apartment houses on the water, it has three wings surrounding a grassy front yard and heated pool. Rooms are done in Danish modern and a blue, brown, and tan color scheme; all have at least a refrigerator but no phone. ⊠ *3960 N. Ocean Blvd., 33483,* ☎ *561/ 276–3032. 17 rooms, suites, and efficiencies. Pool. No credit cards.*

Delray Beach

26 *2 mi south of Gulf Stream.*

What began as an artists' retreat and a small settlement of Japanese farmers is now a sophisticated beach town with a successful local historic-preservation movement. Atlantic Avenue, the main drag, has been transformed into a 1-mi stretch of palm-dotted brick sidewalks, almost entirely lined with stores, art galleries, and dining establishments. Running east–west and ending at the beach, it's a pleasant place for a stroll day or night. Another lovely pedestrian way begins at the edge of town, across Northeast 8th Street (George Bush Boulevard), along the big broad swimming beach that extends north and south of Atlantic Avenue.

Municipal Beach (⊠ Atlantic Ave. at Rte. A1A) has a boat ramp and volleyball court.

The chief landmark along Atlantic Avenue is the Mediterranean Revival **Colony Hotel** (⊠ 525 E. Atlantic Ave., ☎ 561/276–4123), still open only for the winter season as it has been almost every year since 1926.

Cason Cottage, a restored Victorian-style home that dates from about 1915, now serves as offices of the Delray Beach Historical Society. The house is filled with relics of the Victorian era, including an old pipe organ donated by descendants of one of the original families to settle Delray Beach. Periodic displays celebrate the town's architectural evolution. The cottage is a block north of the cultural center. ⊠ *5 N.E. 1st St.,* ☎ *561/243–0223.* ☜ *Free.* ☉ *Tues.–Fri. 11–4.*

The **Old School Square Cultural Arts Center,** just off Atlantic Avenue, houses several museums in restored school buildings dating from 1913 and 1926. The **Cornell Museum of Art & History** offers an ever-changing array of art exhibits. ⊠ *51 N. Swinton Ave.,* ☎ *561/243– 7922.* ☜ *Donation welcome.* ☉ *Tues.–Sat. 11–4, Sun. 1–4.*

Florida seems an odd place for the ★**Morikami Museum and Japanese Gardens.** At this 200-acre cultural and recreational facility, a display in a building modeled after a Japanese imperial villa recalls the Yamato Colony, an agricultural community of Japanese settlers who came to Florida in 1905. Gardens include the only known collection of bonsai Florida plants. There are also programs and exhibits in a lakeside museum and theater, as well as a nature trail, picnic pavilions, a library and audiovisual center, and snack bar. The on-site Cornell Cafe is a pleasant retreat serving light Asian fare. ⊠ *4000 Morikami Park Rd.,* ☎ *561/495–0233.* ☜ *Park free; museum $4.25, free Sun. 10–noon.* ☉ *Park daily sunrise–sunset; museum Tues.–Sun. 10–5; café Tues.–Sun. 11–3.*

Dining and Lodging

$$–$$$ ✕ **Damiano's at the Tarrimore Home.** Dinner is an intimate affair at this sophisticated restaurant in an Old Florida home. Nothing on the menu is ordinary. The eclectic cuisine from around the world often incorporates local ingredients and always with a twist. Consider the escargots tossed in mint and garlic oil and served in a nest of phyllo dough or the sweet Vidalia and green onion soup; or try the lobster potpie with nuggets of Florida lobster plus peas and carrots in a light cream sauce or oven-roasted yellowtail snapper served with thin slices of Florida lemon, capers, and a chardonnay sauce. ⊠ *52 N. Swinton Ave.,* ☎ *561/272–4706. AE, MC, V.*

$–$$ ✕ **Blue Anchor.** Unbelievably, this pub was actually shipped from En-
★   gland, where it stood for 150 years as the old Blue Anchor Pub, in London's historic Chancery Lane. There it was a regular watering hole for many famous Englishmen, including Winston Churchill. The Delray Beach incarnation still cooks up authentic British pub fare: ploughman's lunch (a chunk of cheddar or Stilton cheese, a chunk of bread, and English pickled onions), steak-and-kidney pie, fish-and-chips, and bangers (sausage) and mash, to name just a few. You can also get delicious hamburgers, sandwiches, and salads. The dessert menu includes an English sherry trifle and a Bailey's Irish Cream pie. English beers and ales are available on tap and in the bottle. ⊠ *804 E. Atlantic Ave.,* ☎ *561/272–7272. AE, MC, V.*

$–$$ ✕ **Boston's on the Beach.** Often a restaurant that's facing a beach re-
★   lies on its location to fill the place up and doesn't worry enough about the food. Not so with Boston's, which is just across the street from the public beach. As you might expect from the name, you'll find good New England clam chowder and several lobster dishes, as well as fresh fish grilled, fried, or prepared just about any other way. All this is presented in an ultra-informal setting. Tables are old and wooden, and walls are decorated with traffic signs and other conversation stoppers, most notably paraphernalia from the Boston Bruins, New England Patriots, and Boston Red Sox, including a veritable shrine to Ted Williams. An outdoor deck upstairs is a terrific place to catch ocean breezes. After dark the place becomes a casual club with live music. ⊠ *40 S. Ocean Blvd. (Rte. A1A),* ☎ *561/278–3364. AE, MC, V.*

$$$–$$$$ ⊞ **Seagate Hotel & Beach Club.** One of the best garden hotels in Palm Beach County, this property offers value, comfort, style, and personal attention. The one-bedroom suite is all chintz and rattan, with many upholstered pieces. All units have at least kitchenettes. The less expensive studios have compact facilities behind foldaway doors, while more expensive units have a separate living room and a larger kitchen. You can dress up and dine in a smart little mahogany- and lattice-trimmed beachfront salon or have the same Continental fare in casual attire in the equally stylish bar. Guests enjoy privileges at the private beach club. ⊠ *400 S. Ocean Blvd., 33483,* ☎ *561/276–2421 or 800/233–3581. 70 1- and 2-bedroom suites. Restaurant, bar, freshwater and saltwater pools, beach. AE, DC, MC, V.*

$$ ⊞ **Harbor House Inn.** These white, two-story 1950s buildings have a privileged location in a quiet residential enclave three blocks east of U.S. 1 and across from the Delray Marina. In addition to two tiny motel rooms, there are 23 efficiencies and one- and two-bedroom apartments with kitchens and a mix of seating generally done in white, beige, tan, and blue. Everything retains a 1950s look, but carpets and upholstery are replaced before they look tired. In a nice touch, matching fabrics are changed by the season: solid blue in summer, blue florals in winter. ⊠ *124 Marine Way, 33483,* ☎ *561/276–4221. 2 rooms, 23 suites. Pool, shuffleboard, coin laundry. MC, V.*

Nightlife and the Arts

THE ARTS

The **Crest Theater** (✉ 51 N. Swinton Ave., ☎ 561/243–7922), in the Old School Square Cultural Arts Center, presents productions in dance, music, and theater.

NIGHTLIFE

The **Back Room Blues Lounge** (✉ 909 W. Atlantic Ave., ☎ 561/243–9110), behind Westside Liquors, has comedy night on Wednesday and live bands Thursday–Saturday. **Boston's on the Beach** (✉ 40 S. Ocean Blvd., ☎ 561/278–3364) presents live reggae music Monday and rock and roll Tuesday–Sunday.

Outdoor Activities and Sports

BIKING

There is a bicycle path in Barwick Park and a special oceanfront lane along Route A1A. **Rich Wagen's Bicycle Shop** (✉ 217 E. Atlantic Ave., ☎ 561/276–4234) rents bikes by the hour or day.

SCUBA DIVING AND SNORKELING

Scuba and snorkeling equipment can be rented from longtime family-owned **Force E** (✉ 660 Linton Blvd., ☎ 561/276–0666). It has PADI affiliation, provides instruction at all levels, and offers charters.

TENNIS

Each winter the **Delray Beach Tennis Center** (✉ 201 W. Atlantic Ave., ☎ 561/243–7380) hosts a professional women's tournament that attracts players like Steffi Graf. The center is also a great place to practice or learn; it has 14 clay courts and five hard courts and offers individual lessons and clinics.

WATERSKIING

Lake Ida Park (✉ 2929 Lake Ida Rd., ☎ 561/964–4420) is an excellent place to water-ski, whether you're a beginner or a veteran. The park has a boat ramp, slalom course, and trick ski course.

Shopping

Street-scaped **Atlantic Avenue** is a showcase for art galleries, shops, and restaurants. In addition to serving lunch and a traditional afternoon tea, the charmingly old-fashioned **Sundy House** (✉ 106 S. Swinton Ave., ☎ 561/272–5678) sells antiques and gifts in the former home of one-time Flagler foreman and first Delray mayor John Shaw Sundy. The structure's beautiful gardens and five gingerbread gables complement Delray's finest wraparound porch.

Boca Raton

🏵 *6 mi south of Delray Beach.*

This upscale town at the south end of Palm Beach County, 30 minutes south of Palm Beach, has a lot in common with its ritzy cousin. For one thing, both reflect the unmistakable architectural presence of Addison Mizner, their principal developer in the mid-1920s. Mizner Park, an important Boca Raton shopping district, bears his name.

Built in 1925 as the headquarters of the Mizner Development Corporation, the structure at **2 East El Camino Real** is a good example of Mizner's characteristic Spanish Revival architectural style, with its wrought-iron grills and handmade tiles.

🕭 Championed by *Beetle Bailey* cartoonist Mort Walker, the **International Museum of Cartoon Art** is the only museum of its kind in the world. It showcases more than 160,000 pieces of art created over two centuries by more than 1,000 artists from more than 50 countries—everything from turn-of-the-century Buster Brown cartoons to the *Road Runner* to Charles Schulz's *Peanuts.* ⊠ *201 Plaza Real,* ☎ *561/391–2200.* ⊠ *$6.* ☉ *Tues.–Sat. 10–6, Sun. noon–6.*

Containing whimsical metal sculptures on the lawn, the **Boca Raton Museum of Art** is a must. The permanent collection includes works by Picasso, Degas, Matisse, Klee, and Modigliani as well as notable pre-Columbian art. ⊠ *801 W. Palmetto Park Rd.,* ☎ *561/392–2500.* ⊠ *$3.*☉ *Weekdays 10–4, weekends noon–4.*

The residential area behind the Boca Raton Museum of Art is known as **Old Floresta.** Developed by Addison Mizner starting in 1925 and landscaped with many varieties of palms and cycads, it includes houses that are mainly in a Mediterranean style, many with upper balconies supported by exposed wood columns.

☾ Hands-on interactive exhibits make the new **Children's Science Explorium** a definite kid pleaser. Children can create their own laser-light shows, explore a 3-D kiosk that illustrates wave motion, and try all kinds of electrifying experiments. There are also wind tunnels, microscopes, and microwave and radiation experiment stations. ⊠ *300 S. Military Trail,* ☎ *561/395–8401.* ⊠ *Free.* ☉ *Weekdays 8 AM–10:30 PM, Sat. 8–5, Sun. 10–5.*

☾ A big draw for kids, the **Gumbo Limbo Nature Center** has four huge saltwater sea tanks and a long boardwalk through dense forest with a 50-ft tower you can climb to overlook the tree canopy. In the spring and early summer, staff members lead nighttime turtle walks to see nesting females come ashore and lay their eggs. ⊠ *1801 N. Ocean Blvd.,* ☎ *561/338–1473.* ⊠ *Donation welcome; turtle tours $3 (tickets must be obtained in advance).* ☉ *Mon.–Sat. 9–4, Sun. noon–4; turtle tours late May–mid-July, Mon.–Thurs. 9 PM–midnight.*

Red Reef Park (⊠ 1400 N. Rte. A1A) offers a beach and playground plus picnic tables and grills. In addition to its beach, **Spanish River Park** (⊠ 3001 N. Rte. A1A) has picnic tables, grills, and a large playground. Popular **South Beach Park** (⊠ 400 N. Rte. A1A) has a concession stand along with its sand and ocean.

The Arts

Caldwell Theatre Company (⊠ 7873 N. Federal Hwy., ☎ 561/241–7432), an Equity regional theater, hosts the multimedia Mizner Festival each April and May and stages four productions each winter. **Jan McArt's Royal Palm Dinner Theatre** (⊠ 303 S.E. Mizner Blvd., Royal Palm Plaza, ☎ 561/392–3755 or 800/841–6765), an Equity theater, presents five or six musicals a year.

Dining and Lodging

$$–$$$$ ✕ **La Vieille Maison.** This French restaurant remains one of the temples of haute cuisine along the Gold Coast. Featuring a stunning courtyard, it occupies a 1920s-era dwelling believed to be an Addison Mizner design. Closets and cubbyholes have been transformed into intimate private dining rooms. Fixed-price, à la carte, Temptations, and Grand menus are available, and all feature Provençal dishes, including *soupe au pistou* (vegetable soup with basil and Parmesan cheese) and venison chop with red currant–pepper sauce and roasted chestnuts. Health-conscious selections are available on all menus. Dessert choices include French sponge cake with lemon cream and strawberries, French apple tart, and a chocolate lover's delight called *L'Indulgence de Chocolat.* ⊠ *770 E. Palmetto Park Rd.,* ☎ *561/391–6701 or 561/737–5677. AE, D, DC, MC, V. Closed early July–Aug.*

FLORIDA'S SEA TURTLES: THE NESTING SEASON

FROM MAY TO OCTOBER it's turtle nesting season all along the Florida coast. During the night female Loggerhead, Kemp's Ridley, and other species of turtles that live way out in the Atlantic or Gulf of Mexico swim to shore. They drag their 100- to 400-pound bodies up the beach, arduously dig a hole with their flippers, drop in about 100 eggs, cover up the hole, and return to sea.

About 60 days later, generally in the middle of the night, the baby turtles hatch. It can take them several days just to make it up to the surface. However, once they burst out of the ground, the little hatchlings must get to the sea as fast as possible, or they will be caught by crabs or birds or become dehydrated by the morning sun.

Instinctively the baby turtles head to the brightest light. It's believed they do this because for millions of years starlight or moonlight reflected on the waves was the brightest light around, and it guided the hatchlings right to water. These days, however, light from buildings along the beach can disorient the baby turtles and cause them to go in the wrong direction. To prevent this, many coastal towns have lighting restrictions during nesting months. These are seriously enforced, and more than one homeowner has been surprised by a police officer at the door requesting that lights be dimmed.

At night volunteers walk the beaches, searching for signs of turtle nests. When they find the telltale scratches in the sand, they cordon off the site, so daytime beach-goers will leave the spots undisturbed. These same volunteers keep an eye on the nests when babies are about to hatch and provide assistance if the hatchlings do get disoriented.

It's a hazardous world for baby turtles. They can die after eating tar balls or plastic garbage or can get eaten by sharks, large fish, or circling birds. Only about one in 1,000 survives to adulthood. Once the baby turtles reach the water, they make their way to warm currents. East coast hatchlings drift into the Gulf Stream and spend several years floating around the Atlantic.

MALES NEVER, EVER return to land, but when females attain maturity, which takes 15–50 years, they come back to shore to lay their eggs. Remarkably, even though they migrate hundreds and even thousands of miles out at sea, most return to the very beach where they were born to deposit their eggs. Sea turtles nest at least twice a season—sometimes as many as 10 times—and then skip a year or two. Each time they nest, they come back to the same tiny stretch of beach. In fact, the more they nest, the more accurate they get, until eventually they return time and again to within a few feet of where they last laid their eggs. Though scientists have studied these incredible navigation skills for some time, they remain a complete mystery. If you want to find out more about sea turtles, check out the website at www.cccturtle.org.

$$–$$$$ ✕ **Ristorante La Finestra.** Belle Epoque lithographs decorate the walls,
★   and though the formal interior is just this side of austere, the cuisine
itself is an extravaganza of taste treats. Start with the Portobello mush-
room with garlic or the roasted red peppers and anchovies. For a main
course try a pasta dish, such as ricotta ravioli with vodka or rigatoni
Bolognese (with ground veal, marinara sauce, and Parmesan). Or
order the scallopini of veal stuffed with crabmeat, lobster, and Gor-
gonzola; the Tuscan fish stew; or the baked jumbo shrimp wrapped in
bacon and stuffed with Swiss cheese. ✉ *171 E. Palmetto Rd.,* ☎ *561/
392–1838. AE, DC, MC, V. No lunch.*

$$–$$$ ✕ **Crab House Seafood Restaurant.** Crowds come here day and night
to dine on fresh Florida seafood and the restaurant's well-known crab
specials. Landlubbers will find chicken, steaks, and salads to satisfy
their fancies. There's a nautical theme to the decor, a wide deck for
outside dining, a raw bar, and a cocktail lounge. ✉ *6909 S.W. 18th
St.,* ☎ *561/750–0498. AE, D, MC, V.*

$$–$$$ ✕ **Mark's at the Park.** Exotic cars pour into valet parking at this lat-
est Mark Militello creation, where eating is only half the fun. Decor
constitutes a whimsical 21st-century interpretation of retro and art deco.
On the outside terrace, furnishings are metal, but wood and fabric reign
indoors, where asymmetrical columns and banquettes with immense
backs and fabric inserts create cozy but noisy dining spaces. If you can
tear your eyes away to focus on the dazzling menu, consider the
chopped Sicilian salad, calamari cakes, or pizza with Maine lobster or
onion, bacon, gorgonzola, and walnuts. For an entrée, try the fusilli
with a roasted eggplant and tomato ragout or the braised lamb shank
with almond and raisin couscous. Desserts are deliciously old-fashioned.
✉ *344 Plaza Real, Mizner Park,* ☎ *561/395–0770. AE, D, MC, V.*

$$–$$$ ✕ **Uncle Tai's.** People flock here for some of the best Szechuan cuisine
on Florida's east coast. House specialties include sliced duck with
snow peas and water chestnuts in a tangy plum sauce, sliced fillet of
snapper stir-fried and sautéed in a rice-wine sauce, and Uncle Tai's fa-
mous Orange Beef Delight—flank steak stir-fried until crispy and then
sautéed with pepper sauce, garlic, and orange peel. Szechuan-style
cooking is extremely hot and spicy, so remember to specify if you want
the chef to go easy on you. ✉ *5250 Town Center Circle,* ☎ *561/368–
8806. AE, MC, V. No lunch.*

$ ✕ **Tom's Place.** "This place is a blessing from God," says the sign over
★   the fireplace, and after braving the long lines and sampling the superb
menu, you will add, "Amen!" That's in between mouthfuls of Tom
Wright's soul food—sauce-slathered ribs, pork chop sandwiches,
chicken cooked in peppery mustard sauce over hickory and oak, sweet
potato pie. Buy a bottle or two of Tom's barbecue sauce ($2.25 a pint)
just as Lou Rawls, Ben Vereen, Sugar Ray Leonard, and a rush of NFL
players have before you. ✉ *7251 N. Federal Hwy.,* ☎ *561/997–0920.
MC, V. Closed Sun., also Mon. May–mid-Nov.*

$$$$ 🏨 **Boca Raton Resort & Club.** Addison Mizner built the Mediterranean-
★   style Cloister Inn here in 1926; it has been added to several times since
to create this sprawling resort with a beach accessible by shuttle.
Rooms in the Cloister are small and warmly traditional; those in the
27-story Tower are in a similar style but larger, while rooms in the Beach
Club are light, airy, and contemporary. Golf villas are, naturally, near
the golf course. The concierge staff speaks at least 12 languages. Win-
ter rates don't include meals, but you can pay extra for MAP (includ-
ing breakfast and dinner). Rooms have been recently refurbished, the
main golf course has been redesigned, and there's a new $10 million
Tennis & Fitness Center. ✉ *501 E. Camino Real, 33431-0825,* ☎ *561/
395–3000 or 800/327–0101,* 🖷 *561/447–5888. 840 rooms, 63 suites,
60 golf villas. 7 restaurants, 3 bars, 5 pools, 36 holes of golf, 40 ten-*

nis courts, basketball, 3 health clubs, beach, boating, fishing. AE, DC, MC, V.

$$ 🏨 **Inn at Boca Teeca.** If golf is your game, this is an excellent place to stay. Inn guests can play the outstanding golf course at the adjoining Boca Teeca Country Club, otherwise available only to club members. Guest rooms are in a three-story building, and most have a patio or balcony. Although the inn is nearly 30 years old, the interior was recently refurbished, and rooms are small but comfortable and contemporary. ✉ 5800 N.W. 2nd Ave., 33487, ☎ 561/994–0400, FAX 561/998–8279. 46 rooms. Restaurant, 27 holes of golf, 6 tennis courts. AE, DC, MC, V.

$$ 🏨 **Ocean Lodge.** The price is right at this small motel because instead of being right on the beach, it's just across the street. Rooms are in a simple two-story building, and all have refrigerators. Eleven rooms also have small kitchenettes with a two-burner stove top. Restaurants are within easy walking distance. ✉ 531 N. Ocean Blvd., 33432, ☎ 561/395–7772, FAX 561/395–0554. 18 rooms. Pool, coin laundry. AE, DC, MC, V.

Outdoor Activities and Sports

BIKING

Plenty of bike trails and quiet streets make for pleasant pedaling in the area; for current information contact the city of Boca Raton's **Bicycle Coordinator** (☎ 561/393–7910).

BOATING

If you ever wanted the thrill of blasting across the water at up to 80 mph, check out **Air and Sea Charters** (✉ 490 E. Palmetto Park Rd., Suite 330, ☎ 561/368–3566). For $80 per person (four-person minimum), you can spend a wild-eyed hour holding on to your life vest aboard an 800-horsepower offshore racing boat. For a more leisurely trip go for Air and Sea's 55-ft catamaran or 45-ft sailboat.

GOLF

Two championship courses and golf programs run by Dave Pelz and Nicklaus/Flick are available at **Boca Raton Resort & Club** (✉ 501 E. Camino Real, ☎ 561/395–3000 or 800/327–0101).

POLO

Royal Palm Polo Sports Club, founded in 1959 by Oklahoma oilman John T. Oxley and now home to the $100,000 International Gold Cup Tournament, has seven polo fields within two stadiums. ✉ 6300 Old Clint Moore Rd., ☎ 561/994–1876. 🎟 $6, box seats $10–$25. ☉ Games Jan.–Apr., Sun. 1 and 3.

SCUBA DIVING AND SNORKELING

Information about dive trips, as well as rental scuba and snorkeling equipment, can be obtained at **Force E** (✉ 877 E. Palmetto Park Rd., ☎ 561/368–0555).

Shopping

Mizner Park (✉ Federal Hwy. between Palmetto Park Rd. and Glades Rd.) is a distinctive 30-acre shopping village with apartments and town houses among its gardenlike spaces. Some three dozen retail stores include the excellent Liberties Fine Books & Music, a Jacobson's specialty department store, seven restaurants with sidewalk cafés, and 12 movie screens. **Town Center** (✉ 6000 W. Glades Rd.) combines a business park with ritzy shopping and great dining. Major retailers include Bloomingdale's, Burdines, Lord & Taylor, Saks Fifth Avenue, and Sears—201 stores and restaurants in all.

THE TREASURE COAST

From south to north, the Treasure Coast encompasses the top end of Palm Beach County plus Martin, St. Lucie, and Indian River counties. Though dotted with towns, this section of coastline is one of Florida's quietest. Most towns are small and laid-back, and there's lots of undeveloped land between them. Vero is the region's most sophisticated town and the one place you'll find clusters of fine-dining establishments and upscale shops. The beaches along here are sought out by nesting sea turtles; you can join locally organized watches, which go out to view the turtles laying their eggs in the sand between late April and August. Remember that you mustn't touch or disturb the turtles or their nests in any way.

Palm Beach Shores

28   *7 mi north of Palm Beach.*

This residential town rimmed by mom-and-pop motels is at the southern tip of Singer Island, across Lake Worth Inlet from Palm Beach. To get between the two, however, you must cross over to the mainland before returning to the beach. The main attraction of this unpretentious middle-class community is its affordable beachfront lodging and its proximity to several nature parks.

Peanut Island, a 79-acre island in the Intracoastal Waterway between Palm Beach Shores and Riviera Beach, is a brand-new recreational park, opened in 1999. The $2.75 million project includes a 20-ft-wide walking path surrounding the entire island, a 19-slip boat dock, a 170-ft T-shape fishing pier, six picnic pavilions, a visitor center, and 20 overnight campsites. To get to the island, you'll have to drive your own boat or catch a water taxi (call for schedules and pickup locations). ✉ *6500 Peanut Island Rd., Riviera Beach,* ☎ *561/966–6600.* ☞ *Free.* ☼ *Sunrise–sunset for noncampers.*

OFF THE   **JOHN D. MACARTHUR BEACH STATE PARK –** Here you will find almost 2
BEATEN PATH   mi of beach, good fishing and shelling, and one of the finest examples of subtropical coastal habitat remaining in southeast Florida. To learn about what you see, take an interpretive walk to a mangrove estuary along the upper reaches of Lake Worth. Or visit the **William T. Kirby Nature Center** (☎ 561/624–6952), open Wednesday–Monday from 9 to 5, which has exhibits on the coastal environment. ✉ *10900 Rte. A1A, North Palm Beach,* ☎ *561/624–6950.* ☞ *$3.25 per vehicle with up to 8 people.* ☼ *8–sunset.*

LOGGERHEAD PARK MARINE LIFE CENTER OF JUNO BEACH – Established by Eleanor N. Fletcher, "the turtle lady of Juno Beach," the center focuses on the natural history of sea turtles. Also on view are displays of coastal natural history, sharks, whales, and shells. ✉ *1200 U.S. 1 (entrance on west side of park), Juno Beach,* ☎ *561/627–8280.* ☞ *Donation welcome.* ☼ *Tues.–Sat. 10–4, Sun. noon–3.*

Dining and Lodging

$$ ✕ **The Galley.** Don't overlook this open-air waterfront restaurant. After a hot day of mansion gawking or beach bumming, there's no better place to chill out. The blender seems to run nonstop, churning out tropical drinks like piña coladas and Goombay Smashes. Old Florida favorites like grouper and conch chowder are mainstays, but there are also a few highbrow entrées (this is Palm Beach County, after all), such as lobster tail or baby sea scallops sautéed in garlic and lemon butter.

This is also a good spot for breakfast. ✉ *98 Lake Dr.,* ☎ *561/848–1492. MC, V. No dinner Mon.–Tues.*

$$ 🏨 **Sailfish Marina.** This long-established one-story motel has a marina
★ with 94 deep-water slips and 15 rooms and efficiencies that open to landscaped grounds. None is directly on the water, but Units 9–11 have ocean views across the blacktop drive. Rooms have peaked ceilings, carpeting, king-size or twin beds, and stall showers; many have ceiling fans. From the seawall you can see fish through the clear inlet water. The motel's staff is informed and helpful, and the proprietors are as promotional as they are friendly. ✉ *98 Lake Dr., 33404,* ☎ *561/844–1724 or 800/446–4577,* 📠 *561/848–9684. 15 units. Restaurant, bar, grocery, pool, dock. AE, MC, V.*

Palm Beach Gardens

㉙ *5 mi north of West Palm Beach.*

About 15 minutes northwest of Palm Beach is this relaxed, upscale residential community widely known for its high-profile golf complex, the PGA National Resort & Spa. Although the town is not on the beach, the ocean is just a 15-minute drive away.

Dining and Lodging

$$–$$$ ✗ **Arezzo.** The pungent smell of fresh garlic tips you off that the food's
★ the thing at this outstanding Tuscan grill at the PGA National Resort & Spa. In this unusually relaxed, upscale resort setting, you can dine in shorts or in jacket and tie. Families are attracted by the affordable prices (as well as the food), so romantics might be tempted to pass Arezzo up. Their loss. Dishes include the usual variety of chicken, veal, fish, and steaks, but there are a dozen pastas, including rigatoni Bolognese (a specialty), and almost as many pizzas. The decor, too, has the right idea: an herb garden in the center of the room, slate floors, upholstered banquettes to satisfy the upscale mood, and butcher paper over yellow table covers to establish the light side. ✉ *400 Ave. of the Champions,* ☎ *561/627–2000. AE, MC, V. Closed Mon. No lunch.*

$$ ✗ **River House.** People keep returning to this waterfront restaurant for the large portions of straightforward American fare; the big salad bar and fresh, slice-it-yourself breads; the competent service; and, thanks to the animated buzz of a rewarded local clientele, the feeling that you've come to the right place. Choices include seafood (always with a daily catch), steaks, chops, and seafood-steak combo platters. Booths and freestanding tables are surrounded by lots of blond wood, high ceilings, and nautical art under glass. The wait on Saturday night in season can be 45 minutes. Reserve one of the 20 upstairs tables, available weekends only; the upstairs is a little more formal and doesn't have a salad bar (bread comes from below), but it does possess a cathedral ceiling. ✉ *2373 PGA Blvd.,* ☎ *561/694–1188. AE, MC, V. No lunch.*

$$$$ 🏨 **PGA National Resort & Spa.** Outstanding mission-style rooms are decorated in deep, almost somber florals, and the rest of the resort is equally richly detailed, from lavish landscaping to limitless sports facilities to excellent dining. The spa is housed in a building styled after a Mediterranean fishing village. Its six outdoor therapy pools, dubbed "Waters of the World," are joined by a collection of imported mineral salt pools; there are 22 private treatments. Golf courses and croquet courts are adorned with 25,000 flowering plants amid a 240-acre nature preserve. Two-bedroom, two-bath cottages with fully equipped kitchens and no-smoking rooms are available, too. ✉ *400 Ave. of the Champions, 33418,* ☎ *561/627–2000 or 800/633–9150. 279 rooms, 60 suites, 80 cottages. 4 restaurants, 2 bars, lake, pool, hot tubs,*

saunas, spa, 90 holes of golf, 19 tennis courts, croquet, racquetball, boating. AE, D, DC, MC, V.

Nightlife

Irish Times (⌧ 9920 Alternate A1A, Promenade Shopping Plaza, ☎ 561/624–1504) is a four-leaf-clover find, featuring a microbrewery. There are live music and live Irish acts Wednesday–Saturday.

Outdoor Activities and Sports

AUTO RACING

Weekly ¼-mi drag racing; monthly 2¼-mi, 10-turn road racing; and monthly AMA motorcycle road racing take place year-round at the **Moroso Motorsports Park** (⌧ 17047 Beeline Hwy., ☎ 561/622–1400).

GOLF

PGA National Resort & Spa (⌧ 1000 Ave. of the Champions, ☎ 561/627–1800) offers a reputedly tough 90 holes.

Shopping

The Gardens mall (⌧ 3101 PGA Blvd.) contains the standards if you want to make sure you're not missing out on anything at home: Bloomingdale's, Burdines, Macy's, Saks Fifth Avenue, and Sears.

Jupiter

30 *12 mi north of Palm Beach Shores.*

This little town is on one of the few parts of the east coast of Florida that do not have an island in front of them. Beaches here are part of the mainland, and Route A1A runs for almost 4 mi along the beachfront dunes.

Take a look at how life once was in the **Dubois Home,** a modest pioneer home dating from 1898. Sitting atop an ancient Jeaga Indian mound 20 ft high and looking onto Jupiter Inlet, it features Cape Cod as well as Cracker design. Even if you arrive when the house is closed, surrounding **Dubois Park** is worth the visit for its lovely beaches and swimming lagoons. ⌧ *Dubois Rd.,* ☎ *no phone.* ⊡ *Donation welcome.* ☉ *Wed. 1–4.*

Permanent exhibits at the **Florida History Center and Museum** review not only modern-day development along the Loxahatchee River but also shipwrecks, railroads, and Seminole, steamboat-era, and pioneer history. ⌧ *805 N. U.S. 1, Burt Reynolds Park,* ☎ *561/747–6639.* ⊡ *$5.* ☉ *Tues.–Fri. 10–4, weekends noon–5.*

The **Jupiter Inlet Lighthouse,** a redbrick Coast Guard navigational beacon designed by Civil War hero General George Meade, has operated here since 1860. Tours of the 105-ft-tall local landmark are given every half hour, and there is also a small museum. Those familiar with the lighthouse may notice a significant change, courtesy of an $858,000 federal grant: the lighthouse is being transformed from bright red to natural brick, which is how it looked from 1860 to 1918. ⌧ *Off U.S. 1,* ☎ *561/747–8380.* ⊡ *Tour $5.* ☉ *Sun.–Wed. 10–4, last tour 3:15.*

Carlin Park (⌧ 400 Rte. A1A) provides beachfront picnic pavilions, hiking trails, a baseball diamond, playground, six tennis courts, fishing sites, and, naturally, a beach. The Park Galley, serving snacks and burgers, is usually open daily 9–5.

Dining and Lodging

$$–$$$$ ✕ **Charley's Crab.** The grand view across the Jupiter River complements
★   the soaring ceiling and striking interior architecture of this marina-side restaurant. You'll have great water views whether you choose to dine

inside or out, and if you eat after dark, you can watch the searching beam of the historic Jupiter Inlet Lighthouse. Come here for expertly prepared seafood, including outstanding pasta choices: *pagliara* with scallops, fish, shrimp, mussels, spinach, garlic, and olive oil; fettuccine *verde* with lobster, sun-dried tomatoes, fresh basil, and goat cheese; and shrimp and tortellini Boursin with cream sauce and tomatoes. Consider also such fresh fish as black grouper, Florida pompano, red snapper, or Gulf Stream yellowfin tuna. Other branches of Charley's are in Boca Raton, Deerfield Beach, Fort Lauderdale, Palm Beach, and Stuart. ⊠ *1000 N. U.S. 1,* ☎ *561/744–4710. AE, D, DC, MC, V.*

$$–$$$ ✕ **Sinclairs Ocean Grill & Rotisserie.** This popular spot in the Jupiter Beach Resort has tall French doors that look out to the pool and tropical greenery. The menu features a daily selection of fresh locally caught fish, such as cashew-encrusted Florida grouper, Cajun-spiced tuna, and mahimahi with pistachio sauce. Landlubbers can choose thick juicy steaks (filet mignon is the house specialty) and a variety of chicken and veal dishes. Sunday brunch is a big draw. ⊠ *5 N. Rte. A1A,* ☎ *561/ 746–2551. AE, MC, V.*

$ ✕ **Lighthouse Restaurant.** Low prices match the plain decor in this coffee shop–style building, but the menu and cuisine are a delightful surprise. You can get chicken breast stuffed with sausage and fresh vegetables, burgundy beef stew, and king crab cakes, and a full-time pastry chef is at work, too. The same people-pleasing formula has been employed since 1936: round-the-clock service (except 10 PM Sunday– 6 AM Monday) and a menu that changes daily to take advantage of the best market buys. Those looking for something less stick-to-the-ribs can order one of the affordable "lite dinners." ⊠ *1510 U.S. 1,* ☎ *561/746–4811. D, DC, MC, V.*

$$$$ 🏨 **Jupiter Beach Resort.** This unpretentious resort is popular with families thanks to plentiful activities and a casual atmosphere. Rooms, which are painted in pastel colors and decorated in floral prints and rattan, are in an eight-story tower. Most rooms have balconies, and higher rooms have excellent ocean views. Taking further advantage of its location, the resort offers turtle watches in season, during which you can see newly hatched turtles make their way to the water for the first time. Snorkeling and scuba equipment and Jet Skis are available for rent, and the restaurant is worth staying in for. ⊠ *5 N. Rte. A1A, 33477,* ☎ *561/746–2511 or 800/228–8810,* 𝔽𝔸𝕏 *561/747–3304. 187 rooms, 28 suites. Restaurant, 2 bars, pool, tennis court, beach, dive shop, recreation room, children's programs, coin laundry, business services. AE, D, MC, V.*

Outdoor Activities and Sports

BASEBALL
Both the **St. Louis Cardinals and Montreal Expos** (⊠ 4751 Main St., ☎ 561/684–6801) train at the $28 million Roger Dean Stadium, which has seating for 7,000 fans and 12 practice fields.

CANOEING
Canoe Outfitters of Florida (⊠ 4100 W. Indiantown Rd., ☎ 561/746– 7053) runs trips along 8 mi of the Loxahatchee River, Florida's only designated Wild and Scenic River. Canoe rental for two people, with drop-off and pickup, costs $30 plus tax. You can also just paddle around for an hour.

GOLF
The **Golf Club of Jupiter at Indian Creek** (⊠ 1800 Central Blvd., ☎ 561/747–6262) offers 18 holes of varying difficulty. **Jupiter Dunes Golf Club** (⊠ 401 Rte. A1A, ☎ 561/746–6654) features 18 holes and a putting green.

Jupiter Island and Hobe Sound

31 *5 mi north of Jupiter.*

Northeast across the Jupiter Inlet from Jupiter is the southern tip of Jupiter Island, which includes a carefully planned community of the same name. Here estates often retreat from the road behind screens of vegetation, while at the north end of the island, turtles come to nest in a wildlife refuge. To the west, on the mainland, is the little community of Hobe Sound.

Within **Blowing Rocks Preserve,** a 73-acre Nature Conservancy holding, you'll find plant communities native to beachfront dune, coastal strand (the landward side of the dunes), mangrove, and hammock (tropical hardwood forests). The best time to visit is when high tides and strong offshore winds coincide, causing the sea to blow spectacularly through holes in the eroded outcropping. Park in the lot; police ticket cars parked along the road. ⊠ *Rte. 707, Jupiter Island,* ☎ *561/744–6668.* ⊑ *$3 donation.* ☉ *Daily 6–5.*

The **Hobe Sound National Wildlife Refuge** actually consists of two tracts: 232 acres of sand pine and scrub oak forest in Hobe Sound and 735 acres of coastal sand dune and mangrove swamp on Jupiter Island. Trails are open to the public in both places. Turtles nest and shells wash ashore on the 3½-mi beach, which has been severely eroded by winter high tides and strong winds. ⊠ *13640 S.E. Federal Hwy., Hobe Sound,* ☎ *561/546–6141;* ⊠ *Beach Rd. off Rte. 707, Jupiter Island.* ⊑ *$5 per vehicle.* ☉ *Daily sunrise–sunset.*

Though on the Hobe Sound National Wildlife Refuge, the appealing ☾ **Hobe Sound Nature Center** is an independent organization. Its museum, which has baby alligators, baby crocodiles, and a scary-looking tarantula, is a child's delight. Interpretive exhibits focus on the environment, and a ½-mi trail winds through a forest of sand pine and scrub oak—one of Florida's most unusual and endangered plant communities. A classroom program on environmental issues is for preschool-age children to adults. ⊠ *13640 S.E. Federal Hwy., Hobe Sound,* ☎ *561/546–2067.* ⊑ *Free.* ☉ *Trail daily sunrise–sunset; nature center weekdays 9–11 and 1–3, call for Sat. hrs, group tours by appointment.*

Once you've gotten to the **Jonathan Dickinson State Park,** follow signs to Hobe Mountain. An ancient dune topped with a tower, it yields a panoramic view across the park's 10,285 acres of varied terrain, as well as the Intracoastal Waterway. The Loxahatchee River, part of the federal government's Wild and Scenic Rivers program, cuts through the park and harbors manatees in winter and alligators year-round. Two-hour boat tours of the river leave four times daily. Among amenities here are bicycle and hiking trails, a campground, and a snack bar. ⊠ *16450 S.E. Federal Hwy., Hobe Sound,* ☎ *561/546–2771.* ⊑ *$3.25 per vehicle with up to 8 people, boat tours $10.* ☉ *Daily 8–sunset.*

Outdoor Activities and Sports

Jonathan Dickinson's River Tours (⊠ Jonathan Dickinson State Park, ☎ 561/746–1466) rents canoes for use around the park.

Stuart

32 *7 mi north of Hobe Sound.*

This compact little town on a peninsula that juts out into the St. Lucie River has a remarkable amount of river shoreline for its size as well as a charming historic district. The ocean is about 5 mi east.

★ Strict architectural and zoning standards guide civic renewal projects in **historic downtown Stuart,** which now claims eight antiques shops, six restaurants, and more than 50 specialty shops within a two-block area. The old courthouse has become the **Cultural Court House Center** (⊠ 80 E. Ocean Blvd., ☎ 561/288–2542), which features art exhibits. The George W. Parks General Store is now the **Stuart Heritage Museum** (⊠ 101 S.W. Flagler Ave., ☎ 561/220–4600). On the National Register of Historic Places, the **Lyric Theatre** (⊠ 59 S.W. Flagler Ave., ☎ 561/220–1942) has been revived for performing and community events; a gazebo features free music performances. For information on downtown, contact the **Stuart Main Street Office** (⊠ 151 S.W. Flagler Ave., 34994, ☎ 561/286–2848).

Dining and Lodging

$$ ✕ **The Ashley.** Although plants hang from the ceiling and art decorates
★ the walls, this restaurant still has elements of the old bank that was robbed three times early in the century by the Ashley Gang (hence the name). The big outdoor mural in the French Impressionist style was paid for by downtown revivalists, whose names are duly inscribed on wall plaques inside. The Continental menu appeals, with lots of salads, fresh fish, and pastas. Crowds head to the lounge for a popular happy hour. ⊠ *61 S.W. Osceola St.,* ☎ *561/221–9476. AE, MC, V. Closed Mon. in off-season.*

$$ ✕ **Jolly Sailor Pub.** In an old historic-district bank building, this eatery is owned by a 27-year British Merchant Navy veteran, which may account for the endless ship paraphernalia. A veritable Cunard museum, it has a model of the *Britannia,* prints of 19th-century side-wheelers, and a big bar painting of the *QE2.* There are a wonderful brass-railed wood bar, a dartboard, and such pub grub as fish-and-chips, cottage pie, and bangers and mash, with Guinness and Double Diamond ales on tap. You can also get hamburgers and salads. ⊠ *1 S.W. Osceola St.,* ☎ *561/221–1111. AE, MC, V.*

$$ 🛏 **The Homeplace.** The house was built in 1913 by pioneer Sam Matthews, who contracted much of the early town construction for railroad developer Henry Flagler. Hardwood floors have been restored, and rooms are individually and quaintly decorated with antiques. The fern-filled dining room and Victorian parlor, full of cushioned wicker, overlook a pool, heated spa, and patio. A full breakfast is included. ⊠ *501 Akron Ave., 34994,* ☎ *561/220–9148. 4 rooms. Pool, hot tub. MC, V.*

$–$$$ 🛏 **HarborFront.** On a quiet site that slopes to the St. Lucie River, this
★ B&B combines an unusual mix of accommodations and imaginative extras, including picnic baskets and conciergelike custom planning. Units are cozy and eclectic, ranging from a spacious chintz-covered suite to a cozy apartment with full kitchen, from rooms that are tweedy and dark to those that are airy and bright with a private deck. Furnishings mix wicker and antiques. From hammocks in the yard you can watch pelicans and herons, or take a full- or half-day sail on the 33-ft sailboat that's tied up to the dock. ⊠ *310 Atlanta Ave., 34994,* ☎ *561/ 288–7289. 6 rooms, 2 suites, 1 cottage, 2 apartments. Hot tub, dock, boating. MC, V.*

Outdoor Activities and Sports

Deep-sea charters are available at the **Sailfish Marina** (⊠ 3565 S.E. St. Lucie Blvd., ☎ 561/283–1122).

Shopping

More than 60 restaurants and shops featuring antiques, art, and fashions have opened along **Osceola Street** in the restored downtown area, with hardly a vacancy.

Hutchinson Island (Jensen Beach)

33 *5 mi northeast of Stuart.*

Unusual care limits development here and prevents the commercial crowding found to the north and south, although there are some high-rises here and there along the shore. The small town of Jensen Beach, part of which is in the central part of the island, actually stretches across both sides of the Indian River. Citrus farmers and fishermen still play a big role in the community, giving the area a down-to-earth feel. Its most notable population is that of the sea turtles; between late April and August more than 600 turtles come to nest along the town's Atlantic beach.

Built in 1875, the **House of Refuge Museum** is the only remaining building of nine such structures erected by the U.S. Life Saving Service (a predecessor of the Coast Guard) to aid stranded sailors. Exhibits include antique lifesaving equipment, maps, artifacts from nearby wrecks, and boat-making tools. ⊠ *301 S.E. Mac Blvd.,* ☎ *561/225–1875.* ☞ *$2.* ☉ *Tues.–Sun. 11–4.*

Run by the Florida Oceanographic Society, the **Coastal Science Center** consists of a coastal hardwood hammock and mangrove forest. Expansion has yielded a visitor center, a science center with interpretive exhibits on coastal science and environmental issues, and a ½-mi interpretive boardwalk. Guided nature walks are offered. ⊠ *890 N.E. Ocean Blvd.,* ☎ *561/225–0505.* ☞ *$3.50.* ☉ *Mon.–Sat. 10–5, nature walks Mon.–Sat. 10:30 and by request.*

The pastel-pink **Elliott Museum** was built in 1961 in honor of Sterling Elliott, inventor of an early automated addressing machine and a four-wheel cycle. The museum features antique automobiles, dolls and toys, and fixtures from an early general store, blacksmith shop, and apothecary shop. ⊠ *825 N.E. Ocean Blvd.,* ☎ *561/225–1961.* ☞ *$6.* ☉ *Daily 10–4.*

Bathtub Beach (⊠ MacArthur Blvd. off Rte. A1A), at the north end of the Indian River Plantation, is ideal for children because the waters are shallow for about 300 ft offshore and usually calm. At low tide bathers can walk to the reef. Facilities include rest rooms and showers.

Dining and Lodging

$$–$$$ ✕ **11 Maple Street.** This 16-table restaurant is as good as it gets on
★ the Treasure Coast. Run by Margee and Mike Perrin, it offers a Continental menu that changes nightly. The soft recorded jazz and the earnest, friendly staff satisfy as fully as the brilliant food served in ample portions. Appetizers might include walnut bread with melted fontina cheese or sautéed conch with balsamic vinegar; among entrées are salmon with leeks, lobster, and blue-crab cake, and porcini mushroom risotto. For dessert look out for cherry *clafouti* (like a bread pudding) and white-chocolate custard with blackberry sauce. ⊠ *3224 Maple Ave.,* ☎ *561/334–7714. Reservations essential. MC, V. Closed Mon.–Tues. No lunch.*

$$–$$$ ✕ **Scalawags.** The look is plantation tropical—coach lanterns, gingerbread, wicker, slow-motion paddle fans—but the top-notch buffets are aimed at today's resort guests. Standouts are the all-you-can-eat Wednesday evening Seafood Extravaganza, with jumbo shrimp, Alaskan crab legs, clams on the half shell, marinated salmon, and fresh catch. A regular menu with a big selection of fish, shellfish, and grills plus a big salad bar is also offered. The main dining room in this second-floor restaurant at the Indian River Plantation Marriott Beach Resort overlooks the Indian River; there is also a private 20-seat wine room and a terrace that looks out on the marina. ⊠ *555 N.E. Ocean Blvd.,* ☎ *561/225–6818. AE, DC, MC, V.*

$$ ✕ **Conchy Joe's.** This classic Florida stilt house full of antique fish mounts, gator hides, and snakeskins dates from the late 1920s—but Conchy Joe's, like a hermit crab sliding into a new shell, only moved up from West Palm Beach in 1983. Under a huge Seminole-built *chickee* (raised wood platform) with a palm through the roof, you find a supercasual atmosphere and the freshest Florida seafood from a menu that changes daily. Staples, however, are the grouper marsala, broiled sea scallop, and fried cracked conch. Try the rum drinks with names like Goombay Smash and Bahama Mama, while listening to steel-band calypso or reggae Wednesday–Sunday. Happy hour is 3–6 daily and during all NFL games. ⊠ *3945 N. Indian River Dr.,* ☎ *561/334–1130. AE, D, MC, V.*

$ ✕ **The Emporium.** Indian River Plantation Marriott Beach Resort's coffee shop is an old-fashioned soda fountain and grill that also serves hearty breakfasts. Specialties include eggs Benedict, omelets, deli sandwiches, and salads. ⊠ *555 N.E. Ocean Blvd.,* ☎ *561/225–3700. AE, DC, MC, V.*

$$$–$$$$ ▥ **Indian River Plantation Marriott Beach Resort.** With a wealth of recreational activities and facilities as well as many restaurants and bars, this 200-acre sprawling yet self-contained resort is an excellent choice for families. Reception, some of the restaurants, and many rooms are in three yellow four-story buildings that form an open courtyard with a large swimming pool. Additional rooms and apartments with kitchens are in numerous other buildings spread around the property. Some overlook the Intracoastal Waterway and the resort's 77-slip marina, while other rooms look out to the ocean or onto tropical gardens. Complimentary tram service runs to key points around the property day and night. ⊠ *555 N.E. Ocean Blvd., Hutchinson Island, Stuart 34996,* ☎ *561/225–3700 or 800/775–5936. 299 rooms, 27 suites, 150 condominiums. 5 restaurants, 4 bars, 4 pools, spa, 18-hole golf course, 13 tennis courts, beach, docks, boating, children's program. AE, DC, MC, V.*

$$–$$$ ▥ **Hutchinson Inn.** Sandwiched among the high-rises, this modest and affordable two-story motel from the mid-1970s has the feel of a B&B thanks to pretty canopies at the entrance and management's friendly attitude. An expanded Continental breakfast is served in the well-appointed lobby or on little tables outside, and you can borrow a book or a stack of magazines to take to your room, where homemade cookies are delivered in the evenings. On Saturday there's a noon barbecue. Motel-style rooms range from small but comfortable to fully equipped efficiencies and seafront suites with private balconies. ⊠ *9750 S. Ocean Dr., 34957,* ☎ *561/229–2000,* ℻ *561/229–8875. 19 rooms, 2 suites. Pool, tennis court, beach. MC, V.* ·

Outdoor Activities and Sports

BASEBALL

The **New York Mets** (⊠ 525 N.W. Peacock Blvd., Port St. Lucie, ☎ 561/871–2115) train at the St. Lucie County Sport Complex.

GOLF

Indian River Plantation Marriott Beach Resort (⊠ 555 N.E. Ocean Blvd., ☎ 561/225–3700 or 800/444–3389) sports 18 holes. The PGA-operated **PGA Golf Club at the Reserve** (⊠ 1916 Perfect Dr., Port St. Lucie, ☎ 407/467–1300 or 800/800–4653) is a public facility scheduled to open its third 18-hole course by early 2000.

Fort Pierce

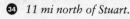 *11 mi north of Stuart.*

This community, about an hour north of Palm Beach, has a distinctive rural feel, focusing on ranching and citrus farming rather than tourism. It has several worthwhile stops for visitors, including those easily seen while following Route 707.

Once a reservoir, 550-acre **Savannahs Recreation Area** has been returned to its natural state. Today the semiwilderness has campsites, a petting zoo, botanical garden, boat ramps, and trails. ⊠ *1400 E. Midway Rd.,* ☎ *561/464–7855.* ☜ *$1 per vehicle.* ☉ *Daily 8–6.*

At the **Heathcote Botanical Gardens,** a self-guided tour takes in a palm walk, Japanese garden, and subtropical foliage. ⊠ *210 Savannah Rd.,* ☎ *561/464–4672.* ☜ *$2.50.* ☉ *Tues.–Sat. 9–5, also Sun. 1–5 Nov.–Apr.*

As the home of the Treasure Coast Art Association, the **A. E. "Bean" Backus Gallery** displays the works of one of Florida's foremost landscape artists. The gallery also mounts changing exhibits and offers exceptional buys on work by local artists. ⊠ *500 N. Indian River Dr.,* ☎ *561/465–0630.* ☜ *Donation welcome.* ☉ *Tues.–Sun. 1–5.*

Highlights at the **St. Lucie County Historical Museum** include historic photos, early 20th-century memorabilia, vintage farm tools, a restored 1919 American La France fire engine, replicas of a general store and the old Fort Pierce railroad station, and the restored 1905 Gardner House. ⊠ *414 Seaway Dr.,* ☎ *561/462–1795.* ☜ *$3.* ☉ *Tues.–Sat. 10–4, Sun. noon–4.*

The 340-acre **Fort Pierce Inlet State Recreation Area** contains sand dunes and a coastal hammock. The park offers swimming, surfing, picnicking, hiking, and walking along a self-guided nature trail. ⊠ *905 Shorewinds Dr.,* ☎ *561/468–3985.* ☜ *$3.25 per vehicle with up to 8 people.* ☉ *Daily 8–sunset.*

The **UDT-Seal Museum** commemorates the site where more than 3,000 navy frogmen trained during World War II. Weapons and equipment are on view, and exhibits depict the history of the UDTs (Underwater Demolition Teams). Numerous patrol boats and vehicles are displayed outdoors. ⊠ *3300 N. Rte. A1A,* ☎ *561/595–5845.* ☜ *$3.25.* ☉ *Mon.–Sat. 10–4, Sun. noon–4.*

Accessible only by footbridge, the **Jack Island Wildlife Refuge** contains 4⅓ mi of trails. The 1½-mi Marsh Rabbit Trail across the island traverses a mangrove swamp to a 30-ft observation tower overlooking the Indian River. ⊠ *Rte. A1A,* ☎ *561/468–3985.* ☜ *Free.* ☉ *Daily 8–sunset.*

The **Harbor Branch Oceanographic Institution** is an internationally recognized diversified research and teaching facility that offers a glimpse into the high-tech world of marine research. Its fleet of research vessels—particularly its two submersibles—operates around the world for NASA, NOAA, and NATO, among other contractors. Visitors can take a 90-minute tour of the 500-acre facility, including aquariums of sea life indigenous to the Indian River Lagoon, exhibits of marine technology, and other learning facilities. There are also lifelike and whimsical bronze sculptures created by founder J. Seward Johnson, Jr., and a gift shop with imaginative sea-related items. ⊠ *5600 Old Dixie Hwy.,* ☎ *561/465–2400.* ☜ *$6.* ☉ *Tours Mon.–Sat. 10, noon, and 2.*

Dining and Lodging

$–$$ ✕ **Mangrove Mattie's.** Since its opening in the late 1980s, this upscale but rustic spot on Fort Pierce Inlet has provided dazzling waterfront views and imaginative nautical decor with delicious seafood. Dine outdoors on the terrace or inside in the cool air-conditioning, and try the coconut-fried shrimp or the chicken and scampi. Or come by during happy hour (weekdays 5–8) for a free buffet of snacks. ✉ *1640 Seaway Dr.,* ☎ *561/466–1044. AE, D, DC, MC, V.*

$–$$ ✕ **Theo Thudpucker's Raw Bar.** Businesspeople dressed for work mingle here with people fresh from the beach wearing shorts. On squally days everyone piles in off the jetty. Specialties include oyster stew, smoked fish spread, conch salad and conch fritters, fresh catfish, and alligator tail. ✉ *2025 Seaway Dr. (South Jetty),* ☎ *561/465–1078. No credit cards.*

$$ 🏠 **Mellon Patch Inn.** This tiny B&B has an excellent location—across the shore road from a beach park, at the end of a canal leading to the Indian River Lagoon. One side of the canal has a bank of attractive new homes; the other has the Jack Island Wildlife Refuge. Images of split-open melons permeate the house—on pillows, crafts, and candies on night tables. Each of the guest rooms has imaginative accessories, art, and upholstery appropriate to its individual theme. The cathedral-ceiling living room features a wood-burning fireplace, and full breakfast is included. ✉ *3601 N. Rte. A1A, North Hutchinson Island 34949,* ☎ *561/461–5231. 4 rooms. Dock, fishing. MC, V.*

$–$$ 🏠 **Harbor Light Inn.** The pick of the pack of lodgings lining the Fort Pierce Inlet along Seaway Drive is this modern nautical-style, blue-trimmed motel. Spacious units on two floors feature kitchen or wet bar and routine but well-cared-for furnishings. Half the rooms have a waterfront porch or balcony. In addition to the motel units there is a set of four apartments across the street (off the water), where in-season weekly rates are $360. ✉ *1156–1160 Seaway Dr., 34949,* ☎ *561/468–3555 or 800/433–0004. 17 rooms, 4 apartments. Pool, fishing, coin laundry. AE, D, DC, MC, V.*

Outdoor Activities and Sports

FISHING

For charter boats and fishing guides, try the **Dockside Inn** (✉ 1152 Seaway Dr., ☎ 561/461–4824).

JAI ALAI

Fort Pierce Jai Alai operates seasonally for live jai alai and year-round for off-track betting on horse-racing simulcasts. ✉ *1750 S. Kings Hwy., off Okeechobee Rd.,* ☎ *561/464–7500 or 800/524–2524.* ✉ *$1.* ◷ *Games Jan.–Apr., Wed. and Sat. 12:30 and 7, Thurs.–Fri. 7, Sun. 1; call to double-check schedule; simulcasts Wed.–Mon. noon and 7.*

SCUBA DIVING

Some 200 yards from shore and ¼ mi north of the UDT-Seal Museum on North Hutchinson Island, the **Urca de Lima Underwater Archaeological Preserve** features the remains of a flat-bottom, round-bellied storeship. Once part of a treasure fleet bound for Spain, it was destroyed by a hurricane. Dive boats can be chartered through the **Dockside Inn** (✉ 1152 Seaway Dr., ☎ 561/461–4824).

Shopping

One of Florida's best discount malls, the **Manufacturer's Outlet Center** (✉ Rte. 70, off I–95 at Exit 65) contains 41 stores offering such brand names as American Tourister, Jonathan Logan, Aileen, Polly Flinders, Van Heusen, London Fog, Levi Strauss, and Geoffrey Beene.

En Route   To reach Vero Beach, you have two options—Route A1A, along the coast, or Route 605 (often called Old Dixie Highway), on the mainland. As you approach Vero on the latter, you'll pass through an ungussied landscape of small farms and residential areas. On the beach route, part of the drive is through an unusually undeveloped section of the Florida coast. Both trips are very relaxing.

Vero Beach

 12 mi north of Fort Pierce.

There's a tranquility to this Indian River County seat, an affluent town with a strong commitment to the environment and the arts. Retirees make up about half the winter population. In the exclusive Riomar Bay area of town, "canopy roads" are shaded by massive live oaks, and a popular cluster of restaurants and shops is just off the beach.

At the **Indian River Citrus Museum,** photos, farm tools, and videos tell about a time when oxen hauled the citrus crop to the railroads, when family fruit stands dotted the roadsides, and when gorgeous packing labels made every crate arriving up north an enticement to visit the Sunshine State. You can also book free citrus tours of actual groves. ⊠ *2140 14th Ave.,* ☎ *561/770–2263.* ⊠ *Donation welcome.* ☉ *Tues.–Sat. 10–4, Sun. 1–4.*

In Riverside Park's Civic Arts Center, the **Center for the Arts** presents a full schedule of exhibitions, art movies, lectures, workshops, and other events, with a focus on Florida artists. ⊠ *3001 Riverside Park Dr.,* ☎ *561/231–0707.* ⊠ *Free.* ☉ *Fri.–Wed. 10–4:30, Thurs. 10–8.*

In addition to a wet lab containing aquariums filled with Indian River Lagoon life, the outstanding 51-acre **Environmental Learning Center** has a 600-ft boardwalk through mangrove shoreline and a 1-mi canoe trail. The center is on the north edge of Vero Beach, on Wabasso Island, but it's a pretty drive and worth the trip. ⊠ *255 Live Oak Dr.,* ☎ *561/589–5050.* ⊠ *Free.* ☉ *Weekdays 9–5, weekends 1–4.*

Humiston Park is just one of the beach-access parks along the east edge of town that have boardwalks and steps bridging the foredune. It has a large children's play area and picnic tables and is across the street from shops. ⊠ *Ocean Dr. below Beachland Blvd.,* ☎ *no phone.* ⊠ *Free.* ☉ *Daily 7 AM–10 PM.*

The Arts

The **Civic Arts Center** (⊠ Riverside Park), a cluster of cultural facilities, includes the Riverside Theatre (⊠ 3250 Riverside Park Dr., ☎ 561/231–6990), which stages six productions each season in its 633-seat performance hall; the Agnes Wahlstrom Youth Playhouse (⊠ 3280 Riverside Park Dr., ☎ 561/234–8052), which mounts children's productions; and the Center for the Arts (⊠ 3001 Riverside Park Dr., ☎ 561/231–0707), which presents art movies and lectures in addition to its other offerings. **Riverside Children's Theatre** (⊠ 3280 Riverside Park Dr., ☎ 561/234–8052) offers a series of professional touring and local productions, as well as acting workshops at the Agnes Wahlstrom Youth Playhouse.

Dining and Lodging

$$–$$$ ✕ **Black Pearl.** This intimate and sophisticated restaurant, one of Vero's trendiest dining picks, has moved to a new riverfront location, and now water views accompany the superb cuisine. The menu emphasizes fresh local ingredients. Specialties include chilled leek-and-asparagus soup, fresh oysters, local fish in parchment paper with fresh vegetable chutney, and panfried veal with local shrimp and vermouth.

✉ *4455 N. Rte. A1A,* ☎ *561/234–4426. AE, MC, V. No lunch weekends.*

$$–$$$ ✕ **Ocean Grill.** Opened by Waldo Sexton as a hamburger shack in 1938,
★ the oceanfront Ocean Grill is now furnished with Tiffany lamps,
wrought-iron chandeliers, and Beanie Backus paintings of pirates and
Seminole Indians. The menu includes black-bean soup, jumbo lump-
crabmeat salad, and at least three kinds of fish every day. The house
drink, the Leaping Limey, a curious blend of vodka, blue curaçao, and
lemon, commemorates the 1894 wreck of the *Breconshire,* which occurred just offshore and from which 34 British sailors escaped. The
bar and some tables look over the water. ✉ *1050 Sexton Plaza (Beachland Blvd. east of Ocean Dr.),* ☎ *561/231–5409. AE, D, DC, MC, V.
Closed 2 wks following Labor Day. No lunch weekends.*

$–$$ ✕ **Pearl's Bistro.** Island-style cuisine is the draw at this laid-back and
less expensive sister restaurant to the Black Pearl (☞ *above*). For
starters try the pasta Rasta, the seafood chowder, or the Jamaican jerk
shrimp. Then move on to grilled Yucatán-spiced local fish, barbecued
ribs, Bahamian shrimp and grouper pepper pot, or blackened New York
strip with peppery rum sauce. ✉ *56 Royal Palm Blvd.,* ☎ *561/778–
2950. AE, MC, V. No lunch Sun.*

$$$–$$$$ 🏨 **Disney's Vero Beach Resort.** Built on 71 oceanfront acres, this
sprawling vacation getaway, which operates both as a time-share and
a hotel, is the classiest resort in Vero Beach. The main four-story build-
ing, three freestanding villas, and six beach cottages are nestled among
tropical greenery. Buildings are painted in pale pastels and sport steeply
pitched gables, and many units have balconies. Bright interiors feature
rattan furniture and tile floors. ✉ *9235 Rte. A1A, 32963,* ☎ *561/234–
2000. 161 rooms, 14 suites, 6 cottages. 2 restaurants, bar, pool, wad-
ing pool, 6 tennis courts, basketball, bicycles, video games. AE, D, DC,
MC, V.*

$$$–$$$$ 🏨 **DoubleTree Guest Suites.** This five-story rose-color stucco hotel is
conveniently located—right on the beach and near restaurants, specialty
shops, and boutiques. One- and two-bedroom suites have patios open-
ing onto a pool or balconies and excellent ocean views. ✉ *3500 Ocean
Dr., 32963,* ☎ *561/231–5666. 55 suites. Bar, 2 pools, wading pool,
hot tub. AE, D, DC, MC, V.*

$$ 🏨 **Captain Hiram's Islander Motel.** Across from the beach, the aqua-
and-white-trim Islander has a snoozy Key West style that contrasts
stylishly with the smart shops it's tucked between. Jigsaw-cut brack-
ets and balusters and beach umbrellas dress up the pool. All rooms feature white wicker, paddle fans hung from vaulted ceilings, and fresh
flowers. It's just right for beachside Vero. ✉ *3101 Ocean Dr., 32963,*
☎ *561/231–4431 or 800/952–5886. 16 rooms, 1 efficiency. Pool. AE,
DC, MC, V.*

Outdoor Activities and Sports

The **Los Angeles Dodgers** (✉ 4101 26th St., ☎ 561/569–4900) train
at Dodgertown, actually in Vero Beach.

Shopping

Along **Ocean Drive** near Beachland Boulevard, a specialty shopping area
includes art galleries, antiques shops, and upscale clothing stores.

Sebastian

36 *7 mi north of Vero Beach.*

One of only a few sparsely populated areas on Florida's east coast, this
little fishing village has as remote a feeling as you'll find anywhere between Jacksonville and Miami Beach. That remoteness adds to the ap-

peal of the recreation area around Sebastian Inlet, where you can walk for miles along quiet beaches.

The **McLarty Treasure Museum,** designated a National Historical Landmark, features displays dedicated to the 1715 hurricane that sank a fleet of Spanish treasure ships. ⊠ *13180 N. Rte. A1A,* ☎ *561/589–2147.* ⊡ *$1.* ☉ *Daily 10–4:30.*

You've really come upon hidden loot when you step into **Mel Fisher's Treasure Museum.** Here you can view some of what was recovered from the Spanish treasure ship *Atocha* and its sister ships of the 1715 fleet. Fisher operates a similar museum in Key West. ⊠ *1322 U.S. 1,* ☎ *561/589–9875.* ⊡ *$5.* ☉ *Mon.–Sat. 10–5, Sun. noon–5.*

Because of the highly productive fishing waters of Sebastian Inlet, at the north end of Orchid Island, the 578-acre **Sebastian Inlet State Recreation Area** is one of the best-attended parks in the Florida state system. On both sides of the high bridge that spans the inlet—from which the views are spectacular—the recreation area attracts plenty of anglers as well as those eager to enjoy the fine sandy beaches (both within the recreation area and outside it), which are known for having the best waves in the state. A concession stand on the north side of the inlet sells short-order food, rents various craft, and has an apparel and surf shop. A boat ramp is available. Not far away along the sea is a dune area that's part of the **Archie Carr National Wildlife Refuge,** a haven for sea turtles and other protected Florida wildlife. ⊠ *9700 S. Rte. A1A, Melbourne Beach,* ☎ *407/984–4852;* ⊠ *1300 Rte. A1A, Melbourne Beach,* ☎ *561/589–9659.* ⊡ *$3.25.* ☉ *Daily 24 hrs, bait and tackle shop daily 7:30–6, concession stand daily 8–5.*

Dining and Lodging

$–$$ ✕ **Capt. Hiram's.** This family-friendly restaurant on the Indian River Lagoon is easygoing, fanciful, and fun—definitely not purposefully hip. As the sign says, NECKTIES ARE PROHIBITED. The place is "real"—full of wooden booths, stained glass, umbrellas on the open deck, and ceiling fans. Don't miss Capt. Hiram's Sandbar, where kids can play while parents enjoy a drink at stools set in an outdoor shower or a beached boat. Choose among seafood brochette, New York strip steak, the fresh catch, and lots of other seafood dishes as well as raw-bar items. The full bar has a weekday happy hour and free hot hors d'oeuvres Friday 5–6. There's nightly entertainment in season. ⊠ *1606 N. Indian River Dr.,* ☎ *561/589–4345. AE, D, MC, V.*

$–$$ ✕ **Hurricane Harbor.** Built in 1927 as a garage and used during Prohibition as a smugglers' den, Hurricane Harbor now draws a year-round crowd of retirees and locals. Guests love the waterfront window seats on stormy nights, when sizable waves break outside in the Indian River Lagoon. The menu features seafood, steaks, and grills, along with lighter fare. On Friday and Saturday nights the Antique Dining Room is opened, with linen, stained glass, and a huge antique breakfront. There's also live music nightly. ⊠ *1540 Indian River Dr.,* ☎ *561/589–1773. AE, D, MC, V. Closed Mon.*

$–$$ ▥ **Captain's Quarters Riverfront Motel.** Five units—four overlooking the Indian River Lagoon and the marina at Capt. Hiram's restaurant and one two-room suite—are all Key West cute. Painted in bright colors with matching fabrics, the rooms have pine and white-wicker furniture and pine plank floors with grass rugs. The adequate bathrooms have large stall showers. Glass doors open to a plank porch, but the porches are all within sight of each other. ⊠ *1606 Indian River Dr., 32958,* ☎ *561/589–4345. 4 rooms, 1 suite. Restaurant. AE, D, MC, V.*

$–$$ 🏨 **Davis House Inn.** Vero native Steve Wild modeled his two-story inn after the clubhouse at Augusta National, and, perhaps surprisingly, it fits right in with Sebastian's fishing-town look. Wide overhung roofs shade wraparound porches. In a companion house that Steve calls the Gathering Room, he serves a complimentary expanded Continental breakfast. Rooms are huge—virtual suites, with large sitting areas— though somewhat underfurnished. Overall, it's a terrific value. ⊠ *607 Davis St., 32958,* ☎ *561/589–4114. 12 rooms. Bicycles. MC, V.*

Outdoor Activities and Sports

CANOEING AND KAYAKING

Bill Rogers Outdoor Adventures (⊠ 1541 DeWitt La., ☎ 561/564–9600) outfits canoe trips down the Sebastian River, along Indian River Lagoon, and through Pelican Island Wildlife Refuge, as well as more distant locations. The concession stand at **Sebastian Inlet State Recreation Area** (⊠ 9700 S. Rte. A1A, Melbourne Beach, ☎ 561/984–4852) rents canoes, kayaks, and paddleboats.

FISHING

The best inlet fishing in the region is at **Sebastian Inlet State Recreation Area** (⊠ 9700 S. Rte. A1A, Melbourne Beach), where the catch includes bluefish, flounder, jack, redfish, sea trout, snapper, snook, and Spanish mackerel. For deep-sea fishing try *Miss Sebastian* (⊠ Sembler Dock, ½ block north of Capt. Hiram's restaurant, ☎ 561/589–3275); $25 for a half day covers rod, reel, and bait. **Sebastian Inlet Marina at Capt. Hiram's** (⊠ 1606 Indian River Dr., ☎ 561/589–4345) offers half- and full-day fishing charters.

WINDSURFING

The **Sailboard School** (⊠ 9125 U.S. 1, ☎ 561/589–2671 or 800/253–6573) provides year-round one-day, weekend, and five-day programs of windsurfing instruction, including boards, for $120 a day, $575 for five days.

PALM BEACH AND THE TREASURE COAST A TO Z

Arriving and Departing

By Bus

Greyhound Lines (☎ 800/231–2222) buses arrive at the station in West Palm Beach (⊠ 100 Banyan Blvd., ☎ 561/833–8534).

By Car

I–95 runs north–south, linking West Palm Beach with Miami and Fort Lauderdale to the south and with Daytona, Jacksonville, and the rest of the Atlantic coast to the north. To get to central Palm Beach, exit at Belvedere Road or Okeechobee Boulevard. Florida's Turnpike runs up from Miami through West Palm Beach before angling northwest to reach Orlando.

By Plane

Palm Beach International Airport (PBIA) (⊠ Congress Ave. and Belvedere Rd., West Palm Beach, ☎ 561/471–7400) is served by **Air Canada** (☎ 800/776–3000), **American/American Eagle** (☎ 800/433–7300), **American Trans-Air** (☎ 800/225–2995), **Canadian Holidays** (☎ 800/661–8881), **Carnival Airlines** (☎ 800/824–7386), **Comair** (☎ 800/354–9822), **Continental** (☎ 800/525–0280), **Delta** (☎ 800/221–1212), **KIWI International Airlines** (☎ 800/538–5494), **Northwest** (☎ 800/225–2525), **Paradise Island** (☎ 800/432–8807), **Republic Air Travel** (☎ 800/233–

0225), **Spirit Airlines** (☎ 561/471–7467), **TWA** (☎ 800/221–2000), **United** (☎ 800/241–6522), and **US Airways/US Airways Express** (☎ 800/428–4322).

BETWEEN THE AIRPORT AND THE TOWNS

Route 10 of **Tri-Rail Commuter Bus Service** (☎ 800/874–7245) runs from the airport to Tri-Rail's nearby Palm Beach airport station daily. **CoTran** (☞ Getting Around by Bus, *below*) Route 4-S operates from the airport to downtown West Palm Beach every two hours at 35 minutes after the hour from 7:35 until 5:35. The fare is $1.

Palm Beach Transportation (☎ 561/689–4222) provides taxi and limousine service from PBIA. Reserve at least a day in advance for a limousine. The lowest fares are $1.50 per mile, with the meter starting at $1.25. Depending on your destination, a flat rate (from PBIA only) may save money. Wheelchair-accessible vehicles are available.

By Train

Amtrak (☎ 800/872–7245) connects West Palm Beach (⊠ 201 S. Tamarind Ave., ☎ 561/832–6169) with cities along Florida's east coast and the Northeast daily and via the *Sunset Limited* to New Orleans and Los Angeles three times weekly. Included in Amtrak's service is transport from West Palm Beach to Okeechobee (⊠ 801 N. Parrott Ave.); the station is unmanned.

Getting Around

The **Downtown Transfer Facility** (⊠ Banyan Blvd. and Clearlake Dr., West Palm Beach), off Australian Avenue at the west entrance to downtown, links the downtown shuttle, Amtrak, Tri-Rail (the commuter line of Miami-Dade, Broward, and Palm Beach counties), CoTran (the county bus system), Greyhound, and taxis.

By Bus

CoTran (Palm Beach County Transportation Authority) buses require exact change. The cost is $1.50, $1 for students, senior citizens, and people with disabilities (with reduced-fare ID); transfers are 20¢. Service operates 5 AM–8:30 PM, though pickups on most routes are 5:30 AM–7 PM. For details call CoTran (☎ 561/233–1111 for Palm Beach; 561/930–5123 for Boca Raton–Delray Beach).

Palmtran (☎ 561/833–8873) is a shuttle system that provides free transportation around downtown West Palm Beach, weekdays 6:30 AM–7:30 PM.

By Car

U.S. 1 threads north–south along the coast, connecting most coastal communities, while the more scenic Route A1A ventures out onto the barrier islands. The interstate, I–95, runs parallel to U.S. 1 but a bit farther inland.

A nonstop four-lane route, Okeechobee Boulevard carries traffic from west of downtown West Palm Beach, near the Amtrak station in the airport district, directly to the Flagler Memorial Bridge and into Palm Beach. Plans are in the works to turn Flagler Drive over for pedestrian use sometime in the next several years.

The best way to get to Lake Okeechobee from West Palm is to drive west on Southern Boulevard from I–95 past the cutoff road to Lion Country Safari. From there the boulevard is designated U.S. 98/441.

By Taxi

Palm Beach Transportation (☎ 561/689–4222) has a single number serving several cab companies. Meters start at $1.25, and the charge is $1.25

per mile within West Palm Beach city limits; if the trip at any point leaves the city limits, the fare is $1.50 per mile. Some cabs may charge more. Waiting time is 25¢ per 75 seconds.

By Train

Tri-Rail (☎ 800/874–7245), the commuter rail system, has six stations in Palm Beach County (13 stops altogether between West Palm Beach and Miami). The round-trip fare is $5, $2.50 for students and senior citizens.

Contacts and Resources

Emergencies

Dial **911** for police or ambulance.

HOSPITALS

The following hospitals have 24-hour emergency rooms: **Good Samaritan Hospital** (✉ Flagler Dr. and Palm Beach Lakes Blvd., West Palm Beach, ☎ 561/655–5511; 561/650–6240 physician referral), **JFK Medical Center** (✉ 5301 S. Congress Ave., Atlantis, ☎ 561/965–7300; 561/642–3628 physician referral), **Palm Beaches Medical Center** (✉ 2201 45th St., West Palm Beach, ☎ 561/694–7124; 561/881–2661 physician referral), **Palm Beach Regional Hospital** (✉ 2829 10th Ave. N, Lake Worth, ☎ 561/967–7800), and **St. Mary's Hospital** (✉ 901 45th St., West Palm Beach, ☎ 561/844–6300; 561/881–2929 physician referral).

LATE-NIGHT PHARMACIES

Eckerd Drug (✉ 3343 S. Congress Ave., Palm Springs, ☎ 561/965–3367) and **Walgreens** (✉ 1688 S. Congress Ave., Palm Springs, ☎ 561/968–8211; ✉ 7561 N. Federal Hwy., Boca Raton, ☎ 561/241–9802; ✉ 1634 S. Federal Hwy., Boynton Beach, ☎ 561/737–1260; ✉ 1208 Royal Palm Beach Blvd., Royal Palm Beach, ☎ 561/798–9048; ✉ 6370 Indiantown Rd., Jupiter, ☎ 561/744–6822; ✉ 20 E. 30th St., Riviera Beach, ☎ 561/848–6464).

Guided Tours

BOAT TOURS

Capt. Doug's (✉ Sebastian Marina, Sebastian, ☎ 561/589–2329) offers three-hour lunch and dinner cruises along the Indian River on board a 35-ft sloop. Cost is $100 per couple, including meal, tips, beer, and wine. **J-Mark Fish Camp** (✉ Torry Island, ☎ 561/996–5357) has 45- to 60-minute airboat rides for $20 per person, with a minimum of two people and a maximum of six; 90- to 120-minute rides for $30 per person include a look at an active eagle's nest. **Jonathan Dickinson's River Tours** (✉ Jonathan Dickinson State Park, 16450 S.E. Federal Hwy., Hobe Sound, ☎ 561/746–1466) runs two-hour guided riverboat cruises daily at 9, 11, 1, and 3 and once a month, at the full moon, at 7. The cost is $12. **Loxahatchee Everglades Tours** (✉ 10400 Loxahatchee Rd., ☎ 561/482–6107) operates airboat tours year-round from west of Boca Raton through the marshes between the built-up coast and Lake Okeechobee. The **Manatee Queen** (✉ Jonathan Dickinson State Park, 16450 S.E. Federal Hwy., Hobe Sound, ☎ 561/744–2191), a 49-passenger catamaran, offers day and evening cruises November–May on the Intracoastal Waterway and into the park's cypress swamps.

Ramblin' Rose Riverboat (✉ 1 N.E. 1st St., Delray Beach, ☎ 561/243–0686) operates luncheon, dinner-dance, and Sunday brunch cruises along the Intracoastal Waterway. The **Spirit of St. Joseph** (✉ 109 Myrtle St., Fort Pierce, ☎ 561/467–2628) offers seven lunch and dinner cruises weekly on the Indian River, leaving from alongside the St. Lucie County Historical Museum. Atlantic Cruises' **Star of Palm Beach** (✉ Phil Foster Park, 900 E. Blue Heron Rd., Palm Beach, ☎ 561/842–0882) runs year-round from Singer Island, each day offering one dinner-dance and three sightseeing cruises on the Intracoastal Waterway. **Water Taxi Scenic Cruises** (✉ Sailfish Marina and Riviera Beach Marina, Palm Beach, ☎ 561/775–2628) offers several different daily sightseeing tours in a 16-person launch. Two are designed to let you get a close-up look at the mansions of the rich and famous. The southern tour features the mansions of Palm Beach, while the northern tour follows the North Palm Beach Canal. There are also a one-hour BYOB sunset cruise and a 2½-hour environmental tour to Munyon Island, which usually includes many dolphin sightings.

ECOTOURS

Contact the **Audubon Society of the Everglades** (✉ Box 16914, West Palm Beach 33461, ☎ 561/588–6908) for field trips and nature walks. **Swampland Tours** (✉ 103 75th Hwy. 78W, Okeechobee 34974, ☎ 941/467–4411), on Lake Okeechobee, operates interpretive boat tours through the National Audubon Society Wildlife Sanctuary.

HISTORICAL TOURS

The **Boca Raton Historical Society** (✉ 71 N. Federal Hwy., Boca Raton, ☎ 561/395–6766) offers afternoon tours of the Boca Raton Resort & Club on Tuesday year-round and to other South Florida sites. The **Fort Pierce Historical Society** (✉ 131 Main St., Fort Pierce, ☎ 561/466–3880) gives walking tours of the town's historic section, past buildings built by early settlers. The **Indian River County Historical Society** (✉ 2336 14th Ave., Vero Beach, ☎ 561/778–3435) conducts walking tours of downtown Vero on Wednesday at 11 and 1 (by reservation). **Old Northwood Historic District Tours** (✉ 501 30th St., West Palm Beach, ☎ 561/863–5633) leads two-hour walking tours that include visits to historic home interiors. They leave Sunday at 2, and a $5 donation is requested. Tours for groups of six or more can be scheduled almost any day.

Visitor Information

Belle Glade Chamber of Commerce (✉ 540 S. Main St., Belle Glade 33430, ☎ 561/996–2745). **Chamber of Commerce of the Palm Beaches** (✉ 401 N. Flagler Dr., West Palm Beach 33401, ☎ 561/833–3711). **Clewiston Chamber of Commerce** (✉ 544 W. Sugarland Hwy., Clewiston 33440, ☎ 941/983–7979). **Glades County Chamber of Commerce** (✉ U.S. 27 and 10th St., Moore Haven 33471, ☎ 941/946–0440). **Indian River County Tourist Council** (✉ 1216 21st St., Box 2947, Vero Beach 32961, ☎ 561/567–3491). **Indiantown and Western Martin County Chamber of Commerce** (✉ 15518 S.W. Osceola St., Indiantown 34956, ☎ 561/597–2184). **Okeechobee County Chamber of Commerce** (✉ 55 S. Parrott Ave., Okeechobee 34974, ☎ 941/763–6464). **Pahokee Chamber of Commerce** (✉ 115 E. Main St., Pahokee 33476, ☎ 561/924–5579). **Palm Beach Chamber of Commerce** (✉ 45 Cocoanut Row, Palm Beach 33480, ☎ 561/655–3282). **Palm Beach County Convention & Visitors Bureau** (✉ 1555 Palm Beach Lakes Blvd., Suite 204, West Palm Beach 33401, ☎ 561/471–3995). **St. Lucie County Tourist Development Council** (✉ 2300 Virginia Ave., Fort Pierce 34982, ☎ 561/462–1535). **Stuart/Martin County Chamber of Commerce** (✉ 1650 S. Kanner Hwy., Stuart 34994, ☎ 561/287–1088). For more information on the Okeechobee area, contact the **U.S. Army Corps of Engineers** (✉ South Florida Operations Office, 525 Ridgelawn Rd., Clewiston 33440-5399, ☎ 941/983–8101).

5 THE FLORIDA KEYS

The Keys are one of America's last frontiers. Here both humans and nature seek refuge in a verdant island chain that stretches raggedly west-southwest across a deep blue-green seascape at the base of the Florida peninsula.

Updated by
Diane P.
Marshall

THE FLORIDA KEYS ARE A WILDERNESS of flowering jungles and shimmering seas, a jade necklace of mangrove-fringed islands dangling toward the tropics. The Florida Keys are also a 110-mi traffic jam lined with garish billboards, hamburger stands, shopping centers, motels, and trailer courts. Unfortunately, in the Keys you can't have one without the other. A river of tourist traffic gushes along U.S. 1 (also called the Overseas Highway), the main artery between Key Largo and Key West. Residents of Monroe County live by diverting that river's flow of green dollars to their own pockets. In the process, the fragile beauty of the Keys—or at least the 45 that are inhabited and linked to the mainland by 43 bridges—has paid an environmental price.

Despite designation as "an area of critical state concern" in 1975 and a subsequent state-mandated development slowdown, rapid growth has continued, and the Keys' natural resources are still in peril. In 1990 Congress established the Florida Keys National Marine Sanctuary, covering 2,800 square nautical mi of coastal waters. Adjacent to the Keys landmass are spectacular, unique, and nationally significant marine environments, including sea-grass meadows, mangrove islands, and extensive living coral reefs. These fragile environments support rich and diverse biological communities possessing extensive conservation, recreational, commercial, ecological, historical, research, educational, and aesthetic values.

The Florida Keys National Marine Sanctuary and Protection Act is intended to protect the coral reefs and restore worsening water quality. But problems continue. Increased salinity in Florida Bay causes large areas of sea grass to die and drift in mats out of the bay. These mats then block sunlight from reaching the reefs, stifling their growth and threatening both the Keys' recreational diving economy and tourism in general.

Other threats to the Keys' charm also loom. As government officials with one hand sign the national marine sanctuary into effect, with the other they bring about the four-laning of U.S. 1 to the mainland, opening the floodgates to increased traffic, population, and tourism. Observers wonder if the four-laning of the rest of U.S. 1 throughout the Keys can be far away and if a trip to paradise will then be worth it.

For now, however, take pleasure as you drive down U.S. 1 along the islands. Most days you can gaze over the silvery blue and green Atlantic and its still-living reef, with Florida Bay, the Gulf of Mexico, and the backcountry on your right (the Keys extend east–west from the mainland). At a few points the ocean and gulf are as much as 10 mi apart. In most places, however, they are within 1–4 mi, and on the narrowest landfill islands, they are separated only by the road.

Things to do and see are everywhere, but first you have to remind yourself to get off the highway. Once you do, rent a boat and find a secluded anchorage and fish, swim, or marvel at the sun, sea, and sky. In the Atlantic you can dive to spectacular coral reefs or pursue dolphin, blue marlin, and other deep-water game fish. Along the Florida Bay coastline you can seek out the bonefish, snapper, snook, and tarpon that lurk in the grass flats and in the shallow, winding channels of the backcountry.

Along the reefs and among the islands are more than 600 kinds of fish. Diminutive deer and pale raccoons, related to but distinct from their mainland cousins, inhabit the Lower Keys. And throughout the islands you'll find such exotic West Indian plants as Jamaica dogwood, pigeon plum, poisonwood, satin leaf, and silver and thatch palms, as well as tropical birds, including the great white heron, mangrove cuckoo, roseate spoonbill, and white-crowned pigeon. Mangroves, with their gracefully bowed prop roots, appear to march out to sea. Day by day they busily add more keys to the archipelago.

With virtually no distracting air pollution or obstructive high-rises, sunsets are a pure, unadulterated spectacle that each evening attracts thousands of tourists and locals to waterfront parks, piers, restaurants, bars, and resorts throughout the Keys.

Another attraction is the weather: In the winter it's typically 10°F warmer than on the mainland; in the summer it's usually 10°F cooler. The Keys also get substantially less rain, around 30 inches annually, compared to an average 55–60 inches in Miami and the Everglades. Most rain falls in quick downpours on summer afternoons, except in June, September, and October, when tropical storms can dump rain for two to four days straight. In winter continental cold fronts occasionally stall over the Keys, dragging overnight temperatures down to the 40s.

The Keys were only sparsely populated until the early 20th century. In 1905, however, railroad magnate Henry Flagler began building the extension of his Florida railroad south from Homestead to Key West. His goal was to establish a rail link to the steamships that sailed between Key West and Havana, just 90 mi across the Straits of Florida. The railroad arrived at Key West in 1912 and remained a lifeline of commerce until the Labor Day hurricane of 1935 washed out much of its roadbed. For three years thereafter, the only way in and out of Key West was by boat. The Overseas Highway, built over the railroad's old roadbeds and bridges, was completed in 1938, and many sections and bridges have recently been widened or replaced.

New and Noteworthy

Hurricane Georges roared through the Florida Keys in September 1998, flooding and ripping apart waterfront hotels, businesses, and parks in Key West and the Middle and Lower keys. In most cases, recovery was swift, with all but a few properties reopening within a few days or weeks. The most long-term visible effects are in the landscaping, once lush with mature trees, sea oats, and palms, but now thin or nonexistent. In one way, visitors will benefit from the storm: Many properties took the opportunity to renovate and upgrade.

Florida State Parks opened two new facilities. After nearly a six-month closing, Windley Key Fossil Reef State Geologic Site, in Islamorada, reopened with the new Alison Fahrer Environmental Education Center and improved trails. In the Middle Keys, Curry Hammock State Park, considered one of the best kayaking areas in the Keys, opened with a wide beach, bathhouse, and picnic tables.

In Key West, the **Historic Seaport at Key West Bight** officially debuted after a $30 million renovation of the 8.5-acre waterfront area. More than 100 land- and sea-based businesses are now open.

Pleasures and Pastimes

Biking

Cyclists are now able to ride all but a tiny portion of the bike path that runs along the Overseas Highway from MM 106 south to the Seven Mile Bridge. The state plans to extend the route throughout the Keys. Some areas have lots of cross traffic, however, so ride with care.

Boating

If it floats, local marinas rent it. For up-close exploration of the mangroves and near-shore islands in Florida Bay, nothing beats a kayak or canoe. You can paddle within a few feet of a flock of birds without disturbing them. Visiting the backcountry islands and inlets of Everglades National Park requires a shallow-draft boat: A 14- to 17-ft skiff with a 40- to 50-horsepower outboard is sufficient. For diving the reef or fishing on the open ocean, you'll need a larger boat with greater horsepower. Houseboats are ideal for cruising the Keys.

Only experienced sailors should attempt to navigate the shallow waters surrounding the Keys with deep-keeled sailboats. On the other hand, small shallow-draft, single-hulled sailboats and catamarans are ideal. Personal water vehicles, such as Wave Runners and Jet Skis, rent by the half hour or hour but are banned in many areas. Flat, stable pontoon boats are a good choice for anyone with seasickness. Those interested in experiencing the reef without getting wet can take a glass-bottom boat trip.

Dining

A number of talented young chefs have settled in the Keys—especially Key West—contributing to the area's image as one of the nation's points of culinary interest. Restaurants' menus, rum-based fruit beverages, and music reflect the Keys' tropical climate and their proximity to Cuba and other Caribbean islands. Better restaurants serve imaginative and tantalizing fusion cuisine that draws on traditions from all over the world.

Florida citrus, seafood, and tropical fruits figure prominently, and Florida lobster and stone crab should be local and fresh from August to March. Also keep an eye out for authentic key lime pie. The real McCoy has a yellow custard in a graham-cracker crust and tastes like nothing else.

Restaurants may close for a two- to four-week vacation during the slow season—between mid-September and mid-November. Check local newspapers or call ahead, especially if driving any distance.

Fishing

These sun-bathed waters are home to 100 species of game fish as well as lobster, shrimp, and crabs. Flats fishing and backcountry fishing are Keys specialties. In flats fishing, a guide poles a shallow-draft outboard boat through the shallow, sandy-bottomed waters while sighting for bonefish and snook to be caught on light tackle, spin, and fly. Backcountry fishing may include flats fishing or fishing in the channels and basins around islands in Florida Bay. Charter boats fish the reef and Gulf Stream for deep-sea fish. Party boats, which can be crowded, carry up to 50 people to fish the reefs for grouper, kingfish, and snapper. Some operators boast a guarantee, or "no fish, no pay" policy.

Scuba Diving and Snorkeling

Diving in the Keys is spectacular. In shallow and deep water with visibility up to 120 ft, you can explore sea canyons and mountains covered with waving sea plumes, brain and star coral, historic shipwrecks, and sunken submarines. The colors of the coral are surpassed only by the brilliance of the fish that live around it. There's no best season for diving, but occasional storms in June, September, and October cloud the waters and make seas rough.

You can dive the reefs with scuba, snuba, or snorkeling gear, using your own boat, renting a boat, or booking a tour with a dive shop. Tours depart two or three times a day, stopping at two sites on each trip. The first trip of the day is usually the best. It's less crowded—vacationers like to sleep in—and visibility is better before the wind picks up in the afternoon. There's also night diving.

If you want to scuba dive but are not certified, take an introductory resort course. Though it doesn't result in certification, it allows you to scuba with an instructor in the afternoon following morning class-room and pool instruction.

Nearly all the waters surrounding the Keys are part of the Florida Keys National Marine Sanctuary and thus are protected. Signs, brochures, tour guides, and marine enforcement agents remind visitors that the reef is fragile and shouldn't be touched.

Exploring the Florida Keys

Finding your way around the Keys isn't hard once you understand the unique address system. Many addresses are simply given as a mile marker (MM) number. The markers themselves are small, green rectangular signs along the side of the Overseas Highway (U.S. 1). They begin with MM 126 a mile south of Florida City and end with MM 0, in Key West. Keys residents use the abbreviation BS for the bay side of U.S. 1 and OS for the ocean side. From Marathon to Key West, residents may refer to the bay side as the gulf side.

The Keys are divided into four areas: the Upper Keys, from Key Largo to the Long Key Channel (MM 106–65) and Ocean Reef and North Key Largo, off Card Sound Road and Route 905, respectively; the Mid-dle Keys, from Conch (pronounced *konk*) Key through Marathon to the south side of the Seven Mile Bridge, including Pigeon Key (MM 65–40); the Lower Keys, from Little Duck Key south through Big Coppitt Key (MM 40–9); and Key West, from Stock Island through Key West (MM 9–0). The Keys don't end with the highway, however; they stretch another 70 mi west of Key West to the Dry Tortugas.

Numbers in the text correspond to numbers in the margin and on the Florida Keys and Key West maps.

Great Itineraries

IF YOU HAVE 3 DAYS

You can fly and then dive; but if you dive, you can't fly for 24 hours, so spend your first morning diving or snorkeling at John Pennekamp Coral Reef State Park in 🎦 **Key Largo** ②. If you aren't certified, take a resort course, and you'll be exploring the reefs by afternoon. After-ward, breeze through the park's visitor center. The rest of the after-noon can be whiled away either lounging around a pool or beach or visiting the Maritime Museum of the Florida Keys. Dinner or cock-tails at a bay-side restaurant or bar will give you your first look at a fabulous Keys sunset. On day two, get an early start to savor the breathtaking views on the two-hour drive to Key West. Along the way make stops at the natural history museum that's part of the Museums of Crane Point Hammock, in **Marathon** ⑧, and Bahia Honda State Park, on **Bahia Honda Key** ⑨, where you can stretch your legs on a forest trail or snorkel on an offshore reef. Once in 🎦 **Key West** ⑫–㉜, you can watch the sunset before dining at one of the island's first-class restau-rants. Spend the next morning exploring beaches, visiting any of the myriad museums, or taking a walking or trolley tour of Old Town be-fore driving back to the mainland.

IF YOU HAVE 4 DAYS

Spend the first day as you would above, overnighting in 🎦 **Key Largo** ②. Start the second day by renting a kayak and exploring the mangroves and small islands of Florida Bay or take an ecotour of the islands in Everglades National Park. In the afternoon stop by the Florida Keys Wild Bird Rehabilitation Center before driving down to 🔟 **Islamorada** ④. Pause to read the inscription on the Hurricane Monument, and before day's end, make plans for the next day's fishing. After a late lunch on day three—perhaps at one of the many restaurants that will prepare your catch for you—set off for 🔟 **Key West** ⑫–㉜. Catch the sunset celebration at Mallory Square, and spend the last day as you would above.

IF YOU HAVE 7 DAYS

Spend your first three days as you would in the four-day itinerary, but stay the third night in 🔟 **Islamorada** ④. In the morning catch a boat to Lignumvitae Key State Botanical Site, before making the one-hour drive to 🔟 **Marathon** ⑧, where you can visit the natural history museum that's part of the Museums of Crane Point Hammock and walk or take a train across the Old Seven Mile Bridge to Pigeon Key. The next stop is just 10 mi away at Bahia Honda State Park, on 🔟 **Bahia Honda Key** ⑨. Take a walk on a wilderness trail, go snorkeling on an offshore reef, wriggle your toes in the beach's soft sand, and spend the night in a waterfront cabin, letting the waves lull you to sleep. Your sixth day starts with either a half day of fabulous snorkeling or diving at Looe Key National Marine Sanctuary or a visit to the National Key Deer Refuge, on **Big Pine Key** ⑩. Then continue on to 🔟 **Key West** ⑫–㉜, and get in a little sightseeing before watching the sunset. The next morning take a walking, bicycling, or trolley tour of town or catch a ferry or seaplane to Dry Tortugas National Park before heading home.

When to Tour the Florida Keys

High season in the Keys is mid-December through March, and traffic on the Overseas Highway is inevitably heavy. From November to the middle of December, crowds are thinner, the weather is superlative, and hotels and shops drastically reduce their prices. Summer, which is hot and humid, is becoming a second high season, especially among families and Europeans. Key West's annual Fantasy Fest is the last week in October; if you plan to attend this popular event, reserve at least six months in advance. Rooms are also scarce the first few weekends of lobster season, which starts in August.

THE UPPER KEYS

The tropical coral reef tract that runs a few miles off the seaward coast accounts for most of the Upper Keys' reputation. This is a diving heaven, thanks to scores of diving options, accessible islands and dive sites, and an established tourism infrastructure.

Yet although diving is king here, fishing, kayaking, and nature touring draw an enviable number of tourists. Within 1½ mi of the bay coast lie the islands of Everglades National Park; here naturalists lead ecotours to see one of the world's only saltwater forests, endangered manatees, dolphins, roseate spoonbills, and tropical bird rookeries. Though the number of birds has dwindled since John James Audubon captured their beauty on a visit to the Keys, bird-watchers won't be disappointed. At sunset flocks take to the skies, and in spring and autumn migrating birds add their numbers. Tarpon and bonefish teem in the shallow waters surrounding the islands, providing food for birds and a challenge to light-tackle fishermen. These same crystal-clear waters attract windsurfers, sailors, and powerboaters.

Dining in the Upper Keys used to be, with one or two exceptions, ho hum. However, within the last five years, half a dozen fine restaurants have opened and are thriving on repeat local customers and word-of-mouth tourist business.

Accommodations are as varied as they are plentiful. The majority are in small waterfront resorts, whose efficiency and one- or two-bedroom units are decorated in tropical colors. They offer dockage and either provide or will arrange boating, diving, and fishing excursions. Depending on which way the wind blows and how close the property is to the highway, noise from U.S. 1 can be bothersome. In high season, expect to pay $65–$165 for an efficiency (in low season, $45–$145). Campground and RV park rates with electricity and water run $22–$48. Some properties require two- or three-day minimum stays during holidays and on weekends in high season. Conversely, discounts are given for midweek, weekly, and monthly stays, and rates can drop 20%–40% April–June and October–mid-December. Keep in mind that salty winds and soil play havoc with anything man-made, and constant maintenance is a must; inspect your accommodations before checking in.

Key Largo

56 mi south of Miami International Airport.

The first Key reachable by car, 30-mi-long Key Largo—named Cayo Largo (long key) by the Spanish—is also the largest island in the chain. Comprising three areas—North Key Largo, Key Largo, and Tavernier—it runs northeast–southwest between Lake Surprise and Tavernier Creek, at MM 95. Most businesses are on the four-lane divided highway (U.S. 1) that runs down the middle, but away from the overdevelopment and generally suburban landscape you can find many areas of pristine wilderness.

❶ One such area is **North Key Largo,** which still contains a wide tract of virgin hardwood hammock and mangrove as well as a crocodile sanctuary (not open to the public). To reach North Key Largo, take Card Sound Road just south of Florida City, or from within the Keys, take Route 905 north.

The 2,005-acre **Key Largo Hammocks State Botanical Site** is the largest remaining stand of the vast West Indian tropical hardwood hammock and mangrove wetland that once covered most of the Keys' upland areas. Among the site's 84 species of protected plants and animals are the endangered American crocodile and the Key Largo wood rat. Concrete skeletons of defunct developments remain but are slowly disappearing under vegetation. To protect the land from further development, state and federal governments are acquiring as much of the hammock as they can. You can take a self-guided tour by picking up a brochure at the park entrance. Better still are the biweekly tours led by Ranger Joseph Nemec, who points out rare species, tells humorous nature stories, and encourages visitors to taste the fruits of native plants. Pets are welcome if on a 6-ft leash. ✉ *1 mi north of U.S. 1 on Rte. 905, OS, North Key Largo,* ☎ *305/451–1202.* 🎟 *Free.* ☉ *Daily 8–5, tours Thurs. and Sun. 10.*

❷ Taking the Overseas Highway from the mainland lands you closer to **Key Largo** proper, abounding with shopping centers, chain restaurants, and, of course, dive shops.

The small but earnest not-for-profit **Maritime Museum of the Florida Keys** depicts the local history of shipwrecks and salvage efforts through

The Florida Keys

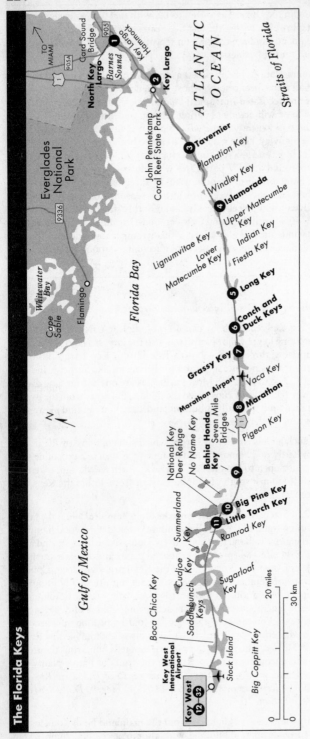

Gulf of Mexico

Everglades National Park

Whitewater Bay

Cape Sable

Flamingo

Florida Bay

TO MIAMI

905

1

Card Sound Bridge

North Key Largo

Key Largo Hammock

Barnes Sound

9336

1

2 Key Largo

ATLANTIC OCEAN

Straits of Florida

John Pennekamp Coral Reef State Park

3 Tavernier

Plantation Key

Windley Key

4 Islamorada

Upper Matecumbe Key

Lignumvitae Key

Lower Matecumbe Key

Indian Key

Fiesta Key

5 Long Key

6 Conch and Duck Keys

7 Grassy Key

Vaca Key

Marathon Airport

8 Marathon

Pigeon Key

Seven Mile Bridges

National Key Deer Refuge

No Name Key

Bahia Honda Key

9

10 Big Pine Key

11 Little Torch Key

Ramrod Key

Summerland Key

Cudjoe Key

Saddlebunch Keys

Boca Chica Key

Sugarloaf Key

Big Pine Key

N

Key West International Airport

Key West

Stock Island

Big Coppitt Key

12 **32**

20 miles

30 km

0

0

retrieved treasures, reconstructed wreck sites, and artifacts in various stages of preservation. Some of the more notable exhibits have come from a fleet of treasure ships wrecked by a hurricane in 1715. A bottle exhibit tells Keys history through more than 200 salvaged bottles, dating from as early as the 1600s. The museum is a labor of love, and its primary purpose is preservation. ⊠ *MM 102.5, BS,* ☎ *305/451–6444.* ▨ *$5.* ☉ *Mon.–Sat. 10–4.*

★ **John Pennekamp Coral Reef State Park** encompasses 78 square mi of coral reefs, sea-grass beds, and mangrove swamps. Its reefs contain 40 of the 52 species of coral in the Atlantic Reef System and more than 650 varieties of fish, and the diving and snorkeling here are famous. A concessioner rents canoes and sailboats and offers boat trips to the reef. Even a landlubber can appreciate the superb interpretive aquarium, exhibits, and video in the visitor center. The park also includes a nature trail through a mangrove forest, two man-made beaches, picnic shelters, a snack bar, and a campground. ⊠ *MM 102.5, OS, Box 487, 33037,* ☎ *305/451–1202.* ▨ *$4 per vehicle plus 50¢ per person, $1.50 per pedestrian or bicyclist.* ☉ *Daily 8–sunset.*

You can see the *African Queen*—the steam-powered workboat on which Katharine Hepburn and Humphrey Bogart rode in the movie of the same name—moored at the **Key Largo Harbor Marina,** next to the Holiday Inn Key Largo Resort. You can even arrange to take an hour-long ride on the classic vessel. Also on display is the *Thayer IV,* a 22-ft mahogany Chris Craft used by Hepburn and Henry Fonda in *On Golden Pond.* Both vessels are in demand at boat shows and occasionally vacate their moorings. ⊠ *MM 99.7, OS,* ☎ *305/451–4655.* ▨ *Boat ride $15.* ☉ *Boat ride by appointment.*

❸ The southernmost part of Key Largo is **Tavernier.** Wood-carver and teacher Laura Quinn brought the **Florida Keys Wild Bird Rehabilitation Center** here in 1991, and nowhere else in the Keys can you see birds so close up. Many are kept for life because of injuries that can't be healed, while others are brought for rehabilitation and then set free. At any time the residents can include ospreys, hawks, pelicans, cormorants, terns, and herons of various types. A short nature trail runs into the mangrove forest (bring bug spray May–October), and a video explains the center's mission. ⊠ *MM 93.6, BS, Tavernier,* ☎ *305/852–4486.* ▨ *Donation welcome.* ☉ *Daily sunrise–sunset.*

Harry Harris County Park (⊠ MM 93, OS, Burton Dr., Tavernier, ☎ 305/852–7161 or 888/227–8136) has play equipment, a small swimming lagoon, a boat ramp, ball fields, barbecue grills, and rest rooms. Though the turnoff is clearly marked on the Overseas Highway, the road to the ocean is circuitous.

Dining and Lodging

$–$$$ ✕ **The Fish House.** Behind the screened, diner-style facade are display
★ cases filled with the freshest catches, which are then baked, blackened, broiled, fried, sautéed, steamed, or stewed as if every night were the finals of a seafood competition (in fact, the Fish House wins many such competitions). The dining room—festooned with nets and fishy Christmas ornaments—is as redolent of the Keys as a Bogart movie. Generous portions come with corn on the cob, new potatoes or rice, and coleslaw; the key lime pie is homemade. You can't beat the fast service and great eats. ⊠ *MM 102.4, OS,* ☎ *305/451–4665. AE, D, MC, V. Closed early Sept.–early Oct.*

$–$$$ ✕ **Frank Keys Cafe.** This contemporary restaurant is hidden in a nat-
★ ural hardwood hammock except at night, when little white lights in the branches mark the spot. The wooden Victorian-style house has a

deep porch for dining alfresco, and the kitchen is skillfully staffed by chef-owner Frank Graves III and returning executive chef Ralph Salvatore. Their fresh-fish dishes remain local favorites. Try the pan-sautéed catch washed in egg, lightly coated, then given a kiss of sherry, or opt for delicate pasta entrées like seafood Mediterranean (sautéed fresh seafood over pesto linguine with a marinara cream sauce). Salvatore enthusiastically welcomes special requests. If he has the ingredients, he'll make it, whatever it is. ⊠ *MM 100, OS,* ☎ *305/453–0310. AE, MC, V. Closed Tues., plus Mon. Easter–Christmas.*

$–$$ ✗ **Anthony's Italian Restaurant & Lounge.** The portly proprietor greets guests at the door or their tables, making sure they are enjoying his hospitality. There's little to be concerned about; the food, faithful to Italian tradition, speaks for itself. The solid kitchen serves veal, chicken, and home-style pasta dishes in a comfortable setting. Spicy mussels marinara are so good you'll want an order to go. Friday and Saturday nights bring live music. ⊠ *MM 97.6, in the median,* ☎ *305/853–1177. AE, D, MC, V.*

$–$$ ✗ **Cafe Largo.** Soothing jazz plays in this intimate bistro-style Italian
★ restaurant. Dinner starts with a basket of focaccia bread and garlic rolls. Next choose one of the chef's specials; they won't disappoint. The chicken garlic—two thin breast cutlets lightly coated and sautéed, then covered in a light sauce of garlic and rosemary—is divine. The penne with shrimp and broccoli has tender shrimp, al dente broccoli, and a hint of garlic. A more than ample wine list, international beers, Italian bottled waters, and, of course, espresso and cappuccino are offered, and the dessert list is short but sweet. ⊠ *MM 99.5, BS,* ☎ *305/451–4885. AE, MC, V. No lunch.*

$–$$ ✗ **Calypso's.** Hidden away on the waterfront at Ocean Bay Marina is one of the best-kept secrets in the Upper Keys. The self-taught cook Todd Lollis consistently takes away a pan full of prizes at local cook-offs thanks to innovative seafood dishes. One example is seafood burritos, a multitaste dish of grilled shrimp, onion, garlic, and green and red peppers mixed with well-seasoned black beans, tomatoes, and cilantro served on a flour tortilla. A select wine list shows he knows his wines, too, but there are no desserts. The setting is Keys casual; plastic outdoor furniture is complemented by paper napkins and plastic cutlery. ⊠ *MM 99.5, OS, 1 Seagate Blvd.,* ☎ *305/451–0600. D, MC, V. Closed Tues.*

$–$$ ✗ **Mrs. Mac's Kitchen.** Hundreds of beer cans, beer bottles, and expired license plates from all over the world decorate the walls of this wood-paneled, screened, open-air restaurant, which offers traditional American sandwiches, burgers, barbecue, and seafood. At breakfast and lunch, the counter and booths fill up early with locals. Regular nightly specials are worth the stop: meat loaf on Monday, Italian on Wednesday, and seafood Thursday–Saturday. The chili is always good, and the beer of the month is $1.50 a bottle. ⊠ *MM 99.4, BS,* ☎ *305/451–3722. No credit cards. Closed Sun.*

$ ✗ **Alabama Jack's.** In 1953 Alabama Jack Stratham opened his open-air seafood restaurant on two barges in an old fishing community 13 mi southeast of Homestead. The spot, something of a no-man's-land, belongs to the Keys in spirit thanks to Card Sound Road. Regular customers include Keys fixtures, Sunday cyclists, local retirees, and boaters, who come to admire tropical birds in nearby mangroves, the occasional crocodile in the canal, the live band on weekends, or simply the food. Favorites include peppery crab cakes, crispy-chewy conch fritters, crunchy breaded shrimp, and homemade tartar sauce. The place closes by 7 or 7:30, when the skeeters come out. ⊠ *58000 Card Sound Rd., Card Sound,* ☎ *305/248–8741. MC, V.*

$ ✕ **Chad's Deli & Bakery.** Each morning Chad, the owner, bakes eight kinds of breads, which he uses to make sandwiches ($5–$6) large enough to feed two hungry adults. Residents recently voted them the best sandwiches in the Upper Keys. If you're not in the mood for one of the regular sandwiches, ranging from certified Angus roast beef to veggie, try the daily special. The menu also features salads, sides, soft drinks, and a choice of two cookies—white-chocolate macadamia nut and chocolate chip—with a whopping 8-inch diameter (75¢–$1). Most orders in this four-table establishment are takeout. ⊠ *MM 92.3, BS,* ☎ *305/853–5566. No credit cards. No dinner.*

$ ✕ **Harriette's Restaurant.** If you're looking for a traditional American eatery, this is it. Little has changed here over the years other than a new mural and a new, bright, island-style paint job. Owner Harriette Mattson still welcomes her guests, and the same wisecracking but efficient waitresses make breakfast and lunch entertaining. Harriette's is famous for breakfast: steak and eggs with hash browns or grits and toast and jelly for $6.95, or old-fashioned hotcakes with butter and syrup and sausage or bacon for $3.75. The comfy, Keys-y eatery is a local institution. ⊠ *MM 95.7, BS,* ☎ *305/852–8689. No credit cards. No dinner.*

$$$$ ☷ **Jules' Undersea Lodge.** In the "not for everyone" category, this novel accommodation caters to well-finned visitors who want a total Keys diving experience. The hotel, a former underwater research lab, is 5 fathoms (30 ft) below the surface. Hence, to be one of the six guests, you have to be a certified diver or take the hotel's three-hour introductory course (an additional $75). Rooms have a shower, telephone, VCR and stereo (no TV), and galley. The lodge is popular with honeymooners. Rates include breakfast, dinner, snacks, beverages, and diving gear. Because of the length of stay underwater, once back on terra firma, you can't fly or make deep dives for 24 hours. ⊠ *MM 103.2, OS, 51 Shoreland Dr., 33037,* ☎ *305/451–2353,* ℻ *305/451–4789. 2 bedrooms, sleeps up to 6. Dining room. AE, D, MC, V.*

$$$$ ☷ **Marriott's Key Largo Bay Beach Resort.** This 17-acre bay-side resort's five lemon-yellow, grill-balconied, and spire-topped stories are sliced between highway and bay and give off an air of warm, indolent days. The facilities are as good as the guest rooms, which feature rattan, paddle fans, and balconies. From some you can watch the sunset sweep across the bay. ⊠ *MM 103.8, BS, 103800 Overseas Hwy., 33037,* ☎ *305/453–0000 or 800/932–9332,* ℻ *305/453–0093. 153 rooms, 20 2-bedroom suites, 6 3-bedroom suites, 1 penthouse suite. Restaurant, 3 bars, pool, beauty salon, hot tub, massage, beach, dive shop, fishing, meeting rooms. AE, D, DC, MC, V.*

$$$–$$$$ ☷ **Westin Beach Resort, Key Largo.** This large resort with lush land-
★ scaping is tucked away in a hardwood hammock. Fourth-floor bay-side rooms afford marvelous water views. Units on the first three floors overlook the woods, except the 230, 330, and 430 series, which face the landscaped parking lot. The spacious, comfortable rooms have tropical decor. Lighted nature trails and boardwalks wind through the woods to a small beach. Two pools, one for adults only, are separated by a coral rock wall and waterfall. Both restaurants overlook the water. ⊠ *MM 96.9, BS, 97000 Overseas Hwy., 33037,* ☎ *305/852–5553 or 800/826–1006,* ℻ *305/852–8669. 190 rooms, 10 suites. 2 restaurants, 2 bars, 2 pools, hot tub, 2 tennis courts, beach, dock, windsurfing, boating, fishing. AE, D, DC, MC, V.*

$$$ ☷ **Kona Kai Resort.** A sidewalk winds between beautifully landscaped
★ cottages to a small beach and marina at this stylish laid-back resort. The garden alone makes it worth staying here, as do rooms with tropical furnishings, toiletries made from fruits and flowers, and Noritake china. This is not your typical first-class resort with staff everywhere

you turn. Privacy is paramount: There are no room phones, and maid service is every fourth morning. Guests trade in their fluffy towels at a linen cabinet as they please. Studios and one- and two-bedroom suites—with full kitchens and original art—are spacious and light filled. Beachfront hammocks and a toasty pool make it easy to while away the day, but there's also plenty to do. Try a paddleboat or kayak, or visit the art gallery, with works by major South Florida artists. Smoking is not permitted, nor are guests under 16. ⊠ *MM 97.8, BS, 97802 Overseas Hwy., 33037,* ☎ *305/852–7200 or 800/365–7829. 11 units. Pool, lighted tennis court, basketball, volleyball, boating, beach, dock. AE, D, MC, V.*

$$–$$$ 🏨 **Marina Del Mar Resort and Marina.** This two- to four-story resort on a deep-water marina caters to sailors and divers. Units have original watercolors by Keys artist Mary Boggs, as well as refrigerators. Suites 502–504 have kitchens (as do studios) and plenty of room for groups. There's a free Continental breakfast in the lobby; live entertainment nightly in Coconuts, a popular restaurant and bar; and spectacular sunrise and sunset views from the fourth-floor observation deck. ⊠ *MM 100, OS, 527 Caribbean Dr., 33037,* ☎ *305/451–4107 or 800/451–3483,* ﬀ *305/451–1891. 52 rooms, 8 suites, 16 studios. Restaurant, bar, pool, 2 tennis courts, exercise room, dock, boating, fishing. AE, D, DC, MC, V.*

$$ 🏨 **Frank's Key Haven Resort.** In a quiet neighborhood under a canopy of graceful, towering gumbo-limbo trees, this lodge, made of beams from Flagler's railroad tracks and imported German concrete, was built in the 1930s to withstand hurricane-force winds. The original owner ran bird-watching tours, and though the enlarged property still offers ecotours, it now caters to divers. The resort has its own dive boat, waterfront, and training pool and offers diving certification as well as diving-lodging packages that include night dives. Screened porches have racks for dive equipment. Rooms vary from one-room efficiencies to one- and two-bedroom apartments and family units. A public area has a TV, half kitchen, and comfy seating. ⊠ *MM 92, BS, 198 Harborview Dr., Tavernier 33070,* ☎ *305/852–3017 or 800/765–5397,* ﬀ *305/852–3880. 14 units. Pool, docks. MC, V.*

$$ 🏨 **Largo Lodge.** No two rooms are the same in this 1950s-vintage adults-
★ only resort, but all are cozy and fully equipped with kitchens, rattan furniture, and screened porches but no phones. The prettiest palm alley you've ever seen sets the mood, while tropical gardens with more palms, sea grapes, and orchids surround the guest cottages. There's 200 ft of bay frontage. Late in the day, wild ducks, pelicans, herons, and other birds come looking for a handout from longtime owner Harriet "Hat" Stokes. If you want a laid-back, top-value tropical hideaway not too far down the Keys, this is it. ⊠ *MM 101.5, BS, 101740 Overseas Hwy., 33037,* ☎ *305/451–0424 or 800/468–4378. 6 apartments, 1 efficiency. Beach, dock. MC, V.*

$ 🏨 **Popp's Motel.** Since 1951 and for four generations, Popp family members have welcomed guests to this small and private motel. Rooms are just yards from a sandy beach, and you can take part in activities galore or relax in a hammock while the kids play on swings. All bedroom units and efficiencies have a kitchen. Though the place is clean and has been updated several times, dark wood paneling and terrazzo floors in some rooms reveal their age. Other than that, it's a gem of a resort. ⊠ *MM 95.5, BS, 95500 Overseas Hwy., 33037,* ☎ *305/852–5201,* ﬀ *305/852–5200. 9 units. Picnic area, beach, dock, playground. AE, MC, V.*

$ ⚠ **America Outdoors.** Reserve early to camp here, especially around holidays and from January to mid-March. A waterfront location and woodsy setting, security, boat ramps and rentals, a sandy beach, store, bait shop, bathhouse, and an adult recreation center make it popular with snowbirds and South Floridians, who come back year after year and weekend after weekend. It's also very clean, orderly, and well managed. Rates for tents are $20–$40, for RVs $33–$55, depending on season, day of week, and services. ⊠ *MM 97.5, BS, 97450 Overseas Hwy., 33037,* ☎ *305/852–8054. 154 sites. Grocery, beach, dock, boating, fishing, coin laundry, recreation room. AE, D, MC, V.*

Nightlife

The semiweekly *Keynoter* (Wednesday and Saturday), weekly *Reporter* (Thursday), and Friday to Sunday editions of the *Miami Herald* are the best sources of information on entertainment and nightlife.

Breezers Tiki Bar (⊠ MM 103.8, BS, ☎ 305/453–0000), in Marriott's Key Largo Bay Beach Resort (☞ Dining and Lodging, *above*), is popular with the smartly coiffed crowd. Office workers join guests for cocktails to toast the sun going down. Walls plastered with Bogart memorabilia remind customers that the classic 1948 Bogart-Bacall flick *Key Largo* was shot in the **Caribbean Club** (⊠ MM 104, BS, ☎ 305/451–9970). An archetype of a laid-back Keys bar, it draws a hairy-faced, down-home group to shoot the breeze while shooting pool but is friendlier than you might imagine. It also has postcard-perfect sunsets. **Coconuts** (⊠ MM 100, OS, 528 Caribbean Dr., ☎ 305/453–9794), in Marina Del Mar Resort (☞ Dining and Lodging, *above*), has blues on Tuesday and nightly entertainment year-round, except Sunday and Monday during football season. The crowd is primarily thirty- and fortysomething. The new **Zappie's Bar and Tackle** (⊠ MM 99.2, BS, ☎ 305/451–0531) goes by the slogan "Live Bait & Live Music." Sorry, this isn't the ultimate pickup spot. The bait refers to fishing bait that's sold in the adjoining shop, Bill's Bait, which has been here for years. There's good, live music on weekends ($3 cover) and on other nights in high season.

Outdoor Activities and Sports

BIKING

Equipment Locker Sport & Cycle (⊠ Tradewinds Plaza, MM 101, OS, ☎ 305/453–0140) rents single-speed adult and children's bikes. Cruisers go for $10 a day, $50 a week. No helmets are available.

FISHING

Sailors Choice (⊠ MM 99.7, OS, ☎ 305/451–1802 or 305/451–0041) runs a party boat daily plus a night trip on Friday and Saturday. The ultramodern 60-ft, 49-passenger boat with air-conditioned cabin leaves from the Holiday Inn docks.

SCUBA DIVING AND SNORKELING

American Diving Headquarters (⊠ MM 105.5, BS, ☎ 305/451–0037) offers certification and dive tours on request, not a schedule, and a Water-Tight Guarantee ensures you'll get your money's worth. The staff is concerned about guests and the environment, the latter demonstrated by a reef ecology and fish identification course. Before getting their toes wet, divers attend lectures and slide presentations to help them get more out of the dive experience. The cost is $55 for a two-tank dive with tank and weight rental, $80 if you need everything; $92 includes a wet suit, suggested in winter.

Amy Slate's Amoray Dive Resort (⊠ MM 104.2, BS, ☎ 305/451–3595 or 800/426-6729) is a full-service dive shop (NAUI, PADI, YMCA, and British BSAC certified) that has accommodations packages and also performs underwater weddings. **Coral Reef Park Co.** (⊠ John Pennekamp Coral Reef State Park, MM 102.5, OS, ☎ 305/451–1621) offers scuba and snorkeling tours of the park. **Quiescence Diving Service, Inc.** (⊠

MM 103.5, BS, ☎ 305/451–2440) sets itself apart in two ways: It limits groups to six to ensure personal attention and offers day, night, and twilight dives an hour before sundown, the time when sea creatures are most active.

WATER SPORTS

Coral Reef Park Co. (⊠ John Pennekamp Coral Reef State Park, MM 102.5, OS, ☎ 305/451–1621) rents boats and equipment for sailing, canoeing, and windsurfing. You can rent a canoe or a one- or two-person sea kayak, even camping equipment, from **Florida Bay Outfitters** (⊠ MM 104, BS, ☎ 305/451–3018). Real pros, they match the right equipment to the right skill level, so even novices feel confident paddling off. Rentals are by the hour, half day, or full day. They also sell lots of accessories.

Islamorada

❹ *MM 90.5–70.*

Early settlers named Islamorada after their schooner, the *Island Home,* but to make the name more romantic, they translated it into Spanish— *isla morada.* The local chamber of commerce prefers to say it means "the purple isles." Early maps show Islamorada as only Upper Matecumbe Key. Historians refer to it as the group of islands between Tavernier Creek at MM 90 and Fiesta Key at MM 70, including Plantation Key, Windley Key, Upper Matecumbe Key, Lower Matecumbe Key, Craig Key, and Fiesta Key. In addition, two islands—Indian Key, in the Atlantic Ocean, and Lignumvitae Key, in Florida Bay—belong to the group.

Claiming they were fed up with a county government more interested in the needs of Key West than the Upper Keys, residents voted for self-incorporation in a controversial election in 1997. Though it's now officially the Village of Isles, some things haven't changed. The area remains a great place to fish. For nearly 100 years, seasoned anglers have recognized these sun-bathed waters as home to a huge variety of game fish as well as lobster, shrimp, and crabs. The rich, the famous, the powerful have all fished here, including Lou Gehrig, Ted Williams, Zane Grey, and presidents Hoover, Truman, Carter, and Bush. More than 150 backcountry guides and 400 offshore captains operate out of this 20-mi stretch.

Activities range from fishing tournaments to historic reenactments. During September and October, Heritage Days feature free lectures on Islamorada history, a golf tournament, and the Indian Key Festival. Holiday Isle Resort sponsors boating, fishing, car, and golf tournaments, as well as bikini and body-building contests.

Between 1885 and 1915 settlers earned good livings growing pineapples on **Plantation Key** (⊠ MM 90.5–86), using black Bahamian workers to plant and harvest their crops. The plantations are gone, replaced by a dense concentration of homes and businesses.

At 16 ft above sea level, **Windley Key** (⊠ MM 86–84) is the highest point in the Keys. Originally two islets, the area was first inhabited by Native Americans, who left middens and other remains, and then by settlers, who farmed and fished in the mid-1800s and called the islets the Umbrella Keys. The Florida East Coast Railway bought the land from homesteaders in 1908, filled in the inlet between the two islands, and changed the name. They quarried rock for the rail bed and bridge approaches in the Keys—the same rock used in many historic South Florida structures, including Miami's Vizcaya and the Hurricane Monument on Upper Matecumbe. Though the Quarry Station stop was destroyed by the 1935 hurricane, quarrying continued until the 1960s. Today a few resorts and attractions occupy the island.

When the Florida East Coast Railway drilled, dynamited, and carved Windley Key's limestone bed, it exposed the once-living fossilized coral reef that was laid down about 125,000 years ago, now visible at the **Windley Key Fossil Reef State Geologic Site.** Five trails lead to old quarrying equipment and cutting pits, where you can stand within a petrified reef and take rubbings of beautifully fossilized brain coral and sea ferns. The new Alison Fahrer Environmental Education Center contains historic, biological, and geological displays. For information contact the Long Key State Recreation Area (☞ Long Key, *below*). ⊠ *MM 85.5, BS,* ☎ *305/664–4815.* ▧ *Education center free, quarry trails $1.50.* ☉ *Education center Thurs.–Mon. 8–5; inquire about quarry tour schedule.*

At **Theater of the Sea,** dolphins, sea lions, stingrays, and tropical fish swim in the 1907 Windley Key railroad quarry, whose huge blasted holes are now filled with seawater. The park features marine-mammal shows, sea-life interaction programs, snorkel ecotours, and cruises. Allow at least two hours to attend the dolphin and sea-lion shows and visit all the exhibits, which include an injured birds of prey display, a "bottomless" boat ride, a shell-life touch tank, a pool where sharks are fed by a trainer, and several small-fish aquariums. For an additional fee, you can even swim with dolphins, sea lions, or stingrays for 30 minutes, after a 15- or 30-minute orientation, and arrange for video or still photos of your experience. ⊠ *MM 84.5, OS, Box 407, 33036,* ☎ *305/664–2431.* ▧ *$15.75; snorkel ecotours $50; swim with dolphins $85, with sea lions $65, with stingrays $50; reservations required with 50% deposit.* ☉ *Daily 9:30–4.*

Upper Matecumbe Key (⊠ MM 84–79) was one of the earliest in the Upper Keys to be permanently settled. Homesteaders were so successful at growing pineapples and limes in the rocky soil that at one time the island had the largest U.S. pineapple crop; however, Cuban pineapples and the hurricane of 1935 killed the industry. Today life centers on fishing and tourism, and the island is lively with homes, charter fishing boats, bait shops, restaurants, stores, nightclubs, marinas, nurseries, and offices.

Somewhere in Time is a small, unlikely combination museum and antiques and jewelry shop crowded with hundreds of interesting artifacts. Nearly every inch of wall and counter space is filled with objects salvaged from merchant and slave ships that used to ply Florida's waters. There are coins from the *Atocha*, rare ceramic containers, original 18th-century maps, cannon, solid silver bars, slave artifacts, religious medallions, rare bottles, and a corny diorama of two infamous English women who were pirates. The owner tells marvelous stories about the objects' provenance. ⊠ *MM 82.7, OS,* ☎ *305/664–9699.* ▧ *Free.* ☉ *Daily 9–5.*

Home to the local chamber of commerce, a **red train caboose** sits at the site where the Florida East Coast Railway had a station and living quarters, before they washed away with the hurricane of 1935. Artifacts ranging from dishes and flatware to uniform buttons and medicine bottles were excavated and are on display. ⊠ *MM 82.5, BS.* ▧ *Free.* ☉ *Weekdays 9–5, Sat. 9–4.*

Beside the highway, the **Hurricane Monument** (⊠ MM 81.6, OS) marks the mass grave of 423 victims of the 1935 Labor Day hurricane. Many of those who perished were World War I veterans who had been working on the Overseas Highway and died when a tidal surge overturned a train sent to evacuate them. The 65-ft by 20-ft Art Deco–style monument, built of Keys coral limestone with a ceramic map of the Keys, depicts wind-driven waves and palms bowing before the storm's fury. Note that the trees bend in the wrong direction.

Tucked away behind the Islamorada library is a small beach on a creek at **Islamorada County Park** (⊠ MM 81.5, BS, ☎ 305/852–7161 or 888/ 227–8136). The water isn't very deep, but it is crystal clear. Currents are swift, making swimming unsuitable for young children, but they can enjoy the playground as well as picnic tables, grassy areas, and rest rooms.

OFF THE
BEATEN PATH

INDIAN KEY STATE HISTORIC SITE – On the ocean side of the Matecumbe islands, 10½-acre Indian Key was inhabited by Native Americans for several thousand years before Europeans arrived, as archaeological excavations here show. The islet was a county seat and base for early 19th-century shipwreck salvagers until an Indian attack wiped out the settlement in 1840. Dr. Henry Perrine, a noted botanist, was killed in the raid. Today his plants overgrow the town's ruins. On the first weekend in October the Indian Key Festival celebrates the Key's heritage. Guided tours are available most days, but even when they're not, you can roam among the marked trails and sites. The island is reachable only by boat—either your own, a rental, or a ferry. Robbie's Marina (☞ *below*), the official concessioner, rents kayaks and boats and operates twice-daily ferry service coordinated with the tours. To arrange for a ranger-led tour if you're using your own or a rental boat, contact Long Key State Recreation Area (☞ Long Key, *below*). Locals like to kayak out from Indian Key Fill (⊠ MM 78.5, BS). ⊠ MM 78.5, OS, ☎ 305/ 664–9814 for ferry service; 305/664–4815 for Long Key State Recreation Area. ⌦ Free, tour $1, ferry (includes tour) $15, $25 with Lignumvitae Key. ☉ Tours Thurs.–Mon. 9 and 1.

LIGNUMVITAE KEY STATE BOTANICAL SITE – A virgin hardwood forest still cloaks this 280-acre bay-side island, punctuated by the home and gardens that chemical magnate William Matheson built as a private retreat in 1919. Access is only by boat—either your own, a rental, or a ferry operated by the official concessioner, Robbie's Marina (☞ *below*), which also rents kayaks and boats. (Kayaking out from Indian Key Fill, at MM 78.5, is popular with locals.) Once on the key you can take a tour with the resident ranger, from whom you can request a list of native and well-naturalized plants. As a courtesy, you should arrange for a tour in advance with Long Key State Recreation Area (☞ Long Key, *below*) if you're using your own or a rental boat. ⊠ MM 78.5, BS, ☎ 305/664– 9814 for ferry service; 305/664–4815 for Long Key State Recreation Area. ⌦ Free, tour $1, ferry (includes tour) $15, $25 with Indian Key. ☉ Tours Thurs.–Mon. 10 and 2.

Though tarpon are known for the exciting fight they put up when hooked, you'd never know it judging by the 50 or so prehistoric-looking specimens that gather around the docks at **Robbie's Marina,** on Lower Matecumbe Key. These fish—some as long as 5 ft—literally eat out of the hands of children who buy a $2 bucket of bait fish. Both kids and adults enjoy watching them. ⊠ MM 77.5, BS, ☎ 305/664–9814 or 877/664–8498. ⌦ Dock access $1. ☉ Daily 8–5:30.

Anne's Beach (⊠ MM 73.5, OS, ☎ 305/852–7161 or 888/227–8136), on Lower Matecumbe Key, has a ½-mi elevated wooden boardwalk that meanders through a natural wetland hammock. Covered picnic areas along the boardwalk provide a place to rest and enjoy the view. Rest rooms are at the north end.

Dining and Lodging

$$–$$$ ✕ **Morada Bay.** The owners of the tony Moorings resort opened this
★ restaurant, which has a bay-front location perfect for sunset watching. Conch architecture is enhanced by the black-and-white Everglades
photos of Clyde Butcher, which line the walls. The contemporary
menu features a died-and-gone-to-heaven shrimp bisque, Portobello
burger, and cumin-seared snapper with roasted red peppers and a
spinach quesadilla. It's a small place (there's often a wait to be seated),
with half a dozen tables inside and a dozen on the porch overlooking
a sandy beach dotted with Adirondack chairs. The melodic tunes of a
guitar player waft out to sea on the breezes Friday to Sunday nights.
Another restaurant with the same name but with fine dining is opening next door. ✉ *MM 81, BS,* ☎ *305/664–0604. AE, MC, V.*

$–$$ ✕ **Islamorada Fish Company.** In one of the prettiest spots in the Keys,
this very casual seafood restaurant has undertaken a major expansion
of its indoor seating area by moving its fish market and retail section
into a new building. Charm will be retained, however, with small um-
brella-covered tables and family-style awning-covered picnic benches
overlooking several islets and the calm waters of Florida Bay. At the
fish market's dock, boats unload the fresh catch, which minutes later
is served fried, grilled, blackened, or broiled. The kitchen staff prepares
good, satisfying, and simple food. Wine, beer, soda, and pink lemonade are served icy cold. ✉ *MM 81.5, BS,* ☎ *305/664–9271. MC, V.*

$–$$ ✕ **Manny & Isa's.** Fewer than a dozen tables are squeezed into the sim-
ple room, where the namesake owners serve always perfect Cuban and
Spanish cuisine. The regular menu is split between traditional Cuban
dishes and local seafood, and there are several fish, chicken, and pork
chop specials, all served with salad and Cuban bread. Succulent fish
fingers served with black beans and rice will set you back only $9.95.
Manny's key lime pies are legendary. On any evening a parade of customers comes through to get them takeout, and speaking of takeout,
many people call ahead for meals to go, to avoid lines on weekends
and in high season. ✉ *MM 81.6, OS, 81610 Old Hwy.,* ☎ *305/664–
5019. AE, D, MC, V. Closed Tues. and mid-Oct.–mid.-Nov.*

$–$$ ✕ **Squid Row.** This affable roadside seafood eatery serves the freshest
★ fish possible, courtesy of the seafood wholesalers who own it. Grouper
comes grilled, divinely flaky, or in bread crumbs and sautéed, served
with citrus butter, and the nightly special bouillabaisse ($23.95) is
simply wonderful. If you finish it by yourself—no cheating—you get
a free slice of key lime pie. The waitstaff will brew a fresh pot of coffee and volunteer to wrap what's left of the flavorful, airy banana bread
that comes at the start of the meal but is best as dessert. There's also
a bar with happy hour 4–7. ✉ *MM 81.9, OS,* ☎ *305/664–9865. AE,
D, DC, MC, V.*

$$$$ ⌂ **Cheeca Lodge.** This 27-acre low-rise resort sits amid tranquil fish-
filled lagoons and gardens. Decorated with high-grade fabrics, carpets,
and furniture, units are washed in oh-so-tropical blue and rich sand.
Suites have kitchens and screened balconies; fourth-floor rooms in the
main lodge have ocean or bay views. The resort is the local leader in
green activism with everything from recycling efforts to ecotours.
Camp Cheeca for kids is fun and educational. ✉ *MM 82, OS, Box
527, 33036,* ☎ *305/664–4651 or 800/327–2888,* FAX *305/664–2893.
139 rooms, 64 suites. 2 restaurants, lobby lounge, 2 pools, saltwater
tidal pool, 9-hole golf course, 6 lighted tennis courts, boating, parasailing, fishing, children's programs, playground. AE, D, DC, MC, V.*

$$$–$$$$ ⌂ **The Moorings.** This onetime coconut plantation on 18 acres is one
★ of the finest places to stay in the Keys. Tucked in a tropical forest, one-,
two-, and three-bedroom cottages and two-story houses are furnished
with wicker and artistic African fabrics and have pristine white kitchens.

Peaked roofs rise behind French doors, lighting is soft, and there are many exquisite touches, from thick towels to extra-deep, cushiony bed-covers. The beach has a scattering of Adirondack chairs and hammocks, complimentary windsurfing and kayaking, and a swimming dock. There's a two-night minimum on one-bedrooms and a one-week minimum on other lodgings. ⊠ *MM 81.6, OS, 123 Beach Rd., 33036,* ☎ *305/664–4708,* FAX *305/664–4242. 18 cottages and houses. Pool, tennis court, beach, windsurfing. MC, V.*

$$ ⊡ **White Gate Court.** Far from the madding crowds of Islamorada's business district, this recently restored resort consists of five wooden cottages laid out on 3 pretty landscaped acres along 200 ft of white-sand beach. Susanne Orias de Cargnelli spent two years restoring and decorating the cottages, which date from the 1940s. The result is a simple, intimate escape, where everyone in the family, including the dog, is welcome. All the units, which sleep either two or four, have a full kitchen, cable TV, direct phone lines, and air-conditioning. Barbecue grills and umbrella-shaded tables, big old palm and native trees create a relaxing mood. ⊠ *MM 76, BS, 76010 Overseas Hwy., 33036,* ☎ *305/664–4136. 7 units. Picnic area, beach, dock, coin laundry. MC, V.*

$ ⊡ **Ragged Edge Resort.** People come to the Keys to get away. The fortunate ones find the Ragged Edge, a come-as-you-are, be-who-you-are kind of place. There are lots of regulars, some of whom have been coming for 20 years. Clean rooms feature pine paneling, chintz, and a tile bath suite, and most have kitchens with irons. Most downstairs units have screened porches, while upper units have large decks, more windows, and beam ceilings. Though the place feels expensive, it's affordable due to a lack of staff and things like in-room phones. Amenities take the form of a thatch-roof observation tower, picnic areas, barbecue pits, and free bikes. There's not much of a beach, but you can swim off the remodeled dock—a virtual rookery when boats don't disturb the pelicans, herons, anhingas, and terns. ⊠ *MM 86.5, OS, 243 Treasure Harbor Rd., 33036,* ☎ *305/852–5389. 10 units. Picnic area, pool, shuffleboard, dock, bicycles. MC, V.*

Nightlife

Holiday Isle Beach Resorts & Marina (⊠ MM 84, OS, ☎ 305/664–2321) is the liveliest spot in the Upper Keys. On weekends, especially during spring break and holidays, the resort's three entertainment areas are mobbed, primarily with the under-30 set, whose IDs are carefully scrutinized. Live bands play everything from reggae to heavy metal. Behind the larger-than-life mermaid is the Keys-easy, over-the-water cabana bar the **Lorelei** (⊠ MM 82, BS, ☎ 305/664–4656). Live nightly sounds are mostly reggae and light rock.

Outdoor Activities and Sports

BOATING

To experience the Keys as they were before the highway intruded, rent a houseboat from **Houseboat Vacations of the Florida Keys** (⊠ MM 85.9, BS, 85944 Overseas Hwy., 33036, ☎ 305/664–4009). The new fleet of 40- to 44-ft boats accommodate from six to eight people and come fully outfitted with safety equipment and necessities—except food—as well as an AM/FM cassette stereo. The three-day minimum runs $595–$890; a week costs $1,025–$1,575. Kayaks, canoes, and 16-ft skiffs are also for hire. **Robbie's Boat Rentals & Charters** (⊠ MM 77.5, BS, 77520 Overseas Hwy., 33036, ☎ 305/664–9814) rents a 15-ft skiff with a 25-horsepower outboard (the smallest you can charter) for $20 an hour, $70 for four hours, and $90 for the day. Boats up to 27 ft are also available, but there's a two-hour minimum. Other than clothes and food, Captains Pam and Pete Anderson of **Treasure Har-**

bor Marine (✉ MM 86.5, OS, 200 Treasure Harbor Dr., 33036, ☎ 305/852–2458 or 800/352–2628) provide everything you'll need for a vacation at sea—linens, safety gear, and, best of all, advice on where to find the best beaches, marinas, and lobster sites. You can rent a vessel bareboat or crewed, with sail or with power. Boats include a 19-ft Cape Dory, 41-ft custom-built ketch, 35-ft Mainship, and 35-ft Chenhwa trawler, as well as Morgans, Watkins, and Hunters. A new 47-ft Tradewind comes with a captain. Rates start at $95 a day, $395 a week. Most business is repeat customers. Marina facilities are basic—water, electric, ice machine, laundry, picnic tables, and shower/rest rooms—and dockage is only $1 a foot.

FISHING

Sandy Moret is one of the most respected and recognizable names in Keys fly-fishing. He operates **Florida Keys Outfitters** (✉ MM 82, BS, ☎ 305/664–5423), home to a store and the Florida Keys Fly Fishing School, which attracts anglers from around the world. Two-day weekend fly-fishing classes, which include classroom instruction, equipment, arrival cocktails, and daily breakfast and lunch, cost $795. Add another $800 for two days of fishing. Guided fishing trips cost $275 for a half day, $400 for a full day. Fishing and accommodations packages (at Cheeca Lodge) are available. The 65-ft party boat **Gulf Lady** (✉ Bud 'n' Mary's Marina, MM 79.8, OS, ☎ 305/664–2628 or 305/664–2461) has a new look, having been rebuilt after being destroyed by a Tropical Storm Mitch tornado. If you take full-day and night trips, the boat can be crowded, so call about loads in advance. Since 1957 Captain Ken Knudsen of the **Hubba Hubba** (✉ Bud 'n' Mary's Marina, MM 79.8, OS, ☎ 305/664–9281) has fished the waters around Islamorada, first taking out guests at his family's hotel when he was 12, later as a licensed backcountry guide. His expertise earned him ranking as one of the top 10 guides in Florida by national fishing magazines, and he fishes what he knows best: bonefish, permit, snook, redfish, trout, and tarpon. Unlike most guides, he offers four-hour sunset trips for tarpon ($300) and two-hour sunset trips for bonefish ($175), as well as half- ($275) and full-day ($375) outings. Prices are for one or two anglers, and tackle and bait are included.

SCUBA DIVING AND SNORKELING

Florida Keys Dive Center (✉ MM 90.5, OS, Box 391, Tavernier 33070, ☎ 305/852–4599 or 800/433–8946) organizes dives from John Pennekamp Coral Reef State Park to Alligator Light. The center has two Coast Guard–approved dive boats, offers scuba training, and is one of the few Keys dive centers to offer Nitrox (mixed gas) diving. Since 1980 **Lady Cyana Divers** (✉ MM 85.9, BS, Box 1157, 33036, ☎ 305/664–8717 or 800/221–8717), a PADI five-star training resort, has operated dives on deep and shallow wrecks and reefs between Molasses and Alligator reefs. The 40- and 55-ft boats provide everything a diver needs, including full bathrooms.

TENNIS

New owners of the four clay and two hard courts at **Islamorada Tennis Club** (✉ MM 76.8, BS, ☎ 305/664–5340) keep the center buzzing year-round. It's popular partly because it's inexpensive (from $12 an hour) and partly because it's well run. Amenities include racket stringing, ball machines, private lessons, a full-service pro shop, night games, and partner pairing.

Shopping

Two former Miami teachers knocked down walls, added a coffee bar, and turned the once tiny **Cover to Cover Books** (✉ MM 90.1, OS, 90130 Old Hwy., ☎ 305/852–1415) into one of the best bookstores in the

Keys. They also sell gifts and jewelry and hold book signings and readings for kids. There is an extensive selection of books, cards, and maps on Florida and the Keys. There's chic shopping at the **Gallery at Morada Bay** (✉ MM 81.6, BS, ☎ 305/664–3650), stocked with blown glass and glassware, furniture and home furnishings, original paintings and lithographs, sculptures, and hand-painted scarves and earrings by top South Florida artists. At **Island Silver & Spice** (✉ MM 82, OS, ☎ 305/664–2714), the first floor is devoted to women's and men's resort wear, a large jewelry section with high-end Swiss watches and marine-theme jewelry, tropical housewares, cards, and toys and games. Climb the wooden stairway to the second floor to browse through tropical bedding and bath goods and a sale section.

A circa-1977 crafts village set in a tropical garden of native plants and orchids, **Rain Barrel** (✉ MM 86.7, BS, ☎ 305/852–3084) represents works by numerous local and national artists and has eight resident artists in separate studios. On the third weekend in March, the largest arts show in the Keys takes place here; some 20,000 visitors view the work of 100 artists and listen to live jazz. A new café offers a primarily vegetarian menu. Such nationally and internationally recognized outdoor artists as sculptor Kendall Van Sant; watercolorists Chet Reneson, Jeanne Dobie, and Kathleen Denis; and painters C. D. Clarke and Tim Borski are represented at the **Redbone Gallery** (✉ MM 81, OS, 200 Industrial Dr., ☎ 305/664–2002). At **Treasure Village** (✉ MM 86.7, OS, 86729 Old Hwy., ☎ 305/852–0511), salvage master Art McKee ran McKee's Treasure Museum in the 1950s. An enormous fabricated lobster by artist Richard Blaes stands in front of the center, where a dozen crafts and specialty shops plus the excellent little Made to Order eat-in and carryout restaurant operate. **World Wide Sportsman** (✉ MM 82.5, BS, ☎ 305/664–4615) is a two-level attraction, lounge, and retail center selling very upscale fishing equipment. It has a pricey art gallery, marina, and departments for clothing and gifts. Black-and-white photos of former U.S. presidents, celebs, and record holders beaming alongside their catches adorn the walls.

Long Key

❺ *MM 70–65.5.*

This island is best known for the **Long Key State Recreation Area.** On the main, ocean side, the Golden Orb Trail leads onto a boardwalk through a mangrove swamp alongside a lagoon, where waterbirds congregate. The park has a campground, picnic area, rest rooms and showers, a canoe trail through a tidal lagoon, and a not-very-sandy beach fronting a broad expanse of shallow grass flats. Bring a mask and snorkel to observe the marine life in this rich nursery area. In 1998 Hurricane Georges flooded the park's ocean side and killed almost all the vegetation. Although the park is open, all repairs and replantings may not be completed by the time you visit. Across the road, near a historical marker partially obscured by foliage, is the **Layton Nature Trail** (✉ MM 67.7, BS), which takes 20–30 minutes to walk and leads through tropical hardwood forest to a rocky Florida Bay shoreline overlooking shallow grass flats. A marker relates the history of the Long Key Viaduct, the first major bridge on the rail line, and the exclusive Long Key Fishing Camp, which Henry Flagler established nearby in 1906 and which attracted sportsman Zane Grey, the noted western novelist and conservationist, who served as its first president. The camp was washed away in the 1935 hurricane and never rebuilt. For Grey's efforts, the creek running near the recreation area was named for him. ✉ *MM 67.5, OS, Box 776, 33001, ☎ 305/664–4815.* 🎫 *$3.25 for 1* *person, plus 50¢ each additional person; canoe rental $4 per hr, $10 per day; Layton Nature Trail free.* ☉ *Daily 8–sunset.*

Dining and Lodging

$–$$ ✕ **Little Italy.** The hearty Italian and seafood dishes here are a great value. Food is consistently good, and prices are consistently low. Recent lunch menu changes added Caesar salads, chicken marsala, stone crabs, and stuffed snapper priced at $3.95–$7.95, including salad, french fries, and bread. Dinner selections are equally tasty and well priced—pasta, chicken, seafood, veal, and steak for $8.50–$13.95. Don't miss the rich, dreamy hot chocolate pecan pie. Breakfast, too, is served, and a light-bites menu features smaller portions. ⊠ *MM 68.5, BS,* ☎ *305/664–4472. AE, D, MC, V.*

$$ ▣ **Lime Tree Bay Resort Motel.** This popular 2½-acre hideaway has attractive wicker- and rattan-furnished guest rooms, tropical art, and cottages with kitchens along with a little beach, nice landscaping, a beautiful pool deck, hammocks, a gazebo, and a covered walkway. The best units are the cottages out back (no bay views) and four deluxe rooms upstairs, which have cathedral ceilings and skylights. The upstairs Tree House, the best bet for two couples traveling together, has a palm tree growing through its private deck. You can swim and snorkel in the shallow grass flats offshore. An on-site concessioner offers water sports, available separately or with an accommodation package. ⊠ *MM 68.5, BS, Box 839, Layton 33001,* ☎ *305/664–4740 or 800/723–4519,* 𝖥𝖠𝖷 *305/664–0750. 30 rooms. Restaurant, picnic area, pool, hot tub, tennis court, horseshoes, shuffleboard, beach, dive shop, snorkeling, windsurfing, boating, jet skiing. AE, D, DC, MC, V.*

$ ◬ **Long Key State Recreation Area.** Situated along the park's narrow, semi-sandy beach are tent and RV sites under tall, shady trees. Fishing in the near-shore flats is superb, yielding bonefish, permit, and tarpon. A new reservation system went into effect in 1998 (you can reserve up to 11 months in advance by phone or in person) along with major upgrades. All sites now have water and electricity, signage has been improved, and campground hostesses are available to answer questions and help out. Sites cost $17, plus $2 for electricity. ⊠ *MM 67.5, OS, Box 776, 33001,* ☎ *305/664–4815. 60 sites. Picnic area, hiking, beach, fishing. D, MC, V.*

Outdoor Activities and Sports

Based at Lime Tree Bay Resort, Captain Elizabeth Jolin's **Lime Tree Water Sports** (⊠ MM 68.5, BS, ☎ 305/664–0052) provides a wide variety of recreational opportunities, including sunset cruises; sailboat, powerboat, kayak, sailboard, and Wave Runner rentals; backcountry fishing trips; and snorkeling and scuba. She also offers PADI diving certification and windsurfing and sailing lessons.

En Route As you cross Long Key Channel, look beside you at the old **Long Key Viaduct.** The second-longest bridge on the former rail line, this 2-mi-long structure has 222 reinforced-concrete arches.

THE MIDDLE KEYS

Stretching from Conch Key to the far side of the Seven Mile Bridge, the Middle Keys contain U.S. 1's most impressive stretch, MM 65–40, bracketed by the Keys' two longest bridges—Long Key Bridge and Seven Mile Bridge, both historic landmarks. Activity centers on the town of Marathon, the Keys' third-largest metropolitan area.

Fishing and diving are the main attractions. In both bay and ocean, the deep-water fishing is superb at places like the Marathon West

Hump, whose depth ranges from 500 to more than 1,000 ft. Anglers successfully fish from a half-dozen bridges, including Long Key Bridge, the old Seven Mile Bridge, and both ends of Toms Harbor. There are also many beaches and natural areas to enjoy in the Middle Keys.

Conch and Duck Keys

❻ *MM 63–61.*

This stretch of islands is rustic. Fishing dominates the economy, and many residents are descendants of immigrants from the mainland South. Across a causeway from Conch Key, a tiny fishing and retirement village, lies Duck Key, an upscale community and resort.

Dining and Lodging

$–$$$ ✕ **Watersedge.** A collection of historic photos on the walls depicts the railroad era, the development of Duck Key, and many of the notables who have visited this eatery at the Hawk's Cay Resort (☞ *below*). Dine in the newly renovated indoor dining room or under the dockside canopy. Soup and a 40-item salad bar are included with dinners. The menu emphasizes seafood, and specialties range from spicy conch chowder, chicken Key West (stuffed with crab and shrimp), and Florida stone-crab claws (in season) to mud pie and coconut ice cream. ✉ *MM 61, OS, Duck Key,* ☎ *305/743–7000. AE, D, DC, MC, V. No lunch mid-Dec.–mid-Apr.*

$$$$ 🏨 **Hawk's Cay Resort.** This rambling Caribbean-style resort, which opened in 1959, has entertained film stars and politicians. Today it's big with families and businesspeople, who enjoy golf on a nearby course, dive trips, volleyball on a sand court overlooking the Atlantic, swimming in the smooth saltwater lagoon or pool, a new fitness center with state-of-the-art equipment, new basketball courts, and a new whirlpool spa. There are programs for kids and teens as well as an interactive, in-the-water educational program called Dolphin Discovery. The light, casual decor comprises lots of wicker and earthy colors. Rooms facing the water are getting makeovers, and construction continues on additional two-bedroom villas. ✉ *MM 61, OS, 33050,* ☎ *305/743–7000 or 800/432–2242,* ℻ *305/743–5215. 160 rooms, 16 suites, 130 two-bedroom villas. 4 restaurants, 2 bars, 2 pools, golf privileges, 8 tennis courts, basketball, health club, volleyball, boating, fishing, video games, children's programs. AE, D, DC, MC, V.*

$$ 🏨 **Conch Key Cottages.** This happy hideout on its own island bridged by a pebbly causeway has a castaway, live-and-let-live mood. Allamanda, bougainvillea, and hibiscus jiggle colorfully, and the beach curves around a mangrove-edged cove. Lattice-trimmed cottages with kitchens, some with two bedrooms, rise up on pilings, old-fashioned in Dade County pine. Cool tile floors, hammocks, and furnishings of reed, rattan, and wicker create an island look. Three cottages face the beach. Though not on the water, the small honeymoon cottage is very charming. If you need a coffee fix, bring your own to prepare, as the closest source is 1½ mi away. Highway noise can be distracting. ✉ *MM 62.3, OS, R.R. 1, Box 424, Marathon 33050,* ☎ *305/289–1377 or 800/330–1577,* ℻ *305/743–8207. 12 units. Pool, beach. D, MC, V.*

Grassy Key

❼ *MM 60–57.*

Local lore has it that this sleepy little key was named not for its vegetation—mostly native trees and shrubs—but for an early settler. It's primarily inhabited by a few families who operate small fishing camps and motels.

The former home of Milton Santini, creator of the original *Flipper* movie, the **Dolphin Research Center** is now home to a colony of about 15 dolphins. A not-for-profit organization offers a half-day program called Dolph*Insight*, which teaches dolphin biology and human–dolphin communications and allows you to touch the dolphins out of the water. A 2½-hour instruction-education program aptly called Dolphin Encounter enables you to do just that in the water for 20 minutes. ⊠ *MM 59, BS, Box 522875, Marathon Shores 33052,* ☎ *305/289–1121.* ⌨ *$12.50, DolphInsight $75, Dolphin Encounter $110.* ⊙ *Daily 9–4, walking tours daily 10, 11, 12:30, 2, and 3:30. Children 5–12 must swim with accompanying, paying adult. Reserve 30 days in advance for all programs.*

OFF THE BEATEN PATH
CURRY HAMMOCK STATE PARK – Comprising upland hammock, wetlands, and mangroves, the state's latest land acquisition open for public use is a jewel. The park covers 260 acres—the largest uninhabited parcel between Key Largo and Big Pine—and is bordered by a sandy beach. There are a new bathhouse and picnic tables, but plans for a campground and entrance fees are still undecided. Locals consider this one of the best areas for kayaking in the Keys. Trails meander under canopies of arching mangroves. Manatees frequent the area, and it's a birding paradise. For now, information is provided by Long Key State Recreation Area (☞ Long Key, *above*). ⊠ *MM 57, OS, Crawl Key,* ☎ *305/664–4815.* ⌨ *Free.* ⊙ *Daily 8–sunset.*

Dining and Lodging

$–$$ ✕ **Grassy Key Dairy Bar.** This little seafood and steak landmark dates from 1959. Locals and construction workers stop here for quick lunches and good company. Despite the name, the only ice cream served is an ice cream pie. To reflect that—and cut down on confusion—the new sign outside says simply GRASSY KEY DB. What they do serve is a popular broiled dolphin with black beans and rice and cheese sauce. Owner-chefs George and Johnny Eigner are also proud of their broiled or grilled fish with wasabi, as well as the fresh-daily homemade bread and fresh-cut beef. On Tuesday night they add Mexican dishes to the menu, and in fall their OctoberFest features German foods, beers, and live entertainment. ⊠ *MM 58.5, OS,* ☎ *305/743–3816. MC, V. Closed Sun.–Mon. No lunch Sat. Apr.–Dec.*

$ 🏨 **Curry Hammock Resort & Marina.** Since the early '60s people have come to the Valhalla Beach Resort Motel, an unpretentious Crawl Key lodging with the waterfront location of a posh resort. In the late '90s the property was split into two resorts, Valhalla Beach Motel (☞ *below*) and Curry Hammock Resort & Marina, with a fence dividing the property. This half has the feel of a friend's beach house. There are a very good beach with hammocks and chaises, a dock from which manatees are frequently sighted, picnic tables, barbecue grills, and kayaks and canoes, a nice touch since the property borders the state's new park, Curry Hammock (☞ *above*), which locals say has one of the Keys' best kayak trails. Family-oriented snorkeling trips to the reefs are offered. There are no phones in rooms. ⊠ *MM 57.5, OS, 56223 Ocean Dr., Crawl Key 33050,* ☎ *305/289–0614. 1 room, 4 efficiencies. Picnic area, beach, dock, boating. MC, V.*

$ 🏨 **Valhalla Beach Motel.** Bruce Schofield runs this motel, which has a few more units than his brother's next door (☞ *above*). Rooms have small refrigerators, while efficiencies have kitchens. The property features a small beach, boat ramp, dock, barbecue grills, canoes and rental fishing boats, and Adirondack chairs. Some things haven't changed, like the palm trees rustling in the wind, clean and simple rooms with TVs but no telephones, and peace and quiet. ⊠ *MM 57.5, OS,*

56243 Ocean Dr., Crawl Key 33050, ☎ 305/289–0616. 4 rooms, 1 suite, 5 efficiencies. Beach, dock, boating. No credit cards.

Marathon

❽ *MM 53–47.5.*

This community is the commercial hub of the Middle Keys. Commercial fishing—still a big local industry—began here in the early 1800s. Pirates, salvors, fishermen, spongers, and later farmers eked out a living, traveling by boat between islands. About half the population were blacks, who burned charcoal for a living. According to local lore, Marathon was renamed after a 1906 hurricane, when a worker commented that it was a marathon task to rebuild the railway across the 6-mi island.

The railroad brought businesses and a hotel, and today Marathon is a bustling town by Keys standards. Yet the town remains laid-back. Fishing, diving, and boating are the primary attractions.

The small **Museums of Tropical Crane Point Hammock**—part of a 63-acre tract that includes the last-known undisturbed thatch-palm hammock—is owned by the Florida Keys Land Trust, a private, nonprofit conservation group. In the **Museum of Natural History of the Florida Keys,** behind a stunning bronze-and-copper door crafted by Roy Butler of Plantation, are a few dioramas, a shell exhibit, and displays on Keys geology, wildlife, and cultural history. Also here is the **Florida Keys Children's Museum,** which has iguanas, fish, and a pirate dress-up room. Outside, on the 1-mi indigenous loop trail, you can visit the remnants of a Bahamian village, site of the restored **George Adderly House,** the oldest surviving example of Conch-style architecture outside Key West. From November to Easter, docent-led tours, included in the price, are available; bring good walking shoes and bug repellent. ⊠ *MM 50.5, BS, 5550 Overseas Hwy., Box 536, 33050, ☎ 305/743–9100.* ☎ *$7.50.* ☉ *Mon.–Sat. 9–5, Sun. noon–5; tours conducted when docents available.*

Sombrero Beach has separate areas for swimmers, jet boats, and windsurfers, as well as a grassy park with barbecue grills, picnic kiosks, showers, rest rooms, a baseball diamond, large playground, and volleyball court. The park is accessible for travelers with disabilities and allows leashed pets. Turn left at the traffic light in Marathon and follow signs to the end. There's a wide bike path from U.S. 1 to the entrance. ⊠ *MM 50, OS, Sombrero Rd., ☎ 305/289–6077 or 888/227–8136.* ☎ *Free.* ☉ *Daily 7:30–sunset.*

OFF THE BEATEN PATH

PIGEON KEY – This 5-acre island under the Seven Mile Bridge was once the site of a railroad work camp and, later, a fish camp, park, and government administration building. Today the focus is on Florida Keys culture, environmental education, and marine research. You can tour on your own, using a free printed walking guide that highlights the restored railroad work-camp buildings, the earliest of which dates from 1908, or take a trolley tour on the hour. Museum exhibits recall the history of the railroad and the Keys, and a 28-minute video captures railroad baron Henry M. Flagler's life. To reach the island, you can either take the shuttle, which departs from the depot on Knight's Key (⊠ MM 47), or walk across a 2.2-mi stretch of the Old Seven Mile Bridge. Bring a picnic and stay the day. ⊠ MM 45, OS, Box 500130, Pigeon Key 33050, ☎ 305/289–0025. ☎ $7.50. ☉ Daily 10–5.

Dining and Lodging

$$–$$$ ✕ **Kelsey's.** This steak and seafood eatery at the Faro Blanco Marine Resort (☞ *below*) is hung with boat paddles inscribed by charter-boat captains and other frequent diners. Entrées like Maryland-style crab cakes and horseradish-encrusted grouper over mashed potatoes are served with fresh-toasted baguettes prepared here daily. You can bring your own cleaned and filleted catch for the chef to prepare. Desserts may include banana pecan delight, white-chocolate mousse, macadamia pie, and key lime cheesecake. ⊠ *MM 48.5, BS,* ☎ *305/743–9018. AE, MC, V. Closed Mon. No lunch.*

$–$$$$ ✕ **Barracuda Grill.** It's right there on the menu: "The owners are cooking for you; pop your head in the kitchen if you'd like to say hello." Guests who do will find Lance and Jan Hill busily preparing an eclectic menu that capitalizes on the local bounty—fresh fish—but is equally represented by tender, juicy aged Angus beef; rack of lamb; and even meat loaf. The latter, Mama's Meatloaf, will not make you think of your childhood. Innovation is in everything but not at the expense of good, solid cooking. Thai Money Bags, a delicate pastry pouch filled with shrimp and veggies, suggests an Asian influence. Ribbiting Frog's Legs, with butter, garlic, and a touch of tomato sauce, screams South Florida. You can't miss on either. The well-thought-out wine list is heavily Californian. ⊠ *MM 49.5, BS,* ☎ *305/743–3314. AE, MC, V. Closed Sun. No lunch.*

$–$$ ✕ **Hurricane Grille.** The same folks who bring you the good food at Key Colony Inn and Little Italy have taken over this restaurant. The menu is packed with good value—rib-sticking seafood, chicken, and steaks—but the best is the shellfish, which comes steamed (clams, crabs, oysters, shrimp, lobster) or raw (clams only) from the moment the doors open until the bar closes, as late as 4 AM. The owners plan to bring in jazz, blues, and rock bands several nights a week. Satellite TV broadcasts sports games, keeping the bar, which takes up half the building, humming. There's indoor and outdoor seating, but the decor, a mishmash of tropical kitsch, is distracting. ⊠ *MM 49.5, BS, 4650 Overseas Hwy.,* ☎ *305/743–2220. AE, MC, V.*

$–$$ ✕ **Island Tiki Bar & Restaurant.** Location, location, location. The new owners of this eatery are taking advantage of its best asset: prime waterfront. The tables and tiki bar overlook the gulf and sunsets. Diners can arrive by boat and tie up at the dock, while those without boats can take a pre- or postprandial sunset cruise. The staff is sharp, and the food—predominantly seafood—is well prepared. She-crab soup ($3.95) has become a local favorite, and jumbo Key West shrimp come four ways, from grilled to *fra diavolo.* ⊠ *MM 54, BS, 12648 Overseas Hwy.,* ☎ *305/743–4191. AE, D, MC, V.*

$–$$ ✕ **Key Colony Inn.** This local institution features chicken, steak, pasta, and veal dishes with an Italian accent. Food is well prepared, and service is friendly and attentive. For lunch there are well-priced fish and steak entrées ($4.50–$6.95) served with fries, salad, and bread. At dinner you can't miss with the seafood Italiano, a light dish of scallops and shrimp sautéed in garlic butter over a bed of linguine with a hint of marinara sauce. ⊠ *MM 54, OS, 700 W. Ocean Dr., Key Colony Beach,* ☎ *305/743–0100. AE, MC, V.*

$ ✕ **7 Mile Grill.** The walls of this open-air diner built in 1954 at the
★ Marathon end of Seven Mile Bridge are lined with beer cans, mounted fish, sponges, and signs describing individual menu items. The prompt, friendly service rivals the great food at breakfast, lunch, and dinner. Favorites on the mostly seafood menu include fresh-squeezed orange juice, creamy shrimp bisque, and fresh grouper and dolphin grilled, broiled, or fried. Don't pass up the authentic key lime pie, which won the local paper's "Best in the Keys" award three years in a row. A wine

license was recently added. ⊠ *MM 47, BS,* ☎ *305/743–4481. No credit cards. Closed Wed., plus Thurs. mid-Apr.–mid-Nov. and at owner's discretion Aug.–Sept.*

$$–$$$$ 🏨 **Faro Blanco Marine Resort.** One of the oldest resorts in the Keys, Faro Blanco has built up a loyal following of repeat guests, thanks to service that's first-rate without being fussy. Before Hurricane Georges, the property stretched on both sides of the highway with guest rooms (most with kitchens); cottages; houseboats; three-bedroom, two-bath condominiums; and two lighthouse apartments. Houseboat accommodations on the ocean side that were heavily damaged by the storm are gradually being replaced. Bay-side properties weathered the storm just fine. A full-service marina and marine repair shop meet boaters' needs, and diving and fishing charters can be arranged. Pets are allowed in all units except condominiums. ⊠ *MM 48.2, BS and OS, 1996 Overseas Hwy., 33050,* ☎ *305/743–9018 or 800/759–3276,* FAX *305/743–2918. 100 units. 3 restaurants, pool, docks, boating, bicycles. AE, MC, V.*

$$–$$$ 🏨 **Seascape Ocean Resort.** If you're looking for an exclusive but un-
★ pretentious hotel in the Middle Keys, look no farther. Nine rooms, three with kitchen, occupy what was once a large, two-story bay-front house that, thanks to a faux stone exterior, wrought-iron grills, and adjacent barn, seems like a villa in Provence. Owned by Sara and Bill Stites, a nationally recognized painter and a magazine photographer, respectively, the 5-acre property has wicker, soothing sea colors, and artistic touches throughout. Rooms are decorated with original artwork and hand-painted headboards and come with fresh fruit, flowers, and specialty soaps. Guests can while away the time at the pool, on the beach, under a shade tree, in a kayak, or in the barn–turned–art studio, where Sara paints. Continental breakfast and afternoon cocktails and hors d'oeuvres are set out for guests to indulge in at leisure. Rooms are non-smoking and have no phones. ⊠ *MM 50.5, OS, 1075 75th St., 33050,* ☎ *305/743–6455 or 800/332–7327,* FAX *305/743–8469. 9 rooms. Pool, beach, dock. AE, MC, V.*

$$ 🏨 **Coral Lagoon.** Surrounded by lush landscaping on a short, deep-water canal, these charming pastel-color duplex cottages each have a hammock on a private sundeck, a kitchen, and king or twin beds and a sofa bed. Units also have central air, ceiling fans, videocassette players ($1 tape rental), wall safes, and hair dryers, and you can take advantage of complimentary morning coffee, tennis rackets, fishing equipment, dockage, and barbecues. For a fee you can also enjoy admission to a private beach club, charter fishing, and scuba and snorkel trips arranged through the Diving Site, a dive shop that also offers certification. ⊠ *MM 53.5, OS, 12399 Overseas Hwy., 33050,* ☎ *305/289–0121,* FAX *305/289–0195. 18 units. Pool, tennis court, dive shop, dock, library. AE, D, MC, V.*

Outdoor Activities and Sports

BIKING

Some of the best paths in the area include those along Aviation Boulevard on the bay side of Marathon Airport, the four-lane section of the Overseas Highway through Marathon, Sadowski Causeway to Key Colony Beach, Sombrero Beach Road to the public beach, and the roads on Boot Key (across a bridge on 20th Street, OS). There's easy cycling at the south end of Marathon, where a 1-mi off-road path connects to the 2 mi of the Old Seven Mile Bridge that go to Pigeon Key.

Equipment Locker Sport & Cycle (⊠ MM 53, BS, ☎ 305/289–1670) rents cruisers for $10 per day, $50 per week and mountain bikes for adults and children.

BOATING

Fish 'n' Fun (✉ MM 53.5, OS, ☎ 305/743–2275), next to the Boat House Marina, rents 18- to 25-ft boats starting at $85 for a half day, $125 for a full day. It also supplies bait, tackle, licenses, and snorkel gear.

FISHING

A pair of 65-ft party boats, **Marathon Lady** and **Marathon Lady III** (✉ MM 53.5, OS, at 117th St., 33050, ☎ 305/743–5580), go on two half-day ($25) trips from the Vaca Cut Bridge, north of Marathon. Those who don't want to pay $200–$350 for a half-day charter or share a party boat with 30 or more other anglers are turning to **Sea Dog Charters** (✉ MM 47.5, BS, ☎ 305/743–8255), next to the 7 Mile Grill. Captain Jim Purcell, a deep-sea specialist for ESPN's *The Outdoorsman,* offers personalized half- and full-day offshore, reef and wreck, tarpon, and backcountry fishing trips as well as combination fishing and snorkeling trips on the 32-ft *Bad Dog* for up to six people. The cost is $59.99 per person for a half day, regardless of whether your group fills the boat, and includes bait, light tackle, licensing, ice, and coolers.

GOLF

Key Colony Beach Par 3 (✉ MM 53.5, OS, 8th St., Key Colony Beach, ☎ 305/289–1533), a nine-hole course near Marathon, charges $7.50 for nine holes, $2 per person for club rental, and $1 for a pull cart. The beauty of this course is that there are no tee times and no rush. Play from 7:30 to dusk. A little golf shop meets basic golf needs.

SCUBA DIVING AND SNORKELING

Hall's Diving Center and Career Institute (✉ MM 48.5, BS, 1994 Overseas Hwy., 33050, ☎ 305/743–5929 or 800/331–4255), next to Faro Blanco Resort, runs two trips a day to Looe Key, Sombrero Reef, Delta Shoal, Content Key, Coffins Patch, the 110-ft wreck *Thunderbolt,* and the new wreck *Adolphus Busch.*

En Route   To cross the broad expanse of water separating the Middle and Lower keys, you'll travel over the **Seven Mile Bridge,** actually 6.79 mi long. Believed to be the world's longest segmental bridge, it has 39 expansion joints separating its cement sections. Each April runners gather in Marathon for the annual Seven Mile Bridge Run. You can look across at what remains of the **Old Seven Mile Bridge,** an engineering marvel in its day that's now on the National Register of Historic Places. It rested on a record 546 concrete piers. No private cars are allowed on the bridge today, but locals like to ride bikes on it to watch the sunset and to reach Pigeon Key.

THE LOWER KEYS

In truth, the Lower Keys include Key West, but since it's covered in its own section and is as different from the rest of the Lower Keys as peanut butter is from jelly, this section comprises just the limestone keys between MM 37 and MM 9. From Bahia Honda Key south, islands are clustered, smaller, and more numerous, a result of ancient tidal waters flowing between the Florida Straits and the gulf. Here you're likely to see more birds and mangroves than other tourists, and more refuges, beaches, and campgrounds than museums, restaurants, and hotels.

The islands are made up of two types of limestone, both more dense than the highly permeable Key Largo limestone of the Upper Keys. As a result, freshwater forms pools rather than percolating, creating watering holes that support Key deer, alligators, fish, snakes, Lower Keys rabbits, raccoons, migratory ducks, Key cotton and silver rice rats, pines, saw palmettos, silver palms, grasses, and ferns. (Many of these animals and plants can be seen in the National Key Deer Refuge on Big Pine Key ☞ *below.*)

Nature was generous with her beauty in the Lower Keys. They're home to both Looe Key National Marine Sanctuary, arguably the most beautiful coral reef tract in the Keys, and Bahia Honda State Park, considered by many one of the best beaches in the world.

Bahia Honda Key

❾ *MM 38–36.*

Bahia Honda translates from Spanish as "deep bay," a good description of local waters. The government owns most of the island, which ★ is devoted to 524-acre **Bahia Honda State Park.** The park was devastated by Hurricane Georges in September 1998 and was closed for three months. Rangers expect to have everything back to normal by late 1999. The Silver Palm Trail leads through a dense—though slightly less dense following the hurricane—tropical forest where you can see rare West Indian plants and several species found nowhere else in the Keys. The park also contains the Keys' only natural sandy beach of notable size; it extends on both gulf and ocean sides and has deep water close to shore. Plenty of year-round activities are available, and there are cabins, a campground, a snack bar, marina, and dive shop. You can get a panoramic view of the island from what's left of the railroad—the Bahia Honda Bridge. ⊠ *MM 37, OS, 36850 Overseas Hwy., 33043, ☎ 305/872–2353.* ⛱ *$2 for 1 person, $4 per vehicle for 2–8 people plus 50¢ per person county surcharge; $2 per vehicle an hour before closing.* ☺ *Daily 8–sunset.*

Lodging

$$ 🏨 **Bahia Honda State Park.** Views from the six bay-front cabin units on stilts are spectacular. Each is completely furnished (no TV or radio); has two bedrooms, full kitchen, and bath; and sleeps six. The park also has 80 popular campsites, suitable for motor homes and tents. Cabins and campsites are very popular, so reserve up to 11 months before your planned visit. ⊠ *MM 37, OS, 36850 Overseas Hwy., 33043, ☎ 305/872–2353. 3 duplex cabins. Picnic area, beach, boating, fishing. MC, V.*

Outdoor Activities and Sports

Bahia Honda Dive Shop (⊠ MM 37, OS, ☎ 305/872–3210), the concessioner at Bahia Honda State Park, operates offshore-reef snorkel trips and boat rentals. Snorkel trips ($22) run almost three hours (with an hour on the reef) and leave daily at 10 and 2 (also at 1, October–November). Rental craft range from a 20-ft pontoon boat and 22-ft center console fishing-dive boat to kayaks.

Big Pine Key

❿ *MM 32–30.*

Known for its concentration of Key deer, this island is the site of the 2,300-acre **National Key Deer Refuge,** established in 1954 to protect the dwindling population of Key deer, a subspecies of the Virginia white-tailed deer. These deer once ranged throughout the Lower and Middle keys, but hunting, habitat destruction, and a growing human population have caused their numbers to decline to around 250. The best place to see Key deer in the refuge is at the end of Key Deer Boulevard (Route 940), along U.S. 1, and on No Name Key, a sparsely populated island just east of Big Pine Key. Deer may turn up along the road at any time of day—especially in early morning and late afternoon. Admire their beauty, but feeding them is against the law. The **Blue Hole**, a quarry left over from railroad days, is the largest body of freshwater in the Keys. From the observation platform and walking trail, you might see alligators, birds, turtles, Key deer, and other wildlife. There are two well-marked trails: the Jack Watson Nature Trail (⅔ mi), named after Jack Watson, an environmentalist and the refuge's first warden; and the Fred Mannillo Nature Trail, one of the most accessible places to see an unspoiled hardwood hammock and subtropical foliage. The latter has a hard surface for wheelchair access. ⊠ *Headquarters, Big Pine Shopping Center, MM 30.5, BS,* ☎ *305/872–2239.* 🎫 *Free.* ☉ *Daily sunrise–sunset; headquarters weekdays 8–5.*

Dining and Lodging

$ ✕ **No Name Pub.** The Upper Keys has Alabama Jack's and the Caribbean Club. The Lower Keys has this ramshackle American-casual establishment, in existence since 1936, or so the staff's shirts read. As long as anyone can remember, locals have come for the cold beer, excellent pizza, and sometimes questionable companionship. In 1998 the pub introduced a full menu, featuring pastas, chicken wings, and, of course, pizza. Inside is poorly lighted, with rough furnishings, a jukebox, and pool table; outside is a garden area. The pub is hard to find but worth the search if you want to experience the Keys as old-timers say they once were; turn north at the Big Pine Key traffic light, right at the fork, left at the four-way stop, and then over a humpback bridge. It's on the left, before the No Name Bridge. ⊠ *MM 30, BS, N. Watson Blvd.,* ☎ *305/872–9115. MC, V.*

$$–$$$ 🏨 **Deer Run.** The most casual of three local B&Bs, this lodging set on 2 wooded beachfront acres is populated by cats, caged tropical birds, and a herd of Key deer, which forage along the beach. Like her fellow innkeepers, longtime Big Pine resident Sue Abbott is caring and informed, well settled and hospitable. Two large oceanfront rooms are furnished with whitewashed wicker and king-size beds. An upstairs unit looks out on the sea through trees. Guests have use of a living room, a 52-ft veranda cooled by paddle fans, hammocks, a large barbecue grill, a hot tub on a deck overlooking the ocean, and water toys. Smokers and children are not welcome. ⊠ *MM 33, OS, 1985 Long Beach Dr., Box 431, 33043,* ☎ *305/872–2015,* 𝔽𝔸𝕏 *305/872–2842. 3 rooms. Hot tub, beach, bicycles. No credit cards.*

$$ 🏨 **The Barnacle.** Hurricane Georges soaked furnishings upstairs and
★ swept away everything on the ground that wasn't bolted down, including the beach, the lush landscaping, and the fences. But B&B owners Tim and Jane Marquis turned the storm into an opportunity. They busily replanted and improved upon what was already the perfect getaway, comprising two rooms in the main house, both on the second floor; one in a cottage with a kitchen; and another, below the house, that opens to the beach. Guest rooms are large, and those in the main house adjoin an atrium, where a hot tub sits in a beautiful garden overlooking sea and sky. Full breakfast is included, as is use of paddleboats and kayaks. As former owners of a diving business, Tim and Jane offer personalized snorkel and dive charters and certifications, as well as fishing excursions. ⊠ *MM 33, OS, 1557 Long Beach Dr., 33043,* ☎ *305/ 872–3298 or 800/465–9100,* 𝔽𝔸𝕏 *305/872–3863. 4 rooms. Hot tub, beach, dock, boating, bicycles, D, MC, V.*

$$ 🏨 **Casa Grande.** Owner Kathleen Threlkeld took advantage of the dam-
★ age done by Hurricane Georges to upgrade everything from the Berber carpeting to the screened porch. The service remains the same at this

popular bed-and-breakfast, whose guests like to sun themselves on the white-sand beach abutting the rocky, shallow shoreline. The lodging is markedly Mediterranean, with a massive Spanish door and mainly contemporary furnishings. Spacious guest rooms have new color TVs, small refrigerators, new air-conditioning, and high open-beam ceilings with paddle fans, and there is a screened, second-story atrium facing the sea. Guests cozy up to the sitting-room fireplace and get to know one another on cool nights. ⊠ *MM 33, OS, 1619 Long Beach Dr., Box 378, 33043,* ☎ *305/872–2878. 3 rooms. Hot tub, beach, dock, boating, bicycles. No credit cards.*

$–$$ 🏕 **Big Pine Key Fishing Lodge.** The five lodge rooms at this family-owned
★   and family-oriented lodge and campground ($24–$31 per site) are one of the Keys' best buys. They feature tile floors, wicker furniture, louvered and screened windows, doors that allow sea breezes to blow through, queen-size beds, a second-bedroom loft, vaulted ceilings, and mini-kitchens. A skywalk joins them with a pool and deck. Over the next few years, the other units in this almost-30-year-old business— either spic-and-span mobile homes or efficiencies—will slowly be replaced with more modern facilities. Immaculately clean tile lines the spacious bathhouse for campers. Separate game and recreation rooms house TVs, organized family-oriented activities, and other amusements, and there is dockage along a 735-ft canal. A three-day minimum is required. ⊠ *MM 33, OS, Box 430513, 33043,* ☎ *305/872–2351,* 🖷 *305/872–3868. 16 rooms, 158 campsites. Pool, Ping-Pong, shuffleboard, dock, billiards, recreation room, video games. D, MC, V.*

Outdoor Activities and Sports

BIKING

A good 10 mi of paved and unpaved roads run from MM 30.3, BS, along Wilder Road, across the bridge to No Name Key, and along Key Deer Boulevard into the National Key Deer Refuge. You might see some Key deer. Stay off the trails that lead into wetlands, where fat tires can do damage.

In addition to selling and repairing bikes, **Big Pine Bicycle Center** (⊠ MM 30, OS, ☎ 305/872–0130) rents old-fashioned single-speed, fat-tired cruisers for adults ($6 per half day, $9 for a full day, and $38 a week) and children ($5, $7, and $30). Helmets, baskets, and locks are included. Ask owner Marty Baird about his favorite places to ride, or show up at the shop Sunday morning at 8 for the free off-road fun ride.

FISHING

Strike Zone Charters (⊠ MM 29.6, BS, 29675 Overseas Hwy., 33043, ☎ 305/872–9863 or 800/654–9560) runs fishing charters on air-conditioned boats at $425 for a half day, $525 for a full day. In addition, sightseeing trips can include time to fish, as well as bait and tackle.

Little Torch Key

⑪ *MM 28–29.*

Primarily a base for divers headed for Looe Key National Marine Sanctuary, a few miles away, this key provides accommodations and diving outfits. The undeveloped backcountry is at your back door, making this an ideal location for fishing and kayaking, too. Nearby **Ramrod Key**, which also caters to divers bound for Looe Key, derives its name from a ship that wrecked on nearby reefs in the early 1800s.

Dining and Lodging

$–$$ ✕ **Montes Restaurant & Fish Market.** It looks like the archetypal island eatery: a gray wood-frame building with screened sides, a canvas roof, wood-plank floors, a tropical mural, and picnic tables. Casually clad, experienced waitresses provide good service. The menu features fish prepared just right, crabs, and shrimp that's steamed, broiled, stuffed, or fried. You can get a traditional fish sandwich or a variation stuffed with crabmeat. ⊠ *MM 25, BS, Summerland Key,* ☎ *305/745–3731. No credit cards.*

$ ✕ **Baby's Smokehouse Grill & Baby's Coffee.** Hurricane Georges didn't leave much of the restaurant, so an expanded indoor/outdoor restaurant with coffee-roasting facility was rebuilt. (Coffee by the cup is sold in a building across the street.) The menu still features lip-smacking veal, beef, ribs, Long Island duck, and chicken that are grilled, roasted, and smoked until they're fall-off-the-bone tender. Baby's uses its own grilling sauces and serves tangy house red and green hot sauces on the side. Lunches come with corn bread or French bread, dinners with corn bread and a baked sweet potato. Save room for Baby's Coffee, freshly roasted on the premises. ⊠ *MM 15, OS, Saddlebunch Keys,* ☎ *305/ 744–9866 or 800/523–2326. AE, MC, V. Closed Mon.–Tues.*

$$$$ 🏨 **Little Palm Island.** The lobby sits beside U.S. 1 on Little Torch Key, **★** but the resort dazzles 3 mi offshore on a palm-fringed island. The 14 thatch-roof villas each have two suites with Mexican-tile baths, Jacuzzis, mosquito netting–draped beds, Mexican and Guatemalan wicker and rattan furniture, minibars, and safes. A second-floor suite on a houseboat adds to the mix, and many suites as well as the restaurant were redone after Hurricane Georges. There are no in-room phones or TVs. Instead, indulge in a fountain-fed pool, a massage in the indoor or outdoor spa, or some terrific snorkeling, diving, and fishing. The food draws yachtfolk from all over, who tie up at the marina come dinner time. The *Lady Bess,* a 72-ft yacht with two large staterooms that sleep four, is available for four-night voyages around the Keys starting at $6,600 (all-inclusive). ⊠ *MM 28.5, OS, 28500 Overseas Hwy., 33042,* ☎ *305/ 872–2524 or 800/343–8567,* 𝖥𝖠𝖷 *305/872–4843. 30 suites. Restaurant, bar, pool, massage, sauna, beach, dock, snorkeling, boating, fishing. AE, D, DC, MC, V.*

$-$$ 🏨 **Parmer's Place.** Each December Parmer's Place sends out 15,000 holiday cards to former guests, many of whom return year after year to stay in the pastel-color, rustic, family-style waterfront cottages and rooms spread over 5 landscaped acres. Most rooms have a deck or balcony, all have cable and a full or half kitchen, and none has a telephone. Complimentary Continental breakfast is served in the family room. Though the property no longer belongs to the Parmers, the new owners don't plan to change anything. ⊠ *MM 29, BS, 565 Barry Ave., 33042,* ☎ *305/872–2157,* 𝖥𝖠𝖷 *305/872–2014. 18 rooms, 12 efficiencies, 13 apartments. Pool, docks, boating. AE, D, MC, V.*

Outdoor Activities and Sports

FISHING

The Grouch Charters (⊠ Summerland Key Cove Marina, MM 24.5, OS, Summerland Key, ☎ 305/745–1172 or 305/872–6100), under Captain Mark André, takes up to six passengers on offshore fishing trips ($350 for a half day, $475 for a full day). He also packages accommodations, fishing, snorkeling, and sightseeing for better deals. The firm's name refers to his original boat, named after his father, whose nickname was Grouch.

SCUBA DIVING AND SNORKELING

Named for the HMS *Looe,* a British warship wrecked in 1744, **Looe Key National Marine Sanctuary** (⊠ MM 27.5, OS, 216 Ann St., Key West 33040, ☎ 305/292–0311), part of the Florida Keys National Marine Sanctuary, contains a 5.3-square-nautical-mi reef. Perhaps the most beautiful and diverse coral community in the region, it has large stands of elk-horn coral on its eastern margin, immense purple sea fans, and abundant populations of sponges and sea urchins. On its seaward side, it has an almost-vertical drop-off to depths of 50–90 ft. Both snorkelers and divers will find the sanctuary a quiet place to observe reef life, except in July, when the annual Underwater Music Festival pays homage to Looe Key's beauty and promotes reef awareness with six hours of music broadcast via underwater speakers. Dive shops and private charters transport hundreds of divers to hear the spectacle, which includes Caribbean, classical, jazz, new age, and, of course, Jimmy Buffett.

Looe Key Dive Center (⊠ MM 27.5, OS, Box 509, Ramrod Key 33042, ☎ 305/872–2215, ext. 2; 305/872–2215, ext. 2; 305/872–2215, ext. 2; or 800/942–5397), the closest dive shop to Looe Key, offers two-day and overnight dive packages. It's part of the full-service Looe Key Reef Resort, which, not surprisingly, caters to divers. The dive boat, a 45-ft Corinthian catamaran, is docked within 100 ft of the hotel, whose guests have free use of tanks, weights, and snorkeling equipment. **Strike Zone Charters** (⊠ MM 29.6, BS, 29675 Overseas Hwy., Big Pine Key 33043, ☎ 305/872–9863 or 800/654–9560) offers dive trips to two sites on Looe Key, resort courses, and various certifications. The outfit uses glass-bottom boats, so accompanying nondivers can experience the reef, too.

En Route   The huge object that looks like a white whale floating over Cudjoe Key (⊠ MM 23–21) is not a figment of your imagination. It's Fat Albert, a radar balloon that monitors local air and water traffic.

KEY WEST

MM 4–0.

Situated 150 mi from Miami and just 90 mi from Havana, this tropical island city has always maintained a strong sense of detachment, even after it was connected to the rest of the United States—by the railroad in 1912 and by the Overseas Highway in 1938.

The U.S. government acquired Key West from Spain in 1821 along with the rest of Florida. The Spanish had named the island Cayo Hueso (Bone Key) after the Native American skeletons they found on its shores. In 1823 Uncle Sam sent Commodore David S. Porter to chase pirates away.

For three decades the primary industry in Key West was wrecking—rescuing people and salvaging cargo from ships that foundered on the nearby reefs. According to some reports, when pickings were lean, the wreckers hung out lights to lure ships aground. Their business declined after 1849, when the federal government began building lighthouses.

In 1845 the army started construction of Fort Taylor, which held Key West for the Union during the Civil War. After the war, an influx of Cuban dissidents unhappy with Spain's rule brought the cigar industry here. Fishing, shrimping, and sponge-gathering became important industries, and a pineapple-canning factory opened. Major military installations were established during the Spanish-American War and World War I. Through much of the 19th century and into the second decade of the 20th, Key West was Florida's wealthiest city in percapita terms.

In 1929 the local economy began to unravel. Modern ships no longer needed to provision in Key West, cigar making moved to Tampa, Hawaii dominated the pineapple industry, and the sponges succumbed to a blight. Then the Depression hit, and the military moved out. By 1934 half the population was on relief. The city defaulted on its bond payments, and the Federal Emergency Relief Administration took over the city and county governments.

By promoting Key West as a tourist destination, federal officials attracted 40,000 visitors during the 1934–35 winter season, but when the 1935 Labor Day hurricane struck the Middle Keys, it wiped out the railroad and the tourist trade.

An important naval center during World War II and the Korean conflict, the island remains a strategic listening post on the doorstep of Fidel Castro's Cuba. It was during the '60s that the fringes of society began moving here and in the mid-'70s that gay guest houses began opening in rapid succession.

In April 1982 the U.S. Border Patrol threw a roadblock across the Overseas Highway just south of Florida City to catch drug runners and illegal aliens. Traffic backed up for miles as Border Patrol agents searched vehicles and demanded that the occupants prove U.S. citizenship. City officials in Key West, outraged at being treated like foreigners by the federal government, staged a mock secession and formed their own "nation," the so-called Conch Republic. They hoisted a flag and distributed mock border passes, visas, and Conch currency. The embarrassed Border Patrol dismantled its roadblock, and now an annual festival recalls the secessionists' victory.

Key West reflects a diverse population: native "Conchs" (white Key Westers, many of whom trace their ancestry to the Bahamas), freshwater Conchs (longtime residents who migrated from somewhere else years ago), gays (who now make up at least 20% of Key West's citizenry), black Bahamians (descendants of those who worked the railroads and burned charcoal), Hispanics (primarily Cuban immigrants), recent refugees from the urban sprawl of mainland Florida, navy and air force personnel, and an assortment of vagabonds, drifters, and dropouts in search of refuge.

Although the rest of the Keys are more oriented to nature and the outdoors, Key West has more of a city feel. Few open spaces remain, as promoters continue to foster fine restaurants, galleries, shops, and museums to interpret the city's intriguing past. As a tourist destination, Key West has a lot to sell—an average temperature of 79°F, quaint 19th-century architecture, and a laid-back lifestyle. There's also a growing calendar of festivals and artistic and cultural events—including the Conch Republic Celebration in April and a Halloween Fantasy Fest. Few cities of its size—a mere 2 mi by 4 mi—offer the joie de vivre of this one.

Yet, as elsewhere, when preservation has successfully revived once-tired towns, next have come those unmindful of style and eager for a buck. Duval Street is becoming showbiz—an open-air mall of T-shirt shops and tour shills. Mass marketers directing the town's tourism have attracted cruise ships, which dwarf the town's skyline, and Duval Street floods with day-trippers who gawk at the earringed hippies with dogs in their bike baskets and the otherwise oddball lot of locals. You can still find fun, but the best advice is to come sooner rather than later.

Old Town

The heart of Key West, this historic area runs from White Street west to the waterfront. Beginning in 1822, wharves, warehouses, chandleries, ship-repair facilities, and eventually in 1891 the U.S. Customs House sprang up around the deep harbor to accommodate the navy's large ships and other sailing vessels. Wealthy wreckers, merchants, and sea captains built lavish houses near the bustling waterfront. A remarkable number of these fine Victorian and pre-Victorian structures have been restored to their original grandeur and now serve as homes, guest houses, and museums. These, along with the dwellings of famous writers, artists, and politicians who've come to Key West over the past 175 years, are among the area's approximately 3,000 historic structures. Old Town also has the city's finest restaurants and hotels, lively street life, and popular nightspots.

A Good Tour

To cover a lot of sights, take the Old Town Trolley, which lets you get off and reboard a later trolley, or the Conch Tour Train. Old Town is also very manageable on foot, bicycle, or moped, but be warned the tour below covers a lot of ground. You'll want either to pick and choose from it or break it into two days. Or pick up a copy of one of several self-guided tours on the area.

Start on Whitehead Street at the **Hemingway House** ⑫, the author's former home, and then cross the street and climb to the top of the **Lighthouse Museum** ⑬ for a spectacular view. Follow Whitehead north to Angela Street and turn right. At Margaret Street, the **City Cemetery** ⑭ has above-ground vaults and unusual headstone inscriptions. Head north on Margaret to Southard Street, turn left, then right onto Simonton Street. Halfway up the block, Free School Lane is occupied by **Nancy Forrester's Secret Garden** ⑮. After touring this tropical haven, return west on Southard to Duval Street and turn right, where you can view the lovely tiles and woodwork in the **San Carlos Institute** ⑯. Return again to Southard Street, turn right, and follow it through Truman Annex to **Ft. Zachary Taylor State Historic Site** ⑰; after viewing the fort, you can take a dip at the beach.

Go back to Simonton Street and walk north, then turn left on Caroline Street, where you can climb to the widow's walk on top of **Curry Mansion** ⑱. A left on Duval Street puts you in front of the **Duval Street Wreckers Museum** ⑲, Key West's oldest house. Continue west into Truman Annex to see the **Harry S Truman Little White House Museum** ⑳, President Truman's vacation residence. Return east on Caroline and turn left on Whitehead to visit the **Audubon House and Gardens** ㉑, honoring the artist-naturalist. Follow Whitehead north to Greene Street and turn left to see the salvaged sea treasures of the **Mel Fisher Maritime Heritage Society Museum** ㉒. At Whitehead's north end is the **Key West Aquarium** ㉓.

By late afternoon you should be ready to cool off with a dip or catch a few rays at the beach. After all, this is Florida, and you can't go home without wiggling your toes in the waves. From the aquarium, head east two blocks to the end of Simonton Street, where you'll find the appropriately named **Simonton Street Beach** ㉔. On the Atlantic side of Old Town is **South Beach** ㉕, named for its location at the southern end of Duval Street. If you've brought your pet, stroll a few blocks east to **Dog Beach** ㉖, at the corner of Vernon and Waddell streets. A little farther east is **Higgs Beach** ㉗, on Atlantic Boulevard between White and Reynolds streets. As the sun starts to sink, return to the north end of Old Town and follow the crowds to Mallory Square, behind the aquarium, to watch Key West's nightly sunset spectacle. For dinner, head east on Caroline Street to **Historic Seaport at Key West Bight** ㉘ (formerly known simply as Key West Bight), a renovated area where there are numerous restaurants and bars.

TIMING

Allow two full days to see all the Old Town museums and homes, especially with a little shopping thrown in. For a narrated trip on the tour train or trolley, budget 1½ hours to ride the loop without getting off, an entire day if you plan to get off and on at some of the sights and restaurants.

Sights to See

㉑ **Audubon House and Gardens.** This three-story dwelling built in the mid-1840s commemorates ornithologist John James Audubon's 1832 visit to Key West. On display are several rooms of period antiques, a children's room, and a large collection of Audubon engravings. Admission includes an audiotape (in English, French, German, and Spanish) for the self-guided tour of the house and tropical gardens, complemented by an informational booklet and signs that identify the rare indigenous plants and trees you'll see. ✉ *205 Whitehead St.,* ☎ *305/294–2116.* ⌨ *$7.50.* ☉ *Daily 9:30–5.*

★ ⑭ **City Cemetery.** Key West's celebrated burial place covers nearly 20 acres. Among its plots are a bronze statue resembling a ship's mast and the graves of more than two dozen sailors killed in the sinking of the battleship U.S.S. *Maine,* recently tidied for the 150th anniversary of the disaster. There are separate plots for Catholics, Jews, and martyrs of Cuba. Interesting headstones abound: DEVOTED FAN OF SINGER JULIO IGLESIAS, GOD WAS GOOD TO ME, and I TOLD YOU I WAS SICK. Although you can walk around the cemetery on your own, the best way to take it in is on a 90-minute tour given by volunteers of the Historic Florida Keys Foundation. Tours leave from the sexton's office, and reservations are requested. ✉ *Margaret and Angela Sts.,* ☎ *305/292–6718.* ⌨ *Free, tour donation $10.* ☉ *Sunrise–6, tours Tues. and Thurs. 9:30.*

⑱ **Curry Mansion.** This 22-room home built in 1899 for Milton Curry, the son of Florida's first millionaire, is an adaptation of a Parisian town house. It has Key West's only widow's walk open to the public. The owners have restored most of the house and turned it into a winning B&B. Take an unhurried self-guided tour; a brochure describes the home's history and contents. ✉ *511 Caroline St.,* ☎ *305/294–5349.* ⌨ *$5.* ☉ *Daily 10–5.*

㉖ **Dog Beach.** Next to Louie's Backyard, this small beach—the only one in Key West where dogs are allowed—has a shore that's a mix of sand and rocks. ✉ *Vernon and Waddell Sts.,* ☎ *no phone.* ⌨ *Free.* ☉ *Daily sunrise–sunset.*

⑲ **Duval Street Wreckers Museum.** Built in 1829 and alleged to be the oldest house in South Florida, the museum was originally home to Francis Watlington, a sea captain and wrecker. He was also a Florida state senator but resigned to serve in the Confederate navy during the Civil War. Six rooms are now open, furnished with 18th- and 19th-century antiques and providing exhibits on the wrecking industry of the 1800s. In an upstairs bedroom, an eight-room dollhouse of Conch design is outfitted with tiny early 19th-century furniture. ✉ *322 Duval St.,* ☎ *305/294–9502.* ⌨ *$4.* ☉ *Daily 10–4.*

⑰ **Ft. Zachary Taylor State Historic Site.** Built between 1845 and 1866, this fort served as a base for the Union blockade of Confederate shipping during the Civil War (more than 1,500 Confederate vessels were detained in Key West's harbor). Today it's a fort within a fort. A moat suggests how the fort originally looked when it was surrounded by water, and a 30-minute tour is included in the admission price. Because of an artificial reef, snorkeling is excellent here, except when the wind blows south–southwest and muddies the water. There are an uncrowded

Key West

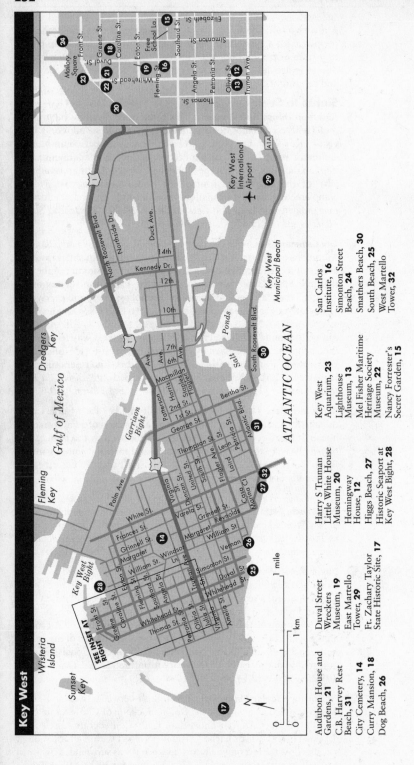

Audubon House and Gardens, **21**
C.B. Harvey Rest Beach, **31**
City Cemetery, **14**
Curry Mansion, **18**
Dog Beach, **26**

Duval Street Wreckers Museum, **19**
East Martello Tower, **29**
Ft. Zachary Taylor State Historic Site, **17**

Harry S Truman Little White House Museum, **20**
Hemingway House, **12**
Higgs Beach, **27**
Historic Seaport at Key West Bight, **28**

Key West Aquarium, **23**
Lighthouse Museum, **13**
Mel Fisher Maritime Heritage Society Museum, **22**
Nancy Forrester's Secret Garden, **15**

San Carlos Institute, **16**
Simonton Street Beach, **24**
Smathers Beach, **30**
South Beach, **25**
West Martello Tower, **32**

beach and an adjoining picnic area with barbecue grills and some shade trees. ⊠ *End of Southard St., through Truman Annex,* ☎ *305/ 292–6713.* ⊠ *$2.50 per person for first 2 people in vehicle plus 50¢ each additional up to $8, $1.50 per pedestrian or bicyclist.* ☉ *Daily 8–sunset, tours noon and 2.*

㉑ Harry S Truman Little White House Museum. On the grounds of Truman Annex, a 103-acre former military parade grounds and barracks, the home served as a winter White House for Presidents Truman, Eisenhower, and Kennedy. It has been restored to its post–World War II glory and contains displays of Truman family memorabilia as well as changing exhibits that have ranged from circa-1951 Truman fashion to the Eisenhower Room's presidential photos. ⊠ *111 Front St.,* ☎ *305/294–9911.* ⊠ *$7.50.* ☉ *Daily 9–5, grounds 8–sunset.*

★ ⑫ Hemingway House. Hemingway bought this house in 1931 and wrote about 70% of his life's work here, including *For Whom the Bell Tolls.* It is now a museum dedicated to the novelist's life and work. Built in 1851, this two-story Spanish-colonial dwelling was the first house in Key West to have running water and a fireplace. Three months after Hemingway died in 1961, local jeweler Bernice Dickson bought the house and two years later opened it as a museum. Of special interest are the huge bed with a headboard made from a 17th-century Spanish monastery gate, a ceramic cat by Pablo Picasso (a gift to Hemingway from the artist), the hand-blown Venetian glass chandelier in the dining room, and the pool. The museum staff gives guided tours rich with anecdotes about Hemingway and his family and feeds the more than 50 feline habitants, descendants of Hemingway's own 50 cats. Tours begin every 10 minutes and take 25–30 minutes; then you're free to explore on your own. ⊠ *907 Whitehead St.,* ☎ *305/294–1575.* ⊠ *$6.50.* ☉ *Daily 9–5.*

㉗ Higgs Beach. This Monroe County park is a popular sunbathing spot. A nearby grove of Australian pines provides shade, and the West Martello Tower provides shelter should a storm suddenly sweep in. ⊠ *Atlantic Blvd. between White and Reynolds Sts.,* ☎ *no phone.* ⊠ *Free.* ☉ *Daily 7 AM–11 PM.*

㉘ Historic Seaport at Key West Bight. In January 1999 the $30 million restoration of structures within this 8.5-acre historic waterfront area was completed, bringing together about 100 businesses: waterfront restaurants, open-air people- and dog-friendly bars, clothing stores, bait shops, docks, a marina, a wedding chapel, the Waterfront Market, the Key West Rowing Club, and dive shops. It's all linked by the 2-mi waterfront Harborwalk, which runs between Front and Grinnell streets, passing big ships, schooners, sunset cruises, fishing charters, and glass-bottom boats. Though it's not as glossy as some waterfront restorations, it's lost much of its funky charm. Additional construction continues on outlying projects.

☝ ㉓ Key West Aquarium. Hundreds of brightly colored tropical fish and other fascinating sea creatures from Key West waters make their home here. A touch tank enables you to handle starfish, sea cucumbers, horseshoe and hermit crabs, even horse and queen conchs—living totems of the Conch Republic. Built in 1934 by the Works Progress Administration as the world's first open-air aquarium, the building has been enclosed for all-weather viewing, though an outdoor area has a small Atlantic shores exhibit, including red mangroves. Guided tours include shark feedings. ⊠ *1 Whitehead St.,* ☎ *305/296–2051.* ⊠ *$8.* ☉ *Daily 10–6, tours 11, 1, 3, and 4:30.*

CLOSE-UP: HEMINGWAY WAS HERE

IN A TOWN WHERE Pulitzer Prize–winning writers are almost as common as coconuts, Ernest Hemingway stands out. Bars and restaurants around the island boast that he ate or drank there, and though he may not have been at all of them, like all legends his larger-than-life image continues to grow.

Hemingway came to Key West in 1928 at the urging of writer John dos Passos and rented a house with wife number two, Pauline Pfeiffer. They spent winters in the Keys and summers in Europe and Wyoming, occasionally taking African safaris. Along the way they had two sons, Patrick and Gregory. In 1931 Pauline's wealthy uncle Gus gave the couple the house at 907 Whitehead Street, now known as Hemingway House and Key West's number one tourist attraction. They renovated the palatial home, added a swimming pool, put in a tropical garden with peacocks, and then in 1935, when the visitor bureau included the house in a tourist brochure, promptly built the high brick wall that surrounds it today.

During his time in Key West, Hemingway penned some of his most important works, including *A Farewell to Arms, To Have and Have Not, Green Hills of Africa,* and *Death in the Afternoon.* His rigorous schedule consisted of writing almost every morning in his second-story studio above the pool, then promptly descending the stairs at midday. By afternoon and evening he was ready for drinking, fishing, swimming, boxing, and hanging around with the boys.

One close friend was Joe Russell, a craggy fisherman and owner of the rugged bar Sloppy Joe's, originally at 428 Greene Street but now at 201 Duval Street. Russell was the only one in town who would cash Hemingway's $1,000 royalty check. Russell and Charles Thompson introduced him to deep-sea fishing, which became fodder for his writing. Another of Hemingway's loves was boxing. He set up a ring in his yard and paid local fighters to box with him as well as refereeing matches at Blue Heaven, then a saloon but now a restaurant, at 729 Thomas Street.

FEELING AT HOME among Key West's characters, Hemingway honed his macho image dressed in cutoffs and old shirts and took on the name *Papa.* In turn, he gave his friends new names and used them as characters in his stories. Joe Russell became Freddy, captain of the *Queen Conch* charter boat in *To Have and Have Not.*

Hemingway stayed in Key West for 12 years before leaving Pauline for wife number three. A foreign correspondent, Martha Gellhorn arrived in town and headed for Sloppy Joe's, intent on meeting him. When the always restless Hemingway packed up to cover the Spanish Civil War, so did she. Though he returned to Pauline occasionally, he finally left her and Key West to be with Martha in 1939. They married a year later and moved to Cuba, and he seldom returned to Key West after that. Pauline and the boys stayed on in the house, which sold in 1951 for $80,000, ten times its original cost.

⑬ Lighthouse Museum. Behind a spic-and-span white picket fence is this 92-ft lighthouse built in 1847 and an adjacent 1887 clapboard house, where the keeper lived. You can climb 88 steps to the top of the lighthouse for a glimpse of the sizable Fresnel lens, installed at a cost of $1 million in the 1860s; a spectacular view of the island town awaits you as well. On display in the keeper's quarters are vintage photographs, ship models, nautical charts, and lighthouse artifacts from all along the Key reefs. ⊠ *938 Whitehead St.,* ☎ *305/294–0012.* 🎫 *$6.* ☉ *Daily 9:30–5, last admission 4:30.*

㉒ Mel Fisher Maritime Heritage Society Museum. Gold and silver bars, coins, jewelry, and other artifacts recovered in 1985 from the Spanish treasure ships *Nuestra Señora de Atocha* and *Santa Margarita* are displayed here. The two galleons foundered in a hurricane in 1622 near the Marquesas Keys, 40 mi west of Key West. In the museum you can lift a gold bar weighing 6.3 troy pounds and see a 77.76-carat natural emerald crystal worth almost $250,000. ⊠ *200 Greene St.,* ☎ *305/ 294–2633.* 🎫 *$6.50.* ☉ *Daily 9:30–5:30, last video 4:30.*

⑮ Nancy Forrester's Secret Garden. Nancy's 30-year-old naturalized garden lost its rain forest–like canopy and many large trees during Hurricane Georges, and as a result some of the delicate undergrowth withered from the strong sun. Renewal took shape quickly, however. Visitors will find a thinner canopy along with many of the same rare palms and cycads, ferns, bromeliads, bright gingers and heliconias, gumbo-limbos strewn with orchids and vines, and a few surprises. Many brides and grooms exchange their vows here and then stay in the garden's cottage ($140–$175, two-day minimum). Picnic tables invite visitors to sit and have lunch. An art gallery features botanical prints and environmental art. ⊠ *1 Free School La.,* ☎ *305/294–0015.* 🎫 *$6.* ☉ *Daily 10–5.*

⑯ San Carlos Institute. This Cuban-American heritage center houses a museum with changing exhibits and a research library focusing on the history of Key West and of 19th- and 20th-century Cuban exiles. The institute was founded in 1871 by Cuban immigrants. Cuban patriot Jose Martí delivered many famous speeches from the balcony of the auditorium, and opera star Enrico Caruso sang in the Opera House, which reportedly has the best acoustics of any concert hall in the South. On weekends you can watch the almost hour-long documentary *Nostalgia Cubano,* about Cuba from the 1930s to 1950s. ⊠ *516 Duval St.,* ☎ *305/294–3887.* 🎫 *$3.* ☉ *Tues.–Sun. 11–5.*

㉔ Simonton Street Beach. This beach facing the gulf is a great place to watch boat traffic in the harbor. Parking, however, is difficult. ⊠ *North end of Simonton St.,* ☎ *no phone.* 🎫 *Free.* ☉ *Daily 7 AM–11 PM.*

㉕ South Beach. On the Atlantic, this stretch of sand, also known as City Beach, is popular with tourists at nearby motels. It has limited parking and a nearby buffet-type restaurant, the South Beach Seafood and Raw Bar. ⊠ *Foot of Duval St.,* ☎ *no phone.* 🎫 *Free.* ☉ *Daily 7 AM– 11 PM.*

New Town

The Overseas Highway splits as it enters Key West, the two forks rejoining to encircle New Town, the area east of White Street to Cow Key Channel. The southern fork runs along the shore as South Roosevelt Boulevard (Route A1A), past municipal beaches, salt ponds, and Key West International Airport. Along the north shore, North Roosevelt Boulevard (U.S. 1) passes the Key West Welcome Center, shopping centers, chain hotels, and fast-food eateries. Part of New Town was created with dredged fill. The island would have continued growing this way had the Army Corps of Engineers not determined in the early 1970s that it was detrimental to the nearby reef.

A Good Tour

Attractions are few in New Town. The best way to take in the sights is by car or moped. Take South Roosevelt Boulevard from the island's entrance to **East Martello Tower** ㉙, near the airport. Continue past the Riggs Wildlife Refuge salt ponds and stop at **Smathers Beach** ㉚ for a dip, or continue west onto Atlantic Boulevard to **C. B. Harvey Rest Beach** ㉛. A little farther along, at the end of White Street, is the **West Martello Tower** ㉜.

TIMING

Allow one to two hours for brief stops at each attraction. If your interests lie in art, gardens, or Civil War history, you'll need three or four hours. Throw in time at the beach, and you can make it a half-day affair.

Sights to See

㉛ **C. B. Harvey Rest Beach.** The city's newest beach and park, named after former Key West mayor and commissioner Cornelius Bradford Harvey, has half a dozen picnic areas, dunes, and a wheelchair and bike path. ⊠ *East side of White Street Pier,* ☎ *no phone.* ⊡ *Free.* ☉ *Daily 7 AM–11 PM.*

★ ㉙ **East Martello Tower.** Housing relics of the U.S.S. *Maine,* the tower also contains a museum operated by the Key West Art and Historical Society. The collection includes Stanley Papio's "junk art" sculptures, Cuban folk artist Mario Sanchez's chiseled and painted wooden carvings of historic Key West street scenes, a Cuban refugee raft, and books by famous writers (including seven Pulitzer Prize winners) who have lived in Key West. Thematic exhibits present a history of the city and the Keys. A circular 48-step staircase in the central tower leads to a platform overlooking the airport and surrounding waters. Hurricane damage to the attractive grounds was extensive, but replanting is under way. ⊠ *3501 S. Roosevelt Blvd.,* ☎ *305/296–3913.* ⊡ *$6.* ☉ *Daily 9:30–5, last admission 4.*

㉚ **Smathers Beach.** This beach features nearly 2 mi of sand. Trucks along the road rent rafts, Windsurfers, and other beach "toys." ⊠ *S. Roosevelt Blvd.,* ☎ *no phone.* ⊡ *Free.* ☉ *Daily 7 AM–11 PM.*

㉜ **West Martello Tower.** The ruins of this Civil War–era fort are home to the Key West Garden Club, which maintains lovely gardens of native and tropical plants. It also holds art, orchid, and flower shows in March and November and leads private garden tours in March. ⊠ *Atlantic Blvd. and White St.,* ☎ *305/294–3210.* ⊡ *Donation welcome.* ☉ *Tues.–Sat. 9:30–3.*

Dining

American

$–$$ ✕ **Pepe's Cafe and Steak House.** Judges, police officers, carpenters, and anglers rub elbows at breakfast in their habitual seats, at tables or dark pine booths under a jumbo paddle fan. Face the street or dine outdoors under a huge rubber tree if you're put off by the naked-lady art on the back wall. Pepe's was established downtown in 1909 (which makes it the oldest eating house in the Keys) and moved here in 1962. Specials change nightly: barbecued chicken, pork tenderloin, ribs, steak, fresh fish, potato salad, red or black beans, and corn bread on

Sunday; meat loaf on Monday; seafood Tuesday and Wednesday; a traditional Thanksgiving every Thursday; prime rib on Saturday; and filet mignon daily. ⊠ *806 Caroline St.,* ☎ *305/294–7192. D, MC, V.*

Caribbean

$ ✕ **Caribe Soul.** This ambitious little restaurant around the corner from Blue Heaven is a welcome addition to Bahama Village's redevelopment. Co-owners Kevin Robinson, who has a catering background, and Michael Weston, who has natural cooking instincts, serve up homestyle Caribbean and soul food that ranges from black-bean soup and yellowtail snapper ($10.50) to chicken livers with rice as well as twice-weekly chitterlings. Entrées come with a choice of two sides: fried green apples, collard greens, sweet potatoes, corn bread, et al. They make and sell their own salsas, relishes, and a cooking base made of eggplant, mango, tomatoes, fresh herbs, and spices. The indoor and outdoor seating is very limited, but they offer takeout and free delivery. Also for sale are southern and Afro-Caribbean cookbooks, including their own, *Using What You've Got.* ⊠ *320 Petronia St,* ☎ *305/296–0094. AE, D, DC, MC, V.*

Contemporary

$$$–$$$$ ✕ **Cafe des Artistes.** Dining doesn't get much better than this. The restaurant was once part of a hotel building constructed in 1935 by C. E. Alfeld, Al Capone's bookkeeper. The look is studiously unhip with its rough stucco walls, old-fashioned lights, and a knotty-pine ceiling. Haitian paintings and Keys scenes by local artists dress the walls. You dine in two indoor rooms or on a rooftop deck beneath a sapodilla tree. Chef Andrew Berman presents a French interpretation of tropical cuisine, using fresh local seafood and produce and light sauces. The wine list is strong on French and California labels. ⊠ *1007 Simonton St.,* ☎ *305/294–7100. AE, MC, V. No lunch.*

$$$ ✕ **Louie's Backyard.** Key West paintings and pastels adorn this oceanfront institution, where you dine outside under a mahoe tree. Executive chef Doug Shook shares Louie's limelight with *chef de cuisine* Annette Foley. The menu changes seasonally. The winter menu might include roast rack of lamb with mint sauce and roasted garlic or grilled sour orange–rubbed grouper with black beans and mango salsa. Louie's key lime pie has a pistachio crust and is served with a raspberry coulis. The best time to come is lunch, when the menu is less expensive and the view is fantastic. For night owls, the Afterdeck Bar serves cocktails on the water until the wee hours. ⊠ *700 Waddell Ave.,* ☎ *305/294–1061. AE, DC, MC, V.*

$$–$$$$ ✕ **Cafe Marquesa.** This intimate restaurant with attentive service and superb food is a felicitous counterpart to the small Marquesa Hotel. Under the direction of chef Susan Ferry, who trained with Norman Van Aken, 10 or so entrées are featured nightly. Though every dish she makes is memorable, the sesame-crusted yellowtail snapper with mango-miso sauce, udon noodles, sautéed spinach, and pineapple-chile salsa has become a requested dish of frequent guests. Some low-fat options are featured, but desserts are quite the contrary. There are also a fine selection of wines and a choice of microbrewery beers. Smoking is not allowed. ⊠ *600 Fleming St.,* ☎ *305/292–1244. AE, DC, MC, V. No lunch.*

$$–$$$ ✕ **Alice's on Duval.** Alice Weingarten earns high praise for an exemplary selection of wines that complement the creative mix of seafood, game, beef, pork, and poultry. The center and each leaf of a jumbo baked artichoke are stuffed with a lovely mixture of bread crumbs, rosemary, lemon, and butter. That appetizer is a fitting precursor to the sizzling Key West yellowtail, with an aromatic blend of Thai red curry and Asian vegetables served over coconut basmati rice. Guests must be totally satisfied or the dish goes back to the kitchen. Surrounded by huge un-

screened windows and a ceiling painted pale blue with white clouds, you'll think you're dining alfresco. The bar has become as popular as the dining room. ✉ *1114 Duval St.,* ☎ *305/292–4888. AE, D, MC, V. No lunch.*

$–$$ ✕ **Rick's Blue Heaven.** The inspired remake of an old blue-on-blue clap-
  ★   board Greek Revival house with peach-and-yellow trim was once a bordello where Hemingway refereed boxing matches and customers watched cockfights. There's still a rooster graveyard out back, as well as a water tower hauled here in the 1920s. Upstairs is an art gallery (check out the zebra-stripe bikes), and downstairs are affordable fresh eats, in both the house and big leafy yard. There are five nightly specials and a good mix of natural and West Indian foods. Top it off with Banana Heaven (banana bread, bananas flamed with spiced rum, and vanilla ice cream). Three meals are served six days a week; Sunday there's a to-die-for brunch. Expect a line—everybody knows how good this is. ✉ *729 Thomas St.,* ☎ *305/296–8666. Reservations not accepted. D, MC, V.*

Cuban

$ ✕ **El Siboney.** This sprawling three-room, family-style restaurant serves traditional Cuban food, including a well-seasoned black-bean soup. Specials include beef stew Monday, pepper steak Tuesday, chicken fricassee Wednesday, chicken and rice Friday, and oxtail stew on Saturday. Always available are roast pork, cassava, paella, and *palomilla* steak. Popular with locals, *sí,* but enough tourists pass through that you'll fit right in even if you have to ask what a "Siboney" is (answer: a Cuban Indian tribe). ✉ *900 Catherine St.,* ☎ *305/296–4184. No credit cards. Closed 2 wks in June.*

Italian

$–$$ ✕ **Mangia Mangia.** Fresh homemade pasta comes *Alfredo,* or with mari-
  ★   nara, meat, or pesto, either in the twinkly brick garden with its specimen palms or in the nicely dressed-up old-house dining room. One of the best restaurants in Key West—and one of its best values—Mangia Mangia is run by Elliot and Naomi Baron, ex–Chicago restaurateurs who found Key West's warmth and laid-back style irresistible. Everything that comes out of the open kitchen is outstanding, especially the pasta, Mississippi mud pie, and made-on-the-premises key lime pie. The wine list, with more than 350 selections, the largest in Monroe County, contains a good selection under $20. ✉ *900 Southard St.,* ☎ *305/294–2469. AE, MC, V. No lunch.*

Pan-Asian

$$–$$$ ✕ **Dim Sum's Far East.** This bright spot in a sophisticated little Asian
  ★   kiosk in gardenlike Key Lime Square serves pan-Asian cuisine and a fusion of classical French and Asian cooking in which the presentation is art and the food is out of this world. The menu features such favorite aromatic dishes as crisply deep-fried whole yellowtail snapper enveloped in a pepper and basil sauce. Nightly specials range from chicken and shrimp in a green Thai curry with essence of cilantro root, lemongrass, and galangal to half duck in a red Thai curry sauce. The setting is intimate and authentic, the service is exemplary, and the selection of beer and wine is good. ✉ *613½ Duval St. (rear),* ☎ *305/294–6230. AE, D, DC, MC, V. No lunch May–late Dec.*

Steak/Seafood

$$ ✕ **Duffy's Steak & Lobster House.** The owners of the elegant Cafe des Artistes (which shares a wall and rest rooms with Duffy's) opened this new American salute to surf and turf. It serves Angus cuts that rival those at good steak houses and lobster and seafood that would make a dedicated seafood restaurant envious. Though the original Duffy's was around when President Truman was a frequent visitor—hence the photo of him on the menu's cover—the look is contemporary and the atmosphere fun. ⊠ *1007 Truman Ave.,* ☎ *305/296–4900. AE, MC, V.*

Lodging

Lodging opportunities rival those found in mainland cities. You'll find historic cottages, restored turn-of-the-century Conch houses, and large resorts. Rates are the highest in the Keys, with a few properties as low as $65, but the majority from $100 to $300 a night.

Guest Houses

$$$$ 🏠 **Paradise Inn.** Renovated cigar makers' cottages and authentically
★ reproduced Bahamian-style houses with sundecks and balconies stand amid a lush tropical garden with a heated pool, lily pond, and whirlpool, light-years from the hubbub of Key West. The only sound disturbing the perfect quiet is the trickling of water from the pool's fountain. Inside, light streams through French doors onto fine earthtone fabrics. Gracious appointments include phones and whirlpools in marble bathrooms, plush robes, polished oak floors, armoires, complimentary fresh breakfast pastries from Louie's Pantry, room safes, and minibars. Suite 205 and the Poinciana Cottage are gilded lilies. One suite is designed for travelers with disabilities. ⊠ *819 Simonton St., 33040,* ☎ *305/293–8007 or 800/888–9648,* 🖷 *305/293–0807. 3 cottages, 15 suites. Pool, hot tub, concierge. AE, D, DC, MC, V.*

$$$–$$$$ 🏠 **Heron House.** Having added full concierge service, newspapers,
★ robes, and valet parking, this place keeps getting better. With four buildings centered on a pool, all slightly different but all Key West–style, it feels like an old town within Old Town. A high coral fence, brilliantly splashed with spotlights at night, surrounds the compound (just a block off Duval Street but quieter by a mile). Neither antiques nor frills is owner Fred Geibelt's thing; superb detailing is. Most units feature a complete wall of exquisitely laid wood, entries with French doors, and bathrooms of polished granite. Some have floor-to-ceiling panels of mirrored glass and/or an oversize whirlpool. An expanded Continental breakfast and complimentary wine and cheese are included. Heron House does not welcome children under 16. ⊠ *512 Simonton St., 33040,* ☎ *305/294–9227,* 🖷 *305/294–5692. 23 rooms. Pool, concierge. AE, DC, MC, V.*

$$$–$$$$ 🏠 **Island City House.** This guest house is actually three buildings: the vintage-1880s Island City House, with a widow's walk; Arch House, a former carriage house; and a 1970s reconstruction of a cigar factory. Arch House features a dramatic carriage entry that opens into a lush courtyard, and though all its suites front on busy Eaton Street, bedrooms in only Numbers 5 and 6 actually face it. Units in Cigar House have porches and decks and are decorated in a plantation style with teak and wicker; those in Island City House have a Victorian flavor. Floors are pine, and ceiling fans and antiques abound. Guests share a private tropical garden and are given free Continental breakfasts. Children are welcome—a rarity in Old Town guest houses. ⊠ *411 William St., 33040,* ☎ *305/294–5702 or 800/634–8230,* 🖷 *305/294–1289. 24 suites. Pool, hot tub, bicycles. AE, D, DC, MC, V.*

$$$ 🏠 **Curry Mansion Inn.** Careful dedication to detail by Key West architect
★ Thomas Pope and much care by owners Al and Edith Amsterdam have made the annex rooms exceptionally comfortable, even if not as detailed as the now rarely used rooms in the circa-1899 main house. Each room has a different tropical pastel color scheme; all have wicker furnishings and handmade quilts. Rooms 1 and 8, honeymoon suites, feature canopy beds and balconies. Eight suites are at the restored James House; Rooms 306 and 308 face south and have beautiful morning

light. Curry Mansion is a historic attraction, with visitors touring the public areas of the house during the day. There are complimentary Continental breakfast and happy hour with an open bar and live piano music; guests also enjoy beach privileges at Pier House Beach Club and Casa Marina. A wheelchair lift is available. ⊠ *511–512 Caroline St., 33040,* ☎ *305/294–5349 or 800/253–3466,* FAX *305/294–4093. 28 rooms, 6 suites. Pool, hot tubs. AE, D, DC, MC, V.*

$$–$$$$ ⬚ **Popular House/Key West Bed & Breakfast.** Local art—large splashy
★ canvases, a mural in the style of Gauguin—hangs on the walls, and tropical gardens and music set the mood. Jody Carlson offers both inexpensive rooms with shared bath (whose rates haven't been raised in more than 10 years) and luxury rooms, reasoning that budget travelers deserve the same good local style (and lavish Continental breakfast) as the rich. Low-end rooms burst with bright yellows and reds; the hand-painted dressers will make you laugh out loud. Spacious third-floor rooms, though, are best (and most expensive), decorated with a paler palette and brilliantly original furniture. There's even one single room. Jody also keeps two friendly resident dogs. ⊠ *415 William St., 33040,* ☎ *305/296–7274 or 800/438–6155,* FAX *305/293–0306. 9 rooms, 4 with bath. Hot tub, sauna. AE, D, DC, MC, V.*

$$–$$$ ⬚ **Center Court Historic Inn & Cottages.** This lodging offers well-priced, charming, restored historical accommodations that seem calm and quiet even though they're only half a block from Duval Street. Units range from rooms with a queen-size bed to efficiency cottages with decks and spas (sleeping from two to six) to studios and fully equipped three-bedroom, two-bath house-size cottages that sleep six. All units are decorated in relaxed tropical style. There are a heated pool, whirlpools, sundeck, and exercise pavilion. Breakfast is included in units without full kitchens. In-room safes are available, and though there's no smoking, pets are welcome. ⊠ *916 Center St., 33040,* ☎ *305/296– 9292 or 800/797-8787,* FAX *305/294–4104. 5 rooms, 5 suites, 2 efficiencies, 6 cottages. Pool, exercise room. AE, D, MC, V.*

$$–$$$ ⬚ **Speakeasy Inn.** This inn derives its name from Prohibition, when Raul Vasquez smuggled liquor from Cuba and taxi drivers pulled up in front to fill suitcases with the bootleg. Painting contractor Thomas Favelli restored the historic house, turning it into one of the best buys in Key West. Spacious studios, suites, and two-bedroom units feature simple tropical decor, queen-size beds, and tables made from 1876 salvaged pine, Saltillo tiles in the bathrooms, kitchenettes, oak floors with throw rugs, and claw-foot tubs in some baths. Some units are wheelchair accessible, and maid and concierge service are provided on request. Guests have beach and pool privileges at the Wyndham Reach. Ironically, though the inn is adjacent to Favelli's other pride and joy, the Key West Havana Cigar Co., there is no smoking in the rooms. Casa 325 Suites, an all-suites property at the opposite end of Duval, is under the same ownership. ⊠ *1117 Duval St., 33040,* ☎ *305/296–2680 or 800/217–4884,* FAX *305/296–2608. 4 suites, 4 studios, 2 2-bedroom units. Concierge. AE, D, MC, V.*

Hostel

$ ⬚ **Hostelling International–Key West.** This financial oasis in a sea of
★ expensive hotels gets high marks for location, comfort, friendliness, amenities, and good value. It is two blocks from the beach in Old Town yet costs only $17 for members of Hostelling International–American Youth Hostels, $20 for nonmembers. Breakfast costs $2, and there's a communal kitchen. When you're not snorkeling ($18.50) or scuba diving ($55, gear included), you can rent bicycles, write letters in the outdoor courtyard, or enjoy a barbecue. ⊠ *718 South St., 33040,* ☎ *305/296–5719,* FAX *305/296–0672. 96 beds in dorm-style rooms with-*

out baths. Bicycles, billiards, recreation room, video games, library, coin laundry. MC, V.

Hotels

$$$$ 🏨 **Cuban Club Suites.** Originally built as a social club for cigar makers, the "club" was rebuilt as a luxury hotel after a 1983 fire. Eight fully equipped town-house units, 900–1,900 square ft, have either two bedrooms and two baths or one bedroom and 1½ baths. Grouped in two buildings that feel like an exclusive apartment complex, they have king-size four-poster beds, queen-size sofa beds, wing chairs, cathedral ceilings, full kitchens, tile counters and floors, and washers and dryers. Wide balconies overlook the excitement of Duval Street. Guests have pool and beach privileges at the Wyndham Reach, and pets are allowed. La Casa de Luces, the club's poor cousin next door, is less elegant but has many winning characteristics. On holidays, the office closes early so most of the staff can be with their families. ✉ *1108 Duval St. (lobby at 422 Amelia St.), 33040,* ☎ *305/296–0465 or 800/432–4849,* 🖷 *305/293–7669. 8 suites. AE, MC, V.*

$$$$ 🏨 **Pier House.** This is Key West's catbird seat. Just off the intersection
★ of Duval and Front streets and an easy walk from Mallory Square, it defines Key West's festive ambience. Weathered-gray buildings, including an original Conch house, flank a courtyard of tall coconut palms and hibiscus blossoms. Most rooms are smaller than in newer hotels, except in the Caribbean Spa section, which has hardwood floors, two-poster plantation beds, and some baths that convert to steam rooms or have whirlpools, and in the Harborview building, whose rooms have private balconies and gulf views. You can gather with locals at the Beach Club's thatch-roof tiki bar. ✉ *1 Duval St., 33040,* ☎ *305/296–4600 or 800/327–8340,* 🖷 *305/296–7569. 142 rooms, 14 suites. 3 restaurants, 4 bars, pool, massage, health club, beach. AE, D, DC, MC, V.*

$$$$ 🏨 **Wyndham's Casa Marina Resort.** Flagler's heirs built 13-acre La Casa Marina in 1921 at the end of the Florida East Coast Railway line. The entire resort revolves around an outdoor patio and lawn facing the ocean. The rich, luxurious lobby has a beamed ceiling, polished Dade County pine floor, artwork, and new island French Provincial furniture. Guest rooms are decorated in yellows and tropical limes with color-coordinated Caribbean shades and linens. Among the best rooms are the two-bedroom loft suites with balconies facing the ocean and the lanai rooms on the ground floor of the main building, which have French doors opening onto the lawn. Rooms for nonsmokers are available. ✉ *1500 Reynolds St., 33040,* ☎ *305/296–3535,* 🖷 *305/296–4633. 311 rooms, 63 suites. 2 restaurants, bar, 2 pools, massage, sauna, 3 tennis courts, exercise room, health club, boating, jet skiing, fishing, bicycles, children's programs. AE, D, DC, MC, V.*

$$$–$$$$ 🏨 **Marquesa Hotel.** This coolly elegant, restored 1884 home is Key West's
★ finest lodging. Guests (typically shoeless in Marquesa robes) relax among richly landscaped pools and gardens against a backdrop of brick steps rising to the villalike suites on the property's perimeter. Elegant rooms contain eclectic antique and reproduction furnishings, dotted Swiss curtains, and botanical-print fabrics. The lobby resembles a Victorian parlor, with antique furniture, Audubon prints, flowers, and wonderful photos of early Key West, including one of Harry Truman in a convertible. Tea is offered poolside. Although the clientele is mostly straight, the hotel is very gay friendly. ✉ *600 Fleming St., 33040,* ☎ *305/292–1919 or 800/869–4631,* 🖷 *305/294–2121. 27 rooms. Restaurant, 2 pools. AE, DC, MC, V.*

$$–$$$ 🏨 **Best Western Key Ambassador Inn.** Every year a third of this com-
★ fortable inn is renovated from carpet to ceiling. The large guest rooms have cheerful Caribbean-style light-color furniture, linens in coordi-

nated tropical colors, and 29-inch color TVs. The 7-acre grounds are well cared for, and the deck-rimmed pool looks over the Atlantic. There is a par course and a covered picnic area with barbecue grills out back. Each room has a small refrigerator and a screened balcony, and most offer ocean and pool views. The bar serves drinks and light dishes. A complimentary Continental breakfast and free weekday newspaper are included. ⊠ *3755 S. Roosevelt Blvd., 33040,* ☎ *305/ 296–3500 or 800/432–4315,* FAX *305/296–9961. 100 rooms. Bar, picnic area, pool, shuffleboard, coin laundry. AE, D, DC, MC, V.*

Motels

$$ ☷ **Harborside Motel & Marina.** The appeal of this ordinary motel is its affordability and its safe, pleasant location between a quiet street and Garrison Bight (the charter boat harbor), between Old Town and New Town. Units are boxy, clean, and basic, with little patios, ceramic-tile floors, phones, and basic color cable TV. Four stationary houseboats each sleep four. Barbecue grills are available. ⊠ *903 Eisenhower Dr., 33040,* ☎ *305/294–2780,* FAX *305/292–1473. 14 efficiencies. Pool, coin laundry. AE, D, DC, MC, V.*

$$ ☷ **Southwinds.** A short walk from Old Town and run by the same friendly folks who operate Harborside Motel & Marina, this pastel 1940s-style motel has mature tropical plantings, all nicely set back from the street a block from the beach. Rooms have basic furnishings. It's as good as you'll find at the price, and though rates have gone up, they drop if demand gets slack. On-premises parking is available. ⊠ *1321 Simonton St., 33040,* ☎ *305/296–2215. 13 rooms, 5 efficiencies. Pool, coin laundry, free parking. AE, D, DC, MC, V.*

Nightlife and the Arts

The Arts

Red Barn Theater (⊠ 319 Duval St. [rear], ☎ 305/296–9911), a professional small theater, performs dramas, comedies, and musicals, including plays by new playwrights. The **Tennessee Williams Fine Arts Center** (⊠ Florida Keys Community College, 5901 College Rd., ☎ 305/ 296–9081, ext. 5), on Stock Island, presents chamber music, dance, jazz concerts, and dramatic and musical plays with major stars, as well as other performing arts events, November–April. The **Waterfront Playhouse** (⊠ Mallory Sq., ☎ 305/294–5015) is a mid-1850s wrecker's warehouse that was converted into a 180-seat, non-Equity community theater presenting comedy and drama December–June.

Nightlife

BARS AND LOUNGES

Capt. Tony's Saloon (⊠ 428 Greene St., ☎ 305/294–1838) is housed in a building that dates from 1851, when it was first used as a morgue and icehouse; later it was Key West's first telegraph station. From 1933 to 1937 the bar was the original Sloppy Joe's. Hemingway was a regular, and Jimmy Buffett got his start here. Live country and rhythm and blues set the scene nowadays, and the rum-based house drink, the Pirates' Punch, still wows those brave enough to try it. Pause for a libation at the open-air **Green Parrot Bar** (⊠ 601 Whitehead St., at Southard St., ☎ 305/294–6133). Built in 1890, the bar is said to be Key West's oldest, a sometimes-rowdy saloon where locals outnumber the tourists, especially on weekends when bands play. **Margaritaville Cafe** (⊠ 500 Duval St., ☎ 305/292–1435) is owned by former Key West resident and recording star Jimmy Buffett, who has been known to perform here. The drink of choice is, of course, a margarita. There's live music nightly.

Called "the last little piece of Old Key West," **Schooner Wharf Bar** (✉ 202 William St., ☎ 305/292–9520) is a laid-back waterside tiki hut where the town's waiters and waitresses hang out. You can hear live music weekends (and sometimes at other times) in the warehouse space next door. **Sloppy Joe's** (✉ 201 Duval St., ☎ 305/294–5717) is the successor to a famous speakeasy named for its founder, Captain Joe Russell. Ernest Hemingway liked to gamble in a partitioned club room in back. Decorated with Hemingway memorabilia and marine flags, the bar is popular with tourists and is full and noisy all the time. Live entertainment plays daily, noon–2 AM. The **Top Lounge** (✉ 430 Duval St., ☎ 305/296–2991) is on the seventh floor of the La Concha Holiday Inn and is one of the best places to view the sunset. (Celebrities, on the ground floor, presents nightly entertainment and serves food.)

DANCE CLUBS
Club Epoch (✉ 623 Duval St., ☎ 305/296–8521) caters to a well-mixed crowd that's wild and eager to party. There are two floors, six bars, a lounge overlooking the dance floor, and a terrace overlooking Duval Street. House dancers set the tone as hip local and celebrity spin masters groove the tunes. It's open nightly, but dancing is Wednesday–Sunday. In the Pier House, **Havana Docks Lounge** (✉ 1 Duval St., ☎ 305/296–4600) has live music nightly in season and live dance music Friday and Saturday nights year-round as well as a nightly sunset celebration with a band.

Outdoor Activities and Sports

Biking

Key West is a cycling town, but if you aren't accustomed to so many bikes, ride carefully. Paved road surfaces are poor, so it's best to ride a fat-tired Conch cruiser. Some hotels rent bikes to guests; others will refer you to a nearby shop and reserve a bike for you.

Keys Moped & Scooter (✉ 523 Truman Ave., ☎ 305/294–0399) rents beach cruisers with large baskets as well as mopeds and scooters. Rates are the lowest in Key West. Look for the huge American flag on the roof. **Moped Hospital** (✉ 601 Truman Ave., ☎ 305/296–3344) supplies balloon-tire bikes with yellow safety baskets, as well as mopeds, tandem mopeds, and scooters for adults and children. Helmets are no charge.

Fishing

Captain Steven Impallomeni works as a flats-fishing guide, specializing in ultralight and fly-fishing for tarpon, permit, and bonefish. Charters on the *Gallopin' Ghost* leave from Murray's Marina (✉ MM 5, Stock Island, ☎ 305/292–9837). **Key West Bait and Tackle** (✉ 241 Margaret St., ☎ 305/292–1961) carries live bait, frozen rigged and unrigged bait, and fishing and rigging equipment. It also has the Live Bait Lounge, where you can unwind and nibble on authentic Texas pork tamales and Louisiana shrimp *boudin* (a highly seasoned sausage) while telling tall tales after fishing.

Golf

Key West Resort Golf Course (✉ 6450 E. College Rd., ☎ 305/294–5232) is an 18-hole course on the bay side of Stock Island. Nonresident fees are $95 for 18 holes (cart included) in season, $65 off-season.

Scuba Diving and Snorkeling

Adventure Charters & Tours (✉ 6810 Front St., Stock Island 33040, ☎ 305/296–0362 or 888/817–0841) offers sail-and-snorkel coral reef adventure tours ($25) aboard the 42-ft trimaran sailboat *Fantasea*, with a maximum of 16 people. There are two daily departures and sometimes one at sunset. **Captain's Corner** (✉ 0 Duval St., 33040, ☎ 305/296–8865), a PADI five star–rated shop, provides dive classes in several languages. All captains are licensed dive masters and/or instructors. A 60-ft dive boat, *Sea Eagle,* and the 48-ft *Sea Hawk* depart twice daily. Reservations are accepted for regular reef and wreck diving.

Shopping

Key West contains dozens of characterless T-shirt shops, but some art galleries and curiosity shops have lots worth toting home.

Arts and Crafts

The oldest private art gallery in Key West, **Gingerbread Square Gallery** (✉ 1207 Duval St., ☎ 305/296–8900) represents mainly Keys artists who have attained national and international prominence. **Haitian Art Co.** (✉ 600 Frances St., ☎ 305/296–8932), containing 4,000 paintings and spirit flags, claims the largest collection of Haitian art outside Haiti, representing a range of artists working in wood, stone, metal, and papier-mâché. **Lucky Street Gallery** (✉ 1120 White St., ☎ 305/294–3973) sells high-end contemporary paintings, watercolors, jewelry, and crafts by internationally recognized Key West–based artists. Exhibits change every two weeks. **Pelican Poop** (✉ 314 Simonton St., ☎ 305/296–3887) sells Caribbean art in a gorgeous setting around a lush, tropical courtyard garden with a fountain and pool. The owners go to the Caribbean every year to buy direct from the artisans, so prices are very attractive. (Hemingway wrote *A Farewell to Arms* while living in the complex's apartment.) **Plantation Pottery** (✉ 521 Fleming St., ☎ 305/294–3143) is not to be missed for its original, never-commercial pottery. Potters Charles Pearson and Timothy Roeder *are* **Whitehead St. Pottery** (✉ 1011 Whitehead St., ☎ 305/294–5067), where they display their porcelain stoneware and raku-fired vessels. They also have a photo gallery where they exhibit Polaroid image transfers and black-and-white photos.

Books

Flaming Maggie's (✉ 830 Fleming St., ☎ 305/294–3931) specializes in books and magazines for and about gays and lesbians and also carries books—and artwork—by or about local authors. It contains a popular coffee bar, too. **Key West Island Bookstore** (✉ 513 Fleming St., ☎ 305/294–2904) is the literary bookstore of the large Key West writers' community. It carries new, used, and rare titles.

Clothes and Fabrics

Since 1964 **Key West Hand Print Fashions and Fabrics** (✉ 201 Simonton St., ☎ 305/294–9535 or 800/866–0333) has been noted for its vibrant tropical prints, yard goods, and resort wear for men and women. It's in the Curry Warehouse, a brick building erected in 1878 to store tobacco. **Tikal Trading Co.** (✉ 129 Duval St., ☎ 305/296–4463) sells its own line of women's clothing of handwoven Guatemalan cotton and knit tropical prints.

Food and Drink

Fausto's Food Palace (✉ 522 Fleming St., ☎ 305/296–5663; ✉ 1105 White St., ☎ 305/294–5221) may be under a roof, but it's a market in the traditional town-square sense. Since 1926 Fausto's has been the spot to catch up on the week's gossip and to chill out in summer—it has the heaviest air-conditioning in town. **Waterfront Market** (✉ 201 William St., ☎ 305/294–8418 or 305/296–0778) purveys health and gourmet foods, deli items, produce, salads, cold beer, and wine. If you're there, be sure to check out the bulletin board. The owners also operate a fish market, bakery, deli, and juice bar.

Gifts and Souvenirs

Like a parody of Duval Street T-shirt shops, the hole-in-the-wall **Art Attack** (⊠ 606 Duval St., ☎ 305/294–7131) throws in every icon and trinket anyone nostalgic for the days of peace and love might fancy: beads, necklaces, medallions, yin-yang banners, harmony bells, and of course Grateful Dead and psychedelic T-shirts. **Fast Buck Freddie's** (⊠ 500 Duval St., ☎ 305/294–2007) is a most unusual department store in that it sells such imaginative items as a noise-activated rat in a trap and a raccoon tail in a bag. There are also crystal, furniture, tropical clothing, and every flamingo item imaginable. In a town with a gazillion T-shirt shops, **Last Flight Out** (⊠ 706A Duval St., ☎ 305/294–8008) stands out for its selection of classic namesake Ts, specialty clothing, and gifts that appeal to aviation types as well as those reaching for the stars. A survivor of Key West's seafaring days, **Perkins & Son Chandlery** (⊠ 901 Fleming St., ☎ 305/294–7635), redolent of pine tar and kerosene, offers one of the largest selections of used marine gear in the Keys, as well as nautical antiques, books, outdoor clothing, and collectibles.

Health and Beauty

Key West Aloe (⊠ 524 Front St., ☎ 305/294–5592 or 800/445–2563) was founded in a garage in 1971; today it produces some 300 perfume, sunscreen, and skin-care products for men and women. You can also visit the factory store (⊠ Greene and Simonton Sts.).

Side Trip

Dry Tortugas National Park

This sanctuary for thousands of birds, 70 mi off the shores of Key West, consists of seven small islands. Its main facility is the long-deactivated Fort Jefferson, where Dr. Samuel Mudd was imprisoned for his alleged role in Lincoln's assassination. For information and a list of authorized charter boats, seaplanes, and water taxis, contact **Everglades National Park** (⊠ 40001 Rte. 9336, Homestead 33034-6733, ☎ 305/242–7700).

A two- to three-hour journey to the park aboard the 100-ft *Yankee Freedom* of the **Yankee Fleet Dry Tortugas National Park Ferry** includes a full breakfast and lunch. On arrival a naturalist leads a 45-minute guided tour, followed by lunch and a free afternoon for swimming, snorkeling (gear included), and exploring. ⊠ *Lands End Marina, 261 Margaret St., Key West 33040,* ☎ *305/294–7009 or 800/634–0939.* 🚢 *$91.* ☉ *Trips daily 8 AM.*

THE FLORIDA KEYS A TO Z

Arriving and Departing

By Airport Shuttle

The **Airporter** (☎ 305/852–3413 or 800/830–3413) operates scheduled van and bus pickup service from all Miami International Airport (MIA) baggage areas to wherever you want to go in Key Largo ($30) and Islamorada ($33). A group discount is given for three or more passengers. Reservations are required. The **SuperShuttle** (☎ 305/871–2000) charges $78 for the first passenger ($15 each additional) for trips to the Upper Keys. To go farther into the Keys, you must book an entire van (up to 11 passengers), which costs $250 to Marathon, $350 to Key West. Super Shuttle requests 24-hour advance notice for transportation back to the airport.

By Boat

Boaters can travel to and along the Keys either along the Intracoastal Waterway (5-ft draft limitation) through Card, Barnes, and Blackwater sounds and into Florida Bay or along the deeper Atlantic Ocean route through Hawk Channel, a buoyed passage. Refer to NOAA Nautical Chart Number 11451 for Miami to Marathon and Florida Bay, Numbers 11445 and 11441 for Marathon to Dry Tortugas. The Keys are full of marinas that welcome transient visitors, but they don't have enough slips for everyone. Make reservations in advance and ask about channel and dockage depth—many marinas are quite shallow.

For information contact **Coast Guard Group Key West** (⊠ Key West 33040, ☎ 305/292–8727 or 305/295–9700; CG on a cellular), which provides 24-hour monitoring of VHF-FM Channel 16. Safety and weather information is broadcast at 7 AM and 5 PM Eastern Standard Time on VHF-FM Channel 16 and 22A. There are three stations in the Keys Islamorada (☎ 305/664–4404), Marathon (☎ 305/743–6778), and Key West (☎ 305/292–8856).

Key West Water Express (☎ 800/650–5397) operates a ferry between Key West and Marco Island, on the mainland's southwest coast. The one-way trip takes three hours.

By Bus

Greyhound Lines (☎ 800/231–2222) runs a special Keys shuttle four times a day between MIA (departing from Concourse E, lower level) and stops throughout the Keys. Fares run from $13 one-way and $26 round-trip for Key Largo to $32 one-way and $60 round-trip for Key West.

By Car

From MIA follow signs to Coral Gables and Key West, which put you on Lejeune Road, then Route 836 west. Take the Homestead Extension of Florida's Turnpike south (toll road), which ends at Florida City and connects to U.S. 1. Tolls from the airport run approximately $1.25. The alternative from Florida City is Card Sound Road (Route 905A), which has a bridge toll of $1.75. Continue to the only stop sign and turn right on Route 905, which rejoins U.S. 1 31 mi south of Florida City.

Avoid flying into Key West and driving back to Miami; there are substantial drop-off charges for leaving a Key West car in Miami.

By Plane

Service between **Key West International Airport** (⊠ S. Roosevelt Blvd., Key West, ☎ 305/296–5439) and Miami, Fort Lauderdale/Hollywood, Naples, Orlando, and Tampa is provided by **American Eagle** (☎ 800/433–7300), **Cape Air** (☎ 800/352–0714), **Comair/Delta Connection** (☎ 800/354–9822), **Gulfstream/Continental Connection** (☎ 800/525–0280), and **US Airways/US Airways Express** (☎ 800/428–4322). **Marathon Airport** (⊠ MM 52, BS, Marathon, ☎ 305/743–2155) connects to Miami via American Eagle.

Getting Around

Chambers of commerce, marinas, and dive shops offer **Teall's Guides,** land and nautical charts that pinpoint popular fishing and diving areas. A complete set can also be purchased for $7.95, postage included, from ⊠ 111 Saguaro La., Marathon 33050, ☎ 305/743–3942.

By Bus

Because of overcrowding, the **City of Key West Department of Transportation** (☎ 305/292–8160) has beefed up its bus system. Four color-coded bus routes cover the entire island from 6:30 AM to 10:30 PM. Stops have signs with the international symbol for bus. Schedules are available on buses and at hotels, visitor centers, and shops. The fare is 75¢ (exact change).

By Car

In Key West's Old Town, parking is scarce and costly ($1.50 per hour at Mallory Square). It's better to take a taxi, rent a bicycle or moped, or park at the Park 'n' Ride and either walk or take the Old Town shuttle (☞ *below*) to get around.

Elsewhere in the Keys, a car is crucial. Gas costs more than on the mainland, so fill your tank in Miami and top it off in Florida City.

Most of the Overseas Highway is narrow and crowded (especially weekends and in high season). Expect delays behind RVs, trucks, cars towing boats, and rubbernecking tourists.

The best Keys road map, published by the Homestead/Florida City Chamber of Commerce, can be obtained for $2 from the **Tropical Everglades Visitor Center** (⊠ 160 U.S. 1, Florida City 33034, ☎ 305/245–9180 or 800/388–9669).

By Limousine

Serving the Keys from Ocean Reef to Key West, **Luxury Limousine** (⊠ ☎ 305/664–0601, 305/367–2329, or 800/664–0124) has luxury sedans and limos that seat up to 10 passengers.

By Shuttle

Park 'n' Ride (⊠ 300 Grinnell St., ☎ 305/293–6426) is a good new option for navigating Old Town. You can park at the city's 24-hour garage at the corner of Caroline and Grinnell streets and take an air-conditioned shuttle that makes an 18-minute circuit through Old Town. The shuttle generally runs 7 AM to 11:30 PM, except when there's little going on, and costs 25¢ each way. Parking runs 50¢ an hour/$3 a day if you use the shuttle, 75¢ an hour/$6 a day if you don't.

By Taxi

In the Upper Keys (MM 94–74), **Village Taxi** (☎ 305/664–8181) charges $2 per mi for vans that hold six. It also makes airport runs. In the Middle Keys, **Cheapo Taxi** (☎ 305/743–7420) rates are $1 for pickup and $1 per mi. Drops beyond MM 61 and MM 40 are $1.50 a mile. **Florida Keys Taxi Dispatch** (☎ 305/296–1800) operates around the clock in Key West. The fare for two or more from the Key West airport to New Town is $5 per person with a cap of $15; to Old Town it's $6 and $20, respectively. Otherwise meters register $1.40 to start, 35¢ for each ⅕ mi, and 35¢ for every 50 seconds of waiting time.

Contacts and Resources

Car Rentals

Avis (☎ 305/743–5428 or 800/831–2847) and **Budget** (☎ 305/743–3998 or 800/527–0700) serve Marathon Airport. Key West's airport has booths for **Alamo** (☎ 305/294–6675 or 800/462–5266), **Avis** (☎ 305/294–4846), **Budget** (☎ 305/294–8868), **Dollar** (☎ 305/296–9921 or 800/800–4000), and **Hertz** (☎ 305/294–1039 or 800/654–3131). **Tropical Rent-A-Car** (⊠ 1300 Duval St., Key West, ☎ 305/294–8136) is based in the city center. **Enterprise Rent-A-Car** (☎ 800/325–8007) has offices in Key Largo, Marathon, and Key West. **Thrifty Car Rental** has an office in Tavernier (⊠ MM 91.8, OS, ☎ 305/852–6088).

Emergencies

Dial **911** for police, fire, or ambulance. If you are a TTD caller, tap the space bar or use a voice announcer to identify yourself. **Keys Hotline** (☎ 800/771–5397) provides information and emergency assistance in six languages. **Florida Marine Patrol** (✉ MM 48, BS, 2796 Overseas Hwy., Suite 100, State Regional Service Center, Marathon 33050, ☎ 305/289–2320; 800/342–5367 after 5 PM) maintains a 24-hour telephone service to handle reports of boating emergencies and natural-resource violations. **Coast Guard Group Key West** (☎ 305/295–9700) responds to local marine emergencies and reports of navigation hazards.

HOSPITALS

The following hospitals have 24-hour emergency rooms: **Fishermen's Hospital** (✉ MM 48.7, OS, Marathon, ☎ 305/743–5533); **Florida Keys Hyperbaric Center** (✉ MM 54, OS, Suite 101, Marathon, ☎ 305/743–9891), for diving accidents; **Lower Florida Keys Health System** (✉ MM 5, BS, 5900 College Rd., Stock Island, ☎ 305/294–5531); and **Mariners Hospital** (✉ MM 88.5, BS, 50 High Point Rd., Plantation Key, ☎ 305/852–4418).

LATE-NIGHT PHARMACIES

The Keys have no 24-hour pharmacies. Hospital pharmacists will help with emergencies after regular retail business hours.

Guided Tours

AIR TOURS

Island Aeroplane Tours (✉ 3469 S. Roosevelt Blvd., Key West Airport, Key West 33040, ☎ 305/294–8687) flies up to two passengers in a 1940 Waco, an open-cockpit biplane. Tours range from a quick six- to eight-minute overview of Key West ($50 for two) to a 50-minute look at the offshore reefs ($200 for two).

BIKE TOURS

Key West Nature Bike Tour (✉ Truman Ave. and Simonton St., Key West, ☎ 305/294–1882) explores the natural, noncommercial side of Key West at a leisurely pace, stopping on back streets and in backyards of private homes to sample native fruits and view indigenous plants and trees. The tours run 90–120 minutes and cost $15 with your own bike, $3 more to rent one.

BOAT TOURS

Coral Reef Park Co. (✉ John Pennekamp Coral Reef State Park, MM 102.5, OS, Key Largo 33037, ☎ 305/451–1621) runs sailing trips on a 38-ft catamaran as well as glass-bottom boat tours. **Everglades Eco-Tours** (✉ Dolphin's Cove, MM 102, BS, Key Largo 33037, ☎ 305/853–5161 or 888/224–6044) operates Everglades and Florida Bay ecology tours ($30 per person, two-person minimum), sunset cruises ($20 per person, two-person mininum), and a private charter evening crocodile tour ($199 for up to four passengers). Bob and Gale Dumouchel have run low-impact ecotours through **Gale Force Charters** (✉ 27960 Porgie Path, Little Torch Key 33042, ☎ 305/745–2868) since 1988. Tours leave from **Sugarloaf Marina** (✉ MM 17, BS, Sugarloaf Key) and venture into the channels and islands of the Great White Heron National Wildlife Refuge aboard the *Gale Force,* a 24-ft Carolina skiff whose shallow draft allows the boat to get really close to nature. It also has a viewing tower. Half-day tours cost $150 for the entire boat, which holds 17 passengers, but they take only six for more personal service; full-day excursions cost $250. All tours include snorkel gear, instruction, narration, coolers with ice, walking tours, and beach time. Fishing, snorkel, and kayak tours are also offered. Captain Mike

Wedeking, a local naturalist at **Reflections Nature Tours** (⊠ Big Pine Key, ☎ 305/872–2896 or 305/304–6785), uses a shallow-draft skiff for close-up wildlife tours and island exploration, concentrating on the birds and animals of the Lower Keys backcountry. There's room for one to three passengers. Rates are $150 half day, $250 full day.

Key Largo Princess (⊠ MM 99.7, OS, 99701 Overseas Hwy., Key Largo 33037, ☎ 305/451–4655) offers two-hour glass-bottom boat trips and sunset cruises on a luxury 70-ft motor yacht with a 280-square-ft glass viewing area, departing from the Holiday Inn docks. **M/V** *Discovery* (⊠ Land's End Marina, 251 Margaret St., Key West 33040, ☎ 305/293–0099) and the 65-ft *Pride of Key West* (⊠ 2 Duval St., Key West 33040, ☎ 305/296–6293) are glass-bottom boats. **Strike Zone Charters** (⊠ MM 29.6, BS, 29675 Overseas Hwy., Big Pine Key 33043, ☎ 305/872–9863 or 800/654–9560) offers glass-bottom boat excursions into the backcountry and to Looe Key. The five-hour Island Excursion ($45) emphasizes nature and Keys history. Besides close encounters with birds, sea life, and vegetation, there's a fish cookout on an island. Snorkel and fishing equipment, food, and drinks are included. This is one of the few nature outings in the Keys with wheelchair access.

Victoria Impallomeni (⊠ 5710 U.S. 1, Key West 33040, ☎ 305/294–9731 or 888/822–7366), noted wilderness guide and authority on the ecology of Florida Bay, invites nature lovers aboard the *Imp II*, a 22-ft Aquasport, for four-hour half-day ($300) and seven-hour full-day ($450) ecotours that frequently include encounters with wild dolphins. While island-hopping, you visit underwater gardens, natural shoreline, and mangrove habitats. Everything is supplied except the picnic. Tours leave from **Murray's Marina** (⊠ MM 5, Stock Island). *Wolf* (⊠ Schooner Wharf, Key West Seaport, end of Greene St., Key West 33040, ☎ 305/296–9653) is Key West's tall ship and the flagship of the Conch Republic. The 74-ft, 44-passenger topsail schooner operates day cruises as well as sunset and starlight cruises with live music.

BUS TOURS

The **Conch Tour Train** (☎ 305/294–5161) is a 90-minute narrated tour of Key West, traveling 14 mi through Old Town and around the island. Board at Mallory Square and Roosevelt Boulevard (just north of the Quality Inn) every half hour (9:30–4:30 from Mallory Square, later at other stops). The cost is $15. **Old Town Trolley** (⊠ 6631 Maloney Ave., Key West, ☎ 305/296–6688) operates 12 trackless trolley-style buses, departing from the Mallory Square and Roosevelt Boulevard depots every 30 minutes (9–4:30 from Mallory Square, later at other stops), for 90-minute narrated tours of Key West. The smaller trolleys go places the train won't fit. You may disembark at any of 12 stops and reboard a later trolley. The cost is $16.

CANOE AND KAYAK TOURS

Adventure Charters & Tours (⊠ 6810 Front St., Stock Island 33040, ☎ 305/296–0362) loads kayaks onto the 42-ft catamaran *Island Fantasea* and heads out to the Great White Heron National Wildlife Refuge for guided kayak nature tours with a maximum of 12 passengers. Half-day trips ($35) depart at 9 and 2. Full-day trips ($100) include snorkeling, fishing, a grilled lunch, drinks, and a sunset. The folks at **Florida Bay Outfitters** (⊠ MM 104, BS, 104050 Overseas Hwy., Key Largo 33037, ☎ 305/451–3018) know Keys waters well. You can take a one- to seven-day canoe or kayak tour to the Everglades or Lignumvitae or Indian Key, or a night trip to neighboring islands. Well-known nature photographer Bill Keogh, who shot and co-authored the beautiful coffee-table book *The Florida Keys: The Natural Wonders of an Island Paradise,* runs **Lost World Expeditions** (⊠ Box 431311, Big

Pine Key 33043, ☎ 305/872–8950 or 305/395–0930). He leads personalized guided kayak nature tours ($45 half day) through the Lower Keys and Key West, with stops at nearby refuges. **Mosquito Coast Island Outfitters and Kayak Guides** (✉ 1107 Duval St., Key West 33040, ☎ 305/294–7178) runs full-day guided sea-kayak natural-history tours around the mangrove islands just east of Key West. The $45-a-day charge covers transportation and supplies, including snorkeling gear. **Reflections Nature Tours** (✉ Big Pine Key, ☎ 305/872–2896 or 305/304–6785) operates daily trips into the Great White Heron National Wildlife Refuge and Everglades National Park. Tours last three hours, and $45 covers granola bars, fruit, raisins, water, a bird-identification sheet, and the use of waterproof binoculars; snorkeling gear is extra. Six-hour tours ($80) that include lunch and overnight trips into the backcountry are also offered.

WALKING TOURS

In addition to publishing several good guides on Key West, the **Historic Florida Keys Foundation** (✉ 510 Greene St., Old City Hall, Key West 33040, ☎ 305/292–6718) conducts tours of the City Cemetery Tuesday and Thursday at 9:30. Sharon Wells of **Island City Strolls** (☎ 305/294–8380) knows plenty about Key West. State historian in Key West for nearly 20 years and owner of a historic-preservation consulting firm, she has authored many works, including the magazine-size guide "The Walking and Biking Guide to Historic Key West," which features 10 self-guided tours of the historic district. It's available free at guest houses, hotels, and Key West bookstores. If that whets your appetite, sign on for one of her walking tours, including "Architectural Strolls," "Literary Landmarks," and "Historic 1847 Cemetery Stroll" (which cost $13–$18 for 1–2 hours), or a personalized excursion ($25 an hour).

"Pelican Path" is a free walking guide to Key West published by the Old Island Restoration Foundation. The tour discusses the history and architecture of 43 structures along 25 blocks of 12 Old Town streets. Pick up a copy at the chamber of commerce.

Lodging Reservations

Key West Vacation Rentals (✉ 525 Simonton St., Key West 33040, ☎ 305/292–7997 or 800/621–9405, FAX 305/294–7501) lists historic cottages, homes, and condominiums for rent. Although it prefers to handle reservations for all types of accommodations in advance, the **Key West Welcome Center** (✉ 3840 N. Roosevelt Blvd., Key West 33040, ☎ 305/296–4444 or 800/284–4482) gets a lot of walk-in business because of its location on U.S. 1 at the entrance to Key West. **Property Management of Key West, Inc.** (✉ 1213 Truman Ave., Key West 33040, ☎ 305/296–7744) offers lease and rental service for condominiums, town houses, and private homes. **Vacation Key West** (✉ 1019 Flagler Ave., Key West 33040, ☎ 305/295–9500 or 800/595–5397) lists all kinds of properties throughout Key West.

Publications

The best of the publications covering Key West is *Solares Hill* (✉ 330-B Julia St., Key West 33040, ☎ 305/294–3602). The weekly is witty, controversial, and tough on environmental issues and gets the best arts and entertainment advertising. The best weekday source of information on Key West is the *Key West Citizen* (✉ 3420 Northside Dr., Key West 33040, ☎ 305/294–6641), which also publishes a Sunday edition. For the Upper and Middle Keys, turn to the semiweekly *Keynoter,* a Knight-Ridder publication. The *Free Press, Reporter,* and *Upper Keys Independent* cover the same area once a week. The *Miami Herald* publishes a Keys edition with good daily listings of local events. The monthly *Southern Exposure* is a good source for gay and lesbian travelers.

Visitor Information

Florida Keys & Key West Visitors Bureau (✉ 402 Wall St., Key West 33040, ☎ 800/352–5397). **Greater Key West Chamber of Commerce (mainstream)** (✉ 402 Wall St., Key West 33040, ☎ 305/294–2587 or 800/527–8539, FAX 305/294–7806). **Islamorada Chamber of Commerce** (✉ MM 82.5, BS, Box 915, Islamorada 33036, ☎ 305/664–4503 or 800/322–5397). **Key Largo Chamber of Commerce** (✉ MM 106, BS, 106000 Overseas Hwy., Key Largo 33037, ☎ 305/451–1414 or 800/822–1088, FAX 305/451–4726). **Key West Business Guild (gay)** (✉ Box 1208, Key West 33041, ☎ 305/294–4603 or 800/535–7797). **Lower Keys Chamber of Commerce** (✉ MM 31, OS, Box 430511, Big Pine Key 33043, ☎ 305/872–2411 or 800/872–3722, FAX 305/872–0752). **Marathon Chamber of Commerce & Visitor Center** (✉ MM 53.5, BS, 12222 Overseas Hwy., Marathon 33050, ☎ 305/743–5417 or 800/842–9580).

6 WALT DISNEY WORLD® AND THE ORLANDO AREA

When Walt Disney chose Central Florida as the site of his Magic Kingdom east, Orlando changed forever. Over the years those who followed Walt have expanded his empire. But today there is plenty of competition as the big entertainment companies play the corporate equivalent of keeping up with the Joneses. It's easy to spend weeks here and still not see everything—and there isn't an ocean-pounded beach in sight.

LONG BEFORE "IT'S A SMALL WORLD" echoed through the palmetto scrub, other theme parks tempted visitors away from the beaches into the scruffy interior of Central Florida. I–4 hadn't even been built when Dick and Julie Pope created Cypress Gardens, which holds the record as the region's oldest continuously running attraction—it celebrated 60 years in 1997. But when the Walt Disney World (WDW) Resort opened with the Magic Kingdom as its centerpiece on October 1, 1971, and was immediately successful, the Central Florida theme-park scene became big business. Disney added Epcot in 1982, Disney–MGM Studios in 1989, and Disney's Animal Kingdom in 1998. Meanwhile, Busch Gardens had steadily expanded, spawning the Busch Entertainment Corporation (BEC). With the 1989 acquisition of Cypress Gardens and SeaWorld, opened in 1973, BEC became the second-largest theme-park owner and operator in the world, right behind the Walt Disney Company. Meanwhile, Universal had also been nibbling at the Mouse's cheese. A year after Disney–MGM, Universal Studios answered with its own movie-theme park. Now we have Universal Studios Escape, an umbrella for Universal Studios Florida, the spectacular new Islands of Adventure theme park, and CityWalk, a shopping, dining, and entertainment complex. Two additional glitzy resort hotels are going up as well.

The problem for visitors with tight schedules or slim wallets is that each park is worth a visit. The Magic Kingdom, Epcot, Disney's Animal Kingdom, and SeaWorld are not to be missed. Of the two movie parks, Universal Studios and Disney–MGM Studios, the former is probably more spectacular. Islands of Adventure will bring out the child in all of us. Cypress Gardens is a 60-minute drive through the dusty remnants of the region's citrus groves.

It is easy to forget that this ever-expanding fantasy world grew up around a sleepy farming town founded as a military outpost, Fort Gatlin, in 1838. Though not on any major waterway, Orlando was surrounded by small spring-fed lakes, and transplanted northerners planted sprawling oak trees to vary the landscape of palmetto scrub and citrus groves. Most tourist development is in southwest Orlando, along the I–4 corridor south of Florida's Turnpike. Orlando itself has become a center of international business, and north of downtown are several handsome, prosperous suburbs, most notably Winter Park, which retains its white-gloves-at-tea Southern charm.

Pleasures and Pastimes

Boating

Orlando is truly a boater's paradise. The Orlando area has one of the highest concentrations of lakes—both large and small—of anywhere in the continental United States. If you decide to tow your boat along, you won't be disappointed, but rental boats are easily available.

You can even take advantage of the huge network of lakes and rivers that run right through Disney property by renting any manner of powerboat or Jet Ski at the various Disney resorts. Another, often overlooked possibility is one of the best: Pack a picnic, rent a low-speed pontoon boat for a few hours, and take a ride up a few lazy rivers at your own pace. It's a great way to unwind after you've been on the ExtraTERRORestrial Alien Encounter one too many times.

Dining

If they batter it, fry it, microwave it, torture it under a heat lamp until it's ready to sign a confession, and serve it with a side of fries, you can find it in Central Florida. Cruise down International Drive or U.S. 192, and you'll probably be convinced that some obscure federal law mandates that any franchise restaurant company doing business in the United States has to have at least one outlet in Orlando. Not all are burger barns, however. Wolfgang Puck has a place here, and even the less lofty restaurant names try to put their best foot forward in Orlando, where food is consumed by millions of international visitors. The McDonald's on International Drive, for example, is the largest in the nation. Restaurateurs build monuments here, so you'll ask, "Hey, why don't they have one of these in our town?" This fiercely competitive dining market even brings out the best from the hometown eateries that predate Disney. The result is that dining choices in Orlando are like entertainment choices. There's simply more than you can sample on any one trip.

Because of the large, international tourist trade and the community's own increasing sophistication, Orlando eateries don't end with fast food. The whole spectrum is available, from the very simplest mom-and-pops to basic ethnic eateries to elaborate restaurants serving excellent food, beautifully presented in lovely surroundings.

Golf
Orlando has been a mecca for professional golfers for decades. Some of the greats, like Arnold Palmer, have established winter homes in the city, and some hometown Orlando boys, like Payne Stewart, have made it to national acclaim. Not surprisingly, the city offers some of the best golfing anywhere, including courses designed by PGA pros and by the elite of professional golf course designers, such as Pete Dye, Tom Fazio, and Robert Trent Jones.

Lodging
The sheer variety of accommodations around Orlando—totaling almost 100,000 hotel rooms—will make your head spin faster than after riding in a Mad Tea Party teacup. Resorts, hotels, motels, B&Bs, campgrounds; on Disney property or off; owned by Disney or not: It's all here. For those who want total immersion in the WDW experience, Disney offers elaborate resorts with themes that span both the years and the globe. For those who just want a relatively cheap place to crash, there are plenty of mom-and-pop and chain motels at a little distance from the main attractions. Moreover, many of these properties have programs and facilities for children that range from good to fabulous.

Shopping
It's only fitting that the world's number one tourist destination should offer excellent shopping. It wasn't always thus, however. Recent years have seen a building bonanza of both retail stores and factory outlets. Every year, it seems, a new mall opens. Disney and Universal have their own shopping "theme parks"—Downtown Disney and CityWalk, respectively—each of which could easily take a day to explore, particularly if you enjoy a relaxing meal at one of their many eateries.

For shopping with a more eclectic feel, the tony shops and bistros of Winter Park's Park Avenue are a must. This elegant little street is home to a number of boutiques as well as the usual assortment of chains: the Gap, Banana Republic, et al. But the real charms here are the little tucked-away shops.

EXPLORING WALT DISNEY WORLD® AND THE ORLANDO AREA

Most visitors spend the majority of their time at the theme parks, largely concentrated southwest of Orlando proper. But Orlando and its upscale neighbor to the north, Winter Park, contain some natural and cultural attractions it would be a shame to miss.

Numbers in the text correspond to numbers in the margin and on the Orlando Area map.

Great Itineraries

IF YOU HAVE 4 DAYS

No stay in the area would be complete without visiting the **Magic Kingdom** ①. On the next day, take your pick between the more sophisticated **Epcot** ② and state-of-the-art **Universal Studios Islands of Adventure** ⑩. On day three, see **Universal Studios Florida** ⑨ or the smaller and more manageable **Disney–MGM Studios** ③. On your fourth day go for **Disney's Animal Kingdom** ④ or **SeaWorld Orlando** ⑧. Be sure to catch fireworks one night and one of the local dinner-show extravaganzas on another.

IF YOU HAVE 6 DAYS

Spend the first four days exploring the theme parks in this order: **Magic Kingdom** ①, **Universal Studios Islands of Adventure** ⑩, **Epcot** ②, and **Disney's Animal Kingdom** ④ or **Universal Studios Florida** ⑨. At night make sure you get to some fireworks, sample at least one of the now-ubiquitous themed dining experiences, and visit Pleasure Island and Church Street Station. After all that theme park-ing, you'll need a rest. Depending on your interests and the ages of your children, use day five to venture into Winter Park, where you can take a leisurely boat tour and visit the **Charles Hosmer Morse Museum of American Art** ㉘, and maybe even the **Orlando Museum of Art** ㉔, or consider the **Orlando Science Center** ㉕ for its great interactive activities before relaxing at your hotel. The sixth day should be for **SeaWorld Orlando** ⑧ or one of the Disney water parks. On your last evening take in a dinner show, perhaps SeaWorld's luau.

IF YOU HAVE 10 DAYS

You'll have time to see *all* the theme parks, but pacing is key. So that go-go Orlando tourism scene doesn't wear you down, intersperse theme-park outings with some low-key sightseeing or shopping. Start with the **Magic Kingdom** ①, staying late the first night for the fireworks. The second day, tackle **Epcot** ② and hit Pleasure Island that evening. Set aside the third day for a visit to slower-paced **SeaWorld Orlando** ⑧, making luau reservations when you enter the park. On your fourth day it's back to Disney—either **Disney–MGM Studios** ③, **Blizzard Beach** ⑤, or **Typhoon Lagoon** ⑦. On your fifth and sixth days take in **Disney's Animal Kingdom** ④ and **Universal Studios Islands of Adventure** ⑩. Have dinner at a restaurant that suits your fancy. On day seven, a day of (relative) rest, enjoy a boat tour through Winter Park and visit the **Orlando Science Center** ㉕ and **Orlando Museum of Art** ㉔, at Loch Haven Park, which has lovely grassy areas good for a picnic. In late afternoon walk around Church Street Station, visit **Terror on Church Street** ㉖, and have dinner. On your eighth day drive out to **Cypress Gardens** ⑪ or **Splendid China** ⑯ and catch a dinner show in the evening. Reserve day nine for **Universal Studios Florida** ⑨. Your last day can be spent hitting a mall or outlet stores for some last-minute shopping or for revisiting your favorite theme park. Leave time to clean up back

276

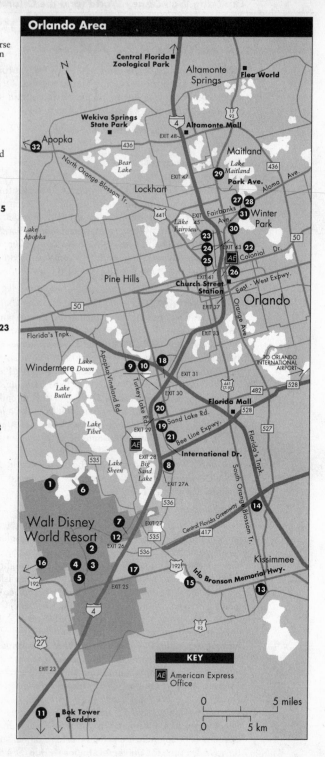

Orlando Area

KEY

AE American Express Office

0   5 miles

0   5 km

at the hotel, and to ease your return to real life, have a bon voyage dinner at a restaurant outside Walt Disney World Resort.

When to Tour Walt Disney World® and the Orlando Area

That the Orlando area is a destination for vacationing families is obvious, but a few important corollaries should be added. If you're traveling without youngsters, try to avoid school-holiday periods. If you have preschoolers, follow the same course; crowds can overwhelm small fry. With schoolchildren, it's nice to avoid prime break times, but it's not always possible—or necessary. Since the parks staff up in peak season, bigger crowds don't always mean longer lines, and busy periods bring longer hours and added entertainment and parades. Nevertheless, to avoid crowds, avoid Christmas, late March, the Easter weeks, and mid-June–mid-August, especially July 4 (it's too hot, anyway). Try to vacation in late May or early June, as soon as the school year ends; in late August; or at Thanksgiving, which is not as busy as other holidays.

Audiences and Ratings

Every visitor leaves the theme parks with a different opinion about what was "the best." Some attractions get raves from all visitors, while others are enjoyed most by young children or older travelers. To take this into account, our descriptions rate each attraction with ★, ★★, or ★★★, depending on the strength of its appeal to the visitor group noted by the italics preceding the stars. "Young children" refers to kids ages 5–7; "very young children" are those (ages four and under) who probably won't meet the height requirements of most thrill rides anyway (for safety reasons). However, since youngsters come in different heights and confidence levels, parents should exercise their judgment when it comes to the scarier rides.

DISNEY THEME PARKS

No doubt about it, the Disney parks have a special magic. You probably know lots about the Magic Kingdom (which is something like California's Disneyland), Epcot, and Disney–MGM Studios, and you've probably heard by now about WDW's new major theme park, Disney's Animal Kingdom, which opened in 1998. But there are also three wonderful water parks—River Country (the oldest), Typhoon Lagoon, and Blizzard Beach.

Magic Kingdom

❶ *Take the Magic Kingdom–U.S. 192 exit (Exit 25) off I–4; from there it's 4 mi along Disney's main entrance road and another mile to the parking lot; be prepared for serious traffic.*

The Magic Kingdom is the heart and soul of the Disney empire. Comparable to California's Disneyland, it was the first Disney outpost in Florida when it opened in 1971, and it is the park that traveled, with modifications, to France and Japan. For a park that wields such worldwide influence, the Magic Kingdom is surprisingly small: At barely 98 acres, it is the tiniest of Walt Disney World Resort's Big Four. However, the unofficial theme song—"It's a Small World After All"—doesn't hold true when it comes to the Magic Kingdom attractions. Packed into seven different "lands" are nearly 50 major crowd pleasers, and that's not counting all the ancillary shops, eateries, live entertainment, cartoon characters, fireworks, parades, and, of course, the sheer pleasure of strolling through the beautifully landscaped and manicured grounds.

The park is laid out on a north–south axis, with Cinderella Castle at the epicenter and the various lands surrounding it in a broad circle. Upon passing through the entrance gates, you immediately discover yourself in **Town Square,** a central connection point that directly segues into **Main Street, U.S.A.,** a boulevard filled with Victorian-style stores and dining spots. Main Street runs due north and ends at the Hub, a large tree-lined circle, known as Central Plaza, in front of Cinderella Castle. Rope Drop, the ceremonial stampede that kicks off each day, occurs at various points along Main Street and the Hub.

As you move clockwise from the Hub, the Magic Kingdom's various lands begin with **Adventureland, Frontierland,** and **Liberty Square.** Next, **Fantasyland** is directly behind Cinderella Castle—in the castle's courtyard, as it were. **Mickey's Toontown Fair** is set off the upper right-hand corner—that's northeast, for geography buffs—of Fantasyland. And **Tomorrowland,** directly to the right of the Hub, rounds out the circle.

Main Street, U.S.A.

With its pastel Victorian-style buildings, antique automobiles oohga-oohga-ing as they stop to offer you a lift, sparkling sidewalks, and atmosphere of what one writer has called "almost hysterical joy," Main Street is more than a mere conduit to the other enchantments of the Magic Kingdom. It is where the spell is first cast.

Although attractions with a capital *A* are minimal on Main Street, there are plenty of inducements to spend more than the 40 minutes most visitors usually take. The Main Street Athletic Shop sells a variety of Team Mickey clothing. The Harmony Barber Shop is the place to have yourself shorn. The Chapeau stocks *Cat in the Hat* fantasies, and the Main Street Gallery, a bright yellow Victorian-style gingerbread building, features animation art and other memorabilia. All sorts of snacks and souvenirs are on sale. If the weather looks threatening, head for the Emporium to purchase those signature mouse-eared umbrellas and bright yellow ponchos with Mickey emblazoned on the back.

City Hall. This is information central, where you can pick up maps and guidebooks and inquire about all things Disney.

Main Street Cinema. Six screens run continuous vintage Disney cartoons in cool, air-conditioned quiet. It's a great opportunity to see the genius of Walt Disney and to meet the endearing little mouse that brought Disney so much fame. *Audience: All ages. Rating:* ★

Walt Disney World Railroad. Step right up to the elevated platform above the Magic Kingdom's entrance for a ride into living history. The 1½-mi track runs along the perimeter of the Magic Kingdom, with much of the trip through the woods. You'll pass Tom Sawyer Island and other attractions; stops are in Frontierland and Mickey's Toontown Fair. Though the ride provides a good introduction to the layout of the park, it's better as relief for tired feet and dragging legs later in the day. *Audience: All ages. Rating:* ★

Adventureland

From the scrubbed brick, manicured lawns, and meticulously pruned trees of the Central Plaza, an artfully dilapidated wooden bridge leads to Adventureland, Disney's version of jungle fever. The landscape artists went wild here: South African cape honeysuckle droops; Brazilian bougainvillea drapes; Mexican flame vines cling; spider plants clone; and three varieties of palm trees sway, all creating a seemingly spontaneous mess.

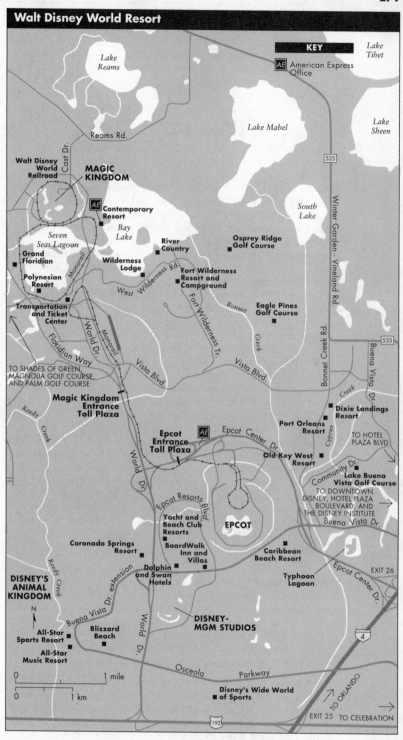

Walt Disney World Resort

KEY

AE American Express Office

Lake Tibet

Lake Reams

Lake Mabel

Lake Sheen

Reams Rd.

Cast Dr.

Walt Disney World Railroad

MAGIC KINGDOM

AE Contemporary Resort

Bay Lake

River Country

Osprey Ridge Golf Course

South Lake

535

Winter Garden - Vineland Rd.

Seven Seas Lagoon

Monorail

Grand Floridian

Polynesian Resort

Wilderness Lodge

West Wilderness Rd.

Fort Wilderness Resort and Campground

Fort Wilderness Tr.

Bonnet

Eagle Pines Golf Course

Creek

Transportation and Ticket Center

World Dr.

Monorail

Floridian Way

Vista Blvd.

Vista Blvd.

Bonnet Creek Rd.

535

Buena Vista Dr.

TO SHADES OF GREEN, MAGNOLIA GOLF COURSE, AND PALM GOLF COURSE

Reedy

Creek

Magic Kingdom Entrance Toll Plaza

World Dr.

Epcot Entrance Toll Plaza

AE

Epcot Center Dr.

Port Orleans Resort

Old Key West Resort

Cypress

Dixie Landings Resort

TO HOTEL PLAZA BLVD.

Creek

Community Dr.

Lake Buena Vista Golf Course

TO DOWNTOWN DISNEY, HOTEL PLAZA BOULEVARD, AND THE DISNEY INSTITUTE

Epcot Resorts Blvd.

EPCOT

Buena Vista Dr.

Yacht and Beach Club Resorts

BoardWalk Inn and Villas

Caribbean Beach Resort

EXIT 26

Coronado Springs Resort

Dolphin and Swan Hotels

Typhoon Lagoon

Epcot Center Dr.

DISNEY'S ANIMAL KINGDOM

N

Buena Vista Dr. extension

World Dr.

DISNEY-MGM STUDIOS

4

All-Star Sports Resort

Blizzard Beach

Reedy Creek

All-Star Music Resort

0   1 mile

0   1 km

Osceola   Parkway

TO ORLANDO

Disney's Wide World of Sports

EXIT 25   TO CELEBRATION

192

Adventureland Challenge. Your mission, should you choose to accept it, is to find the Golden Idol of Adventureland. Upon receiving a map of the area, you are given a riddle that will help you find it. *Audience: Older children and adults. Rating:* ★

Enchanted Tiki Room Under New Management. In its original incarnation as the Enchanted Tiki Birds, this was Disney's first Audio-Animatronics attraction. Now updated, it includes the avian stars of recent Disney animated films: Zazu from *The Lion King* and *Aladdin*'s Iago. The boys take you on a tour of the original attraction while cracking lots of in-jokes. A holdover from the original is the ditty "In the Tiki, Tiki, Tiki, Tiki, Tiki Room," which is second only to "It's a Small World" as the Disney song you love to hate. *Audience: All ages. Rating:* ★

Jungle Cruise. During this ride you cruise through three continents and along four rivers—the Congo, the Nile, the Mekong, and the Amazon—past all manner of animals from bathing elephants to slinky pythons. The canopied launches are loaded, the safari-suited guides make a point of checking their pistols, and the *Irrawady Irma* or *Mongala Millie* is off for another "perilous" journey. The guide's spiel is surprisingly funny, with just the right blend of cornball humor and gentle snideness. *Audience: All ages. Rating:* ★★★

Pirates of the Caribbean. This boat ride is classic Disney: memorable vignettes, incredible detail, a gripping story, and catchy music whose relentless yo-ho-ing can only be eradicated by "It's a Small World." One of the pirate's "Avast, ye scurvy scum!" is the sort of greeting your kids will proclaim for the next week—which gives you an idea of the ride's impact. Emerging from a pitch-black time tunnel, you're literally in the middle of a furious battle. A pirate ship, cannons blazing, is attacking a stone fortress. Cannonballs splash into the water just off your bows, and Audio-Animatronics pirates hoist the Jolly Roger while brave soldiers scurry to defend the fort—to no avail. *Audience: All ages. Rating:* ★★

Swiss Family Treehouse. Based on the classic novel by Johann Wyss about the adventures of the Robinson family, who were shipwrecked on the way to America, the tree house shows what you can do with a big banyan and a lot of imagination. The rooms are furnished with patchwork quilts and mahogany furniture. Disney detail abounds: The kitchen sink is made of a giant clamshell; the boys' room, strewn with clothing, has two hammocks instead of beds; and an ingenious system of rain barrels and bamboo pipes provides running water in every room. *Audience: All ages; toddlers unsteady on their feet may have trouble with the stairs. Rating:* ★★

Frontierland

Frontierland, in the northwest quadrant of the Magic Kingdom, invokes the American frontier. The period seems to be the latter half of the 19th century, and the West is being won by Disney staffers dressed in checked shirts, leather vests, cowboy hats, and brightly colored neckerchiefs. Banjo and fiddle music twang from tree to tree, and guests walk around munching on the biggest drumsticks you've ever seen.

Big Thunder Mountain Railroad. As any true roller-coaster lover can tell you, this three-minute ride is relatively tame; despite the posted warnings, you won't stagger off, you won't throw up, and you won't vow never to subject yourself to the experience again. The thrills are there, however, thanks to the intricate details and stunning scenery along every inch of the 2,780-ft-long wooden track. Set in gold rush days, the runaway train rushes and rattles past 20 Audio-Animatronics figures—including donkeys, chickens, a goat, and a grizzled old miner surprised in his bathtub. *Audience: All but young children. No pregnant women* *or guests with back, neck, or leg braces; minimum height: 40". Rating:* ★★★

Country Bear Jamboree. Wisecracking, cornpone Audio-Animatronics bears joke, sing, and play country music and 1950s rock and roll in this stage show. *Audience: All ages. Rating:* ★★★

Diamond Horseshoe Saloon Revue. "Knock, knock." "Who's there?" "Ya." "Ya who?" "Yaaahooo!" And they're off, with another rip-roaring, raucous, corny, nonstop, high-kicking, elbow-jabbing, song-and-dance-and-fiddling show staged in a re-creation of an Old West saloon. In the evening the entertainment changes to a quartet of singing cowpokes who lead the audience in a campfire sing-along. *Audience: All ages. Rating:* ★★

Splash Mountain. At Rope Drop, the hordes hoof it to this incredibly popular log-flume ride. Based on the animated sequences in Disney's 1946 film *Song of the South,* it features Audio-Animatronics creations of Brer Rabbit, Brer Bear, Brer Fox, and a menagerie of other Brer beasts (including Brer Frog and a Heckle and Jeckle duo of Brer Crows). You get one heart-stopping pause at the top—just long enough to grab the safety bar—and then the boat plummets down a long, sharp flume drop right into a gigantic briar patch. *Audience: All but very young children. No pregnant women or guests with back, neck, or leg braces; minimum height: 40". Rating:* ★★★

Tom Sawyer Island. The island—actually two islands connected by an old-fashioned swing bridge—is a natural playground, all hills and trees and rocks and shrubs. Some guidebooks suggest that parents sit this one out on the porch of Aunt Polly's Dockside Inn, sipping lemonade; we say, why let the kids have all the fun? Most attractions are on the main island. The mystery cave is an almost-pitch-black labyrinth where the wind wails in a truly spooky fashion. Injun Joe's Cave is all pointy stalactites and stalagmites with lots of columns and crevices from which to jump out and startle younger sisters and brothers. Harper's Mill is an old-fashioned grist mill, and a rustic playground sits in a clearing at the top of the hill. *Audience: All ages. Rating:* ★★★

Liberty Square

The weathered siding gives way to neat clapboard and solid brick, the mesquite and cactus are replaced by stately oaks and masses of azaleas, and the rough-and-tumble Western frontier gently slides into Colonial America. Liberty Square picks up where Frontierland leaves off, continuing around the shore of Rivers of America and forming the western boundary of Fantasyland.

Hall of Presidents. This multimedia tribute to the Constitution caused quite a sensation when it opened because it was here that the first refinements of the Audio-Animatronics system of computerized robots could be seen. Now surpassed by Epcot's American Adventure, it's still well worth attending, as much for the spacious, air-conditioned theater as for the two-part show. It starts with a film, narrated by writer Maya Angelou, that discusses the Constitution as the codification of the spirit that founded America. The second half is a roll call of all 42 U.S. presidents. Each chief executive rises and responds with a nod—even those who blatantly attempted to subvert the Constitution. The detail is lifelike, right down to the brace on Franklin Delano Roosevelt's leg. *Audience: Older children and adults. Rating:* ★★★

Haunted Mansion. Part walk-through, part ride on a "doom buggy," this eight-minute buggy ride is scary but not terrifying, and the special effects are a howl. Catch the glowing bats' eyes on the wallpaper; the strategically placed gusts of damp, cold air; the wacky inscriptions on the tombstones; and the dancing ghosts. *Audience: All but young children. Rating:* ★★★

Liberty Belle **Riverboat.** A real old-fashioned steamboat, the *Liberty Belle* is authentic, from its calliope whistle and the gingerbread trim on its three decks to the boilers that produce the steam that drives the big rear paddle wheel. The trip is slow and not exactly thrilling, but it's a relaxing break for all concerned. *Audience: All ages. Rating:* ★

Mike Fink Keelboats. They're short and dumpy, and you have to sit on a bench, wedged tightly between fellow visitors. *Audience: All ages. Rating:* ★

Fantasyland

Many of the rides here are for children, and the lines move slowly. If you're traveling without young kids, skip this area, with the possible exception of Cinderella's Golden Carrousel.

Cinderella Castle. At 180 ft, this castle is more than 100 ft taller than Disneyland's Sleeping Beauty Castle and, with its elongated towers and lacy fretwork, immeasurably more graceful.

Cinderella's Golden Carrousel. The whirling, musical heart of Fantasyland, this antique merry-go-round has 90 prancing horses, each one completely different. The rich notes of the band organ—no calliope here—play favorite tunes from Disney movies. *Audience: All ages. Rating:* ★★

Dumbo the Flying Elephant. Jolly Dumbos fly around a central column, each pachyderm packing a couple of kids and a parent. A joystick controls each Dumbo's vertical motion, making him ascend or descend at will. Doesn't sound like much? It's one of Fantasyland's most popular rides. Alas, the ears do not flap. *Audience: Young children and the young at heart. Rating:* ★

It's a Small World. Visiting the Magic Kingdom and not stopping here—why, the idea is practically un-American! Moving somewhat slower than a snail, barges inch through several brightly colored barnlike rooms, each representing a continent and each crammed with musical moppets dressed in various national costumes and madly singing the theme song, "It's a Small World After All." But somehow by the time you reach the end of the 11-minute trip, you're grinning and humming, too—as has been the case with almost everyone who's gone on the ride since it debuted at the 1964–65 New York World's Fair. *Audience: All ages. Rating:* ★★

Legend of the Lion King. Unlike many Magic Kingdom stage shows, this one does not draw on human talent. Simba, Mufasa, Scar, and the rest are played by "humanimals," Disneyspeak for bigger-than-life-size figures that are manipulated by human "animateers" hidden from audience view. The preshow consists of the "Circle of Life" overture from the film. *Audience: All ages. Rating:* ★★

Mad Tea Party. In this ride based on the 1951 Disney film about a girl named Alice who tumbles into Wonderland, you hop into oversize pastel-color teacups and whirl for two minutes around a giant platter. If the centrifugal force hasn't shaken you up too much, check out the soused mouse that pops out of the teapot centerpiece. *Audience: All ages. Rating:* ★

The Many Adventures of Winnie the Pooh. The famous honey-lover and his exploits in the Hundred Acre Wood are the theme for this newcomer, debuting summer 1999. *Audience: All ages.*

Peter Pan's Flight. Aboard two-person magic sailing ships with brightly striped sails, you soar into the skies above London en route to Never Land. Adults enjoy the dreamy views of London by moonlight. *Audience: All ages. Rating:* ★★

Skyway to Tomorrowland. This cable car takes off on its one-way aerial trip to Tomorrowland from an enchanted attic perched above the trees in a far corner of Fantasyland not far from It's a Small World. Can anyone say "photo opportunity"? *Audience: All ages. Rating:* ★

Snow White's Scary Adventures. What was previously an unremittingly frightening, three-minute, indoor spook-house ride, whose dwarfs might as well have been named Anxious and Fearful, has been toned down somewhat. However, there's still no shortage of the evil queen, her nose wart, and her cackle, and the trip is still packed with scary moments. But the Prince and Snow White have joined the cast, and there's an honest-to-goodness kiss followed by a happily ever-after ending, which might even have you heigh-ho-ing on your way out. *Audience: All ages; toddlers may be scared. Rating:* ★★

Mickey's Toontown Fair

For a company that owes its fame to a certain endearing, big-eared little fellow, Walt Disney World Resort is astonishingly mouse-free. Until, that is, you arrive here, a concentrated dose of adulation built in 1988 and originally named Mickey's Birthdayland to celebrate the Mouse's Big Six-O. Due to its popularity with the small-fry set, it was retained year after year under the appellation Mickey's Starland. The area is now an official Magic Kingdom land. The 3-acre niche set off to the side of Fantasyland is like a scene from a cartoon, and everything is child size. Its pastel houses are positively lilliputian, with miniature driveways, toy-size picket fences, and signs scribbled with finger paint. The best way to arrive is on the Walt Disney World Railroad, the old-fashioned choo-choo that also stops at Main Street and Frontierland.

Barnstormer at Goofy's Wiseacres Farm. Traditional red barns and farm buildings form the backdrop here. The real attraction is the Barnstormer, a kid-size roller coaster that's housed in a 1920s crop-dusting biplane. *Audience: Young children. Rating:* ★★

Donald's Boat. A cross between a tugboat and a leaky ocean liner, the *Miss Daisy* is actually a water play area. *Audience: Young children and their families. Rating:* ★★

Mickey's Country House. This slightly goofy architectural creation is right in the heart of Toontown Fairgrounds. Inside, a radio in the living room is "tooned" to scores from Mickey's favorite football team, from Duckburg University, while his clothes are neatly arranged in his bedroom beside Mickey's baby pictures and a photo of Minnie. *Audience: All ages, although teens may be put off by the terminal cuteness. Rating:* ★★

Minnie's Country House. A peek inside this baby blue and pink house reveals Minnie's lively lifestyle. In addition to her duties as editor of *Minnie's Cartoon Country Living* magazine, the Martha Stewart of the mouse set also quilts, paints, and gardens. *Audience: All ages, although teens may be put off. Rating:* ★★

Toon Park. Another play area, this spongy green meadow is filled with foam topiary in the shapes of goats, cows, pigs, and horses. Kids can jump and hop on interactive lily pads to hear animal topiaries moo, bleat, and whinny. *Audience: Young children, mainly. Rating:* ★

Toontown Hall of Fame. Check out the blue-ribbon winning entries from the Toontown Fair. *Audience: Young children. Rating:* ★★

Tomorrowland

The stark, antiseptic future forecasted in the original design of Tomorrowland had become embarrassingly inaccurate by the mid-'90s. Bare concrete, plain white walls, and outdated rides said more about Eisenhower-era aesthetics (or lack thereof) than third-millennium progress.

To revitalize what had become the least appealing area of the Magic Kingdom, Disney artists and architects created new facades, restaurants, and shops for an energized Future City, which is more similar in mood to the themed villages of the other lands. And this time around the creators showed that they had learned their lesson: Rather than predict a tomorrow destined for obsolescence, they focused instead on "the future that never was"—the future envisioned by sci-fi writers and moviemakers in the '20s and '30s, when space flight, laser beams, and home computers belonged in the world of fiction, not fact. As the millennium approaches, the Jetson-esque styling has a retro feel that lends it fresh chicness . . . for now.

Astro-Orbiter. The superstructure of revolving planets has come to symbolize the new Tomorrowland as much as Dumbo represents Fantasyland. Despite the spiffy new look, though, the ride is still just the old Starjets, something like Dumbo for grown-ups but with Buck Rogers–style vehicles rather than elephants. You can control the altitude if not the velocity. *Audience: All ages. Rating:* ★★

Buzz Lightyear's Space Ranger Spin. You're seated in a fast-moving vehicle equipped with a laser gun and can choose from four interactive games to help Disney's macho space man save the universe. As Buzz likes to say, "To infinity—and beyond!" *Audience: Young children. Rating:* ★★

Carousel of Progress. This 20-minute show in a revolving theater, first seen at the 1964–65 World's Fair and updated many times since then, traces the impact of technological progress from the turn of this century into the near future. In each decade an Audio-Animatronics family sings the praises of the new gadgets that technology has wrought. The preshow, on overhead video monitors, details the design of the original carousel and features Walt Disney himself singing the theme song, "There's a Great Big Beautiful Tomorrow"—very fitting for the new Tomorrowland. *Audience: All ages. Rating:* ★

ExtraTERRORestrial Alien Encounter. This ride is probably the single scariest attraction in all Walt Disney World Resort, engendering start-to-finish screams among teens and ashen faces and tears among younger children who decide to brave it (despite copious posted warnings). Playing on Tomorrowland's Future City theme, this attraction has guests enter what is ostensibly the city's convention center to watch a test of a new teleportation system. The attempt fails, however, and the resulting catastrophe consists of a very close encounter with an "extraTERRORrestrial" creature, complete with realistic sound effects, smoke, and several seconds of complete darkness. *Audience: All but young children. Rating:* ★★

Skyway to Fantasyland. You can pick up the brightly colored cable cars right outside Space Mountain for the commute to the far western end of Fantasyland. The silence aloft is quite pleasant after the hubbub on the ground. *Audience: All ages. Rating:* ★

Space Mountain. Its needlelike spires and 180-ft-high, gleaming white-concrete cone are a Magic Kingdom icon. Inside you'll find a roller coaster that may well be the world's most imaginative. The ride only lasts two minutes and 38 seconds and attains a top speed of a mere 28 mph, but the devious twists and drops, and the fact that it's all in the dark so that you can never see where you're going, make it seem twice as long and four times as thrilling. Try and grab the very front car. Many people of all ages adore this ride, but a significant number dislike it, too. *Audience: All but young children. No pregnant women or guests with back, neck, or leg braces; minimum height: 44". Rating:* ★★★

Timekeeper. This time-traveling adventure is hosted by TimeKeeper, a C-3PO clone whose frenetic personality is given voice by Robin Williams, and Nine-Eye, a slightly frazzled droid, who's a graduate of MIT (that would be the Metropolis Institute of Time Travel). Along the way, you meet famous inventors and visionaries of the machine age, such as Jules Verne and H. G. Wells. Don't plan on a relaxing voyage, however; there are no seats in the theater—only rails to lean on. *Audience: All ages. Rating:* ★★

Tomorrowland Speedway. Be prepared for instant addiction among kids: brightly colored Mark VII model gasoline-powered cars swerve around the four 2,260-ft tracks with much vroom-vroom-vroom-ing. But there's way too much waiting. *Audience: Older children (minimum height: 52" to drive; be sure to check your youngster's height before lining up). Rating:* ★

Tomorrowland Transit Authority—TTA. All aboard for a nice, leisurely ride around the perimeter of Tomorrowland, circling the Astro-Orbiter and eventually gliding through the middle of Space Mountain. Like the old WEDway People Mover, of which this is a redo, the TTA is smooth and noiseless, thanks to an electromagnetic linear induction motor that has no moving parts, uses little power, and emits no pollutants. It's Disney's look at the future of mass transit. *Audience: All ages. Rating:* ★

Entertainment

Beginning at 3 every day, the 15-minute-long **daily parade** proceeds through Frontierland and down Main Street; there are floats, balloons, cartoon characters, dancers, singers (usually lip-synching to music played over the PA system), and much waving and cheering. It's pleasant, and young children love it. **Main Street Electrical Parade,** a 20-minute nighttime extravaganza of twinkling floats, waving characters, and singing-and-prancing human escorts runs only during holiday periods and during the summer. **Fantasy in the Sky** is the Magic Kingdom fireworks display. Heralded by a dimming of all the lights along Main Street, a single spotlight illuminates the top turret of the Cinderella Castle and—poof!—Tinker Bell emerges in a shower of pixie dust to fly over the treetops and the crowds. Her disappearance signals the start of the fireworks. It's a great show and well worth waiting around for.

Epcot

➋ *Take the Epcot–Downtown Disney exit (Exit 26) off I–4.*

Walt Disney World was created because of Walt Disney's dream of EPCOT, the Experimental Prototype Community of Tomorrow. Disney envisioned a future in which nations coexisted in peace and harmony, reaping the miraculous harvest of technological achievement. He suggested the idea as early as October 1966, saying, "EPCOT will be an experimental prototype community of tomorrow that will take its cue from the new ideas and new technologies that are now emerging from the creative centers of American industry." The permanent community that he envisioned has not yet come to be. Instead, we have Epcot (the *Center* was dropped from the park's name in 1994)—which opened in 1982, 16 years after Disney's death—a showcase, ostensibly, for the concepts that would be incorporated into the real-life Epcots of the future.

Epcot is that rare paradox—an educational theme park—and a very successful one, too. Although rides have been added over the years to amuse young 'uns, the thrills are mostly for the mind. Consequently, Epcot is best for older children and adults.

The two parts of Epcot are separated by the 40-acre World Showcase Lagoon. The northern half, **Future World,** is where the monorail drops you off and is the official entrance. The southern half, at whose International Gateway the trams from the Dolphin and Swan hotels and

Disney's Yacht and Beach Club and BoardWalk resorts drop you off, is **World Showcase**.

Future World

Future World is made up of two concentric circles of pavilions. The inner core is composed of the Spaceship Earth geosphere and, just beyond it, the large, computer-animated Fountain of Nations, bracketed by the crescent-shape Innoventions East and West. This is also the site of the new Ice Station Cool, a re-created igloo where you can sample Coca-Cola products from around the world. The monorail circles the park overhead, serving as an unofficial dividing line between the inner core and the pavilions beyond.

The outer ring comprises seven pavilions. On the east side they are, in order, the Universe of Energy, Wonders of Life, Horizons (currently closed, perhaps for good), and Test Track. With the exception of the Wonders of Life, the pavilions present a single, self-contained ride and an occasional post-ride showcase; a visit rarely takes more than 30 minutes, but it depends on how long you spend in the post-ride area. On the west side there are the Living Seas, the Land, and Journey into Imagination. Like the Wonders of Life, these blockbuster exhibits contain both rides and interactive displays; count on spending at least 1½ hours per pavilion—and wanting to stay longer.

Innoventions. In this two-building, 100,000-square-ft attraction, live stage demonstrations, hands-on displays, and exhibits highlight new technology that affects daily living. Each major exhibition area is presented by a leading manufacturer. **Innoventions East** appeals more strongly to adults, with manufacturers such as General Electric, Hammacher Schlemmer, and Honeywell displaying products for the home of the not-too-distant future. There's also a hands-on display of Apple software that keeps your kids entertained—provided they can get to a computer. **Innoventions West**, hugely popular with preteens, features an enormous display of Sega toys and games. *Audience: All ages, although young children may be bored. Rating:* ★★★

Journey into Imagination. The Journey into Imagination ride is currently being redone, but there are still plenty of things to do at this pavilion.

Honey, I Shrunk the Audience is one of the most popular attractions in Epcot. This 3-D adventure utilizes the futuristic "shrinking" technologies demonstrated in the hit films that starred Rick Moranis. Just be prepared to laugh and scream your head off, courtesy of the special in-theater effects, moving seats, and 3-D film technology. Don't miss this one. *Audience: All but very young children. Rating:* ★★★

No other theme park has anything that compares with Journey into Imagination's **Image Works**, an electronic fun house crammed with interactive games and wizardry that will give your imagination a real workout. *Audience: All ages. Rating:* ★★★

The Land. Shaped like an intergalactic greenhouse, the enormous skylighted The Land pavilion dedicates 6 acres and a host of attractions to everyone's favorite topic: food. You can easily spend two hours exploring here.

Circle of Life is a film featuring three stars of *The Lion King*—Simba the lion, Timon the meerkat, and Pumbaa the waddling warthog—in an enlightening and powerful message about protecting the world's environment for all living things. *Audience: All ages, although some toddlers may nap. Rating:* ★★

Food Rocks is a rowdy concert in which recognizable rock-and-roll performers in the shape of favorite foods (the Peach Boys, Chubby Cheddar, and Neil Moussaka, to name a few) sing about the joys of nutrition. *Audience: Children and their parents. Rating:* ★

The main event is a boat ride called **Living with the Land,** piloted by an informative, overalls-clad guide. You cruise through three biomes—rain forest, desert, and prairie ecological communities—and into an experimental greenhouse that demonstrates how food sources may be grown in the future, not only on this planet but also in outer space. *Audience: Teens and adults. Rating:* ★★★

Living Seas. On Epcot's western outer ring is the first satellite pavilion, Living Seas, a favorite among children. Epcot is known for its imaginative fountains; the one at Living Seas flings surf in a never-ending wave against a rock garden beneath the stylized marquee. Time and technology have caught up with the 5.7-million-gallon aquarium at the pavilion's core—thrilling when it first opened—so that what was once revolutionary has now been equaled by top aquariums around the country.

The two-level **Sea Base Alpha,** a typical Epcot playground, contains six modules, each dedicated to a specific subject: the history of robotics, ocean exploration, ocean ecosystems, dolphins, porpoises, and sea lions. *Audience: All but young children. Rating:* ★★★

The three-minute **Seacabs,** a shuttle to Sea Base Alpha, is simply too short. In addition to watching the aquarium's full-time denizens, you may catch sight of a diver, testing out the latest scuba equipment, surrounded by a cloud of parrot fish. Afterward you may want to circumnavigate the tank at your own speed on an upper level, pointing out barracudas, stingrays, sea turtles, and even sharks. *Audience: All but young children. Rating:* ★★★

Spaceship Earth. Balanced like a giant golf ball waiting for some celestial being to tee off, the multifaceted silver geosphere of Spaceship Earth is to Epcot what the Cinderella Castle is to the Magic Kingdom. Everyone likes to gawk at the golf ball, but here are some truly jaw-dropping facts: It weighs 1 million pounds, measures 164 ft in diameter and 180 ft in height—aha! you say, it's not really a sphere!

The **Spaceship Earth ride** explores human progress and the continuing search for better forms of communication. Scripted by science fiction writer Ray Bradbury and narrated by Jeremy Irons (who replaced Walter Cronkite), the journey begins in the darkest tunnels of time. It proceeds through history and ends poised on the edge of the future. Special effects, animated sets, and audience-enclosing laser beams are used to create the experience. *Audience: All ages, but persons who experience anxiety in dark, narrow, or enclosed spaces should not ride. Rating:* ★★★

Test Track. This small-scale version of a General Motors test track is finally open. The main draw is the ride itself, billed as "the longest and fastest ride in Walt Disney World history." A six-passenger Test Track vehicle takes you on a heart-pounding trip through seven different tests: hill climbing, suspension, brakes, environmental, handling, barriers, and, finally, high speed. *Audience: All but young children. No pregnant women or guests with back, neck, or leg braces; minimum height: 40". Rating:* ★★★

Universe of Energy. The first of the pavilions on the left, or east, side of Future World occupies a large, lopsided pyramid sheathed in thousands of mirrors—solar collectors that power the attraction within.

One of the most technologically complex shows at Epcot, **Ellen's Energy Adventure** features the popular comedienne Ellen DeGeneres as a woman who dreams she's a contestant on *Jeopardy!*, only to discover that all the categories are about a subject she knows nothing about—energy. With help from Bill Nye the Science Guy, she (and you) get a "crash course" in Energy 101. The exhibit combines a ride, three films, the largest Audio-Animatronics animals ever built, 250 prehistoric trees, and enough cold, damp fog to make you think you've been transported to the inside of a defrosting refrigerator. *Audience: All ages. Rating:* ★★★

Wonders of Life. A towering statue of a DNA double helix stands outside the gold-crowned dome of one of the most popular wonders of Epcot. The attraction takes an amusing but serious and educational look at health, fitness, and modern lifestyles.

Walt Disney World Resort's first flight simulator—**Body Wars**—takes visitors on a bumpy platelet-to-platelet ride through the human circulatory system. *Audience: All but young children. No pregnant women or guests with heart, back, or neck problems or motion sickness; minimum height: 40". Rating:* ★★★

The theater housing **Cranium Command** seats 200 at a shot. Combining a fast-paced movie with an elaborate set, this engaging show looks at how the cranium manages to make the heart, the uptight left brain, the laid-back right brain, the stomach, and an ever-alert adrenal gland all work together as their host, a 12-year-old boy, suffers the slings and arrows of a typical day. *Audience: All ages. Rating:* ★★★

The **Fitness Fairground,** an educational playground that teaches both adults and children about good health, takes up much of Wonders of Life. There are games in which you can test your golf and tennis prowess, pedal around the world on a stationary bicycle while watching an ever-changing view on video, and guess your stress level at an interactive computer terminal. *Audience: All ages. Rating:* ★★★

Starring Martin Short as a man in search of his origins, *The Making of Me* is a valuable film on human conception and childbearing, using both animation and actual footage from a live birth to explain where babies come from. Some scenes are explicit, but all the topics are handled with gentle humor and great delicacy. Children tend to be dumbstruck, and many adults find the film affecting enough to get out the handkerchiefs for a quick swipe at overflowing eyes. *Audience: All ages. Rating:* ★★★

World Showcase

The 40-acre World Showcase Lagoon is 1⅓ mi around, but in that space you circumnavigate the globe, or at least explore it, in pavilions representing 11 countries in Europe, Asia, North Africa, and the Americas. (There is also an area, though no pavilion, representing Africa, which features African entertainment and shopping.) In each pavilion native food, entertainment, art and handicrafts, and usually a multimedia presentation showcase the particular culture and people; architecture and landscaping re-create well-known landmarks.

American Adventure. The pavilion's superlative attraction is a 100-yard dash through history called the **American Adventure.** To the music of a piece called "The Golden Dream," performed by the Philadelphia Orchestra, it combines evocative sets, the world's largest rear-projection screen (72 ft wide), enormous movable stages, and 35 Audio-Animatronics players, which are some of the most lifelike ever created. *Audience: All ages. Rating:* ★★★

While waiting for the American Adventure show to begin, you can read the quotes on the walls of the **Hall of Presidents.** Directly opposite the pavilion, on the edge of the lagoon, is the **America Gardens Theatre,** the venue for concerts and shows of the Yankee Doodle Dandy variety.

Canada. "Oh, it's just our Canadian outdoors," said a typically modest native guide upon being asked the model for the striking rocky chasm and tumbling waterfall that represent just one of the high points of Canada. The top attraction is the CircleVision film *O Canada!* And that's just what you'll say after the stunning opening shot of the Royal Canadian Mounted Police literally surrounding you as they circle the screen. *Audience: All ages, although no strollers permitted and toddlers have to be held aloft to see. Rating:* ★★★

China. A shimmering red-and-gold three-tier replica of Beijing's Temple of Heaven towers over a serene Chinese garden, an art gallery displaying treasures from the People's Republic, a spacious emporium devoted to Chinese goods, and two restaurants. The *Wonders of China,* a sensational panorama of the land and people, is dramatically portrayed on a 360-degree CircleVision screen. *Audience: All ages, although no strollers permitted and small children have to be held aloft to see. Rating:* ★★★

France. You don't need the scaled-down model of the Eiffel Tower to tell you that you've arrived in France, specifically Paris. There are the poignant accordion music wafting out of concealed speakers, the trim sycamores pruned in the French style to develop signature knots at the end of each branch, and the delicious aromas surrounding the Boulangerie Pâtisserie bakeshop. The intimate Palais du Cinema, inspired by the royal theater at Fontainebleau, screens the film *Impressions de France,* an homage to the glories of the country. Shown on five screens spanning 200 degrees in an air-conditioned sit-down theater, the film takes you to vineyards at harvesttime, Paris on Bastille Day, the Alps, Versailles, Normandy's Mont-St-Michel, and the stunning châteaus of the Loire Valley. *Audience: Adults. Rating:* ★★★

Germany. This jovial make-believe village distills the best folk architecture from all over that country. You'll hear the hourly chimes from the specially designed glockenspiel on the clock tower, musical toots and tweets from multitudinous cuckoo clocks, folk tunes from the spinning dolls and lambs sold at Der Teddybär, and the satisfied grunts of hungry visitors chowing down on hearty German cooking. The four-times-a-day oompah band show in the Biergarten restaurant is also performed twice a day in the courtyard. Germany boasts the most shops of any pavilion. *Audience: Adults and older children. Rating:* ★★

Italy. The star here is the Piazza San Marco, complete with a re-creation of Venice's Doge's Palace that's accurate right down to the gold leaf on the ringlets of the angel perched 100 ft atop the campanile, gondolas tethered to a seawall stained with age, and Romanesque columns, Byzantine mosaics, Gothic arches, and stone walls that have all been carefully antiqued to look historic. *Audience: Adults and older children. Rating:* ★★

Japan. A brilliant vermilion torii gate, derived from the design of Hiroshima Bay's much-photographed Itsukushima Shrine, epitomizes the striking yet serene mood here. Disney horticulturists deserve a hand for their achievement in constructing out of all-American plants and boulders a very Japanese landscape, complete with rocks, pebbled streams, pools, and hills. At sunset or during a rainy dusk, the sharp edges of the evergreens and twisted branches of the corkscrew willows frame a perfect Japanese view of the five-story winged pagoda that is the heart of the pavilion. The peace is occasionally disturbed by performances of traditional Japanese drumming or by demonstrations of traditional Japanese crafts, such as snipping brown rice toffee into intricate shapes. *Audience: Adults and older children. Rating:* ★★★

Mexico. Housed in a spectacular Maya pyramid surrounded by a tangle of tropical vegetation, Mexico contains an exhibit of pre-Columbian art, a restaurant, and, of course, a shopping plaza, where you can unload many, many pesos. True to its name, the **El Río del Tiempo** boat ride takes you on a trip down the river of time. Your journey from the jungles of the Yucatán to modern-day Mexico City is enlivened by video images of feathered Toltec dancers, by Audio-Animatronics Spanish-colonial dancing puppets, and by film clips of the cliff divers in Acapulco, the speed boats in Manzanillo, and snorkeling around Isla Mujeres. *Audience: All ages. Rating:* ★

Morocco. You don't need a magic carpet to be instantaneously transported into an exotic culture—just walk through the pointed arches of the Bab Boujouloud Gate. Koutoubia Minaret, a replica of the prayer tower in Marrakesh, acts as Morocco's landmark. Traditional, winding alleyways, each corner bursting with carpets, brasses, leather work, and other North African craftsmanship, lead to a beautifully tiled fountain and lush gardens. You can take a guided tour of the pavilion by inquiring of any cast member, check out the ever-changing exhibit in the **Gallery of Arts and History,** and entertain yourself examining the wares at such shops as Casablanca Carpets, Jewels of the Sahara, Brass Bazaar, and Fez House. *Audience: Adults and older children. Rating:* ★★

Norway. Here you'll find rough-hewn timbers and sharply pitched roofs, softened and brightened by bloom-stuffed window boxes, figured shutters, and lots of smiling blond and blue-eyed young Norwegians, all eager to speak English and show off their country. The pavilion complex contains a 14th-century stone fortress that mimics Oslo's Akershus, cobbled streets, rocky waterfalls, and a wood-stave church, modeled after one built in 1250, with wooden dragons glaring from the eaves. The church houses an exhibit called *To the Ends of the Earth,* which tells the story of two early 20th-century polar expeditions by using vintage artifacts. It all puts you in the mood to handle the merchandise in the pavilion's shops: wood carvings, glass artworks, and beautifully embroidered woolen sweaters, which sell briskly despite Florida's heat. Norway also has a dandy boat ride: **Maelstrom,** in which dragon-headed longboats take a voyage through time that, despite its scary name and encounters with evil trolls, is actually more interesting than frightening. *Audience: All ages. Rating:* ★★

United Kingdom. Never has it been so easy to cross the English Channel. A pastiche of "There will always be an England" architecture, the United Kingdom rambles between the elegant mansions lining a London square to the bustling, half-timbered shops of a village High Street to the thatched-roof cottages of the countryside. Their thatch is made of plastic broom bristles in consideration of local fire regulations. And of course there's a pair of the scarlet phone booths that used to be found all over Great Britain, now on their way to being historic relics. The pavilion has no single major attraction. Instead, you can wander through shops selling tea and tea accessories, Welsh handicrafts, Royal Doulton figurines, and woolens and tartans from Pringle of Scotland. *Audience: Adults and older children. Rating:* ★★★

Entertainment

Above the lagoon every night, about a half hour before closing, don't miss the spectacular **IllumiNations** sound-and-light show, with fireworks, lasers, and lots of special effects to the accompaniment of a terrific score. Best viewing spots are on the bridge between France and the United Kingdom, the promenade in front of Canada and Norway, and the bridge between China and Germany.

Disney–MGM Studios

❸ *Take the Epcot–Downtown Disney exit (Exit 26) off I–4.*

When Walt Disney Company chairman Michael Eisner opened Disney–MGM Studios in May 1989, he welcomed visitors to "the Hollywood that never was and always will be." Inspired by southern California's highly successful Universal Studios tour, an even more successful version of which is just down I–4, Disney-MGM combined Disney detail with MGM's motion picture expertise. The result is an amalgamation that blends theme park with fully functioning movie and television production center, breathtaking rides with instructional tours, nostalgia with high-tech wonders.

Although some attractions will interest young children, Disney–MGM Studios is best for teenagers old enough to catch all the cinematic references. Surprisingly, the entire park is rather small—only 110 acres, a quarter the size of Universal Studios—with not even 20 major attractions. When the lines are minimal, the park can be easily covered in a day with time for repeat rides.

Hollywood Boulevard

With its palm trees, pastel buildings, and flashy neon, Hollywood Boulevard paints a rosy picture of Tinseltown in the 1930s. The sense of having walked right onto a movie set is enhanced by the Art Deco storefronts, strolling brass bands, and roving actors dressed in costume and playing everything from would-be starlets to nefarious agents. Like Main Street, Hollywood Boulevard has souvenir shops and memorabilia collections galore. Oscar's Classic Car Souvenirs & Super Service Station is crammed with fuel-pump bubble-gum machines and other automotive knickknacks. At Sid Cahuenga's One-of-a-Kind antiques and curios store, you might find and acquire Liberace's table napkins or autographed stars' photos. Down the street at Cover Story, have your picture put on the cover of a major magazine.

Great Movie Ride. Housed in a fire-engine-red pagoda replica of Grauman's Chinese Theater, this 22-minute tour captures great moments in film—from Gene Kelly clutching that immortal lamppost as he sings the title song from *Singin' in the Rain* to some of the slimier characters from *Alien*. Disney cast members dressed in 1920s newsboy costumes usher you onto open trams, and you're off—through Audio-Animatronics, scrim, smoke, and Disney magic. *Audience: All but young children, for whom it may be too intense. Rating:* ★★★

Sunset Boulevard

This avenue pays tribute to famous Hollywood monuments.

Rock 'n' Roller Coaster. This is the first WDW attraction (opened mid-1999) to feature a high-speed launch and multiple complete inversions. The twists and turns are accentuated by a synchronized rock soundtrack that resonates from speakers mounted in each vehicle. *Audience: Teens and adults. No guests with heart, back, or neck problems or motion sickness; minimum height: 44". Rating:* ★★★

Theater of the Stars. The wildly popular *Beauty and the Beast—Live* *on Stage* takes place in a re-creation of the famed Hollywood Bowl. The long-running production is a skillful condensation of the animated film. *Audience: All ages. Rating:* ★★★

Twilight Zone Tower of Terror. Ominously overlooking Sunset Boulevard is a 13-story structure that's reputedly the now-deserted Hollywood Tower Hotel. You take an eerie stroll, especially at night, through the dimly lighted lobby and decaying library to the boiler room before boarding the hotel's giant elevator. As you head upward past seemingly deserted hallways, ghostly former residents appear around you, until suddenly—faster than you can say, "Where's Rod Serling?"—the creaking vehicle abruptly plunges downward in a terrifying 130-ft free-fall drop, and then it does it all over again! *Audience: Older children and adults. No pregnant women or guests with heart, back, or neck problems; minimum height: 40". Rating:* ★★★

Animation Courtyard

Backstage Pass to . . . This walking tour covers an exhibit of props, costumes, and sets from the latest Disney film, combined with a look at filmmaking techniques. *Audience: Older children and adults. Rating:* ★★

Magic of Disney Animation. This approximately 30-minute self-guided tour through the Disney animation process is one of the funniest and most engaging attractions at the park. More than any other backstage tour, more than any other revelation of stunt secrets, this tour truly takes you inside the magic as you follow the many steps of animation from concept to charisma. From a designated lobby in the Animation Courtyard, you segue into the Disney Animation Theater for a hilarious eight-minute film in which Walter Cronkite and Robin Williams explain animation basics. From the theater you follow walkways with windows overlooking the working animation studios, where you see salaried Disney artists at their drafting tables doing everything you just learned about. Their desks are strewn with finished drawings of Simba, Scar, Aladdin, Genie, and other famous characters, and you can peer over their shoulders at soon-to-be-famous characters. This is better than magic—this is real. *Audience: All but toddlers. Rating:* ★★★

Studios Backlot Tour. This combination tram ride and walking tour takes you on a 60-minute exploration of the back-lot building blocks of movies: set design, costumes, props, lighting, and special effects. At Catastrophe Canyon, the tram bounces up and down in a simulated earthquake, an oil tanker explodes in gobs of smoke and flame, and a water tower crashes to the ground, touching off a flash flood. *Audience: All but young children. Rating:* ★★★

Voyage of the Little Mermaid. A boxy building on Mickey Avenue invites you to join Ariel, Sebastian, and the underwater gang in this stage show, which condenses the movie into a marathon presentation of the greatest hits. *Audience: All ages. Rating:* ★★

Walt Disney Theater. Tucked behind the *Voyage of the Little Mermaid* is this movie theater, which usually runs ***The Making of . . . ,*** a behind-the-scenes look at Disney's latest smash hit. Each film was produced for the Disney Channel, so if you're a subscriber, you may have already seen it. Programs have included *The Lion King, Toy Story,* and *The Hunchback of Notre Dame. Audience: All ages. Rating:* ★

New York Street

Backlot Theater. This is where Disney animated films are brought to life. The productions rival Broadway in scope; in fact, the first show to be performed in the Backlot's original locale, near the Brown Derby restaurant, was *Beauty and the Beast: Live on Stage,* a small-scale prototype for what eventually became the Broadway musical. *Audience: All ages. Rating:* ★★

GOOSEBUMPS HorrorLand Fright Show. Children who are die-hard *Goosebumps* fans will love this attraction, a magic show in which frightfully scary illusions come to life. Among the ghouls in the cast are the Executioner, who performs the "Terror of the Tower" and instructs the audience to "hold on to your heads," and the Amazing Amaz-O (the Master of Magic and Wizard of Wonder). *Audience: Children ages 10 and older. Rating:* ★★

Honey, I Shrunk the Kids Movie Set Adventure. Let the kids run free in this state-of-the-art playground based on the movie about lilliputian kids in a larger-than-life world. They can slide down a gigantic blade of grass, crawl through caves, and climb a mushroom mountain. *Audience: Children and those who love them. Rating:* ★★★

Jim Henson's MuppetVision 3-D. You don't have to be a Miss Piggyphile to get a kick out of this combination 3-D movie and musical revue. The theater was constructed especially for this show, with special effects built into the walls. *Audience: All ages. Rating:* ★★★

Echo Lake

In the center of this idealized California is cool, blue Echo Lake, an oasis fringed with trees and benches and ringed with landmarks: pink-and-aqua restaurants trimmed in chrome, presenting sassy waitresses and television sets at the tables; Min and Bill's Dockside Diner, which offers fast food in a shipshape atmosphere; and Gertie, a Sinclair gas station dinosaur that dispenses ice cream, Disney souvenirs, and the occasional puff of smoke in true magic-dragon fashion.

ABC Sound Studio One Saturday Morning. This show is a delightful, multifaceted demonstration of the use of movie sound effects. Volunteer Foley artists dash around trying to coordinate their sound effects with the short movie being shown simultaneously. "Foley artist," the movie name for sound effects specialists, was named for Jack Foley, the man who created the system. *Audience: All ages. Rating:* ★★★

Doug Live! A handful of lucky volunteers perform alongside Patti Mayonnaise, Pork Chop, and the Gang in a mix of live theater and animation. Each show is flavored differently by the volunteer cast. *Audience: Children ages 6–15.*

Indiana Jones Epic Stunt Spectacular! Don't leave Disney–MGM Studios without seeing this 30-minute show featuring the stunt choreography of veteran coordinator Glenn Randall (*Raiders of the Lost Ark, Indiana Jones and the Temple of Doom, E.T.,* and *Jewel of the Nile* are among his credits). Presented in a 2,200-seat amphitheater, it teaches how the most breathtaking movie stunts are pulled off, with the help of audience participants (go ahead, volunteer!). Arrive early because the theater does fill to capacity. *Audience: All but young children. Rating:* ★★★

Star Tours. Although the flight-simulator technology used for this ride was long-ago surpassed by other thrill rides, most notably Universal Studios' *Back to the Future . . . The Ride,* Star Tours is still a pretty good trip. Guarded by an otherworldly metallic monster, Star Tours is inspired by the *Star Wars* films. Piloted by characters R2D2 and C-3PO, the 40-passenger StarSpeeder that you board is supposed to take off on a routine flight to the moon of Endor. But with R2D2 at the helm, things quickly go awry. *Audience: Older children and adults. No pregnant women or guests with heart, back, or neck problems or motion sickness; no children under three, and children under seven must be accompanied by an adult. Rating:* ★★★

Entertainment

The **daily parade** that wends its way up Hollywood Boulevard is also usually tied to the latest Disney hit film, such as *Aladdin, Toy Story,*

Hercules, and *Mulan,* with all the characters from the films appearing in larger-than-life incarnations. The fireworks in Disney-MGM may be the best in the World: Mickey appears as the Sorcerer's Apprentice in **Fantasmic!,** presented on Friday and Saturday nights and nightly in summer and during year-end holidays.

Disney's Animal Kingdom

❹ *Take the Magic Kingdom–U.S. 192 exit (Exit 25) off I–4.*

Humankind's enduring love for animals is the inspiration for Disney's fourth theme park in Orlando, which opened in the spring of 1998. At 500 acres, the largest of all Disney theme parks worldwide and five times the size of the Magic Kingdom, Disney's Animal Kingdom explores the story of all animals—real, imaginary, and extinct—in a development that's part wildlife park, part entertainment complex. In true Disney fashion, it is home to carefully re-created and dramatic landscapes, rides, peppy musical shows, shops, and eateries—augmented by an earnest educational undercurrent that fosters in children and adults alike a renewed appreciation for wild beasts and their efforts for survival.

The park is laid out very much like its oldest sibling; its focal point is the spectacular **Tree of Life,** in **Safari Village.** From there, all the other "lands" are laid out like the spokes of a wheel. At the entrance is the **Oasis,** and to its right is **DinoLand U.S.A.** The northeast corner houses **Asia** (the newest land), while **Africa** is on the northwest side. South of Safari Village, immediately west of the Oasis, is **Camp Minnie-Mickey,** a character greeting and show area.

Opening time for this park is earlier than the others (7 AM) and for good reason: That's when many of the animals are most likely to be up and around. Make sure you arrive early, or you may miss out on some of the best reasons to go.

The Oasis

At this lush entrance garden that houses Guest Relations, you'll feel cool mist, smell the aroma of flowers, and see playful animals amid a miniature landscape of streams and grottoes, waterfalls, and glades.

Safari Village

Primarily the site of the Tree of Life, this land also houses some visitor services, such as the baby-care center and lost and found.

Discovery River. Take a boat trip around the river, either to or from Asia, traveling past the forbidding Dragon Rocks and mythical monsters, which may be too intense and frightening for young children. *Audience: All but young children. Rating:* ★★

Tree of Life. The park centerpiece is an imposing 14 stories high and 50 ft wide at its base and features intricate carvings of animal forms symbolizing the richness of life on earth. Once inside, you get a bug's-eye view of life in the whimsical adventure *It's Tough to Be a Bug!*—modeled after the animated film *A Bug's Life. Audience: All ages. Rating:* ★★★

DinoLand U.S.A.

Just as it sounds, this is the place to come in contact with creatures prehistoric.

Boneyard. Youngsters can slide, bounce, and slither around this archaeological dig site–cum–playground. *Audience: Young children and their families. Rating:* ★★

Countdown to Extinction. When a carload of guests rouses a cantankerous Carnotaurus (Car-no-*taw*-rus) from his Cretaceous slumber, it's show time on this thrill ride. You travel back 65 million years on a twisting start-stop adventure and try to save the "terrible lizards" as a massive asteroid hurtles toward Earth. Exciting Audio-Animatronics brings dinosaurs to life. *Audience: Preteens to adults; minimum height: 46". Rating:* ★★★

Cretaceous Trail. Walk through a re-creation of a primeval forest containing some of the survivors of the dinosaur age, such as soft-shell turtles and Chinese alligators. *Audience: All ages. Rating:* ★

Theater in the Wild. The theater features *Journey into the Jungle Book,* a live musical stage show based on the classic Disney animated film. *Audience: All ages. Rating:* ★★★

Asia

Opened in 1999, this land features a typical rural village and an exotic rain forest. Groupings of trees grow from a crumbling tiger shrine and two massive towers, one representing Thailand, the other Nepal.

Caravan Stage. This outdoor show area presents *Flights of Wonder,* spectacular demonstrations of skill by falcons, hawks, and other rare and fascinating birds, which swoop down over the audience. *Audience: All but toddlers, who might be frightened by the flying birds. Rating:* ★★

Kali River Rapids. The most thrilling Asia adventure, this raft trip takes you on a run down the Chakranadi River, through a huge bamboo tunnel and a series of sharp twists and turns, and past rain forests and temple ruins. *Audience: Older children and adults. No guests with heart, back, or neck problems or motion sickness; minimum height: 44". Rating:* ★★★

Maharajah Jungle Trek. Get an up-close view of jungle animals along this trail, and at the end walk through an aviary set with a lotus pool. *Audience: Older children and adults. Rating:* ★★

Africa

Predominately an enclave for wildlife from the continent, this largest of the lands is an area of forests and grasslands. The focus is on live animals; you'll have to go to Camp Minnie-Mickey to find the Lion King. **Harambe,** on the northern banks of Discovery River, is Africa's starting point. Inspired by the small town of Lamu, Kenya, this coastal "village" features Swahili architecture, food, and shopping with African themes.

Conservation Station. Take the Wildlife Express steam train (or walk) to this unique center, where you can meet animal experts, learn about worldwide efforts to protect endangered species and their habitats, and hear about the park's behind-the-scenes operations, about Disney's own conservation programs, and about how to connect with efforts in your own community. This is a good trip for young children, who may be frightened by the up-close animal encounters on Kilimanjaro Safari. At **Affection Station,** getting face to face with animals is far less threatening; here you are able to meet and touch small critters. *Audience: All ages. Rating:* ★★★

Kilimanjaro Safaris. A re-created African safari in the United States (or even Florida, for that matter) may not be a new idea, but this one goes a step beyond merely observing zebras and lions and the like. Open-sided safari vehicles take you over some 100 acres of savanna, forest, rivers, and rocky hills to see herds of African animals. Watch out for ivory poachers! The safari also includes a race to save elephants from their would-be killers, dramatizing the very real dangers facing the pachyderms' wild relatives. To get the most of your adventure, do this early in the day, when the animals are awake. *Audience: All but very young* *children, who may be frightened. Rating:* ★★★

Pangani Forest Exploration Trail. Take a nature walk among streams and waterfalls to see lowland gorillas, hippos (viewed from under the water), meerkats, warthogs, and exotic birds. *Audience: All ages, although young children may be bored. Rating:* ★★★

Camp Minnie-Mickey

This Adirondack-style land is a meet-and-greet area where characters from *The Lion King, The Jungle Book,* and other Disney favorites gather for picture taking and autographs. Very small children may be frightened by the larger-than-life renditions of Simba, Scar, et al., but everyone else will have a blast. Live performances are also staged here.

Campside Circle. This outdoor theater-in-the-round presents *Festival of the Lion King* on huge moving stages. *Audience: All ages. Rating:* ★★★

Grandmother Willow's Grove. This is the venue for *Colors of the Wind,* a show featuring live animals and Pocahontas as your official hostess. *Audience: All ages. Rating:* ★★★

Entertainment

Twice daily, the **March of the ARTimals** winds through Safari Village. Accompanied by African-themed music, it's a parade unlike any other in the Disney theme parks. Animals come to life with the assistance of colorful costumes, stilts, and other props.

The Disney Water Parks

Blizzard Beach

❺ Blizzard Beach promises the seemingly impossible—a seaside playground with an alpine theme. The Disney Imagineers have gone all out to create a ski resort in the midst of a tropical lagoon. Playing with the snow-in-Florida motif, there are lots of puns and sight gags.

The park centers on **Mt. Gushmore,** a "snowcapped" mountain with all sorts of ways, such as toboggan and sled runs, to get down. At the base of the mountain, there are a sandy beach featuring the obligatory wave pool, a lazy river, and play areas for both young children and preteens.

Mt. Gushmore's big gun is **Summit Plummet,** which Disney bills as "the world's tallest, fastest free-fall speed slide." From the top it's a wild 55-mph plunge straight down to a splash landing at the base of the mountain. **Teamboat Springs** is a "white-water raft ride" in which six-passenger rafts zip along a twisting series of rushing waterfalls. Of course, no water park would be complete without a flume ride; enter **Snow Stormers**—actually three flumes that descend from the top of Mt. Gushmore along a switchback course of ski-type slalom gates. Slightly less adventurous swimmers, take note: There are rides for you, too.

River Country

❻ Imagine a mountain in Utah's red-rock country. Put a lake at the bottom and add a verdant fuzz of maples and pines here and there on the sides. Then plant some big water slides among the greenery and call it a "good ol' fashioned swimmin' hole." That's **River Country.** The first of Walt Disney World Resort's water parks, it adjoins the Fort Wilderness Resort and Campground. Although larger, glitzier Typhoon Lagoon is balmy and tropical, this is rustic and rugged. In summer come first thing in the morning or in late afternoon to avoid crowds.

Walking from the dressing rooms brings you to the massive **pool,** bright blue and concrete-paved, like something out of a more modern Midwest; there are a couple of short, steep water slides here. **Bay Cove** is the roped-off corner of Bay Lake that's the main section of River Country. Rope swings hang from a rustic boom, and there are various other woody contraptions from which kids dive and cannonball. **White Water Rapids,** a series of short chutes and swirling pools, allows you to descend the mountain in jumbo inner tubes at a leisurely pace.

Typhoon Lagoon

❼ Four times the size of River Country, **Typhoon Lagoon** offers a full day of activities: bobbing in 4-ft waves in a surf lagoon the size of two football fields, speeding down arrow-straight water slides and around twisty storm slides, and bumping through white-water rapids. The park is popular; in fact, in summer and on weekends it often reaches capacity (7,200) by mid-morning. If you must go in summer, head out for a few hours during the dreamy late afternoons or when the weather clears up after a thundershower. (Typically, rainstorms drive away the crowds, and lots of people simply don't come back.) If you plan to make a whole day of it, avoid weekends—Typhoon Lagoon is big among locals as well as tourists.

Activities include snorkeling in **Shark Reef,** a 360,000-gallon tank (closed November–April) containing an artificial coral reef and 4,000 real tropical fish. Mellow folks can float in inner tubes along 2,100-ft **Castaway Creek,** which circles the entire park. It takes about 30 minutes to do the circuit; you can stop as you please along the way. If you want to get scared out of your wits in three seconds flat, slide down **Humunga Kowabunga,** with a drop of more than 50 ft. A children's area, **Ketchakiddie Creek,** replicates adult rides on a smaller scale (children must be accompanied by an adult). It's Disney's version of a day at the beach—complete with lifeguards in spiffy red-and-white-stripe T-shirts.

Tips for Making the Most of Your Visit

- Arrive at the theme parks early—30–45 minutes before opening—so you can check belongings into lockers, rent strollers, and otherwise take care of business before everyone else. Then you'll be able to see the parks at their most pleasant, without a lot of waiting.

- See the three-star attractions first thing in the morning, at the end of the day, or during a parade, being careful not to get stuck on the wrong side of the parade route.

- Whenever possible, eat in a restaurant that takes reservations, bring your own food discreetly (a big time *and* money saver), or have meals before or after mealtime rush hours (from 11 AM to 2 PM and again from 6 to 8 PM). Or leave the theme parks altogether for a meal in one of the hotels.

- Spend afternoons in high-capacity sit-down shows or catching live entertainment—or leave the park for a swim in your hotel pool.

- If you plan to take in Typhoon Lagoon, Blizzard Beach, or River Country, go early in your visit (but not on a weekend). You may like it so much you'll want to go again.

- If a meal with the characters is in your plans, save it for the end of your trip, when your youngsters will have become accustomed to these large, looming figures.

- Familiarize yourself with all age and height restrictions to avoid having younger children get excited about rides they're too short or too young to experience. Most rides have premeasured signs at the entrance to the queuing area, so even if you don't know how tall your child is, you won't have to wait in line before finding out.

- Call ahead to check on operating hours and parade times, which vary greatly throughout the year.

Walt Disney World Resort A to Z

Admission Fees

Visiting Walt Disney World Resort is not cheap, especially if you have a child or two along. Everyone 10 and older pays adult prices; reductions are available for children ages three through nine. Children under three get in free. No discounted family tickets are available.

TICKETS AND PASSES

In Disneyspeak, "ticket" refers to a single day's admission to the Magic Kingdom, Epcot, Disney–MGM Studios, or Disney's Animal Kingdom. If you want to spend two or three days at WDW, you have to buy a separate ticket each day. A ticket is good in the park for which you buy it only on the day you buy it. If you buy a one-day ticket and later decide to extend your visit, you can apply the cost of it toward the purchase of any "pass" (passes being Disneyspeak for multiday, multipark admission media). Exchanges can be made at City Hall in the Magic Kingdom and at Guest Relations in Epcot, Disney-MGM, and Disney's Animal Kingdom.

If you want to spend more than three days, you have several options. Prices and combinations change often, so be sure to call for the most up-to-date information. A **Park Hopper** pass allows unlimited visits to the four major parks on any four or five days, with any combination of parks on a day. The five-, six-, or seven-day **All-in-One Hopper** pass includes unlimited visits to the four main theme parks on any five, six, or seven days, plus unlimited admission—dated from first entry to WDW—to WDW's minor attractions, including Blizzard Beach, Disney's Wide World of Sports, Pleasure Island, River Country, and Typhoon Lagoon.

Though these passes don't represent a tremendous savings over the cost of one-day tickets, depending on the parks you plan to see and the number of days you have, they can save you some money as well as time spent in line. Be warned that it's not easy to "do" more than one park in a day, but if you want to take in the attractions of, say, the Magic Kingdom and then nip over for dinner at Epcot's World Showcase, park hopability may be attractive. In fact, if you plan to visit the minor parks or go to Typhoon Lagoon or Blizzard Beach more than once, it may pay to buy an All-in-One Hopper pass even if you're staying only four days. Remaining days may be used anytime in your lifetime. A variety of annual passes are also available, at a cost only slightly more than an All-in-One Hopper pass; if you plan to visit twice in a year, these are a good deal.

Guests at Disney resorts can also purchase **Length of Stay Passes,** which are good from the time of arrival until midnight of the departure day. Buy them at the front desks of all resorts or in Guest Relations at the four theme parks. Prices are based on the number of room nights. The pass is good for all four theme parks, as well as the three water parks and Pleasure Island. In addition, E tickets are available to resort guests, for use on certain evenings each month when the Magic Kingdom is closed to everyone else; these tickets must be used in conjunction with a multiday pass used that day.

PRICES

WDW changes its prices at least once a year and without much notice. At press time rates (including 6% tax) were as follows:

One-day ticket: $44.52 adults, $36.04 children.

Park Hopper:	Four days	$172.78 adults, $137.80 children.
	Five days	$200.34 adults, $160.06 children.
All-in-One Hopper:	Five days	$236.40 adults, $188.70 children.
	Six days	$263.96 adults, $210.95 children.
	Seven days	$290.46 adults, $232.15 children.

Blizzard Beach and Typhoon Lagoon: $28.57 adults, $22.79 children.

River Country: $16.91 adults, $13.25 children.

Pleasure Island: $20.09 18 and over.

Disney's Wide World of Sports (does not include events): $8.48 adults, $7.16 children.

Tickets and passes to all Walt Disney World Resort parks can be purchased at park entrances, at admission booths at the Transportation and Ticket Center (TTC), in all on-site resorts (if you're a registered guest), and at the Walt Disney World kiosk at Orlando International Airport (second floor, main terminal). American Express, Visa, and MasterCard are accepted, as are cash, personal checks (with ID), and traveler's checks. Many offices of the American Automobile Association (AAA) sell discounted tickets. Check with your local office. Tickets are also available in local Disney stores, so you may want to purchase them at home before you leave. Some tickets, especially multiday passes, are available at hotels and stores off WDW property. Though these outlets may not save you much, if any, money, they could very well save time waiting in line at the park.

Getting Around

Walt Disney World Resort has its own transportation system, which can get you wherever you want to go. It's fairly simple once you get the hang of it.

BY BOAT

Motor launches connect WDW destinations on lakes and waterways. Specifically, they operate between the Epcot resorts (except the Caribbean Beach) and Disney–MGM Studios and between the Magic Kingdom, Wilderness Lodge, Grand Floridian, the Fort Wilderness Resort and Campground, and the Polynesian and Contemporary resorts.

BY BUS

Buses provide direct service from every on-site resort to both major and minor theme parks, and express buses go direct between the major theme parks. You can go directly from or make connections at the TTC to Downtown Disney, Epcot, and the Epcot resorts, including the Yacht and Beach clubs, BoardWalk Inn, Caribbean Beach Resort, the Swan, and the Dolphin, as well as to Disney's Animal Kingdom and the Animal Kingdom resorts (the All-Star and Coronado Springs resorts).

BY MONORAIL

The elevated monorail serves many important destinations. It has two loops: one linking the Magic Kingdom, the TTC, and a handful of resorts, including the Contemporary, Polynesian, and Grand Floridian; the other looping from the TTC direct to Epcot.

BY TRAM

From the Epcot resort area, trams operate to the International Gateway of the park's World Showcase.

Monorails, launches, buses, and trams all operate from early in the morning until at least midnight. (Hours are shorter when the park closes earlier.) Officially, charges for transportation are included in the price of a multiday pass or are available for a small fee. In reality, however, IDs are rarely checked, and you can generally hop on the monorail even if you're only visiting for a day.

Guided Tours

Reservations for many **Disney tours** (☎ 407/939–8687) can be made up to six weeks in advance, up to 60 days for the tour at Disney's Animal Kingdom.

A good way to get a feel for the layout of the Magic Kingdom and what goes on behind the scenes is to take the **Keys to the Kingdom** tour, a 3½- to 4-hour guided orientation tour ($45 adults and children 16 and up, not including park admission; no younger children allowed). Tours leave from City Hall daily between 9:15 and 9:30. The **Family Magic tour** ($25 adults, $15 children) is a scavenger hunt in which your tour guide encourages you to find things that have disappeared. Meet at City Hall at 9:30.

Several of the behind-the-scenes Epcot tours, led by knowledgeable Disney cast members and open to guests 16 and older, offer close-up views of the phenomenal detail involved in the planning and maintenance of Epcot. **Hidden Treasures** ($75, including park admission and lunch) is a comprehensive guide to all 11 international pavilions. For $35 plus park admission, the two-hour **Hidden Treasures of World Showcase East,** which runs on Tuesday, offers a look at the eastern half of World Showcase. Like its eastern cousin, **Hidden Treasures of World Showcase West** takes two hours and costs $35 plus park admission. However, it runs on Saturday and features the other half of the countries. The three-hour **Gardens of the World** ($35 plus park admission) runs Tuesday and Thursday; it explains World Showcase's realistic replicas of exotic plantings. **Behind the Seeds** ($6 adults, $4 children), 45-minute guided tours of the greenhouses and aquacell areas in Future World's the Land pavilion, covers the same topics as the Living with the Land boat ride but in much more detail—and you have the chance to ask questions. Tours run every half hour 9:30–4:30, and reservations can be made behind the Green Thumb Emporium.

If you want to learn more about the animation process, take Disney–MGM Studio's 2½-hour **Inside Animation** tour ($45; admission not required), offered on Tuesday and Thursday. At the end of the tour, you get to go backstage and paint your own animation cel.

At Disney's Animal Kingdom, **Backstage Safari** ($60 plus park admission) takes an in-depth look at animal conservation every Monday, Wednesday, and Friday 9:30–12:30, stopping at the animal hospital and other behind-the-scenes areas.

Opening and Closing Times

Operating hours for the Magic Kingdom, Epcot, Disney–MGM Studios, and Disney's Animal Kingdom vary widely throughout the year and change for school and legal holidays. In general, the longest days are during prime summer months and over the year-end holidays, when the Magic Kingdom is open to midnight (later on New Year's Eve), Epcot is open to 11 PM, and Disney–MGM Studios is open until 9 PM. At other times Epcot and Disney-MGM are open until 8 and the Magic Kingdom until 7—but there are variations, so call ahead.

Disney's Animal Kingdom opens at the early hour of 7 AM and closes at 8 PM. Note that, in general, the Magic Kingdom, Epcot's Future World (World Showcase opens at 11), and Disney–MGM officially open at 9. The parking lots open at least an hour earlier. Arriving at the Magic Kingdom turnstiles before the official opening time, you can breakfast in a restaurant on Main Street, which opens before the rest of the park, and be ready to dash to one of the popular attractions in other areas as soon as officially possible. Arriving in Epcot, Disney–MGM Studios, or Disney's Animal Kingdom, you can make dinner reservations before the crowds arrive and take in some of the attractions and pavilions well before the major crowds descend, at about 10.

Parking

Every theme park has a parking lot—and all are huge. Always write down exactly where you park your car and take the note with you. (Repeating "Goofy, Goofy, Goofy" or something similar as a reminder of your Disney-themed locations doesn't always help; by the end of the day you'll be so goofy with eating and shopping and riding that you'll be thinking, "Sleepy, Sleepy, Sleepy.") Parking area trams deliver you to the park entrance. For each lot the cost is $5 for cars and $6 for RVs and campers (free to WDW resort guests with ID). At Typhoon Lagoon, River Country, and Blizzard Beach, parking is free.

Visitor Information

For general information contact **Walt Disney World Information** (☎ 407/824–4321) or the central **WDW switchboard** (☎ 407/824–2222). For accommodations and shows, call **WDW Central Reservations** (☎ 407/934–7639). For **dining reservations** at Walt Disney World there's a single phone number: ☎ 407/939–3463. To inquire about resort facilities, call the individual property.

For specific information call the attraction or department directly: **Disney–MGM Studios TV-show tapings** (☎ 407/560–4651), **Kinder-Care** child care (☎ 407/827–5444 for in-room; 407/827–5437 for drop-off), **learning programs** (☎ 407/354–1855), **Pleasure Island** (☎ 407/934–7781), **water parks** (☎ 407/560–9283).

THEME PARKS BEYOND DISNEY

Theme parks grow so well in the sandy Central Florida soil that you might almost imagine a handful of seeds scattered across the fertile I–4 belt, waiting for the right combination of money and vision to nurture them into the next . . . Walt Disney World. The magic touch may well show up at the just-expanded Universal Studios Escape complex. However, existing theme parks, including the Busch parks—SeaWorld and Cypress Gardens—are growing, too. Although you used to be able to do a whole park—any park—in about six hours, a thorough visit now can barely be contained in a day. As competition sharpened and tastes grew more sophisticated, a sort of me-too mentality became prevalent. If one park has a flight simulator attraction, then all parks must have one (the best are Disney–MGM Studio's Star Tours and Universal Studios' *Back to the Future* . . . The Ride). Ditto for Broadway-style music-and-dance shows. Every park also has a sophisticated children's play area, with ball crawls, bouncing rooms, and the like.

Luckily some of the parks have banded together to match Walt Disney World Resort's multipark pass system. Busch parks offer discounts on visits to additional Busch parks, and Universal has followed suit. In addition, there's the Orlando FlexTicket—valid for admission to SeaWorld, Universal Studios Florida, Universal Studios Islands of Adventure, and Wet 'n Wild—even Busch Gardens (☞ Chapter 7), if you like. Also look for second-day-free offers, especially off season.

SeaWorld Orlando

❽ *Near the intersection of I–4 and the Bee Line Expressway; take I–4 to Exit 27A or 28 and follow signs.*

At 135 acres, SeaWorld is the world's largest zoological park and is devoted entirely to the mammals, birds, fish, and reptiles living in the ocean and its tributaries. Every attraction is designed to demonstrate the beauty of the marine world and how it is threatened by human thoughtlessness. Yet the presentations are rarely dogmatic, never pedantic, and almost always memorable as well as enjoyable. The park rivals Disney properties for squeaky-cleanliness, courteous staff, and clever attention to details and beats them hands down when it comes to crowd management and lines. Because there are more exhibits and shows than rides, you can go at your own pace without that hurry-up-and-wait feeling.

SeaWorld is organized around a 17-acre central lake. As you enter, the lake is to your right. You can orient yourself by the Sky Tower, whose revolving viewing platform is generally visible even above the trees; it's directly opposite Shamu Stadium. Schedule your day around the show times printed on your map, which will enable you to see it all in the time you have.

Among SeaWorld's educational programs are **Backstage Explorations, Animal Lover's Adventure, Animal Training Discoveries, To the Rescue, Wild Arctic,** and the **Sharks Tour,** in which SeaWorld trainers discuss animal behavior and training techniques. Register at the guided tour center to the left of the Guest Relations information center at the park entrance.

Atlantis Bayside Stadium. In an intense themed show on the central lagoon, SeaWorld's water-ski team displays awesome athletic prowess, executing extraordinary stunts and eye-opening jumps and displaying expert skiing ability. *Audience: All ages. Rating:* ★★★
Journey to Atlantis. SeaWorld has never been a destination for thrill-seeking, ride-hungry teens, but this new attraction may just change some adolescent attitudes about spending a day with Shamu. Combining elements of a high-speed water ride and roller coaster with state-of-the-future special effects, it plunges you into the world of Greek mythology and down two of the fastest, steepest drops anywhere. You will get soaked, so bring a change of clothes (including underwear). *Audience: Older children and adults. Not recommended for pregnant women or guests with heart problems or a fear of dark, enclosed spaces; minimum height: 42″. Rating:* ★★★
Key West at SeaWorld. This laid-back area resembles Key West, that southernmost Florida outpost famous for spectacular sunsets and a Caribbean atmosphere. Here you can feed nearly two dozen Atlantic bottle-nosed dolphins with fish purchased nearby, and at the nightly sunset celebration kids can get their faces painted and have their pictures taken with a larger-than-human-size Shamu or Dolly Dolphin. The music has a reggae beat, and even the dolphins seem to get into the party. *Audience: All ages. Rating:* ★★★
Key West Dolphin Stadium. The show here spotlights bottle-nosed dolphins and a couple of false killer whales, who wave, leap, and do back flips as the crowd oohs and aahs. In one sequence a trainer rides on one of their backs and gets torpedoed into the air. One lucky child from the audience acts as a helper; to get yours picked, come early and

ask one of the stadium attendants. *Audience: All ages. Rating:* ★★★

Manatees: The Last Generation? After a short film, you can watch manatees splash about in their 300,000-gallon tank. Keep an eye out for mama manatees and their nursing calves. *Audience: All ages. Rating:* ★★★

Pacific Point Preserve. The fun-loving California sea lions and harbor and fur seals on these 2½ acres literally sing for their supper. *Audience: All ages. Rating:* ★★★

Penguin Encounter. Go during a dolphin or sea lion show to visit this refrigerated re-creation of Antarctica at its least crowded time. The exhibit is home to 17 species of penguins; a Plexiglas wall on the viewers' side of the tank lets you see that the penguins are as graceful in the water as they are awkward on land. A similar viewing area housing puffins and murres is just as entertaining. *Audience: All ages. Rating:* ★★

Sea Lion & Otter Stadium. Wildly inventive, multilevel balconies (used as diving boards) and staircases (used as water slides) form the set for *Clyde and Seamore Take Pirate Island.* The comedy features breakdancing sea lions, an environmentally sensitive otter, and a heroic walrus that lumbers in and saves the day from blundering, littering humans. Chances are you'll roar as loud as the mammals themselves. *Audience: All ages. Rating:* ★★★

SeaWorld Theater. Between Penguin Encounter and the central lagoon, this theater features **Pets on Stage,** a show starring animals adopted from the humane society. *Audience: All ages. Rating:* ★★

Shamu: Close Up! For unprecedented up-close-and-personal underwater viewing of the breeding and nursery area, this is the place to be. Follow the signs around to the underground viewing stations for a unique glimpse of favorite whale pastimes: tummy-rubbing and back-scratching. The 1.7-million-gallon outdoor tanks are on the same level as the main pool in Shamu Stadium and have similar Plexiglas walls and viewing setups. *Audience: All ages. Rating:* ★★★

Shamu Stadium. Home to SeaWorld's orca mascot, the stadium is hands down the most popular feature in the park. Several shows daily showcase the whales' acrobatic, spectator-drenching antics. Fantastic flips and jumps are combined with video footage of orcas in the wild and gently educational factoids. In the slightly funkier nighttime *Shamu Rocks America,* the famous orca jumps to the beat of "God Bless the USA." As at the other shows, take the splash zone seriously, and bring a change of clothes to the park, just in case. *Audience: All ages. Rating:* ★★★

Shamu's Happy Harbor. Little ones love to scramble around this 3-acre outdoor play area with crawlable, climbable, explorable, bounceable, and get-wet activities. *Audience: Toddlers through grade-schoolers. Rating:* ★★

Stingray Lagoon. Buy a batch of smelts so you can feed the rays and stroke their velvety skin as they flap up to you for a snack. *Audience: All ages. Rating:* ★★★

Terrors of the Deep. Videos and walk-through Plexiglas tunnels let you get acquainted with the world's largest collection of such dangerous sea creatures as eels, barracuda, venomous and poisonous fish, and sharks. *Audience: All ages. Rating:* ★★★

Tropical Reef. In this soothing indoor attraction, more than 30 separate aquariums are aswim with tropical fish from around the world. Each display seems more beautiful and imaginative than the next. *Audience: All ages. Rating:* ★★★

Wild Arctic. This pseudo–ice station combines a bumpy simulated helicopter ride with educational exhibits about some of the Arctic's most deceptively cuddly predators. At above- and below-water viewing sta-

.tions you can take your time watching beluga whales blowing bubble rings, polar bears cavorting with their toys, and walruses hoisting themselves onto the ice with a groan. To get here, follow the crowds across the bridge to Shamu Stadium; while they're watching the orca perform, you can sneak in without a wait. There's a nonmoving option for those too small for or not interested in the jostling ride. *Audience: All ages. Minimum height: 42" for motion option. Rating:* ★★★

SeaWorld Orlando Information

✉ *7007 Sea Harbor Dr., Orlando 32821,* ☎ *407/351–3600 or 800/327–2424.* ✆ *$44.52 adults, $36.04 children 3–9; educational programs $5 adults, $4 children 3–9; parking $5 per car, $7 per RV or camper.* ☉ *Daily 9–7, until as late as 10 summer and holidays; educational programs daily 9–3, every 30 mins.*

Universal Studios Florida

❾ *Near the intersection of I–4 and Florida's Turnpike. If you're heading eastbound on I–4, take Exit 29; turn left onto Sand Lake Rd. and right onto Turkey Lake Rd. If you're heading west on I–4, take Exit 30B and follow the signs.*

Universal Studios Florida is a theme park with plenty of personality, a personality that can be summed up in one word: attitude. It's saucy, sassy, and hip and geared to those who like their attractions loud and scary. A prime example is the special effects–laden disaster ride *Twister*, whose opening was postponed after real tornadoes devastated areas around Orlando in early 1998. Contrast that with the *Beetlejuice Graveyard Revue*, a new take on the Grateful Dead, which features a funky Dracula belting "I'm Gonna Wait 'til the Midnight Hour." E.T., Tickli Moot, and other inventions of Steven Spielberg, Universal's genius on call, round out the vast cast of characters that give Universal its pizzazz. They've even figured out a way to keep people entertained while they wait in line; from arcade games at Nickelodeon to news shows on overhead screens in the *Jaws* line, Universal makes the most of its video connection.

The 444 acres of Universal Studios are a bewildering conglomeration of stage sets, shops, reproductions of New York and San Francisco, and anonymous soundstages housing theme attractions as well as genuine moviemaking paraphernalia. On the map, these sets are neatly divided into six neighborhoods surrounding a huge blue lagoon, which is the setting for the **Dynamite Nights Stunt Spectacular,** a shoot-'em-up stunt show (performed on water skis, no less!) presented nightly at 7. As you walk around the park, however, expect to get lost, and if you do, just ask directions of the nearest staffer.

With Disney–MGM Studios just down the road, is Universal worth the visit? The answer is an unqualified yes. Attractions here are geared more to teenagers and adults than to the stroller set. (Most rides are too frightening for young children.)

The Front Lot

This is essentially a scene setter and the place to find many services. The main drag, the Plaza of the Stars, stretches from the marble-arch entrance gateway straight down to the other end of the lot.

Production Central

This area is composed of six huge warehouses containing working soundstages, as well as several attractions. Follow Nickelodeon Way left from the Plaza of the Stars.

Alfred Hitchcock's 3-D Theatre. This is a dandy 40-minute multimedia tribute to the master of suspense (young children may be frightened). *Audience: All but young children. Rating:* ★★★

Funtastic World of Hanna-Barbera. This combination simulator ride–video–interactive display at the corner of Nickelodeon Way and Plaza of the Stars is always crowded. Using Hanna-Barbera animated characters (Yogi Bear, the Jetsons, the Flintstones), it shows how cartoons are made and gives you eight minutes of thrills in the process. *Audience: All but young children. No pregnant women or guests with heart, back, or neck problems or motion sickness; minimum height: 40". Rating:* ★★★

Hercules & Xena: Wizards of the Screen. Based on an animated film that was in turn based on the popular TV shows starring Kevin Sorbo and Lucy Lawless, this attraction explores the magic of special effects. First the Creature Lab, with help from the audience, brings to life the monsters from the film. Then it's on to a lesson in digital visual effects. Finally, sound is integrated with the visuals, and everything is put together to create the finished product. It's quite entertaining to see how it all turns out, especially if you're lucky enough to participate. *Audience: All but very young children. Rating:* ★★

Nickelodeon Studios. This 30-minute tour shows how a television show is produced. The banks of lights, concrete floors, and general warehouse feel go a long way toward demystifying movie magic, but it's exactly that behind-the-scenes perspective that makes the tour interesting. About 90% of Nick's shows are made on its pair of soundstages. This attraction is really big with the elementary school set, so if you don't have any with you or if no shows are taping, you may want to skip it. *Audience: All ages. Rating:* ★★

New York

Here the Big Apple is rendered with surprising detail, right down to the cracked concrete and slightly stained cobblestones. The **Blues Brothers Bluesmobile** regularly cruises the neighborhood, and musicians hop out to give impromptu performances at 70 Delancey.

Kongfrontation. A thriller, this very popular five-minute ride puts you on a tram for a joyous, scream-filled encounter with the beast. *Audience: Older children and adults. No pregnant women or guests with heart, back, or neck problems or motion sickness; minimum height: 40" to ride alone. Rating:* ★★

Twister. Here's your chance to see a tornado up close and personal, in the form of an ominous five-story-high funnel cloud that circulates some 2 million cubic ft of air around the theater and creates a terrifying freight-train sound. *Wizard of Oz* fans will want to click their heels three times in the hope that they can go home—or at least make it out of the theater. *Audience: All but young children. Rating:* ★★★

San Francisco/Amity

This area combines two sets. One part is the wharves and warehouses of San Francisco's Embarcadero and Fisherman's Wharf district, with cable-car tracks and the distinctive redbrick Ghirardelli chocolate factory; the other is the New England fishing village terrorized by the shark in *Jaws*.

Beetlejuice's Graveyard Revue. A live 25-minute sound-and-light spectacle, this stars the ghoul of the same name, from the 1991 movie starring Michael Keaton, along with a graveyard rock-and-roll call that includes an earring-clad Dracula and Frankenstein on bass. The show is carried off with lots of noise, smoke, and wit. *Audience: Older children and adults. Rating:* ★★★

Earthquake—The Big One. This is another headliner in Universal's "adrenaline alley." The preshow reproduces choice scenes from the movie *Earthquake,* then takes you onto San Francisco Bay Area Rapid Transit subway cars to ride out an 8.3 Richter-scale tremor and its consequences: fire, flood, blackouts. Unlike Disney–MGM Studios' Catastrophe Canyon, this ride has no "safe" seats. It lasts 20 minutes, and lines are always long. *Audience: All but young children. No pregnant women or guests with heart, back, or neck problems or motion sickness; minimum height: 40" to ride alone. Rating:* ★★★

Jaws. Stagger out of San Francisco into Amity, and you can stand in line for this terror-filled boat trip with explosions, noise, shaking, and gnashing of sharp shark teeth. *Audience: All but young children. No pregnant women or guests with heart, back, or neck problems or motion sickness. Rating:* ★★★

Wild, Wild, Wild West Stunt Show. Presented in a covered amphitheater at the very end of Amity Avenue, this extravaganza involves trapdoors, fistfights, bullwhips, water gags, explosions, shoot-outs, horseback riding, and jokes that skewer every other theme park in Central Florida. *Audience: All but young children. Rating:* ★★★

Expo Center
The southeastern corner of the park contains a treasure trove of attractions.

AT&T at the Movies. Here you can play high-tech computer games. *Audience: All ages. Rating:* ★★

Back to the Future . . . The Ride. Universal's flight simulator ride is a flight simulator ride to beat all others, even (probably) those yet to be built. A one-of-a-kind seven-story Omnimax screen surrounds your DeLorean-shape simulator so you lose all sense of perspective as you rush backward and forward in the space-time continuum—and there are no seat belts. You may have to wait up to two hours for this five-minute ride unless you make a beeline here first thing in the morning. *Audience: Older children and adults. No pregnant women or guests with heart, back, or neck problems or motion sickness; minimum height: 40". Rating:* ★★★

A Day in the Park with Barney. America's most famous purple dinosaur sings and does his shtick, and there are plenty of nifty things to play with once the show is over. *Audience: Young children and their families. Rating:* ★★

E.T. Adventure. This trip aboard bicycles mounted on a movable platform takes you through fantastic forests and across the moon in an attempt to help the endearing extraterrestrial find his way back to his home planet. You can wait hours to ride on busy days and (almost) be glad you did. *Audience: All ages. No guests with heart, back, or neck problems or motion sickness. Rating:* ★★★

Fievel's Playland. For toddlers and preschool-age children, this is a true gift. Based on the adventures of Steven Spielberg's mighty, if miniature, mouse, this gigantic playground incorporates a four-story net climb, tunnel slides, water play areas, ball crawls, a 200-ft water slide, and a harmonica slide that plays music when you slide along the openings. *Audience: Young children and their families. Rating:* ★★

Hollywood
Angling off to the right of Plaza of the Stars, Rodeo Drive forms the backbone of Hollywood.

Gory, Gruesome & Grotesque Horror Make-Up Show. Although young children may be frightened, older kids and teens love this production, showing as it does what goes into and oozes out of the most mangled monsters in movie history. *Audience: Preteens to adults. Rating:* ★★

Lucy: A Tribute. This walk-through collection of Lucille Ball's costumes and other memorabilia plus trivia quizzes and short spots from the series is best for real fans of the ditzy redhead. *Audience: Adults. Rating:* ★

Terminator 2 3-D. Arnold said he'd be back, and he is (along with the popular film's other main characters) in this exciting 3-D adventure that's among the theme-park world's most technologically advanced. Set in the years 1996 and 2029, *T23-D* takes the audience into the future through a mix of live action and filmed sequences shot especially for this attraction. *Audience: All but young children. Rating:* ★★★

Universal Studios Florida Information

Tickets are available at the entrance, by mail from the park, and by mail through Ticketmaster (☎ 800/745–5000); discounted tickets are available at the Orlando/Orange County Convention & Visitors Bureau. ✉ *1000 Universal Studios Plaza, Orlando 32819-7610,* ☎ *407/ 363–8000; 888/331–9108; 407/363–8265 TTY.* ✆ *One day: $44.52 adults, $36.04 children 3–9; two-day combination with Islands of Adventure: $84.74 adults, $68.84 children 3–9; parking: $6 cars, $8 campers.* ☉ *Daily 9–7, until as late as 10 summer and holidays.*

Universal Studios Islands of Adventure

❿ *Near the intersection of I–4 and Florida's Turnpike. Take Exit 30 to Kirkman Rd.*

Universal Studios Escape's second theme park, which opened in May 1999, is the permanent home of some of the world's most beloved characters, from the Cat in the Hat, Popeye, and Sinbad to Spider-Man, the Incredible Hulk, and the Jurassic Park dinosaurs. Like its neighbors, this newest theme park is subdivided into sections, connected by walkways and watercraft. In addition to **Port of Entry,** the park's gateway, the five themed islands are **Seuss Landing, the Lost Continent, Jurassic Park, Toon Lagoon,** and **Marvel Super Hero Island.** Since the park is new, ratings are tentative.

Seuss Landing

This whimsical 10-acre island is the only place in the world where the books of Dr. Seuss come to life.

Caro-Seuss-El. Seven different Seussian characters, totaling 54 mounts, are featured in this elaborate carousel. Each figure offers guest-activated interactive animation, a new concept in carousel rides. *Audience: All ages. Rating:* ★★

Cat in the Hat: Ride Inside. Take a cleverly chaotic journey through the pages of Dr. Seuss's most famous book. You'll experience more than 130 effects and 30 Animatronic characters. *Audience: All ages. Rating:* ★★

If I Ran the Zoo. At this totally interactive playground, divided into three areas—Hedges, Water, and the New Zoo—children can be entertained by strange animals from the books of Dr. Seuss. *Audience: Young children. Rating:* ★★

One Fish, Two Fish, Red Fish, Blue Fish. On this colorful ride, you can steer a Seussian-style fish 15 ft up or down in the air while traveling counterclockwise through myriad water spouts and streams. You'll need to guide your fish wisely if you wish to keep from getting wet. *Audience: Young children. Rating:* ★★

Sylvester McMonkey McBean's Very Unusual Driving Machines. Based on *The Sneetches,* Dr. Seuss's popular tale about discrimination, this elevated indoor-outdoor attraction (slated to open in late fall 1999) is actually two rides in one. Choose between Star-Belly and Plain-Belly sides, each offering a different experience. Bumper cars travel throughout Seuss Landing and pass through six show scenes. You can honk your horn, control the speed of your vehicle, and bump the cars ahead of them, setting off honks, beeps, and screeches. *Audience: All ages.*

Lost Continent

This area represents a land believed to have existed in the mists of time. A visit transports you through time, past a crumbling statue of Poseidon, the Greek god of the sea, toward a revered city buzzing with humanity.

Dueling Dragons. This is no ordinary roller coaster. You whiz through the trees of a medieval forest and over Dragon Lake on one of two tracks that are entwined over, under, and around each other and encounter five inversions, three near misses, and top speeds of 55–60 mph. All the while your legs dangle freely. *Audience: Teens and adults. No pregnant women or guests with heart, back, or neck problems. Rating:* ★★★

Eighth Voyage of Sinbad. Seven voyages were not enough for Sinbad. So he strikes out again on his continuing search for enormous riches, encountering life-threatening perils along the way. Staged in a 1,700-seat theater, this edge-of-your-seat stunt show features six water explosions and 50 pyrotechnic effects. *Audience: Older children and adults. Rating:* ★★★

Poseidon's Fury: Escape from the Lost City. The Keeper is extremely pleased to welcome you, his unexpected guests, to his cavernous retreat. After all, it's been hundreds, perhaps thousands of years since he's had anyone to whom he could tell his story of the city that disappeared into the sea. Eventually the multimedia presentation becomes a battle between Poseidon (water) and his archenemy, Zeus (fire), and the "weapons" consist of more than 350,000 gallons of water and 200 flame effects, including 25-ft exploding fireballs. *Audience: Older children and adults. Rating:* ★★★

Jurassic Park

In this land you come face to face with some of the most lifelike animatronic creatures ever created, "living, breathing" dinosaurs. Those known as Spitters actually spit water on you as you make your way through the lush, tropical island.

Camp Jurassic. In this park-within-a-park, kids and adults alike may explore the caves, mines, and decks that hold secrets of the past. *Audience: Older children and adults. Rating:* ★★

Discovery Center. Get close to skeletal remains of a massive T. rex and laboratories where biochemists develop the technology to bring these prehistoric creatures to life. One of the many demonstration areas shows a seemingly realistic raptor being hatched. *Audience: Older children and adults. Rating:* ★★

Jurassic Park River Adventure. You'll discover that you have become the prey of a terrifying Tyrannosaurus rex as the beast comes within inches of your face. A treacherous 85-ft plunge straight down is the longest, fastest, steepest water descent ever built. *Audience: All but young children. No pregnant women or guests with heart, back, or neck problems. Rating:* ★★★

Pteranodon Flyers. Get a prehistoric bird's-eye view of the Jurassic Park compound as you soar through the air on the back of one of these gentle flying dinosaurs. *Audience: All ages. Rating:* ★

Triceratops Encounter. An opportunity to pet a "living" dinosaur is offered at the feed and control stations of the resident 24-ft-long, 10-ft-high triceratops. Trainers teach about the family history, emotional state, and feeding habits of the creature, who responds with realistic blinks and muscle flinches when touched. *Audience: All ages. Rating:* ★★

Toon Lagoon

Here's your chance to leap into the Sunday funnies and romp around the animated universe with some pretty famous characters—more than 150 in all—in an environment that melts the boundaries between imagination and reality.

Dudley Do-Right's Ripsaw Falls. Based on the popular 1960s cartoon *Rocky and Bullwinkle,* this ride is wet and wild, as riders try to help Dudley rescue Nell from Snidely Whiplash. The culmination is a drop through the rooftop of a ramshackle dynamite shack and an explosive dive 15 ft below water level into a 400,000-gallon lagoon. It is the first flume ever to send riders plummeting 75 ft at nearly 50 mph beneath the water's surface. *Audience: All but young children. No pregnant women or guests with heart, back, or neck problems. Rating:* ★★★

Popeye & Bluto's Bilge-Rat Barges. First comes a bumping, churning, twisting, turning white-water raft ride with a top speed of 16 ft per second. Next you're spun into Octopus Grotto for an encounter with an 18-ft-tall, 14-ft-wide creature with five 10- to 12-ft tentacles bulging with water. Finally, you're whirled into a fully operational boat wash, where you may get completely soaked. *Audience: All but young children. No pregnant women or guests with heart, back, or neck problems or motion sickness. Rating:* ★★★

Popeye's Boat, the *Olive.* From bow to stern dozens of participatory activities are featured in this family-friendly interactive playground. Toddlers enjoy crawling in Swee' Pea's Playpen, while older children attempt to drench unsuspecting Bilge-Rat Barges riders at Cargo Crane. *Audience: Young children. Rating:* ★★

Marvel Super Hero Island

At this island, state-of-the-art technology is incorporated with popular comic book heroes and villains.

Amazing Adventures of Spider-Man. Combining moving vehicles, filmed 3-D action, live action, and special effects, this revolutionary ride starts with a tour of the *Daily Bugle,* where Peter Parker, a.k.a. Spider-Man, works as a reporter. Evil villains use their antigravity gun to steal the Statue of Liberty, and you are drafted as part of a civilian force to help Spider-Man retrieve the national treasure. Speeding through the street set, you're swept into a battle between good and evil. *Audience: All but young children. No pregnant women or guests with heart, back, or neck problems. Rating:* ★★★

Dr. Doom's Fearfall. You learn about Dr. Doom's new creation, a machine that purges fear, as you board this ride. With feet dangling, you're fired to the top of either of two 200-ft towers of menacing steel and then sent plummeting to the ground at unthinkable speed. The drop is fast and steep. There isn't even a chance to scream! *Audience: Older children and adults. No pregnant women or guests with heart, back, or neck problems or motion sickness. Rating:* ★★★

Incredible Hulk Coaster. This roller coaster blasts from 0 to 40 mph in two seconds, followed by a complete inversion 100 ft from the ground, during which you're weightless. Next come seven rollovers before you're plunged into two deep subterranean enclosures. *Audience: Older children and adults. No pregnant women or guests with heart, back, or neck problems. Rating:* ★★★

Universal Studios Islands of Adventure Information

Tickets are available at the entrance, by mail from the park, and by mail through Ticketmaster (☎ 800/745–5000). ✉ *1000 Universal Studios Plaza, Orlando 32819-7610,* ☎ *407/363–8000; 888/331–9108; 407/363–8265 TTY.* 💻 *One day: $44.52 adults, $36.04 chil-*

dren 3–9; two-day combination with Universal Studios Florida: $84.74 adults, $68.84 children 3–9; parking: $6 cars, $8 campers.

Cypress Gardens

⑪ *Take I–4 to Exit 23 (U.S. 27S) and follow signs.*

A botanical garden, amusement park, and waterskiing circus rolled into one, Cypress Gardens is a uniquely Floridian combination of natural beauty and utter kitsch. A 45-minute drive from Walt Disney World Resort, the park now encompasses more than 200 acres and contains more than 8,000 varieties of plants gathered from 75 countries. More than half the grounds are devoted to flora, ranging from natural landscaping to cutesy-poo topiary to chrysanthemum cascades. Even at a sedate pace, you can see just about everything in six hours.

Boardwalk Aviary. At this interactive encounter, you can learn about birds native to Florida. *Audience: All ages. Rating:* ★★★

Botanical Gardens. The plantings here are naturalized, and a saunter on winding paths beneath shady live oaks or the quiet chamber created by a giant banyan's roots provides a welcome respite. *Audience: Older children and adults. Rating:* ★★★

Botanical Gardens Cruise. This float through cypress-hung canals passes hoop-skirted southern belles, flowering shrubs, 27 species of palm, and the occasional baby alligator. Doing this as soon as you arrive in Cypress Gardens gives you a sense of the place. *Audience: All ages. Rating:* ★★★

Exhibition Gardens. The path leading from the ski stadiums to the amusement-park area meanders through this expanse of landscaping, whose philosophy is heroic in intent and hilariously vulgar in execution. *Audience: All ages. Rating:* ★★

Nature's Boardwalk. Take a leisurely stroll through this area with exhibits on animal habitats. *Audience: All ages. Rating:* ★★★

Pontoon Lakes Cruise. Narrated pontoon-boat cruises show off the scenery around Lakes Eloise, Summit, and LuLu. *Audience: All ages. Rating:* ★★

Southern Crossroads. Many of the park's attractions are here: the huge walk-through **Wings of Wonder: The Butterfly Conservatory** (★★); the ice show at **the Palace** (★★★); **Tampa's Electric Bright House** (★★), a museum showcasing electricity; **Carousel Cove** (★), with ball rooms and bouncing pads plus a lovely old carousel; **Cypress Junction** (★★★), one of the nation's most elaborate model railroad exhibits; Crossroads Arena (★★★), home to a rotating collection of circus-theme acts from acrobats to trained birds; **Cypress Roots** (★), a clapboard shack chock-full of memorabilia about the Gardens' founders, Dick and Julie Pope; and **When Radios Were Radios** (★★), a museum of antique radios. **Kodak's Island in the Sky** (★★★), a 153-ft-high revolving platform, provides aerial views of the park.

Water Ski Stadiums. Don't miss one of Cypress Gardens' true specialties, the stunt-filled water-ski revue. Unlike the splashy song-and-dance extravaganzas at other parks, the show at Cypress Gardens is purely athletic—and those sitting in the front rows don't get wet here! *Audience: All ages. Rating:* ★★★

Cypress Gardens Information

✉ *Box 1, Cypress Gardens 33884,* ☎ *941/324–2111; 800/237–4826; 800/282–2123 in FL.* 🎟 *$33.87 adults, $15.85 children 6–17; parking $4 regular, $5 preferred.* ☉ *Daily 9:30–5:30, longer during peak seasons.*

AWAY FROM THE THEME PARKS

Once you've exhausted the theme parks, or been exhausted by them, you can turn your attention to a wealth of other area offerings. Though you'll find plenty of other recreational activities of interest to kids, there are also museums and parks and gardens galore, highlighting the cultural and natural heritage of this part of the South.

Kissimmee

10 mi east of Walt Disney World Resort; take I–4 Exit 25A.

Although Kissimmee is primarily known as the gateway to Walt Disney World, its non-WDW attractions just might tickle your fancy.

⑫ **DisneyQuest.** At this totally interactive venue, you can learn animation techniques, create your own toys or a wild self-portrait, take a virtual jungle cruise, or play video games. You decide how much to do by purchasing a credit card that debits itself each time you use it. ⊠ *Downtown Disney West Side,* ☎ *407/828–4600.* ⚏ *$14–$45 cards available.* ⊙ *Daily 10:30 AM–midnight.*

⑬ **Flying Tigers Warbird Air Museum.** Old war birds never die—they just become attractions. This working aircraft restoration facility is nicknamed Bombertown USA because most planes here are bombers. Once they are operational, they are usually flown away by private collectors, but the museum also houses a permanent collection of about 30 vintage planes in its hangar, with a few big ones out on the tarmac. ⊠ *231 Hoagland Blvd.,* ☎ *407/933–1942.* ⚏ *$8 adults, $6 children 5–12.* ⊙ *Mon.–Sun. 9–5:30.*

⑭ **Gatorland.** Long before Walt Disney World, there was this campy attraction, which has endured since 1949 without much change, despite major competition. Through the monstrous aqua gator-jaw doorway—a definite photo op—lie thrills and chills in the form of thousands of alligators and crocodiles, swimming and basking in the Florida sun. The newest addition, **Jungle Crocs,** features rare and deadly crocodiles, and don't miss the **Gator Jumparoo Show.** There's also a **Gator Wrestling Cracker-style Show,** and though there's no doubt who's going to win the match, it's still fun to see the handlers take on those tough guys with the beady eyes. In the educational **Snakes of Florida Show,** high drama is provided by the 30–40 rattlesnakes that fill the pit around the speaker. ⊠ *14501 S. Orange Blossom Trail, between Orlando and Kissimmee,* ☎ *407/855–5496 or 800/393–5297.* ⚏ *$16.93 adults, $9.95 children 10–12, $7.48 children 3–9, 1 child free with each full-paying adult.* ⊙ *Daily 9–sunset.*

⑮ **Haunted Mansion.** As you walk through two floors and the attic, you'll find vampires, open crypts, skeletons, and live and animated spooks behind quirky twists and turns. ⊠ *4710 W. Irlo Bronson Memorial Hwy.,* ☎ *407/396–6661.* ⚏ *$9.63 adults, $6.42 children 2–12.* ⊙ *Mon.–Sat. noon–11, Sun. 4–11.*

⑯ **Splendid China.** West of I–4 and Walt Disney World is this attraction that's more a superlative open-air museum than a theme park. Here you can stroll among painstakingly re-created versions of China's greatest landmarks—such as the Dalai Lama's **Potala Palace,** the **Great Wall,** and the Forbidden City's **Imperial Palace**—and watch artisans demonstrate traditional Chinese woodworking, weaving, and other crafts, while tinkling meditative music plays in the background. It took $100 million and 120 Chinese craftspeople working for two years and using, whenever possible, historically accurate building materials and techniques to create the 60-plus replicas. Both man-made structures and natural phenomena are represented—some life-size, others greatly reduced in scale (the bricks in the Great Wall, for example, are only 2 inches long). To appeal to theme-park savvy Western visitors, live entertainment and a playground are also on the grounds, and the shops and restaurants of the Chinatown section are a cut above those at typical theme parks. The park is at its most magical at night. ⊠ *3000 Splendid China Blvd.,* ☎ *407/397–8800 recording; 407/396–7111 voice; 800/244–6226.* ⬜ *$26.99 adults, $16.99 children 5–12; parking and Chinatown free.* ☉ *Daily 9:30–7, later in peak seasons, Chinatown shops and restaurants until 9.*

🔟 **Water Mania.** All the requisite rides and slides are at this 36-acre park—without Walt Disney World Resort aesthetics. However, it's the only water park around to have **Wipe Out,** a surfing simulator, where you grab a body board and ride a continuous wave form. The giant Pirate Ship in the **Rain Forest,** one of two children's play areas, is equipped with water slides and water cannons. The **Abyss,** similar to Wet 'n Wild's Black Hole (☞ Near International Drive, Orlando, *below*), is an enclosed tube slide through which you twist and turn on a one- or two-person raft for 300 ft of deep-blue darkness. You'll also find a sandy beach, a picnic area, snack bars, gift shops, and periodic concerts, which can be enjoyed while floating in an inner tube. The park is just east of I–4 at Exit 25. ⊠ *6073 W. Irlo Bronson Memorial Hwy.,* ☎ *407/239–8448, 407/396–2626, or 800/527–3092.* ⬜ *$24.95 adults, $17.95 children 3–9 (½ price after 3, after 4 in summer); parking $4.* ☉ *Nov.–late Feb., daily 11–5; Mar., late Apr.–May, and mid-Sept.–Oct., daily 10–5; early–mid-Apr. and Memorial Day weekend, daily 10–7; June–late Aug., weekdays 9:30–7, weekends 9:30–8; late Aug.–early Sept., daily 9:30–6.*

OFF THE BEATEN PATH | **BOK TOWER GARDENS –** For those in need of a back-to-nature fix, this appealing but often overlooked sanctuary of plants, flowers, trees, and wildlife is definitely worth a trip. Shady paths meander through pine forests in this peaceful world of silvery moats, mockingbirds and swans, blooming thickets, and hidden sundials. The majestic 200-ft Bok Tower is constructed of coquina (from seashells) and pink, white, and gray marble and houses a carillon with 57 bronze bells that ring every half hour after 10 AM. Each day at 3 there is a 45-minute recital, which may include Early American folk songs, Appalachian tunes, Irish ballads, or Latin hymns. There are also moonlight recitals. To reach the gardens, take I–4 Exit 23 and head south along U.S. 27, away from the congestion of Orlando and past quite a few of Central Florida's citrus groves. ⊠ *Burns Ave. and Tower Blvd., Lake Wales,* ☎ *941/676–1408.* ⬜ *$4 adults, $1 children 5–12, free Sat. if you arrive 8 AM–9 AM; Pinewood House $5 suggested donation.* ☉ *Daily 8–6, Pinewood House tours Sept. 15–May 15, Tues. and Thurs. 12:30 and 2, Sun. 2.*

Near International Drive, Orlando

7 mi northeast of Walt Disney World Resort; take I–4 Exit 28 or 29, unless otherwise noted.

Between WDW and downtown Orlando are several attractions that kids adore. Unfortunately they may put some wear and tear on parents.

⑱ **Mystery Fun House.** There are a variety of ways to attack this place. You can just bring your quarters to the video arcade (for which there's no admission charge) or pay to walk through the 18-chamber **Mystery Maze**, which comes with the warning that it is "90% dark" and full of gory and distorted images. Outside, there's the 18-hole **Jurassic Golf**, a basic putt-putt course, laid out flat and simple, with, as you might expect, a dinosaur motif. The real highlight is the **Starbase Omega** laser-tag game. Take I–4 Exit 30B (Universal Studios). Turn right (north) on Kirkman Road and right again on Major Boulevard. ✉ *5767 Major Blvd.,* ☎ *407/351–3355.* ⌨ *Maze $10.95, miniature golf $4.95, laser game $9.95, all 3 $19.95.* ⊘ *Mon.–Sat. 10 AM–11 PM, until midnight in peak seasons.*

⑲ **Ripley's Believe It or Not! Museum.** A 10-ft-square section of the Berlin Wall, a pain and torture chamber, a Rolls-Royce constructed entirely of matchsticks—these and almost 200 other oddities speak for themselves in this museum-cum-attraction in the heart of tourist territory. It is said that the fruits of Robert Ripley's explorations are to reality what Walt Disney World is to fantasy. ✉ *8201 International Dr.,* ☎ *407/363–4418 or 800/998–4418.* ⌨ *$10.95 adults, $7.95 children 4–12.* ⊘ *Daily 9 AM–midnight.*

⑳ **Wet 'n Wild.** Now owned by Universal, this park is probably best known for its outrageous water slides, especially the **Black Hole**—a 30-second, 500-ft, twisting, turning ride on a two-person raft through total darkness propelled by a 1,000-gallon-a-minute blast of water. There's also an elaborate **Kid's Park**—for those 4 ft and under—full of miniature versions of the bigger rides. The **Bubba Tub** is a six-story triple-dip slide with a tube big enough for the entire family. Teens like the Top 40 concerts that take place frequently in summer. The park has snack stands, but visitors are allowed to bring their own food and picnic around the pool or on the lakeside beach. Combination tickets with other parks are available. Take I–4 Exit 30A and make a left. ✉ *6200 International Dr.,* ☎ *407/351–3200.* ⌨ *$24.95 adults, $19.95 children 3–9 (half price after 3, after 5 in peak season); parking $4 cars, $6 RVs.* ⊘ *Daily 10–5, until 9 in summer; call for exact hours.*

㉑ **WonderWorks.** Just up the street, the Ripley's Believe It or Not! building seems to be sinking into the ground, but true to Orlando tradition, this newer attraction one-ups the competition: It's sinking into the ground upside down. If the strange sight of a topsy-turvy facade complete with upended palm trees and simulated FedEx box doesn't catch your attention, the swirling "dust" and piped-out creaking sounds will. Inside, the upside-down theme continues only as far as the lobby. After that, it's a playground of 75 interactive experiences and demonstrations, some educational (similar to those at a science museum) and others just pure entertainment. Exhibits range from interactions with natural disasters and optical illusions to a mock electric chair, climbing wall, and virtual sports games. ✉ *Pointe*Orlando, International Dr.,* ☎ *407/352–8655.* ⌨ *$12.95 adults, $9.95 children 4–12.* ⊘ *Daily 10–11, longer in peak seasons.*

Downtown Orlando

15 mi northeast of Walt Disney World Resort; take I–4 Exit 41 if you're heading westbound, Exit 40 if eastbound, or Exit 43 for Loch Haven Park sights.

Downtown Orlando is a dynamic community that's constantly growing and changing. Here you'll find new buildings under construction, interesting museums, and bustling Church Street Station. Numerous parks, many of which surround lakes, provide pleasant relief from the tall office buildings. One such is Lake Eola, which has a delightful playground at one end and a walkway around its circumference that invites strolling. Just a few steps from downtown's tourist meccas are delightful residential neighborhoods with brick-paved streets and live oaks dripping with Spanish moss.

㉒ Harry P. Leu Gardens. The former estate of citrus entrepreneur Harry P. Leu provides a quiet respite from the artificial world of the theme parks. On the grounds' 50 acres are a collection of historical blooms, many varieties of which were established before 1900. ⊠ *1920 N. Forest Ave.,* ☎ *407/246–2620.* ⊠ *$4 adults, $1 children 6–16.* ☉ *Garden daily 9–6; guided house tours daily 10–3:30.*

㉓ Orange County Historical Museum. On Loch Haven Park, this storehouse of Orlando memorabilia, photographs, and antiques features displays of Native American and native Floridian culture, a country store, Victorian parlor, and print shop. Call for an update on the always-changing traveling exhibits. **Fire Station No. 3,** an actual 1926 brick firehouse behind the museum, houses antique fire trucks, fire-fighting memorabilia, and collectibles. ⊠ *812 E. Rollins St.,* ☎ *407/897–6350.* ⊠ *$4 adults, $2 children 6–12.* ☉ *Mon.–Sat. 9–5, Sun. noon–5.*

㉔ Orlando Museum of Art. The draw at this Loch Haven Park museum is the first-class **Art Encounter,** created with the help of Walt Disney World. Young children love it. Hands-on activities, such as dressing up in colorful handwoven clothing from South America, stimulate imaginations and enhance children's understanding of the works in the galleries. There's also a rather limited art collection, including 19th-and 20th-century American art. ⊠ *2416 Mills Ave.,* ☎ *407/896–4231.* ⊠ *$4 adults, $2 children 4–11.* ☉ *Tues.–Sat. 9–5, Sun. noon–5; tours Sept.–May, Wed. and Sun. 2; Art Encounter Tues.–Fri. and Sun. noon–5, Sat. 10–5.*

㉕ Orlando Science Center. With all the high-tech glitz and imagined worlds of the theme parks, which are closer to where most tourists stay, is it worth visiting this reality-based science museum in Orlando proper? Absolutely. The action-packed 207,000-square-ft, four-level building is the perfect antidote to long lines and overwhelming gimmickry. The 10 themed display halls house a multitude of exciting hands-on exhibits covering mechanics, electricity and magnetism, math, health and fitness, nature, the solar system, and light, lasers, and optics. Walk through an enormous open mouth (literally) and take a journey through the human body (figuratively). Raise a suspended VW bug with the help of a lever and learn about physics while you're showing off (you don't need to tell the kids it's educational if you don't want). The **Dr. Phillips CineDome,** a movie theater with a giant eight-story screen, offers large-format Iwerks films, planetarium programs, and, on weekends, laser-light shows. In addition, the **Darden Adventure Theater** features the center's in-house performance troupe, the Einstein Players. ⊠ *777 E. Princeton St.,* ☎ *407/514–2000.* ⊠ *Exhibits $9.50 adults, $6.75 children 3–11; CineDome films $6 adults, $4.50 children; both $12 adults, $9.50 children; exhibits plus 2 CineDome experiences $14.25 adults, $11 children; parking $3.50.* ☉ *Mon.–Thurs. 9–5, Fri.–Sat. 9–9, Sun. noon–5.*

㉖ Terror on Church Street. Take a 30-minute walking tour through this showcase of horror in the heart of downtown, just a few blocks east of Church Street Station. The high-tech labyrinth features 23 scenes from horror films, with live actors and state-of-the-art sound effects. ⊠ *Church St. and Orange Ave.,* ☎ *407/649–3327.* 🎟 *$12 adults, $10 children 17 and under.* ☉ *Sun.–Thurs. 7 PM–midnight, Fri.–Sat. 7 PM– 1 AM.*

Winter Park

20 mi northeast of WDW; take I–4 Exit 45 and head east 3 mi on Fair-banks Ave.

You can spend a pleasant day in this upscale town shopping at chic boutiques, eating at a cozy café, visiting museums, and taking in the scenery along Park Avenue, with its hidden alleyways that lead to peaceful nooks and crannies. Away from the avenue, moss-covered trees form a canopy over brick streets, and old estates surround canal-linked lakes.

㉗ **Central Park.** This lovely, shady green space with a stage and gazebo is Winter Park's gathering place, often the scene of concerts. If you don't want to browse in the shops across the street, a rest on a bench or a stroll through the park is a delightful alternative. ⊠ *Park Ave.*

㉘ **Charles Hosmer Morse Museum of American Art.** Here you'll see many works of Louis Comfort Tiffany, including immense stained-glass windows, lamps, watercolors, and desk sets. A new attraction, the 8,000-square-ft Tiffany Chapel was originally built for the 1893 World's Fair. ⊠ *445 Park Ave. N,* ☎ *407/645–5311.* 🎟 *$3 adults, $1 students.* ☉ *Tues.–Sat. 9:30–4, Sun. 1–4.*

㉙ **Holocaust Memorial Resource and Education Center of Central Florida.** Exhibits depicting major events of the Holocaust are arranged in chronological order and include a large number of photographs and audiovisual presentations. The museum also contains a library and archives. ⊠ *851 N. Maitland Ave., Maitland,* ☎ *407/628–0555.* 🎟 *Free.* ☉ *Mon.–Thurs. 9–4, Fri. 9–1.*

㉚ **Mead Gardens.** The 55 acres in this unusual park have been intentionally left to grow as a natural preserve. Walkers and runners are attracted to the trails that wind around the creek. ⊠ *S. Denning Ave.,* ☎ *407/599–3334.* 🎟 *Free.* ☉ *Daily 8–sunset.*

㉛ **Rollins College.** This private liberal arts school was once Mister (Fred) Rogers's neighborhood—yes, he's an alumnus. You'll see the **Knowles Memorial Chapel,** built in 1932, and the **Annie Russell Theatre,** a 1931 building that's often the venue for local theatrical productions. The **Cornell Fine Arts Museum** houses a small but interesting collection of 19th- and 20th-century American and European paintings, decorative arts, and sculpture. ⊠ *End of Holt Ave.,* ☎ *407/646–2526.* 🎟 *Museum free.* ☉ *Museum Tues.–Fri. 10–5, weekends 1–5.*

OFF THE
BEATEN PATH

CENTRAL FLORIDA ZOOLOGICAL PARK - If you're expecting a grand metro zoo, this will disappoint. However, there is a respectable display of about 230 animals tucked under pine trees, and like the city of Orlando, 22 mi south, it continues to grow. Children love the **Animal Adventure,** containing domestic and farm animals to pet and feed. Take I–4 Exit 52. ⊠ *3755 N. U.S. 17–92, Sanford,* ☎ *407/323–4450.* 🎟 *$7 adults, $3 children 3–12.* ☉ *Daily 9–5; pony rides weekends 10–4.*

WEKIVA SPRINGS STATE PARK - Where the tannin-stained Wekiva River meets the crystal-clear Wekiva headspring, you'll find this 6,400-acre park that's well suited to camping, hiking, picnicking, swimming, canoeing, fishing, and watching for alligators, egrets, and deer. Though it can be crowded on weekends, on weekdays it's Walden Pond, Florida style. Take I–4 Exit 49 and turn left on Route 434 and right on Wekiva Springs Road. ⊠ *1800 Wekiva Circle, Apopka,* ☎ *407/884–2009.* ⌫ *$3.25 per vehicle.* ☉ *Daily 8–sunset.*

Mount Dora

32 *35 mi northwest of Orlando and 50 mi north of WDW; take U.S. 441 (Orange Blossom Trail in Orlando) north or take I–4 to Exit 48, then take Rte. 436 west to U.S. 441, and follow the signs.*

Built around the unspoiled Lake Harris chain of lakes, the quaint valley community of Mount Dora has a slow and easy pace, a rich history, New England–style charm, and excellent antiquing. Although the population is under 8,000, there is plenty of excitement here. The first weekend in February is the annual Mount Dora Art Festival. Attracting more than 200,000 visitors over a three-day period, it is one of Central Florida's major outdoor events. During the year there are a sailing regatta, a bicycle festival, and a crafts fair, or you can take in the historic buildings along Donnelly Street or 5th Avenue any time of year.

DINING

Because tourism is king here, casual dress is the rule, and few restaurants require fancier attire. Reservations are always a good idea in a city where the phrase "Bus drivers eat free" could be emblazoned on the coat of arms. If you don't have reservations, the entire Ecuadorean soccer team or the Platt City High School senior class may arrive moments before you and keep you waiting a long, long time. Save that experience for the theme parks.

For restaurants within Walt Disney World Resort, reservations are especially easy to make, thanks to its **central reservations line** (☎ 407/ 939–3463). In addition, you can make reservations for the very popular Epcot restaurants at any of the WorldKey Information System terminals in the park.

Orlando is not big, but getting to places is frequently complicated, so always call for directions. Almost everything can be reached from I–4, so if you know the right exit, you can at least start looking in the right neighborhood. Some of the smaller, hungrier restaurant operators may offer to come get you. The other benefit of the competitive restaurant market is that prices have remained cheaper than elsewhere in Florida.

Epcot

English

$$ ✕ **Rose and Crown.** If you are an Anglophile and you love nothing more than a good, thick beer, this friendly pub is the place to soak up both the suds and the British street culture. "Wenches" serve up simple pub fare, such as steak-and-kidney pie and fish-and-chips. Dark wood floors, sturdy pub chairs, and brass lamps create a warm, homey atmosphere. At 4, a traditional tea is served. All things considered, it's one of the best bets in Epcot.

French

$$–$$$ ✕ **Bistro de Paris.** The great secret at the France pavilion—and, indeed,
★ in all of Epcot—is this bistro, around the back of Les Chefs de France and upstairs. The sophisticated menu changes regularly and contains

exciting offerings that reflect the cutting edge of French cooking. The dining salon is serene—and often filled with well-dressed French people, the mark of a successful transplant.

$$–$$$ ✕ **Les Chefs de France.** To create this sparkling French café-restaurant,
★ three of France's most famous culinary artists came together: Paul Bocuse, who operates one restaurant north of Lyon and two in Tokyo; Gaston Lenôtre, noted for his pastries and ice creams; and Roger Vergé, proprietor of France's celebrated Mougins, near Cannes. The three developed the menu, trained the chefs, and sometimes look in—apparently not as frequently as they should, according to some reviewers—to make sure the food and service stay up to snuff. Start with a chicken-and-duck pâté in a pastry crust, follow with a classic coq au vin or the roasted red snapper in pastry with a creamy lobster sauce, and end with chocolate-doused, ice-cream-filled pastry shells.

German

$$ ✕ **Biergarten.** In this popular spot, Oktoberfest runs 365 days a year. The cheerful—some would say raucous—atmosphere is what you would expect in a place with an oompah band. Waitresses in typical Bavarian garb serve *breseln,* hot German pretzels made fresh daily on the premises. Other classic German fare in the one-price buffet includes sauerbraten and bratwurst. Patrons pound stout pitchers of beer and wine on their long communal tables—even when the yodelers, singers, and dancers aren't egging them on.

Italian

$$–$$$ ✕ **L'Originale Alfredo di Roma Ristorante.** This is the most popular
★ restaurant at Epcot, and its namesake dish, made with mountains of butter flown in from Italy, is one of the principal reasons. The restaurant was created, with the help of Disney, by the descendants of Alfredo de Lelio, who in 1914 founded Rome's Alfredo all'Augusteo restaurant and invented the now-classic dish—fettuccine sauce with cream, butter, and loads of freshly grated, imported Parmesan cheese. But the true secret to the dish here is the butter. Insiders say the only Parmesan used is what your waiter sprinkles on at the table. During dinner the Italian waiters skip around singing Italian songs and bellowing arias, a show in itself.

Japanese

$$–$$$ ✕ **Mitsukoshi.** This complex of dining areas overlooking tranquil gardens is actually three restaurants. Yakitori House, a gussied-up fast-food stand in a small pavilion modeled on a teahouse in Kyoto's Katsura Summer Palace, offers broiled skewers of chicken basted with teriyaki sauce and *gyudon* (paper-thin beef simmered in a spicy sauce and served with noodles). At the Tempura Kiku, two dozen diners sit around a central counter and watch the chefs prepare sushi, sashimi, tempura, batter-dipped deep-fried shrimp, scallops, and vegetables. In the five Teppanyaki Dining Rooms, chefs skillfully chop vegetables, meat, and fish at lightning speed and then stir-fry them at grills set into communal dining tables.

Mexican

$$–$$$ ✕ **San Angel Inn.** The lush, tropical surroundings—cool, dark, and almost surreal—make this restaurant in the courtyard inside the Mexican pavilion perhaps the most exotic at WDW. It's popular among Disney execs as well as tourists, who treasure the respite it offers, especially when the humid weather outside makes Central Florida feel like equatorial Africa. Candlelit tables are companionably close together, and the restaurant is open to a midnight-blue "sky" in the inside of the pavilion and filled with the music of folksingers, guitars, and marimbas. On the roster of authentic dishes, one specialty is mole *poblano* (chicken

simmered until tender in a rich sauce of different kinds of chilies, green tomatoes, ground tortillas, cumin, and 11 other spices mixed with cocoa).

Moroccan

$$–$$$ ✕ **Marrakesh.** This is the least popular of the World Showcase restaurants, not because the food isn't good—it is—but because the average American hasn't heard much about Moroccan cuisine. The food is mildly spicy and relatively inexpensive, and Disney has taken it quite seriously, bringing in Chef Abrache Lahcen, who was personally recommended by King Hassan II of Morocco. Try the couscous, the national dish of Morocco, served with vegetables; or *bastilla* (an appetizer made of alternating layers of sweet-and-spicy pork and a thin pastry, redolent of almonds, saffron, and cinnamon). Belly dancers and a three-piece Moroccan band set a North African mood that feels like the set of *Casablanca.*

Scandinavian

$$ ✕ **Restaurant Akershus.** Norway's tradition of seafood and cold meat dishes is highlighted at the *koldtboard* (Norwegian buffet) in this restaurant, comprising four dining rooms that occupy a copy of Oslo's Akershus Castle. Hosts and hostesses explain the dishes and suggest which ones go together, then send you off to the buffet table for the first of several trips. First you go for appetizers, which usually consist of herring done several ways. Then go for cold seafood such as gravlax, a cured salmon served with mustard sauce, and *fiskepudding,* a seafood mousse with herb dressing. Pick up cold salads and meats on your next trip, and on your last foray, fill up on hot lamb, veal, or venison. The selection of desserts, offered à la carte, includes cloudberries (a delicate fruit that grows on the tundra in season).

Elsewhere in Walt Disney World Resort

American/Casual

$$ ✕ **Planet Hollywood.** Patrons come to see the movie memorabilia assembled by owners Schwarzenegger, Stallone, Willis, and the biggest showman among the partners, restaurateur Robert Earl. Outside there's a souvenir shop, where you can buy T-shirts while you wonder when you'll actually get inside. The wait, once a guaranteed two hours at peak periods, has abated somewhat, except when movies at the multiplex next door let out. If you want to save time, go mid-afternoon on a weekday: The menu doesn't change. Food is secondary to the 20,000-square-ft building complete with an indoor waterfall; it cost $15 million, as much as a theme-park attraction. The menu is built around fresh, healthful dishes like turkey burgers, smoked and grilled meats, unusual pastas and salads, and a wide range of desserts. Among the better offerings are a creole pizza with shrimp, chicken, and Cajun sausage, and a tasty $7.50 burger, a bargain in these parts. ⊠ *Downtown Disney West Side, at entrance to Pleasure Island,* ☎ *407/827–7827. Reservations not accepted. AE, DC, MC, V.*

$–$$ ✕ **Official All-Star Cafe.** We've always maintained that you can't go wrong with cuisine created by renowned gastronomic experts Shaquille O'Neill, Monica Seles, Joe Montana, Tiger Woods, Andre Agassi, Wayne Gretzky, and Ken Griffey, Jr. And for an atmosphere that brings the dining experience to its zenith, we can't think of anything better than 16 big-screen TVs playing nonstop sports clips as loud rock music blares, spotlights roam around the room, and strobe lights periodically blind you. If you agree, you're going to love this celeb-brand eatery. The food, ranging from burgers to steaks to pasta, is nothing special. Among the best offerings are Wayne's Cracked Ribs (barbecued spare ribs), Shaq's Slammin' Smoked Turkey Sandwich, and Bull Penne

Pasta. The best dessert is the Banana Split Decision Cheesecake. At $5.95, the white-chocolate-chip cookie may be the most expensive cookie in North America. ⊠ *Disney's Wide World of Sports,* ☎ 407/827–8326. *AE, MC, V.*

$–$$ ✕ **Rainforest Café.** People start lining up half an hour before the 11
★ AM opening of this 30,000-square-ft jungle fantasy. A pump system creates periodic "rain storms," and a 3½-story man-made volcano, forming the roof, erupts frequently, shaking the tables. The food, an eclectic mix of American fare with imaginative names, is also an attraction. Eyes of the Ocelot is a nice meat loaf topped with sautéed mushrooms. Other good choices are Rasta Pasta (bow-tie pasta with grilled chicken and pesto sauce) and Mojo Bones (tender oven-roasted ribs with barbecue sauce). The big, gleaming neon SAVE THE RAINFOREST globe in the fountain does resemble the Hard Rock Cafe's, but this place puts its money where its slogan is, donating to groups working to save forest land and buying none of its beef from deforested South American ranch land. ⊠ *Downtown Disney Marketplace,* ☎ 407/827–8500; ⊠ *Disney's Animal Kingdom,* ☎ 407/938–9100. *AE, D, DC, MC, V.*

Cajun/Creole

$–$$ ✕ **House of Blues.** From the outside, this cavernous rusted-tin building looks like an old factory, but it's a ruse. What we really have here is a darn good little southern-cookin' restaurant and bar with a separate concert hall just up the sidewalk. The interior architecture, which looks like an old church converted into an eatery, is more inspired than the exterior. There's even an angelic fresco over the bar. The best menu items include catfish, pork chops, and the New Orleans–style étouffée. A gospel Sunday brunch is righteous—and so popular you'll need reservations. Suffused with the buzz of tourists and the patented Downtown Disney if-you're-here-you-must-be-cool attitude, the place gets even noisier when the live music plays (11 PM–2 AM), but lunches can be almost serene. ⊠ *Downtown Disney West Side,* ☎ 407/934–2583. *Reservations essential for Sun. brunch, not accepted weekday lunches. AE, D, MC, V.*

Contemporary

$$$$ ✕ **Victoria and Albert's.** Servers work in male-female pairs, calling them-
★ selves Victoria and Albert and reciting specials in tandem. This will either seem incredibly silly to you, or, if you are a true Disney believer, strike your fancy. Unfortunately, if you are in the former category, you can't really shoo the thespians-servers away. But the cuisine will wow you nevertheless. The intimate, lavish, and romantic Victorian-themed room, considered Disney's top restaurant in its top hotel by many Disney execs, has a domed ceiling, fabric-covered walls, marbleized columns, and lots of flowers. A harpist adds an ethereal touch. The seven-course, prix-fixe menu ($80–$110) changes day to day. Appetizers might include velvety veal sweetbreads or artichokes in a lusty *duxelles* (mushroom-based) sauce. Entrées range from sautéed breast of duck to well-prepared sirloin. Kosher and vegetarian meals can be ordered in advance. One seating (7–7:45) is offered nightly. ⊠ *Grand Floridian, Magic Kingdom Resort Area,* ☎ 407/939–3463. *Reservations essential. Jacket required. AE, MC, V.*

$$$–$$$$ ✕ **Citrico's.** In true Disney style, the totally made up name of this worthy hotel culinary centerpiece alludes to the citrus-oriented cuisine, part of a well-choreographed gastronomic fantasy. Central in the bright and cheery design is the now-popular "performance-style" kitchen, where diners can watch Chef Roland Muller's minions do their magic. Aggressively friendly servers explain everything except how citrus is picked, but don't expect to be overwhelmed with citrus choices. Although there is a tasty citrus-and-chicken-sausage appetizer, an oak-grilled salmon entrée with citrus couscous, and excellent assorted citrus desserts, the menu is not quintessential Florida. Instead it leans toward innovations like tender pan-roasted halibut and six-hour braised veal shank. ⊠ *Grand Floridian, Magic Kingdom Resort Area,* ☎ *407/939–3463. AE, MC, V.*

$$–$$$$ ✕ **California Grill.** Disney marketing executives cite this restaurant as
★ an example of the culinary revolution that Dieter Hannig, vice president of food and beverage for the resort, is bringing about: More high-quality restaurants are serving original, one-of-a-kind menus. The Grill, which flies in 23 varieties of tomatoes every day from a special farm in California, is a shining example of Hannig's master plan. Manager George Miliotes says the strategy is "fresh food, simply prepared," but those words hardly do justice to some of the excellent offerings, like the wood-oven pizza garnished with fresh veggies, the pan-seared tuna steaks, or the hearty grilled pork tenderloin. The restaurant is smoke free. ⊠ *Contemporary Resort, Magic Kingdom Resort Area,* ☎ *407/939–3463. AE, MC, V.*

$–$$$ ✕ **Artist Point.** The Wilderness Lodge—a huge, jauntily brawny hunt-
★ ing-lodge-style hotel—is definitely worth a look, and a meal here should be on your short list of things to do, if only for a good excuse to see the place. The northwestern salmon sampler is a good start, but you might also try the smoked duck breast, maple-glazed steak, sautéed elk sausage, or pan-fried rainbow trout, which probably traveled farther to get here than you did. Most meats are hardwood grilled. The house specialty is the "trail dust shortcake," a buttermilk biscuit with strawberries, vanilla-bean ice cream, and whipped cream. ⊠ *Wilderness Lodge, Magic Kingdom Resort Area,* ☎ *407/939–3463. AE, MC, V.*

$–$$$ ✕ **Wolfgang Puck Café.** You almost need a road map to find all the
★ parts of this elegant eatery. There's a Wolfgang Puck Express in Downtown Disney Marketplace, which serves excellent light fare like wood-fired minipizzas, in addition to the main Puckarama complex, which also has a Puck Express. However, this Express is attached to a two-story restaurant with semicasual dining and a sushi bar downstairs and the main café upstairs. It's upstairs where you'll find the more formal setting *and* menu, but downstairs is a good choice if you want to sample the famous Puck fare without going too upscale. Here Art Deco furnishings are complemented by a great lakefront view. Must-tries include the pizzas, with toppings like grilled chicken or salmon, and various inspired pastas with sublime sauces laced with chunks of lobster, salmon, or chicken. Don't let the highbrow reputation fool you; Puck's menu also contains down-home favorites like garlic mashed potatoes and, for children, a peanut butter and marshmallow "samich." ⊠ *Downtown Disney West Side,* ☎ *407/938–9653. AE, MC, V.*

Continental

$$$–$$$$ ✕ **Arthur's 27.** Though the 27th-floor view is breathtaking, you may be even more lightheaded when you get your check. Handle the fiscal traumas up front with one of three prix-fixe dinner options. If you order à la carte, you'll probably leave behind a couple of bills with Ben Franklin's picture on them. What you get, however, is a formal dining experience lasting from two to three hours—time to savor the haute cuisine and the sun setting behind the Epcot dome. All entrées come with some kind of heavenly sauce, like the herb-rich garlic sauce with roast loin of lamb. Desserts include a chocolate cake to die for. Word has it that efforts to make the restaurant a little less formal are being made. ⊠ *Buena Vista Palace Resort and Spa, 1900 Buena Vista Dr., Lake Buena Vista,* ☎ *407/827–3450. Reservations essential. AE, D, DC, MC, V.*

Cuban

$–$$$ ✕ **Bongos Cuban Café.** The menu at this Cuban eatery, tucked inside a two-story building shaped like a pineapple, won't make any of the chefs along Miami's Calle Ocho jealous, but it does contain a relatively solid array of choices typical of Cuban eateries in Orlando. There's a decent but pricey paella and a fine rice and chicken casserole jazzed up with other morsels, such as lobster or black beans. Other familiar Cuban offerings include arroz con pollo, *churrasco* (skirt steak), and tasty ham croquettes. The eclectic wine list ranges from a Chilean chardonnay by the glass to Louis-Jadot Pouilly-Fuissé. Try one of three varieties of flan for dessert along with good Cuban coffee, also available at a walk-up bar outside. There's live music at night. ⊠ *Downtown Disney West Side,* ☎ *407/828–0999. Reservations not accepted. AE, D, DC, MC, V.*

Italian

$$–$$$$ ✕ **Portobello Yacht Club.** Operated by Chicago's venerable Levy brothers, this eatery has a much better lineage than the one Disney made up—that the building was the home of Merriweather Adam Pleasure, eponym of Pleasure Island. Of course, Pleasure is fictitious, but pleasurable dining is not. Start with something simple—chewy sourdough bread with roast garlic. Then move on to spaghettini *alla Portobello* (a stick-to-your-ribs pasta dish with scallops, clams, shrimp, mussels, tomatoes, garlic, Portobello mushrooms, and herbs). There's always a fresh-catch special, and a wood-oven pizza has been added—not quite as good as Wolfgang Puck's, but tasty. This is a good spot for a late meal; it's open until midnight. ⊠ *Pleasure Island,* ☎ *407/934–8888. AE, MC, V.*

Mediterranean

$$–$$$$ ✕ **Spoodles.** Chef David Reynoso, a native of Mexico who studied in
★   the United States and Italy, has blended all the best foods of the Mediterranean into a taste that can be sampled through the tapas-style menu (small portions on small plates, and a lot of them). Perhaps the best dish is *rotollo,* a Moroccan flat bread rolled up like a burrito and filled with succulent roasted vegetables, hummus, cucumbers, and *tzatziki* (a yogurtlike sauce). High recommendations also go to the barbecued Moroccan beef skewers with raisin and almond couscous, the spicy black mussel and pepperoni soup with Greek orzo and tomato fennel broth, and the duck sausage pizza. Fittingly, desserts are pan-Mediterranean, too. A $21 sampler lets you taste them all. ⊠ *Board-Walk Inn, Epcot Resort Area,* ☎ *407/939–3463. AE, MC, V.*

Mexican

$–$$ ✕ **Chevy's.** It defies logic to think you'd find anything original across from hotel row, where garish neon signs advertise "bargain" T-shirts and gasoline sells for 20¢ a gallon more than in Orlando. Sure enough, Chevy's is a chain out of California, occupying an ersatz cantina that looks like every Mexican restaurant in every suburb. But the food is a real shocker: it's good—really good. The menu promises that everything is made from fresh ingredients, and it's not just Tourism World hyperbole. Try the hot tamales, a simple dish made perfect by a fresh cornmeal shell and the piquant taste of the chicken, pork, or beef. The menu also includes some gringo creativity, like chicken with Dijon mustard wrapped in a tortilla; a huge burrito made with barbecue and black beans; and a good selection of high-calorie desserts like flan and some fetching cream pies. The screaming-kid quotient is high here, but no more so than at any other establishment at Exit 27. ⊠ *1547 Rte. 535, Lake Buena Vista,* ☎ *407/827–1052. AE, MC, V.*

Seafood

$$–$$$$ ✕ **Fulton's Crab House.** Run by Levy Restaurants, the Chicago com-
★ pany that also operates the nearby Portobello Yacht Club, this nauti-
cal eatery in a faux riverboat is a first-class fish house. Docked in a
man-made lagoon near an entrance to Pleasure Island, it provides
lovely views from the windows lining its three dining decks, matched
by polished, unhurried service. As the name implies, crab is the spe-
cialty, and just like the tourists who consume it, the crab at Fulton's
flies in daily from all over North America. Dungeness crab from the
Atlantic banks, Alaskan king crab, Florida stone crab: It's all served
fresh. A crab sampler offers a taste of just about every variety on the
menu. Other standouts include grilled tuna steak and panfried oysters
served in the shell with spinach and smoked chunks of bacon, but lis-
ten, too, for the chef's recommendations. Steaks and chicken are also
available. ⊠ *Downtown Disney Marketplace,* ☎ *407/934–2628. AE,
MC, V.*

$$–$$$ ✕ **Flying Fish.** One of Disney's better new restaurants, this fine fish house
was created by Martin Dorf, who is also responsible for the Califor-
nia Grill and Citrico's (☞ *above*). The Flying Fish sampler appetizer—
peekytoe crab cakes, seared rare tuna, and barbecued rock shrimp—says
a lot about the kitchen's abilities with seafood. The best of the house
specialties are the potato-wrapped Florida red snapper served with leek-
fennel fondue and the fennel-crusted yellowfin tuna with roasted-egg-
plant mashed potatoes and a lobster-nectar-and-olive tapenade.
Chocolate lovers should save room for Lava Cake, a fine chocolate cake
served warm with a liquid chocolate center, topped with pomegranate
ice cream. There's also a carefully considered wine list, with many choices
available by the glass. ⊠ *Disney's BoardWalk, Epcot Resort Area,* ☎
407/939–3463.

International Drive, Orlando

Take I–4 Exit 28 or 29.

American/Casual

$–$$$ ✕ **Beeline Diner.** As you might expect from its location in the Peabody
Orlando, this slick 1950s-style diner with red-vinyl counter seats is not
exactly cheap, but the salads, sandwiches, and griddle foods are tops.
They do the greatest combo ever—thick, juicy burgers; fries; and heav-
enly milk shakes—just right. Though very busy at times, it can be fun
for breakfast or a late-night snack. And for just a little silver, you get
to play a lot of old tunes on the jukebox. ⊠ *Peabody Orlando, 9801
International Dr.,* ☎ *407/352–4000. AE, D, DC, MC, V.*

Chinese

$$–$$$ ✕ **Ming Court.** Even though this place is on International Drive, a truly
great wall designed to look like a dragon's back blocks out the hubbub and gives an enclosed courtyardlike serenity to this Chinese palace
of a restaurant. A pool with carp greets you at the entrance, and the
elegance continues inside, where you can look out through glass walls
over a beautifully arranged series of floating gardens. The prices are
probably a little higher than what you're used to paying at your local
strip mall, but then the food is probably better, too. Expertly prepared
versions of Chinese restaurant standards are accompanied by some
slightly more unusual dishes like mango chicken and jalapeño beef. Tasteful presentations, ample quantities, and attentive service add to the pleasure of dining here. ⊠ *9188 International Dr.,* ☎ *407/351–9988. AE,
D, DC, MC, V.*

Contemporary

$–$$ ✕ **Cafe Tu Tu Tango.** Multiple kitchens here bombard you with different courses, which arrive in waves if you follow the house custom and order a series of appetizers. Actually, you end up doing this anyway, since the entrées are appetizer size. The menu gives the address—on International Drive—a new meaning. Try the Cajun chicken egg rolls, for instance, with blackened chicken, Greek goat cheese, creole mustard, and tomato salsa, if you want to get a compendium of the world cuisines at one go. For added atmosphere, artists paint at easels while diners watch and sip drinks like the Matisse margarita and the Renoir rum runner. ⊠ *8625 International Dr.,* ☎ *407/248–2222. Reservations not accepted. AE, D, DC, MC, V.*

Thai

$–$$ ✕ **Siam Orchid.** One of Orlando's several elegant Asian restaurants, Siam Orchid occupies a gorgeous structure a bit off I-Drive. Waitresses, who wear costumes from their homeland, serve authentic fare, such as Siam wings (a chicken wing stuffed to look like a drumstick) and *plalad prig* (a whole, deep-fried fish covered with a sauce flavored with red chilies, bell peppers, and garlic). If you like your food spicy, say "Thai hot" and grab a fire extinguisher. ⊠ *7575 Republic Dr.,* ☎ *407/351–0821. AE, DC, MC, V.*

Universal Studios CityWalk, Orlando

Take I–4 Exit 29B if you're heading westbound, 30A if eastbound.

American/Casual

$–$$ ✕ **Hard Rock Cafe Orlando.** We're not saying the Hard Rock hierarchy felt the heat from Johnny-come-lately House of Blues (HOB), which often sells out its live concerts, but we do know that the new Hard Rock offers concert seating for 2,000, big enough to bring in big-name talent that will give HOB and Planet Hollywood a run for their money. The largest Hard Rock in the world, it's still loaded down with memorabilia and still attracts a lot of Universal visitors as well as Orlando Magic players. And, yes, food is even served here. Best bets are the pig sandwich, made of pork shoulder hickory-smoked for 14 hours, and the ⅓-pound cheeseburger with all the trimmings. This place is a rock club and proud of it, so don't go if you can't tolerate noise, which approaches the level of a 747 at takeoff. That noise, incidentally, is by design; it helps the tables turn over faster. Take I–4 Exit 30. ⊠ *5800 S. Kirkman Rd.,* ☎ *407/351–7625. Reservations not accepted. AE, D, DC, MC, V.*

$–$$ ✕ **Jimmy Buffett's Margaritaville.** Even casual Buffett fans can probably guess the top two menu items: a cheeseburger, as in the song "Cheeseburger in Paradise," and the Ultimate Margarita, of "Margaritaville" fame. To our knowledge, he hasn't yet had a hit about that fried fish platter or the stone crab claws, but they're just as tasty. This place doesn't really re-create Key West—though it's usually filled with boisterous and semisober people—but it does try for that Keys feeling. A giant plastic replica of a seaplane adorns the restaurant, along with other Keys-y memorabilia. On special occasions, the Buff-man himself makes an appearance, but most of the time you'll have to be content with a Jimmy Buffett sound-alike who covers most of the middle-aged island boy's songs along with some taped Buffett performances played on big screens hanging from the ceiling. In an effort to be truly thoughtful, management has included an extensive gift shop where you can browse while waiting for a table. ⊠ *Universal Studios Plaza,* ☎ *407/224–9255. Reservations not accepted. AE, D, DC, MC, V.*

Jamaican

$–$$ ✕ **Bob Marley's, A Tribute to Freedom.** With live music that runs almost nonstop all day long, this informal restaurant and reggae club seems more like a tribute to tolerance—that is, how loud a noise the human ear can tolerate. Suffice it to say, you will need to scream your order to your dreadlock-wearing server, assuming he or she will lean over next to your mouth when you speak. The good news is that the music is quite fine, involving mostly reggae musicians from Jamaica. And if you can get over the decibel level, the food is quite tasty. Typical entrées include Jamaican patties (spicy meat patties of pork, lamb, and other meats). The more health-conscious can get a veggie patty, also spicy but minus the meat. Other authentic Jamaican treats include jerk chicken, a spicy grilled treat served on a stick. For an appetizer, go for the Jamin' Platter, which features not only chips and dip but some fresh veggies (to dip) and a few morsels of homemade bread, and you'll probably want to reach for the authentic Jamaican beer, Red Stripe, early and often. ✉ *1000 Universal Studios Plaza,* ☎ *727/224–2262. Reservations not accepted for parties of fewer than 6. AE, D, DC, MC, V.*

Downtown Orlando

Take I–4 Exit 41 if you're heading westbound, Exit 40 if eastbound, unless otherwise noted.

Contemporary

$$$–$$$$ ✕ **Manuel's on the 28th.** How's this for one-upmanship? For a decade
★ Arthur's 27 was Orlando's loftiest restaurant in terms of altitude, with a spot on the 27th floor of the Buena Vista Palace. In 1994 Manuel's on the 28th—as in the 28th floor of the downtown Nations Bank building—opened its doors and was almost immediately hailed by local dining critics as a culinary landmark. In many cases, restaurants with a view offer only that, but the cuisine here is excellent, with stellar offerings like seared loin of lamb in a cayenne and scotch-whiskey sauce, wood-roasted chicken and lobster in coconut-lime sauce, and hickory-grilled Muscovy duck breast with plum-ginger sauce. ✉ *390 N. Orange Ave.,* ☎ *407/246–6580. AE, D, DC, MC, V. Closed Sun.–Mon. No lunch.*

$–$$$ ✕ **Harvey's Bistro.** In the Nations Bank building, within walking distance of the arena and the Centroplex, this clubby café with panel walls and white tablecloths has collected an enthusiastic business crowd at lunch and concert-, theater-, and arena-goers after dark. The menu offers a good selection of bistro and comfort foods. Soups are good, as are the oven-roasted saffron scallops, the duck cassoulet with white and black beans, and the thin-crust pizza with caramelized onions, fresh spinach, and goat cheese. ✉ *390 N. Orlando Ave.,* ☎ *407/246–6560. AE, D, DC, MC, V. Closed Sun. No lunch Sat.*

Eastern European

$$ ✕ **Café Europa.** It tells you something about Orlando's diverse dining when you can sip a hot bowl of borscht in a cozy Eastern European eatery next door to a Hooter's restaurant. Although this quaint little place with flagstone walls and artificial vines hanging from the ceiling may not make you swear you're in Budapest, the food makes a great European sojourn for the palate, and the quiet, sedate atmosphere makes a great change of pace from Orlando's hype and hoopla. The chef does wonderful things with potatoes, including excellent dumplings, which look like round morsels of pasta but have a lighter texture. They are served with beef Stroganoff and Hungarian goulash, both hearty, well-seasoned versions of these traditional stews. Good desserts include home-

made apple strudel and cookies. Take I–4 Exit 38 or 39. ⊠ *Church Street Marketplace, 55 W. Church St.,* ☎ *407/872–3388. AE, DC, MC, V.*

French

$$–$$$$ ✕ **Le Provence Bistro Français.** This charming two-story restaurant in the heart of downtown does a fine imitation of an out-of-the-way bistro on the Left Bank in Paris. Reasonable prices and first-rate service add to the delightful surroundings and excellent food. For lunch try the *salade Niçoise* (with fresh grilled tuna, French string beans, and hard-boiled eggs) or the cassoulet *toulousain* (a hearty mixture of white beans, lamb, pork, and sausage). At dinner you can choose between a six-course prix-fixe menu, a less pricey four-course version, or à la carte options. ⊠ *50 E. Pine St.,* ☎ *407/843–1320. AE, DC, MC, V. Closed Sun. No lunch Sat.*

Elsewhere in Orlando

Contemporary

$$–$$$ ✕ **Chatham's Place.** In Florida, grouper is about as ubiquitous as
★ Coca-Cola, but to discover its full potential, try the grouper here, sautéed in pecan butter and flavored with a hint of cayenne. It's a strong contender for the best dish served in Orlando today. A close second is another house specialty—pan-roasted rack of lamb flavored with a touch of rosemary. Perennially on the best lists of virtually every Florida publication that has a mailing permit, Chatham's was started by two brothers who were Culinary Institute of America grads. Sadly, the surviving brother sold it after the other died. The good news is that the new owners, including chef Tony Lopez, haven't let the standards drop. The decor is adequate but does little to ameliorate the nondescript office-building setting. Nevertheless, the food is worthy of a palace, and the service is as good as it gets in Central Florida. Take I–4 Exit 29. ⊠ *7575 Dr. Phillips Blvd.,* ☎ *407/345–2992. AE, D, DC, MC, V.*

Cuban

$–$$ ✕ **Numero Uno.** To the followers of this long-popular Latin restaurant,
★ the name is quite appropriate. Downtowners have been filling the place at lunch for years. It bills itself as "the home of paella," and that's probably the best dish. If you have time and a good appetite, try the paella *Valenciana* (with yellow rice, sausage, chicken, fish, Spanish spices, and a side order of plantains), which takes an hour and 15 minutes on special order. If you don't have that long, go for traditional Cuban fare like shredded flank steak or the dish that half of Latin America eats daily: arroz con pollo. Take I–4 Exit 34 or 35A. ⊠ *2499 S. Orange Ave.,* ☎ *407/841–3840. AE, D, DC, MC, V.*

French

$$$–$$$$ ✕ **La Coquina.** This restaurant bills itself as French with an Asian influence, and if you sample the pheasant and truffle wonton with foie gras and chives, you'll think this culture combo is quite worthwhile. The hotel culinary staff uses this restaurant as a showcase for its skills, and if you want a closer look, there's a special chef's table dining experience—your party eats in the kitchen—which can be arranged through the restaurant manager. The best meal here is Sunday brunch, whose generous selection of goodies makes the price ($38) seem like a bargain. Take I–4 Exit 27. ⊠ *Hyatt Regency Grand Cypress, 1 Grand Cypress Blvd.,* ☎ *407/239–1234. AE, D, DC, MC, V. Closed in summer.*

$$ ✕ **Le Coq au Vin.** Though Louis Perrotte could run a stuffed-shirt
★ kind of place—his food is as expertly prepared as any you'll find in town—instead he chooses the self-effacing route, running a modest lit-

tle kitchen in a small but charming house in south Orlando. Perrotte and his wife, Magdalena, who acts as hostess, make the place warm and homey, and it is usually filled with friendly Orlando residents. The traditional French fare roused *Vogue*'s restaurant critic to raves: homemade chicken liver pâté, fresh rainbow trout with champagne sauce, and Long Island duck with green peppercorns. For dessert try crème brûlée and pat yourself on the back for discovering a place that few tourists know about. Ask to be seated in the main dining room—it's the center of action. Take I–4 Exit 34 or 35. ✉ *4800 S. Orange Ave.,* ☎ *407/851–6980. AE, DC, MC, V. Closed Mon.*

Italian

$$ ✕ **Gargi's Italian Restaurant.** When Amtrak rolls by on the nearby tracks, it seems like you're still on the *Earthquake* ride at Universal Studios. If you don't mind a tremor or two, you're in for some of the best pasta in Florida at this mom-and-pop eatery across the street from a quiet lake. If you crave old-fashioned spaghetti and meatballs, lasagna, or manicotti made with sauces that you know have been simmering all day, this storefront hole-in-the-wall is the place. If you want more than basic pasta, try some of the specialties, like the veal marsala or tasty shrimp with marinara sauce and peppers over linguine. The place is notorious for slow service—but worth it. Take I–4 Exit 42. ✉ *1421 N. Orange Ave.,* ☎ *407/894–7907. AE, MC, V. Beer and wine only. Closed Sun.*

Steak

$$–$$$ ✕ **White Horse Saloon.** Cattle ranchers would love this, the only hoedown kind of place we know of in a top-notch hotel. They would be mighty pleased at the way this western-theme saloon in the Hyatt Regency Grand Cypress sells its products: You can get a barbecued half chicken for 20 bucks or pay a dollar more for prime rib. If you want to go for the 28-ounce beef worshiper's cut—that's 1½ pounds of corn-fed beef—it's $46. All entrées come with sourdough bread, baked or mashed potatoes, and your choice of creamed spinach or corn on the cob. A hearty, hot apple pie with cinnamon-raisin sauce awaits those desperadoes who can still handle dessert. You also get music with your victuals. The Hand-Picked Trio, which has been here for years, plays in the evenings. Take I–4 Exit 27. ✉ *Hyatt Regency Grand Cypress, 1 Grand Cypress Blvd.,* ☎ *407/239–1234. AE, DC, MC, V.*

$–$$$ ✕ **Linda's La Cantina.** This place takes beef very seriously, as you can tell by the disclaimer on the menu: "We cannot be responsible for steaks cooked medium-well and well done." Despite that stuffy-sounding caveat, this down-home eatery has been a favorite among locals since the Eisenhower administration, thanks to its straightforward approach to well-prepared, tender beef. The menu is short and to the point, including about a dozen steak dishes and just enough ancillary items to fill up a page. Among the best is the La Cantina large T-bone—more beef than most can handle, for $22. With every entrée you get a heaping order of spaghetti or a baked potato. Take I–4 Exit 41 if you're heading westbound, Exit 40 if eastbound. ✉ *4721 E. Colonial Dr.,* ☎ *407/894–4491. AE, D, MC, V.*

Vietnamese

$ ✕ **Little Saigon.** The friendly folks here love to introduce novices to
★   their healthy and delicious national cuisine. Sample the spring rolls or the summer rolls (spring roll filling in a soft wrapper). Then move on to the grilled pork and egg, served atop rice and noodles, or the traditional soup, filled with noodles, rice, vegetables, and your choice of either chicken or seafood; ask to have extra meat in the soup if you're hungry, and be sure they bring you the mint and bean sprouts to sprin-

kle in. If you're unfamiliar with the cuisine, request an English-speaking waiter. Take I–4 Exit 41 if you're heading westbound, Exit 40 if eastbound. ⊠ *1106 E. Colonial Dr.,* ☏ *407/423–8539. MC, V. Beer and wine only.*

Outlying Towns

Contemporary

$ ✕ **Dexter's.** This hip college bar is so nondescript on the outside that the facade almost blends into the coin laundry next door. But inside you'll find a popular, trendy eatery and winery sophisticated enough to offer its own wine label and publish a monthly newsletter for those who appreciate a good vintage. Much of the clientele comes from Rollins College, a block away, and the SoHo-like menu reflects that. If you are over 40, however, you won't feel out of place. One of the best entrées is chicken tortilla pie (a stack of cheese-laden tortillas that's more spaceship than pie). Jazz is frequently featured at night. Take I–4 Exit 45. If you're not up for an evening among the young coeds, try Dexter's of Thornton Park, in the trendy, gentrified Thornton Park neighborhood, just east of downtown Orlando. You may be the only tourist there. ⊠ *200 W. Fairbanks Ave., Winter Park,* ☏ *407/629–1150;* ⊠ *808 E. Washington St., Orlando,* ☏ *407/648–2777. Reservations not accepted. AE, D, DC, MC, V.*

Continental

$$$$ ✕ **Chalet Suzanne.** If you like to drive, are on your way south, or are
★   visiting Cypress Gardens or Bok Tower Gardens, consider making time for a scrumptious and relaxing meal at this family-owned country inn. Because of its charm and originality, Chalet Suzanne has earned praise from restaurant critics and might provide one of the most memorable dining experiences of your stay. Expanded bit by quirky bit since it opened in the 1930s, this unlikely inn looks like a small Swiss village plopped in the middle of orange groves by way of the Mediterranean. Come for the traditional six-course dinner or for a sophisticated breakfast of eggs Benedict or Swedish pancakes with lingonberries. Sitting in the antiques-filled dining room and watching turtles play in the lake or ibis meander on the lawn is the perfect way to start your day. Take I–4 Exit 23. The restaurant is about 2 mi south of the Cypress Gardens turnoff on U.S. 27. ⊠ *3800 Chalet Suzanne Dr., Lake Wales,* ☏ *941/676–6011. AE, DC, MC, V. Closed Mon. in summer.*

Italian

$$–$$$ ✕ **Enzo's on the Lake.** Enzo's is one of Orlando foodies' favorite
★   restaurants, even though it's on a tacky stretch of highway filled with used-car lots. The Roman charmer who owns the place, Enzo Perlini, has turned a rather ordinary lakefront house into an Italian villa. It's worth the trip, about 30 minutes from I-Drive, to sample the antipasti. Mussels, cooked in a heady broth of white wine and garlic, and the mild *buffalo* mozzarella cheese, flown in from Italy, make equally good starters. The *bucatini à la Enzo* (sautéed bacon, mushrooms, and peas served over long hollow noodles) is a very popular house specialty. Take I–4 Exit 49. ⊠ *1130 S. U.S. 17–92, Longwood,* ☏ *407/834–9872. AE, DC, MC, V. Closed Sun.*

$$ ✕ **La Scala.** Mirrored walls and gracious, sophisticated decor make this one of the area's most romantic restaurants. The fact that owner Joseph del Vento, a former opera singer who once worked in New York's Tre Scalini, breaks into song every so often only adds to the charm. For pasta, order the dish called Chop, Chop, Chop (fresh seafood sautéed table-side, doused in marinara sauce, and served over fettuccine). Take

I–4 Exit 48. ⊠ *205 Loraine Dr., Altamonte Springs,* ☎ *407/862–3257. AE, DC, MC, V. Closed Sun. No lunch Sat.*

Seafood

$$ ✕ **Gina's on the Water.** The waterfront location is almost a technicality;
★ the postage stamp–size Crane's Roost Lake is actually across the street.
But guests don't come for the proximity to the water. They come because the Italian seafood restaurant is one of the best way-too-small eateries around. It serves all sorts of tasty tuna, grouper, snapper, and salmon entrées, as well as some decent landlubber options. Traditional Italian pasta dishes are dispensed from an open-air, stage-front-style upstairs kitchen, while a quiet downstairs bar area affords views of the lake or the current football game (on several TVs). Save room for the tiramisu. Take I–4 Exit 48. ⊠ *309 N. Lake Blvd., Altamonte Springs,* ☎ *407/834–5880. AE, D, MC, V.*

LODGING

Your basic options come down to properties that are (1) owned and operated by Disney on WDW grounds, (2) not owned or operated by Disney but on Disney property, and (3) not on WDW property. There are advantages to each. If you are coming to Orlando for only a few days and are interested solely in the Magic Kingdom, Epcot, and the other Disney attractions, the resorts on Disney property—whether or not they're owned by Disney—are the most convenient. But if you plan to spend time sightseeing in and around Orlando, it makes sense to look into the alternatives. On-site hotels are generally more expensive, though there are now some moderately priced establishments on Disney property. But Orlando is not huge, and even apparently distant properties are only a half hour's drive from Disney entrance gates. As a rule, the greater the distance from Walt Disney World Resort, the lower the room rates.

Reservations should be made several months in advance—as much as a year in advance for the best rooms during high season (historically, Christmas vacation, summer, and from mid-February through the week after Easter). Many hotels and attractions offer discounts up to 40% from September to mid-December. Orlando lodging prices tend to be a little higher than elsewhere in Florida, but in all but the smallest motels there is little or no charge for children under 18 who share a room with an adult.

In WDW: Disney-Owned Properties

For locations of these properties, *see* the Walt Disney World Resort map. Reservations may be booked through **WDW Central Reservations** (⊠ Box 10100, Lake Buena Vista 32830, ☎ 407/934–7639); for same-day reservations contact the number listed for the individual property.

Magic Kingdom Resort Area
Take I–4 Exit 24C, 25B, or 26B.

$$$$ 🏨 **Grand Floridian.** As you'll see from the rates, this is what Disney
★ considers its top hotel. It appears to have been transported brick by brick from some Victorian-era coastal hot spot to the shores of the Seven Seas Lagoon. Actually, the gabled red roof, brick chimneys, rambling verandas, and delicate gingerbread are grand-old yet brand-new. Serious attention was paid to each detail, from the crystal chandeliers and stained-glass domes to the ornate balconies and aviary. Although equipped with every modern convenience, the moss-green and salmon-pink rooms, with Victorian wallpaper and wall hangings, have real vin-

tage charm, especially the attic nooks. ☎ *407/824–3000,* FAX *407/824–3186. 900 rooms, 90 suites. 6 restaurants, 3 lobby lounges, pool, beauty salon, hot tub, 2 tennis courts, croquet, health club, volleyball, beach, boating, waterskiing, baby-sitting, children's programs, playground, coin laundry, laundry service, concierge. AE, MC, V.*

$$$$ 🏨 **Polynesian Resort.** If it weren't for the kids in Mickey Mouse caps, you might think you were in Fiji. A three-story tropical atrium fills the lobby. Orchids bloom alongside coconut palms and banana trees, and water cascades from volcanic rock fountains. Rooms offer two queen-size beds and a twin bed in the living room, accommodating five. Lagoon-view rooms—which overlook the Electrical Water Pageant—are the most peaceful and the priciest, and most units have a balcony or patio. Both pools—one an extravagantly landscaped, free-form affair with rocks and caverns—are beloved by children; for quiet, head for the beach. Monorail, bus, and motor launch lines network at this always-popular resort. ☎ *407/824–2000,* FAX *407/824–3174. 848 rooms, 5 suites. 3 restaurants, lobby lounge, snack bar, 2 pools, volleyball, beach, boating, waterskiing, baby-sitting, children's programs, playground, coin laundry, laundry service, concierge floor. AE, MC, V.*

$$$–$$$$ 🏨 **Contemporary Resort.** Even though this awkwardly modern, 15-story, flat-top pyramid is old enough for current parents to have dreamed of riding into it on the monorail when they were kids, it remains current. Looking like an intergalactic docking bay, the ideally situated resort bustles from dawn to after midnight. Half the rooms are in the Tower, the main building, and you'll have to pay extra for their spectacular views. Those in front look out on Cinderella Castle and Space Mountain, flaming sunsets, and the fireworks show; those in back have ringside views of the Electrical Water Pageant and sunrise over misty Bay Lake. All have a small terrace. ☎ *407/824–1000,* FAX *407/824–3539. 972 rooms, 36 suites. 3 restaurants, 2 lobby lounges, snack bar, 3 pools, beauty salon, 6 tennis courts, health club, shuffleboard, volleyball, beach, boating, waterskiing, baby-sitting, children's programs, playground, coin laundry, laundry service, concierge. AE, MC, V.*

$$$–$$$$ 🏨 **Wilderness Lodge.** This seven-story hostelry was modeled after the
★ turn-of-the-century lodges of national parks out west. Of course, Disney does everything bigger and grander than does history. Supported by great tree trunks, the towering five-story lobby features a huge three-sided fireplace made of rocks from the Grand Canyon, illuminated by enormous tepee-shape chandeliers. Rooms have western motifs—leather chairs, patchwork quilts, and cowboy art. Each has a balcony or a patio and two queen beds or, on request, a queen and two bunk beds. The hotel's showstopper is its Fire Rock Geyser, a sort of faux Old Faithful, near the large pool, which itself begins as a hot spring in the lobby. Motor launches and buses connect here. ☎ *407/824–3200,* FAX *407/824–3232. 728 rooms, 31 suites. 2 restaurants, 2 lobby lounges, pool, wading pool, beach, boating, waterskiing, bicycles, baby-sitting, children's programs, coin laundry, laundry service. AE, MC, V.*

$–$$$$ ⚠ **Fort Wilderness Resort and Campground.** For a calm spot amid the
★ theme-park storm, go no farther than the 700 acres of scrubby pine and tiny streams known as Fort Wilderness, on Bay Lake and about a mile from the Wilderness Lodge. Sports facilities abound, bike trails are popular, and a marina rents sailboats. Bringing a tent or RV is one of the cheapest ways to stay on WDW property, especially since sites, with outdoor grills and picnic tables, accommodate up to 10. If you don't have your own RV and don't want to camp out, you can rent one of the fully equipped, air-conditioned trailers, known as Wilderness Homes; they're perfectly comfortable. Larger trailers accommodate four grown-ups and two youngsters; the bedroom has a double bed and a bunk bed, and the living room has a double sleeper sofa or

Murphy bed. Smaller trailers, without the bunk beds, sleep four. Both types come with full kitchen, dishes, linens, a comfortable bathroom, daily housekeeping services, an outdoor grill and picnic table, and cable TV. ☎ 407/824–2900. *783 campsites, 408 60- and 80-ft trailers. Cafeteria, grocery, snack bar, 2 pools, 2 tennis courts, basketball, horseback riding, shuffleboard, volleyball, beach, boating, bicycles, playground, coin laundry. AE, MC, V.*

Epcot Resort Area
Take I–4 Exit 25B or 26B.

$$$$ 🏨 **BoardWalk Inn and Villas.** This Disney hotel brings back all the cotton-candy enchantment of America's great amusement piers. The most
★   famous was at Atlantic City, re-created by Disney at its BoardWalk area. As part of the complex, WDW's noted architectural master, Robert A. M. Stern, has designed this inn, WDW's smallest and most intimate deluxe hotel, which features 19th-century New England architecture. The pool complex includes a 200-ft water slide in the form of a classic wooden roller coaster. Bus, tram, and motor launch lines access the parks, and you can walk to Epcot. ☎ 407/939–5100 Inn; 407/939–6200 Villas, ℻ 407/939–5150. *378 rooms, 20 suites, 383 villas. 3 restaurants, lobby lounge, pool, tennis court, croquet, exercise room, shops, nightclub, baby-sitting, laundry service, concierge, convention center. AE, MC, V.*

$$$$ 🏨 **Yacht and Beach Club Resorts.** Straight out of a Cape Cod summer,
★   these two properties on a 25-acre lake are coastal inns on a grand Disney scale. The five-story Yacht Club recalls turn-of-the-century New England seacoast resorts, with its hardwood floors, lobby full of gleaming brass and polished leather, oyster-gray clapboard facade, and evergreen landscaping; there's even a lighthouse on its pier. Rooms are similarly nautical, with white-and-blue naval flags on the bedspreads and a small ship's wheel on the headboard. Drawing on similar inspiration is the blue-and-white three- to five-story Beach Club, where a croquet lawn and cabana-dotted white-sand beach set the scene. Guest rooms are summery, with wicker and pastel furnishings. Both establishments are refreshingly unstuffy, just right for families. ☎ 407/934–8000 for beach; 407/934–7000 for yacht, ℻ 407/934–3850 for beach; 407/934–3450 for yacht. *1,213 rooms, 112 suites. 4 restaurants, 3 lobby lounges, snack bar, 3 pools, beauty salon, 2 tennis courts, croquet, health club, volleyball, beach, boating, baby-sitting, laundry service, concierge. AE, MC, V.*

$$–$$$ 🏨 **Caribbean Beach Resort.** Talk about tropical punch! Awash in dizzy-
★   ing Caribbean colors, this smashing hotel was the first of Disney's moderately priced accommodations. Just east of Epcot and Disney–MGM Studios and surrounding 42-acre Barefoot Bay, this property comprises five palm-studded "villages" named for Caribbean islands. Each has its own pool (one even has a pirate fort), but all share a white-sand beach. Bridges over the lake connect to the 1-acre path-crossed Parrot Cay, where there's a play area. A 1-mi-long promenade circling the lake is favored by bikers, joggers, and romantic strollers. At the resort's hub, a complex called Old Port Royale, decorated with pirates' cannons and tropical birds, has stores, a food court, and a tropical lounge. Bus lines network to all parks. ☎ 407/934–3400, ℻ 407/934–3288. *2,112 rooms. Restaurant, food court, lobby lounge, 7 pools, wading pool, hot tub, jogging, beach, boating, bicycles, baby-sitting, playground, coin laundry, laundry service. AE, MC, V.*

$$–$$$ 🏨 **Coronado Springs Resort.** This moderately priced hotel serves two
★   constituencies. Because of its on-property 95,000-square-ft convention center, it's popular with business groups. But its casual southwestern architectural style; its lively Mexican-style Pepper Market food court;

and its elaborate swimming pool complex, complete with a Maya pyramid overlooking the big water slide, attract a good number of family vacationers as well. The hotel is close to both Epcot and Disney's Animal Kingdom. ☎ 407/939–1000, FAX 407/939–1001. 1,967 rooms. *2 restaurants, bar, food court, 4 pools, beauty salon, health club, boating, bicycles, laundry service, convention center. AE, MC, V.*

Downtown Disney/Lake Buena Vista/ WDW Resort Area
Take I–4 Exit 27.

$$$ 🏨 **Dixie Landings Resort.** Disney's Imagineers drew inspiration from the Old South for this sprawling, moderately priced resort northwest of Downtown Disney and Lake Buena Vista. Rooms, in three-story plantation-style mansions and rustic two-story bayou dwellings, are all the same size and accommodate up to four in two double beds. Elegantly decorated, they have wooden armoires and gleaming brass faucets. Guest registration looks like a steamboat interior, and a 3½-acre old-fashioned swimming-hole complex called Ol' Man Island is, in fact, a pool with slides, rope swings, and an adjacent play area. ☎ 407/934–6000, FAX 407/934–5777. 2,048 rooms. *Restaurant, food court, lobby lounge, 6 pools, wading pool, hot tub, boating, baby-sitting, playground, coin laundry, laundry service. AE, MC, V.*

$$$ 🏨 **Port Orleans Resort.** Disney's version of New Orleans's French Quarter emulates the charm and romance of the original. Ornate row houses with wrought-iron balconies overgrown with vines are clustered around squares lushly planted with magnolias. Walking on the lamp-lighted sidewalks that edge the complex's alleyways, you might find yourself on Bourbon Street, since routes are named for French Quarter thoroughfares. The food court serves up such Crescent City specialties as jambalaya and beignets (fritters), in addition to standards, and Bonfamille's Café offers varied Louisiana-style fare. Kids love the large, free-form Doubloon Lagoon, one of Disney's most exotic pools. ☎ 407/934–5000, FAX 407/934–5353. 1,008 rooms. *Restaurant, food court, lobby lounge, pool, wading pool, hot tub, croquet, boating, bicycles, baby-sitting, coin laundry, laundry service, concierge. AE, MC, V.*

All-Star Village
Take I–4 Exit 25B.

$–$$ 🏨 **All-Star Sports and All-Star Music Resorts.** What could Americans possibly love more than Mickey Mouse? Sports and music, perhaps. The buildings here carry out five sports themes (baseball, football, tennis, surfing, and basketball) and five music themes (Broadway, country, jazz, rock, and calypso). Don't worry about being able to tell them apart; gargantuan exterior ornamentation defines each theme. Stairwells shaped like giant bongos frame Calypso, while at Sports, you'll find 30-ft tennis rackets striking balls the size of small cars. These resorts mark Disney's entry into the economy-priced hotel market, and so, beneath the elaborate packaging, they're basically well-maintained motels. Each room has two double beds, a closet rod, an armoire, and a desk. The End Zone and Intermission food courts offer a predictable selection of fast foods. In 1999 the equally huge All-Star Movies made its premiere with similar facilities and appropriately themed architecture. ☎ 407/939–5000 for sports; 407/939–6000 for music, FAX 407/ 939–7333 for sports; 407/939–7222 for music. 1,920 rooms at each. *2 bars, 2 food courts, 4 pools, baby-sitting, playground, coin laundry, laundry service. AE, MC, V.*

In WDW: Other Hotels

For locations of these properties, *see* the Orlando Lodging map. Epcot Resort Area hotels are also noted on the Walt Disney World Resort map.

Epcot Resort Area
Take I–4 Exit 25B or 26B.

$$$$ ★ ⊡ **Walt Disney World Dolphin.** Two mythical 56-ft sea creatures bracket the 27-story glass pyramid—one of the tallest structures at WDW—that is the central part of this Michael Graves–designed hotel. Though this pyramid hardly qualifies as a Wonder of the World, it's a wonder nonetheless. Outside, a waterfall cascades down from seashell to seashell into a 54-ft-wide clamshell supported by giant dolphin sculptures. Inside, the fabric-draped lobby resembles a giant sultan's tent, and monkey-shape chandeliers are matched by equally jocular palm tree–shape lamps in rooms. The best units overlook Epcot and its nightly fireworks. The Grotto Pool features a high-speed water slide. ⊠ *1500 Epcot Resorts Blvd., Lake Buena Vista 32830-2653,* ☎ *407/934–4000 or 800/227–1500,* FAX *407/934–4884. 1,369 rooms, 140 suites. 7 restaurants, 3 lobby lounges, 4 pools, beauty salon, 4 tennis courts, exercise room, beach, boating, children's programs, concierge. AE, D, MC, V.*

$$$$ ⊡ **Walt Disney World Swan.** Facing its twin, the Dolphin, across Crescent Lake, this is another example of the postmodern "Learning from Las Vegas" school of entertainment architecture characteristic of Michael Graves. Two 45-ft swans grace the rooftop of this coral-and-aquamarine hotel, connected to the Dolphin by a covered causeway. Guest rooms, in a 12-story main building and two seven-story wings, are quirkily decorated with floral and geometric patterns, pineapples painted on furniture, and exotic bird-shape lamps. Rooms are a bit plusher than at the Dolphin, but the price reflects that. A quiet piano bar near the lobby is actually a coffee bar. ⊠ *1200 Epcot Resorts Blvd., Lake Buena Vista 32830,* ☎ *407/934–3000 or 800/248–7926,* FAX *407/934–4499. 758 rooms. 4 restaurants, 3 lobby lounges, 2 pools, 4 tennis courts, health club, beach, boating, baby-sitting, concierge. AE, DC, MC, V.*

Downtown Disney/Lake Buena Vista/ WDW Resort Area
Take I–4 Exit 27.

$$$–$$$$ ★ ⊡ **Hilton at WDW Resort.** An ingeniously designed waterfall tumbles off the covered entrance and into a stone fountain surrounded by palm trees so hefty you'd think they were on steroids. Another fountain adorns the lobby, which is enlivened by shell-shape cornices and two large tanks of tropical fish. Although not huge, guest rooms in bright yellow and mauve are cheery, cozy, and contemporary. Prices vary dramatically from one location, floor, and season to another. A seafood buffet in the lobby (around 6 PM) tantalizes with wonderful smells of shrimp and salmon. The Vacation Station, a hotel within a hotel, is aimed at kids. ⊠ *1751 Hotel Plaza Blvd., 32830,* ☎ *407/827–4000 or 800/782–4414,* FAX *407/827–6369. 787 rooms, 27 suites. 7 restaurants, lobby lounge, 3 pools, outdoor hot tub, health club, baby-sitting, children's program, coin laundry, laundry service, business center. AE, DC, MC, V.*

$$$–$$$$ ⊡ **Royal Plaza.** The hotel bills itself as the place where Burt Reynolds and Barbara Mandrell (apparently experts on fine hotels) stay when in Orlando. We frankly can't understand why. It's nice and comfortable and convenient, but it is not to die for. You can book the suites

Note: For Disney-owned accommodations, see the Walt Disney World Resort map.

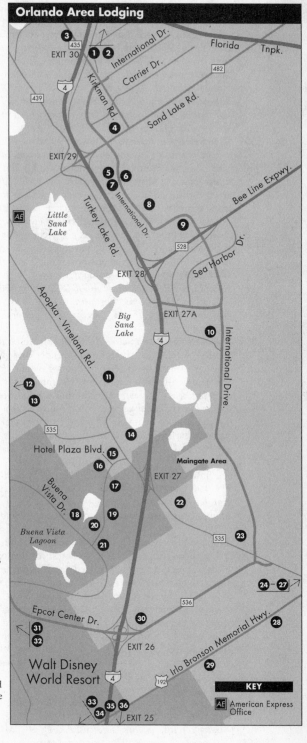

Orlando Area Lodging

where the two celebrities stay—with photos, gold records, and other memorabilia they donated. Otherwise, you'll get a comfortable but not extravagant unit decorated in earth tones with multicolor bedspreads. Each has a terrace or balcony, and the best overlook the pool. The casual, lively hotel is popular with families. If you're a golfer, you'll like the advance-reservation privileges at five nearby courses. ⊠ *1905 Hotel Plaza Blvd., 32830,* ☎ *407/828–2828 or 800/248–7890,* ℻ *407/828–8046. 394 rooms, 21 suites. Restaurant, 2 bars, grill, pool, hot tub, sauna, 4 tennis courts, baby-sitting, children's program, laundry service. AE, D, DC, MC, V.*

$$$–$$$$ 🏨 **Travelodge at Downtown Disney.** The word *Travelodge* may not conjure up visions of unparalleled luxury, but you may be surprised here. The lobby, for instance, has achieved the kind of manufactured rainforest look that virtually every Central Florida hotel strives for. Deep green bird-of-paradise–pattern carpet, lush plants, a winding two-story staircase, and big, broad wicker chairs lend a warm feeling. Though otherwise unexceptional, this is a quality property and a good choice for families. Guest rooms are decorated with touches of brass and hues of baby blue, peach, and soft green. Each comes with a king-size or two double beds and private balcony. For nightly entertainment—and great vistas of Epcot—head for Topper's, on the 18th floor. ⊠ *2000 Hotel Plaza Blvd., 32830,* ☎ *407/828–2424 or 800/348–3765,* ℻ *407/828–8933. 325 rooms. Restaurant, lobby lounge, snack bar, pool, wading pool, playground, coin laundry, laundry service. AE, D, DC, MC, V.*

$$$ 🏨 **DoubleTree Guest Suites.** It's probably no accident that there's no ★ picture of the hotel's exterior—lavender and pink with dark blue awnings—on the brochure. The interior is another story. Comfortable one- and two-bedroom suites are decorated in tasteful hues, with gray carpeting and blond wood furniture. Each bedroom has either a king-size bed or two doubles, and living rooms have a foldout sofa, so it's possible to sleep 10 if you can stand a spring break–style crowd. Units come with a TV in each room plus another in the bathroom, a fridge, wet bar, and coffeemaker; microwaves are available on request. The smallish lobby has a charming feature—a small aviary with birds from South America and Africa. ⊠ *2305 Hotel Plaza Blvd., 32830,* ☎ *407/934–1000 or 800/222–8733,* ℻ *407/934–1011. 239 suites. Restaurant, bar, ice cream parlor, lobby lounge, pool, wading pool, hot tub, 2 tennis courts, exercise room, coin laundry, laundry service. AE, DC, MC, V.*

$$–$$$ 🏨 **Buena Vista Palace Resort and Spa at WDW Resort.** The rumor that ★ this renamed property was in a contest for the longest hotel name is untrue. Several resorts here added "at Walt Disney World Resort" to their names when Downtown Disney was rechristened. The sand-color tower, the largest hotel at Lake Buena Vista, looks a little like an insurance company, but don't be fooled. It's a very elegant hotel featuring the largest health and beauty spa in the area. Upper-floor rooms in the main hotel are more expensive; the best ones look out toward Epcot's Spaceship Earth. Suites in the adjacent Island Resort accommodate up to eight. All rooms have balconies or patios. ⊠ *1900 Buena Vista Dr., 32830,* ☎ *407/827–2727 or 800/327–2990,* ℻ *407/827–6034. 1,014 rooms. 4 restaurants, 4 lobby lounges, patisserie, snack bar, 2 pools, wading pool, hot tub, spa, 3 tennis courts, health club, volleyball, baby-sitting, children's program, playground, coin laundry, laundry service, business services. AE, D, DC, MC, V.*

$$–$$$ 🏨 **Grosvenor Resort.** The nondescript pink high-rise across from Downtown Disney looks like a VA hospital on the outside but is quite pleasant on the inside. Offering a wealth of facilities and comfortable rooms for a fair price, this member of the Best Western chain is a good

deal in the neighborhood. Rooms are average in size but colorfully decorated and filled with amenities. Blond wood furniture and rose-color carpeting give them a homey feeling, while spacious public areas have Colonial-Caribbean decor. Baskerville's, festooned with Sherlock Holmes memorabilia, hosts a Saturday murder-mystery dinner show. ⊠ *1850 Hotel Plaza Blvd., 32830,* ☎ *407/828–4444 or 800/624–4109,* ℻ *407/828–8192. 629 rooms, 6 suites. 2 restaurants, cafeteria, lobby lounge, 2 pools, wading pool, hot tub, 2 tennis courts, basketball, volleyball, playground, coin laundry, laundry service. AE, DC, MC, V.*

$$ 🏨 **Courtyard by Marriott at WDW Resort.** A 14-story atrium accented with gazebos, white-tile trim, and tropical gardens creates a tranquil place to enjoy a gourmet breakfast under white umbrellas. By evening activity has shifted to the Tipsy Parrot, the hotel's welcoming bar. Guest rooms are Marriott-modern and feature handy coffeemakers. ⊠ *1805 Hotel Plaza Blvd., 32830,* ☎ *407/828–8888 or 800/223–9930,* ℻ *407/827–4623. 323 rooms. Restaurant, lobby lounge, 2 pools, wading pool, hot tub, exercise room, playground, coin laundry, laundry service. AE, DC, MC, V.*

Orlando

International Drive
Take I–4 Exit 28 or 29.

If you plan to visit other attractions besides Walt Disney World, the sprawl of newish hotels, restaurants, and shopping malls known as International Drive—"I-Drive" to locals and "Florida Center" in formal parlance—makes a convenient base. Parallel to I–4, it's just a few minutes south of downtown Orlando. It's also near SeaWorld, Universal Studios, Wet 'n Wild, and several popular dinner theaters.

$$$$ 🏨 **Peabody Orlando.** At 11 AM, the celebrated Peabody ducks exit a
★ private elevator into the marble-floor lobby and waddle across a red carpet to the little marble fountain where they pass the day: Eat your heart out, Donald. At 5 the marching mallards repeat the ritual in reverse. Built by the owners of the landmark Peabody Hotel in Memphis, this 27-story structure looks like three high-rise offices from afar, but don't be put off by its austere exterior. The interior is impressive and handsome. The most panoramic of the oversize beige-and-cream rooms have views of WDW. Across from the Orange County Convention Center, the hotel attracts rock stars and other performers, conventioneers, and duck lovers. An additional 800 rooms will be added by 2000. ⊠ *9801 International Dr., 32819,* ☎ *407/352–4000 or 800/732–2639,* ℻ *407/351–9177. 891 rooms. 3 restaurants, 2 lobby lounges, pool, wading pool, hot tub, spa, golf privileges, 4 tennis courts, health club, baby-sitting, concierge. AE, D, DC, MC, V.*

$$$–$$$$ 🏨 **Summerfield Suites Hotel.** "Time to go to bed, kids—yes!—in your own room." How many times have you wanted to say that on your vacation? Sleeping from four to eight people, the one- and two-bedroom units at the all-suites Summerfield are a great option for families. Parents relish the chance for a little peace, and youngsters enjoy the feeling of grown-up privacy and, more important, the chance to control their own TV fate—there's a box in each room. Two-bedroom units, the most popular, have fully equipped kitchens, plus a living room with TV and VCR. Plush landscaping manages to give the place a secluded feel even though it's on International Drive. ⊠ *8480 International Dr., 32819,* ☎ *407/352–2400 or 800/830–4964,* ℻ *407/352–4631. 146 suites. Grocery, lobby lounge, pool, wading pool, hot tub, exercise room, coin laundry, laundry service. AE, D, DC, MC, V.*

$$$ 🏨 **Parc Corniche Resort.** A good bet for golf enthusiasts, the resort is framed by a Joe Lee–designed course. Each of the one- and two-bedroom suites is decked out in pastels and tropical patterns and has a patio or balcony with a golf course view, as well as a kitchen. The largest accommodations, with two bedrooms and two baths, can sleep six. A complimentary Continental breakfast is served daily, and SeaWorld is only a few blocks away. ⊠ *6300 Parc Corniche Dr., 32821,* ☎ *407/ 239–7100 or 800/446–2721,* ℻ *407/239–8501. 90 1-bedroom suites, 120 2-bedroom suites. Restaurant, lobby lounge, pool, wading pool, hot tub, 18-hole golf course, baby-sitting, playground, coin laundry, laundry service. AE, D, DC, MC, V.*

$$–$$$$ 🏨 **Embassy Suites International Drive South.** Another of the all-suite chain of hotels, this member has an expansive lobby with marble floors, pillars, hanging lamps, and old-fashioned ceiling fans. Tropical gardens with mossy rock fountains and palm trees add to the atrium's distinctive southern ambience. Elsewhere, ceramic tile walkways and brick arches complement the tropical mood. ⊠ *8978 International Dr., 32819,* ☎ *407/352–1400 or 800/433–7275,* ℻ *407/ 363–1120. 244 suites. Restaurant, lobby lounge, indoor pool, hot tub, sauna, steam room. AE, D, DC, MC, V.*

$$–$$$ 🏨 **Enclave Suites at Orlando.** With three 10-story buildings surrounding an office, restaurant, and recreation area, this all-suite lodging is less a hotel than a condominium complex. What you would spend for a room in a fancy hotel gets you a complete apartment here, with significantly more space than you'll find in other all-suite hotels. Accommodating up to six, the units have full kitchens, living rooms, two bedrooms, and small terraces. ⊠ *6165 Carrier Dr., 32819,* ☎ *407/351– 1155 or 800/457–0077,* ℻ *407/351–2001. 352 suites. Grocery, 1 indoor and 2 outdoor pools, hot tub, tennis court, exercise room, playground, coin laundry, laundry service. AE, D, DC, MC, V.*

$$ 🏨 **Wynfield Inn–Westwood.** If you don't want a room with just the bare essentials yet don't have the budget for luxury, this two-story motel is a find. The staff is friendly and helpful and acts more like the do-anything-to-please staff of an independent motel. Complimentary coffee and tea are served daily. ⊠ *6263 Westwood Blvd., 32821,* ☎ *407/ 345–8000 or 800/346–1551,* ℻ *407/345–1508. 299 rooms. Restaurant, bar, 2 pools, coin laundry, laundry service. AE, D, DC, MC, V.*

$ 🏨 **Fairfield Inn by Marriott.** This understated, few-frills three-story hotel—the Marriott Corporation's answer to the Motel 6 and Econolodge chains—is a natural for single travelers or small families on a tight budget. It's squeezed between International Drive and the highway and doesn't have the amenities of top-of-the-line Marriott properties, but nice perks such as complimentary coffee and tea, free local phone calls, and cable TV give a sense of being at a much fancier property. ⊠ *8342 Jamaican Ct., 32819,* ☎ *407/363–1944 or 800/228–2800,* ℻ *407/363–1944. 134 rooms. Pool. AE, D, DC, MC, V.*

Downtown Disney/Lake Buena Vista Area
Take I–4 Exit 27.

In addition to the Disney-owned and non-Disney-owned resorts clustered on Disney property not far from Downtown Disney, there are a number of nearby hotels unaffiliated with Walt Disney World Resort. Just outside the park's northernmost entrance, they tend to be sprawling, high-quality resorts catering to WDW vacationers.

$$$$ 🏨 **Hyatt Regency Grand Cypress Resort.** On more than 1,500 acres,
★   Orlando's most spectacular resort offers virtually every facility and then some—even a 45-acre nature preserve. Golf facilities, including a high-tech golf school, are first class. The huge, 800,000-gallon pool resembles

an enormous grotto, has a 45-ft water slide, and is fed by 12 water-falls. A striking 18-story atrium is filled with tropical plants, ancient Chinese sculptures, and live tropical birds. Accommodations are divided between the Hyatt Regency Grand Cypress and the Villas of Grand Cypress. There's just one drawback: the king-size conventions the resort commonly attracts. *Hyatt Regency Grand Cypress: ⊠ 1 Grand Cypress Blvd., 32836, ☎ 407/239–1234 or 800/233–1234, ℻ 407/239–3800. 750 rooms. Villas of Grand Cypress: ⊠ 1 N. Jacaranda Dr., 32836, ☎ 407/239–4700 or 800/835–7377. 146 villas. 5 restaurants, 4 lobby lounges, 2 pools, 4 hot tubs, massage, driving range, 45 holes of golf, 12 tennis courts, croquet, health club, horseback riding, jogging, boating, bicycles, baby-sitting, children's program, laundry service. AE, D, DC, MC, V.*

$$$–$$$$ 🏨 **Vistana Resort.** Consider this peaceful resort if you're interested in tennis. Its clay and all-weather courts can be used without charge, and private or semiprivate lessons are available for a fee. It's also a good bet if your family is large or you're traveling with friends. Spread over 95 landscaped acres, the spacious, tastefully decorated villas and town houses have two bedrooms each plus a living room and all the comforts of home, including a full kitchen and a washer and dryer. ⊠ *8800 Vistana Center Dr., 32821, ☎ 407/239–3100 or 800/877–8787, ℻ 407/239–3111. 1,300 units. 2 restaurants, grocery, lobby lounge, 7 pools, 5 wading pools, 7 hot tubs, miniature golf, 13 tennis courts, basketball, 2 health clubs, shuffleboard, baby-sitting, children's program. AE, D, DC, MC, V.*

$$–$$$$ 🏨 **Embassy Suites Resort Lake Buena Vista.** Some locals have been shocked by the wild turquoise, pink, and yellow facade of this otherwise typical example of the all-suite chain. Clearly visible from I–4 and just 1 mi from WDW, 3 mi from SeaWorld, and 7 mi from Universal Studios, it has become something of a local landmark. The atrium lobby, loaded with tropical vegetation and soothed by the sounds of a rushing fountain, is a great place to enjoy the complimentary breakfast and evening cocktails. ⊠ *8100 Lake Ave., Lake Buena Vista 32836, ☎ 407/239–1144, 800/257–8483, or 800/362–2779, ℻ 407/239–1718. 280 suites. Restaurant, deli, lobby lounge, indoor-outdoor pool, wading pool, hot tub, tennis court, basketball, exercise room, shuffleboard, volleyball, baby-sitting, children's program, playground. AE, D, DC, MC, V.*

$$ 🏨 **Perri House.** Exactly 1 mi from the Magic Kingdom as the crow flies,
★ this B&B on a serene side road is unique in build-it-bigger-and-they-will-come Orlando. Part hostelry and part bird preserve, Perri House is an Audubon Society–recognized bird sanctuary, complete with observation paths, a pond, feeding station, and a small birdhouse museum. About 200 trees and more than 1,500 bushes have been planted—many awaiting the addition of birdhouses. Here you can awaken to the cries of bobwhites, downy woodpeckers, red-tail hawks, and an occasional bald eagle. Nick and Angi Perretti planned and built the circular house so that each room has an outside entrance. Four birdhouse vacation cottages are planned. ⊠ *10417 Centurion Ct., Lake Buena Vista 32830, ☎ 407/876–4830 or 800/780–4830, ℻ 407/876–0241. 8 rooms. Pool, hot tub. AE, D, DC, MC, V.*

$–$$$ 🏨 **Holiday Inn SunSpree Resort Lake Buena Vista.** Proving that if chil-
★ dren are happy, their parents are happy, this place is as kid-oriented as it gets. Upon arrival, you check in and so do your little ones—at their own registration desk. Off the lobby are a small theater; the CyberArcade; a buffet restaurant, where kids accompanied by adults eat free at their own little picnic tables; and Camp Holiday, a free supervised program (beeper rental available). The family-friendly focus continues in the guest rooms, many of them Kidsuites. A playhouse-style

room within a larger room, each Kidsuite has a fun-inspiring theme: magic castles, tree houses, igloos, space capsules, etc. (At night, Max, the hotel's raccoon mascot, will even tuck kids in.) Add a fridge, microwave, and coffeemaker, and you have a reasonably priced alternative to typical suites that still provides some privacy. ⊠ *13351 Rte. 535, 32821,* ☎ *407/239–4500 or 800/366–6299,* ℻ *407/239–7713. 507 rooms. Restaurant, bar, grocery, lobby lounge, pool, wading pool, 2 hot tubs, basketball, exercise room, Ping-Pong, theater, video games, children's program, playground, coin laundry, laundry service. AE, D, DC, MC, V.*

$–$$ ⊞ **Riu Orlando Hotel.** After traipsing through theme parks and malls, what many visitors want most is to lounge around their living room just as they do at home. This six-story complex lets you do just that: It provides a living room full of big couches, with a better-than-at-home big-screen TV fitted with a Nintendo unit. The hotel, which looks like a brown-brick office building from the outside but is quite comfortable inside, is now operated by a Spanish hotel chain. ⊠ *8688 Palm Pkwy., 32836,* ☎ *407/239–8500 or 888/222–9963,* ℻ *407/239–8591. 167 rooms. Restaurant, lobby lounge, pool, hot tub, health club. AE, D, DC, MC, V.*

Universal Studios CityWalk

Take I–4 Exit 29B if you're heading westbound, 30A if eastbound.

$$$–$$$$ ⊞ **Portofino Bay Hotel.** How far was Universal willing to go to make its first on-property lodging (managed by Loews Hotels) seem like the Italian resort after which it was modeled? That the architecture is an exact copy of the little bay-front Italian village, complete with the same type of bright-color stucco buildings, isn't surprising. But although at the real Portofino Bay, Italian fishermen mend their nets along the waterfront, at Universal's Portofino Bay, imitation Italian fishermen have been hired to mend nets around a 1-acre man-made lake with 40 faux fishing boats—just for atmosphere. Some Italian touches make more sense, like gelato machines at the pool, a wood-fired pizzeria, and great Italian cuisine. With 42,000 square ft of meeting space, the hotel caters to conventions but is also heavy on amenities for individual travelers, including poolside cabanas with fax machines and internet hookups, lest you lose touch with the office. For about $300 a night, you can get a "butler villa" with your own butler to mix your drinks, fix your bed, and unpack your suitcases. ⊠ *1000 Universal Studios Plaza, 32819,* ☎ *407/224–7117. 750 rooms and suites. 2 restaurants, bar, pizzeria, pool, spa, health club, meeting rooms. AE, D, DC, MC, V.*

Kissimmee

Take I–4 Exit 25A unless otherwise noted.

If you're looking for anything remotely quaint, charming, or sophisticated, move on. The U.S. 192 strip—also known as the Irlo Bronson Memorial Highway, the Spacecoast Parkway, and Kissimmee—is a neon-and-plastic theme park crammed with mom-and-pop motels, bargain-basement hotels, and cheap restaurants. But if all you want is a decent room, this is wonderland. Room rates start at $20 a night—lower at the right time of year, if you can cut the right deal—with most costing from $30 to $70 a night, depending on facilities and proximity to Walt Disney World.

$$$–$$$$ ⊞ **Marriott's Orlando World Center.** To call this hotel massive would be an understatement—more than 1,500 rooms with another 500 on the way by the end of 1999. The lineup of amenities and facilities seems endless—a plus for tourists that mitigates the presence of all those conventioneers, who largely pay the freight here. One of the four pools is Florida's largest, and the lobby is a huge, opulent atrium, adorned with 16th-century Asian artifacts. Take I–4 Exit 26A. ⊠ *8701 World Center Dr., 32821,* ☎ *407/239–4200 or 800/228–9290,* FAX *407/238–8777. 1,501 rooms, 85 suites. 5 restaurants, 2 lobby lounges, 1 indoor and 3 outdoor pools, wading pool, beauty salon, 4 hot tubs, 18-hole golf course, miniature golf, 7 tennis courts, health club, volleyball, baby-sitting, children's program, coin laundry, laundry service. AE, D, DC, MC, V.*

$$–$$$ 🖬 **Inn at Maingate.** This sleek, twin-towered seven-story hotel, just a
★ few minutes from WDW's front door, has cheerful guest rooms, large bathrooms, and plenty of extras. It's not fancy, but it is perfectly adequate. The best rooms are those with a view of the pool. ⊠ *3011 Maingate La., 34747,* ☎ *407/396–1400 or 800/239–6478,* FAX *407/396–0660. 577 rooms, 6 suites. Restaurant, deli, lobby lounge, pool, hot tub, 2 tennis courts, basketball, exercise room, jogging, baby-sitting, coin laundry, laundry service. AE, D, DC, MC, V.*

$$–$$$ 🖬 **Sheraton Inn Lakeside.** This comfortable, if undistinguished, resort, a complex of 15 two-story balconied buildings spread over 27 acres by a small man-made lake, offers quite a few recreational facilities. The nondescript beige rooms are available in the standard two double beds or one king-size bed configurations, and each has a refrigerator and safe. ⊠ *7769 W. Irlo Bronson Memorial Hwy., 34747,* ☎ *407/396–2222 or 800/848–0801,* FAX *407/239–2650. 651 rooms. 2 restaurants, deli, lobby lounge, 3 pools, wading pool, miniature golf, 4 tennis courts, boating, fishing, children's program, coin laundry, laundry service. AE, D, DC, MC, V.*

$$ 🖬 **Residence Inn by Marriott on Lake Cecile.** Of the all-suite hotels on U.S. 192, this complex of four-unit town houses is probably the best. One side of the complex faces the highway; the other overlooks an attractive lake, where you can sail, water-ski, jet-ski, and fish. (Watersport rentals are operated by vendors next door to the hotel.) Forty of the units are penthouses accommodating four, with complete kitchens, small living rooms, loft bedrooms, and fireplaces. All others accommodate two and are similar to studio apartments but still have full kitchens and fireplaces. ⊠ *4786 W. Irlo Bronson Memorial Hwy., 34746,* ☎ *407/396–2056 or 800/468–3027,* FAX *407/396–2296. 160 units. Pool, hot tub, basketball, playground, coin laundry, laundry service. AE, D, DC, MC, V.*

$–$$$ 🖬 **Quality Suites Maingate East.** This hotel is an excellent option for a large family or group of friends. The spacious green-and-mauve rooms, designed to sleep between 6 and 10, come equipped with a microwave, refrigerator, and dishwasher. Suites have two bedrooms with two double beds each and a living room with a double pullout couch. A complimentary Continental breakfast is offered, and free beer and wine are served afternoons at the poolside bar. As an added bonus, guests get one free admission per suite to Cypress Gardens, Water Mania, or Splendid China. ⊠ *5876 W. Irlo Bronson Memorial Hwy., 34746,* ☎ *407/396–8040 or 800/848–4148,* FAX *407/396–6766. 225 units. Restaurant, bar, lobby lounge, pool, wading pool, hot tub, playground, laundry service. AE, D, DC, MC, V.*

$–$$$ 🖬 **Radisson Resort Parkway.** This bright, spacious Radisson may offer
★ the best deal in the neighborhood: attractive setting, good facilities, and competitive prices. Its delicatessen comes in handy when you want to assemble a picnic. Generously proportioned rooms are decked out in tropical patterns, with pastel colors and pineapple shapes carved in white, wooden furniture. Rooms with the best view and light face the pool. ⊠ *2900 Parkway Blvd., 34746,* ☎ *407/396–7000 or 800/634–4774,* FAX *407/396–6792. 712 rooms, 6 suites. Restaurant, deli, 2 lobby*

lounges, snack bar, 2 pools, wading pool, 2 hot tubs, sauna, 2 tennis courts, exercise room, volleyball, coin laundry, laundry service. AE, D, DC, MC, V.

$–$$ ⊞ **Best Western Kissimmee.** You certainly can't complain about the price at this hotel overlooking a nine-hole, par-3 executive golf course. Not surprisingly, this independently owned and operated three-story lodging is a hit with golf-loving senior citizens as well as families. The pools in the garden courtyard are amply shaded to protect tender skin from the sizzling sun. Spacious rooms are done in soft pastels, with light wood furniture and attractive wall hangings. Units with king-size beds and kitchenettes are available. ⊠ *2261 E. Irlo Bronson Memorial Hwy., 34744,* ☎ *407/846–2221 or 800/944–0062,* 🆁🅰🆇 *407/846– 1095. 285 rooms. Restaurant, bar, lobby lounge, picnic area, 2 pools, playground. AE, D, DC, MC, V.*

$ ⊞ **Park Inn International.** The Mediterranean-style architecture of this property on Cedar Lake is not likely to charm you off your feet, but the friendly staff might. Ask for a room as close to the water as possible. ⊠ *4960 W. Irlo Bronson Memorial Hwy., 34741,* ☎ *407/396– 1376 or 800/327–0072,* 🆁🅰🆇 *407/396–0716. 192 rooms. Restaurant, grocery, pool, hot tub, beach, coin laundry. AE, D, DC, MC, V.*

$ ⊞ **Record Motel.** There are campgrounds in these parts that cost more than this simple property—the kind of mom-and-pop operation with few frills and the type of rock-bottom rates that made U.S. 192 famous. Remodeled, clean rooms with free HBO and ESPN, Continental breakfast, and a solar-heated pool are the basic attractions here. What the place lacks in luxuries and ambience, it more than makes up for with the friendliness of its staff, which will gladly direct you to equally inexpensive restaurants. In that sense, this is a piece of Old Florida that is fading away. ⊠ *4651 W. Irlo Bronson Memorial Hwy., 34746,* ☎ *407/396–8400 or 800/874–4555,* 🆁🅰🆇 *407/396–8415. 57 rooms. Pool. AE, D, MC, V.*

$ ⊞ **Sevilla Inn.** This family-operated motel built in 1985 and expanded
★ in 1990 is one of the best buys in the Orlando area. Stucco and wood on the outside, the three-story building has up-to-date rooms with colorful bedspreads, tasteful wall hangings, and cable TV. If you need a place just to drop your bags and get some rest between theme parks, this is a good bet. The pool area, encircled by palm trees and tropical shrubs, looks like something you'd find in a much fancier resort. ⊠ *4640 W. Irlo Bronson Memorial Hwy., 34746,* ☎ *407/396–4135 or 800/367–1363,* 🆁🅰🆇 *407/396–4942. 50 rooms. Pool, coin laundry. AE, D, MC, V.*

Orlando Suburbs

Travel farther afield, and you can get more comforts and facilities for the money, and maybe even some genuine Orlando charm—of the warm, cozy, one-of-a-kind country inn variety.

$$$ ⊞ **Chalet Suzanne.** This quiet, family-owned B&B is a world away from the world of Disney. A 40-minute drive past RV parks and orange groves brings you to this little country inn with a style you can't put your finger on. Constructed over time since the 1930s, buildings resemble a Swiss village but are painted in tropical pink and aqua and accented with Near Eastern tiles. The grounds contain everything from a serene Autograph Garden (lined with tiles made by guests) to a soup cannery. Some of the lovely antiques-dotted guest rooms have original tile baths, while others have been redone with whirlpools. The best look out on lake or garden. But perhaps the biggest treat is a meal in the inn's elegant restaurant; luckily, breakfast is included. Take I–4 Exit 23 and

U.S. 27 south. ✉ *3800 Chalet Suzanne Dr., Lake Wales 33853,* ☎ *941/ 676–6011 or 800/433–6011,* FAX *941/676–1814. 30 rooms. Restaurant, bar, lake, pool, badminton, croquet, volleyball, private airstrip. AE, DC, MC, V.*

$$$ ⛆ **Embassy Suites Orlando–North.** What makes this hotel different from others in its chain is its location on the edge of Crane's Roost Lake. Otherwise, suites are up to the high Embassy Suites standard and look out on a lush, tropical atrium. Although the sound of the waterfalls is soothing, the same can't be said for that of the conventioneers at the tables around them. So for guaranteed quiet, choose a suite on an upper floor. Accommodations are spacious and flawlessly kept, the staff friendly and helpful, and the complimentary cooked-to-order break-fast makes a great send-off for your busy day. Take I–4 Exit 48. ✉ *225 E. Altamonte Dr., Altamonte Springs 32701,* ☎ *407/834–2400 or 800/362–2779,* FAX *407/834–2117. 277 suites. Restaurant, lobby lounge, indoor pool, exercise room, coin laundry, laundry service, business services. AE, D, DC, MC, V.*

$$–$$$ ⛆ **Park Plaza Hotel.** Small and intimate, this 1922-vintage establish-ment feels almost like a private home, with such nice touches as a com-plimentary breakfast brought to your room. The key to a special stay is a front garden suite. These open onto a long balcony usually abloom with impatiens and bougainvillea, perfect for people-watching. Balconies are so covered with shrubs and ferns that they are somewhat private, inspiring more than a few romantic interludes, a member of manage-ment confided. This old-fashioned hotel is definitely not for people who want recreational facilities or other amenities—nor is it suitable for young children. Aside from these things, the only downside is the proximity of Amtrak. If you feel the earth move while on a romantic getaway, it could be your companion, or it could just be the train. Take I–4 Exit 45. ✉ *307 Park Ave. S, Winter Park 32789,* ☎ *407/647–1072 or 800/ 228–7220,* FAX *407/647–4081. 27 rooms. Restaurant, lobby lounge, jog-ging, laundry service. AE, DC, MC, V.*

NIGHTLIFE AND THE ARTS

The powers that be have finally embraced the fact that about half of Disney's 13 million travelers per year are adults without children. So Disney's nightlife has taken on a new identity. Meanwhile, Orlando keeps up with the quickened pace on Church Street and Orange Av-enue, a post-teen and tourist hangout that stretches for several blocks. Not to miss out on the action (and the profits), Universal opened the much-postponed CityWalk entertainment complex in 1999.

The Arts

Check out the local fine arts scene in the *Orlando Weekly,* a local en-tertainment magazine, or "Calendar," which is printed every Friday in the *Orlando Sentinel,* both available at newsstands. For some rea-son local theater has the mistaken impression it presents Broadway-caliber shows, and tickets are often overpriced. To make prices even steeper, traveling Broadway shows actually do come to the Carr Per-forming Arts Centre.

Orlando has an active agenda of dance, classical music, opera, and the-ater, much of which takes place at the **Carr Performing Arts Centre** (✉ 401 W. Livingston St., ☎ 407/849–2577). The **Civic Theater of Cen-tral Florida** (✉ 1001 E. Princeton St., ☎ 407/896–7365) presents a va-riety of shows, with evening performances Wednesday–Saturday and Sunday matinees. **Orange County Convention and Civic Center** (✉ South end of International Dr., ☎ 407/345–9800) is sometimes the venue for local concerts by top artists. The downtown **Orlando Arena** (✉ W. Amelia St., ☎ 407/849–2020) plays host to many big-name performers. During the school year **Rollins College** (✉ Winter Park, ☎ 407/646–2233) has a choral concert series that is open to the public and usually free. The last week in February internationally recognized artists appear at the **Bach Music Festival** (☎ 407/646–2182), a tradition for more than 60 years. Also at the college, the **Annie Russell Theater** (☎ 407/646–2145) has a regular series of student productions.

Nightlife

Bars, Lounges, and Nightclubs

WALT DISNEY WORLD RESORT

Every WDW hotel has its quota of bars and lounges pushing specialty drinks in all colors of the rainbow. Jazz trios and bluesmen, DJs and rockers tune up and turn on their amps after dinner's done. And you can drink later here than off-property—WDW clubs serve as late as 2:45 AM. But there's plenty to do beyond your hotel. One cluster of nightspots is found at Disney's BoardWalk. Downtown Disney is another, much larger area, that actually comprises three shopping-dining-entertainment districts: the Marketplace, Pleasure Island, and West Side. They keep building big-bucks, celebrity-backed eatery-drinkeries with elaborate themed architecture and outrageous neon consumption, and people keep coming. You could easily stay up half the night for weeks on end.

The **Laughing Kookaburra** (✉ Buena Vista Palace, Lake Buena Vista, ☎ 407/827–3722) has been a consistent favorite among hospitality employees due to its drink specials, young crowd, and entertainment. Live rock and roll and comedy are performed nightly.

Disney's BoardWalk, across Crescent Lake from the Yacht and Beach Club Resorts, recalls a turn-of-the-century amusement complex by the shore, complete with restaurants, clubs, souvenir sellers, surreys, saltwater taffy vendors, and shops. When the lights go on after sunset, the mood is festive—a nice, nostalgic setting for plentiful diversions and a romantic stroll. In true Disney fashion, the sports motif at the **ESPN Club** (☎ 407/939–1177) is carried into every nook and cranny. The main dining area looks like a sports arena, there's a TV and radio broadcast booth, and more than 70 TV monitors are located throughout the facility, even in the rest rooms. The setting is rugged and boisterous at **Jellyrolls** (☎ 407/560–8770), which features comedians at dueling grand pianos and a sing-along piano bar made interesting by all the conventioneers. The cover charge varies depending on the day of the week.

Many Disney clubs are at **Pleasure Island,** a 6-acre after-dark entertainment complex, connected to the rest of Downtown Disney by footbridges. It's better than you might expect. Despite its location on Disney property, the entertainment has real grit and life. In addition to eight clubs, you'll find a few restaurants and shops. A pay-one-price admission gets you into all the clubs and shows. Children accompanied by an adult are admitted to all clubs except Mannequins.

Adventurer's Club is supposed to re-create a private club of the 1930s. Much of the entertainment is found in looking at exotic accent pieces that clutter the walls, the rest is in watching actors lead sing-alongs and share tall tales from their adventures. **BET SoundStage Club** is backed by Black Entertainment Television and pays tribute to all genres of black music—from BET's Top 10 to old R&B to hip-hop—a blend that's attracted legions of locals who proclaim this the funkiest nightspot in Central Florida (and perhaps also the loudest). **Comedy Warehouse** stars a gifted troupe of comedians, who perform various improv games based on audience suggestions. Each of the evening's seven performances is different. At **8trax,** groove to the recorded music of Donna Summer or the Village People while light reflects from disco balls. Guests at **Mannequins Dance Palace** love the high-tech New York–style atmosphere, complete with Top 40 hits; a revolving dance floor; elaborate lighting; suggestive, over-the-top Disney dancers; and such special effects as bubbles and snow. With decor reminiscent of a '30s speakeasy, the **Pleasure Island Jazz Company** presents nightly performances by accomplished soloists or six- or seven-piece bands. The tapas bar is well stocked, and you can get assorted wines by the glass. The **Rock & Roll Beach Club** throbs with live rock music of the 1950s and 1960s. **Wildhorse Saloon** is a retro western hangout that hits the bull's-eye with daily (and nightly) dance lessons, kickin' barbecue, and up-and-coming country singers. Yeee-ha! ⊠ *Off Buena Vista Dr. (I–4 Exit 27),* ☎ *407/934–7781 or 407/824–2222.* 🎫 *$19.99, shops and restaurants free.* ⊗ *Clubs daily 7 PM–2 AM, shops daily 10 AM–1 AM, restaurants usually daily 11:30 AM–midnight.*

The newest addition to the mass of shopping and entertainment that is Downtown Disney, **Downtown Disney West Side** (⊠ Off Buena Vista Dr., ☎ 407/824–4321 or 407/824–2222) opened in 1997, and new attractions are opening all the time. A 24-screen AMC cinema shows the same movies you could see at home. For something a little different, drop by for a beer and a *baba-lu* at Gloria Estefan's **Bongos Cuban Café** (☎ 407/828–0999). **Cirque du Soleil** (☎ 407/939–7600) features the progressive circus known worldwide for its avant-garde stagings, costumes, and choreography. Shows featuring 72 performers are scheduled twice daily, five days a week, in a 70,000-square-ft custom-made theater. Adjacent to the **House of Blues** (HOB) restaurant (☎ 407/934–2583), which itself showcases cool blues starting at 11, HOB's up-close-and-personal concert venue brings local and nationally known artists playing everything from reggae to rock to R&B.

UNIVERSAL STUDIOS ESCAPE

Universal Studios CityWalk (☎ 888/331–9108) is the newest kid in Orlando's ever-expanding world of nighttime diversions, containing stores, dining and drinking establishments, and a 20-screen multiplex with stadium seating. **Bob Marley's, A Tribute to Freedom** is a loud reggae club/restaurant with more than a touch of Jamaica. **CityWalk's Latin Quarter** combines food and entertainment from 21 Latin American countries in a 20,000-square-ft venue with two open-air kitchens, a nightclub, a dance studio, and a Latin cultural center. Each evening Latin rock bands and costumed dance troupes move to south-of-the-border sounds, with dance instructors on hand to help the rhythmically challenged. The **Groove** is Universal's answer to Pleasure Island's Mannequins, with wild lighting, visual effects, disco chrome, and funk music that will have you shakin' your groove thang all night long. The world's largest **Hard Rock Cafe** includes the chain's first dedicated live concert venue. (Sadly, the cool, guitar-shape original Hard Rock is being turned into a hotel.) **Jimmy Buffett's Margaritaville** should prove popular with Parrotheads and margarita drinkers. Expect long lines at the **Motown Cafe,** where tribute groups perform floor shows emulating the Miracles, Supremes, Four Tops, et al. Race fans will want to check out the **NASCAR Cafe,** the only NASCAR-sanctioned specialty restaurant featuring full-size stock cars and racing memorabilia. Having teamed up with the Hard Rock Cafe, the NBA and WNBA see a demand for the basketball-theme **NBA restaurant.** An exact duplicate of the New Orleans favorite, **Pat O'Brien's** blows into Orlando with its signature drink, the Hurricane, as well as dueling pianos and a "flaming fountain" patio.

ORLANDO

Outside Walt Disney World Resort, there's lots going on, much of it at Church Street Station but plenty in freestanding clubs as well. Nightclubs in Orlando proper have significantly more character than those in the areas around Walt Disney World Resort, but they close earlier.

Howl at the Moon (⊠ Church St. Marketplace, 55 W. Church St., 2nd floor, ☎ 407/841–4695 or 407/841–9118) encourages its patrons to warble along to the pop classics of yesteryear or campy favorites like the "Time Warp" and "Hokey Pokey" (turn yourself around). Piano players keep the music rolling in the evening, and the World's Most Dangerous Wait Staff adds to the entertainment. No food is served, but the management encourages you to bring your own or order out; several nearby restaurants deliver. There's a cover charge of $2–$4 Wednesday–Saturday; Sunday–Tuesday it's free. **Mulvaney's** (⊠ 27 W. Church St., ☎ 407/872–3296) is downtown's most frequented Irish pub. Seven nights a week the wood-paneled bar is packed with pub crawlers fond of simple fare, imported ales, and authentic Irish folk music. Two big pluses are no cover and live entertainment every night. The hypercool **Rat Pack's on the Avenue** (⊠ 25 S. Orange Ave., ☎ 407/649–8829 office; 407/649–4803 concert line) answers Orlando's demand for a real swing club.

Refreshingly free of stand-up comedians, lively **Sak Comedy Lab** (⊠ 380 W. Amelia Ave., ☎ 407/648–0001) is home to Orlando's premier comedy troupe, deserving of their regular first-place finishes in a national improv competition. They play to sold-out audiences Tuesday–Sunday. Cowboys of all ages come to **Sullivan's Entertainment Complex** (⊠ 1108 S. Orange Blossom Trail [U.S. 441], ☎ 407/843–2934), a longtime country-and-western dance hall, to strut their stuff. Big-name performers entertain on occasion, a house band plays Thursday and Saturday, and hours and cover charges vary. At **Zuma Beach** (⊠ 46 N. Orange Ave., ☎ 407/648–8363), a sun-and-surf-theme dance club, up to 1,200 young adults a night take advantage of the club's "alternative formatting"—from techno pop to Latin carnival nights. The cover is $6.

In the **Church Street Station** entertainment complex, the old-fashioned saloons, dance halls, dining rooms, and shopping arcades are almost Disneyesque in their attention to detail. Unlike much of what you see at WDW, however, this place doesn't just look authentic—it is. The train on the tracks is an actual 19th-century steam engine; the whistling calliope was specially rebuilt to blow its original tunes. Just about everything down to the cobblestones that clatter under the horse-drawn carriages is the real McCoy. For a single admission you can wander freely and stay as long as you wish. Food and drink cost extra and are not cheap. Parts of the complex are open during the day, but the place is usually quiet then; the pace picks up at night, especially on weekends, with crowds thickest from 10 to 11.

Quiet **Apple Annie's Courtyard** offers recorded easy-listening music from Jimmy Buffett to James Taylor. The immensely popular trilevel **Cheyenne Saloon and Opera House** was, in fact, an opera house and is now full of moose racks, steer horns, buffalo heads, and Remington rifles. The seven-piece country-and-western band that plays here darn near brings the house down. **Crackers Oyster Bar,** behind the Orchid Garden, is a good place to get a meal of fresh Florida seafood and pasta or slam down a few oysters with a beer chaser. Relaxed and wood-paneled, **Lili**

Marlene's Aviators Pub and Restaurant feels like an English pub and has the best food on Church Street—hearty, upscale, and very American steaks, ribs, and seafood. There is no cover. Iron latticework, arched ceilings, Victorian lamps, and stained-glass windows are out of place at the Orchid Garden Ballroom, where the original '30s and '40s music was replaced with the more popular '50s–'60s theme. Phineas Phogg's Balloon Works plays Top 40 tunes on a sound system that will blow your argyle socks off. It draws a good-looking yuppie tourist crowd and a few locals intrigued by the no-cover admission; the place is jammed by midnight. Rosie O'Grady's Good Time Emporium, the original bar on Church Street, is a turn-of-the-century saloon with dark wood, brass trim, a full Dixieland band, banjo shows, tap dancers, and vaudeville singers. ⊠ *129 W. Church St.,* ☎ *407/422–2434.* ⊠ *$17.95 adults, $11.95 children 4–12.* ☉ *Daily 11 AM–2 AM.*

Dinner Shows

For a single price these hybrid eatery-entertainment complexes deliver a theatrical production and a multicourse dinner. Performances run the gamut from jousting to jamboree tunes and tend to be better than the rather forgettable meal. Unlimited beer, wine, and soda are usually included, but mixed drinks (often *any* drinks before dinner) will cost you extra. What the shows lack in substance and depth they make up for in color and enthusiasm; children often love them. Shows have seatings between 7 and 9:30—usually one or two performances a night, but an extra show can be added during peak tourist periods—and at most you sit with strangers at long tables. Always call and make reservations in advance, especially for weekends and shows at Walt Disney World Resort.

WALT DISNEY WORLD RESORT

Staged at rustic Pioneer Hall, the **Hoop-Dee-Doo Revue** may be corny, but it is also the liveliest show in Walt Disney World. A troupe of jokers called the Pioneer Hall Players stomp their feet, wisecrack, and otherwise make merry while the audience chows down on barbecued ribs, fried chicken, corn on the cob, strawberry shortcake, and all the fixin's. Shows during busy seasons sell out months in advance. ⊠ *Fort Wilderness Resort,* ☎ *407/939–3463 in advance; 407/824–2803 day of show.* ⊠ *$38 adults, $19.50 children 3–11. AE, MC, V.*

At the outdoor barbecue that is the **Polynesian Luau,** the entertainment is in keeping with the colorful South Pacific setting. There are two shows nightly, plus an earlier wingding for children called Mickey's Tropical Luau, in which Disney characters do a few numbers decked out in South Seas garb. ⊠ *Polynesian Resort,* ☎ *407/939–3463 in advance; 407/824–1593 day of show.* ⊠ *Polynesian Luau $38 adults, $19.50 children 3–11; Mickey's Tropical Luau $33 adults, $16 children 3–11. AE, MC, V.*

AROUND ORLANDO

The **Aloha! Polynesian Luau Dinner and Show,** at SeaWorld's Bimini Bay Café, is an Anheuser-Busch family version of *Blue Hawaii.* Scantily clad dancers undulate across the floor, bearing lei-draped platters of roast pig, mahimahi, piña coladas, and hula pie. Reservations may be made the same day, either at the luau reservations counter in the information center at the entrance or by telephone. Although the restaurant is inside the park, you don't have to pay park admission to attend the feast. ⊠ *SeaWorld, Orlando,* ☎ *407/351–3600 or 800/227–8048.* ⊠ *$35.95 adults, $25.95 children 8–12, $15.95 children 3–7. D, MC, V.*

An elaborate palace outside, **Arabian Nights** is more like an arena within, with seating for more than 1,200. The show features eerie fog, an Arabian princess, and a buffoonish genie, but the real stars are the 54 fabulous horses that perform in acts representing horse-loving cultures from around the world: bareback acrobatics by Gypsies, an intricate western square dance on horseback, a chariot race, and Walter Farley's Black Stallion. The three-course dinners are of prime rib or vegetarian lasagna. ⊠ *6225 W. Irlo Bronson Memorial Hwy., Kissimmee,* ☎ *407/239–9223; 800/553–6116; 800/533–3615 in Canada.* ⬛ *$36.95 adults, $23.95 children 3–11. AE, D, MC, V.*

Returning to gangland Chicago of 1931, **Capone's Dinner and Show** comes complete with mobsters and their dames. The evening begins in an old-fashioned ice cream parlor; say the secret password, and you'll be ushered inside Al Capone's private Underworld Cabaret and Speakeasy. Dinner is an unlimited Italian buffet heavy on pasta. ⊠ *4740 W. Irlo Bronson Memorial Hwy., Kissimmee,* ☎ *407/397–2378.* ⬛ *$35.99 adults, $18 children 4–12. AE, D, MC, V.*

In **King Henry's Feast,** jesters, jugglers, dancers, magicians, and singers ostensibly fete Henry VIII as he celebrates his birthday in this Tudor-style building. Saucy wenches serve forth potato-leek soup, salad, and chicken and ribs. ⊠ *8984 International Dr., Orlando,* ☎ *407/351–5151 or 800/883–8181.* ⬛ *$35.95 adults, $22.95 children 3–11. AE, D, MC, V.*

Broadway musicals are performed at **Mark Two** throughout the year except during the Yuletide holidays, when there are musical revues chockablock with Broadway tunes. For about two hours before curtain, you can order from the bar and help yourself at buffet tables laden with institutional-grade food; dessert arrives during intermission. Unlike other dinner theaters, the Mark Two offers only tables for two and four. The theater is west of I–4 Exit 44. ⊠ *Edgewater Center, 3376 Edgewater Dr., Orlando,* ☎ *407/843–6275 or 800/726–6275.* ⬛ *$29–$41 adults, $18–$30 children under 12. AE, D, MC, V.*

In **Medieval Times,** no fewer than 30 charging horses and a cast of 75 knights, nobles, and maidens perform in a huge, ersatz-medieval manor house. The two-hour tournament includes sword fights, jousting matches, and other games, and the bill of fare is heavy on meat and potatoes. ⊠ *4510 W. Irlo Bronson Memorial Hwy., Kissimmee,* ☎ *407/ 239–0214 or 800/229–8300.* ⬛ *$37.95 adults, $22.95 children 3–12. AE, D, MC, V.*

At **Sleuths Mystery Dinner Show,** your four-course meal is served up with a healthy dose of conspiracy. Each of the seven whodunit performances rotated throughout the year stops short of revealing the perpetrator. You get to question the characters and attempt to solve the mystery. ⊠ *7508 Universal Blvd., Orlando,* ☎ *407/363–1985 or 800/ 393–1985.* ⬛ *$38.11 adults, $24.33 children 3–11. AE, D, MC, V.*

Held in the 22-acre Fort Liberty complex, **Wild Bill's Wild West Dinner Show** is a mixed bag of Native American dances, an authentic Texas lariat master, and country-and-western hijinks. The chow, served by a rowdy chorus of cavalry recruits, is beef soup, fried chicken, corn on the cob, and pork and beans. No smoking is allowed in the showroom. ⊠ *5260 W. Irlo Bronson Memorial Hwy., Kissimmee,* ☎ *407/351–5151 or 800/883–8181.* ⬛ *$36.95 adults, $22.95 children 3–11. AE, DC, MC, V.*

Movies

If you didn't come to Orlando just to see a "regular" movie at one of the megaplexes, check out the impressive **Muvico Pointe 21** (✉ Pointe*Orlando, 9101 International Dr., Orlando, ☎ 407/903–0555). It not only has 21 screens and stadium seating but also a six-story theater for IMAX 3-D films, which are viewed with state-of-the-art liquid-crystal headsets.

OUTDOOR ACTIVITIES AND SPORTS

Orlando is the place to visit if you want to be outside. You'll find just about every outdoor sports opportunity here—unless it involves a ski lift—that you'll find anywhere else in the country. The city also holds a hot ticket as a professional sports town. In addition to hosting the NBA Magic, Orlando lays claim to the Walt Disney Speedway. **Disney's Wide World of Sports** (☎ 407/363–6600) accommodates tournament-type events in more than 30 individual and team sports; presents other annual events, such as Harlem Globetrotter basketball games; serves as the spring-training home of the Atlanta Braves; and offers participatory sports—basketball, softball, and track and field events—for visiting groups.

Auto Racing

The Indy 200 is held in late January at the **Walt Disney Speedway** (✉ Adjacent to Disney's Wide World of Sports, ☎ 407/839–3900 tickets, 407/939–7810 vacation packages). The facility has a 1-mi tri-oval track and accommodates 51,000 fans. If you've always wanted to actually ride in or even drive a NASCAR-style stock car on a real race track, head to the **Richard Petty Driving Experience** (✉ Walt Disney Speedway, ☎ 800/237–3889). Depending on what you're willing to spend—and the cost ranges from $89.99 to $2,200—you can do everything from being a passenger for three laps to taking 1½ days of lessons, culminating in your very own solo behind the wheel. Though even the cheapest option works out to $30 per mi—nearly the cost of a New York City cab ride and somewhat less dangerous—it's a one-of-a-kind experience.

Basketball

The NBA **Orlando Magic** (✉ Box 76, 600 W. Amelia St., Orlando 32801, ☎ 407/839–3900) play in the Orlando Arena, which is two blocks west of the I–4 Amelia Street exit. A new WNBA team, the **Orlando Miracle** (✉ 600 W. Amelia St., Orlando 32801, ☎ 407/916–2255) started playing at the Orlando Arena in 1999.

Biking

The most scenic bike riding in Orlando is on Walt Disney World Resort property, along roads that take you past forests, lakes, golf courses, and Disney's wooded resort villas and campgrounds. Orlando, on the other hand, hasn't been much of a bicyclist's town, with no bike trails to speak of and a tough stand on riding bikes on sidewalks. But things have changed. The city now has two good bike trails that have been created from former railroad lines. The **West Orange Trail** runs some 19 mi through western Orlando and a neighboring town, Apopka. The best place to access the trail is at **Clarcona Horseman's Park** (✉ 3535 Damon Rd., Apopka, ☎ 407/654–5144). The 3.5-mi **Cady Way Trail**, connecting east Orlando with the well-manicured suburb of Winter Park, has water fountains and shaded seating en route. The best place to access the trail is at the small park at its west end, immediately east of the parking lot of **Orlando Fashion Square** (✉ 3201 E. Colonial Dr.; I–4 Exit 41).

Fishing

Central Florida is covered with freshwater lakes and rivers teeming with all kinds of fish, especially largemouth black bass, but also perch, catfish, sunfish, and pike. To fish in most Florida waters—but not at Walt Disney World Resort—anglers over 16 need a fishing license, available at bait-and-tackle shops, fishing camps, most sporting-goods stores, and Wal-Marts and Kmarts.

WALT DISNEY WORLD RESORT

Fishing without a guide is permitted in the canals around the Dixie Landings and Port Orleans resorts and at Fort Wilderness Resort and Campground. **Bay Lake Fishing Trips** (☎ 407/824–2621) takes two-hour fishing excursions on regularly stocked Bay Lake and Seven Seas Lagoon.

AROUND ORLANDO

Top fishing waters include Lake Kissimmee, the Butler and Conway chains of lakes, and Lake Tohopekaliga (also known as Lake Toho). You can arrange for a guide through one of the excellent area fishing camps. **East Lake Fish Camp** (✉ 3705 Big Bass Rd., Kissimmee, ☎ 407/348–2040) is on East Lake Tohopekaliga. **Red's Fish Camp** (✉ 4715 Kissimmee Park Rd., St. Cloud, ☎ 407/892–8795) is on West Lake Tohopekaliga. **Richardson's Fish Camp** (✉ 1550 Scotty's Rd., Kissimmee, ☎ 407/846–6540) is also on West Lake Tohopekaliga.

Golf

Golf is extremely popular in Central Florida. Be sure to reserve tee times well in advance.

Golfpac (✉ Box 162366, Altamonte Springs 32701, ☎ 407/260–2288 or 800/327–0878) packages golf vacations and prearranges tee times at more than 40 courses around Orlando. Rates vary based on hotel and course, and 60–90 days' advance notice is recommended to set up a vacation.

WALT DISNEY WORLD RESORT

Walt Disney World has five championship 18-hole courses—all on the PGA Tour route: **Eagle Pines** (Bonnet Creek Golf Club), **Lake Buena Vista** (Lake Buena Vista Dr.), **Magnolia** (Shades of Green), **Osprey Ridge** (Bonnet Creek Golf Club), and the **Palm** (Shades of Green). Except for **Oak Trail** (Shades of Green), a nine-hole layout for novice and preteen golfers, these courses are among the busiest and most expensive ($100–$130) in the region.

The three original Disney courses—Lake Buena Vista, Magnolia, and the Palm—have the same fees and discount policies regardless of season and are slightly less expensive than Eagle Pines and Osprey Ridge, whose fees change during the year. All offer a twilight discount rate, $45–$68, which goes into effect at anywhere from 2 to 4, depending on the season.

AROUND ORLANDO

Greens fees at most non-Disney courses fluctuate with the season. A twilight discount applies after 2 in busy seasons and after 3 during the rest of the year; the discount is usually half off the normal rate.

You can only play at Arnold Palmer's **Bay Hill Golf Resort** (✉ 9000 Bay Hill Rd., Orlando, ☎ 407/876–2429 or 888/422–9445) if you're invited by a member or stay at the club's on-property hotel, but room rates that include a round of golf run as low as $189 per person in summer. The course at the **Black Bear Golf Club** (✉ 24505 Calusa Blvd., Eustis, ☎ 352/357–4732) was designed by Pete Dye. **Cypress Creek Country Club** (✉ 5353 Vineland Rd., Orlando, ☎ 407/351–2187) is a demanding course with 16 water holes and lots of trees. The **Falcon's**

Fire Golf Club (⊠ 3200 Seralago Blvd., Kissimmee, ☎ 407/239–5445) course was designed by Rees Jones. **Grand Cypress Resort** (⊠ 1 N. Jacaranda Dr., Orlando, ☎ 407/239–1909 or 800/297–7377) has 45 holes of golf. **Mission Inn Resort** (⊠ 10400 Rte. 48, Howey-in-the-Hills, ☎ 352/324–3885 or 800/874–9053) features two courses. Overlooking Lake Minneola, **Palisades Country Club** (⊠ 16510 Palisades Blvd., Clermont, ☎ 352/394–0085) has a Joe Lee–designed course. The exceptionally long course at **Southern Dunes Golf Club** (⊠ 2888 Southern Dunes Blvd., Haines City, ☎ 941/421–4653 or 800/632–6400) is great for low handicappers. **Timacuan Golf and Country Club** (550 Timacuan Blvd., Lake Mary, ☎ 407/321–0010) has a two-part course designed by Ron Garl—an open front nine with lots of sand and a heavily wooded back nine. The low-key nine-hole **Winter Park Municipal Golf Club** (⊠ 761 Old England Ave., Winter Park, ☎ 407/623–3339) is incredibly inexpensive; greens fees are $8.75.

Horseback Riding

Fort Wilderness Resort and Campground (☎ 407/824–2832) offers tame trail rides through backwoods. Children must be over nine, and adults must be under 250 pounds. Daily trail rides cost $23 for 45 minutes; times vary according to season, and reservations are required.

Running

Walt Disney World has several scenic jogging trails. Pick up maps at any Disney resort. At the **Caribbean Beach Resort** (☎ 407/934–3400), there is a 1½-mi promenade around Barefoot Bay. **Fort Wilderness Resort and Campground** (☎ 407/824–2900) has a 2⅓-mi course with plenty of fresh air and woods as well as numerous exercise stations along the way. Orlando has two excellent bike trails (☞ Biking, *above*) that are also good for jogging.

Water Sports

Marinas at the Caribbean Beach Resort, Contemporary Resort, Dixie Landings Resort, Downtown Disney Marketplace, Fort Wilderness Resort and Campground, Grand Floridian, Polynesian Resort, Port Orleans Resort, Wilderness Lodge, and Yacht and Beach clubs rent Sunfish, catamarans, motor-powered pontoon boats, pedal boats, and tiny two-passenger Water Sprites—a hit with kids—for use on their nearby waters: Bay Lake, Seven Seas Lagoon, Lake Buena Vista, Club Lake, or Buena Vista Lagoon. The Polynesian Resort marina also rents outrigger canoes, and Fort Wilderness rents canoes for paddling along the placid canals in the area. To sail or water-ski on Bay Lake or the Seven Seas Lagoon, stop at the Fort Wilderness, Contemporary, Polynesian, or Grand Floridian marinas.

SHOPPING

Factory Outlets

The International Drive area is filled with outlet stores. At the northern tip of I-Drive, **Belz Factory Outlet World** (⊠ 5401 W. Oak Ridge Rd., Orlando) is the area's largest collection of outlets—more than 180—in two malls and four nearby annexes. All the dinnerware, flatware, glassware, and cookware you can imagine is at **Dansk Factory Outlet** (⊠ 5247 International Dr., Orlando), and all of it is at discount prices. Many of these items are seconds, limited editions, and discontinued styles.

Flea Markets

Flea World (⊠ 3 mi east of I–4 Exit 50 on Lake Mary Blvd., then 1 mi south on U.S. 17–92, between Orlando and Sanford) claims to be

America's largest flea market under one roof. More than 1,600 booths sell only new merchandise—everything from car tires and pet tarantulas to gourmet coffee, leather lingerie, and beaded evening gowns. It's open Friday–Sunday 9–6. Kids love **Fun World,** next door, which offers miniature golf, arcade games, go-carts, bumper cars, bumper boats, kiddie rides, and batting cages.

On weekends **Renninger's Twin Markets** (⊠ U.S. 441, Mount Dora) hosts hundreds of dealers at flea and antiques markets. There's even more to see on the third weekend of each month between March and October, when Antique Fairs attract about 500 dealers. The biggest shows—Extravaganzas—take place the third weekend of November, January, and February. These three-day antiques festivals draw 1,400 dealers. Depending on the day of the week, entrance to Extravaganzas costs $3–$10, but the other markets are free.

Shopping Districts and Malls

WALT DISNEY WORLD RESORT

Shopping is an integral part of the Disney experience, going far beyond the surfeit of Disney trinkets you can find in every park. (And be warned: Disney merchandisers had a plan when they routed the exits of some attractions through gift shops, prompting many a young rider to ask, "Can I have . . .?") The area known as Downtown Disney contains two shopping-entertainment areas with plenty of just about everything. **Downtown Disney Marketplace,** a pleasant complex of shops, includes the **World of Disney** (☎ 407/828–1451), the Disney superstore to end all Disney superstores, and the **LEGO Imagination Center** (☎ 407/828–0065), featuring an impressive backdrop of elaborate Lego sculptures and piles of colorful Lego pieces waiting for kids and their parents to construct something. Among the standouts over at **Downtown Disney West Side** are **Guitar Gallery** (☎ 407/827–0118), which sells videos, music books, accessories, and guitars, guitars, and more guitars; **Magnetron** (☎ 407/827–0108), which, as the name implies, offers you a choice of 20,000 magnets; **Starabilia's** (☎ 407/827–0104), a good place to window-shop for expensive autographed items and other memorabilia; and the enormous **Virgin Megastore** (☎ 407/828–0222), with a music, video, and book selection as large as its prices.

UNIVERSAL STUDIOS ESCAPE

Universal Studios CityWalk (☎ 888/331–9108) brings themed shopping experiences along with its cornucopia of restaurants, clubs, bars, and cafés. Retailers include Quiet Flight (a surf shop), All Star Collectibles, Dapy, Glow! (glow-in-the-dark and black-light merchandise), Endangered Species, Elegant Illusions (carrying paste jewelry), and the Universal Studios Store (packed with Universal merchandise and apparel).

ORLANDO

Church Street Exchange (⊠ Church Street Station, 129 W. Church St.) is a decorative, brassy Victorian-theme marketplace with more than 40 specialty shops. The necessities, such as a 24-hour grocery and pharmacy, post office, bank, and cleaners, are all at **Crossroads of Lake Buena Vista** (⊠ Rte. 535 and I–4, Lake Buena Vista), across from Downtown Disney Marketplace. While you shop, your offspring can entertain themselves at Pirate's Cove Adventure Golf. **Florida Mall** (⊠ 8001 S. Orange Blossom Trail), 4½ mi east of I–4 and International Drive, is the largest mall in Central Florida. It includes Sears, JCPenney, Burdines, Gayfers, Dillards, 200 specialty shops, seven theaters, and one of the better food courts around. At **Mercado Mediterranean Village** (⊠ 8445 International Dr.), there are more than 60 specialty shops and a clean, quick, and large food court, which offers a selection of cuisines from around the world. **Orlando Fashion Square** (✉ 3201 E. Colonial Dr.), 3 mi east of I–4 Exit 41, has 165 shops, including Burdines, JCPenney, Sears, Camelot Music, the Disney Store, the Gap, and Lerner. **Pointe*Orlando** (✉ 9101 International Dr.) is across from the Orange County Convention Center. It's home to 70 specialty shops, including A/X Armani Exchange, Abercrombie & Fitch, and a mighty impressive F.A.O. Schwarz, as well as WonderWorks (a kid-paced participatory science and fun lab), the Muvico Pointe 21 theater, and such restaurants as Johnny Rockets.

ORLANDO SUBURBS

The airy, spacious, two-level **Altamonte Mall** (✉ 451 Altamonte Ave., Altamonte Springs) contains Sears, Gayfers, Burdines, and JCPenney department stores and 175 specialty shops. The New England–style village of **Mount Dora** is recognized as the "antiques capital of Florida" because of its dozens of galleries and antiques shops and its many weekend art, antiques, and crafts shows. **Old Town** (✉ 5770 W. Irlo Bronson Memorial Hwy., Kissimmee) is a shopping-entertainment complex featuring a 1909 carousel, a Saturday-night classic-car rally, and more than 70 specialty shops in a re-creation of a turn-of-the-century Florida village. **Park Avenue** (✉ Winter Park) has a collection of chic boutiques and bistros and is the perfect place for a romantic evening stroll.

WALT DISNEY WORLD® AND THE ORLANDO AREA A TO Z

Arriving and Departing

By Bus

Greyhound Lines (☎ 800/231–2222) buses stop in Orlando (✉ 555 N. John Young Pkwy., ☎ 407/292–3422).

By Car

From I–95, which runs down Florida's east coast, you can turn off onto I–4 just below Daytona; it's about 50 mi from there to Orlando. If you're taking I–75 down through the middle of the state, get off at Wildwood and take Florida's Turnpike for about 50 mi. The scenic Beeline Expressway, a toll road, links Orlando and Cocoa Beach, about an hour away.

By Plane

More than 20 scheduled airlines and more than 30 charter firms operate in and out of **Orlando International Airport** (☎ 407/825–2001), providing direct service to more than 100 cities in the United States and overseas. The most active carriers are Delta and United. Other airlines include America West, American, British Airways, Continental, Northwest, TWA, US Airways, and Virgin Atlantic.

BETWEEN THE AIRPORT AND THE HOTELS

Find out in advance whether your hotel offers a free airport shuttle; if not, ask for a recommendation.

Lynx (✉ 1200 W. South St., Orlando, ☎ 407/841–8240) operates public buses between the airport and the main terminal downtown. Though the cost is very low, other options are preferable since the terminal is far from most hotels used by theme-park vacationers.

Mears Transportation Group (☎ 407/423–5566) meets you at the gate, helps you with your luggage, and whisks you away, either in an 11-passenger van, a town car, or a limo. Vans run to and along U.S. 192 every 30 minutes; prices range from $12.50 one-way to $22 round-trip for adults. Limo rates run around $50–$60 for a town car that accommodates three or four and $90 for a stretch limo that seats six. **Town & Country** (☎ 407/828–3035) charges $30–$40 one-way for up to seven, depending on the hotel.

Taxis take only a half hour to get from the airport to most hotels used by WDW visitors. They charge about $25 to the International Drive area, about $10 more to the U.S. 192 area.

By Train
Amtrak (☎ 800/872–7245) operates the *Silver Star* and the *Silver Meteor* to Florida. Both stop in Winter Park (✉ 150 Morse Blvd.), Orlando (✉ 1400 Sligh Blvd.), and Kissimmee (✉ 416 Pleasant St.). The Auto Train carries cars between Sanford and Lorton, Virginia (just south of Washington, D.C.).

Getting Around

Although the public transportation in Orlando could use some work and taxis are expensive because of the distances involved, it is by no means absolutely necessary to rent a car in Orlando.

If you are staying at a Walt Disney World Resort hotel or if you buy a multiday pass, your transportation within WDW is free.

Outside, just about every hotel and even many motels are linked to one of several private transportation systems that shuttle travelers back and forth to most area attractions for only a few dollars. However, if you want to visit the major theme parks outside Walt Disney World Resort, venture off the beaten track, or eat where most tourists don't, a rental car is essential. And if you are traveling with your family, you may spend more on these shuttles, which charge by the head, than on a rental car: Orlando offers some of the lowest rental-car rates in the United States.

By Bus
If you are staying along International Drive, in Kissimmee, or in Orlando proper, you can ride public buses to get around the immediate area. To find out which bus to take, ask your hotel clerk or call **Lynx** (☎ 407/841–8240).

By Car
The most important artery in the Orlando area is I–4. This interstate highway, which links the Atlantic Coast to Florida's Gulf of Mexico, ties everything together, and you'll invariably receive directions in reference to it. The problem is that I–4, though considered an east–west expressway in our national road system (where even numbers signify an east–west orientation and odd numbers a north–south orientation), actually runs north and south in the Orlando area. So when the signs say east, you are usually going north, and when the signs say west, you are usually going south.

Another main drag is International Drive, also known as I-Drive, which has many major hotels, restaurants, and shopping centers. You can get onto International Drive from I–4 Exits 28, 29, and 30A. The other main road, U.S. 192, cuts across I–4 at Exits 25A and 25B. This highway goes through the Kissimmee area and crosses WDW property, taking you to the Magic Kingdom's main entrance.

By Shuttle
Scheduled service and charters linking just about every hotel and major attraction in the area are available from **Gray Line of Orlando** (☎ 407/422–0744) and **Mears Transportation Group** (☎ 407/423–5566). In

addition, many hotels run their own shuttles especially for guests; to arrange a ride, ask your hotel concierge, inquire at the front desk, or phone the company directly.

One-way fares are usually $6–$7 per adult, a couple of dollars less for children ages 4–11, between major hotel areas and the WDW parks. Round-trip excursion fares to Cypress Gardens are $27 per person, including admission.

By Taxi

Taxi fares start at $2.45 and cost $1.40 for each mile thereafter. Call **Yellow Cab** (☎ 407/699–9999) or **Town & Country** (☎ 407/828–3035). Sample fares are as follows: to WDW's Magic Kingdom, about $20 from International Drive, $11–$15 from U.S. 192; to Universal Studios, $6–$11 from International Drive, $25–$30 from U.S. 192; to downtown Orlando's Church Street Station, $20–$25 from International Drive, $30–$40 from U.S. 192.

Contacts and Resources

Emergencies

Dial **911** for police or ambulance. All the area's major theme parks (and some of the minor ones) have first-aid centers.

HOSPITALS

Hospital emergency rooms are open 24 hours a day. The most accessible hospital in the International Drive area is the **Orlando Regional Medical Center/Sand Lake Hospital** (✉ 9400 Turkey Lake Rd., ☎ 407/351–8500).

LATE-NIGHT PHARMACIES

Eckerd Drug (✉ 908 Lee Rd., off I–4 at Lee Rd. exit, Orlando, ☎ 407/644–6908) and **Walgreens** (✉ 6201 International Dr., opposite Wet 'n Wild, Orlando, ☎ 407/345–8311; ✉ 4578 S. Kirkman Rd., north of Universal Studios, Orlando, ☎ 407/293–8458; ✉ 5935 W. Irlo Bronson Memorial Hwy., Kissimmee, ☎ 407/396–2002).

Guided Tour

One of the most popular—and enduring—tours in the Orlando area is Winter Park's **Scenic Boat Tour,** which leaves hourly from the dock at the end of Morse Avenue. During the one-hour tour you'll get to see lifestyles of the rich and famous—Central Florida–style. The boat cruises by some of the area's most expensive waterfront homes. ✉ *312 E. Morse Blvd., Winter Park,* ☎ *407/644–4056.* ✑ *$6 adults, $3 children 2–11.* ◷ *Daily 10–4.*

Visitor Information

Kissimmee/St. Cloud Convention and Visitors Bureau (✉ 1925 E. Irlo Bronson Memorial Hwy., Kissimmee 34744, ☎ 407/847–5000 or 800/327–9159). **Orlando/Orange County Convention & Visitors Bureau** (✉ 6700 Forum Dr., Suite 100, Orlando 32821-8087, ☎ 407/363–5800). **Winter Park Chamber of Commerce** (✉ Box 280, Winter Park 32790, ☎ 407/644–8281).

7 THE TAMPA BAY AREA

This section of Florida is unusually diverse. Tampa is a bustling city. Across Tampa Bay, on Florida's west coast, the pace on the beaches of Clearwater and St. Petersburg and in the peaceful downtown area of St. Pete is slower. To the north are extensive nature preserves, parks, and tiny communities. South of Tampa, along the gulf, are several quiet burgs and sophisticated Sarasota, a well-known upscale winter resort.

Updated by
Rowland
Stiteler

ALTHOUGH GLITZY MIAMI seems to hold the trendiness trump card and Orlando is the place your kids will want to visit annually until they hit middle school, the Tampa Bay area has that elusive quality that many attribute to the "real Florida." The state's second-largest metro area is less fast-lane than its biggest (Miami) or even Orlando, but its strengths are just as varied, from broad cultural diversity to a sunset-worshipping beach culture. Florida's third-busiest airport, a vibrant business community, world-class beaches, and superior hotels and resorts—many of them historic—make this an excellent place to spend a week or a lifetime.

Native Americans were the sole inhabitants of the region for many years. (Tampa is a Native American word meaning "sticks of fire.") Spanish explorers Juan Ponce de León, Pánfilo de Narváez, and Hernando de Soto passed through in the mid-1500s, and the U.S. Army and civilian settlers arrived in 1824. The Spanish-American War was very good to Tampa, enabling industrialist Henry Plant to create an economic momentum that his successors have kept up through the entire 20th century. A military presence remains in Tampa at MacDill Air Force Base, the U.S. Operations Command.

Today the region offers astounding diversity. Terrain ranges from the rolling, pine-dotted northern reaches to the coast's white-sand beaches and barrier islands. Communities run the gamut as well. Tampa is a full-fledged city with a high-rise skyline and highways jammed with traffic. Across the bay lies the peninsula that contains Clearwater and St. Petersburg. The compact St. Petersburg downtown, which contains interesting restaurants, shops, and museums, is on the southeast tip of the peninsula, facing Tampa. Inland is largely classic American suburbia. If it weren't for the palm trees, you could be on the outskirts of Kansas City. The peninsula's western periphery is rimmed by barrier islands with beaches, quiet parks, and little, laid-back beach towns. To the north are communities that celebrate their ethnic heritage and, farther still, mostly undeveloped land dotted with crystal-clear rivers and springs and nature preserves. To the south lie resort towns, including Sarasota, which fills up in winter with snowbirds escaping the cold.

New and Noteworthy

Centro Ybor, a dining-and-entertainment complex in, you guessed it, the center of Ybor City is slated to open in late 2000. Tampa's biggest hotel news in a decade is the coming of the downtown **Marriott Waterside Hotel,** adjacent to the Tampa Convention Center and near the cruise-ship berths and the Florida Aquarium. The 710-room, 15-story hotel, set to open in March 2000, has been designed as a convention hotel, with a 50,000-square-ft conference center, but lots of amenities and fine restaurants should make it a great place for vacationers, too.

Pleasures and Pastimes

Beaches

Every barrier island from Clearwater to Venice has excellent swimming beaches facing out on the Gulf of Mexico. As on Florida's Atlantic coast, the farther south you go, the more turquoise and tropical the water appears. Don't swim in Tampa Bay, Sarasota Bay, or the inland waterway, however, all of which have been polluted by boaters, marinas, and industry. In addition, there have been rare shark attacks in Tampa Bay (none fatal in recent years), something you never hear about in the gulf itself.

Biking

The 36-mi-long Pinellas Trail, a paved route that follows the path of a former railroad, makes it possible to bike all the way from Tarpon Springs, at the north end of Pinellas County, to a spot not far north of the Sunshine Skyway Bridge, at the south end of the county. You get the flavor of all sorts of neighborhoods and an amalgam of suburbs on this carless highway. The trail, which is also popular with in-line skaters, has spawned all sorts of trail-side businesses, such as bike-rental and repair shops and health food–oriented cafés. There are also many lovely rural areas to bike through and plenty of places to rent bikes, should you want to pedal along the streets. However, be wary of traffic in downtown Tampa and on the congested areas of the Pinellas Trail, which still needs more bridges for crossing over busy streets.

Canoeing

Several inland rivers offer superb canoeing, and outfits at different points along their shores rent equipment and lead guided tours.

Dining

Fresh seafood is plentiful, and raw bars serving oysters, clams, and mussels are everywhere. Combine that with the region's ethnic diversity, and varied and interesting dining options are the result. Tampa's many Cuban and Spanish restaurants serve fresh seafood, perhaps in a spicy paella, along with black beans and rice. Tarpon Springs adds a hearty helping of such classic Greek specialties as moussaka and baklava. In Sarasota, the emphasis is on fine dining—both food and service—no matter what the cuisine.

Many restaurants, from family neighborhood spots to very expensive places, offer extra-cheap early bird menus for seatings before 6 PM. These are even more prevalent off-season, from May to October.

Fishing

Anglers flock to southwest Florida's coastal water to catch tarpon, king-fish, speckled trout, snapper, grouper, sea trout, snook, sheepshead, and shark. You can charter a fishing boat or join a group on a party boat for full- or half-day outings. Avoid fishing in polluted Tampa Bay.

Exploring the Tampa Bay Area

Whether you feel like walking on white-sand beaches, watching sponge fishermen, or wandering through upscale shopping districts, you'll find something to your liking in the remarkably diverse Tampa Bay area. Bright, modern Tampa is the area's commercial center, the only place in the metro area that truly feels urban. Peninsular St. Petersburg lies across the bay with a variety of attractions, including some good beach life. Tarpon Springs, to the northwest, was settled by Greek mariners and is still Greek in flavor. The Manatee Coast, to the north, is quite rural, with extensive nature preserves. To the south are Bradenton, which has several museums; Sarasota, a sophisticated resort town; and small, canal-crossed Venice.

Numbers in the text correspond to numbers in the margin and on the Tampa/St. Petersburg and Bradenton/Sarasota maps.

Great Itineraries

IF YOU HAVE 3 DAYS

Florida Aquarium ①, in downtown ▨ **Tampa** ①–⑧, and **Busch Gardens** ⑤, 8 mi northeast of the city, are probably the two most popular attractions in the area. You'll need a half day for the aquarium and a full day for Busch Gardens. Then it's on to ▨ **Sarasota** ㊲–㊹ and highlights such as the **Ringling Museums** ㊲ and **Bellm's Cars & Music of Yesterday** ㊳.

IF YOU HAVE 4 DAYS

Start your time in **Tampa** ①–⑧ with a half day at the **Florida Aquarium** ①. Then it's just a short drive to **Ybor City** ②, where you can rest your feet over lunch before an hour or two of strolling through the shops. **Busch Gardens** ⑤ will take your whole second day and is worth a visit whether your preference is going on thrilling rides or seeing animals in their natural settings. One of the best spots for a day at the beach is pristine **Fort De Soto State Park** ⑯, a perfect place for a picnic. Art lovers and circus buffs can spend their last day in **Sarasota** ㊲–㊹, traipsing through the **Ringling Museums** ㊲ and **Bellm's Cars & Music of Yesterday** ㊳, a delight if you love antique cars or music boxes.

IF YOU HAVE 10 DAYS

With this much time you can linger five days in **St. Petersburg** ⑨–⑲, which is centrally located for several engaging half- and full-day trips. You could easily spend a full day in downtown **Tampa** ①–⑧. Start with a morning visit to the spectacular **Florida Aquarium** ①; then head to **Ybor City** ② for a bit of exploring and lunch, and end the day with a visit to the **Tampa Museum of Art** ③. The next three attractions, clustered together northeast of Tampa, can be reached by car in 45–60 minutes from St. Petersburg. Spend a day at **Busch Gardens** ⑤, getting there early if you plan to see it all. If your family is into water slides, set aside another day for **Adventure Island** ⑥, Busch Gardens' water-park cousin. On days that Adventure Island is closed or on a rainy afternoon or morning, visit the **Museum of Science and Industry** ⑦, or pick from the fascinating selection of museums in downtown St. Petersburg. Spend a day around **Tarpon Springs** ㉔–㉖, a quaint Greek village and the self-described sponge capital of the world. **Fort De Soto State Park** ⑯ and Caladesi Island State Park and nearby Honeymoon Island State Park, outside **Dunedin** ㉓, are all excellent choices for a day at the beach.

Sarasota ㊲–㊹ is a convenient base for the second part of your stay. One day drive up to **Bradenton** ㉜–㊱ and take in its sights. If you feel like a boat ride, begin or end the day with a trip to **Egmont Key** ㊱. In Sarasota allow about three hours to cover both the **Ringling Museums** ㊲ and **Bellm's Cars & Music of Yesterday** ㊳. In the afternoon you might stop by the **Sarasota Jungle Gardens** ㊴, especially nice for children. On another day visit the **Marie Selby Botanical Gardens** ㊵, quieter but still tropical, and give yourself a couple of hours to shop at St. Armand's Circle on Lido Key. **Venice** ㊺ makes an enjoyable half- or full-day trip, and, of course, sprinkle in some time on the beach.

When to Tour the Tampa Bay Area

Winter and spring are high season here, and the level of activity in hotels and restaurants is double what it is in the off-season. In summer there are huge, showy thunderstorms on many afternoons, and temperatures hover around 90°F during the day. If you don't like equatorial humidity levels, you're in the wrong place at the wrong time. Luckily the mercury drops to the mid-70s at night, and beach towns have a consistent on-shore breeze that starts just before sundown, which enabled civilization to survive here before air-conditioning was invented.

NORTH AND WEST AROUND TAMPA BAY

The core of the northern bay is the cities of Tampa, St. Petersburg, and Clearwater. A semitropical climate and access to the gulf make Tampa an ideal port for the cruise industry; currently, Carnival and Holland America depart from the Port of Tampa. In addition, the waters around Clearwater and St. Pete are often filled with pleasure and commercial craft, including literally dozens of boats offering various types of day trips, as well as night trips featuring what the purveyors euphemistically call "Las Vegas action": gambling in international waters.

It's fitting that an area with a thriving international port should also be populated by a wealth of nationalities. The center of the Cuban community is the east Tampa enclave of Ybor City, while north of St. Petersburg, in Dunedin, the heritage is Scottish. North of Dunedin, Tarpon Springs has supported a large Greek population for decades and is the largest producer of natural sponges in the world.

Inland, to the east of Tampa, it's all suburban sprawl, freeways, shopping malls, and—the main draw—Busch Gardens.

Tampa

84 mi southwest of Orlando.

The west coast's crown jewel as well as its business and commercial hub, Tampa has numerous high-rises and heavy traffic, but amid the bustle are all the delights you'd expect to find in a big city. The region's greatest concentration of restaurants, nightlife, stores, and cultural events are here, as are some appealing extras.

★ ☺ ❶ The $84 million **Florida Aquarium** is no overpriced fishbowl. It's a dazzling architectural landmark with an 83-ft-high multitier glass dome, a worthy addition to the cruise-ship terminal district that surrounds it. More than 4,300 specimens of fish, other animals, and plants representing 550 species native to Florida are housed here, with occasional visits by such rare creatures as an albino alligator with blue eyes. Visitors follow the path of a drop of water from the freshwater springs and limestone caves of an aquifer through rivers and wetlands to beaches and open seas. Four major exhibit areas reflect the variety of Florida's natural habitats—springs and wetlands, bay and barrier beach, coral reef, and the Gulf Stream and open ocean. The centerpiece is a full-scale replica of a Florida coral reef in a 500,000-gallon tank ringed with viewing windows, including an awesome 43-ft-wide panoramic opening. Part of the tank is an acrylic tunnel through an underwater thicket of elk-horn coral teeming with tropical fish, where a dark cave reveals sea life you can ordinarily glimpse only on night dives. If you want to throw an all-out banquet, ask about the catered group dinners offered among the fish tanks, a popular local pastime in Tampa social circles. ✉ *701 Channelside Dr.,* ☎ *813/273–4000.* 🎫 *$11.95.* ⊙ *Daily 9:30–5.*

★ ❷ Whether your interests run to spicy food, boutique shopping, or Latin music, **Ybor City,** Tampa's Cuban enclave, has it all. With antique brick streets and wrought-iron balconies, this historic and lively neighborhood is one of only three National Historic Landmark districts in Florida. Cubans brought their cigar-making industry to Ybor (pronounced *ee*-bore) City in 1866, and the smell of cigars—hand-rolled by Cuban immigrants—still drifts through the heart of this east Tampa area. These days the neighborhood is emerging as Tampa's hot spot, as empty cigar factories are transformed into trendy boutiques, art galleries, restaurants, and nightclubs, which offer as wide a range of entertainment styles as you'll find in Miami's sizzling South Beach district. There's even a microbrewery. Take a stroll past the ornately tiled **Columbia** restaurant and the stores lining 7th Avenue, or step back to the past at **Ybor Square** (✉ 1901 13th St.), a restored cigar factory

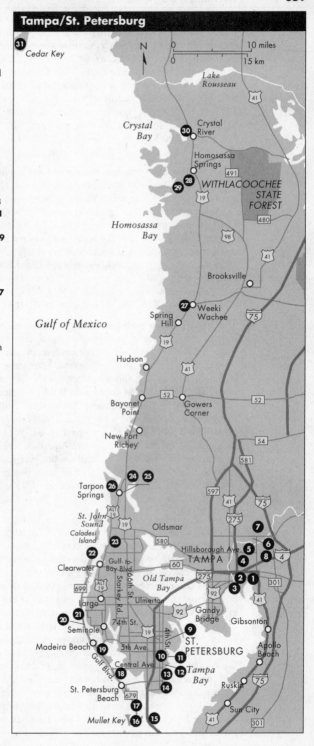

Tampa/St. Petersburg

listed on the National Register of Historic Places that now houses boutiques, offices, and restaurants. By late 2000 a new multivenue dining-and-entertainment palace, **Centro Ybor** (⊠ 7th Ave.), developed
by the company that did Coconut Grove's CocoWalk, is set to open
in the heart of Ybor. A visit to the **Ybor City State Museum** (⊠ 1818
9th Ave.) provides a look at the history of the cigar industry. The museum is open Tuesday–Saturday 9–noon and 1–5, and admission costs
$2. Free guided walking tours of the area enable you to see artisans
hand-roll cigars following time-honored methods. ⊠ *Between Nuccio*
Pkwy. and 22nd St. from 7th to 9th Aves., ☎ *813/248–3712 for tours.*
☉ *Tours Thurs. and Sat. 10:30, also Jan.–Apr., Tues. 10:30.*

❸ The 35,000-square-ft **Tampa Museum of Art** has a permanent collection of more than 7,000 works, including the most comprehensive collection of Greek, Roman, and Etruscan antiquities in the southeastern
United States and an excellent collection of 20th-century American art.
In addition, it presents more than 15 special exhibitions annually. The
Florida Gallery showcases the state's well-known and emerging artists,
and a sculpture garden and 7-acre park are also here. Through December
1999 the museum is featuring the Princess Diana Collection of Gowns,
including the popular "John Travolta" dress. This is the exhibit's first
stop on an international tour. ⊠ *600 N. Ashley Dr.,* ☎ *813/274–8130.*
⊠ *$5.* ☉ *Mon.–Tues. and Thurs.–Sat. 10–5, Wed. 10–9, Sun. 1–5.*

❹ The 24-acre **Lowry Park Zoo** features exotic creatures from four continents in their natural habitats. Get in touch with gentle animals at
the petting zoo. Check out the Asian Domain and its varied primates,
from chimpanzees to woolly monkeys. Spot some fancy flying in the
free-flight bird aviary, and come face to face with alligators, panthers,
bears, and red wolves at the Florida Wildlife Center, a special sanctuary for native Floridian animals. The latest addition is a special walk-
in lorikeet aviary, in which visitors can feed and pet the colorful little
birds. This is also a good place to get a close look at Florida's legendary
manatees, as the zoo's Manatee and Aquatic Center is one of the most
extensive in the state. If you get here and discover your kids really wanted
to go to a theme park, fear not. The adjacent Fun Forest at Lowry Park
has rides as well as that all-important venue for the nurturing of American youth—an arcade. ⊠ *7530 North Blvd.,* ☎ *813/932–0245.* ⊠
$8.50. ☉ *Daily 9:30–5.*

★ ☕ **❺** More than 3,400 animals are just part of the attraction of **Busch Gar-**
dens, a sprawling, immaculately manicured site combining a zoolike
setting with a theme park. Themed sections attempt to capture the spirit
of turn-of-the-century Africa, and a monorail ride simulates an African
safari—taking in free-roaming zebras, giraffes, rhinos, lions, and other
exotic animals. The 335-acre park also has live entertainment, animal
exhibits, shops, restaurants, games, and thrill rides. The pulse-pump-
ing Kumba and Montu are among the largest and fastest roller coasters in the Southeast, both reaching speeds of more than 60 mph and
g-forces that challenge the most ardent roller-coaster freak. If these aren't
fast enough, try your stomach on Gwazi, which opened in summer 1999
and features a 90-ft drop and more than 70,000 ft of track. Akbar's
Adventure Tours is a simulator trek featuring narration and images of
actor Martin Short. You can also take a beer-tasting class (after all,
Anheuser-Busch owns the park). Allow from six to eight hours to *do*
Busch Gardens, but parents take note: This is not the ideal attraction
for little kids. Although there's a small area of rides for little ones and
the animals hold universal appeal, major rides are too wild for toddlers and young grade-schoolers—and the admission price for kids approaches that for adults. Besides, except for buying beer, you're an

"adult" at age 10 here anyway. Busch Gardens is 8 mi northeast of downtown Tampa and 2 mi east of I–275 (Exit 33). ⊠ *3000 E. Busch Blvd.,* ☎ *813/987–5082.* ⊡ *$41.15, parking $4–$6.* ☉ *Daily 10–6, later in summer and holidays.*

Water slides, pools, and artificial-wave pools create a 25-acre water wonderland at **Adventure Island,** a corporate cousin of Busch Gardens. This place features creative, if geographically incorrect, rides like the Key West Rapids and the Tampa Typhoon. Never mind that there are no rapids in the real Key West and that *typhoon* is a term used only in Pacific regions; Tampa Hurricane just wouldn't have had that alliterative allure. Along with a championship volleyball complex, you'll find cafés, snack bars, changing rooms, and video games. The complex is less than a mile north of Busch Gardens. ⊠ *10001 Malcolm McKinley Dr.,* ☎ *813/987–5660.* ⊡ *$24.45.* ☉ *Late Mar.–late Oct., daily 10–5.*

❼ The **Museum of Science and Industry (MOSI)** is a fun and stimulating scientific playground where you learn by doing as well as by seeing. At the Gulf Coast Hurricane Exhibit you can experience what a hurricane and its 74-mph winds feel like (and live to write home about it). Butterfly Encounter is a 6,400-square-ft interactive garden inhabited by free-flying butterflies; the GTE *Challenger* Learning Center offers simulated flights; and the 100-seat Saunders Planetarium, Tampa Bay's only planetarium, has afternoon and evening shows daily, one of them a trek through the universe. There's also an impressive IMAX theater, where films are projected on a 360-degree, eight-story dome. The museum is a mile north of Busch Gardens. ⊠ *4801 E. Fowler Ave.,* ☎ *813/987–6300.* ⊡ *$11.* ☉ *Daily 9–5, longer in peak season.*

If you've brought your body to Tampa but your heart's in Vegas, you can satisfy that urge to hang around a poker table at 4 in the morning at the **Seminole Indian Casino.** The casino offers poker tables, high-stakes bingo, and gaming machines. For those who feel compelled to add a cultural angle to a trip to the tables, the **Seminole Indian Museum and Cultural Center** (☎ 813/620–3077) next door features demonstrations of Seminole skill in beadwork and carving, with all sorts of mementos for sale. There's even an alligator-wrestling show, but not at 4 AM. ⊠ *5223 N. Orient Rd.,* ☎ *813/621–1302 or 800/282–7016.* ⊡ *Free.* ☉ *Casino daily 24 hrs.; museum/cultural center Mon.–Sat. 9–5, Sun. 10–4.*

Dining and Lodging

$$$–$$$$ ✕ **Armani's.** Atop the Hyatt Regency Westshore (☞ *below*), this
★ award-winning northern Italian restaurant has a great view of bay and city and almost as good a sunset view as you'll find along the gulf. Romantic lighting highlights the sophisticated almond-and-black decor. Service is impeccable, and the food incredible. A feast in itself, the antipasto bar changes nightly. Pasta is excellent, and someone at your table should order the veal Armani (with mushrooms, cream, and cognac in black and white truffle sauce), the signature dish. Another standout is the chicken *rollatini,* thin chicken fillets rolled around mozzarella and fresh spinach. (Sunday brunch is also served.) Popular with celebrities, the restaurant has often made the top-20 list of *Florida Trend* magazine, a publication that's notoriously tight-fisted with its kudos. ⊠ *6200 Courtney Campbell Causeway,* ☎ *813/281–9165. AE, DC, MC, V.*

$$$–$$$$ ✕ **Bern's Steak House.** Though the building has been variously described
★ as a "warehouse" and a "bordello" by local dining critics, chef-owner Bern Lexer didn't set out to be an architect or interior designer. He set out to own the best restaurant in Tampa, and most locals feel he has

done just that. Lexer ages his own beef, grows his own organic vegetables, roasts his own coffee, and even maintains his own saltwater fish tanks. The 212-page wine list offers some 7,000 selections (including 1,800 dessert wines), ranging from $10 to $10,000 a bottle. Dinners are served in many small rooms filled with memorabilia, gaudy to some folks, quaint to others. After dinner most guests move upstairs to intimate glass-enclosed rooms for to-die-for desserts. If you want dessert in a more casual atmosphere, or perhaps just a sandwich and some roasted-on-the-premises coffee, head up the block to the new annex, SideBern's (⊠ 1002 S. Howard Ave.). ⊠ *1208 S. Howard Ave.,* ☎ *813/251–2421. AE, DC, MC, V. No lunch.*

$$ ✕ **Castaway.** In something of a restaurant district on the east side of Tampa Bay's Courtney Campbell Causeway (three minutes west of Tampa International Airport), Castaway offers bay views without charging a premium for them. The specialty of this midprice, casual restaurant is fresh local seafood—grilled, broiled, or blackened—but the menu also includes grilled steaks and several pasta dishes. You can choose to dine inside or outside on the expansive deck, which is particularly popular for lunch and at sunset. Don't worry: The jets dipping down over the bay on their final approach are just far enough away to avoid a noise problem. ⊠ *7720 Courtney Campbell Causeway,* ☎ *813/281–0770. DC, MC, V. No lunch Sun.*

$$ ✕ **Columbia.** A Spanish fixture in Ybor City since 1905, this magnif-
★ icent structure with ceramic murals, high archways, and ornate railings occupies an entire city block and contains several airy, spacious dining rooms and a sunny atrium. In the years before the techno music bars and female impersonator clubs, when Ybor City was something less than vibrant and trendy, this restaurant pretty much carried the neighborhood on its big shoulders, drawing downtown business people whose families had eaten here for generations. They still come. Specialties include paella (a version that many consider the best in Florida), black-bean soup, and the infamous Columbia 1905 salad (with ham, olives, cheese, and garlic). There's flamenco dancing nightly in the main dining room, which looks like it could be in a Spanish castle. Like just about every other retail business in Ybor, you can acquire and smoke hand-rolled cigars here—in the bar. ⊠ *2117 E. 7th Ave.,* ☎ *813/248–4961. AE, DC, MC, V.*

$–$$ ✕ **Cafe Winberie.** This charming and sophisticated café with lots of sidewalk seating under a big red awning has become a focal point of the Old Hyde Park Village shopping district. Although sitting outside and tasting your way down the wine list makes for a wonderful spring afternoon, you'll want to dine indoors from May to November unless you come from someplace even hotter and more humid than Tampa. The menu includes a bit of everything: southwestern, vegetarian, Mediterranean, Thai, and classic American. Main-course choices include salmon baked in parchment (perhaps the best item on the menu), vegetarian chili with a triple-grain medley, char-grilled sirloin with cognac-mustard sauce, and a Mediterranean-style pasta with sun-dried tomatoes, Kalamata olives, and roasted garlic. Save room for dessert. The chocolate fondue is fun to share, and the key lime pie is outstanding. Lunch brings sandwiches, including a worthwhile Cuban pork sandwich, and light salads. ⊠ *1610 W. Swann Ave.,* ☎ *813/253–6500. AE, MC, V.*

$–$$ ✕ **Colonnade.** The nautical decor suits the wharf-side location of this popular family restaurant. Seafood—particularly grouper, salmon, shrimp, and lobster—is a specialty, but chicken is also well prepared. ⊠ *3401 Bayshore Blvd.,* ☎ *813/839–7558. AE, DC, MC, V.*

$–$$ ✗ **Kojak's House of Ribs.** Family-run since the door opened here in 1978, this casual eatery has been voted a Tampa favorite year after year in local newspaper and magazine polls. Day and night the three indoor dining rooms and the outdoor dining terrace are crowded with guests digging into mouthwatering platters of tender barbecued ribs. There's chicken on the menu, too, and heaping sides of coleslaw and potato salad. ⊠ *2808 Gandy Blvd.,* ☎ *813/837–3774. Reservations not accepted for fewer than 6. No credit cards. Closed Mon.*

$ ✗ **Cactus Club.** The cuisine is billed as southwestern, but it's served with a Florida twist; shrimp fajitas, for instance, are a specialty. Other standouts include the baby-back ribs and a tasty Texas Pie (otherwise known as pizza) with a thin, crispy crust—try the Laredo, with a tangy tomato-pesto sauce. For devoted carnivores, there's the Blues Burger, and, not surprisingly, the house drink is the Ultimate Margarita. The sidewalk café is lovely in winter and spring but brutal in summer, when it's best to opt for indoor seating. ⊠ *1601 Snow Ave., Old Hyde Park Village,* ☎ *813/251–4089. AE, DC, MC, V.*

$ ✗ **Mise en Place.** Discussion among food critics about what's the best
★ Tampa restaurant usually comes down to two places: Bern's Steak House and Mise en Place. Across from the University of Tampa, this new American bistro is so popular that its owners, Marty and Marianne Blitz, have become local celebrities. The changing menu is replete with Floribbean dishes—like creative takes on swordfish or grouper. But there are some markedly un-Florida, un-Caribbean dishes, too—everything from roast duck and rack of lamb to an occasional venison appearance. Marty's forte is combining seemingly incompatible ingredients to make a masterpiece. His best combo: shrimp, manchego cheese, and chorizo grits with Puerto Rican red-bean salsa—a little United Nations on one plate. The Blitzes also operate 442, an ultracool jazz club next door, which serves appetizers from the Mise en Place kitchen. You can also get this great cuisine to go at the Mise en Place Market (⊠ 2616 S. MacDill Ave.). ⊠ *442 W. Kennedy Blvd.,* ☎ *813/254–5373. Reservations not accepted for fewer than 6. AE, D, DC, MC, V. Closed Sun.*

$$$–$$$$ 🏨 **Saddlebrook Resort Tampa.** With 45 tennis courts and 36 holes of golf, this is arguably one of Florida's premier resorts of its type. Its heavily wooded grounds sprawl over 480 acres just 15 mi north of Tampa. Varied accommodations include many one- and two-bedroom, two-bath suites with kitchens. ⊠ *5700 Saddlebrook Way, Wesley Chapel 33543,* ☎ *813/973–1111 or 800/729–8383,* 🅵🅰🆇 *813/773–4504. 790 units. 3 restaurants, 2 bars, pool, wading pools, saunas, driving range, 36 holes of golf, 45 tennis courts, health club, fishing, bicycles. AE, DC, MC, V.*

$$$–$$$$ 🏨 **Wyndham Harbour Island Hotel.** Even though this 12-story hotel is on a 177-acre island in Tampa Bay, it's just an eight-minute walk or an even shorter drive to downtown Tampa, with both the Tampa Convention Center and the Garrison Seaport a stone's throw away. So it's not surprising that many units have terrific views of the water or the downtown skyline. Dark wood paneling and substantial furniture in the elegant lobby set the scene for attentive service. There is a full-service marina, and hotel guests may use the extensive health and fitness center and 20 tennis courts at the Harbour Island Athletic Club, next door. This is a good choice for travelers who want to be downtown without actually being in the midst of downtown. ⊠ *725 S. Harbour Island Blvd., 33602,* ☎ *813/229–5000,* 🅵🅰🆇 *813/229–5322. 299 units. Restaurant, bar, pool, dock, boating, fishing, bicycles. AE, DC, MC, V.*

$$$ 🏨 **Embassy Suites Hotel–Tampa/Airport/Westshore.** In this modern 16-story hotel midway between Tampa International Airport and downtown, all rooms are suites, and each has a kitchen. A complimentary breakfast is served. ⊠ *555 N. Westshore Blvd., 33609,* ☎ *813/875–1555,* FAX *813/287–3664. 221 suites. Restaurant, bar, pool, saunas, health club, airport shuttle. AE, DC, MC, V.*

$$$ ⊞ **Hyatt Regency Westshore.** As its name implies, this large 14-story luxury hotel sits on the west shore of Tampa Bay and is convenient to Tampa International and downtown Tampa, too. The most upscale hotel in the vicinity of the airport, it has a marble-accented lobby and a scattering of Spanish-style villas with private terraces. In addition to its bay views, the hotel also has a spectacular perch above a grassy, protected salt marsh and bird sanctuary. Though considered one of Tampa's best business hotels, the Hyatt has the amenities and, of course, views to attract vacationers as well. ⊠ *6200 Courtney Campbell Causeway, 33607,* ☎ *813/874–1234,* FAX *813/286–9864. 445 rooms. 3 restaurants, 3 bars, 2 pools, 2 tennis courts, exercise room, jogging, racquetball, boating, fishing. AE, D, DC, MC, V.*

$$ ⊞ **Holiday Inn Busch Gardens.** Renovated extensively in 1998, this well-maintained, family-oriented motor inn is a mile west of Busch Gardens, across the street from University Square Mall, Tampa's largest. ⊠ *2701 E. Fowler Ave., 33612,* ☎ *813/971–4710 or 800/206–2747,* FAX *813/977–0155. 395 rooms, 7 suites. Restaurant, bar, pool, exercise room. AE, DC, MC, V.*

$ ⊞ **Tahitian Inn.** Comfortable rooms and budget prices are the draws at this two-story family-run motel. It's five minutes from Tampa Stadium and 20 minutes from Busch Gardens. ⊠ *601 S. Dale Mabry Hwy., 33609,* ☎ *813/877–6721,* FAX *813/877–6218. 79 rooms. Coffee shop, pool. AE, DC, MC, V.*

Nightlife and the Arts

THE ARTS

Occupying 9 acres along the Hillsborough River, the 290,000-square-ft **Tampa Bay Performing Arts Center** (⊠ 1010 W. C. MacInnes Pl., ☎ 813/229–7827 or 800/955–1045) is one of the largest such complexes south of the Kennedy Center in Washington, D.C. Included are the 2,500-seat Carol Morsani Theater, a 900-seat playhouse, and a 300-seat theater, which feature opera, concerts, drama, and ballet, including the **Tampa Ballet** (☎ 813/229–7827). The **Tampa Convention Center** (⊠ 333 S. Franklin St., ☎ 813/274–8511) hosts concerts throughout the year. In a restored 1926 movie palace that's a nationally registered historic sight, the **Tampa Theater** (⊠ 711 N. Franklin St., ☎ 813/274–8981) mounts shows, musical performances, and films.

NIGHTLIFE

The biggest concentration of nightclubs, as well as the widest variety, is found along 7th Avenue in Ybor City. It becomes a little like Bourbon Street and a little like Miami's South Beach after the sun goes down. For cry-in-your-cabernet blues, sail down to the **Blue Ship Club & Cafe** (⊠ 1910 E. 7th Ave., ☎ 813/248–6097), in Ybor City, any Wednesday. On Friday and Saturday nights crowds head to the noisy, boisterous **Dallas Bull** (⊠ 8222 U.S. 301N, ☎ 813/985–6877) to stomp to down-home country sounds. Dance the night away at **Frankie's Patio Bar & Grill** (⊠ 1920 E. 7th Ave., ☎ 813/248–3337), which has entertainment Friday and Saturday. You probably won't bump into the Reverend Jerry Falwell at the **Pleasure Dome** (⊠ 1430 E. 7th Ave., ☎ 813/247–2711), in Ybor City, but you will see a good number of men on stage who feel pretty darn comfortable wearing women's clothes and singing Streisand songs. **Skippers Smokehouse** (⊠ 910 Skipper Rd., ☎ 813/971–0666), a restaurant and oyster bar, has live reggae and blues. The bar at the **Wyndham Harbour Island Hotel** (⊠ Harbour Island, ☎ 813/229–5000) has a great bay view and a big-screen TV.

Outdoor Activities and Sports

CANOEING

Just south of Tampa, **Canoe Outpost** (⊠ 18001 U.S. 301S, Wimauma, ☎ 813/634–2228) offers half-day, full-day, and overnight canoe trips on several area waters, including the Little Manatee River. But be warned: It's closed Wednesday.

DOG RACING

Tampa Greyhound Track (⊠ 8300 N. Nebraska Ave., ☎ 813/932–4313) holds dog races from July to December.

FOOTBALL

NFL football comes in the form of the **Tampa Bay Buccaneers** (⊠ 4201 N. Dale Mabry Hwy., ☎ 813/870–2700 or 800/282–0683), who play at Raymond James Stadium.

GOLF

Babe Zaharias Golf Course (⊠ 11412 Forest Hills Dr., ☎ 813/932–8932) has an 18-hole public course plus a driving range and a pro available for lessons. **Bloomingdale Golfers Club** (⊠ 4113 Great Golfers Pl., ☎ 813/653–1823) has 18 holes, a driving range, and a pleasant restaurant. At the well-known **Saddlebrook Resort Tampa** (⊠ 5700 Saddlebrook Way, Wesley Chapel, ☎ 913/973–1111), there are 36 holes, a driving range, golf shop, and on-site pro.

HORSE RACING

Tampa Bay Downs (⊠ Race Track Rd. off Rte. 580, Oldsmar, ☎ 813/855–4401) holds Thoroughbred races from mid-December to early May.

ICE HOCKEY

The NHL's **Tampa Bay Lightning** (⊠ 401 Channelside Dr., ☎ 813/229–2658) plays at the 21,500-seat Ice Palace, a classy $153 million downtown waterfront arena. It's near the Florida Aquarium and close enough to both Ybor City and Hyde Park to venture to either spot for lunch or dinner before a hockey match.

TENNIS AND RACQUETBALL

The **City of Tampa Tennis Complex** (⊠ Hillsborough Community College, ☎ 813/870–2383), across from Raymond James Stadium, has 12 clay courts and 16 hard courts. Four are lighted for night play. The complex also has four racquetball courts.

Shopping

For bargains stop at the **Big Top** (⊠ 9250 Fowler Ave.), open weekends 8–5, where vendors hawk new and used items at more than 600 booths. More than 120 shops, department stores, and eateries are found in the area's biggest super mall, **Brandon Town Center** (⊠ Grand Regency and Rte. 60), an attractively landscaped complex near I–75, eight minutes from downtown. **Old Hyde Park Village** (⊠ Swan Ave. near Bayshore Blvd.) is one of those gentrified shopping districts you'll find in every major American city, a place where stores like Williams-Sonoma and Brooks Brothers are mixed in with bistros and sidewalk cafés. The **Shops on Harbour Island** (⊠ 601 S. Harbour Island Blvd.) is a waterfront marketplace with stores, restaurants, and a food court.

St. Petersburg

21 mi west of Tampa.

St. Petersburg and the Pinellas Suncoast form the thumb of the hand jutting out of Florida's west coast, holding in Tampa Bay. There are two distinct parts of St. Petersburg—the downtown and cultural area, centered on the bay, and the beach area, a string of barrier islands facing the gulf that includes St. Pete Beach, Treasure Island, and Madeira Beach. Causeways link beach communities to the mainland peninsula.

⑨   **Sunken Gardens** is one of Florida's most colorful attractions. Walk through an aviary full of tropical birds; stroll among more than 50,000 exotic flowers and other plants; stop to smell the rare, fragrant orchids; and take a peek into the antiques store. You'll also find gator wrestling and macaw bird shows several times a day. In 1999 the owners were thinking of selling the place to a nudist colony, so it's best to call before you drop by. ⊠ *1825 4th St. N,* ☎ *727/896–3186.* 🎟 *$14.* 🕐 *Daily 10–5.*

The largest collection of Holocaust memorabilia outside the United States Holocaust Memorial Museum, in Washington, D.C., is found at the **⑩** downtown **Holocaust Memorial Museum & Education Center.** It features a prisoner transport railcar exhibit similar to the one in Washington as well as an extensive collection of photographs and artifacts. ⊠ *55 5th St. S,* ☎ *727/820–0100.* 🎟 *$6.* 🕐 *Weekdays 10–5, weekends noon–5.*

Outstanding examples of European, American, pre-Columbian, and **⑪** Far Eastern art line the walls of the **Museum of Fine Arts.** There are also photographic exhibits. ⊠ *255 Beach Dr. NE,* ☎ *727/896–2667.* 🎟 *$6.* 🕐 *Tues.–Sat. 10–5, Sun. 1–5.*

⑫ Learn about the region from prehistory to the present at the **St. Petersburg Museum of History.** Exhibits depict primitive shell tools, European settlement, the railroad era and Victorian Florida, the growth of tourism, the Great Depression, and the renewal of tourism since the 1940s. There is also an interesting display on commercial aviation. ⊠ *335 2nd Ave. NE,* ☎ *727/894–1052.* 🎟 *$5.* 🕐 *Mon.–Sat. 10–5, Sun. 1–5.*

The world's most extensive collection of originals by Spanish surreal-**⑬** ist Salvador Dali is found at the **Salvador Dali Museum.** Valued at more than $125 million, it includes 94 oils, more than 100 watercolors and drawings, and 1,300 graphics, sculptures, photographs, and objets d'art, including floor-to-ceiling murals. The downside is that you essentially have to walk through a gift shop to get to the galleries. The upside is the frequent tours led by docents, whose insights provide for a richer experience. The salient question, of course, is how the world's largest collection of Dali art ended up here. It's simple. A rich northern industrialist (one of a popular class of characters in Florida history), in this case Ohio magnate A. Reynolds Morse, was looking for a tourism-oriented destination as a site for a museum after his huge personal collection of Dali art began to overflow his mansion (Morse was a personal friend of Dali for decades). The good people of St. Petersburg made Mr. Morse feel wanted, and the museum was established here as a result. ⊠ *1000 3rd St. S,* ☎ *727/823–3767.* 🎟 *$8.* 🕐 *Mon.–Sat. 9:30–5:30, Sun. noon–5:30.*

☺ **⑭** In **Great Explorations!** you'll never hear, "Don't touch." The museum is hands-on in every room: the Body Shop, where you can explore health; the Think Tank, featuring mind-stretching puzzles; the Touch Tunnel, a 90-ft-long, pitch-black crawl-through maze; and Phenomenal Arts, where you can play a Moog synthesizer and explore neon-filled tubes that glow when touched. This is a big venue for school field trips; if you want to avoid them, come after 3 weekdays. ⊠ *800 2nd Ave. NE,* ☎ *727/821–8885.* 🎟 *$6.* 🕐 *Mon.–Sat. 10–8, Sun. noon–6.*

★ **⑮** It costs $1 to travel southbound on the **Sunshine Skyway,** the 4-mi-long bridge connecting Pinellas and Manatee counties, a section of

I–275. But it's money well spent. The roadway is 183 ft above Tampa Bay at its highest point, and the view out over the bay is spectacular. You'll see the several small islands that dot the bay if you're heading southeast, St. Petersburg Beach if you're going northwest.

⑯ Actually spread over six small islands, or keys, 900-acre **Fort De Soto State Park** lies at the mouth of Tampa Bay. It has 7 mi of beaches, two fishing piers, picnic and camping grounds, and a historic fort. The fort for which it's named was built on the southern end of Mullet Key to protect sea lanes in the gulf during the Spanish-American War. Roam the fort or wander the beaches of any of the islands within the park. ⊠ *Rte. 682 (54th Ave. S),* ☎ *727/866–2484.* ▧ *Free.* ☉ *Daily sunrise–sunset.*

⑰ On the southern end of St. Petersburg Beach, **Pass-A-Grille Beach** has
⑱ parking meters, a snack bar, rest rooms, and showers. **St. Petersburg Municipal Beach** (⊠ 11260 Gulf Blvd.) is a free beach on Treasure Is-
⑲ land. There are dressing rooms, metered parking, and a snack bar. **Maximo Park Beach** (⊠ 34th St. and Pinellas Point Dr. S, Madeira Beach) is on Boca Ciega Bay. It's unguarded, but there is a picnic area with grills, tables, shelters, and a boat ramp.

Dining and Lodging

$$–$$$$ ✕ **Marchand's Grill.** In what was the Pompeii Room when the Vinoy
★ Hotel, now the Renaissance Vinoy Resort (☞ *below*), opened in 1925, this wonderful eatery has frescoed ceilings and a spectacular view of Tampa Bay and the nearby boat docks. Happily, the atmosphere is matched by the great food, prepared by Tom Chin, named 1999 Chef of the Year by the Tampa Bay chapter of the American Culinary Federation. The imaginative menu contains lobster quesadillas with roasted tomato salsa and sweet pea guacamole as well as macadamia nut–crusted grouper with citrus papaya salsa. The wine list is quite extensive, too. Being a hotel restaurant, Marchand's serves breakfast, lunch, and dinner. ⊠ *501 5th Ave. NE,* ☎ *727/822–2785. AE, DC, MC, V.*

$–$$ ✕ **Apropos Bistro.** Sit indoors or out at this little harbor-front café open all day. For breakfast try the delicious blueberry pancakes. For lunch choose a light salad or one of the appealing sandwiches—filet mignon, tarragon chicken club, or ginger-marinated pork loin. Dinner entrées feature salads; grilled meats, including a great New York strip; pastas; and fish, including seared sesame tuna. ⊠ *300 2nd Ave., at beginning of pier,* ☎ *727/823–8934. MC, V. Closed Mon.*

$–$$ ✕ **Cafe Lido.** Sitting at the end of the St. Petersburg Pier is this peaceful place with red-and-white-checked tablecloths and pretty water views. Pizzas baked in a wood-burning oven are a specialty. Rigatoni à la vodka, the signature dish, headlines the pastas, and there are some nicely prepared veal dishes. ⊠ *800 2nd Ave. NE,* ☎ *727/898–5800. AE, MC, V.*

$–$$ ✕ **Hurricane Seafood Restaurant.** Everyone loves this seafood joint on historic Pass-A-Grille Beach for its steamed shrimp, homemade crab cakes, and grilled, broiled, or blackened grouper. One of the few places in St. Petersburg with live jazz (from Wednesday to Sunday), it also has a disco next door, Stormy's at the Hurricane. Check out the Keys Club for terrific live piano and specialty martinis. Crowds descend on the third-floor sundeck to see those gorgeous sunsets. ⊠ *807 Gulf Way,* ☎ *727/360–9558. MC, V.*

$ ✕ **Ted Peters Famous Smoked Fish.** A Pinellas County beach-culture institution, this place is popular with flip-flop-wearing fishermen who like to sit on the picnic benches, soak up a beer or three, and sample the wonderful smoked fish. The menu is limited to mackerel, mullet, and salmon, but all are smoked and seasoned to perfection and served with heaping helpings of German potato salad. The smoked fish spread, available to go, is incredible, too. Though all seating is outdoors, it's covered to protect you from those guaranteed summer-afternoon rainstorms. ⊠ *1350 Pasadena Ave. S, Pasadena,* ☎ *727/381–7931. No credit cards. Closed Tues. No dinner.*

$$$$ 🏨 **Don CeSar Beach Resort.** Still echoing with the ghosts of Scott and Zelda Fitzgerald, this sprawling, sybaritic, beachfront "Pink Palace" has long been a Gulf Coast landmark because of its remarkable architecture. Steeped in turn-of-the-century elegance, the hotel was a veterans' hospital during World War II and was vacant for a decade before local history lovers saved it from demolition in the late '60s. Be sure to ask the staff about the ghosts, which some locals swear they've seen in the halls at night. The resort offers some great amenities, such as a full-service spa. New one-bedroom suites are found in the Don CeSar Beach House, less than a half mile from the main building. Far more casual than the main hotel, the Beach House has a great beach bar of its own. ⊠ *3400 Gulf Blvd., St. Petersburg Beach 33706,* ☎ *727/ 360–1881,* FAX *813/367–3609. 275 rooms, 20 suites. 3 restaurants, 3 bars, 2 pools, 2 spas, exercise room, beach, boating, jet skiing, parasailing, children's programs, meeting rooms. AE, DC, MC, V.*

$$$$ 🏨 **Renaissance Vinoy Resort.** Though rooms in the original 1925 hotel building, listed on the National Register of Historic Places, have more character, all of the spacious units here—slated to be completely refurbished for the millennium—are comfortable and stylish. They come with three phones, two TVs, minibars, hair dryers, and bathrobes. The resort overlooks Tampa Bay, and a tiny beach does adjoin the property; in addition, transportation is provided to ocean beaches 20 minutes away. Other offerings include a Ron Garl–designed golf course with a stunning clubhouse, a big marina, and tours that include the downtown museums, making this a great base for seeing old downtown St. Petersburg. As a bonus, you can dine on excellent food in beautiful surroundings in the hotel's main dining room. ⊠ *501 5th Ave. NE, 33701,* ☎ *727/894–1000,* FAX *727/822–2785. 360 rooms. 5 restaurants, 2 bars, 2 pools, 18-hole golf course, 14 tennis courts, croquet, health club, dock, boating, business services. AE, DC, MC, V.*

$$ 🏨 **Mansion House.** Built at the end of the 19th century, this charming wood-frame house, now a bed-and-breakfast, is rumored to have been the home of the first mayor of St. Petersburg. Its first and second floors have five individually decorated and inviting rooms, but the most appealing might be the Carriage Room, which has a cathedral ceiling and an old-fashioned four-poster bed. Breakfast (included in the rate) is served in the dining room every morning. A pleasant 15-minute walk from the Pier on Tampa Bay, this B&B is within walking distance of restaurants, shops, and art galleries. ⊠ *105 5th Ave., 33701,* ☎ FAX *727/821–9391. 6 rooms. Dining room, library. AE, MC, V.*

$–$$ 🏨 **Islands's End Cottages.** These simply decorated, little one-bedroom cottages have water views and full kitchens. Outdoors, attractive wooden walkways lead to latticework sitting areas and peaceful gazebos. The grounds are nicely landscaped, and you can walk to the beach, restaurants, and shops. Grills are available if you want to barbecue. ⊠ *1 Pass-A-Grille Way, St. Petersburg Beach 33706,* ☎ *727/ 360–5023,* FAX *727/367–7890. 6 cottages. Fishing. MC, V.*

The Arts

THE ARTS

The **St. Petersburg Concert Ballet** (⊠ 400 12th St. S, ☎ 727/892–5767) performs throughout the year, mostly at the Bayfront Center.

NIGHTLIFE

Carlie's (✉ 5641 49th St., ☎ 813/527–5214) is hopping on Friday and Saturday nights, with plenty of dancing to live local bands. At the popular **Cha Cha Coconuts** (✉ City Pier, ☎ 727/822–6655), crowds drop in to catch live contemporary music every night. **Coliseum Ballroom** (✉ 535 4th Ave. N, ☎ 727/892–5202) offers ballroom dancing on some Wednesday afternoons and Saturday nights. Call ahead to check before going. **Harp & Thistle** (✉ 650 Corey Ave., St. Petersburg Beach, ☎ 727/360–4104) presents live Irish music Wednesday–Sunday. **Hurricane Lounge** (✉ 807 Gulf Way, Pass-A-Grille Beach, ☎ 727/360–9558) is a nice place to watch the sun go down and listen to jazz. Weekend crowds pack the noisy, boisterous **Joyland Country Music Night Club** (✉ 11225 U.S. 19, ☎ 727/573–1919).

Outdoor Activities and Sports

BASEBALL

One of Major League Baseball's newest teams, the **Tampa Bay Devil Rays** (✉ 1 Tropicana Dr., ☎ 727/825–3120) began playing at 45,000-seat Tropicana Field in 1998. They hold their spring training at **Lang Stadium** (✉ 1st St. and 2nd Ave., ☎ 813/822–3384).

DOG RACING

Dog races are held January–June at **Derby Lane** (✉ 10490 Gandy Blvd., ☎ 813/576–1361).

GOLF

You'll find 18 holes and a practice range at **Mainlands Golf Course** (✉ 9445 Mainlands Blvd. W, ☎ 727/577–4847). **Mangrove Bay Golf Course** (✉ 875 62nd Ave. NE, ☎ 727/893–7800) offers a driving range as well as 18 holes.

Shopping

Florida has never been known as the Great Bookstore State, being oriented more to activities of the outdoor variety. A notable exception is **Haslam's** (✉ 2025 Central Ave., ☎ 727/822–8616), a family-owned emporium that's been doing business at the same location, just north of downtown St. Petersburg, for 66 years. An attraction unto itself, the store carries more than 300,000 volumes, from cutting-edge bestsellers to ancient tomes. If you value a good book or simply like to browse, you could easily spend an afternoon here, and many people do.

John's Pass Village and Boardwalk (✉ 12901 Gulf Blvd., Madeira Beach) features a collection of shops and restaurants in an old-style fishing village, where you can pass the time watching pelicans cavorting and dive-bombing for food. The five-story bay-front **Pier** (✉ 800 2nd Ave. NE), near the Museum of Fine Arts, looks like an inverted pyramid; inside are numerous shops and eating spots. On weekends between 8 and 4, some 2,000 vendors set up a flea market on 100 acres at the **Wagonwheel** (✉ 7801 Park Blvd., Pinellas Park).

Clearwater

12 mi north of St. Petersburg.

This sprawling town has many residential areas and small shopping plazas. There's a semiquaint downtown area on the mainland, but the draw is the beaches along the barrier islands offshore.

When pelicans become entangled in fishing lines, locals sometimes carry them to the nonprofit **Suncoast Seabird Sanctuary,** which is dedicated to the rescue, repair, recuperation, and release of sick and injured birds. At times there are between 500 and 600 land and seabirds in residence, including pelicans, egrets, herons, gulls, terns, cranes, ducks, owls, and cormorants. Many are kept in open-air pens while they recover. The sanctuary backs up to the Indian Rocks Beach. ⊠ *18328 Gulf Blvd., Indian Shores,* ☎ *727/391–6211.* ☒ *Donation welcome.* ☉ *Daily sunrise–sunset, tours Wed. and Sun. 2.*

㉑ **Indian Rocks Beach** (⊠ Off Rte. 8, south of Clearwater Beach) attracts mostly couples. Connected to downtown Clearwater by Memorial
㉒ Causeway, **Clearwater Beach** is on a narrow island between Clearwater Harbor and the gulf. It's a popular hangout for teens and college students. Facilities include a marina, concessions, showers, rest rooms, and lifeguards.

Dining and Lodging

$–$$ ✕ **Kaiko Japanese Restaurant.** Step up to the counter or grab a table and settle down for some terrific Japanese food. Traditionally prepared sushi and *makimono* (rolled sushi) are specialties here, and the large appetizer menu gives everyone a chance to try a variety of items, including fried tofu, vegetable sushi, and sashimi. The menu also includes teriyaki-grilled seafood, beef, and chicken. Entrées are accompanied by miso soup, a small salad, and rice. Try the fried ice cream for dessert. ⊠ *7245 McMullen Booth Rd.,* ☎ *727/791–6640. MC, V.*

$–$$ ✕ **Le Petit Cafe.** The atmosphere is very casual in this corner spot at the end of a strip mall, but the delightful cuisine is pure French. Try the grilled lamb chops with cucumber-watercress sauce or the vegetable quiche. Daily and nightly specials are scrawled on a chalkboard. In the morning choose a delicate pastry, buttery croissant, or freshly made waffle. ⊠ *1465 Ft. Harrison Ave. S,* ☎ *727/442–9177. MC, V. Closed Mon.*

$$$ 🏨 **Belleview Biltmore Resort & Spa.** This charming Victorian resort,
★ built in 1896 and on the National Register of Historic Places, is thought to be the world's largest wooden structure. In 1998 the resort completed a massive "renovation" that was actually a step back into the past. A previous owner had modernized, replacing a beautiful entrance and main foyer dominated by natural wood floors and ornate woodwork walls with forgettable '70s decor. Today the painstaking restoration has revived the feel of a century ago. Units, which vary from extracozy little rooms to spacious suites, are off creaky corridors that seem to extend for miles. The resort is a 21-acre enclave overlooking a narrow part of Clearwater Bay, with high-rise condos nearby. Although the spa was built recently, it beautifully matches the Victorian opulence of the rest of the hotel. ⊠ *25 Belleview Blvd., 34616,* ☎ *727/442–6171,* FAX *727/441–4173. 292 rooms. 3 restaurants, 2 bars, 1 indoor and 1 outdoor pool, saunas, spa, 18-hole golf course, 4 tennis courts, health club, boating, bicycles, playground. AE, D, DC, MC, V.*

$$$ 🏨 **Sheraton Sand Key Resort.** This is a supreme spot for those searching for sun, sand, and surf. Set on 10 well-manicured acres, the nine-story, T-shape resort contains many rooms with excellent gulf views as well as others that look out over an adjacent park. All rooms have balconies or patios. Considered one of the top corporate meeting and convention hotels in the Clearwater area, it has amenities—like a beautiful private beach—that make it ideal for leisure travelers, too. ⊠ *1160 Gulf Blvd., Clearwater Beach 33515,* ☎ *727/595–1611,* FAX *727/596–8488. 390 rooms. Restaurant, bar, pool, wading pool, 3 tennis courts, health club, beach, windsurfing, boating, playground. AE, DC, MC, V.*

$$–$$$ 🏨 **Best Western Sea Wake Inn.** This white, concrete six-story hotel won't win any architectural awards, but it is right on the beach. Rooms are nicely decorated, and many have excellent views of the gulf. Some rooms have refrigerators. ⊠ *691 S. Gulfview Blvd., 34630,* ☎ *727/443–*

7652, FAX 727/461–2836. *110 rooms. Restaurant, bar, pool, beach, fishing. AE, DC, MC, V.*

The Arts

Ruth Eckerd Hall (⊠ 1111 McMullen Booth Rd., ☎ 727/791–7400) hosts many national performers of ballet, opera, and music—pop, classical, or jazz.

Outdoor Activities and Sports

BASEBALL

The **Philadelphia Phillies** (⊠ Seminole St. and Greenwood Ave., ☎ 727/441–8638) get ready for the season at Jack Russell Memorial Stadium.

BIKING

Lou's Bicycle Center (⊠ 8990 Seminole Blvd., Largo, ☎ 727/398–2743) offers rentals, quick repairs, and new bikes for sale, and it's close to the Pinellas Trail.

GOLF

Clearwater Golf Park (⊠ 1875 Airport Dr., ☎ 727/447–5272) has 18 holes and a driving range. **Largo Municipal Golf Course** (⊠ 12500 131st St. N, Largo, ☎ 727/587–6724) is an 18-hole course.

TENNIS

Shipwatch Yacht & Tennis Club (⊠ 11800 Shipwatch Dr., Largo, ☎ 727/596–6862) has 12 clay courts, 10 with lights for night play.

Shopping

Hamlin's Landing (⊠ 401 2nd St. E, Indian Rocks Beach) has several shops and restaurants in a Victorian-style setting along the Intracoastal Waterway.

Dunedin

23 *3 mi north of Clearwater.*

If the sound of bagpipes played by men in kilts appeals to you, head to this town, named by two Scots in the 1880s. In March and April the Highland games and the Dunedin Heather and Thistle holidays pay tribute to the town's Celtic heritage. Dunedin also has a nicely restored historic downtown area—only about five blocks long—that has become a one-stop shopping area for antiques hunters and is also lined with gift shops and good, nonchain eateries.

OFF THE BEATEN PATH **CALADESI ISLAND AND HONEYMOON ISLAND STATE PARKS –** Sharing an entrance and a parking lot, these two parks are just a few hundred yards from one another. However, whereas Honeymoon Island is right where you park, Caladesi Island is off the coast across Hurricane Pass and is accessible only by boat. One of Florida's few undeveloped barrier islands, 600-acre Caladesi Island has a beach on the gulf side, mangroves on the bay side, and a self-guided nature trail winding through the island's interior. Because it is so popular with locals, most of whom have their own boats, don't expect it to feel secluded on weekends. Park rangers are available to answer questions. A good spot for swimming, fishing, shelling, boating, and studying nature, the park has boardwalks, picnic shelters, bathhouses, and a concession stand. If you want to skip the ferry ride to Caladesi Island, you can stay at Honeymoon Island, also an excellent state park and beach. It has the same elements as Caladesi, but a bridge connects it to the mainland. ⊠ *Dunedin Causeway to Honeymoon Island, then board ferry,* ☎ *727/734–5263.* 🎫 *Parking $4, ferry $3.50.* ☉ *Daily 8–sunset, ferry hourly 10–5 in fair weather.*

Dining and Lodging

$$ ✕ **Bon Appetit.** This restaurant with views of the Intracoastal Water-
★   way and the gulf is known for its creative cuisine. European-trained
chef-owners Peter Kreuziger and Karl Heinz Riedl change the menu
twice a month and offer salads and light entrées as well as fresh seafood
and more ambitious fare, such as peppered quail and scallops with figs
and raisins on fettuccine. This is an excellent place to catch a sunset.
In fact, a private 300-seat dining room upstairs is named the Sunset
Room, or if you've got the budget for a party of 40 or so, you can dine
aboard the restaurant's own yacht, the *Bon Appetit.* ⊠ *148 Marina
Plaza,* ☎ *727/733–2151. AE, MC, V.*

$$ ✕ **Cité Grille.** The varied menu at this upscale eatery ranges from fried
calamari and oysters served with a piquant salsa to wonderfully fresh
trout sautéed with capers, almonds, and shrimp to grilled New York
strip with a brandied peppercorn-cream sauce. Unusual vegetarian selections include *poblano*-chile pesto linguine, vegetable almond rice pilaf,
and eggplant *rollatini.* The outdoor patio is a little more casual than
the austere but classy interior. ⊠ *461 Main St.,* ☎ *727/733–5449. AE,
MC, V.*

$–$$ ✕ **Casa Tina.** Chef-owner Javier Avila, whose credentials include a stint
★   as partner in a popular restaurant in Mazatlán, Mexico, named this
place for his wife. He apparently wants to keep her thin, because the
focus is on "healthy" and relatively low-fat Mexican dishes. No lard
or animal stock is used in the salsas or bean dishes, for instance. Try
Avila's versions of such standards as enchiladas (with veggies or
chicken) or chile *rellenos,* which, unlike most everyone else's, are not
battered and fried, but presented in beautiful roasted green poblano
peppers. If you want to try a dish to tell the folks back home about,
sample the cactus soup—not as daring as it sounds. Nothing will stick
your tongue except perhaps the spicy flavor, created with tender pieces
of cactus, cilantro, tomatoes, onions, lime, and *queso fresco* cheese. A
note on the menu implies that service can be slow, especially when this
place is crowded, which it often is. The wait is worth it. ⊠ *369 Main
St.,* ☎ *727/734–9226. AE, MC, V. Closed Mon.*

$–$$ ☷ **Inn on the Bay.** A good value, this modest four-story motel has com-
fortable rooms and a small number of two-bedroom units. Check to
see if you can get one with an excellent gulf view. The inn has a fishing pier and rents bicycles, and good beaches and water-sports rentals
are nearby, as is the ferry to Caladesi Island State Park. ⊠ *1420
Bayshore Blvd., 34698,* ☎ *727/734–7689. 41 rooms. Restaurant, bar,
pool, fishing, bicycles. AE, MC, V.*

Outdoor Activities and Sports

BASEBALL

The **Toronto Blue Jays** (⊠ 373 Douglas Ave., north of Rte. 88, ☎ 727/
733–9302) hold spring training at Grant Field.

GOLF

Dunedin Country Club (⊠ 1050 Palm Blvd., ☎ 727/733–7836) offers
18 holes, a driving range, and a pro shop.

Tarpon Springs

10 mi north of Dunedin.

This tiny town tucked into a little harbor at the mouth of the Anclote
River was settled by Greek immigrants at the end of the 19th century,
who brought with them the generations-old craft of sponge diving. Although bacterial and market forces seriously hurt the industry in the
'40s, today sponging has returned, but mostly as a focal point for tourism.
The docks along Dodecanese Boulevard, the main waterfront street,

are now a tourist district filled with quaint old buildings housing all sort of shops and eateries. Tarpon Springs' other key street is Tarpon Avenue, about a mile south of Dodecanese. This old central business district has become an antiques hunter's paradise.

㉔ Don't miss **St. Nicholas Greek Orthodox Church,** a replica of St. Sophia's in Istanbul and an excellent example of New Byzantine architecture. ⊠ *36 N. Pinellas Ave.* ⊡ *Donation welcome.* ☉ *Daily 9–5.*

㉕ No, **Spongeorama** is not some warped presentation of what happens to your brain on drugs. It's a museum/cultural center that shows and tells you more than you ever imagined about how a lowly sea creature, the sponge, created the industry that built this quaint little fishing (actually sponging) village. Visitors see a film about these much-sought-after creatures from the phylum *porifera* and how they helped the town prosper at the turn of the century. You'll probably come away converted to (and loaded up with) natural sponges and loofahs. ⊠ *Dodecanese Blvd. off Rte. 19,* ☎ *727/943–9509.* ⊡ *Free.* ☉ *Daily 10–5.*

㉖ Two public **Tarpon Springs beaches** have lifeguards in spring and summer: **Howard Park Beach** (⊠ Sunset Dr.) and **Sunset Beach** (⊠ Gulf Rd.), which has rest rooms, picnic tables, grills, and a boat ramp.

Dining and Lodging

$–$$ ✕ **Louis Pappas' Riverside Restaurant.** This waterside restaurant has
★ a little bit of an institutional feel to it, even though it offers a great view of the Anclote River and the docks where shrimp and sponge-diving boats gather. What has made it a local favorite for generations is the consistent quality of its food. Here you can sample well-prepared Greek favorites like moussaka, Greek meatballs, *stifado* (a Greek stew made with lamb), *spanakopita* (white cheese and spinach baked into phyllo pastry), and dolmades (grape leaves stuffed with rice and ground lamb). If you want a more esoteric Greek specialty, try the marinated octopus. There's also an excellent selection of such Florida classics as stone crab and the ubiquitous grouper. The main dining room can get crowded, but a more accessible and informal restaurant under the same roof offers virtually the same menu. ⊠ *10 W. Dodecanese Blvd.,* ☎ *727/937–5101. AE, DC, MC, V. No lunch Sun.*

$–$$ ✕ **Tarpon Avenue Grill.** This quaint little spot, formerly a French bistro, has reopened as an eclectic American restaurant, keeping two things from its previous incarnation, the phone number and the house specialty: French onion soup. Other standouts include the blackened "VooDoo" shrimp and a fresh local fish of the day. The restaurant is housed in an ancient brick building across from the old train depot in the heart of the town's historic/antiques district. If you want to walk off your meal, hop on the bicycle trail that replaced the train tracks just outside the restaurant; you can walk all the way to St. Petersburg if you like—30 mi south. ⊠ *200 E. Tarpon Ave.,* ☎ *727/942–3011. AE, MC, V.*

$ ✕ **Leo's Pizza.** Because of its unspectacular and implicitly limited
★ name, it's easy to walk right past Leo's without ever trying the food. That would be a mistake. What you've got here is a little piece of New York City transplanted to Florida; everybody in the kitchen seems to be from up north and of Italian descent. The pizza is wonderful, but entrées are in a class of their own, including a chicken *cacciatore* and sausage and peppers parmigiana that are nothing short of incredible. The best dish of all, however, is the grouper *française,* battered and sautéed with lemon butter and white wine and served over linguine. You can finish your tour of the extensive menu with an exquisite Ital-

DIVING FOR SPONGES

ANIMALS THAT SWIM or slither around in Florida's semitropical waters have a vaunted place in state folklore. Several have been chosen as team mascots—the Miami Dolphins, Florida Marlins, and the University of Florida Gators, to name a few—a sign of the impact these animals have had on the state. But no aquatic creature has had a greater impact on the Tampa Bay area than the sponge.

Unlike the reputedly intelligent dolphin, the sponge is no genius. It's hard to be when you consist of only one cell. The sponge that divers retrieve from the seabed or that you reach for in the shower is actually a colony of millions of the one-cell organisms bound together in an organic matrix that makes up a soft, flexible lump.

As you'll learn if you visit Tarpon Springs' aging and modest Spongeorama, sponge diving predates the birth of Christ, and the first Greek sponge seekers actually worshiped the god Poseidon. For the past millennium or so, the spongers have been devoutly Greek Orthodox, and today many sponge boats carry a small shrine to St. Nicholas, the patron saint of mariners. The divers' deep devotion to their religion—and to Greek culture—resulted in the development of Tampa Bay's own little Greek village.

Sponge gathering actually began in the Florida Keys circa 1850, but it gathered momentum around Tampa Bay after 1905, when George Cocoris brought to Florida the first mechanical diving apparatus, complete with a brass-helmeted diving suit and pump system that enabled divers to stay in 75–100 ft of water for two hours at a time. Cocoris and those who worked with him soon discovered a particularly marketable variety of sponge: the Rock Island wool sponge, so named because it resembles fine wool and is found in abundance around Rock Island, off Florida's west coast. When word of Cocoris's success got back to Greece, more sponge-diving families headed west, and within a decade or so, several thousand of his fellow Greeks had settled around Tarpon Springs to share in its prosperity.

BY THE 1930S Tarpon Springs was the largest U.S. sponging port, but in the late '40s and early '50s, a sponge blight and the growing popularity of synthetic sponges nearly wiped out the local industry. Still, the hardy Greeks held on. They discovered that tourists were drawn more by the town's Hellenic culture than by the sponges sold in the dockside markets. In the ensuing 40 years Tarpon Springs' waterfront area has been turned into a delightful tourist district filled with Greek restaurants, Greek pastry shops, and Greek art galleries. And should you choose to see divers pull sponges from the seabed, you can book passage on one of the glass-bottom boats that leave hourly from the town docks.

And so the town owes its success to the humble sponge. Yet although you'll find bronze statues of sponge divers, with the exception of Spongeorama there is no tribute to the monocellular creature itself. Perhaps a future Florida ball team will choose the "Fightin' Sponges" as its mascot.

ian cheesecake. ⊠ *510 W. Dodecanese Blvd.,* ☎ *727/943–9517;* ⊠ *2876 Alt. U.S. 19, Palm Harbor,* ☎ *727/781–3456. AE, MC, V. Closed Mon.*

$$$–$$$$ ⊡ **Westin Innisbrook Resort.** This 600-acre resort added a massive new
★   pool and water-slide complex in 1998, designed to make what was once considered a corporate-meeting-and-golf retreat more family friendly. Grounds are beautifully maintained, and guest suites are in 28 two-story lodges tucked in the trees between golf courses. All units are roomy, and all have kitchens; some have balconies or patios as well. Once fairly remote, the Innisbrook has built in enough restaurant and lounge choices to make it self-contained, though today the area around it offers plenty of competition. The children's program is excellent. ⊠ *U.S. 19, Box 1088, 34684,* ☎ *727/942–2000,* FAX *727/942–5576. 1,000 units. 4 restaurants, 5 bars, 6 pools, saunas, driving range, 4 18-hole golf courses, miniature golf, putting green, 13 tennis courts, health club, jogging, racquetball, nightclub, children's programs, playground. AE, DC, MC, V.*

Outdoor Activities and Sports

Westin Innisbrook Resort (⊠ U.S. 19, ☎ 727/942–2000) offers 72 holes of golf as well as privileges at another course off property, driving ranges, and putting greens, plus opportunities for off-property sports like deep-sea fishing.

THE MANATEE COAST

The coastal area north of Tampa is aptly called the Manatee Coast. Of these gentle vegetarian water mammals, distantly related to elephants, only 1,200 are alive today, and they are threatened by development and speeding motorboats. In fact, many manatees that survive today have massive scars on their backs from run-ins with boat propellers. Extensive nature preserves and parks have been created to protect them and other wildlife indigenous to the area and are among the best spots to view manatees in the wild. Although they are far from mythical beauties, it is believed that manatees inspired ancient mariners' tales of mermaids.

U.S. 19 is the prime route through rural manatee country, and traffic flows freely once you've left the congestion of St. Petersburg, Clearwater, and Palm Harbor. If you are planning a day trip from the bay area, pack a picnic lunch before leaving, since most of the sights are outdoors.

Weeki Wachee

27 mi north of Tarpon Springs.

㉗   The highlight here is **Weeki Wachee Spring,** which flows at the remarkable rate of 170 million gallons a day with a constant temperature of 74°F. The spring has long been famous for its live mermaids, who wear bright costumes that were clearly not the work of Mother Nature. Nowadays a clever breathing apparatus makes possible performances of Weeki Wachee's 50th anniversary show, *Tails of Yesterday,* and the long popular *The Little Mermaid* in the underwater theater. A nature trail threads through the subtropical wilderness, and a jungle boat cruises to view local wildlife. A petting zoo and an exotic-birds-of-prey show have been added in recent years. You'll need four hours to see everything. ⊠ *U.S. 19 and Rte. 50,* ☎ *352/596–2062.* 🎟 *$16.95.* ☉ *Daily 10–4.*

Outdoor Activities and Sports

The 48 holes at **World Woods Golf Club** (✉ 17590 Ponce de León Blvd., Brooksville, ☎ 352/796–5500) are some of the best in Florida; the club also has a 22-acre practice area with a four-sided driving range and a 2-acre putting course.

Homosassa Springs

20 mi north of Weeki Wachee.

㉘ At the **Homosassa Springs State Wildlife Park** you may see manatees, but the main attraction is the Spring of 10,000 Fish, a clear spring with many species of fish that can be easily watched through a floating glass observatory. A walk along the park's paths leads you to alligator, other reptile, and exotic-bird shows. The park is also a refuge and rehabilitation center where ailing animals are nursed back to health. Among the species you can see are bobcats, western cougars, white-tailed deer, black bears, pelicans, herons, snowy egrets, river otters, and even a hippopotamus or two, though no one tries to pass them off as being Florida natives like the other animals. Jungle boat cruises on the Homosassa River are available across Fish Bowl Drive from the entrance. In 1998 a restaurant was added in the main visitor reception building. ✉ *1 mi west of U.S. 19 on Fish Bowl Dr.,* ☎ *352/628–2311.* ☑ *$7.95.* ☉ *Daily 9–5:30.*

㉙ The **Yulee Sugar Mill State Historic Site,** the ruined remains of a 5,100-acre sugar plantation owned by Florida's first U.S. senator, David Levy Yulee, makes for pleasant picnicking. ✉ *Rte. 490A,* ☎ *352/795–3817.* ☑ *Free.* ☉ *Daily sunrise–sunset.*

Dining and Lodging

$–$$ ✕ **K. C. Crump Restaurant.** This 1870 Old Florida residence on the Homosassa River was restored and opened as a restaurant serving steaks, poultry, and seafood in 1987. In addition to the large, airy dining rooms, there are outdoor dining, a lounge, and a dock on the river, in case you prefer to arrive by boat. ✉ *11210 Hall's River Rd.,* ☎ *352/628–1500. AE, MC, V.*

$ ▦ **Homosassa River Retreat.** On the banks of the Homosassa River, with two docks and nearby boat and pontoon rentals, this resort of one- and two-bedroom cottages with kitchens is well situated for outdoor adventuring. ✉ *10605 Hall's River Rd., 34446,* ☎ *352/628–7072. 9 cottages. Docks, coin laundry. MC, V.*

$ ▦ **Howard Johnson Riverside Inn.** Even though it's now a Howard Johnson, this little inn is still rustic. The setting is intimate—tucked beside the Homosassa River and across from Monkey Island, where a group of monkeys makes the place seem like the set of a Disney movie. In addition to having its own restaurant and lounge, the Riverside is within walking distance of three local restaurants, and two others are accessible by boat. ✉ *5297 Cherokee Way, 34446,* ☎ *352/628–2474,* FAX *352/628–5208. 70 rooms. Restaurant, bar, pool, tennis court. AE, MC, V.*

$ ▦ **Ramada Inn Downtown.** This is a simple motor inn with king-size beds in most rooms. It accepts pets. ✉ *U.S. 19 at Rte. 490A, 34448,* ☎ FAX *352/628–4311. 104 rooms. Restaurant, bar, pool, 4 tennis courts, playground. AE, D, DC, MC, V.*

Crystal River

7 mi north of Homosassa Springs.

㉚ The **Crystal River National Wildlife Refuge** is a U.S. Fish and Wildlife Service sanctuary for the endangered manatee. The main spring, around which manatees congregate in winter (generally from November to March), feeds crystal-clear water into the river at 72°F year-round. In warmer months, when manatees scatter, the main spring is still fun for a swim. Though accessible only by boat, the refuge provides neither tours nor boat rentals. For these, contact marinas in the town of Crystal River. ⊠ *1502 S. Kings Bay Dr.,* ☎ *352/563–2088.* ⊠ *Free.* ☉ *Daily 9–4, office weekdays 7:30–4.*

Dining and Lodging

$ ✕ **Charlie's Fish House Restaurant.** This popular, no-frills seafood spot serves fish caught locally as well as oysters, crab claws, and lobster. It's accessible by boat. ⊠ *224 U.S. 19N,* ☎ *352/795–3949. AE, MC, V.*

$$ ⊞ **Plantation Inn & Golf Resort.** Set on the banks of Kings Bay, this rustic two-story plantation-style resort sits on 232 acres near several nature preserves and rivers. ⊠ *9301 W. Fort Island Trail, 34423,* ☎ *352/795–4211 or 800/632–6262,* FAX *352/795–1368. 194 rooms. Restaurant, bar, pool, saunas, driving range, 27 holes of golf, putting green, tennis, horseshoes, shuffleboard, boating, fishing. AE, DC, MC, V.*

$–$$ ⊞ **Best Western Crystal River Resort.** This cinder-block roadside motel is close to Kings Bay and its manatee population. A marina is steps away, and dive boats depart for scuba and snorkeling excursions. Only two rooms view the water: 114 and 128, but all the units are nestled under large oak trees that make the place feel like the Old South. ⊠ *614 N.W. U.S. 19, 34428,* ☎ *352/795–3171,* FAX *352/795–3179. 96 rooms, 18 efficiencies. Restaurant, bar, pool. AE, DC, MC, V.*

Outdoor Activities and Sports

BOATING

The **Kayak Shack** (300 N. U.S. 19, ☎ 352/564–1334) rents craft for exploring the wildlife refuge. Boat rentals are available at the **Twin Rivers Marina** (2880 N. Seebreeze Point, ☎ 352/795–3552).

GOLF

Plantation Inn & Golf Resort (⊠ 9301 W. Fort Island Trail, ☎ 352/795–7211) features 27 holes, a lighted driving range, and a putting green.

Cedar Key

57 mi northwest of Crystal River; follow Rte. 24 southwest from U.S. 19 to the end.

Up in the area known as the Big Bend, Florida's long, curving coastline north of Tampa, you won't find many beaches. You will find an idyllic collection of small cays and a little island village tucked in among the marshes and scenic streams feeding the Gulf of Mexico. Once a strategic port for the Confederate States of America, remote Cedar Key is today a commercial fishing center.

Change is in the air, however. Though the town used to be a well-kept secret with sparse tourism, it's becoming increasingly popular as a getaway, thanks in part to the spring and fall art festivals that take over the streets of the quaint little downtown area. Today there are no fewer than a dozen commercial galleries, a sign that Cedar Key is now attracting travelers who carry platinum credit cards and have an affinity for sun-dried tomatoes. It's also become a favorite of the college crowd, as it's only an hour from the main campus of the University of Florida, in Gainesville. Though the island can seem like an MTV location event on weekends, the upside of this popularity is the popping up of some creative bars and restaurants, several on a Cannery Row–style pier a block from downtown.

③ The **Cedar Key Historical Society Museum** features photographs and exhibits that focus on the area's development and includes displays of Native American artifacts. ✉ *Rte. 24 and 2nd St.,* ☎ *352/543–5549.* 💲 *$1.* ⊙ *Mon.–Sat. 11–5, Sun. 2–5.*

Dining and Lodging

$$–$$$ ✕ **Island Room.** On the ground floor of a waterfront condo complex, this place has a good gulf view, which makes it like virtually every other restaurant in the downtown area. What sets it apart, however, is excellent upscale cuisine, including such treats as grouper *piccata,* linguine *vongoli* (with local clams sautéed in oil with garlic and fresh herbs), and a very worthy crab bisque. For breakfast try the crab Benedict or the oysters Rockefeller omelet. All the food here is available for takeout, so you can call ahead for the makings of a gourmet beach picnic. ✉ *Cedar Cove Beach and Yacht Club, 10 E. 2nd St.,* ☎ *352/543–6520. MC, V.*

$–$$ ✕ **Pat's Red Luck Cafe.** Nobody at this restaurant seems to know how it got its strange name, but they do know how to serve up some great food, including what you'd expect in a small fishing town—fried shrimp, grouper, and oysters—and what you wouldn't—tasty crepes with blueberries and bananas, smoked salmon with capers, and a decent spinach salad with honey-mustard dressing. On the town dock, this place has a good view of the gulf. ✉ *On the dock,* ☎ *352/543–6840. MC, V.*

$–$$ 🏨 **Island Place.** Gulf views are the big attraction at this waterfront condo-style hotel, and all the guest rooms have them. The units, which have one bedroom and one bath or two bedrooms and two baths, are set up for those who might want to stay in this lovely town a while; they come with full kitchens (including microwave and dishwasher) and dining room areas. For those who don't want to cook, each room has a ring binder with menus from all the town's restaurants, all of which will either deliver or prepare takeout for you to pick up. ✉ *1st and C Sts., 32625,* ☎ *352/543–5306 or 800/780–6522. 27 1-bedroom suites, 3 two-bedroom suites. Pool, saunas. MC, V.*

$ 🏨 **Park Place Motel.** Views of the gulf are lovely from the private balconies off many units at this three-story motel within walking distance of stores and restaurants. On the top floor are bilevel units with sleeping lofts, but there's no elevator. ✉ *211 2nd St., at A St., 32625,* ☎ *352/543–5737 or 800/868–7963. 34 rooms. MC, V.*

SOUTH OF TAMPA BAY

The southern end of Tampa Bay is anchored by Bradenton and Sarasota, two cities bordered by a string of barrier islands with fine beaches. Sarasota County has no less than 35 mi of gulf beaches, as well as two state parks, 22 municipal parks, and more than 30 golf courses, many open to the public.

Sarasota has a thriving cultural scene, thanks mostly to John Ringling, founder of the Ringling Brothers Barnum & Bailey Circus, who chose this area for the winter home of his circus and his family. Bradenton, to the north, maintains a lower profile, while Venice, a few miles south on the Gulf Coast, claims some of Sarasota County's best beaches and the world's only clown college.

Bradenton

49 mi south of Tampa.

This city on the Manatee River is home to some 20 mi of beaches and is well sited for access to fishing, both fresh- and saltwater. It also has its share of golf courses and historic sites dating to the mid-1800s.

㉜ The **Manatee Village Historical Park** is the real thing. It consists of an 1860 courthouse, 1887 church, 1903 general store and museum, and 1912 settler's home. The Old Manatee Cemetery, which dates to 1850, contains the graves of early Manatee County settlers. An appointment is necessary for a cemetery tour. ⊠ *Rte. 64 at 6th Ave. E,* ☎ *941/749–7165.* ☞ *Free.* ☉ *Sept.–June, weekdays 9–4:30, Sun. 1:30–4:30; July–Aug., weekdays 9–4:30.*

㉝ Showcased at the **South Florida Museum and Bishop Planetarium and Parker Manatee Aquarium** are Florida artifacts, including displays relating to Native American culture and an excellent collection of Civil War objects. The museum is also home to Snooty, the oldest living manatee in captivity. He likes to shake hands and perform other tricks at feeding time in his 60,000-gallon home. At the domed Bishop Planetarium you can see star shows and laser-light displays. ⊠ *201 10th St.,* ☎ *941/746–4132.* ☞ *$7.50.* ☉ *Tues.–Sat. 10–5, Sun. noon–5; star shows Tues.–Sun. 1 and 4.*

Hernando de Soto, one of the first Spanish explorers, set foot in Florida in 1539 near what is now Bradenton; that feat is commemorated at

★ **㉞** the **De Soto National Memorial.** In the high season (late December–early April) park employees dressed in 16th-century costumes demonstrate period weapons and show how European explorers prepared and preserved food for their journeys over the untamed land. Films, demonstrations, and a short nature trail are on the grounds. ⊠ *75th St. NW,* ☎ *941/792–0458.* ☞ *Free.* ☉ *Daily 9–5.*

㉟ **Anna Maria Island,** Bradenton's barrier island to the west, has a number of worthwhile beaches. Manatee Avenue connects the mainland to the island via the **Palma Sola Causeway,** adjacent to which is a long, sandy beach fronting Palma Sola Bay. There are boat ramps, a dock, and picnic tables. **Anna Maria Bayfront Park** (⊠ N. Bay Blvd., adjacent to municipal pier) is a secluded beach fronting both the Intracoastal Waterway and the Gulf of Mexico. Facilities include picnic grounds, a playground, rest rooms, showers, and lifeguards. In the middle of the island, **Manatee County Beach** (⊠ Gulf Dr. at 44th St., Holmes Beach) is popular with all ages. It has picnic facilities, a snack bar, showers, rest rooms, and lifeguards. **Cortez Beach** (⊠ Gulf Blvd., Bradenton Beach) is popular with those who like their beaches without facilities—nothing but sand, water, and trees. **Coquina Beach,** at the southern end of the island, is big with singles and families. Facilities here include a picnic area, boat ramp, playground, refreshment stand, rest rooms, showers, and lifeguards. Just across the inlet on the northern tip of Longboat Key, **Greer Island Beach** is accessible by boat or via North Shore Boulevard. The secluded peninsula has a wide beach and excellent shelling but no facilities.

㊱ Off the northern tip of Anna Maria Island lies **Egmont Key.** On it is **Fort Dade,** a military installation built in 1900 during the Spanish-American War, as well as Florida's sixth-brightest lighthouse. The primary inhabitant of the 2-mi-long island is the threatened gopher tortoise, and shellers as well as nature lovers will find the trip rewarding. The only way to get here, however, is by boat, either the *Miss Cortez,* an excursion boat (☞ Guided Tours *in* The Tampa Bay Area A to Z, *below*),

Bradenton/Sarasota

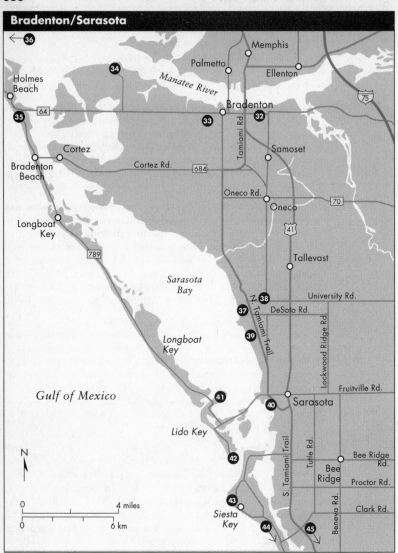

or a rented runabout, readily available throughout the Tampa Bay area. One note of caution: In addition to the tortoises, you'll find some huge rattlesnakes on the island. Do *not* venture off the trails.

OFF THE
BEATEN PATH **GAMBLE PLANTATION AND CONFEDERATE MEMORIAL STATE HISTORIC SITE** – Built in 1850, this, the only pre–Civil War plantation house in South Florida, still displays some of the original furnishings. The Confederate secretary of state took refuge here when the Confederacy fell to Union forces. ✉ *3708 Patten Ave., Ellenton,* ☎ *941/723–4536.* ⌑ *$3.* ☉ *Thurs.–Mon. 8–5, tours 9:30, 10:30, 1, 2, 3, and 4.*

Dining and Lodging

$–$$ ✕ **Crab Trap and Crab Trap II.** Rustic decor, ultrafresh seafood, gator tail, and wild pig are among the trademarks of these casual and very popular restaurants. ✉ *U.S. 19 at Terra Ceia Bridge, Palmetto,* ☎ *941/722–6255;* ✉ *4814 Memphis Rd., Ellenton,* ☎ *941/729–7777. D, MC, V.*

$$–$$$ ⌑ **Silver Surf.** For a great location it's hard to beat this bright, white two-story spot. The beach and heated pool are right out front, and many restaurants are just a short walk away. Units range from simple rooms with a small refrigerator to larger efficiencies with a full kitchen. Rooms are simply decorated but comfortable, and many have great ocean views. ✉ *1301 Gulf Dr., Bradenton Beach 34217,* ☎ *941/778–6626. 10 rooms, 20 efficiencies. Pool, beach. AE, MC, V.*

$$ ⌑ **Holiday Inn Riverfront.** This Spanish Mediterranean–style motor inn near the Manatee River is easily accessible from I–75 and U.S. 41. One-third of the rooms are suites. ✉ *100 Riverfront Dr. W, 34205,* ☎ *941/747–3727,* FAX *941/746–4289. 153 units. Restaurant, bar, pool, exercise room. AE, DC, MC, V.*

$–$$ ⌑ **Duncan House.** This two-story, wood-frame Victorian B&B is just across the street from the beach. Inviting rooms are individually decorated by a loving owner with attention to detail. Although a condo on the beach prevents a straight-on ocean view, you can see the water from some rooms. A full breakfast is included in the rate. ✉ *1703 Gulf Dr., Bradenton Beach 34217,* ☎ *941/778–6858. 6 rooms. Pool. AE, MC, V.*

Outdoor Activities and Sports

BASEBALL
The **Pittsburgh Pirates** (✉ 17th Ave. W and 9th St., ☎ 941/748–4610) have spring training at McKechnie Field.

BIKING
Ringling Bicycles (✉ 3606 Manatee Ave., ☎ 941/749–1442) rents bicycles by the hour and the day.

GOLF
The excellent county-owned 18-hole **Buffalo Creek Golf Course** (✉ 8100 Erie Rd., Palmetto, ☎ 941/776–2611), designed by Ron Garl, resembles a Scottish links course. **Manatee County Golf Course** (✉ 6415 53rd Ave. W, ☎ 941/792–6773) features a driving range as well as 18 holes of golf. **Peridia Golf & Country Club** (✉ 4950 Peridia Blvd., ☎ 941/753–9097) has 18 holes and a driving range.

Shopping
Some vendors at the **Red Barn** (✉ 1707 1st St. E), a flea market in the requisite big red barn, do business during the week (often Tuesday–Sunday 10–4), but the number of vendors skyrockets to 1,000 on weekends, when many open as early as 8.

Sarasota

16 mi south of Bradenton.

Despite its circus reputation, Sarasota is a sophisticated resort town with cultural events scheduled year-round. Across the water from Sarasota lie the barrier islands of **Siesta Key, Longboat Key,** and **Lido Key,** with myriad beaches, shops, hotels, condominiums, and houses.

★ ○ ③⑦ Decades ago circus tycoon John Ringling found this area an ideal spot for his clowns and performers to recuperate from their months of travel while preparing for their next journey. Along Sarasota Bay, Ringling built himself a fancy home, patterned after the Palace of the Doges in Venice, Italy. Today the **Ringling Museums** include that **mansion,** as well as his **art museum** (with a world-renowned collection of Rubens paintings and 17th-century tapestries) and a **museum of circus memorabilia.** ☒ ½ *mi south of Sarasota-Bradenton Airport on U.S. 41,* ☎ *941/359–5700.* ☒ *$8.50.* ☉ *Daily 10–5:30.*

③⑧ You could say they are rocking and rolling at **Bellm's Cars & Music of Yesterday.** On display are both 175 restored antique automobiles—including Rolls-Royces, Pierce Arrows, and Auburns—and more than 1,200 old-time music makers, such as hurdy-gurdies, calliopes, and music boxes. ☒ *5500 N. Tamiami Trail,* ☎ *941/355–6228.* ☒ *$8.* ☉ *Daily 9:30–5:30.*

○ ③⑨ It takes a couple of hours to stroll through the 10-acre spread of tropical plants at the **Sarasota Jungle Gardens.** Also on site are a petting zoo and playground, a shell and butterfly museum, and reptile and bird shows. ☒ *3701 Bayshore Rd.,* ☎ *941/355–5305.* ☒ *$9.* ☉ *Daily 9–5; shows 10, noon, 2, and 4.*

④⓪ At the 9-acre **Marie Selby Botanical Gardens,** you can stroll through a world-class display of orchids, see air plants and colorful bromeliads, and wander through 14 garden areas along Sarasota Bay. There is also a small museum of botany and art in a gracious restored mansion. ☒ *811 S. Palm Ave.,* ☎ *941/366–5730.* ☒ *$8.* ☉ *Daily 10–5.*

○ ④① The 135,000-gallon shark tank at **Mote Marine Aquarium** lets you see its inhabitants from above and below the water's surface. Additional tanks show off sharks, rays, and other marine creatures native to the area. A neat touch tank lets you handle rays, guitar fish, horseshoe crabs, and sea urchins. ☒ *1600 City Island Park, Lido Key,* ☎ *941/388–4441.* ☒ *$8.* ☉ *Daily 10–5.*

④② **South Lido Park** (☒ Ben Franklin Dr., Lido Key), at the southern tip of the island, has one of the largest and best beaches in the region. The sugar-sand beach offers little for shell collectors, but the interests of others are served well, resulting in a mix of people. Try your luck at fishing, take a dip in the waters of the bay or gulf, roam the 130-acre park, or picnic as the sun sets through the Australian pines into the water. Facilities include nature trails, a canoe trail, volleyball court, playground, horseshoe pits, rest rooms, and picnic grounds.

④③ **Siesta Beach** (☒ 600 Beach Rd., Siesta Key) and its 40-acre park contain nature trails, a concession stand, soccer and softball fields, picnic facilities, a playground, rest rooms, a fitness trail, and tennis and volleyball courts. Only 14 acres, **Turtle Beach** (☒ Turtle Beach Rd., Siesta Key) is a beach park that's popular with families. It includes boat ramps, horseshoe pits, picnic and play facilities, a recreation building, rest rooms, and a volleyball court. ④④

OFF THE
BEATEN PATH

MYAKKA RIVER STATE PARK – With 28,900 acres, this outstanding wildlife preserve is absolutely lovely and great for bird-watching and gator sighting. Tram tours explore natural hammocks, airboat tours whiz over the lake, and there are hiking trails and bike rentals. ⊠ *17 mi southeast of Sarasota on Rte. 72,* ☎ *941/365–0100.* ⊠ *$2 for 1 person, $4 per vehicle for 2–8 people; tours $7.* ☉ *Daily 8–sunset.*

Dining and Lodging

$$$–$$$$
★

✕ **Bijou Cafe.** Wood, brass, and sumptuous green carpeting surround diners in this 1920 gas station turned restaurant. Chef-owner Jean Pierre Knaggs's Continental specialties include superb crab cakes with *rémoulade* sauce, crispy roast duckling with orange-lingonberry and port wine–cherry sauce, horseradish-encrusted salmon, rack of lamb for two, and crème brûlée. An extensive international wine list includes vintages ranging from an Australian cabernet-shiraz blend to a South African merlot, and of course, numerous selections from France and California. ⊠ *1287 1st St.,* ☎ *941/366–8111. AE, DC, MC, V.*

$$$–$$$$
★

✕ **Cafe L'Europe.** On fashionable St. Armand's Circle, this greenery- and art-filled café specializes in Continental cuisines, featuring fresh veal and seafood. Menus change frequently but might include fillet of sole Picasso, Dover sole served with a choice of fruits, or Wiener schnitzel sautéed in butter and topped with anchovies, olives, and capers. ⊠ *431 St. Armand's Circle, Lido Key,* ☎ *941/388–4415. AE, DC, MC, V.*

$$–$$$

✕ **Marina Jack.** Eat in the restaurant overlooking Sarasota Bay, or from Wednesday through Sunday take a dinner cruise on the *Marina Jack II,* a paddle wheeler that cruises for two romantic hours with entertainment. Fresh seafood prevails in both places. ⊠ *2 Marina Plaza,* ☎ *941/365–4232. MC, V.*

$$–$$$

✕ **Michael's on East.** Prices are reasonable despite the elegant setting of this favorite in downtown Sarasota. The cuisine is contemporary, ranging from penne with grilled summer vegetables and black olives to grilled fillet of beef served with a house specialty—mashed potatoes. A light menu is served in the intimate bar, where there's always piano music or jazz in the evening. The lunch menu includes unusual sandwiches—grilled Portobello mushrooms with Gouda, for example—and an excellent assortment of fresh salads. ⊠ *1212 East Ave. S,* ☎ *941/ 366–0007. AE, MC, V.*

$$–$$$

✕ **Ophelia's on the Bay.** Sample mussel soup, eggplant crepes, roast duck, and fresh pompano in parchment, among other things, at this waterfront restaurant. ⊠ *9105 Midnight Pass Rd., Siesta Key,* ☎ *941/ 349–2212. AE, D, DC, MC, V. No lunch.*

$$
★

✕ **Columbia.** This classic on trendy St. Armand's Circle offers most of the same elements that make its 95-year-old mother restaurant in Ybor City the great Florida institution it is. The menu is essentially the same, reflecting great Spanish and Cuban cooking, and includes a fine paella and superb black-bean soup. There are even nightly entertainment and dancing in the patio area. If you somehow failed to get Columbia checked off your must-visit list when you were in Tampa, this makes a worthy substitute. Snag a copy of the restaurant cookbook to take home to the folks in Akron. ⊠ *411 St. Armand's Circle, Lido Key,* ☎ *941/388– 3987. AE, DC, MC, V.*

$–$$

✕ **Patrick's.** A longtime favorite among locals, this upscale sports bar attracts crowds that belly up to the bar after work and end up staying for steak sandwiches, juicy cheeseburgers, meat loaf, pizza, pasta, and char-grilled steaks. This joint is the closest thing to a New York City bar that you'll find south of the World Trade Center. Weekends are also busy, and Sunday brunch is popular. ⊠ *1400 Main St.,* ☎ *941/952– 1170. AE, MC, V.*

$-$$ ✕ **Trolley Station.** Even after you arrive, it's not at all obvious why this popular lunch spot is called what it is. The restaurant actually started out at another location, near a trolley stop, and featured a train-station motif inside. When it moved, it dropped the railway look but kept the name. Offerings range from a salad and baked-potato bar to roast beef, fish, chicken, and pasta. Prices are reasonable. ⊠ *3550 Clark Rd.,* ☎ *941/923–2721. MC, V.*

$$$$ ⊞ **Colony Beach and Tennis Resort.** If tennis is your game, this is the
★ place to stay—such tennis greats as Björn Borg make the Colony their home court, and for good reason. Ten courts are clay hydrosurfaced (the others are hard), and the pros are all USPTA-certified. They run clinics and camps at all levels, do video analyses of your game, and will play with guests when no one else is available. They even have scaled-down rackets for children. Other activities include ecology-oriented trips and deep-sea fishing. All accommodations are suites, some sleeping up to eight; private beach houses that open onto sand and sea are also available. ⊠ *1620 Gulf of Mexico Dr., Longboat Key 34228,* ☎ *941/ 383–6464; 800/237–9443; 800/282–1138 in FL;* ℻ *941/383–7549. 235 suites. 3 restaurants, 2 bars, pool, 21 tennis courts, health club, boating, children's programs. AE, D, MC, V.*

$$$$ ⊞ **Resort at Longboat Key Club.** This beautifully landscaped 410-acre property is one of *the* places to golf in the state and one of the top tennis resorts in the country. Water is the test on both golf courses, which have excellent pro shops, lessons, and clinics. Tennis courts are Har-Tru–surfaced. Hobie Cats, kayaks, Sunfish, deep-sea charters, and ecology trips are also available. Suites, for four or six, have huge private balconies overlooking a golf course, beach, or private lagoon where manatees and bottlenose dolphins are occasionally seen. ⊠ *301 Gulf of Mexico Dr., Box 15000, Longboat Key 34228,* ☎ *941/383– 8821; 800/237–8821; 800/282–0113 in FL;* ℻ *941/383–0359. 232 suites. 5 restaurants, pool, driving range, 45 holes of golf, putting greens, 38 tennis courts, exercise room, beach, library, meeting rooms. AE, DC, MC, V.*

$$$–$$$$ ⊞ **Radisson Lido Beach Resort.** This classy beachfront resort has superb views of the gulf. Units are decorated in soft-blue and pink-pastel print fabrics. All have a refrigerator, and many have a full kitchen. Beachfront minisuites, at the western end of the building, have balconies. A large rectangular pool is right on the beach. ⊠ *700 Ben Franklin Dr., Lido Beach 34236,* ☎ *941/388–2161,* ℻ *941/388–3175. 116 units. Restaurant, bar, pool, beach. AE, DC, MC, V.*

$$$ ⊞ **Hyatt Sarasota.** The Hyatt is contemporary in design and conveniently located in the heart of the city, across from the Van Wezel Performing Arts Hall. All the spacious rooms overlook Sarasota Bay or the marina. ⊠ *1000 Blvd. of the Arts, 34236,* ☎ *941/953–1234,* ℻ *941/952–1987. 297 rooms. 2 restaurants, bar, pool, sauna, health club, dock, boating. AE, DC, MC, V.*

$$ ⊞ **Best Western Midtown.** This three-story motel is clean, comfortable, and very affordable during its off-season, from mid-April through early February. Set back from U.S. 41 and somewhat removed from traffic noise, it is within walking distance of a shopping center and several restaurants—including the popular Michael's on East—and is central to area attractions and downtown. Rooms, which have seating areas, are done in pale pastel fabrics and blond wood. ⊠ *1425 S. Tamiami Trail, 34239,* ☎ *941/955–9841,* ℻ *941/954–8948. 100 rooms. Pool. AE, DC, MC, V.*

Nightlife and the Arts

THE ARTS

Among the many theaters in Sarasota, the $10 million **Asolo Center for the Performing Arts** (✉ 5555 N. Tamiami Trail, ☎ 941/351–8000) mounts productions nearly year-round. The small, professional **Florida Studio Theatre** (✉ 1241 N. Palm Ave., ☎ 941/366–9000) presents contemporary dramas, comedies, and musicals. **Golden Apple Dinner Theatre** (✉ 25 N. Pineapple Ave., ☎ 941/366–5454) serves up a standard buffet along with musicals and comedies. A long-established community theater, the **Players of Sarasota** (✉ U.S. 41 and 9th St., ☎ 941/365–2494) has launched such performers as Montgomery Clift and Pee-Wee Herman. The troupe performs comedies, thrillers, and musicals. **Theatre Works** (✉ 1247 1st St., ☎ 941/952–9170) presents professional non-Equity productions at the Palm Tree Playhouse. The **Van Wezel Performing Arts Hall** (✉ 777 N. Tamiami Trail, ☎ 941/953–3366) is easy to find—just look for the purple shell rising along the bay front. It hosts some 200 performances each year, including Broadway plays, ballet, jazz, rock concerts, symphonies, children's shows, and ice-skating.

The **Florida West Coast Symphony Center** (✉ 709 N. Tamiami Trail, ☎ 941/953–4252) hosts several area music groups that perform in Manatee and Sarasota counties regularly: the Florida West Coast Symphony, Florida String Quartet, Florida Brass Quintet, Florida Wind Quintet, and New Artists String Quartet. The **Sarasota Concert Band** (✉ Van Wezel Performing Arts Hall, 777 N. Tamiami Trail, ☎ 941/955–6660) includes 50 players, many of them full-time musicians. The group performs monthly concerts.

Celebrating its 40th season in 1999, the **Sarasota Opera** (✉ 61 N. Pineapple Ave., ☎ 941/953–7030) performs from February through March in a historic theater downtown. Internationally known artists sing the principal roles, supported by a professional chorus of 24 young apprentices.

The **Sarasota Film Society** (✉ 506 Burns La., ☎ 941/364–8662) operates year-round, showing foreign and art films daily at 2, 5:45, and 8 at the Burns Court Cinema.

NIGHTLIFE

Michael's On East (✉ 1212 East Ave. S, ☎ 941/366–0007) features light piano during the dinner hour, but jazz aficionados begin dropping in about 10 to listen to the mellow tunes of the light jazz bands that play here on weekends and even more frequently during the season. The **Patio** (✉ St. Armand's Circle, Lido Key, ☎ 941/388–3987), a casual lounge in the Columbia restaurant, has live music Wednesday–Sunday.

Outdoor Activities and Sports

BASEBALL

The **Cincinnati Reds** (✉ 2700 12th St., ☎ 941/954–7699) have spring training at Ed Smith Stadium.

BIKING

CB's (✉ 1249 Stickney Point Rd., ☎ 941/349–4400) rents bikes hourly and daily.

CANOEING

At **Myakka River State Park** (✉ 17 mi southeast of Sarasota on Rte. 72, ☎ 941/361–6511), you can rent canoes, paddles, and life vests.

DOG RACING

The greyhounds run from late December through April at the **Sarasota Kennel Club** (⊠ 5400 Bradenton Rd., ☎ 941/355–7744).

FISHING

Flying Fish at Marina Jack's (⊠ U.S. 41 on bay front, ☎ 941/366–3373) has several boats that can be chartered for deep-sea fishing and offers scheduled group trips.

GOLF

Bobby Jones Golf Course (⊠ 1000 Circus Blvd., ☎ 941/955–8097) has 18 holes and a driving range. **Forest Lakes Golf Club** (⊠ 2401 Beneva Rd., ☎ 941/922–1312) features a practice range and 18 holes. Known for its golf, the **Resort at Longboat Key Club** (⊠ 301 Gulf of Mexico Dr., Longboat Key, ☎ 941/383–8821) offers 45 holes and several putting greens, but the golf facilities are for resort guests or club members only.

TENNIS

If you love tennis and aren't staying at one of the tennis resorts, you might want to play at the **Forest Lakes Racket Club** (⊠ 2401 Beneva Rd., ☎ 941/922–1312), which has six courts.

WATER SPORTS

Don and Mike's Boat and Jet Ski Rental (⊠ 482 Blackburn Point Rd., ☎ 941/966–4000) has water skis, Jet Skis, pontoon boats, and instruction for all activities.

Shopping

St. Armand's Circle (⊠ Lido Key) is a cluster of oh-so-exclusive shops and restaurants.

Venice

45 *18 mi south of Sarasota.*

This small town is crisscrossed with even more canals than the city for which it was named. Venice beaches are good for shell collecting, but they're best known for their wealth of sharks' teeth and fossils, washed up from the ancient shark burial grounds just offshore.

Nakomis Beach (⊠ Albee Rd., Casey Key) is one of two notable beaches on the island. Just north of North Jetty Park, it offers rest rooms, a concession stand, picnic equipment, play areas, two boat ramps, a volleyball court, and fishing. **North Jetty Park** (⊠ Albee Rd., Casey Key), at the south end of the key, is a favorite for family outings, and fossil hunters may get lucky here. Facilities include rest rooms, a concession stand, play and picnic equipment, horseshoes, and a volleyball court. **Caspersen Beach** (⊠ Beach Dr., South Venice) is the county's largest park. It has a nature trail, fishing, picnicking, rest rooms, and lots of beach for those who prefer space to a wealth of amenities. At **Blind Pass Beach** (⊠ Manasota Beach Rd., Manasota Key), you can fish and swim but will find no amenities. **Manasota Beach** (⊠ Manasota Beach Rd., Manasota Key) has a boat ramp, picnic area, and rest rooms. **Englewood Beach,** near the Charlotte–Sarasota county line, is popular with teenagers, although beachgoers of all ages frequent it. In addition to a wide and shell-littered beach, there are barbecue grills, picnic facilities, boat ramps, a fishing pier, a playground, and showers. There's a $1 charge for parking.

The Arts

Venice Little Theatre (⊠ 140 W. Tampa Ave., ☎ 941/488–1115) is a community theater offering comedies, musicals, and a few dramas during its October–May season.

Dining and Lodging

$$ ✕ **Sharky's on the Pier.** Gaze out on the beach and sparkling waters while dining on fresh, grilled seafood at this popular and very casual eatery. Catches of the day can be broiled, blackened, grilled, or fried—your choice. There's an outdoor veranda and tables indoors as well. ⊠ *1600 S. Harbor Dr.,* ☎ *941/488–1456. AE, MC, V.*

$$–$$$ 🏨 **Inn at the Beach.** Across the street from the beach, this little one- and two-story resort is popular with families. Some of the one- and two-bedroom suites, which contain full kitchens and spacious living rooms, have views of the gulf. Others look out on tropical gardens. ⊠ *725 Venice Ave., 34285,* ☎ *941/484–8471,* 📠 *941/484–0593. 47 suites. Shuffleboard. AE, DC, MC, V.*

$$ 🏨 **Days Inn.** This simple but well-kept motel is on the main business route through town—but it's only 10 minutes from the beach. Rooms are comfortable, and pets are allowed. ⊠ *1710 S. Tamiami Trail, 34293,* ☎ *941/493–4558,* 📠 *941/493–1593. 73 rooms. Restaurant, pool. AE, MC, V.*

Outdoor Activities and Sports

BIKING

Bicycles International (⊠ 744 Tamiami Trail S, ☎ 941/497–1590) rents its varied stock weekly as well as hourly and daily.

FISHING

Gulfwater Marine (⊠ 215 Tamiami Trail S, ☎ 941/484–9044) is a good place to try for deep-sea fishing.

GOLF

Bird Bay Executive Golf Course (⊠ 602 Bird Bay Dr. W, ☎ 941/485–9333) has 18 holes. **Plantation Golf & Country Club** (⊠ 500 Rockley Blvd., ☎ 941/493–2000) boasts 36 holes and a driving range.

Shopping

If you like flea markets, check out the **Dome** (⊠ Rte. 775 west of U.S. 41), where dozens of sheltered stalls sell new and recycled wares. It's open October–August, Friday–Sunday 9–4.

THE TAMPA BAY AREA A TO Z

Arriving and Departing

By Bus

Service to and throughout the state is provided by **Greyhound Lines** (☎ 800/231–2222; 813/229–2112 in Tampa; 727/898–1496 in St. Petersburg; 941/955–5735 in Sarasota).

By Car

I–75 spans the region from north to south. Once you cross the Florida border from Georgia, it should take about three hours to reach Tampa and another hour to reach Sarasota. If coming from Orlando, you're likely to drive west into Tampa on I–4.

By Plane

Several carriers serve **Tampa International** (☎ 813/870–8700), 6 mi from downtown, including **Air Canada** (☎ 800/776–3000), **Air Jamaica** (☎ 800/523–5585), **American** (☎ 800/433–7300), **Bahamasair** (☎ 800/222–4262), **British Airways** (☎ 800/247–9297), **Canadian Holidays**

(☎ 800/661–8881), **Cayman Airlines** (☎ 800/422–9626), **Continental** (☎ 800/956–6680), **Delta** (☎ 800/241–4141), **Mexicana** (☎ 800/531–7921), **Northwest** (☎ 800/225–2525), **Southwest** (☎ 800/435–9792), **TWA** (☎ 800/222–2000), **United** (☎ 800/241–6522), **US Airways** (☎ 800/428–4322), and **Virgin Atlantic** (☎ 800/862–5621). **Central Florida Limousine** (☎ 813/396–3730) provides airport service to and from Hillsborough and Polk counties. The **Limo** (☎ 727/572–1111 or 800/282–6817) serves Pinellas County. Expect taxi fares to be about $12–$25 for most of Hillsborough County and about twice that for Pinellas County.

St. Petersburg–Clearwater International (☎ 727/535–7600) is only about 9 mi from downtown St. Petersburg, but if you're coming from many areas of the country, you may have to supply your own plane, as scheduled service is limited and charters and corporate jets outnumber airlines with recognizable names. However, **American TransAir** (☎ 800/435–9282) does connect to selected cities in the Midwest and West; **Sunjet** (☎ 800/478–6538) offers regular service to Newark, New Jersey; and Canadian travelers have two options from Toronto: **Air Transat** (☎ 800/655–8284) and **Canada 3000** (☎ 800/993–4378).

Sarasota's airport, **Sarasota-Bradenton** (☎ 941/359–5200), lies just north of the city. It is served by American, Continental, Delta, Northwest, TWA, United, and US Airways. Transportation to and from the airport is provided by **Airport Shuttle** (☎ 941/355–9645) and **West Coast Executive Sedan** (☎ 941/359–8600). The average cab fare between the airport and downtown is $16–$25.

By Train
Amtrak (☎ 800/872–7245) trains run from the Northeast, Midwest, and much of the South to the Tampa station.

Getting Around

By Bus
Around Tampa, the **Hillsborough Area Regional Transit** (HART; ☎ 813/254–4278) serves the county. Around St. Petersburg, **Pinellas Suncoast Transit Authority** (PSTA; ☎ 727/530–9911) serves Pinellas County. In Sarasota the public transit company is **Sarasota County Area Transit** (SCAT; ☎ 941/951–5850).

By Car
I–75 and U.S. 41 (which runs concurrently with the Tamiami Trail for much of the way) stretch the length of the region. U.S. 41 links the business districts of many communities, so it's best to avoid it and all bridges during rush hours, 7–9 and 4–6. U.S. 19 is St. Petersburg's major north–south artery; traffic can be heavy, and there are many lights, so use a different route when possible.

I–275 heads west from Tampa across Tampa Bay to St. Petersburg, swings south, and crosses the bay again on its way to Terra Ceia, near Bradenton. Along this last leg—the Sunshine Skyway and its stunning suspension bridge—you'll get a bird's-eye view of bustling Tampa Bay.

The Bayshore Boulevard Causeway also yields a spectacular view of Tampa Bay, and Route 679 takes you along two of St. Petersburg's most pristine islands, Cabbage and Mullet keys. Route 64 connects I–75 to Bradenton and Anna Maria Island. Route 789 runs over several slender barrier islands, past miles of blue-green gulf waters, beaches, and waterfront homes. The road does not connect all the islands, however; it runs from Holmes Beach off the Bradenton coast south to Lido Key, then begins again on Siesta Key and again on Casey Key south of Osprey, and runs south to Nokomis Beach.

Contacts and Resources

Emergencies
Dial **911** for police and ambulance.

HOSPITALS
There are 24-hour emergency rooms at **Bayfront Medical Center** (⊠ 701 6th St. S, St. Petersburg), **Manatee Memorial Hospital** (⊠ 206 2nd St. E, Bradenton), **Sarasota Memorial Hospital** (⊠ 1700 S. Tamiami Trail, Sarasota), and **University Community Hospital** (⊠ 3100 E. Fletcher Ave., Tampa).

LATE-NIGHT PHARMACY
Eckerd Drug (⊠ 11613 N. Nebraska Ave., Tampa, ☎ 813/978–0775).

Guided Tours

AIR TOURS
Tours of the bay area and the Gulf Coast, given by **Helicopter Charter & Transport Co.** (⊠ 9000 18th St., Tampa, ☎ 813/933–2686), leave from Tampa International. **West Florida Helicopters** (⊠ Albert Whitted Airport, St. Petersburg, ☎ 727/823–5200) offers bay-area tours.

BOAT TOURS
On **Captain Memo's Pirate Cruise** (⊠ Clearwater Beach Marina, Clearwater Beach, ☎ 727/446–2587), crew members dressed as pirates take visitors on sightseeing and sunset cruises in a replica of a 19th-century sailing ship. A floating casino comes to life aboard the **Europa SeaKruz** (⊠ John's Pass Village, Madeira Beach, ☎ 727/393–2885 or 800/688–7529), which offers a six-hour cruise that also includes dining and nightclub-style entertainment. The **Miss Cortez** (⊠ Cortez, ☎ 941/794–1223) departs for Egmont Key from just north of Bradenton every Tuesday, Thursday, and Sunday. **Myakka Wildlife Tours** (⊠ Myakka River State Park, Rte. 72 southeast of Sarasota, ☎ 941/365–0100) runs four daily hour-long tours of the wildlife sanctuary aboard the *Gator Gal,* a large airboat. Visitors can take a sightseeing cruise of Tarpon Springs' historic sponge docks and see an actual diver at work on the seabed aboard the glass-bottom boats of **St. Nicholas Boat Line** (⊠ 693 Dodecanese Blvd., Tarpon Springs, ☎ 727/942–6425). The **Starlite Princess and Starlite Majestic** (⊠ Hamlin's Landing, Indian Rocks Beach, ☎ 727/595–1212), an old-fashioned paddle wheeler and a sleek yacht-style vessel, respectively, both make sightseeing and dinner cruises.

Visitor Information
Cedar Key Chamber of Commerce (⊠ Box 610, Cedar Key 32625, ☎ 352/543–5600). **Greater Clearwater Chamber of Commerce** (⊠ 128 N. Osceola Ave., Clearwater 34615, ☎ 727/461–0011). **Greater Dunedin Chamber of Commerce** (⊠ 301 Main St., Dunedin 34698, ☎ 727/736–5066). **Greater Tampa Chamber of Commerce** (⊠ Box 420, Tampa 33601, ☎ 813/228–7777; 813/223–1111, ext. 44; 813/223–1111, ext. 44 Visitors Information Department). **Gulf Beaches on Sand Key Chamber of Commerce** (⊠ 501 150th Ave., Madeira Beach 33701, ☎ 727/595–4575 or 727/391–7373). **St. Petersburg Chamber of Commerce** (⊠ 100 2nd Ave. N, St. Petersburg 33701, ☎ 727/821–4069). **St. Petersburg/Clearwater Area Convention & Visitors Bureau** (⊠ 14450 46th St. N, Suite 108, St. Petersburg 33762, ☎ 727/582–7892). **Sarasota Convention and Visitors Bureau** (⊠ 655 N. Tamiami Trail, Sarasota 34236, ☎ 941/957–1877 or 800/522–9799). **Tampa/Hillsborough Convention and Visitors Association** (⊠ 111 Madison St., Suite

1010, Tampa 33601-0519, ☎ 800/826–8358; 800/448–2672 for information and hotel reservations; 800/284–0404 for vacation packages). **Tarpon Springs Chamber of Commerce** (✉ 210 S. Pinellas Ave., Suite 120, Tarpon Springs 34689, ☎ 727/937–6109). **Treasure Island Chamber of Commerce** (✉ 108th Ave., Treasure Island 33706, ☎ 727/367–4529).

8 SOUTHWEST FLORIDA

Still somewhat less discovered than its neighbors to the north and east, this diverse section of Florida has plenty to do. Fort Myers, a sleepy city built along a river, has a number of interesting museums. Sanibel and Captiva, two nearby barrier islands, are known for their exceptional shell-filled beaches. In Naples you find fine cuisine and equally fine shopping. And all this is wrapped up in a delightful subtropical climate.

Updated by
Pamela
Acheson

THE SOUTHWEST FLORIDA COAST is often called "Florida's Florida" because its natural subtropical environment has made it a favorite vacation spot for Florida natives as well as visitors. There's lots to do here, and although much activity centers on sun and surf, there are several distinctly different travel destinations in a relatively compact area.

Fort Myers is a small and pretty inland city built along the Caloosahatchee River. It got its nickname, "the City of Palms," from the hundreds of towering royal palms that inventor Thomas Edison planted along McGregor Boulevard, the main residential street and site of his winter estate. Edison's idea caught on, and there are now more than 2,000 royal palms on McGregor Boulevard alone.

Off the coast west of Fort Myers, more than 100 coastal islands range in length from just a few feet to more than 16 mi. Here you'll find Sanibel and Captiva, two thoughtfully developed resort islands. Connected to the mainland by a 3-mi causeway, Sanibel is known for its world-class shelling, fine fishing, beachfront resorts (mostly at the south end of the island), and its wildlife refuge. You won't be able to see most of the houses, which are shielded by tall Australian pines, but the beaches and tranquil gulf waters are readily accessible.

Just southwest of Fort Myers is Estero Island, home of busy Fort Myers Beach, and farther south, Lover's Key State Park, Florida's newest.

Down the coast still farther is Naples, once a small fishing village and now a thriving and sophisticated town—something like a smaller version of Palm Beach. There are a number of fine restaurants and several upscale shopping complexes, including the gracious, tree-lined 3rd Street South area. The number of golf courses per capita in Naples is said to be the highest in the world, a 1,200-seat performing arts hall attracts world-class performers, and the town is the west-coast home of the Miami City Ballet. Unlike Palm Beach, the Naples area offers easy access to its many miles of sun-drenched white beach.

East of Naples stretches the Big Cypress National Preserve, and a half hour south is Marco Island, with several large resorts, good beaches, restaurants, and shops. Farther southeast is Everglades City, the western gateway to Everglades National Park (☞ Chapter 2).

Pleasures and Pastimes

Beaches
Southwest Florida has gorgeous, long white-sand beaches, both along the coast and on many barrier islands. Many beaches, particularly on Sanibel and Captiva, are prime shelling spots. Waters in this part of the Gulf of Mexico are often the soft aquamarine blue found in the tropics.

Canoeing
Sanibel Island's J. N. "Ding" Darling National Wildlife Refuge is a popular spot for canoeing. There are also many opportunities to canoe inland in the less developed areas of the region; several outfits offer half- and full-day trips and overnighters.

Dining
In this part of Florida seafood reigns supreme. Expect ample fresh fish on the menu. A particular treat is a succulent claw of the native stone crab, usually served with drawn butter or a tangy mustard sauce and

in season from mid-October through mid-May. (Luckily, stone crabs are not killed to harvest their claws, and they regenerate the limbs before the next season, so they are not in danger of being overcrabbed.) Naples is home to many fine dining establishments, where you can mingle with the very social winter people and experience the latest in culinary trends. Throughout southwest Florida many restaurants offer discount-price early bird menus with seating before 6 PM.

Golf

The area has one of the highest concentrations of courses in the nation. In fact, Naples currently has 45 courses (new ones open all the time), and *Golf Digest* named it the "Golf Capital of the World."

Shopping

Prepare to shell out some cash for at least one kitschy crustacean creation. As one of the world's premier shelling grounds, Sanibel Island has numerous shops seriously selling shells (try to say that three times fast)—from lamps to jewelry. However, Sanibel also has its share of appealing boutiques showcasing delicate jewelry and fashionable resort wear. Naples has the fanciest shopping in southwest Florida, and here you'll find many unique but expensive shops carrying gift items, men's and women's clothing, shoes, linens, and lingerie as well as numerous art galleries.

Exploring Southwest Florida

Vacationers to southwest Florida tend to spend most of their time outdoors—swimming, sunning, shelling, or playing tennis or golf. Fort Myers is the only major inland destination; it is situated along a winding river and has a number of interesting museums. The offshore barrier islands vary from tiny undeveloped islands to popular vacation spots with numerous hotels and restaurants. Sanibel and Captiva, connected to each other and to the mainland by causeways, offer beaches known for shelling and a superb wildlife preserve. Naples is a sophisticated town with art galleries, fine dining, and upscale shopping and rapid development along its north shore. A bit farther south is Marco Island, where you can take an airboat to see tight clusters of tiny undeveloped islands. Although high-rises line much of Marco Island's waterfront, many natural areas have been preserved, including the tiny fishing village of Goodland, an outpost of Old Florida.

Numbers in the text correspond to numbers in the margin and on the Southwest Florida map.

Great Itineraries

IF YOU HAVE 2 DAYS

⛏ **Fort Myers** ① is a good base for a short visit. It's not directly on the beach, but its central location makes day trips easy. On the morning of your first day, visit Thomas Edison's Winter Home, in downtown Fort Myers, and then take beautiful McGregor Boulevard to **Sanibel Island** ⑥ for the rest of the day. Once on the island, stop by the Bailey-Matthews Shell Museum and the J. N. "Ding" Darling National Wildlife Refuge before heading to Bowman's Beach for shelling and swimming the rest of the afternoon. The next day drive down I–75 to **Naples** ⑩, where you can check out Caribbean Gardens' tropical flora and exotic wildlife. Those with a soft spot for teddy bears should stop by the Teddy Bear Museum of Naples before hitting Old Naples for some shopping and relaxing on the nearby beach.

IF YOU HAVE 4 DAYS

With a little extra time for getting around, you'll be able to stay near the water, on **Sanibel Island** ⑥. Spend your first day shelling and swimming, with a stop at the Bailey-Matthews Shell Museum. On day two, head into **Fort Myers** ① to Thomas Edison's Winter Home and Henry Ford's Mangoes. Then drive to Babcock Wilderness Adventures, northeast of the city, for a swamp-buggy ride. Why not spend your third day back on Sanibel, dividing your time between the beach and the J. N. "Ding" Darling National Wildlife Refuge? You could even try early morning or evening bird-watching. On day four, drive south to **Naples** ⑩ and the sights mentioned in the two-day itinerary, or for even more wildlife, head to the Corkscrew Swamp Sanctuary, a nature preserve east of **Bonita Springs** ⑨.

IF YOU HAVE 10 DAYS

An extended stay will enable you to move your base from area to area and explore each in more depth by adding the following activities to those listed above. With two days in the 🖪 **Fort Myers** ① area, you can get a taste of southern viticulture at the Eden Vineyards Winery and Park, or if the Babcock Wilderness Adventures has whetted your ecological appetite, head to the Calusa Nature Center and Planetarium. An extra day on 🖪 **Sanibel Island** ⑥ allows you to visit an isolated key, such as **Cabbage Key** ⑤ or the little town of Boca Grande, on **Gasparilla Island** ④. For the second half of your trip, relocate to 🖪 **Naples** ⑩, stopping on the way at Lover's Key State Park for sensational shelling along 2½ mi of white-sand beach. When you reach Naples, you can combine beach activities with days of wandering through art galleries and shops in Old Naples. The Caribbean Gardens and the Corkscrew Swamp Sanctuary are good bets for kids; to try your hand at paddling, rent a canoe or kayak at the Naples Nature Center.

When to Tour Southwest Florida

In winter this is one of the warmest areas of the United States, though there is occasional cold weather. From January through April you may find it next to impossible to find a hotel room in this hugely popular destination. Fewer people visit in the off-season, but there really is no bad time to come. Ocean breezes keep the coast cool even in summer.

FORT MYERS AND NORTH

Fort Myers is one of the prettiest cities in Florida. The broad, flat Caloosahatchee River forms its northern shoreline, and water views soften the businesslike cluster of downtown office buildings. Between rows of stately palms you can catch glimpses of old southern mansions. North of Fort Myers are several small fishing communities, including Port Charlotte, on the north side of the Caloosahatchee River, and Punta Gorda, at the convergence of the Peace River and Charlotte Harbor.

Fort Myers

❶ *90 mi southeast of Sarasota, 140 mi west of Palm Beach.*

Although the nearest beach is a half hour away, there is still plenty to do in this small, inviting inland city that stretches along the Caloosahatchee River. The town is best known as the winter home of inventors Thomas A. Edison and Henry Ford.

One of the region's most scenic stretches of highway, **McGregor Boulevard** is lined with majestic palm trees, some planted by Thomas Edison. It runs from downtown to the Gulf of Mexico.

★ **Thomas A. Edison's Winter Home,** Fort Myers's premier attraction, contains a laboratory, botanical gardens, and a museum. A remarkable showpiece, the house was donated to the city by Edison's widow. As a result, the laboratory is not merely reconstructed but just as Edison

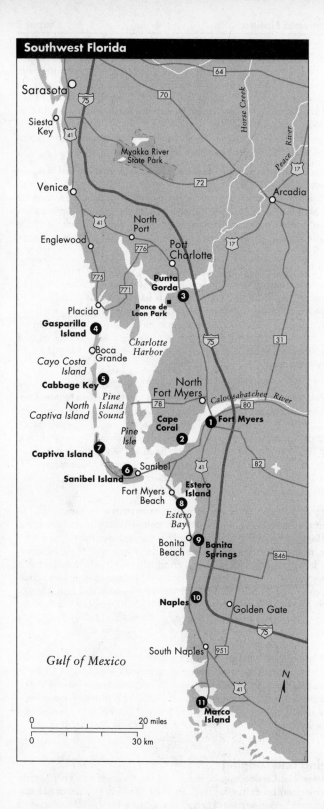

Southwest Florida

Sarasota

Siesta Key

Venice

Englewood

North Port

Port Charlotte

Punta Gorda ③

Ponce de Leon Park

Placida

Gasparilla Island ④

Boca Grande

Cayo Costa Island

Cabbage Key ⑤

North Captiva Island

Charlotte Harbor

Pine Island Sound

Pine Island

Pine Isle

Captiva Island ⑦

Sanibel ⑥

Sanibel Island

Fort Myers Beach

North Fort Myers

Cape Coral ②

Fort Myers ①

Estero Island ⑧

Estero Bay

Bonita Beach

Bonita Springs ⑨

Naples ⑩

Golden Gate

South Naples

Gulf of Mexico

Marco Island ⑪

Myakka River State Park

Horse Creek

Peace River

Arcadia

Caloosahatchee River

0   20 miles

0   30 km

left it. The property straddles McGregor Boulevard about a mile west of U.S. 41, near downtown. The inventor spent his winters on the 14-acre estate, developing the phonograph and teletype, experimenting with rubber, and planting some 600 species of plants collected around the world. Next door is **Mangoes,** the more modest winter home of fellow inventor and longtime friend automaker Henry Ford. It is said that the V-8 engine was primarily designed on the back porch. ✉ *2350 Mc-Gregor Blvd.,* ☎ *941/334–3614.* ✇ *Edison home and Mangoes (combined) $11.* ✲ *Tours Mon.–Sat. 9–4, Sun. noon–4.*

Housed in a restored railroad depot, the **Fort Myers Historical Museum** showcases the area's history dating to 800 BC. Displays include prehistoric Calusa artifacts, a reconstructed *chickee* hut, canoes, clothing and photos from Seminole settlements, and the Ethel Cooper collection of decorative glass. A favorite attraction is the *Esperanza,* a 1930s private rail car. ✉ *2300 Peck St.,* ☎ *941/332–5955.* ✇ *$4.* ✲ *Tues.–Sat. 9–4.*

🖑 Kids can't wait to get their hands on all the wonderful interactive exhibits at the **Imaginarium,** where the rule is definitely "Please touch!" There are more than 60 exhibits at this hands-on museum-aquarium combo, and children can learn about the environment, physics, anatomy, weather, and other science topics. Check out the marine life in the aquariums, touch pool, living reef tank, outdoor lagoon, 3-D theater, and butterfly garden. ✉ *2000 Cranford Ave.,* ☎ *941/337–3332.* ✇ *$6.* ✲ *Tues.–Sat. 10–5.*

For a look at frequently changing exhibits on wildlife, fossils, and Florida's native animals and habitats, head to the **Calusa Nature Center and Planetarium.** Rustic boardwalks lead through subtropical wetlands, an aviary, and a village. There are snake and alligator demonstrations several times daily. The planetarium offers star shows, laser-light shows, and Cinema-360 films in its 90-seat theater. ✉ *3450 Ortiz Ave.,* ☎ *941/275–3435.* ✇ *Nature center $4, planetarium $3, laser-light and music shows $3.* ✲ *Nature center Mon.–Sat. 9–5, Sun. 11–5; planetarium shows Wed.–Sun. 1:30 and 3.*

To catch a glimpse of Florida's most famous marine mammal, head to **Manatee Park.** When gulf waters are cold—usually from November to March—the gentle sea cows tend to congregate in the warm waters here, near the outflow of a power plant. Pause at any of the observation decks and watch for bubbles. Periodically you'll see a manatee come up for air. Don't be surprised at how big they are; fully grown manatees can weigh hundreds of pounds! ✉ *1½ mi east of I–75 on Rte. 80,* ☎ *941/694–3537 viewing update, 941/432–2004 office.* ✇ *Parking 75¢ per hr to maximum of $3 per day.* ✲ *Apr.–Sept., daily 8–8; Oct.–Mar., daily 8–5.*

OFF THE BEATEN PATH

EDEN VINEYARDS WINERY AND PARK – Even connoisseurs can't resist a stop here, reputed to be the southernmost bonded winery in the United States. Besides offering half a dozen kinds of traditional wine, the vineyard puts its own spin on the trade with carambola (starfruit) wine. The family-owned winery offers tours and tastings. Reservations are needed for groups of 12 or more. ✉ *10 mi east of I–75 on Rte. 80, Alva,* ☎ *941/728–9463.* ✇ *$2.50; complimentary tasting.* ✲ *Daily 11–4.*

Dining and Lodging

$$$ ✕ **Peter's La Cuisine.** Smack in the middle of downtown Fort Myers,
★ two blocks off the river, is this charming restaurant in a restored brick building. The dining room's extra-high ceiling gives a spacious feel, and exposed brick walls, dim lighting, crisp linen tablecloths and napkins,

THE WEST INDIAN MANATEE: FLORIDA'S LARGEST MAMMAL

OK, SO THEY WON'T WIN any beauty contests. Florida's West Indian manatees, also known as sea cows, are absolutely enormous aquatic mammals. The average adult male is about 10 ft long and weighs in at around a thousand pounds, so it should come as no surprise that their closest relative is the elephant. (What may surprise you, however, is the speculation that sightings of "mermaids" were actually manatees.) Yet despite their mass, these creatures somehow manage a sweet appeal. Their big lump of a body has wrinkly grey-brown skin, a tiny paddle-shape tail, two little flippers, and a stubby, pug-nose face that is at once whiskery and winsome.

In spite of their giant size, sea cows are entirely harmless. In fact, they are extremely docile. Moving very slowly, they sometimes submerge and rest, coming up for a breath of fresh air every three to five minutes. These completely herbivorous animals spend the day grazing along the floor and surface of a body of water in search of aquatic greenery. Consummate munchers, the gentle giants can consume close to 15 percent of their body weight in plants each day!

Male manatees take about nine years to reach adulthood, while females take only five. Baby manatees stay with their mothers for as long as two years.

Although sea cows have no natural enemies and can live to be 60 years old, only about 2,500 are left in all of the United States. As an endangered species, they are protected under U.S. federal law by the 1973 act of the same name as well as by the Marine Mammal Protection Act of 1972 and the Florida Manatee Sanctuary Act of 1978. Florida waterways have manatee zones with restricted, no-wake speed limits, yet each year too many manatees are still wounded and killed by watercraft and their propellers. Others die from eating fishing line, plastic, or fish hooks, while development continues to swallow up the manatees' natural habitats.

MANATEES LIVE IN SHALLOW, slow-moving waters, such as quiet rivers, peaceful saltwater bays, and calm coastal canals. To see them, look in both coasts' Intracoastal Waterway from spring to fall. In the winter, the creatures search for warmer waters, heading to inland springs or even to the heated outflow of a power plant (☞ Manatee Park). Spotting them can be tricky. Since manatees usually travel together in a long line with their bodies mostly submerged, look for something resembling drifting coconuts. Also look for concentric circles in the water, a signal that manatees are about to surface.

Several organizations are intent on helping manatees. The Save the Manatee Club, which operates under the auspices of the U.S. Fish and Wildlife Service, welcomes new members. If you choose to "adopt" a sea cow, you'll receive a picture of "your" manatee, a little history about him or her, a handbook about manatees, and a certificate of adoption. A newsletter includes periodic updates about your adoptee. For more information contact the Save the Manatee Club and Adopt a Manatee (✉ 500 N. Maitland Avenue, Maitland 32751, ☎ 800/432–5646, www.savethemanatee.org).

and a refined atmosphere provide a pleasant background for Continental cuisine with a contemporary twist. After dinner wander upstairs for a cordial and some great blues. ⊠ *2224 Bay St.,* ☎ *941/332–2228. AE, MC, V. No lunch weekends.*

$$–$$$ ✕ **Prawnbroker Restaurant and Fish Market.** Ads for this restaurant
★ urge you to scratch and sniff—there is no odor, the ad reads, because truly fresh seafood has none. The dyed-in-the-wool establishment has an abundance of fish and shellfish seemingly just plucked from gulf waters and prepared just about any way you want. Culinary landlubbers will find good choices here, too. This place is almost always crowded, and for good reason. ⊠ *13451 McGregor Blvd.,* ☎ *941/489–2226. AE, MC, V. No lunch.*

$$–$$$ ✕ **The Veranda.** An imaginative assortment of Continental cuisine infused with a southern accent is turned out in this sprawling turn-of-the-century home. The menu includes Bourbon Street filet mignon, rack of lamb with rosemary sauce, salmon over a bed of julienne vegetables, and a southern-fried seafood sampler. Sconces and antique oil paintings line the pale yellow walls of this popular place for business and government bigwigs. Courtyard dining is also available. ⊠ *2122 2nd St.,* ☎ *941/332–2065. AE, DC, MC, V. Closed Sun. No lunch Sat.*

$ ✕ **Mel's Diner.** During peak hours you have to wait for a table, but it's
★ worth it at this 1950s-style diner with black-and-white tiles on the floor and comfortable booths. Try the real mashed potatoes, homemade soups, spicy chili, and blue-plate specials. For dessert the popular mile-high pies hit the spot. ⊠ *4820 Cleveland Ave.,* ☎ *941/275–7850. No credit cards.*

$ ✕ **Miami Connection.** If you hunger for choice chopped liver, lean but tender corned beef, and a chewy bagel, this kosher-style deli can fill the bill. The sandwiches are huge. It is, as a local restaurant critic aptly said, "the real McCohen." ⊠ *11506 Cleveland Ave.,* ☎ *941/936–3811. No credit cards. No dinner.*

$$–$$$ 🏨 **Amtel Marina Hotel & Suites.** This modern, 25-story high-rise takes a commanding spot in the downtown skyline, rising tall above the river and yacht basin. Well-furnished rooms have panoramic views of the water or the city. Restaurants, the Harborside Convention Center, and Thomas Edison's home are all within walking distance. ⊠ *2500 Edwards Dr., 33901,* ☎ *941/337–0300 or 800/833–1620,* ℻ *941/479–4180. 406 rooms, 23 suites. Restaurant, bar, pool, hot tub, tennis court, exercise room, dock, video games. AE, DC, MC, V.*

$$ 🏨 **Radisson Inn Fort Myers.** Families like this popular hotel's recreational facilities and restaurant as well as its convenient location—close to I-75, just 7 mi south of downtown Fort Myers, and only 12 mi from Fort Myers Beach. Units, many with balconies, are in both a two- and a five-story building, and an inviting courtyard dotted with palm trees surrounds the free-form pool. ⊠ *12635 Cleveland Ave., 33907,* ☎ *941/936–4300,* ℻ *941/936–2058. 181 rooms, 11 suites. Restaurant, bar, pool, tennis court, horseshoes, volleyball, billiards. AE, DC, MC, V.*

Nightlife and the Arts

THE ARTS

The **Barbara B. Mann Performing Arts Hall** (⊠ 8099 College Pkwy. SW, ☎ 941/481–4849) presents plays, concerts, musicals, and dance programs. Call or check the Friday entertainment section of the local newspapers for upcoming events. The **Broadway Palm Dinner Theater** (⊠ 1380 Colonial Blvd., ☎ 941/278–4422) serves up buffet dinners along with some of Broadway's best comedies and musicals.

NIGHTLIFE

Those in the know come to the **Brick Bar** (⊠ 2224 Bay St., ☎ 941/332–2228), above Peter's La Cuisine restaurant, for blues music seven nights a week. The **Laugh-In Comedy Cafe** (✉ College Plaza, College Pkwy. and Winkler Rd., ☎ 941/338–6127) features MTV, HBO, and Comedy Network comedians every Friday and Saturday. **Shoeless Joe's Sports Cafe** (✉ Holiday Inn Select, 13051 Bell Tower Dr., ☎ 941/482–2900) has big-screen TVs for watching your favorite sports.

Outdoor Activities and Sports

BASEBALL

The **Boston Red Sox** (✉ 2201 Edison Ave., ☎ 941/334–4700) play in Fort Myers during their spring-training sojourn. The **Minnesota Twins** (✉ Lee County Sports Complex, 1410 Six Mile Cypress Pkwy., ☎ 941/768–4278) play exhibition games in March and April.

BIKING

The best path in Fort Myers is along Summerlin Road; for rentals call **Trikes & Bikes & Mowers** (✉ 3224 Fowler St., ☎ 941/936–4301).

FISHING

Party-boat and private fishing charters can be arranged at **Deebold's Marina** (✉ 1071 San Carlos Blvd., ☎ 941/466–3525).

GOLF

You'll find a driving range and an 18-hole course at the **Eastwood Golf Club** (✉ 4600 Bruce Herd La., ☎ 941/275–4848). The **Fort Myers Country Club** (✉ 3591 McGregor Blvd., ☎ 941/936–2457) offers golf lessons and an 18-hole course. A practice range and 18-hole course can be found at the **Palm Lakes Country Club** (✉ Lehigh Acres, ☎ 941/369–8216), southeast of town.

SAILING

For sailing lessons or bareboat or captained sail cruises, contact **Fort Myers Yacht Charters** (✉ Port Sanibel Yacht Club, South Fort Myers, ☎ 941/540–8050). **Southwest Florida Yachts** (✉ 3444 Marinatown La. NW, ☎ 941/656–1339 or 800/262–7939) has a fleet of sailboats for charter and also offers lessons.

Shopping

The **Bell Tower Shops** (✉ U.S. 41 and Daniels Pkwy., South Fort Myers), an outdoor shopping center catering to upscale tastes, has about 50 boutiques and specialty shops, a Saks Fifth Avenue and a Jacobson's, and 20 movie screens. Historic downtown **1st Street** features several charming restaurants and many unique shops, as well as street musicians and artists. At **Royal Palm Square** (✉ Colonial Blvd. between McGregor Blvd. and U.S. 41), more than two dozen shops and restaurants are set amid waterways and tropical foliage. For discounted prices, go to **Sanibel Factory Outlets** (✉ McGregor Blvd. and Summerlin Rd.), containing more than 55 brand-name outlets, including Dexter, Van Heusen, Maidenform, Coach, Jones New York, and Corning/Revere.

Just east of Fort Myers, **Fleamasters Fleamarket** (1 mi west of I–75 Exit 23 on Rte. 82) features covered walkways and hundreds of vendors selling new and used items. It's open Friday–Sunday 8–4.

Cape Coral

❷ *13 mi from Fort Myers via North Fort Myers.*

Though this relaxed residential community is just across the Caloosahatchee River from Fort Myers, to reach it you have to head north to North Fort Myers and then swing back southwest along the river.

★ ⏾ Nature walks, bubblebins, Xeriscape displays, mazes, optical tricks, mind-benders, and brain twisters are just some of the appealing attractions for kids at the **Children's Science Center.** ⊠ 2915 N.E. Pine Island Rd., ☎ 941/997–0012. ▧ $4. ◷ Weekdays 9:30–4:30, weekends noon–5.

⏾ **Sun Splash Family Waterpark** has more than two dozen wet and dry attractions, including three large water slides; the Lilypad Walk, where you step from one floating "lily pad" to another; an arcade; Squirtworks, a special play area for very young children; and Cape Fear, the park's newest and fastest tube slide. ⊠ 400 Santa Barbara Blvd., ☎ 941/574–0558. ▧ $10.50. ◷ Mid-Mar.–mid-May, Fri. 11–5, weekends 10–5; mid-May–late May, Wed.–Fri. 11–5, weekends 10–5; June–late Aug., Mon.–Wed. and Fri. 10–6, Thurs. and Sat. 10–9; late Aug.–Oct., weekends 10–5.

OFF THE
BEATEN PATH

ECHO – Educational Concerns for Hunger Organization is a small Christian ministry group striving to solve the world's hunger problems. It offers tours of its gardens (which feature the largest collection of tropical food plants in Florida), walks through a simulated rain forest, and looks at crops such as sesame and rice grown without soil. ⊠ 17430 Durrance Rd., North Fort Myers, ☎ 941/543–3246. ▧ Donation welcome. ◷ Tours Tues., Fri., and Sat. at 10 or by appointment.

Dining and Lodging

$–$$ ✗ **Cape Crab and SteakHouse.** Crabs are the specialty here. Try them Maryland style—heaped on a tablecloth of newspaper and with a mallet on the side. Don't want to whack out your frustrations on your dinner? A more refined second dining room has linen tablecloths and a piano player. The menu for both rooms carries 11 crab dishes, shrimp, fish, chicken, pizza, and a pasta du jour. ⊠ Coralwood Mall, Del Prado Blvd., ☎ 941/574–2722. AE, MC, V.

$ ✗ **Siam Hut.** Thai music pings and twangs in the background while your taste buds do the same. Specialties are *pad thai* (a mixture of noodles, crushed peanuts, chicken, shrimp, egg, bean sprouts, and scallions) and crispy Siam rolls (spring rolls stuffed with ground chicken, bean thread, and vegetables). You can have it fiery hot or extra mild. ⊠ Coral Pointe Shopping Center, 1873 Del Prado Blvd., ☎ 941/772–3131. AE, MC, V.

$$ ▥ **Cape Coral Golf & Tennis Resort.** Aimed at golf and tennis enthusiasts, this resort is a good value. The main clubhouse houses reception areas and two restaurants, while comfortably furnished rooms are in a two-story motel-like building. Understated decor reflects the sporty atmosphere. ⊠ 4003 Palm Tree Blvd., 33904, ☎ 941/542–3191 or 800/648–1475, ℻ 941/542–4694. 199 rooms, 1 suite. 3 restaurants, bar, pool, driving range, 27 holes of golf, putting green, 8 tennis courts. AE, DC, MC, V.

$$ ▥ **Quality Inn–Nautilus.** Conveniently near parks, beaches, restaurants, and malls, this downtown motel offers no-smoking and wheelchair-accessible rooms with complimentary breakfast and newspaper. Pets are permitted. ⊠ 1538 Cape Coral Pkwy., 33904, ☎ 941/542–2121, ℻ 941/542–6319. 142 rooms. Bar, pool, shuffleboard. AE, DC, MC, V.

Outdoor Activities and Sports

GOLF

Cape Coral Golf & Tennis Resort (⊠ 4003 Palm Tree Blvd., ☎ 941/542–7879) features 27 holes of golf, a lighted driving range, and a putting green. **Coral Oaks Golf Course** (⊠ 1800 N.W. 28th Ave., ☎ 941/283–4100) has an 18-hole course and a practice range.

Cape Coral Golf & Tennis Resort (⊠ 4003 Palm Tree Blvd., ☎ 941/542–3191) offers eight lighted Har-Tru courts. **Lochmoor Country Club** (⊠ 3911 Orange Grove Blvd., North Fort Myers, ☎ 941/995–0501) has two Har-Tru clay courts; lessons are available.

Shopping

The **Shell Factory** (⊠ 2787 N. Tamiami Trail, North Fort Myers, ☎ 941/995–2141) claims to have the world's largest display of seashells and coral.

Punta Gorda

❸ *30 mi north of Cape Coral, 23 mi north of Fort Myers.*

This small town is at the mouth of the Peace River, where it empties into Charlotte Harbor. Although both it and its slightly larger neighbor, Port Charlotte, are on the water, they are not on the ocean, and the closest beach is about 20 minutes away. This is a good destination if you're interested in canoeing, walking through the Florida wilderness, and most of all, escaping the crowds.

The **Florida Adventure Museum** features mounted animal specimens from Africa and North America, as well as a rotating exhibit on local artifacts. A variety of programs entertain and educate the kids. ⊠ *260 W. Retta Esplanade,* ☎ *941/639–3777.* ⊠ *$1.* ☉ *Weekdays 10–5, Sat. 10–3.*

OFF THE BEATEN PATH

BABCOCK WILDERNESS ADVENTURES – To see what Florida looked like centuries ago, visit the 90,000-acre Babcock Crescent B Ranch, southeast of Punta Gorda and northeast of Fort Myers. During the 90-minute excursion you ride in a swamp buggy (converted school buses, mostly) through a variety of ecosystems, the most unusual and fascinating of which is the Telegraph Cypress Swamp. Along the way an informative and amusing guide describes the social and natural history of the area while everyone watches out for alligators, wild pigs, all sorts of birds, and other denizens of the wild. The tour also takes in the ranch's bison herd as well as some snakes and southern mountain lions in captivity. Photo ops abound, and reservations are essential. ⊠ *8000 Rte. 31,* ☎ *941/489–3911.* ⊠ *$17.95.* ☉ *Tours daily, with varying schedules, weather permitting.*

Dining and Lodging

$$ ✕ **Salty's Harborside.** Although seafood is the specialty, including some of the freshest mahimahi and grouper around, you'll also find grilled filet mignon, rosemary chicken, and various salads. The dining room looks out on the boats docked at Burnt Store Marina (☞ below) and Charlotte Harbor. ⊠ *Burnt Store Rd.,* ☎ *941/639–3650. AE, DC, MC, V.*

$$–$$$$ ⊡ **Burnt Store Marina Resort.** For boating, golfing, and getting away from it all, this sprawling resort and marina do the trick. Modern one- and two-bedroom apartments are situated along a relatively undeveloped stretch of vast Charlotte Harbor. All have kitchens, and some face the water. ⊠ *3150 Matecumbe Key Rd., 33955,* ☎ *941/575–4488 or 800/859–7529. 39 1-bedroom suites, 1 2-bedroom suite. Restaurant, bar, pool, 27 holes of golf, 6 tennis courts, boating. AE, DC, MC.*

Outdoor Activities and Sports

The **Texas Rangers** (⊠ Charlotte County Stadium, Rte. 776, Port Charlotte, ☎ 941/625–9500) play games during spring training.

CANOEING

With several Florida locations, **Canoe Outpost** (✉ 2816 N.W. Rte. 661, Arcadia, ☎ 941/494–1215) conducts all-day and overnight canoe trips, camping equipment included. The outfit has riverside picnic-camping areas just for their customers, some with great hiking trails. Up the Peace River, about 25 mi from Punta Gorda, **Canoe Safari** (✉ 3020 N.W. Rte. 661, Arcadia, ☎ 941/494–7865) runs half- and full-day trips plus overnights, including camping equipment.

FISHING

For half- and full-day deep-sea fishing trips, call **King Fisher Charter** (✉ Fishermen's Village, ☎ 941/639–0969).

GOLF

The **Burnt Store Marina Resort** (✉ 3150 Matecumbe Key Rd., ☎ 941/637–6633) features 27 holes of golf, and lessons are available. There are 18 holes to play at the **Deep Creek Golf Club** (✉ 1260 San Cristobal Ave., Port Charlotte, ☎ 941/625–6911).

TENNIS

Port Charlotte Tennis Club (✉ 22400 Gleneagles Terr., Port Charlotte, ☎ 941/625–7222) offers four lighted hard-surface courts.

THE BARRIER ISLANDS

Forming a backward *J*, dozens of islands curve toward Fort Myers and Cape Coral, separated from the mainland by Pine Island Sound. Though Sanibel and Captiva, the most visited spots, are reached by a causeway, you need a boat to reach many of the other islands. (If you cut through Pine Island Sound, you have a good chance of being escorted by bottle-nosed dolphins.) Many of the tiny and uninhabited islands are excellent spots for bird-watching and nature walks.

The tourist-pampering hotels on Sanibel and Captiva have a few counterparts in such neighboring islands as Cabbage Key and Pine Island, which have older properties and a sleepier atmosphere. When exploring the beaches, keep one eye on the sand; shelling is a major pursuit in these parts.

South of Pine Island Sound's barrier islands and 18 mi southwest of downtown Fort Myers is Estero Island, home of casual Fort Myers Beach. A causeway connects the southern tip of Estero Island to the northern end of Lover's Key.

Gasparilla Island (Boca Grande)

❹ *43 mi northwest of Fort Myers, 23 mi southwest of Punta Gorda.*

Before roads to southwest Florida were even talked about, wealthy northerners came by train to spend the winter at the **Gasparilla Inn**, built in 1912 in Boca Grande on Gasparilla Island. Although condominiums and modern sprawl creep up on the rest of Gasparilla, much of the town of Boca Grande looks as it has for a century or more. The mood is set by the old Florida homes, many made of wood, with wide, inviting verandas and wicker rocking chairs. The island's relaxed atmosphere is disrupted only in the spring, when tarpon fishermen descend with a vengeance on Boca Grande Pass, considered among the best tarpon-fishing spots in the world.

Cabbage Key

❺ *5 mi south of Boca Grande.*

You'll have to take a boat from Bokeelia, on Pine Island, to get to this island, which sits at Mile Marker 60 on the Intracoastal Waterway. Here, atop an ancient Calusa Indian shell mound, is the friendly, six-room **Cabbage Key Inn,** built by novelist and playwright Mary Roberts Rinehart in 1938. The inn also offers several guest cottages, a marina, and a dining room papered with thousands of dollar bills, signed and posted by patrons over the years.

Sanibel and Captiva Islands

23 mi southwest of downtown Fort Myers.

❻ Popular **Sanibel Island** and its quieter northern neighbor, Captiva, are reached via the Sanibel Causeway. There is a $3 round-trip bridge toll (collected on the way over), but avid shell collectors and nature enthusiasts will get their money's worth, for Sanibel's beaches are rated among the best shelling grounds in the world. For the choicest pickings, arrive as the tide is going out or just after a storm—you'll probably see plenty of other shell seekers with the telltale "Sanibel stoop."

❼ **Captiva Island** has more private development than Sanibel, and its resorts reflect this sense of seclusion. Resorts and restaurants are clustered at the northern end of Captiva and the southern end of Sanibel. In between are residential areas and a wildlife refuge.

At Sanibel's southern tip, **Old Lighthouse Beach** is especially good for shell collecting, attracting a mix of families, shellers, and singles. The adjacent, historic wooden **Sanibel Lighthouse,** a frequently photographed landmark, was built in 1884, when the entire island was a nature preserve. The lighthouse is not open to the public. Rest rooms are available. ⊠ *Periwinkle Way, Sanibel,* ☎ *no phone.* 🅿 *Parking 75¢ per hr.*

★ For a walk through history, stop by the charming **Sanibel Historical Village and Museum,** and follow a boardwalk as it winds through examples of the island's architectural past. Check out a post office built in 1927, a garage with a Model T Ford, the Old Bailey Store, and the 1913 Rutland House Museum, which contains historical documents, old photographs, and a Calusa Indian exhibit. ⊠ *950 Dunlop Rd., Sanibel,* ☎ *941/472–4648.* 🅿 *Donation welcome.* ☉ *Nov.–Aug., Wed.– Sat. 10–4.*

Gulfside City Park has a lesser-known and less populated beach, ideal for those who seek solitude and shells and who do not require facilities. ⊠ *Algiers La. off Casa Ybel Rd., Sanibel,* ☎ *no phone.* 🅿 *Parking 75¢ per hr.*

Tarpon Bay Road Beach is a quiet beach good for shelling. ⊠ *Tarpon Bay Rd. off Sanibel-Captiva Rd., Sanibel,* ☎ *no phone.* 🅿 *Parking 75¢ per hr.*

★ As though to one-up the nearby beaches, the **Bailey-Matthews Shell Museum** contains more than a million shells from around the world in colorful and lovingly created displays. The centerpiece, a 6-ft revolving globe, shows visitors where in the world the museum's shells are found. Novice collectors can identify their beach finds by comparing their own shells with the numerous local specimens displayed. ⊠ *3075 Sanibel-Captiva Rd., Sanibel,* ☎ *941/395–2233.* 🅿 *$5.* ☉ *Tues.–Sun. 10–4.*

Footpaths, winding canoe routes, and the 5-mi dirt Wildlife Drive meander through the beautiful **J. N. "Ding" Darling National Wildlife**

Refuge. Visitors can drive, walk, bicycle, canoe, kayak, or ride a specially designed open-air tram with a naturalist on board. With 6,000 acres, the area covers more than half of the island and is home to raccoons, otters, alligators, and numerous exotic birds, such as roseate spoonbills, egrets, ospreys, and herons. Walk among sea grape, wax and salt myrtles, red mangroves, sabal palms, and other flora native to Florida, or explore from the water (guided tours available), discovering the life that teems where the mangroves seem to wade just off the shore. An observation tower along the road is a prime bird-watching site, especially in the early morning and just before dusk. ⊠ *1 Wildlife Dr., Sanibel,* ☎ *941/472–1100.* ☞ *$5 per car, $1 for pedestrians/bicyclists alone or as a family, duck stamp $15 (covers all national wildlife refuges), tram $8.* ☉ *Visitor center mid-Nov.–mid-Apr., daily 9–5; mid-Apr.–mid-Nov., Mon.–Sat. 9–4; Wildlife Dr. Sat.–Thurs. sunrise–sunset.*

Bowman's Beach, on Sanibel's northwest end, is mainly a family beach. ⊠ *Bowman Beach Rd., Sanibel,* ☎ *no phone.* ☞ *Parking 75¢ per hr.*

Turner Beach, on the southern tip of Captiva, is a quiet beach. Parking is quite limited. ⊠ *Captiva Dr., Captiva,* ☎ *no phone.* ☞ *Parking 75¢ per hr.*

North Captiva Beach is, not surprisingly, on the north end of Captiva. The beach is peaceful, and there's limited space for parking. ⊠ *Captiva Dr., Captiva,* ☎ *no phone.* ☞ *Parking 75¢ per hr.*

Dining and Lodging

$$–$$$ ✕ **Bellini's.** Dine inside this charming house or outside under the canvas canopy on the breezy patio. People come to drink the famous frozen peach Bellini and eat from the definitely Italian menu. For starters try fresh mozzarella or fried calamari and then move on to chicken marsala, grilled veal chops, fettuccine carbonara, sausages with peppers over linguine, or grouper cooked with tomatoes, white wine, and garlic. There's a piano bar in the adjoining cocktail lounge. ⊠ *11521 Andy Rosse La., Captiva,* ☎ *941/472–6866. DC, MC, V. No lunch.*

$$–$$$ ✕ **Bubble Room.** It's hard to say which is more eclectic here, the atmosphere or the menu. Waiters and waitresses wearing scout uniforms race amid an array of colored Christmas lights, movie photos, electric trains, and memorabilia from the '30s and '40s. Get started stuffing yourself on the oddly juxtaposed salty, cheesy Bubble Bread and sweet sticky buns, followed by such items as the Eddie Fisherman (poached fresh grouper) or prime ribs Weissmuller (aged prime rib). Chances are you'll be too full for the enormous desserts—brought out by servers in a dizzying display—but they can be wrapped to go. The red velvet cake is an unforgettable meal in itself. ⊠ *15001 Captiva Dr., Captiva,* ☎ *941/472–5558. AE, DC, MC, V.*

$$–$$$ ✕ **Green Flash.** Good food, a casual atmosphere, and terrific views of quiet waters dotted with little green islands make this an incredibly popular stop. The restaurant is set right at the edge of Pine Island Sound on one of Captiva Island's narrowest sections. Seafood is the specialty, but there's a bit of everything on the menu, from shrimp in beer batter to pork tenderloin Wellington to grilled swordfish to pasta primavera. Kids like the children's menu, and everyone likes the key lime pie and the chocolate mousse, which comes with both ice cream *and* raspberry sauce! ⊠ *15183 Captiva Dr., Captiva,* ☎ *941/472–3337. AE, DC, MC, V.*

$$–$$$ ✕ **Jean-Paul's French Corner.** Food critics have been praising this long-time favorite ever since it first opened its doors way back in 1979. The food here is finely seasoned with everything but the highfalutin atti-

tude often dished up in French establishments. Excellent onion soup, salmon in a creamy dill sauce, veal medallions in a cream sauce with mushrooms, and roast duckling in fruit sauce are among the few but well-prepared choices on the menu. ⊠ *708 Tarpon Bay Rd., Sanibel,* ☎ *941/472–1493. MC, V. Closed Sun. No lunch.*

$$–$$$ ✕ **Thistle Lodge.** Many tables in this dimly lighted restaurant facing the gulf have great waterfront views. Fresh oysters, the house specialty appetizer, come with corn bread and andouille sausage, baked in a wine and herb sauce, baked in a seafood walnut stuffing, or baked with spinach, bacon, and Parmesan cheese. Gulf crab cakes may be the most popular entrée, but the grilled catch of the day, filet mignon, and seafood grill aren't far behind. ⊠ *2255 W. Gulf Dr., Sanibel,* ☎ *941/ 472–9200. AE, MC, V.*

$$ ✕ **McT's Shrimphouse and Tavern.** This lively and informal gathering spot features a host of fresh seafood specialties, including numerous oyster and mussel appetizers, shrimp prepared all kinds of ways, and all-you-can-eat shrimp and crab. Landlubbers will enjoy the black-bean soup, prime rib, and blackened chicken. There's always a dessert du jour, but most people end up choosing the Sanibel mud pie, a delicious concoction heavy on the Oreos. ⊠ *1523 Periwinkle Way, Sanibel,* ☎ *941/472–3161. AE, DC, MC, V.*

$–$$$ ✕ **Tarpon Bay Cafe.** The decor is predictably Eastern and spare in this excellent, authentic Japanese restaurant and sushi bar. Sashimi, sushi, *nigiri-zushi* (sushi-rice balls with a topping), *temaki-zushi* (sushi hand-rolled into a cone), and *makimono-zushi* (raw fish rolled in rice and wrapped in seaweed) are all available from the sushi bar, but the menu also includes seaweed salad, fried dumplings, seafood and vegetable tempura, and sukiyaki or salmon *nabe* (salmon and vegetables cooked in miso broth) prepared for two. Choose the green-tea ice cream or banana tempura for dessert. ⊠ *630 Tarpon Bay Rd., Sanibel,* ☎ *941/ 472–6300. AE, DC, MC, V. Closed Sun.*

$–$$ ✕ **Sanibel Brew Pub.** Hammerhead stout, palmetto honey ale, and pelican light are just some of the bubbly brews made at Sanibel's only brew pub. If you can't decide, order the "sampler"—6-ounce glasses of five craft-brewed beers—so everyone at your table can have a taste. Also good news is that there's fine chow here, too. The menu includes a corned beef or grouper Reuben, hamburger, grilled cheese sandwich, shrimp in tomato sauce over linguine, fried chicken baskets, stuffed shrimp, and grilled fresh catch of the day. ⊠ *1547 Periwinkle Way, Sanibel,* ☎ *941/395–2030. AE, MC, V.*

$–$$ ✕ **Sunshine Cafe.** Shorter on ambience than taste, this busy, efficient eatery turns out very good food and provides plenty of alternatives for lighter appetites. Sit out on the porch and start with grilled Portobello pita pizza with rosemary Gorgonzola sauce, artichokes, and chorizo sausage, followed by sesame seed–crusted tuna over greens tossed with wasabi and soy vinaigrette. For dessert indulge in the mixed berry cobbler with ice cream. ⊠ *Captiva Village Square, Captiva Dr., Captiva,* ☎ *941/472–6200. AE, MC, V.*

$ ✕ **Lighthouse Cafe.** Sanibel's oldest restaurant looks pretty much like a plain old coffee shop, but it consistently wins the local award for best breakfast on the island. Whole-wheat pancakes, fresh-baked muffins, frittatas, and bubbly mimosas bring people in the morning and beyond, since breakfast is served until closing. Hamburgers, grilled cheese sandwiches, and fresh salads are popular luncheon and dinner items. People also stop by just for a slice of the superb cheesecake. ⊠ *362 Periwinkle Way, Sanibel,* ☎ *941/472–0303. MC, V. No dinner off-season.*

$$$$ ⚐ **Casa Ybel Resort.** This time-share property faces the gulf on 23 acres of tropical grounds, complete with palms, ponds, a footbridge, and gazebos dotting the lawns. Early in this century this was the site of a lodge, and buildings are in a Victorian style meant to replicate the originals. Contemporary one- and two-bedroom apartments with full kitchens are brightly furnished in tropical prints, and big screened-in porches look out to the beach. There is a well-respected restaurant on site. ⊠ *2255 W. Gulf Dr., Sanibel 33957,* ☎ *941/472–3145 or 800/276–4753,* FAX *941/472–2109. 40 1-bedroom units, 74 2-bedroom units. Restaurant, bar, pool, 6 tennis courts, shuffleboard, beach, windsurfing, boating, bicycles, video games, baby-sitting, playground. AE, DC, MC, V.*

$$$$ ⚐ **Sanibel Harbour Resort & Spa.** People come to this high-rise resort
★ at the last mainland exit before the causeway for its spa and racquet club, but one look at the sweeping views of island-studded San Carlos Bay and you'll be tempted just to sit on your porch and daydream. Resist the temptation and substitute another. Wander through the woods and across a pond to the exceptional spa, where you can choose from more than 60 treatments for relaxation and reenergizing. Rent a kayak for a peaceful paddle or take a wildlife-viewing, fishing, shelling, or sunset cruise. Alas, the beach is on the Inland Waterway, not the gulf, but there is a large free-form pool and free transportation to Sanibel Island. The Kids Klub keeps children busy, and the staff is exceptionally helpful. ⊠ *17260 Harbour Pointe Dr., Fort Myers 33908,* ☎ *941/466–4000 or 800/767–7777,* FAX *941/466–2150. 240 rooms, 80 2-bedroom condominiums. 3 restaurants, 3 bars, lobby lounge, snack bar, 1 indoor and 3 outdoor pools, beauty salon, 11 hot tubs, massage, saunas, spa, steam rooms, 13 tennis courts, basketball, health club, racquetball, beach, docks, boating, jet skiing, fishing, baby-sitting. AE, DC, MC, V.*

$$$$ ⚐ **Sanibel's Seaside Inn.** A pleasant alternative to large full-service resorts is this quiet inn right on the beach. Choose from studios, one- to three-bedroom units, and individual cottages. All are decorated in bright tropical prints and have rattan furniture. Some units have much better views than others so be sure to ask. Outdoor grills are available. Since the Seaside Inn is a South Seas Resort, guests have access to the facilities at other properties in the group. ⊠ *541 E. Gulf Dr., Sanibel 33957,* ☎ *941/472–1400 or 800/831–7384,* FAX *941/481–4947. 12 rooms, 20 suites. Picnic area, pool, shuffleboard, beach, bicycles, coin laundry. DC, MC, V.*

$$$$ ⚐ **South Seas Plantation Resort and Yacht Harbour.** This 330-acre prop-
★ erty at Captiva's far end is both busy and peaceful. In keeping with the spirit of the island, low-rise accommodations—from hotel rooms to villas to cottages and private homes—are tucked around the property. Tracts of grassy dune and mangrove forest, sea turtle patrols, posted manatee signs, and a nature center show that the natural world is respected here. So is recreation. Choose from activities on land (such as golf and tennis), sea (sailing lessons to island cruises), and air (even parasailing). Go shelling at dawn or strolling at sunset along 2½ mi of beach. From the posh restaurant's servers to the kids' program's counselors, the staff is generally five star. Rates can drop as much as 40% off-season. ⊠ *5400 Plantation Rd., Box 194, Captiva 33924,* ☎ *941/472–5111 or 800/227–8482,* FAX *941/472–7541. 138 units, 482 suites. 4 restaurants, 3 bars, deli, ice cream parlor, snack bar, 18 pools, beauty salon, hot tub, massage, 9-hole golf course, putting green, 21 tennis courts, exercise room, shuffleboard, beach, docks, windsurfing, boating, jet skiing, parasailing, waterskiing. AE, DC, MC, V.*

$$$ 🏨 **Shalimar Motel.** Well-maintained grounds and an inviting beach make this small property appealing. Units (all with full kitchen) are in small two-story cottages set back from the beach amid tropical greenery. There are barbecue facilities and a courtyard pool. ✉ *2823 W. Gulf Dr., Sanibel 33957,* ☎ *941/472–1353 or 800/645–4092,* FAX *941/472–6430. 21 efficiencies, 10 1-bedroom units, 2 2-bedroom units. Pool, shuffleboard, beach. DC, MC, V.*

$$–$$$ 🏨 **Waterside Inn.** Palm trees and white sand set the scene at this quiet vacation spot comprising bright white one- and two-story buildings just at the edge of the beach. Modestly furnished rooms and efficiencies have balconies or patios and at least a partial view of the gulf. There is an additional charge for maid service, and several housekeeping cottages are available. ✉ *3033 W. Gulf Dr., Sanibel 33957,* ☎ *941/472–1345,* FAX *941/472–2148. 4 rooms, 10 efficiencies, 8 cottages. Pool, shuffleboard, beach. AE, MC, V.*

Outdoor Activities and Sports

BIKING

On Sanibel, rent bicycles by the hour at **Bike Route** (✉ 2330 Palm Ridge Rd., ☎ 941/472–1955). On Captiva, rent bikes by the hour or day from **Jim's Bike & Scooter Rental** (✉ 11534 Andy Rosse La., ☎ 941/472–1296).

BOATING

Boat House of Sanibel (✉ Sanibel Marina, 634 N. Yachtman Dr., Sanibel, ☎ 941/472–2531) has powerboats for rent. **Jensen's Marina** (✉ Captiva, ☎ 941/472–5800) rents little powerboats perfect for fishing and shelling.

CANOEING AND KAYAKING

Tarpon Bay Recreation (✉ 900 Tarpon Bay Rd., Sanibel, ☎ 941/472–8900) offers canoes, kayaks, and equipment for exploring the wildlife refuge.

FISHING

Fishing is popular in this part of the world, and anglers head out to catch mackerel, pompano, grouper, reds, snook, bluefish, and shark. Call **Captain Pat Lovetro** (✉ Sanibel Marina, 634 N. Yachtman Dr., Sanibel, ☎ 941/472–2723) for half-day, six-hour, and full-day trips.

GOLF

You can rent golf clubs and take lessons as well as play at the **Dunes** (✉ 949 Sandcastle Rd., Sanibel, ☎ 941/472–2535), which has 18 holes.

TENNIS

The **City Recreation Complex** (✉ 3840 Sanibel-Captiva Rd., Sanibel, ☎ 941/472–0345) has five lighted tennis courts. At the **Dunes** (✉ 949 Sandcastle Rd., Sanibel, ☎ 941/472–3522), there are seven clay courts and two tennis professionals ready to give lessons.

Shopping

The largest cluster of shops on Sanibel, **Periwinkle Place** (✉ 2075 Periwinkle Way) has 55 shops and several restaurants. **Aboriginals** (✉ 2340 Periwinkle Way, ☎ 941/395–2200) sells textiles, baskets, pottery, and jewelry from Native Americans, Australians, and Africans. At **She Sells Sea Shells** (✉ 1157 Periwinkle Way, ☎ 941/472–6991), everything imaginable is made from shells, from decorative mirrors and lamps to Christmas ornaments.

Estero Island (Fort Myers Beach)

❽ *18 mi southwest of Fort Myers.*

This laid-back island lined with motels, hotels, and restaurants serves as one of Fort Myers's more frenetic ocean playgrounds. The marina at the north end of the island is the starting point for much boating, including sunset cruises, sightseeing cruises, and deep-sea fishing. At the southern tip a causeway leads to the entrance of Lover's Key State Park.

Lynn Hall Memorial Park is in the more commercial northern part of Estero Island. The shore slopes gradually into the usually tranquil and warm gulf waters, providing safe swimming for children. Since the beach is for the most part lined with houses, condominiums, and hotels, you're never far from civilization. A number of nightspots and restaurants are also close. There are picnic tables, barbecue grills, playground equipment, a free fishing pier, and a bathhouse with rest rooms. ⊠ *Estero Blvd.,* ☎ *no phone.* ⊠ *Parking 75¢ per hour.* ☉ *Daily 7 AM–10 PM.*

<table>
<tr><td>OFF THE
BEATEN PATH</td><td>

LOVER'S KEY STATE PARK – Florida's newest state park is a combination of the former Lover's Key State Recreation Area and the Carl E. Johnson Park and now encompasses two islands and several uninhabited islets. Nearly $5 million has been spent on renovations, improvements, and environmental protection. Bike, hike, or walk on trails that wind through the park's 700 acres, go shelling on 2½ mi of beaches, or rent a canoe or kayak. Watch for osprey, bald eagles, herons, ibis, pelicans, and roseate spoonbills. Sign up for one of the special excursions to observe manatees, dolphins, or loggerhead turtles. A romantic gazebo on the beach holds 100 people and can be rented for weddings. There are also rest rooms, picnic tables, a snack bar, and showers. ⊠ *8700 Estero Blvd.,* ☎ *941/463–4588.* ⊠ *$5.* ☉ *Daily 8–sunset.*

</td></tr>
</table>

Dining and Lodging

$$ ✕ **Mucky Duck.** Yes, there are two restaurants by this name—one on the Captiva waterfront, the other a slightly more formal restaurant in Fort Myers Beach. Both concentrate on fresh, well-prepared seafood. The bacon-wrapped barbecued shrimp is popular, and local grouper prepared any number of ways is the house specialty. ⊠ *2500 Estero Blvd.,* ☎ *941/463–5519;* ⊠ *Andy Rosse La., Captiva,* ☎ *941/472–3434. MC, V.*

$$ ✕ **Snug Harbor.** You can watch boats coming and going whether you sit inside or out at this dockside restaurant on stilts. The secret of its success is absolutely fresh seafood, courtesy of the restaurant's private fishing fleet. This place is a favorite of year-round residents and seasonal visitors alike. ⊠ *645 San Carlos Blvd.,* ☎ *941/463–4343. AE, MC, V.*

$$$–$$$$ 🛏 **Best Western Pink Shell Beach Resort.** Set on 12 acres, this beachfront and family-focused resort's accommodations range from cottages on stilts to rooms and apartments in a five-story building. There are children's, social, and recreation programs. ⊠ *275 Estero Blvd., 33931,* ☎ *941/463–6181,* FAX *941/463–1229. 146 rooms, 62 suites. 3 pools, 2 tennis courts, shuffleboard, volleyball, beach, windsurfing, jet skiing, parasailing, fishing, children's programs. AE, MC, V.*

$$–$$$$ 🛏 **Grand View.** Views from the upper floors of this 15-story beachfront high-rise can be stupendous. The gulf seems to stretch forever, and sunsets are quite a show. Other units look out on Estero Bay or, from some lower-floor units, gardens. All units have a separate bedroom and living room, a fully equipped kitchen, a sofa sleeper in the living room, and a balcony, making this a good place for families. The

resort is just north of Lover's Key State Park. ✉ *8701 Estero Blvd.,*
33931, ☎ *941/765–4422 or 800/723–4944. 78 1-bedroom suites.*
Pool, beach, boating, bicycles. MC, V.

$$–$$$ 🏨 **Outrigger Beach Resort.** This informal, family-oriented resort is set
on a wide beach overlooking the gulf. Rooms and efficiencies are decorated in bright prints. Views vary, so ask when making reservations.
The resort also has a broad sundeck, tiki huts to sit under to escape
the heat, sailboats, and a beachfront pool. ✉ *6200 Estero Blvd.,*
33931, ☎ *941/463–3131 or 800/749–3131. 112 rooms, 32 suites. Pool,*
shuffleboard, volleyball, beach, jet skiing, bicycles. MC, V.

Outdoor Activities and Sports

BIKING

Fun Rentals (✉ 1901 Estero Blvd., ☎ 941/463–8844) rents bicycles
by the day and the week.

FISHING

Getaway Bait (✉ 1091 San Carlos Blvd., ☎ 941/466–3200) rents fishing equipment, sells bait, and can arrange half- and full-day charters.

GOLF

The **Bay Beach Golf Club** (✉ 7401 Estero Blvd., ☎ 941/463–2064) offers 18 holes, a practice range, and lessons.

TENNIS

You'll find six Har-Tru clay courts plus private and group lessons at
the **Bay Beach Racquet Club** (✉ 120 Lenell St., ☎ 941/463–4473).

NAPLES AREA

Driving U.S. 41 south from Fort Myers, you'll pass through Bonita
Springs on your way to the Naples and Marco Island area, sandwiched
between the Big Cypress Swamp and the Gulf of Mexico.

The land east of Naples is undeveloped all the way to Fort Lauderdale.
Most of it is swampland and forms the northern border of the Florida
Everglades—making it excellent territory for visiting nature preserves
and parks. It's worth the 90-minute drive to see the Ah-Tha-Thi-Ki Museum and the rest of the Big Cypress Seminole Reservation (☞ Chapter 3), not only for the interesting museum and Indian village but also
for the scenery along the way—acres of breeze-swept swamp grass
stretching off to the horizon.

Naples itself is a major vacation spot, having sprouted a bevy of high-
end restaurants and shops. A similar but not as thorough change has
occurred on Marco Island, once a quiet fishing community.

Bonita Springs

🟢 *24 mi south of Fort Myers.*

Though the town is not on the gulf, there are several sizable, popular
beaches to its west and south. **Bonita Beach** is the southern gateway
to Lover's Key State Park (☞ Estero Island, *above*).

The **Everglades Wonder Gardens,** one of the first attractions of its kind
in the state, captures the feral beauty of untamed Florida. Zoological
gardens contain Florida panthers, black bear, crocodiles and alligators,
tame Florida deer, flamingos, and trained otters and birds. There's also
an eclectic natural history museum on site. ✉ *Old U.S. 41,* ☎ *941/*
992–2591. 💵 *$9.* ⏰ *Daily 9–5.*

Bonita Springs Public Beach, at the south end of Bonita Beach, has picnic tables and nearby refreshment stands and shopping. ⊠ *Bonita Beach Rd.,* ☎ *no phone.* ☛ *Parking 75¢ per hour.*

Popular **Barefoot Beach Preserve,** between Naples and Bonita, has picnic tables, a nature trail, refreshment stands, and other comforts. ⊠ *Lely Beach Rd.,* ☎ *no phone.* ☛ *Parking 75¢ per hr.*

OFF THE
BEATEN PATH

CORKSCREW SWAMP SANCTUARY – To get a feel for what this part of Florida was like before civil engineers began draining the swamps, drive 13 mi east of Bonita Springs (30 mi northeast of Naples) to this 11,000-acre sanctuary. Managed by the National Audubon Society, it protects 500-year-old trees and endangered birds, such as wood storks, which often nest high in the bald cypress. Visitors taking the 1¾-mi self-guided tour along the boardwalk, which takes about two hours, may glimpse alligators, graceful wading birds, and air plants that cling to the sides of trees. ⊠ *16 mi east of I–75 on Rte. 846,* ☎ *941/348–9151.* ☛ *$6.50.* ☉ *Dec.–Apr., daily 7–5; May–Nov., daily 8–5.*

Outdoor Activities and Sports

BIKING

You can rent bicycles at **Bonita Beach Bike** (⊠ 4892 Bonita Beach Rd., ☎ 941/947–6377).

BOATING

Bonita Beach Resort Motel (⊠ 26395 Hickory Blvd., ☎ 941/992–2137) rents motorboats by the hour or day.

CANOEING

Estero River Tackle and Canoe Outfitters (⊠ 20991 Tamiami Trail S, Estero, ☎ 941/992–4050) provides rental canoes and equipment for use on the meandering Estero River.

DOG RACING

There is dog racing year-round at the **Naples/Fort Myers Greyhound Track** (⊠ 10601 Bonita Beach Rd., ☎ 941/992–2411).

GOLF

Pelican's Nest Golf Course (⊠ 4450 Pelican's Nest Dr. SW, ☎ 941/947–4600) features 27 holes bordered by swamp and thick vegetation.

Naples

🔟 *21 mi south of Bonita Springs.*

Naples is fast becoming Florida's west-coast version of Palm Beach. Twenty-story condominiums now line much of the north shore, and many sophisticated (and pricey) restaurants have opened, as have a number of upscale shopping areas, including tree-lined 3rd Street South. Though golf, tennis, and miles of beach draw visitors to this area year-round, the winter months are by far the most crowded, and it can be difficult to find a room or get a reservation at the popular restaurants.

In the 1800s, houses in South Florida were often built of tabby, a cement-type material created from sand and seashells. For a fine example of this construction, stop by the **Palm Cottage,** built in 1895 and one of the last remaining tabby homes in southwest Florida. The interior, now housing a little museum, is decorated in a historically accurate style and contains the simple furnishings found in very rural southwest Florida in the 19th century. ⊠ *137 12th Ave. S,* ☎ *941/261–8164.* ☛ *Free.* ☉ *Tues.–Fri. 10–4, Sun. 2–4.*

Teddy bear lovers of all ages delight in the more than 3,000 teddy bears on display at the **Teddy Bear Museum of Naples.** Built by oil heiress and area resident Frances Pew Hayes, the $2 million museum also has a reading library—stocked with books just about bears—and a life-size Three Bears House. ⊠ *2511 Pine Ridge Rd.,* ☎ *941/598–2711.* ◰ *$6.* ☉ *Mon. and Wed.–Sat. 10–5, Sun. 1–5.*

Originally a botanical garden planted in the early 1900s, **Caribbean Gardens & Zoological Park,** a 52-acre junglelike educational park, now houses exotic wildlife, including African lions, mandrills, Bengal tigers, lemurs, antelope, and monkeys. The Primate Expedition Cruise takes you through islands of monkeys and apes living in their natural habitat. There are elephant demonstrations and alligator feedings, and kids particularly enjoy the petting zoo. ⊠ *1590 Goodlette Rd.,* ☎ *941/ 262–5409.* ◰ *$13.95.* ☉ *Daily 9:30–5:30.*

On 13 acres bordering a tidal lagoon teeming with wildlife, the **Naples Nature Center** includes an aviary, a wildlife rehabilitation clinic, a natural science museum with a serpentarium, and a 3,000-gallon marine aquarium. Free guided walks and miniboat tours are scheduled several times daily, and there are canoes and kayaks for rent. ⊠ *1450 Merrihue Dr.,* ☎ *941/262–0304.* ◰ *$6.* ☉ *Daily 9–4:30.*

To get a feel for the history of the area, stop by the **Collier County Museum,** where exhibits capture important developments since the Calusa Indians lived here. ⊠ *Airport Rd. at U.S. 41,* ☎ *941/774–8476.* ◰ *Free.* ☉ *Weekdays 9–5.*

Stretching along Gulf Shore Boulevard, **Lowdermilk Park** has more than 1,000 ft of beach, volleyball courts, a playground, rest rooms, showers, a pavilion, vending machines, and picnic tables. No alcoholic beverages or fires are permitted. ⊠ *Gulf Shore Blvd. at Banyan Blvd.,* ☎ *no phone.* ◰ *Parking 75¢ per hr.* ☉ *Daily 7–sunset.*

Clam Pass Park is a glistening stretch of particularly pristine white sand. A 3,000-ft boardwalk winds through tropical mangroves to the beach. ⊠ *Seagate Dr.,* ☎ *941/353–0404.* ◰ *Free.* ☉ *Daily 8–sunset.*

Delnor-Wiggins Pass State Recreation Area is a well-maintained park comprising 100 acres, with sandy beaches, lifeguards, barbecue grills, picnic tables, boat ramp, observation tower, rest rooms with wheelchair access, lots of parking, bathhouses, and showers. Fishing is best in Wiggins Pass, at the north end of the park. Alcohol is prohibited. ⊠ *West end of 111th Ave. N,* ☎ *no phone.* ◰ *$3.25 per vehicle with up to 8 people, boat launching $1.* ☉ *Daily 7–sunset.*

Dining and Lodging

$$–$$$ ✕ **Bistro 821.** The decor of this popular restaurant is spare but sophisticated. Fairly bright, the long, narrow room is mostly white and black. Entrées range from marinated leg of lamb with basil mashed potatoes to snapper baked in parchment, wild-mushroom pasta, vodka penne, risotto, and a seasonal vegetable plate. The menu accommodates appetites of all sizes, with little plates, big plates, and half portions. ⊠ *821 5th Ave. S,* ☎ *941/261–5821. Reservations essential on weekends. AE, DC, MC, V. No lunch.*

$$–$$$
★ ✕ **Cloyde's Steak & Lobster House.** As the name says, steak and seafood are the highlights here, as are great service and a glittering waterfront view. This choice restaurant is in the upscale Village on Venetian Bay, a collection of expensive shops and sophisticated restaurants. Dine on fresh Maine lobster, blackened New York strip, Florida grouper, grilled gulf shrimp, or one of the nightly specials, and spend some time re-

viewing the impressive wine list. ⊠ *4050 Gulf Shore Blvd.,* ☎ *941/ 261–0622. Reservations essential in season. AE, MC, V. No lunch.*

$$–$$$ ✕ **Ristorante Ciao.** One block north of 5th Avenue's "Restaurant
★ Row," this elegant, award-winning northern Italian restaurant is packed all winter long. Veal is excellent: Try the veal piccata, veal marsala, or whatever the nightly special is. A hearty minestrone or the garlicky Caesar salad is a good bet for a first course, and the extensive wine list includes some fine Italian selections. ⊠ *835 4th Ave. S,* ☎ *941/263–3889. AE, D, DC, MC, V. No lunch.*

$$–$$$ ✕ **Terra.** This is one of the most popular restaurants in Old Naples.
★ There's a long bar on one side of the room and tables on the other, some lining a bank of sliding-glass doors, making it feel like a sunroom. Additional tables on an outdoor terrace overlook 3rd Avenue. The Mediterranean-inspired menu features such starters as seafood risotto cakes, sea scallops and prosciutto on grilled Tuscan bread, and a hearty bean soup. Grilled pork sausage, wild-mushroom lasagna, Mediterranean seafood stew, and herb-encrusted tuna are some of the excellent entrées, while tasty side dishes include tomato-basil polenta, roasted elephant garlic, and ratatouille. ⊠ *1300 3rd St. S,* ☎ *941/262–5500. AE, MC, V.*

$$ ✕ **Tommy Bahama's Tropical Cafe.** When you're in the mood for ultracasual, this is the place to be. The Caribbean decor and laid-back island atmosphere make it quite a switch from the typically trendy Naples restaurant. Day and night, crowds fill up the outside deck and the inside dining room and bar to dine on sandwiches, hamburgers, conch fritters, and grilled fish, and to partake of Tommy's famous Bungalow Brew. ⊠ *1220 3rd St. S,* ☎ *941/643–6889. AE, MC, V.*

$$ ✕ **Truffles.** This longtime favorite closed its doors several years ago after
★ 20 years in business, but there was so much complaining that the owners brought it back in a different location. Thankfully the menu is just what everyone remembers: tuna Caesar, linguine with peas and prosciutto, crispy fish, and Reuben sandwiches. Southern-fried chicken is the special on Sunday, and Truffles' original meat loaf is the Tuesday highlight. The much-loved desserts are back, too. Try the poppyseed cake, raspberry Grand Marnier cake, or the unbeatable chocolate mousse cake. ⊠ *8920 Tamiami Trail N,* ☎ *941/597–8119. AE, MC, V.*

$ ✕ **California Pizza Kitchen.** Everything sparkles in this restaurant with
★ a black-and-white tile floor and mirrored wall. Settle into a big booth, sit at a table, or grab a seat at the counter and dine on delightful, very affordable Italian cuisine. The menu boasts close to 30 pizzas (roasted garlic chicken, mixed-grill vegetarian, and the BLT are good choices), but there are also salads big enough for a meal, two terrific soups (potato leek and white-corn tortilla) that come in the same bowl (they sit side by side), and a full page of pasta dishes. It's tough, but try to save room for dessert. Hot apple crisp à la mode is a winner. ⊠ *5555 Tamiami Trail N,* ☎ *941/566–1900. AE, MC, V.*

$ ✕ **Old Naples Pub.** From Robinson Court walk up a few stairs to this comfortable pub, open 11 until late at night. Sample from 20 kinds of beer and the not-so-traditional pub menu, with fish-and-chips, burgers, bratwurst, pizza, and chicken Caesar salad as well as a selection of snacks: nachos, fries smothered in chili, and cheese-stuffed, deep-fried jalapeños. There's piano entertainment Monday–Saturday. ⊠ *255 13th Ave. S,* ☎ *941/649–8200. AE, MC, V.*

$$$$ ☷ **Edgewater Beach Hotel.** At the north end of fashionable Gulf Shore Boulevard stands this compact, high-rise waterfront resort. The brightly decorated units are either one- or two-bedroom suites and have full kitchens and either patios or balconies. Many have exquisite views of the gulf. Dine by the pool or in the elegant restaurant, or enjoy piano music in the lounge during happy hour. Shopping, golf, and tennis are close by. Some units are being converted to time-shares. ⊠ *1901 Gulf Shore Blvd. N, 33940,* ☎ *941/403–2000; 800/821–0196; 800/282–3766 in FL;* ℻ *941/262–1243. 124 suites. Restaurant, bar, pool, exercise room, beach, bicycles. AE, DC, MC, V.*

$$$$ ⊞ **La Playa Beach & Racquet Inn.** Nestled between a bay and the gulf, this large hotel stretches along the beach. Rooms and efficiencies are in a three-story low-rise. Additional rooms, some with limited kitchen facilities, and some suites are in a much newer 14-story high-rise. All have patios or balconies with excellent gulf views. Kayaks are available. ⊠ *9891 Gulf Shore Blvd., 33963,* ☎ *941/597–3123,* ℻ *941/597–6278. 187 rooms, 4 suites. 2 restaurants, bar, 2 pools, shuffleboard, volleyball, beach, boating. AE, MC, V.*

$$$$ ⊞ **Registry Resort.** Inside this high-rise hotel are an elegant marble-and-oak lobby and deep-colored guest rooms that feel more like someone's house than a hotel. Outside are unique, free-form swimming pools with waterfalls. Walk through a mangrove forest to 3 mi of glistening white beach, or take an open-air tram. Try canoeing around a lagoon. The Caddymaster service arranges tee times at the area's finest golf clubs months in advance, and the tennis program is especially strong. The outstanding Sunday brunch has table after table of exquisitely prepared selections. Most guests dress up for it. ⊠ *475 Seagate Dr., 33940,* ☎ *941/597–3232,* ℻ *941/566–7919. 395 rooms, 29 suites, 50 villas. 4 restaurants, 2 bars, 3 pools, golf privileges, 10 tennis courts, health club, bicycles, shops, children's programs. AE, DC, MC, V.*

$$$$ ⊞ **Ritz-Carlton.** Equally fabulous hotel rooms can be had elsewhere, but the extensive network of lavishly appointed public rooms is astounding, with a dozen meeting rooms of varying shapes and sizes and an estimable collection of 19th-century European oils. Though you might feel a little uncomfortable traipsing through the lobby in tennis shoes, you will be graciously welcomed. Guests have access to a nearby 27-hole golf course. ⊠ *280 Vanderbilt Beach Rd., 33941,* ☎ *941/598–3300,* ℻ *941/598–6690. 435 rooms, 28 suites. 4 restaurants, 2 bars, pool, saunas, golf privileges, 6 tennis courts, health club, beach, windsurfing, boating, children's programs. AE, D, DC, MC, V.*

$$$–$$$$ ⊞ **Trianon Old Naples.** Stay right in the heart of Old Naples at this small luxury inn. In a residential section of town but within walking distance of many shops and restaurants, the three-story pink stucco building with wrought-iron balconies is surrounded by manicured lawns. Inside, the elegant lobby has high ceilings and a working fireplace and is decorated with antique furniture and glittery chandeliers. Rooms are large, with green-and-pink bedspreads, heavy draperies, and pale cream walls. All have seating areas as well as spacious contemporary bathrooms. A Continental breakfast is included in the rate. ⊠ *955 7th Ave. S, 34102,* ☎ *941/453–9600,* ℻ *941/261–0025. 55 rooms, 3 suites. Pool. AE, D, DC, MC, V.*

$$–$$$ ⊞ **Best Western Naples Inn & Suites.** You'd never know you were anywhere near busy U.S. 41 at this two-story spot, which is set back in lush tropical gardens with waterfalls. It is a ½-mi walk to gulf beaches and an easy walk to shops and restaurants. ⊠ *2329 9th St. N, 33940,* ☎ *941/261–1148 or 800/528–1234,* ℻ *941/262–4684. 50 rooms, 30 suites. Restaurant, bar, 2 pools, shuffleboard. AE, D, DC, MC, V.*

$$ ⊞ **Holiday Inn.** Although this two-story motel is on a major highway, it's set back from the road, and rooms are behind the restaurant, bar, and pool, making them very quiet. Landscaping is well maintained, the location is convenient if you plan to sightsee, and rooms are clean and comfortable. The bar is popular at happy hour. ⊠ *1100 9th St. N, 34102,* ☎ *941/262–7146,* ℻ *941/261–3809. 137 rooms. Restaurant, bar, pool. AE, D, DC, MC, V.*

Nightlife and the Arts

THE ARTS

Naples is the cultural capital of this stretch of coast. The **Naples Philharmonic Center for the Arts** (⌧ 5833 Pelican Bay Blvd., ☎ 941/597–1111) has two theaters and two art galleries offering a variety of plays, concerts, and exhibits year-round. It's home to the 80-piece Naples Philharmonic, which presents both classical and pop concerts; the Miami Ballet Company also performs during its winter season. Though the **Naples Players** (⌧ 701 5th Ave. S, ☎ 941/263–7990) have moved to a more central location right on 5th Avenue, they still offer winter and summer seasons—winter shows often sell out well in advance.

NIGHTLIFE

The casual **Backstage Tap & Grill** (⌧ 5535 U.S. 41N, ☎ 941/598–1300) has great guitar and flute combos Thursday, Friday, and Saturday. **Club Zanzibar** (⌧ 475 Seagate Dr., ☎ 941/597–3232), at the Registry Resort, is a light and airy multilevel nightclub where DJs pump out Top 40 hits from 9 PM until 2 AM. It's packed on weekends. Live jazz can be found weekends at **Meson Olé** (⌧ 2016 Tamiami Trail N, ☎ 941/649–6616). The upstairs lounge at **Seawitch** (⌧ 179 Commerce St., Vanderbilt Beach, ☎ 941/566–1514) overlooks Vanderbilt Bay and is a relaxing spot for casual dining. Bands play Top 40 music Tuesday–Sunday. Seawitch's sister restaurant, **Witch's Brew** (⌧ 4836 Tamiami Trail N, ☎ 941/261–4261), is a lively location for nightly entertainment. There is a happy hour weekdays 4–6 and excellent Continental cuisine.

Outdoor Activities and Sports

BIKING

Try the **Bicycle Shoppe of Naples** (⌧ 8789 Tamiami Trail N, ☎ 941/566–3646) for rentals by the hour, day, or week.

BOATING

Port-O-Call (⌧ 550 Port-O-Call Way, ☎ 941/774–0479) rents 16- to 25-ft powerboats.

FISHING

If you want to attempt to catch some fish, ask for Captain Tom at **Deep Sea Charter Fishing** (⌧ Boat Haven, ☎ 941/263–8171). The **Lady Brett** (⌧ Tin City, ☎ 941/263–4949) makes fishing and sightseeing trips twice daily.

GOLF

The **Ironwood Golf Club** (⌧ 205 Charity Ct., ☎ 941/775–2584) has an 18-hole course, a practice range, lessons, and rentals. At the relatively young **Lely Flamingo Island Club** (⌧ 8004 Lely Resort Blvd., ☎ 941/793–2223 or 800/388–4653), 54 holes of golf are accompanied by a driving range. **Naples Beach Hotel & Golf Club** (⌧ 851 Gulf Shore Blvd. N, ☎ 941/261–2222) features 18 holes, a golf pro, and a putting green. **Naples Golf Center** (⌧ 7700 E. Davis Blvd., ☎ 941/775–3337) has a 300-yard driving range and offers private and group lessons by a PGA teaching staff; it even has computerized swing analysis. At **Riviera Golf Club** (⌧ 48 Marseille Dr., ☎ 941/774–1081), you'll find 54 holes and a driving range.

TENNIS

Cambier Park Tennis Courts (⌧ 775 8th Ave. S, ☎ 941/434–4694) offers clinics and play on nine hard-surface and five Har-Tru courts; 11 are lighted. **Naples Racquet Club** (⌧ 100 Forest Hills Blvd., ☎ 941/774–2442) has seven Har-Tru clay courts.

Shopping

The largest shopping area is **Old Naples,** with more than 100 shops and restaurants. Shoppers stroll along broad, tree-lined walkways in an eight-block area bordered by Broad Avenue on the north and 4th Street South on the east. **Old Marine Market Place at Tin City** (✉ 1200 5th Ave. S), in a collection of former fishing shacks along Naples Bay, has more than 40 boutiques, artisans' studios, and souvenir shops with everything from scrimshaw to Haitian art. The classy **Village on Venetian Bay** (✉ 4200 Gulf Shore Blvd.) has more than 60 shops and restaurants built over the bay. **Waterside Shops** (✉ Seagate Dr. and U.S. 41) is built around a courtyard with a series of waterways. Anchored by a Saks Fifth Avenue boutique and Jacobson's department store, Waterside houses more than 50 shops and several eating places.

Gattle's (✉ 1250 3rd St. S, ☎ 941/262–4791) is the place for beautifully made (and pricey) linens. **Marissa Collections** (✉ 1167 3rd St. S, ☎ 941/263–4333) showcases designer women's wear, including Louis Féraud, Donna Karan, and Calvin Klein. Stop at **Mettlers** (✉ 1258 3rd St. S, ☎ 941/434–2700) for high-fashion men's and women's sportswear, including full lines of clothing by Giorgio Armani and Polo. At the **Mole Hole** (✉ 1201 3rd St. S, ☎ 941/262–5115), every surface is covered with gift items large and small, from glassware to paperweights to knick-knacks.

Marco Island

⑪ *20 mi south of Naples.*

Another island connected to the mainland by causeways, this one stubbornly retains its isolated feeling despite the high-rises that line parts of its shore. Many natural areas have been preserved, and the fishing village of **Goodland** resists tourism-induced change. Surfing, sunning, swimming, golf, and tennis are the primary activities.

Tigertail Beach is on the southwest side of the island. Facilities include parking, a concession stand, a picnic area, sailboat rentals, volleyball, rest rooms, and showers. ✉ *480 Hernando Ct.,* ☎ *941/642–0818.* 🚗 *Parking 75¢ per hr.* ☉ *Daily sunrise–sunset.*

Resident's Beach is right in the middle of the south side of the island. Facilities include parking, a concession stand, picnic areas, rest rooms, and showers. ✉ *618 Collier Blvd.,* ☎ *no phone.* 🚗 *Parking 75¢ per hr.* ☉ *Daily sunrise–sunset.*

Dining and Lodging

$$–$$$ ✗ **Bistro Cucina.** The most sophisticated restaurant in Marco, this
★ bistro has been busy since the day it opened. Prints and plants here and there add warmth to the somewhat spare decor, but the stars here are the mostly Italian cuisine and the friendly but professional service. Plain white plates provide the perfect background for the creative presentation of your order. Colorful sauces, perfectly sliced vegetables and fruits, and sprigs of herbs are turned into edible works of art. Start with the mixed green salad, which comes topped with slices of mango and bits of Gorgonzola cheese, or the Portobello mushroom with spinach and roasted red peppers. Next you might try grilled lamb chops or linguine with clams, but be sure to look at the wine list, which also includes a number of microbrews. ✉ *241 N. Collier Blvd.,* ☎ *941/394–5533. Jacket required in season. AE, MC, V. No lunch.*

$$–$$$ ✕ **Old Marco Inn.** This turn-of-the-century home is now a beautifully
★ decorated spot for intimate dinners. The menu covers a cross section
of cuisines—such old-world German specialties as Wiener schnitzel and
sauerbraten with red cabbage and potato pancake plus grilled steaks,
chops, ribs, and a welcome selection of fresh Florida seafood. The piano
bar opens nightly at 8. ⊠ *100 Palm St.,* ☎ *941/394–3131. Jacket required in season. AE, MC, V. No lunch weekends.*

$$ ✕ **Cafe de Marco.** This cozy little award-winning bistro serves some
of the best food on the island. It specializes in combining fresh local
fish with original sauces, so listen carefully to the selections of the day.
Landlubbers can enjoy steaks, chicken, and pasta. ⊠ *244 Royal Palm
Dr.,* ☎ *941/394–6262. AE, DC, MC, V. Closed Sun.*

$$$$ 🏨 **Marco Island Hilton Beach Resort.** With fewer than 300 rooms and
wisely apportioned public areas, the Hilton is smaller than the other
big-name resorts in the area, and facilities tend to be a little less
crowded. All the rooms in this 11-story beachfront hotel are spacious
and have private balconies with unobstructed gulf views, a sitting
area, wet bar, and refrigerator. There is golf nearby. ⊠ *560 S. Collier
Blvd., 33937,* ☎ *941/394–5000 or 800/443–4550,* ☎ *941/394–5251.
270 rooms, 28 suites. 2 restaurants, bar, snack bar, pool, 3 tennis
courts, health club, beach, windsurfing, parasailing, waterskiing. AE,
D, DC, MC, V.*

$$$$ 🏨 **Marriott's Marco Island Resort and Golf Club.** A circular drive leads
to this big beachfront resort hotel and its manicured grounds. Large
rooms are plush, have good to exceptional water views from their bal-
conies, and come with a multitude of amenities, including coffeemaker,
small refrigerator, movie channels, and minibar. Serious shell seekers
will delight in the beachside shell-washing spigot, and golf (the resort's
own course) is 10 minutes by tram. ⊠ *400 S. Collier Blvd., 33937,* ☎
941/394–2511 or 800/438–4373, ☎ *941/394–4645. 736 rooms, 6 suites,
30 lanais, 8 villas. 6 restaurants, 2 bars, 3 pools, 18-hole golf course,
miniature golf, 16 tennis courts, health club, beach, windsurfing, boat-
ing, waterskiing, bicycles, children's programs. AE, DC, MC, V.*

$$$–$$$$ 🏨 **Radisson Suite Beach Resort.** There's something for everyone at this
full-service beachfront property designed for families. Tastefully dec-
orated rooms and one- and two-bedroom suites in this medium high-
rise contain fully equipped kitchens. Though rooms are a bit tight, suites
have plenty of space. ⊠ *600 S. Collier Blvd., 33937,* ☎ *941/394–4100
or 800/333–3333,* ☎ *941/394–0419. 55 rooms, 214 suites. 3 restau-
rants, 2 bars, pool, exercise room, beach, parasailing, bicycles, video
games, children's programs. AE, DC, MC, V.*

Outdoor Activities and Sports

BIKING
Rentals are available at **Island Cycle** (⊠ 845 Bald Eagle Dr., ☎ 941/
394–8400).

FISHING
Factory Bay Marina (⊠ 1079 Bald Eagle Dr., ☎ 941/642–6717) has
fishing-boat rentals as well as offshore charters.

SAILING
For sailing lessons or bareboat or captained sail cruises, contact **Marco
Island Sea Excursions** (⊠ 1281 Jamaica Rd., ☎ 941/642–6400).

SOUTHWEST FLORIDA A TO Z

Arriving and Departing

By Boat

Key West Water Express (☎ 800/650–5397) operates a ferry between Marco Island and Key West that takes three hours one-way.

By Bus

Greyhound Lines (☎ 800/231–2222) has service to Fort Myers (✉ 2275 Cleveland Ave., ☎ 941/334–1011) and Naples (✉ 2669 Davis Blvd., ☎ 941/774–5660).

By Car

I–75 spans the region from north to south. Once you cross the border into Florida, it's about five hours to Fort Myers and another hour to Naples. Alligator Alley, a section of I–75, is a two-lane toll road (75¢ at each end) that runs from Fort Lauderdale through the Everglades to Naples. The trip takes about two hours.

By Plane

The area's main airport is **Southwest Florida International Airport** (☎ 941/768–1000), about 12 mi southwest of Fort Myers, 25 mi north of Naples. It is served by **Air Canada** (☎ 800/776–3000), **American Eagle** (☎ 800/433–7300), **American TransAir** (☎ 800/225–2995), **America West** (☎ 800/235–9292), **Cape Air** (☎ 800/352–0714), **Carnival** (☎ 800/824–7386), **Continental** (☎ 800/525–0280), **Delta** (☎ 800/221–1212), **Midwest Express** (☎ 800/452–2022), **Northwest** (☎ 800/225–2525), **Spirit** (☎ 800/772–7117), **TWA** (☎ 800/221–2000), **United** (☎ 800/241–6522), and **US Airways** (☎ 800/428–4322). A taxi to Fort Myers, Sanibel, or Captiva costs about $30; it's about twice that to Naples. Other transportation companies include **AAA Airport Transportation** (☎ 800/872–2711), **Personal Touch Limousines** (☎ 941/549–3643), and **Sanibel Island Limousine** (☎ 941/472–8888).

The **Naples Airport** (☎ 941/643–6875), a small facility east of downtown, is served by American Eagle, **Atlantic Southeast Airlines** (☎ 800/282–3424), and **US Airways Express** (☎ 800/428–4322). Shuttle service to Naples is generally $15 to $25 per person. Once you have arrived, call **Naples Taxi** (☎ 941/643–2148), or for Marco Island try **Marco Transportation, Inc.** (☎ 941/394–2257).

Getting Around

By Bus

The **Lee County Transit System** (☎ 941/275–8726) serves most of the county.

By Car

I–75 and U.S. 41 run the length of the region. U.S. 41, also known as the Tamiami Trail, goes through downtown Fort Myers and Naples and is also called Cleveland Avenue in the former and 9th Street in the latter. McGregor Boulevard (Route 867), Fort Myers's main road, heads southwest toward Sanibel-Captiva. San Carlos Boulevard runs southwest from McGregor Boulevard to Fort Myers Beach, and Pine Island–Bayshore Road (Route 78) leads from North Fort Myers through northern Cape Coral onto Pine Island.

Contacts and Resources

Emergencies

Dial **911** for police or ambulance.

HOSPITALS

The following hospitals have 24-hour emergency rooms: **Lee Memorial Hospital** (⊠ 2776 Cleveland Ave., Fort Myers), **Naples Community Hospital** (⊠ 350 7th St. N, Naples), and **North Collier Hospital** (⊠ 1501 Imokolee Rd., Naples).

LATE-NIGHT PHARMACIES

Walgreens (⊠ 70703 College Pkwy., Fort Myers, ☎ 941/939–2142; ⊠ 8965 Tamiami Trail N, North Naples, ☎ 941/597–8196).

Guided Tours

AIR TOURS

Boca Grande Seaplane Service (⊠ 375 Park Ave., Boca Grande, ☎ 941/964–0234) operates sightseeing tours in the Charlotte Harbor area. **Classic Flight** (⊠ Fort Myers Jet Center, 501 Danley Rd., Fort Myers, ☎ 941/939–7411) flies an open cockpit biplane for sightseeing tours of the Fort Myers area.

BOAT TOURS

Adventure Sailing Charters (⊠ South Seas Plantation Rd., Captiva, ☎ 941/472–7532) offers captained half- and full-day sailing cruises and sunset cruises for groups of six or fewer. The best way to see the cluster of small, undeveloped, protected islands known as the Ten Thousand Islands is on an airboat tour run by **Airboat Experience of the Everglades** (⊠ 5 Papaya St., Goodland, Marco Island, ☎ 941/642–3141). Though there aren't actually 10,000, the scenery and wildlife are nevertheless remarkable. You'll probably see many birds, including pelicans and hawks, as well as dolphins swimming alongside the boat. As part of its natural history–based pontoon boat tour, **Calusa Coast Outfitters Educational Tours** (⊠ Fish Tale Marina, 7225 Estero Blvd., Fort Myers Beach, ☎ 941/332–0709) has underwater microphones that enable you to hear the whistles and other sounds made by dolphins. (A historical/archaeological walking tour of the Mound Key Archaeological Site is also offered.) At the South Seas Plantation marina, **Captiva Cruises** (⊠ Sanibel-Captiva Rd., Captiva, ☎ 941/472–5300) runs shelling, photo safari, nature, and sunset cruises to and around the out islands of Cabbage Key, Useppa Island, Cayo Costa, and Gasparilla Island. **Estero Bay Boat Tours** (⊠ 5231 Mamie St., Bonita Springs, ☎ 941/992–2200) takes you on guided tours of waterways once inhabited by the Calusa Indians. You'll see birds and other wildlife and may even spot some manatees or dolphins.

Island Rover (⊠ Snug Harbor, Fort Myers Beach, ☎ 941/691–7777), a 72-ft schooner, takes morning, afternoon, and sunset sails in the Gulf of Mexico. **Jammin' Sailboat Cruises** (⊠ 416 Crescent St., Fort Myers Beach, ☎ 941/463–3520) offers 2½-hour champagne cruises and four-hour shrimp-and-seafood cruises on a 30-ft sailboat. Call for reservations. **J. C.'s Cruises** (⊠ Fort Myers Yacht Basin, 2313 Edwards Dr., Fort Myers, ☎ 941/334–7474) explores the Caloosahatchee and Orange rivers of Lee County. From mid-November through mid-April, there are a variety of cruises along the Caloosahatchee River conducted on the *Capt. J. P.,* a stern paddle wheeler, and there is a manatee-watching cruise on a smaller boat. Brunch, lunch, and dinner cruises are available. **King Fisher Cruise Lines** (⊠ Fishermen's Village, 1200 W. Retta Esplanade, Punta Gorda, ☎ 941/639–0969) has half-day, full-day, and sunset cruises in Charlotte Harbor, the Peace River, and the Intracoastal Waterway. One of the best ways to see the J. N. "Ding" Darling National Wildlife Refuge is by taking a canoe or kayak tour with **Tarpon Bay Recreation** (⊠ 900 Tarpon Bay Rd., Sanibel, ☎ 941/472–8900). The knowledgeable naturalist guides can help you see so much more of what's there among the mangroves and under the water's surface.

TRAIN TOUR

Take a narrated sightseeing, dinner, jazz, or murder-mystery excursion aboard the old-fashioned **Seminole Gulf Railway** (⊠ Colonial Station, Fort Myers, ☎ 941/275–6060). Daytime trips, which run Wednesday, Saturday, and Sunday, travel between Fort Myers and Bonita Springs or include a scenic Caloosahatchee bridge crossing.

TROLLEY TOUR

Naples Trolley Tours (☎ 941/262–7300) has five narrated tours daily, covering more than 100 points of interest. You can pick it up at 25 places around town, including the Coastland Mall (⊠ 1900 9th St. N). The tour ($12) lasts about 1¾ hours, but you can get off and reboard at no extra cost.

Visitor Information

The following are open weekdays 9–5: **Charlotte County Chamber of Commerce** (⊠ 2702 Tamiami Trail, Port Charlotte 33950, ☎ 941/627–2222), **Lee County Visitor and Convention Bureau** (⊠ 2180 W. 1st St., Fort Myers 33901, ☎ 941/338–3500 or 800/533–4753), **Naples Area Chamber of Commerce** (⊠ 3620 Tamiami Trail N, Naples 33940, ☎ 941/262–6141), and **Sanibel-Captiva Chamber of Commerce** (⊠ Causeway Rd., Sanibel 33957, ☎ 941/472–1080).

9 THE PANHANDLE

Sometimes referred to as the Panhandle because of its long, skinny shape, northwestern Florida has some of the state's most beautiful beaches, but all is not fun in the sun. Tree-shrouded highways lead nature lovers to natural springs, historic landmarks, and secluded state parks more reminiscent of the Deep South than the state's southern reaches.

FLORIDA'S THIN, GREEN NORTHWEST CORNER snuggles up between the Gulf of Mexico and the Alabama and Georgia state lines. Known as the Panhandle, it's sometimes called "the other Florida," since instead of palm trees, what thrives here are the magnolias, live oaks, and loblolly pines common in the rest of the Deep South. As South Florida's season is winding down in May, action in the northwest is just picking up. The area is even in a different time zone: the Apalachicola River marks the dividing line between eastern and central times.

Updated by
Nancy Orr

Others call this section of the state "Florida's best-kept secret." Until World War II, when activity at the Panhandle air bases took off, it really was. But by the mid-1950s, the 100-mi stretch along the coast between Pensacola and Panama City was dubbed the "Miracle Strip" because of a dramatic rise in property values. In the 1940s this beachfront land sold for less than $100 an acre; today that same acre can yield tens of thousands of dollars. Still, the movers and shakers of the area felt this sobriquet fell short. So to convey the richness of the region, with its white sands and sparkling green waters, swamps, bayous, and flora, they coined the phrase "Emerald Coast."

It's a land of superlatives: It has the biggest military installation in the western hemisphere (Eglin Air Force Base), many of Florida's most beautiful beaches, and the most productive fishing waters in the world (off Destin). It has resorts that outglitz those on the Gold Coast, campgrounds where possums invite themselves to lunch, and every kind of lodging in between. Students of the past can wander the many historic districts or visit archaeological digs. For sports enthusiasts there's a different golf course or tennis court for each day of the week, and for nature lovers there's a world of hunting, canoeing, biking, and hiking. And anything that happens on water happens here: surfing, scuba diving, and plenty of fishing, both from a deep-sea charter boat and the end of a pier.

Pleasures and Pastimes

Beaches

Thanks to restrictions against commercial development imposed by Eglin Air Force Base (AFB) and the Gulf Islands National Seashore, the Emerald Coast has been able to maintain several hundred miles of unspoiled beaches. A 1998 study by the University of Maryland's Laboratory for Coastal Research named Perdido Key State Recreation Area, St. Joseph Peninsula State Park, and St. George Island State Park among the top 20 beaches in the United States.

Biking

Some of the nation's best bike paths run through northwest Florida's woods and dunelands, particularly on Santa Rosa Island, where you can pedal for nearly 20 mi and never lose sight of the water. Eglin AFB Reservation presents cyclists with tortuous wooded trails.

Canoeing

The Panhandle is often referred to as the "canoe capital of Florida," and both beginners and veterans get a kick out of canoeing the area's abundant waterways. The shoals and rapids of the Blackwater River in the Blackwater River State Forest, 40 mi northeast of Pensacola, challenge even seasoned canoeists, while the gentler currents of sheltered marshes and inlets are less intimidating.

Dining

Because the gulf is only an hour's drive from any spot in the Panhandle, restaurants from modest diners to elegant cafés feature seafood, most served the same day it is hauled out of the water. Native fish such as grouper, red snapper, amberjack, catfish, and mullet are the regional staples. Prices are generally reasonable, but if you visit during the off-season, watch for dining discounts, such as two-for-one meal deals and early bird specials.

Fishing

Options range from fishing for pompano, snapper, marlin, and grouper in the saltwater of the gulf to angling for bass, catfish, and bluegill in freshwater. Deep-sea fishing is immensely popular on the Emerald Coast, so there are boat charters aplenty. A day costs about $575, a half day about $300.

Exploring the Panhandle

There are sights to see in the Panhandle, but sightseeing is not the principal activity here. The area is better known for its ample opportunities for such sports as fishing and diving and for just plain relaxing.

Pensacola, with its antebellum homes and historic landmarks, is a good place to start your trek through northwest Florida. After exploring the museums and preservation districts, head east on U.S. 98 to Fort Walton Beach, the Emerald Coast's largest city, and to neighboring Destin, where sportfishing is king. Continuing along the coast, you'll find the quiet family-friendly beaches of South Walton, where the contrast between the sugar-white quartz-crystal sand and emerald water is stunning.

The next resort center along the coast is Panama City Beach, while to the far southeast is Apalachicola, an important oyster-fishing town. Just south of Apalachicola, St. George Island is a 28-mi-long barrier island bordered by the gulf and Apalachicola Bay. Inland, a number of interesting towns and state parks lie along I–10 on the long eastward drive to the state capital, Tallahassee.

Numbers in the text correspond to numbers in the margin and on the Panhandle map.

Great Itineraries

IF YOU HAVE 3 DAYS

History and nature are the two biggest calling cards of this part of the Sunshine State. Visit 🖼 **Fort Walton Beach** ③ or Eglin Air Force Base, depending on whether your heart lies on the seas or in the skies. Kids might enjoy a stop at the Indian Temple Mound and Museum. On day two drive to the capital, 🖼 **Tallahassee** ⑭, and soak up some of Florida's past. On day three you can make a trip to nearby **Wakulla Springs State Park** ⑯, where you'll find one of the world's deepest springs.

IF YOU HAVE 5 DAYS

Start with a visit to the Palafox Historic District in 🖼 **Pensacola** ① and spend the day enjoying a glimpse of Old Florida, as well as visiting the National Museum of Naval Aviation. Next move on to 🖼 **Fort Walton Beach** ③ and stop by Eglin Air Force Base and the antebellum mansion at the Eden State Gardens, set amid moss-draped live oaks. Be sure to spend an afternoon at the Grayton Beach State Recreation Area, one of the most scenic spots along the Gulf Coast. Moving inland, go spelunking at the **Florida Caverns State Park** ⑬ before heading to 🖼 **Tallahassee** ⑭. From there you can make day trips to **Wakulla Springs**

State Park ⑯ and **St. Marks Wildlife Refuge and Lighthouse** ⑰, where you can hike, swim, or have a leisurely picnic.

IF YOU HAVE 7 DAYS

From a base in 🔀 **Pensacola** ①, take a couple of side trips: to the Gulf Islands National Seashore, paying special attention to Fort Pickens, and to the Zoo in Gulf Breeze. Swing north to Milton, do the walking tour of its historic downtown, and then spend two days taking an Adventures Unlimited canoe trip on the Blackwater River and roughing it in an outdoor cabin. Proceed to 🔀 **DeFuniak Springs** ⑪, where must-sees are the quaint Walton DeFuniak Public Library and the Chautauqua Winery. Head south to 🔀 **Destin** ④ for a day of deep-sea fishing or a shopping spree at Silver Sands. Wind up your expedition through the other Florida at the beaches and amusement parks of 🔀 **Panama City Beach** ⑦, via an afternoon's stopover at the award-winning planned community of **Seaside** ⑥.

AROUND PENSACOLA BAY

In the years since its founding, Pensacola has come under the control of five nations, earning this fine, old southern city its nickname, "the City of Five Flags." Spanish conquistadors, under the command of Don Tristan de Luna, landed on the shores of Pensacola Bay in 1559, but discouraged by a succession of destructive tropical storms and dissension in the ranks, de Luna abandoned the settlement two years after its founding. In 1698 the Spanish once again established a fort at the site, and during the early 18th century control jockeyed back and forth among the Spanish, the French, and the British. Finally, in 1819 Pensacola passed into U.S. hands, though during the Civil War it was governed by the Confederate States of America and flew yet another flag.

The city itself has many historic sights, while across the bay lies Santa Rosa Island, where pristine coastline provides a delightful setting for beaching and other recreational activities.

Pensacola

❶ *59 mi east of Mobile, Alabama.*

Historic Pensacola consists of three distinct districts—Seville, Palafox, and North Hill—though they are easy to explore as a unit. Stroll down streets mapped out by the British and renamed by the Spanish, such as Cervantes, Palafox, Intendencia, and Tarragona. Be warned, though, that it is best to stick to the beaten path; Pensacola is a port town and can get rough around the edges, especially at night.

The best way to orient yourself is to stop at the **Pensacola Visitor Information Center** (✉ 1401 E. Gregory St., ☎ 850/434–1234), at the foot of the Pensacola Bay Bridge. Here you can pick up maps of the self-guided historic district tours.

The **Seville** historic district is the site of Pensacola's first permanent Spanish colonial settlement. Its center is Seville Square, a live-oak-shaded park bounded by Alcaniz, Adams, Zaragoza, and Government streets. Roam these brick streets past honeymoon cottages and bay-front homes. Many of the buildings have been converted into restaurants, commercial offices, and shops.

Within the Seville district is the **Historic Pensacola Village,** a complex comprising more than a half dozen museums and other buildings. The **Museum of Industry,** housed in a late-19th-century warehouse, hosts permanent exhibits dedicated to the lumber, maritime, and shipping

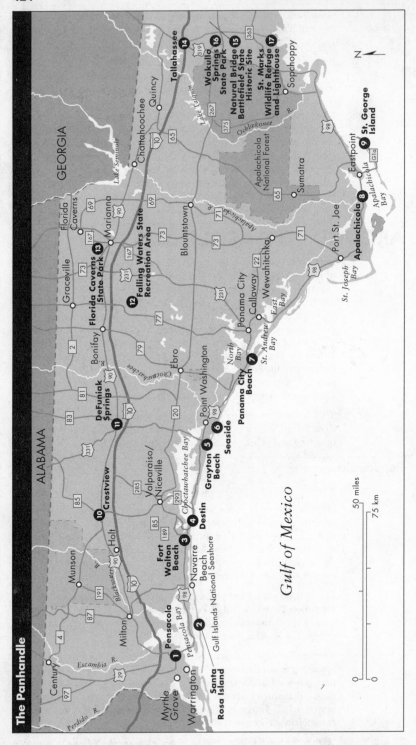

industries—once mainstays of Pensacola's economy. A reproduction of a 19th-century streetscape is displayed in the **Museum of Commerce,** and the city's historical archives are kept in the **Pensacola Historical Museum**—which was once one of Florida's oldest churches. Also in the village are the **Julee Cottage Museum of Black History, Dorr House, Lavalle House,** and **Quina House.** Strolling through the area gives you a good look at many architectural styles, but to enter the museums you must purchase an all-inclusive ticket, which also includes admission to the T. T. Wentworth Jr. Florida State Museum (☞ *below*).

Palafox Street is the main stem of the **Palafox Historic District,** which was the commercial and government hub of Old Pensacola. Note the Spanish Renaissance–style **Saenger Theater,** Pensacola's old movie palace, and the **Bear Block,** a former wholesale grocery with wrought-iron balconies that are a legacy from Pensacola's Creole past. On Palafox between Government and Zaragoza streets is a **statue of Andrew Jackson** that commemorates the formal transfer of Florida from Spain to the United States in 1821. While in the area, stop by the **Wall South,** in Veterans Memorial Park, just off Bayfront Parkway near 9th Avenue. The ¾-scale replica of the Vietnam Memorial in Washington, D.C., honors the more than 58,000 men and women who lost their lives in the Vietnam War.

In the days of the horse-drawn paddy wagon, the two-story mission revival building housing the **Pensacola Museum of Art** served as the city jail. Now it offers international fine art, rotating its two exhibits about every six weeks. ⊠ *407 S. Jefferson St.,* ☎ *850/432–5682.* ⊠ *$2, free Tues.* ☉ *Tues.–Fri. 10–5, Sat. 10–4, Sun. 1–4.*

☾ A former City Hall dating to 1908 now houses the **T. T. Wentworth Jr. Florida State Museum.** It has an eclectic mixture of exhibits that children find especially intriguing—particularly the shrunken heads. ⊠ *330 S. Jefferson St.,* ☎ *850/444–8905.* ⊠ *$6.* ☉ *Mon.–Sat. 10–4.*

For Civil War memorabilia stop by the **Civil War Soldiers Museum.** It holds a large number of items pertaining to Civil War medicine as well as an equally impressive collection of Civil War books. ⊠ *108 S. Palafox St.,* ☎ *850/469–1900.* ⊠ *$5.* ☉ *Tues.–Sat. 10–4:30.*

Pensacola's affluent families, many made rich in the turn-of-the-century timber boom, built their homes in the **North Hill Preservation District,** where British and Spanish fortresses once stood. Residents still occasionally unearth cannonballs in their gardens. North Hill occupies 50 blocks, with more than 500 homes in Queen Anne, neoclassic, Tudor Revival, and Mediterranean styles. Take a drive through this community, but remember these are private residences. Places of general interest include the 1902 Spanish mission–style **Christ Episcopal Church; Lee Square,** where a 50-ft obelisk stands as a tribute to the Confederacy; and **Fort George,** an undeveloped parcel at the site of the largest of three forts built by the British in 1778.

The **Pensacola Naval Air Station,** established in 1914, is the nation's oldest such facility. On display in its **National Museum of Naval Aviation** (☎ 850/452–3604) are more than 150 aircraft that played an important role in aviation history. Among them are the NC-4, which in 1919 became the first plane to cross the Atlantic; the famous World War II fighter, the F6 *Hellcat;* and the *Skylab Command Module.* Other attractions include a 14-seat flight simulator and a new IMAX theater featuring footage of the Blue Angels Flight Demonstration Team. ⊠ *1750 Radford Blvd.,* ☎ *850/452–2311; 850/453–2024 for IMAX theater.* ⊠ *Free, IMAX film $4.50.* ☉ *Daily 9–5.*

Dating from the Civil War, **Fort Barrancas** now has picnic areas and a ½-mi woodland nature trail on its grounds. The fort is part of the Gulf Islands National Seashore, maintained by the National Park Service. ⊠ *Navy Blvd.,* ☎ *850/455–5167.* 🎫 *Free.* ☉ *Dec.–Jan., Wed.–Sun. 10:30–4; Feb.–Nov., daily 9:30–5.*

OFF THE BEATEN PATH	**THE ZOO –** The local zoo, near Gulf Breeze, is home to more than 700 animals, including many endangered species. Kids especially enjoy the glass windows in the commissary, where they can see food being prepared for the animals. A tall platform offers viewers face-to-face meetings with the giraffes. ⊠ *5701 Gulf Breeze Pkwy., Gulf Breeze,* ☎ *850/932–2229.* 🎫 *$9.75.* ☉ *Summer, daily 9–5; winter, daily 9–4.*

Dining and Lodging

$$–$$$ ✕ **Jamie's Wine Bar and Restaurant.** This formerly French restaurant
★   has changed more than its menu. Though it's still in a historic cottage, it's swapped its old antiques-filled rooms for an art deco decor. The fare is a combination of Continental, Floribbean, and Asian cuisines. Game meats are the house specialties, and the menu changes often. The wine list has more than 200 labels. ⊠ *424 E. Zaragoza St.,* ☎ *850/ 434–2911. AE, D, MC, V. Closed Sun. No lunch Mon.*

$–$$ ✕ **McGuire's Irish Pub.** You probably don't want to spend $100 for a hamburger, but you can here. You can also spend $5.95. It depends on whether you want your burger topped with caviar and served with champagne. Beer is brewed right on the premises, and the wine cellar features more than 8,000 bottles. Menu items range from Irish-style corned beef and cabbage to a hickory-smoked rib roast. In an old firehouse, the pub is replete with antiques, moose heads, Tiffany-style lamps, and Erin-go-bragh memorabilia. More than 125,000 dollar bills signed and dated by the pub's patrons flutter from the ceiling. ⊠ *600 E. Gregory St.,* ☎ *850/433–6789. AE, D, DC, MC, V.*

$–$$ ✕ **Mesquite Charlie's.** Saddle up and head on over to this Wild West saloon, complete with brick walls, arched doorways, mounted game, and a second-floor balcony overlooking the lobby. All that's missing are the swinging doors. The 32-ounce porterhouse is large enough to satisfy a posse of cowboys, but there are also smaller selections for dainty appetites. All are charbroiled with 100% mesquite charcoal and seasoned with natural spices. ⊠ *5901 N. W St.,* ☎ *850/434–0498. AE, D, MC, V.*

$$ 🏨 **Pensacola Grand Hotel.** Although the hotel was completely renovated following the 1998 hurricane season, the lobby remains a tribute to years past. Formerly the 1912 Louisville & Nashville train depot, the hotel still has intact ticket and baggage counters, and old railroad signs remind guests of the days when steam locomotives chugged up to these doors. A canopied two-story galleria leads to a 15-story tower where you leave the past behind and enjoy all the amenities of deluxe accommodations. Bilevel penthouse suites have snazzy wet bars and whirlpool baths. ⊠ *200 E. Gregory St., 32501,* ☎ *850/433–3336 or 800/348–3336,* 🗎 *850/432–7572. 202 rooms, 10 suites. Restaurant, bar, pool, exercise room, library, business services, airport shuttle. AE, D, DC, MC, V.*

$$ 🏨 **Residence Inn by Marriott.** Opened in 1998, this all-suites hotel in the downtown area is perfect for travelers with long-term business needs and for families interested in Pensacola's historical attractions. The fully equipped kitchens, complimentary breakfast, and evening social hour are almost as good as being home. ⊠ *601 E. Chase St., 32501,* ☎ *850/ 432–0202,* 🗎 *850/438–7965. 78 suites. Pool, tennis court, exercise room. AE, D, DC, MC, V.*

$–$$ ⊞ **New World Inn.** If a small, warm, and cozy inn sounds appealing,
★   this is the place for you. Located in the downtown historic area just
two blocks from Pensacola Bay, it contains furnishings that reflect the
five periods of Pensacola's past: French and Spanish provincial, Early
American, antebellum, and Queen Anne. Reputed to be the favored
hideout for visiting celebrities, the inn displays photos of famous guests
(Lucille Ball, Shirley Jones, Charles Kuralt) in the front hall. Exquisite
baths are handsomely appointed. Continental breakfast is served. ⊠
600 S. Palafox St., 32501, ☎ *850/432–4111,* ℻ *850/432–6836. 14
rooms, 1 suite. Restaurant, bar. AE, MC, V.*

Nightlife and the Arts

THE ARTS

Productions at the restored 1926 **Saenger Theatre** (⊠ 118 S. Palafox
St., ☎ 850/433–6737) include touring Broadway shows and three locally staged operas a year. The **Pensacola Little Theatre** (⊠ 400 S. Jefferson St., ☎ 850/432–2042) presents plays and musicals during a fall–
spring season. **Pensacola's Symphony Orchestra** (☎ 850/435–2533)
offers five concerts each season at the Saenger Theatre.

NIGHTLIFE

After dark, **McGuire's Irish Pub** (⊠ 600 E. Gregory St., ☎ 850/433–6789)
particularly welcomes those of Irish descent. If you don't like crowds,
stay away from McGuire's on Friday night and on nights when Notre
Dame games are televised. **Mesquite Charlie's** (⊠ 5901 N. W St., ☎ 850/
434–0498) offers country music and all the western trappings. The **Seville
Quarter** (⊠ 130 E. Government St., ☎ 850/434–6211) has seven fabulous bars and features music from disco to Dixieland; it's Pensacola's
equivalent of the New Orleans French Quarter.

Outdoor Activities and Sports

CANOEING AND KAYAKING

Canoe and kayak rentals for exploring the Blackwater River (the
state's only pristine sand-bottom river) are available from **Blackwater
Canoe Rental** (⊠ 6974 Deaton Bridge Rd., Milton, ☎ 850/623–0235
or 800/967–6789), northeast of Pensacola off I–10 Exit 10. **Adventures
Unlimited** (⊠ Rte. 87, 12 mi north of Milton, ☎ 850/623–6197 or 800/
239–6864), on Coldwater Creek, provides a variety of light watercraft
as well as camping accommodations.

DOG RACING

Rain or shine, year-round there's live racing at the **Pensacola Greyhound
Track.** Lounge and grandstand areas are fully enclosed and air-condi-
tioned and have instant-replay televisions throughout. ⊠ *951 Dog Track
Rd., West Pensacola,* ☎ *850/455–8595 or 800/345–3997.* ⊡ *$2.50.*
☉ *Racing Tues.–Wed. and Fri.–Sat. 7, also weekends 1.*

FISHING

Fishing tackle is available at the **Rod and Reel Marina** (⊠ 10045 Sin-
ton Dr., ☎ 850/492–0100), a mile west of Blue Angel Parkway off Gulf
Beach Highway. In a pinch you can drop a line from **Old Pensacola
Bay Bridge.**

GOLF

There are several outstanding golf courses in and around Pensacola.
The **Sportsman of Perdido** (⊠ 1 Doug Ford Dr., ☎ 850/492–1223)
has an 18-hole course. **Tiger Point Golf & Country Club** (⊠ 1255 Country Club Rd., Gulf Breeze, ☎ 850/932–1333 or 800/477–4833) has
36 holes.

TENNIS

Tennis courts are available in more than 30 locations in the Pensacola area; among them is the **Pensacola Racquet Club** (⊠ 3450 Wimbledon Dr., ☎ 850/434–2434).

Shopping

Cordova Mall (⊠ 5100 N. 9th Ave.) is anchored by four department stores, plus specialty shops and a food court. **Harbourtown Shopping Village** (⊠ 913 Gulf Breeze Pkwy., Gulf Breeze) has trendy shops and the ambience of a wharf-side New England village.

Santa Rosa Island

② *5 mi south of Pensacola via U.S. 98 to Rte. 399 (Bob Sikes) Bridge.*

The site of beaches, natural areas, and the town of Pensacola Beach, this barrier island draws visitors for more than seascapes and water sports. It's also a must for cyclists and bird-watchers. Since 1971 more than 280 species of birds, from the common loon to the majestic osprey, have been spotted here. Two caveats for visitors: "Leave nothing behind but your footprints," and "Don't pick the sea oats" (natural grasses that help keep the dunes intact).

Dotting the 150-mi stretch between Destin and Gulfport, Mississippi, is **Gulf Islands National Seashore** (☎ 850/934–2600), managed by the National Park Service. A number of good beach and recreational spots are part of the national seashore along this beautiful stretch of island coast, including the **Santa Rosa Day Use Area** (⊠ 10 mi east of Pensacola Beach). Check with the park service for any restrictions that might apply.

At the western tip of the island and part of the Gulf Islands National Seashore, **Fort Pickens** dates to 1834. Constructed of more than 21 million locally made bricks, the fort once served as the prison of Apache chief Geronimo, who was reportedly fairly well liked by his captors. Other attractions are a beach, nature exhibits, a museum, a large campground, and a visitor center. ⊠ *Ranger station at Ft. Pickens Rd.,* ☎ *850/934–2635.* ☞ *$6 per car.* ☉ *Daily 8:30–sunset.*

At **Pensacola Beach** (⊠ 5 mi south of Pensacola, ☎ 850/932–2258), beachcombers and sunbathers, sailboarders and sailors keep things going at a fever pitch in and out of the water.

Dining and Lodging

$$–$$$ ✕ **Flounder's Chowder and Ale House.** Combine a casual atmosphere, a gulf-front view, and a fruity tropical libation and you're all set for a night of "floundering" at its best. An eclectic collection of antiques and objets d'art contributes to the overall funkiness. The house specialty is seafood charbroiled over a flaming hardwood fire, but the extensive menu offers something for everyone. After dinner, dance beneath the stars at the Jamaican-style beach bar. ⊠ *800 Quietwater Beach Blvd.,* ☎ *850/932–2003. AE, D, DC, MC, V.*

$$$ 🏨 **Perdido Sun.** This high-rise is the perfect expression of gulf-side resort living. One-, two-, and three-bedroom decorator-furnished units all have seaside balconies with spectacular water views. You can choose to make this your home away from home—accommodations include fully equipped kitchens—or you can pamper yourself with daily maid service. ⊠ *13753 Perdido Key Dr., Pensacola Beach 32507,* ☎ *850/ 492–2390 or 800/227–2390,* FAX *850/492–4135. 93 units. Indoor and outdoor pools, spa, health club, beach. AE, D, MC, V.*

$$–$$$ ⊡ **Hampton Inn Pensacola Beach.** The exterior's pink-and-green color scheme is reminiscent of Miami Beach's Art Deco buildings, and the easygoing Florida style continues inside. Directly on the gulf and centrally located, this lodging is within walking distance of several popular restaurants and shops. All rooms are oversize, have gulf views, and include refrigerator, microwave, and HBO. Gulf-front rooms have private balconies. There's an evening cocktail hour, and an expansive Continental breakfast buffet is served. ⊠ *2 Via de Luna, Pensacola Beach 32561,* ☎ *850/932–6800 or 800/320–8108,* F䄀X *850/932–6833. 181 rooms. Bar, 2 pools, exercise room, beach. AE, D, MC, V.*

Outdoor Activities and Sports

FISHING

For a full- or half-day deep-sea charter, try the **Moorings Marina** (⊠ 655 Pensacola Beach Blvd., Pensacola Beach, ☎ 850/432–9620).

GOLF

The **Club at Hidden Creek** (⊠ 3070 PGA Blvd., Navarre, ☎ 850/939–4604) has 18 holes.

WATER SPORTS

When you rent a sailboat, Jet Ski, or catamaran from **Bonifay Water Sports** (⊠ 460 Pensacola Beach Blvd., Pensacola Beach, ☎ 850/932–0633), you'll also receive safety and sailing instructions.

THE GULF COAST

From Pensacola southeast to St. George Island, travelers on U.S. 98 will find a number of towns strung along the shoreline, each with its own personality and offerings. The twin cities of Destin and Fort Walton Beach seemingly merge into one sprawling destination and continue to spread as new condominiums, resort developments, shopping centers, and restaurants crowd the skyline each year.

The view changes drastically farther along the coast as you enter the quiet stretch known as the Beaches of South Walton. Here building restrictions prohibit high-rise developments, and the majority of dwellings are privately owned homes, most of which are available to vacationers. A total of 19 beach communities cluster along this quiet strip off U.S. 98. Many are little more than a wide spot in the road, and all are among the least known and least developed in the entire Gulf Coast area, even though the University of Maryland's Laboratory for Coastal Research ranked Grayton Beach among the country's top 20 beaches for years.

Seaside, a town less than 20 years old, is a thriving planned community with old-fashioned Victorian architecture, brick streets, and a quaint shopping village. Continuing southeast on U.S. 98, you'll find Panama City Beach, its "Miracle Strip" crammed with every teenager's dream—from the carnival-like amusement parks to junk food vendors to T-shirt shops by the dozens. Farther east, an alternative to neon-lighted tourist havens is the quiet blue-collar town of Apalachicola, Florida's main oyster fishery. Here many oystermen still fish by hand, using long-handled tongs to bring in their catch.

Cross the Apalachicola Bay via the Bryant Patton Bridge to St. George Island. This unspoiled 28-mi-long barrier island offers some of the world's most scenic beaches, including St. George Island State Park, which has the longest beachfront of any state park in Florida.

Fort Walton Beach

❸ *46 mi east of Pensacola.*

This coastal town dates from the Civil War but had to wait more than 75 years to come into its own. Patriots loyal to the Confederate cause organized Walton's Guard (named in honor of Colonel George Walton, onetime acting territorial governor of West Florida) and camped at a site on Santa Rosa Sound, later known as Camp Walton. In 1940 fewer than 90 people lived in Fort Walton Beach, but within a decade the city became a boomtown, thanks to New Deal money for roads and bridges and the development of Eglin Field during World War II. The military is now Fort Walton Beach's main source of income, but tourism runs a close second.

Encompassing 728 square mi of land, **Eglin Air Force Base** (⊠ Rte. 85, ☎ 850/882–3931) includes 10 auxiliary fields and a total of 21 runways. Jimmie Doolittle's Tokyo Raiders trained here, as did the Son Tay Raiders, a group that made a daring attempt to rescue American POWs from a North Vietnamese prison camp in 1970.

★ The collection at the **Air Force Armament Museum,** just outside the Eglin Air Force Base's main gate, contains more than 5,000 air-force armaments from World Wars I and II and the Korean and Vietnam wars. Included are uniforms, engines, weapons, aircraft, and flight simulators; larger craft such as transport planes are exhibited on the grounds outside. A 32-minute movie about Eglin's history and its role in the development of armaments plays continuously. ⊠ *Rte. 85, Eglin Air Force Base,* ☎ *850/882–4062.* ▣ *Free.* ☉ *Daily 9:30–4:30.*

John C. Beasley State Park (☎ no phone) is Fort Walton Beach's seaside playground on Okaloosa Island. A boardwalk leads to the beach, where you'll find covered picnic tables, changing rooms, and freshwater showers. Lifeguards are on duty in summer.

☾ Kids especially enjoy the **Indian Temple Mound and Museum,** where they can learn all about the prehistoric peoples who inhabited northwest Florida up to 10,000 years ago. The funerary masks and weaponry on display are particularly fascinating. The museum is adjacent to the 600-year-old **National Historic Landmark Temple Mound,** a large earthwork built over saltwater. ⊠ *139 Miracle Strip Pkwy. (U.S. 98),* ☎ *850/833–9595.* ▣ *$2.* ☉ *Sept.–May, weekdays 11–4, Sat. 9–4; June–Aug., Mon.–Sat. 9–4.*

☾ When the weather drives you off the beach, the **Gulfarium** is a great place to spend your time. Its main attraction is its Living Sea, a 60,000-gallon tank that simulates conditions on the ocean floor. It also features performances by trained porpoises, sea-lion shows, and marine-life exhibits. Don't overlook the extensive gift shop, where you can buy anything from conch shells to beach toys. ⊠ *U.S. 98E,* ☎ *850/244–5169.* ▣ *$14.* ☉ *Mid-May–mid-Sept., daily 10–6; mid-Sept.–mid-May, daily 10–4.*

Dining and Lodging

$$–$$$ ✕ **Pandora's.** On the Emerald Coast the name Pandora's is synony-
★ mous with prime rib. The weather-beaten exterior gives way to a warm and cozy interior with alcoves and tables for four that lend an air of intimacy. You can order your prime rib regular or extra cut; fish aficionados should try the char-grilled yellowfin tuna, bacon wrapped and topped with Jamaican sauce. The mood turns a bit more gregarious in the lounge, where there is live entertainment several evenings a week. ⊠ *1120 Santa Rosa Blvd.,* ☎ *850/244–8669. AE, D, DC, MC, V.*

$–$$ ✕ **Staff's.** Sip a Tropical Depression or a rum-laced Squall Line while you peruse a menu tucked into the centerfold of a tabloid-size newspaper filled with snippets of local history, early photographs, and family memorabilia. Since 1931 people have been coming to this garage-turned-eatery for steaks broiled as you like them and seafood dishes like freshly caught Florida lobster and char-grilled amberjack. The grand finale is a trip to the delectable dessert bar; try a generous wedge of cherry cheesecake. ⊠ *24 Miracle Strip Pkwy. SE,* ☎ *850/243–3482. AE, D, MC, V.*

$$–$$$ ▥ **Radisson Beach Resort.** This U-shape hotel consists of a seven-story tower flanked by three-story wings. Rooms have a pastel green-and-peach decor and face either gulf or pool, though even poolside rooms have a bit of a sea view. ⊠ *1110 Santa Rosa Blvd., 32548,* ☎ *850/243–9181,* FAX *850/243–7704. 388 rooms. 2 restaurants, 2 bars, 4 pools, 2 tennis courts, exercise room, beach. AE, D, DC, MC, V.*

$$–$$$ ▥ **Ramada Plaza Beach Resort.** Activity here revolves around a pool with a grotto and swim-through waterfall; there's also an 800-ft private beach. Tower rooms include refrigerators. ⊠ *1500 Miracle Strip Pkwy. SE, 32548,* ☎ *850/243–9161,* FAX *850/243–2391. 335 rooms. 3 restaurants, 3 bars, 3 pools, exercise room, beach. AE, D, MC, V.*

Nightlife and the Arts

THE ARTS

The **Okaloosa Symphony Orchestra** (☎ 850/244–3308) performs a series of concerts featuring guest artists at the **Fort Walton Beach Civic Auditorium** (⊠ U.S. 98W).

The **Northwest Florida Ballet** (⊠ 101 S.E. Chicago Ave., ☎ 850/664–7787) has a repertoire of the classics and performs throughout the Panhandle.

NIGHTLIFE

Catch the action at **Cash's Faux Pas Lounge** (⊠ 106 Santa Rosa Blvd., ☎ 850/244–2274), where anything goes.

Outdoor Activities and Sports

BIKING

Eglin Air Force Base Reservation has plenty of challenging, twisting wooded trails. Biking here requires a $3 permit, which can be obtained from the Jackson Guard (⊠ 107 Rte. 85N, Niceville, ☎ 850/882–4164). Rentals are available from **Bob's Bicycle Center** (⊠ 415 Mary Esther Cutoff, ☎ 850/243–5856).

FISHING

Get outfitted with tackle at **Stewart's Outdoor Sports** (⊠ 4 S.E. Eglin Pkwy., ☎ 850/243–9443).

GOLF

The **Fort Walton Beach Golf Club** (⊠ Rte. 189, ☎ 850/833–9529), which has 36 holes, is rated as one of Florida's best public layouts. **Shalimar Pointe Golf & Country Club** (⊠ 302 Country Club Dr., Shalimar, ☎ 850/651–1416) has 18 holes.

SCUBA DIVING

You can arrange for diving lessons or excursions at the **Scuba Shop** (⊠ 348 Miracle Strip Pkwy., ☎ 850/243–1600).

TENNIS

You can play tennis on seven Rubico and two hard courts at the **Fort Walton Racquet Club** (⊠ 1819 Hurlburt Field Rd., ☎ 850/862–2023). The **Municipal Tennis Center** (⊠ 45 W. Audrey Dr., ☎ 850/833–9588) has 12 lighted Laykold courts and four practice walls.

Shopping

Stores in the **Manufacturer's Outlet Center** (⊠ 127 and 255 Miracle Strip Pkwy.) offer well-known brands of clothing and housewares at a substantial discount. There are four department stores in the **Santa Rosa Mall** (⊠ 300 Mary Esther Cutoff, Mary Esther), as well as 118 other shops and 15 bistro-style eateries.

Destin

❹ *8 mi east of Fort Walton Beach.*

Fort Walton Beach's neighbor lies on the other side of the strait that connects Choctawhatchee Bay with the Gulf of Mexico. Destin takes its name from its founder, Leonard A. Destin, a Connecticut sea captain who settled his family here sometime in the 1830s. For the next 100 years Destin remained a sleepy little fishing village until the strait, or East Pass, was bridged in 1935. Then recreational anglers discovered its white sands, blue-green waters, and abundance of some of the most sought-after sport fish in the world. More billfish are hauled in around Destin each year than from all other gulf fishing ports combined, giving credence to its nickname, "the world's luckiest fishing village." But you don't have to be the rod-and-reel type to love Destin. There's plenty to entertain the sand-pail set as well as senior citizens, and there are many gourmet restaurants.

☾ In addition to a seasonal water park, **Big Kahuna's Lost Paradise** has year-round family attractions, including 54 holes of miniature golf, two go-cart tracks, an arcade, a kiddy land with a scaled-down Ferris wheel and merry-go-round, and an amphitheater. ⊠ *U.S. 98E,* ☏ *850/837–4061.* ▭ *Grounds free, water park $27.50, miniature golf $6.50, go-carts $8.50.* ☉ *Mid-Sept.–May, Fri.–Sat. 10 AM–11:30 PM; June–mid-Sept., daily 10 AM–11:30 PM. Water park closed mid-Sept.–April.*

OFF THE
BEATEN PATH

FRED GANNON ROCKY BAYOU STATE RECREATION AREA – To the north of Destin is a quiet park offering picnic areas, nature trails, boat ramps, and uncrowded campsites with electrical and water hookups. It's secluded yet easy to find, and it's a great venue for serious bikers. ⊠ *Rte. 20 east of Niceville,* ☏ *850/833–9144.* ▭ *$2 per vehicle for day use; campsites $8.56, with electricity $10.70.* ☉ *Daily 8–sunset.*

Dining and Lodging

$$–$$$ ✕ **Flamingo Café.** This café serves up two different atmospheres for tropical dining. Indoors you'll find freshly starched white linen and refined elegance, while the outdoor patio is more casual. Either way there's a panoramic view of Destin harbor from every seat in the house, and boaters are welcome to tie up at the dock. The cuisine is Floribbean—a mixture of Caribbean and Florida cuisines. Though known for his special snapper and grouper dishes, the chef also turns out a delicious grilled swordfish with papaya-chutney butter, wilted spinach, black beans, and roasted sweet peppers. ⊠ *414 U.S. 98E,* ☏ *850/837–0961. AE, D, DC, MC, V. No lunch.*

$$–$$$ ✕ **Marina Café.** A harbor-view setting, impeccable service, and uptown
★   ambience have earned this establishment a reputation as one of the finest dining experiences on the Emerald Coast. The decor's oceanic motif is expressed in shades of aqua, green, and sand accented with marine tapestries and sea sculptures. The chef calls his cuisine contemporary Continental, offering diners a choice of classic creole, Mediterranean, or Pacific Rim dishes. One regional specialty is the award-winning black pepper–crusted yellowfin tuna with braised spinach and spicy soy

sauce. The menu changes daily, and the wine list is extensive. ✉ *404 U.S. 98E,* ☎ *850/837–7960. AE, D, DC, MC, V. No lunch.*

$–$$ ✗ **Porterhouse Grill.** Not too many places offer fried green beans as an appetizer, but this restaurant does. An original recipe created by the owner's mother, fresh beans are lightly battered (in her secret recipe), quickly fried, and totally delicious. Steaks are all certified Black Angus beef marinated in a special sauce and cooked over a mesquite grill. ✉ *3600 Emerald Coast Pkwy.,* ☎ *850/837–9410. AE, D, DC, MC, V.*

$$$–$$$$ 🏨 **Henderson Park Inn.** Tucked discreetly away at the end of a quiet road bordering Henderson Beach State Park, this bed-and-breakfast has become Destin's premier getaway for couples seeking elegance and pampering. A green mansard roof and Shaker shingle siding are reminiscent of Queen Anne–era architecture and complement the inn's Victorian-era furnishings. Each romantic room is furnished with a four-poster, canopied, or iron bed draped with fine linen. Plush robes, refrigerators, ice makers, and microwaves are standard in all rooms, which also feature a private patio or balcony for admiring the gulf's clear emerald water and smashing sunsets. ✉ *2700 U.S. 98E, 32541,* ☎ *850/837–4853 or 800/336–4853,* 🖷 *850/654–0405. 35 rooms. Restaurant, pool, beach. AE, MC, V.*

$$–$$$ 🏨 **Holiday Inn Destin.** You can lounge on sugar-white sands, get to several golf courses with ease, and walk to some of Destin's amusement parks. Common areas jazzed up with skylights and greenery are spacious and eye-pleasing. Standard motel appointments don't vary much, but prices do, depending on the view. ✉ *U.S. 98E, 32541,* ☎ *850/837–6181,* 🖷 *850/837–1523. 230 rooms. Restaurant, bar, 2 pools, beach. AE, D, DC, MC, V.*

$$–$$$ 🏨 **Sandestin Beach Resort.** This 2,600-acre resort of villas, cottages,
★ condominiums, and an inn seems to be a town unto itself. All rooms have a view, either of the gulf, Choctawhatchee Bay, a golf course, lagoon, or natural wildlife preserve. This resort accommodates an assortment of tastes, from the simple to the extravagant, and offers special rates September–March. ✉ *9300 U.S. 98W, 32541,* ☎ *850/267–8000 or 800/277–0800,* 🖷 *850/267–8222. 175 rooms, 250 condos, 275 villas. 4 restaurants, 11 pools, 63 holes of golf, 16 tennis courts, health club, beach, dock, pro shops. AE, D, DC, MC, V.*

$$ 🏨 **Bluewater Bay Resort.** This upscale resort is 12 mi north of Destin
★ via the Mid-Bay Bridge on the shores of Choctawhatchee Bay. Popular for its 36 holes of championship golf (on courses designed by Jerry Pate and Tom Fazio), it offers vacation rentals ranging from motel rooms to villas to patio homes. *1950 Bluewater Blvd., Niceville 32578,* ☎ *850/897–3613 or 800/874–2128,* 🖷 *850/897–2424. 100 units. Restaurant, bar, 4 pools, 36 holes of golf, 19 tennis courts, playground. AE, D, DC, MC, V.*

Nightlife

Nightown (✉ 140 Palmetto St., ☎ 850/837–6448) has a dance floor with laser lights and a New Orleans–style bar with a live band. At **Yesterday's** (✉ 1079 U.S. 98E, ☎ 850/837–1954), you can relive a jukebox Saturday night with an evening of '60s-style rock and roll.

Outdoor Activities and Sports

FISHING

East Pass Charters (✉ East Pass Marina, 288 U.S. 98E, ☎ 850/664–0039) has a deep-sea charter service for avid sportsmen as well as pontoon rentals for leisurely cruising close to shore. You can always pier-fish from the 3,000-ft-long **Destin Catwalk,** along the East Pass Bridge.

GOLF

Bluewater Bay Resort (✉ 1950 Bluewater Blvd., Niceville, ☎ 850/897–3241 or 800/874–2128), 6 mi east of Niceville on Route 20E, has 36 holes of championship golf on courses designed by Jerry Pate and Tom Fazio. The **Indian Bayou Golf & Country Club** (✉ Airport Rd. off U.S. 98, ☎ 850/837–6192) offers a 27-hole course. The 18-hole, Fred Couples–designed **Kelly Plantation Golf Club** (✉ 34851 Emerald Coast Pkwy., ☎ 850/659–7600) runs along Choctawhatchee Bay. For sheer number of holes, the **Sandestin Beach Resort** (✉ 9300 U.S. 98W, ☎ 850/267–8211) tops the list with 63.

SCUBA DIVING

Diving and snorkeling instruction and outings are available through **Aquanaut Scuba Center, Inc.** (✉ 500 U.S. 98W, ☎ 850/837–0359).

TENNIS

Sandestin Beach Resort (✉ 9300 U.S. 98W, ☎ 850/267–7110), one of the nation's five-star tennis resorts, has 16 courts with grass, hard, and Rubico surfaces. The **Destin Racquet & Fitness Center** (✉ 995 Airport Rd., ☎ 850/837–7300) has six Rubico courts.

Shopping

The **Market at Sandestin** (✉ 9375 U.S. 98W) has 33 upscale shops that peddle such goods as gourmet chocolates and designer clothes in an elegant minimall with boardwalks. **Silver Sands Factory Stores** (✉ 5021 U.S. 98E) is one of the Southeast's largest. More than 100 shops feature top-name merchandise that ranges from gifts to kids' clothes to menswear.

Grayton Beach

⑤ *18 mi east of Destin.*

The 26-mi stretch of coastline between Destin and Panama City Beach is referred to as the Beaches of South Walton because of its amazing beaches. But all is not sun and fun. Surprisingly for such a small area, there are enough award-winning restaurants to make selecting a dinner spot the day's most challenging decision. Accommodations consist primarily of private home rentals, the majority of which are managed by local real estate firms (☞ Contacts and Resources *in* the Panhandle A to Z, *below*). Also scattered along Route 30A are a few small artistic boutiques, where you'll find unique hand-painted furniture, jewelry, and contemporary gifts and clothing. Inland, thick pine forests and hardwoods surround the area's 14 lakes, giving anglers ample opportunities to drop a line.

Grayton Beach, the oldest community in this area, has reached its 100-year mark. You can still see some of the old weathered cypress homes scattered along sandy streets. The town has made some minor concessions to growth in the way of a small market and a couple of restaurants in its single-road "downtown" district. Don't expect much more. Stringent building restrictions, designed to protect the pristine beaches, will always ensure that Grayton maintains its small-town feel and look.

★ The 1,133-acre **Grayton Beach State Recreation Area** is one of the most scenic spots along the Gulf Coast, offering salt marshes, rolling dunes covered with sea oats, crystal-white sand, and contrasting blue-green waters. The park has facilities for swimming, fishing, snorkeling, and camping. ✉ *357 Main Park Rd.*, ☎ *850/231–4210.* ☞ *$3.25 per vehicle with up to 8 people.* ⊙ *Daily 8–sunset.*

OFF THE
BEATEN PATH

EDEN STATE GARDENS – Scarlett O'Hara might be at home here on the lawn of an antebellum mansion set amid an arcade of moss-draped live oaks. Furnishings in the spacious rooms date as far back as the 17th century. The surrounding gardens are beautiful year-round, but they're nothing short of spectacular in mid-March, when the azaleas and dogwoods are in full bloom. ⊠ *Rte. 395, Point Washington,* ☎ *850/231–4214.* ⛫ *Gardens $2, mansion tour $1.50.* ☉ *Daily 8–sunset, mansion tours Thurs.–Mon. hourly 9–4.*

Dining

$$–$$$$ ✕ **Criollas.** This restaurant continues to win award after award with its inventive, contemporary, and constantly changing cuisine. You might choose to experience Island Hopping—a four-course dinner focusing on a particular Caribbean region. The region varies from month to month, so returning diners can sample a different cuisine each visit. ⊠ *Rte. 30A,* ☎ *850/267–1267. D, MC, V. Closed Sun.–Mon. Sept.–Apr. No lunch.*

$–$$ ✕ **Picolo Restaurant & Red Bar.** You could spend weeks here just taking in all the eclectic memorabilia dangling from the ceiling and tacked to every available square inch of wall. Marilyn Monroe posters, 1970s album covers, signs, flags, colored lights, dolls, shoes, Broadway *Playbills,* and just about anything else you could think of add a degree of artistic funkiness. The equally contemporary menu is small, changes daily, and is very Floridian. A baked eggplant dish stuffed with shrimp, crawfish, and grilled vegetables is a popular entrée. Live blues and jazz can be heard nightly. ⊠ *70 Holtz Ave.,* ☎ *850/231–1008. No credit cards. No lunch.*

Nightlife

The **Red Bar** (⊠ 70 Holtz Ave., ☎ 850/231–1008), the local watering hole, is elbow to elbow on Friday and Saturday nights when red-hot bands serve up blues and jazz.

Outdoor Activities and Sports

The **Santa Rosa Golf & Beach Club** (⊠ Rte. 30A, Santa Rosa Beach, ☎ 850/267–2229) has 18 holes.

Shopping

Gaffrey Art Gallery (⊠ Rte. 30A, 3 mi west of Grayton Beach) sells hand-painted furniture and furniture handmade by the Gaffrey family. **Wild Women Art Gallery** (⊠ Rte. 30A, 3 mi west of Grayton Beach), which features "art for the wild at heart," carries adorable hand-painted children's furniture, prints, artwork, and glass. Under the shade trees of Grayton Beach, **Magnolia House** (⊠ Magnolia St.) offers gift items, clothing, bath lotions, and accessories for the home. **Monet, Monet** (⊠ 100 E. Rte. 30A) features garden sculpture, ornamental planters, fine gardening tools, and plants.

Seaside

❻ *2 mi east of Grayton Beach.*

This community of Victorian-style homes is so reminiscent of a storybook town that producers chose it for the set of the 1998 film *The Truman Show,* starring Jim Carrey. The brainchild of Robert Davis, the town was designed to promote a neighborly, old-fashioned lifestyle. Pastel-color homes with white picket fences, front-porch rockers, and captain's walks are set amid redbrick streets, and all are within walking distance of the town center and its unusual cafés and shops. Seaside's popularity continues to soar, and the summer months can be quite crowded. If you're seeking a little solitude, you might prefer visiting during the off-season—between Labor Day and Memorial Day.

Dining and Lodging

$$–$$$ ✕ **Bud & Alley's.** This beachside bistro has been a local favorite since 1986. Indoors the atmosphere is down to earth, with hardwood floors, ceiling fans, and 6-ft windows looking onto a herb garden. A screened-in porch provides the perfect setting for admiring the orange sunsets common in the fall. Daily salad specials are tangy introductions to such entrées as sesame-seared rare tuna on wild greens and rice-wine vinaigrette with soy dipping sauce. ✉ *Rte. 30A,* ☎ *850/231–5900. MC, V. Closed Tues. and Jan.*

$$–$$$ ✕ **Cafe Thirty-A.** In a beautiful Florida-style home with high ceilings
★   and a wide veranda, this restaurant has a casual yet elegant atmosphere, bolstered by white linen tablecloths and impeccable service. The menu changes nightly and includes such entrées as wood oven–roasted, spiced king salmon with fennel slaw and roasted new potatoes. Even if you're not a southerner, you should try the appetizer of grilled Georgia quail with creamy grits and sage fritters. With nearly 20 creative varieties, the martini menu alone is worth the trip. ✉ *3899 E. Rte. 30A, Seagrove Beach,* ☎ *850/231–2166. MC, V. No lunch Sun.*

$$$$ 🛏 **Seaside.** One- to six-bedroom porticoed faux-Victorian cottages are
★   furnished down to the vacuum cleaners, and decor reflects the owners' personalities. Gulf breezes blowing off the water remind you of the unspoiled sugar-white beaches a short stroll away. ✉ *Rte. 30A, 32459,* ☎ *850/231–2992, 800/277–8696, or 800/475–1841,* FAX *850/ 231–4196. 250 units. 3 pools, 6 tennis courts, badminton, croquet, boating, bicycles. AE, D, MC, V.*

$$–$$$ 🛏 **Josephine's Inn.** These charming accommodations offer gulf-view rooms with four-poster beds, fireplaces, and claw-foot tubs. The daily country-style breakfast is delicious. ✉ *101 Seaside Ave., 32459,* ☎ *850/ 231–1939 or 800/848–1840,* FAX *850/231–2446. 7 rooms, 2 suites. AE, MC, V.*

Outdoor Activities and Sports

An 8-ft-wide pathway covering 18 mi of scenic Route 30A winds past freshwater lakes, woodlands, and beaches. Bike rentals are available at **Big Daddy's Bikes and Beachsports** (✉ 4471 Rte. 30A, Seagrove Beach, ☎ 850/231–3811).

Shopping

Seaside's central square and open-air market, along Route 30A, offer a number of unique and whimsical boutiques carrying clothing, jewelry, and arts and crafts. **Perspicasity,** the beachside open-air market, sells simply designed women's clothing and accessories perfect for easy, carefree beach-town casualness. At **Ruskin Place Artist Colony,** in the heart of Seaside, a collection of small shops and artists' galleries features everything from toys and pottery to fine works of art.

Panama City Beach

❼ *21 mi southeast of Seaside.*

In spite of the shoulder-to-shoulder condominiums, motels, and amusement parks that make it seem like one big carnival ground, this coastal resort has a natural beauty that excuses its overcommercialization. The incredible white sands, navigable waterways, and plentiful marine life that attracted Spanish conquistadors bring family vacationers today.

At the **Panama City Beaches** (☎ 800/722–3224), public beaches along the Miracle Strip combine with the plethora of video-game arcades, miniature golf courses, sidewalk cafés, souvenir shops, and shopping centers to lure people of all ages.

Ⓒ Enjoy dozens of rides at **Miracle Strip Amusement Park,** from a traditional Ferris wheel to a roller coaster with a 65-ft drop. ✉ *12000 Front Beach Rd.,* ☎ *850/234–5810.* ☞ *$16.* ☉ *Apr.–May, Fri.–Sat. 6 PM– 11:30 PM; June–Labor Day, Sun.–Fri. 6 PM–11:30 PM, Sat. 1 PM–1:30 AM.*

Ⓒ There are 6 acres of water rides at **Shipwreck Island,** from speedy slides and tubes to the Lazy River. ✉ *12000 Front Beach Rd.,* ☎ *850/234– 0368.* ☞ *$19.* ☉ *Mid-Apr.–May, weekends 10:30–5; June–Labor Day, daily 10:30–5.*

Ⓒ Come to **Gulf World** to see bottle-nosed dolphin, sea lions, and otters perform. ✉ *15412 Front Beach Rd.,* ☎ *850/234–5271.* ☞ *$14.88.* ☉ *Feb.–May and Sept.–Oct., daily 9–3; June–Aug., daily 9–7; Nov.– Dec., holidays 9–3.*

★ Ⓒ At the eastern tip of Panama City Beach, the **St. Andrews State Recreation Area** includes 1,260 acres of beaches, pinewoods, and marshes. There are complete camping facilities here, as well as ample opportunities to swim, pier-fish, or hike the dunes along clearly marked nature trails. You can board a ferry to **Shell Island**—a barrier island in the Gulf of Mexico that offers some of the best shelling north of Sanibel Island. An artificial reef creates a calm, shallow play area that is perfect for young children. ✉ *4607 State Park La.,* ☎ *850/233–5140.* ☞ *$4 per vehicle with up to 8 people.* ☉ *Daily 8–sunset.*

Dining and Lodging

$$–$$$ ✕ **Capt. Anderson's.** Come early to watch the boats unload the catch of the day on the docks, and be among the first to line up to eat in this noted restaurant. The atmosphere is nautical, with tables made of hatch covers. The Greek specialties aren't limited to feta cheese and shriveled olives; charcoal-broiled fish and steaks have a prominent place on the menu as well. ✉ *5551 N. Lagoon Dr.,* ☎ *850/234–2225. AE, D, DC, MC, V. Closed Nov.–Jan.; Sun. May–Sept. No lunch.*

$–$$ ✕ **Billy's Steamed Seafood Restaurant, Oyster Bar, and Crab House.** Roll up your sleeves and dig into some of the gulf's finest blue crabs and shrimp seasoned to perfection with Billy's special recipe. Homemade gumbo, crawfish, and the day's catch as well as a variety of sandwiches and burgers round out the menu. Indoor and outdoor dining are available at this very casual spot. ✉ *3000 Thomas Dr.,* ☎ *850/ 235–2349. AE, D, DC, MC, V.*

$–$$ ✕ **Boar's Head.** An exterior that looks like an oversize thatch-roof cottage sets the mood for dining in this ersatz-rustic restaurant and tavern. Prime rib has been the number one people-pleaser since the house opened in 1978, but blackened seafood and broiled shrimp with crabmeat stuffing are popular, too. ✉ *17290 Front Beach Rd.,* ☎ *850/234– 6628. AE, D, DC, MC, V. No lunch.*

$$$–$$$$ 🏨 **Edgewater Beach Resort.** Luxurious one-, two-, and three-bedroom ★ units in beachside towers and golf-course villas are elegantly furnished with wicker and rattan. The resort centerpiece is a Polynesian-style lagoon pool with waterfalls, reflecting ponds, footbridges, and more than 20,000 species of tropical plants. ✉ *11212 Front Beach Rd., 32407,* ☎ *850/235–4044 or 800/874–8686,* ℻ *850/233–7529. 520 units. Restaurant, bar, golf, 12 tennis courts, shuffleboard, beach, recreation room. D, DC, MC, V.*

$$–$$$ 🏨 **Marriott's Bay Point Resort.** Renovated in January 1999, this pink-★ stucco property on the shores of Grand Lagoon exudes sheer elegance. Wing chairs, camel-back sofas, and Oriental carpets in the common areas recall an English manor house, as do the Queen Anne guest room furnishings. Gulf view or golf view—take your pick. Kitchen-equipped villas are a mere tee-shot away from the hotel, and a 200-slip marina serves boating enthusiasts. ⊠ *4200 Marriott Dr., 32408,* ☎ *850/234–3307 or 800/874–7105,* ℻ *850/234–0305. 355 rooms, 82 suites. 4 restaurants, 4 bars, indoor pool, 3 outdoor pools, hot tub, 2 golf courses, 10 tennis courts, health club, beach, dock, boating, fishing. AE, D, MC, V.*

$–$$$ 🏨 **Boardwalk Beach Resort.** This mile of beachfront has been staked out by a group of four family-oriented hotels: Howard Johnson, Four Points by Sheraton, Gulfwalk, and Beachwalk inns. It's not as glitzy as some of its neighbors, but the reasonable prices are hard to beat. All share the long beach, and group parties are given regularly by all four hotels. Each has its own pool. Refrigerators and microwaves are available in some rooms. ⊠ *9450 S. Thomas Dr., 32408,* ☎ *850/234–3484 or 800/224–4853,* ℻ *850/233–4369. 628 units. 8 restaurants, 3 bar/grills, 4 pools, beach, playground. MC, V.*

Nightlife and the Arts

THE ARTS

Broadway touring shows, top-name entertainers, and concert artists are booked into the **Marina Civic Center** (⊠ 8 Harrison Ave., Panama City, ☎ 850/769–1217).

NIGHTLIFE

Pineapple Willy's (⊠ 9900 S. Thomas Dr., ☎ 850/235–0928) alternately features big-band and rock music for a postcollege crowd.

Outdoor Activities and Sports

CANOEING

Rentals for a trip down Econofina Creek, "Florida's most beautiful canoe trail," are supplied by **Econofina Creek Canoe Livery** (⊠ Strickland Rd. north of Rte. 20, Youngstown, ☎ 850/722–9032).

DOG RACING

There's pari-mutuel betting year-round and live greyhound racing five nights and two afternoons a week at the **Ebro Greyhound Park.** Simulcasts of Thoroughbred racing from the Miami area are also shown throughout the year. Schedules change periodically, so call for details. ⊠ *Rte. 20 at Rte. 79, Ebro,* ☎ *850/535–4048.* 🎫 *$1, clubhouse $2.*

GOLF

The **Hombre Golf Club** (⊠ 120 Coyote Pass, ☎ 850/234–3673) has an 18-hole course. **Marriott's Bay Point Resort** (⊠ 100 Delwood Beach Rd., ☎ 850/235–6937 or 800/874–7105), open to the public, has 36 holes.

TENNIS

The tennis center at **Marriott's Bay Point Resort** (⊠ 100 Delwood Beach Rd., ☎ 850/235–6910) has 10 Har-Tru tennis courts.

Shopping

Stores in the **Manufacturer's Outlet Center** (⊠ 105 W. 23rd St., Panama City) offer well-known brands at a substantial discount. The **Panama City Mall** (⊠ U.S. 231 and Rte. 77, Panama City) has a mix of more than 100 franchise shops and national chain stores.

Apalachicola

8 *65 mi southeast of Panama City Beach.*

Meaning "land of the friendly people" in the language of its original Native American inhabitants, Apalachicola lies on the Panhandle's southernmost bulge. Settlers began arriving in 1821, and by 1847 the southern terminus of the Apalachicola River steamboat route was a bustling port town. Though the town is now known as the "Oyster Capital of the World," oystering only became king after the sponge colonies were depleted and the sponge industry moved down the coast. So if you like oysters or you want to go back in time to the Old South of Gothic churches and spooky graveyards, Apalachicola is a good place to start. Drive by the **Raney House,** circa 1850, and **Trinity Episcopal Church,** built from prefabricated parts in 1838.

Stop in at the **John Gorrie State Museum,** which honors the physician credited with inventing ice making and air-conditioning. Exhibits of Apalachicola history are displayed here as well. ⊠ *Ave. D and 6th St.,* ☎ *850/653-9347.* ⌖ *$1.* ☉ *Thurs.–Mon. 9–5.*

Dining and Lodging

$$–$$$ ✕ **Magnolia Grill.** A culinary treasure tucked away in an unimposing Florida-style cottage, this restaurant has a cozy, intimate dining room as well as a screened-in porch favored by those who prefer a more casual setting. The number of regular menu selections is astounding, and nightly specials often add another dozen or so items. One specialty is pastry-encased snapper Pontchartrain, with artichoke hearts, shrimp, and fresh almond slices in a creamy scampi sauce. Visit the dessert case for key lime pie or another of chef Eddie's homemade treats. ⊠ *133 Ave. E,* ☎ *850/653-8000. MC, V. Closed Sun. and 2½ wks following Thanksgiving. No lunch.*

$–$$ ✕ **Boss Oyster.** Eat your oysters fried, Rockefeller, or on the half shell at this laid-back eatery overlooking the Apalachicola River. Eat 'em alfresco at picnic tables or inside in the anything-goes atmosphere of the rustic dining room. If you're allergic to seafood, don't worry. The menu also features such staples as steak and pizza. ⊠ *123 Water St.,* ☎ *850/653-9364. AE, D, DC, MC, V.*

$–$$ ✕ **Gibson Inn.** You can hobnob with Apalachicola aristocracy as you dine in a serene, Edwardian setting at the town's traditional hotel. The dining room's a bit formal—crisp, creased linen tablecloths and fresh-cut flowers on the tables—and the food's impeccable. Sip a margarita in the adjacent bar. Then sample grouper Rockefeller; shrimp, scallop, and crab Dijon; or oysters Remick, in a horseradish-laced chili sauce with chopped Swiss cheese. ⊠ *51 Ave. C,* ☎ *850/653-2191. AE, MC, V.*

$$–$$$ ☷ **Coombs House Inn.** Nine fireplaces and an ornate oak staircase with leaded-glass windows on the landing lend authenticity to this restored 1905 mansion. No two guest rooms are alike, but all are appointed with Victorian-era settees, poster or sleigh beds, English chintz curtains, and Asian rugs on polished hardwood floors. Continental breakfast is served in the dining room. ⊠ *80 6th St., 32320,* ☎ *850/653-9199,* ⅸ *850/653-2785. 19 rooms. Bicycles. AE, MC, V.*

$–$$ ☷ **Gibson Inn.** One of a few inns on the National Register of Historic Places still operating as a full-service facility, this turn-of-the-century hostelry in the heart of downtown is easily identified by its wraparound porches, fretwork, and captain's watch. Rooms are furnished with period pieces, such as four-poster beds, antique armoires, and pedestal lavatories that have wide basins and porcelain fixtures. ⊠ *51 Ave. C, 32329,* ☎ *850/653-2191,* ⅸ *850/653-9097. 31 rooms, 4 suites. Restaurant, bar. AE, MC, V.*

St. George Island

❾ *8 mi southeast of Apalachicola.*

Pristine St. George Island sits 5 mi out into the Gulf of Mexico just south of Apalachicola. Accessed via the Bryant Patton Bridge off U.S. 98, the island is bordered by both the Apalachicola Bay and the gulf, offering vacationers the best of both. The rich bay is an angler's dream, while the snowy-white beaches and crystal-clear gulf waters satisfy even the most finicky beachgoer. You can indulge in bicycling, hiking, canoeing, and snorkeling, or find a secluded spot for reading, gathering shells, or bird-watching.

Accommodations on St. George Island mostly take the form of privately owned, fully furnished single-family homes, which allow for plenty of privacy (☞ Contacts and Resources *in* the Panhandle A to Z, *below*).

St. George Island State Park, on the east end of the island, has 9 mi of undeveloped beaches and dunes—the longest beachfront of any state park in Florida. Sandy coves, salt marshes, oak forests, and pines provide shelter for a variety of wildlife, including such birds as bald eagles and ospreys. ☎ *850/927–2111.* 🎫 *$3.25 per vehicle with up to 8 people.* ☉ *Daily 8–sunset.*

Dining

$$ ✕ **Oyster Cove Seafood Bar & Grill.** This blue-and-white cottage, tucked in among the trees, yields scenic views of the Apalachicola Bay through its large windows. Mediterranean grouper and shrimp Dijon are two of the restaurant's favored seafood dishes, but the house specialty is East Bay steak, a tender rib eye grilled with oysters and Spanish onions. Sometimes the restaurant closes from mid-November to mid-February; it's best to call ahead to check at that time of year. ⊠ *E. Pine and E. 2nd Sts.,* ☎ *850/927–2600. AE, MC, V. No lunch.*

$ ✕ **Blue Parrot.** You'll feel like you're sneaking in the back door as you climb the side stairs leading to an outdoor deck overlooking the gulf. Or if you can, grab a table indoors. During special event weekends, the place is packed, and service may be a little slow. The food is hard to beat if you're not looking for anything fancy. Baskets of shrimp, oysters, and crab cakes—fried or char-grilled and served with fries—are more than one person can handle. Daily specials are on the blackboard. ⊠ *216 W. Gorrie Dr.,* ☎ *850/927–2987. AE, MC, V.*

LOWER ALABAMA

Near Florida's border with Alabama, in "Lower Alabama," as the locals have labeled it, are several towns worth visiting. Small and unassuming, they often have surprising cultural attributes, such as the voluminous collections at the Robert L. F. Sikes Public Library in Crestview and the Walton-DeFuniak Public Library in DeFuniak Springs. The area also has its share of geologic oddities, such as the plunging pit of the Falling Waters Sink.

Crestview

❿ *33 mi north of Destin on Rte. 85.*

This is the sort of small town where the mayor rides shotgun with the police patrol on a Saturday night and folks enjoy the simpler pleasures, such as roller skating and playing softball. At 235 ft above sea level (quite high by Florida standards), Crestview was dubbed by surveyors of the Louisville & Nashville Railroad Company, which completed a line through northwest Florida in 1882. There has been a settlement of sorts here since the days of the conquistadors, when it was a cross-roads on the Old Spanish Trail.

The **Robert L. F. Sikes Public Library** (✉ 805 James Lee Blvd., ☎ 850/682–4432) and its research center, housed in an imposing Greek Revival building, contain more than 44,000 volumes as well as the private papers of its eponym, a former U.S. congressman.

Dining and Lodging

$ ✗ **McLain's Family Restaurant.** Assorted Wal-Mart art, piped-in country music, and a fireplace with a raised hearth give this mom-and-pop establishment a folksy feel that carries right over to the menu. The owners offer an all-you-can-eat buffet for lunch and dinner, always with a poached or broiled entrée. All steaks are hand-cut. On weekends a seafood buffet draws customers from as far away as Alabama. ✉ *2680 S. Rte. 85,* ☎ *850/682–5286. AE, D, MC, V.*

$ 🏨 **Crestview Holiday Inn.** This simple sandstone-and-stucco motel has typical Florida decor: shell-shape ceramic lamps, seashell-print bedspreads, and oceanic art on the walls. It's a bit south of downtown and is the *in* place for local wedding receptions. ✉ *Rte. 85 and I–10, Box 1358, 32536,* ☎ *850/682–6111,* FAX *850/689–1189. 120 rooms. Restaurant, bar, pool. AE, D, DC, MC, V.*

DeFuniak Springs

⑪ *28 mi east of Crestview.*

In 1848 the Knox Hill Academy was founded in this small town, and for more than half a century it was the only institution of higher learning in northwest Florida. In 1885 the town was chosen as the location for the New York Chautauqua educational society's winter assembly. The Chautauqua programs were discontinued in 1922, but DeFuniak Springs attempts to revive them, in spirit at least, by sponsoring a countywide Chautauqua Festival in April.

By all accounts the 16-ft by 24-ft **Walton-DeFuniak Public Library** is Florida's oldest library continuously operating in its original building. Opened in 1887 and added to over the years, it now contains nearly 30,000 volumes, including some rare books, many older than the structure itself. The collection also includes antique musical instruments and impressive European armor. ✉ *3 Circle Dr.,* ☎ *850/892–3624.* ☉ *Mon. 9–7, Tues.–Fri. 9–6, Sat. 9–3.*

The **Chautauqua Winery** (✉ I–10 and U.S. 331, ☎ 850/892–5887) opened in 1989, and its award-winning wines have earned raves from oenophiles nationwide. Take a free tour to see how ancient art blends with modern technology; then retreat to the tasting room.

Falling Waters State Recreation Area

⑫ *35 mi east of DeFuniak Springs.*

This is the site of one of Florida's most recognized geological features—the Falling Waters Sink. The 100-ft-deep cylindrical pit provides the background for a waterfall, and there's an observation deck for viewing this natural phenomenon. ✉ *Rte. 77A, Chipley,* ☎ *850/638–6130.* 🏷 *$3.25 per vehicle with up to 8 people.* ☉ *Daily 8–sunset.*

Florida Caverns State Park

⓭ *13 mi northeast of Falling Waters off I–10 on U.S. 231.*

Take a ranger-led spelunking tour to see an array of stalactites, stalagmites, and "waterfalls" of solid rock at this expansive park. There are also hiking trails, campsites, and areas for swimming and canoeing on the Chipola River. ✉ *Rte. 167, Marianna,* ☎ *850/482–9598.* *Park $3.25 per vehicle with up to 8 people, caverns $4.* ⏲ *Daily 8–sunset; cavern tours daily 9:30–4.*

TALLAHASSEE

⓮ *61 mi southeast of Florida Caverns.*

I–10 rolls east over the timid beginnings of the Appalachian foothills and through thick pines into the state capital, with its canopies of ancient oaks and spring bowers of azaleas. Home to Florida State University, the city has more than a touch of the Old South.

Tallahassee maintains a tranquil atmosphere quite different from the sun-and-surf hedonism of the major coastal towns. Vestiges of the city's colorful past are found throughout; for example, in the Capitol Complex, the turn-of-the-century Old Capitol building is strikingly paired with the New Capitol skyscraper. Tallahassee's tree-lined streets are particularly memorable—among the best canopied roads are St. Augustine, Miccosukee, Meridian, Old Bainbridge, and Centerville, all dotted with country stores and antebellum plantation houses.

Downtown

A Good Walk

The downtown area is compact enough so that most sights can be seen on foot, though it's also served by a free, continuous shuttle trolley. Start at the Capitol complex, which contains the **Old Capitol** and its counterpoint, the **New Capitol.** Across the street from the older structure is the restored **Union Bank Building,** and two blocks west of the new statehouse you'll find the **Museum of Florida History,** with exhibits on many eras of the state's history and prehistory.

If you really want to get a feel for old Tallahassee, walk the **Downtown Tallahassee Historic Trail** as it wends its way from the Capitol complex through several of the city's historic districts.

TIMING

You can't do justice to the Capitol complex and downtown area in less than two hours. Allow four hours to walk the 8-mi stretch of the historic trail. If you visit between March and April, you'll find flowers in bloom and the Springtime Tallahassee festival in full swing.

Sights to See

Downtown Tallahassee Historic Trail. A route originally mapped and documented by an eager Eagle Scout as part of a merit-badge project, this trail has since become a Tallahassee sightseeing staple. The starting point is the New Capitol, at whose visitor center you can pick up maps and descriptive brochures. You'll walk through the **Park Avenue and Calhoun Street historic districts,** which will take you back to Territorial days and the era of postwar reconstruction. The trail is dotted with landmark churches and cemeteries, along with outstanding examples of Greek Revival, Italianate, and Prairie-style architecture. Some houses are open to the public, including the **Brokaw-McDougall House,** which is a superb example of the Greek Revival and Italianate styles, and the **Meginnis-Monroe House,** which served as a field hospital during the Civil War and is now an art gallery.

Museum of Florida History. Here the long, intriguing story of the state's past—from mastodons to space shuttles—is told in lucid and entertaining ways. ⊠ *500 S. Bronough St.,* ☎ *850/488–1484.* ▣ *Free.* ☉ *Weekdays 9–4:30, Sat. 10–4:30, Sun. noon–4:30.*

★ **New Capitol.** This modern skyscraper looms up 22 stories directly behind the low-rise Old Capitol. On a clear day you can catch a panoramic view of Tallahassee and the surrounding countryside from the top floor. To pick up information about the area, stop at the Florida Visitors Center, on the plaza level. ⊠ *Duvall St.,* ☎ *850/488–6167.* ▣ *Free.* ☉ *Visitor center weekdays 8–5; self-guided or guided tours weekdays 8–5, weekends 9–3.*

★ **Old Capitol.** The centerpiece of the Capitol complex, this pre–Civil War structure has been added to and subtracted from several times. Its restored jaunty red-and-white-striped awnings and combination gas-electric lights make it look much as it did in 1902. Inside, historically accurate legislative chambers and exhibits offer an interesting peek into the past. ⊠ *S. Monroe St. at Apalachee Pkwy.,* ☎ *850/487–1902.* ▣ *Free.* ☉ *Self-guided or guided tours weekdays 9–4:30, Sat. 10–4:30, Sun. noon–4:30.*

Union Bank Building. Chartered in 1833, this is Florida's oldest bank building. Since it closed in 1843, it has played many roles, from ballet school to bakery. It has been restored to what is thought to be its original appearance and currently houses Florida A&M's Black Archives Extension, which depicts black history in Florida. ⊠ *Calhoun St. at Apalachee Pkwy.,* ☎ *850/487–3803.* ▣ *Free.* ☉ *Weekdays 9–4.*

Away from Downtown

Sights to See

Lake Jackson Mounds State Archaeological Site. Here are waters to make bass fishermen weep. For sightseers, Indian mounds and the ruins of an early 19th-century plantation built by Colonel Robert Butler, adjutant to General Andrew Jackson during the siege of New Orleans, are found along the shores of the lake. ⊠ *3600 Indian Mounds Rd.,* ☎ *850/922–6007.* ▣ *Free.* ☉ *Daily 8–sunset.*

Maclay State Gardens. In spring the grounds are afire with azaleas, dogwood, and other showy or rare plants. Allow half a day to wander past the reflecting pool, into the tiny walled garden, and around the lakes and woodlands. The Maclay residence, furnished as it was in the '20s; picnic areas; and swimming and boating facilities are open to the public. ⊠ *3540 Thomasville Rd.,* ☎ *850/487–4556.* ▣ *$3.25 per vehicle with up to 8 people.* ☉ *Daily 8–sunset.*

San Luis Archaeological and Historic Site. This museum focuses on the archaeology of 17th-century Spanish mission and Apalachee Indian town sites. In its heyday, in 1675, the Apalachee village here had a population of at least 1,400. Threatened by Creek Indians and British forces in 1704, the locals burned the village and fled. Visitors may take self-guided tours. ⊠ *2020 W. Mission Rd.,* ☎ *850/487–3711.* ▣ *Free.* ☉ *Weekdays 9–4:30, Sat. 10–4:30, Sun. noon–4:30.*

☾ **Tallahassee Museum of History and Natural Science.** At this museum a working 1880s pioneer farm offers daily hands-on activities for children, such as soap making and blacksmithing. A boardwalk meanders through the 52 acres of natural habitat that make up the zoo, which is home to such varied animals as panthers, bobcats, white-tailed deer, and black bears. Also on site are nature trails, a one-room schoolhouse dating to 1897, and an 1840s southern plantation manor, where you can usually find someone cooking on the weekends. ⊠ *3945 Museum Rd.,* ☎ *850/576–1636.* 🎟 *$6.* ☉ *Mon.–Sat. 9–5, Sun. 12:30–5.*

Dining and Lodging

$$–$$$ ✕ **Andrew's 2nd Act.** Part of a smart complex in the heart of the po-
   ★   litical district, this place serves up classic cuisine: elegant and under-
        stated. For dinner, the tournedos St. Laurent and the peppered New
        York strip are both flawless. Seafood lovers can feast on the day's fresh
        catch. ⊠ *228 S. Adams St.,* ☎ *850/222–3444. AE, DC, MC, V.*

$$–$$$ ✕ **Chez Pierre.** You'll feel as if you've entered a great aunt's old plan-
        tation home in this restored 1920s house set back from the road in his-
        toric Lafayette Park. Its warm cozy rooms, gleaming hardwood floors,
        and large French doors separating dining areas create an intimate
        atmosphere that's the perfect setting for authentic French cuisine. Try
        the tournedos of beef or one of the special lamb dishes. ⊠ *1215
        Thomasville Rd.,* ☎ *850/222–0936. AE, MC, V.*

 $–$$ ✕ **Barnacle Bill's.** The seafood selection is whale size, and it's steamed
   ★   to succulent perfection before your eyes, with fresh vegetables on the
        side. This popular hangout is famous for pasta dishes and home-
        smoked fish, too. Children eat for free on Sunday. ⊠ *1830 N. Mon-
        roe St.,* ☎ *850/385–8734. AE, DC, MC, V.*

   $ ✕ **Nicholson's Farmhouse.** The name says a lot about this friendly, in-
        formal country place with an outside kitchen and grill. Hand-cut steaks
        and chops are specialties of the house. ⊠ *From U.S. 27 follow Rte. 12
        toward Quincy and look for signs,* ☎ *850/539–5931. AE, D, MC, V.
        BYOB. Closed Sun.–Mon. No lunch.*

$$–$$$ 🏨 **Governors Inn.** Only a block from the Capitol, this plushly restored
   ★   historic warehouse is abuzz during the week with politicians, press, and
        lobbyists. It's a perfect location for business travelers and on weekends
        for tourists who want to visit downtown sites. Rooms are a rich blend
        of mahogany, brass, and classic prints. The VIP treatment includes air-
        port pickup, breakfast, cocktails, robes, shoe shine, and a daily paper.
        ⊠ *209 S. Adams St., 32301,* ☎ *850/681–6855; 800/342–7717 in FL;*
        FAX *850/222–3105. 40 units. Airport shuttle, free valet parking. AE,
        D, DC, MC.*

  $$ 🏨 **DoubleTree Hotel Tallahassee.** This upscale hotel a mere two blocks
        from the Capitol hosts heavy hitters from the worlds of politics and
        media. Since it's also an easy walk to the Florida State University cam-
        pus, it welcomes plenty of FSU fans during football season. ⊠ *101 S.
        Adams St., 32301,* ☎ *850/224–5000,* FAX *850/513–9516. 243 rooms.
        Restaurant, bar, pool, exercise room. AE, D, DC, MC, V.*

 $–$$ 🏨 **Shoney's Inn.** The quiet courtyard with its own pool and the darkly
        welcoming cantina (where a complimentary Continental breakfast is
        served) convey the look of old Spain. Rooms are furnished in heavy
        Mediterranean style. ⊠ *2801 N. Monroe St., 32303,* ☎ *850/386–8286,*
        FAX *850/422–1074. 112 rooms. Bar, pool. AE, D, DC, MC.*

Nightlife and the Arts

The Arts
Florida State University annually hosts 400 concerts and recitals given
year-round by its School of Music (☎ 850/644–4774), performances
of the **Tallahassee Symphony Orchestra** (☎ 850/224–0461) from October through April, and countless productions by its top theater program (☎ 850/644–6500). The **Monticello Opera House** (⊠ U.S. 90E,
Monticello, ☎ 850/997–4242) presents concerts and plays in a restored

1890s gaslight-era playhouse. The **Tallahassee Little Theatre** (⊠ 1861 Thomasville Rd., ☎ 850/224–8474) has a five-production season that runs from September through May.

Nightlife

Dave's CC Club (⊠ Sam's La. off Bradfordville Rd., ☎ 850/894–0181), legendary among blues clubs, hosts some of the world's finest blues on Friday and Saturday nights.

Outdoor Activities and Sports

Killearn Country Club & Inn (⊠ 100 Tyron Circle, ☎ 850/893–2144) has 27 holes of golf.

Side Trips

South to the Gulf

South of the capital and east of the Ochlockanee River are several fascinating natural and historical sites. Since they're near each other, you can string several together on an excursion from Tallahassee.

⑮ **Natural Bridge Battlefield State Historic Site** marks the spot where in 1865 Confederate soldiers stood firm against a Yankee advance on St. Marks. The Rebs held, saving Tallahassee—the only southern capital east of the Mississippi that never fell to the Union. Ten miles southeast of Tallahassee, the site is a good place for a hike and a picnic. If you visit the first week in March, you can watch a reenactment of the battle. ⊠ *Natural Bridge Rd. off Rte. 363, Woodville,* ☎ *850/922–6007.* ▨ *Free.* ⊘ *Daily 8–sunset.*

★ ⑯ Known for containing one of the deepest springs in the world, **Wakulla Springs State Park** remains relatively untouched, retaining the wild and exotic look it had in the 1930s, when Tarzan movies were made here. Take a glass-bottom boat deep into the lush, jungle-lined waterways to catch glimpses of alligators, snakes, nesting limpkins, and other waterfowl. An underground river flows into a pool so clear that you can see the bottom, more than 100 ft below. The park is 15 mi south of Tallahassee on Route 61. ⊠ *250 Wakulla Park Dr., Wakulla Springs,* ☎ *850/922–3632.* ▨ *$3.25 per vehicle with up to 8 people, boat tour $4.50.* ⊘ *Daily 8–sunset, boat tours hourly 9–4.*

⑰ As its name suggests, **St. Marks Wildlife Refuge and Lighthouse** is of both natural and historical interest. The once-powerful Fort San Marcos de Apalache was built here in 1639, and stones salvaged from the fort were used in the lighthouse, which is still in operation. In winter the refuge is home to thousands of migratory birds. The visitor center has information on more than 75 mi of marked trails. Twenty-five miles south of Tallahassee, the refuge can be reached via Route 363. ⊠ *1255 Lighthouse Rd., St. Marks,* ☎ *850/925–6121.* ▨ *$4 per car.* ⊘ *Refuge daily sunrise–sunset; visitor center weekdays 8–4:15, weekends 10–5.*

Spreading north of Apalachicola and west of Tallahassee and U.S. 319 is the **Apalachicola National Forest** (☎ 850/643–2282). Here you can camp, hike, picnic, fish, or swim.

CANOEING

Contact **TNT Hideaway** (⊠ U.S. 98 at the Wakulla River, near St. Marks, ☎ 850/925–6412), 18 mi south of Tallahassee, to canoe the Wakulla River.

DINING

$ ✗ **Wakulla Springs Lodge and Conference Center.** On the grounds of Wakulla Springs State Park, this facility serves three meals a day in a sunny, spartan room that seems little changed from the 1930s. Schedule lunch here to sample the famous bean soup, home-baked muffins, and a slab of pie. ⊠ *550 Wakulla Park Dr., Wakulla Springs,* ☎ *850/ 224–5950. MC, V.*

THE PANHANDLE A TO Z

Arriving and Departing

By Bus
The principal common carrier throughout the region is **Greyhound Lines** (☎ 800/231–2222), with stations in Crestview (☎ 850/682–6922), DeFuniak Springs (☎ 850/892–5566), Fort Walton Beach (☎ 850/243– 1940), Panama City (☎ 850/785–7861), Pensacola (☎ 850/476– 4800), and Tallahassee (☎ 850/222–4240).

By Car
The main east–west arteries across the top of the state are I–10 and U.S. 90. Pensacola is about an hour's drive east of Mobile. Tallahassee is 3½ hours west of Jacksonville.

By Plane
The **Pensacola Regional Airport** is served by **Comair** (800/354–9822), **Continental** (☎ 800/523–3273), **Delta** (800/221–1212), and **US Airways** (☎ 800/428–4322). A trip from the airport via **Yellow Cab** (☎ 850/ 433–1143) costs about $10 to downtown and $20 to Pensacola Beach.

Fort Walton Beach/Eglin AFB Airport/Okaloosa County Air Terminal is served by **AirTran** (☎ 800/825–8726), **Atlantic Southeast** (☎ 800/282– 3424), **Northwest** (☎ 800/225–2525), and **US Airways Express** (☎ 800/ 428–4322). A ride from the Fort Walton Beach airport via **Checker Cab** (☎ 850/244–4491) costs $12 to Fort Walton Beach and $20 to Destin. **Bluewater Car Service** (☎ 850/897–5239) charges $14 to Fort Walton Beach and $22 to Destin.

Panama City–Bay County Airport is served by Atlantic Southeast, **Northwest Airlink** (☎ 800/225–2525), and US Airways Express. **Yellow Cab** (☎ 850/763–4691) charges about $15–$27 to the beach area, depending on the location of your hotel. **DeLuxe Coach Limo Service** (☎ 850/763–0211) provides van service to downtown Panama City and to Panama City Beach for $1.25 per mile.

Tallahassee Regional Airport is served by Atlantic Southeast, Comair, Continental, Delta, and US Airways Express. **Yellow Cab** (☎ 850/ 222–3070) travels to downtown for $12–$15. Some Tallahassee hotels provide free shuttle service.

By Train
Amtrak (☎ 800/872–7245) has a Los Angeles–Panhandle route; its stops include Pensacola, Crestview, and Chipley.

Getting Around

By Boat
The Emerald Coast is accessible to yacht captains and sailors from the Intracoastal Waterway, which turns inland at Apalachicola and runs through the bays around Panama City to Choctawhatchee Bay and into Santa Rosa Sound.

By Car

It takes about four hours from Pensacola to Tallahassee. Driving along I–10 can be monotonous, but U.S. 90 piques your interest by routing you along the main streets of several county seats.

U.S. 98 snakes eastward along the coast, splitting into 98 and 98A at Inlet Beach before rejoining at Panama City and continuing down to Port St. Joe and Apalachicola. The view of the gulf from U.S. 98 can leave you oohing and ahing if the sun is out to distract you. If not, the fast-food restaurants, sleazy bars, and tacky souvenir stores are a little too noticeable.

Route 399 between Pensacola Beach and Navarre Beach takes you down Santa Rosa Island, a spit of duneland that juts out into the turquoise and jade waters of the Gulf of Mexico. It's a scenic drive if the day is clear; otherwise, it's a study in gray.

Major north–south highways that weave through the Panhandle are (from east to west) U.S. 231, U.S. 331, Route 85, and U.S. 29. From U.S. 331, which runs over a causeway at the east end of Choctawhatchee Bay between Route 20 and U.S. 98, the panorama of barge traffic and cabin cruisers on the twinkling waters of the Intracoastal Waterway will get your attention.

Contacts and Resources

Emergencies

Dial **911** for police or ambulance.

HOSPITALS

The following hospitals have 24-hour emergency rooms: **Columbia Fort Walton Beach Medical Center** (⊠ 1000 Mar-Walt Dr., Fort Walton Beach, ☎ 850/862–1111), **Columbia Gulf Coast Medical Center** (⊠ 449 W. 23rd St., Panama City, ☎ 850/769–8341), **Columbia West Florida Regional Medical Center** (⊠ 8383 N. Davis Hwy., Pensacola, ☎ 850/494–4000), and **Tallahassee Memorial Hospital** (⊠ Magnolia Dr. and Miccosukee Rd., Tallahassee, ☎ 850/681–1155).

Lodging Reservations

In the Beaches of South Walton, two of the larger vacation-rental management companies that handle furnished rentals and offer free vacation guides are **Abbott Resorts** (☎ 800/336–4853) and **Rivard of South Walton** (☎ 800/423–3215). On St. George Island, fully furnished homes can be rented through **Coldwell Banker Suncoast Realty** (☎ 800/341–2121) and **Prudential Resort Realty** (☎ 800/332–5196).

Visitor Information

Offices below are open from between 8 and 9 to between 4 and 5 unless otherwise stated. **Apalachicola Bay Chamber of Commerce** (⊠ 99 Market St., Apalachicola 32320, ☎ 850/653–9419) is open weekdays 9:30–4, Saturday 10–3. **Beaches of South Walton Visitor Information Center** (⊠ U.S. 331 and U.S. 98, Santa Rosa Beach 32459, ☎ 850/267–1216 or 800/822–6877) is open daily 8:30–6. **Crestview Area Chamber of Commerce** (⊠ 502 S. Main St., Crestview 32536, ☎ 850/682–3212) is open weekdays. **Destin Chamber of Commerce** (⊠ 1021 U.S. 98E, Destin 32541, ☎ 850/837–6241 or 850/837–0087) is open weekdays. **Emerald Coast Convention & Visitors Bureau** (⊠ 1540 Miracle Strip Pkwy. SE, Fort Walton Beach 32549, ☎ 850/651–7122 or 800/322–3319) is open daily. **Niceville/Valparaiso/Bay Area Chamber of Commerce** (⊠ 170 John Sims Pkwy., Valparaiso 32580, ☎ 850/678–2323) is open weekdays. **Panama City Beach Convention & Visitor Bureau** (⊠ 12015 W. Front Beach Rd., Panama City Beach 32407, ☎

850/233–6503 or 800/722–3224) is open daily. **Pensacola Visitor Information Center** (✉ 1401 E. Gregory St., Pensacola 32501, ☎ 850/434–1234 or 800/874–1234) is open daily. **Tallahassee Area Convention and Visitors Bureau** (✉ 200 W. College Ave., Tallahassee 32302, ☎ 850/413–9200 or 800/628–2866) is open weekdays. **Walton County Chamber of Commerce** (✉ 95 W. Circle Dr., DeFuniak Springs 32433, ☎ 850/892–3191) is open weekdays.

10 NORTHEAST FLORIDA

The northeast section of Florida is extraordinarily diverse. Narrow barrier islands run along the entire coast, all with beautiful beaches. Coastal cities and towns have vastly different characters—from remote Amelia Island to the cultivated city of Jacksonville to historic St. Augustine. Farther south lie the auto-racing mecca of Daytona Beach, quiet New Smyrna Beach, and bustling Cocoa Beach. Head inland and you'll find university towns, horse country, and a vast national forest.

Updated by
Pamela
Acheson

I N NORTHEASTERN FLORIDA YOU'LL FIND some of the oldest settlements in the state—indeed in all of the United States—though this region didn't get much attention until the Union army came through during the Civil War. The soldiers' rapturous accounts of the mild climate, pristine beaches, and lush vegetation captured the imagination of folks up north. First came the speculators and the curiosity seekers. Then the advent of the railroads brought more permanent settlers and the first wave of winter vacationers. Finally, the automobile transported the full rush of snowbirds, seasonal residents escaping from harsh northern winters. They still come, to sop up sun on the beach, to tee up in this year-round golfers' paradise, to bass-fish and bird-watch in forests and parks, and to party in the clubs and bars of Daytona (which has the dubious honor of replacing Fort Lauderdale as a top spring break destination).

This region of Florida is an area of remarkable diversity. Tortured, towering live oaks, plantations, and antebellum-style architecture recollect the Old South. The mossy marshes of Silver Springs and the St. Johns River look as untouched and junglelike today as they did generations ago. Horse farms around Ocala resemble Kentucky's bluegrass country or the hunt clubs of Virginia. St. Augustine is a showcase of early U.S. history, and Jacksonville is a young but sophisticated metropolis. Yet these are all but light diversions from northeastern Florida's primary draw—absolutely sensational beaches. Hugging the coast are long, slender barrier islands whose entire eastern sides comprise a broad band of spectacular sand. Except in the most populated areas, development has been modest, and beaches are lined with funky, appealing little towns.

New and Noteworthy
World Golf Village, a stunning but somewhat commercial complex dedicated to golf, continues to grow. Having opened its first course in 1998, it plans to add a second by late 1999, joining a golf academy, resort and conference center, and hall of fame.

Pleasures and Pastimes

Beaches
Beaches in northeastern Florida are luxuriously long. Some are hard-packed white sand, while others have slightly reddish sand with a fine, sugary texture. Surf is normally gentle, and many areas are safe for swimming. The very fragile dunes, held in place by sea grasses, are responsible for protecting the shore from the sea. Florida law mandates that you neither pick the sea oats nor walk on or play in the dunes. A single afternoon of careless roughhousing can destroy a dune forever.

The area's most densely developed beaches, with rows of high-rise condominiums and hotels, are in Daytona and Cocoa Beach. Elsewhere, coastal towns are still mostly small and laid-back, and beaches are crowded only on summer weekends.

Canoeing
Opportunities for canoeing are excellent here. Inland, especially in Ocala National Forest, sparkling-clear spring "runs" may be mere tunnels through tangled jungle growth. Grassy marshes near the coast and the maze of shallow inlets along the inland waterway side of Canaveral National Seashore are other favored canoeing spots.

Dining

The ocean, the Intracoastal Waterway, and numerous lakes and rivers are teeming with fish, and so naturally seafood is prominent on local menus. In coastal towns catches often come straight from the restaurant's own fleet. Shrimp, snapper, swordfish, and grouper are especially popular.

Fishing

From cane-pole fishing in a roadside canal to throwing a line off a pier to deep-sea fishing from a luxury charter boat, options abound. There's no charge (or a nominal one) to fish from many causeways, beaches, and piers. Deep-sea fishing charters are available up and down the coast.

Skydiving

Deland is the skydiving capital of the world. Spectators can watch high-flying competitions, while those interested in swooping down from an airplane that's thousands of feet up can try tandem jumping.

Exploring Northeast Florida

Much of this region's tourist territory lies along the Atlantic coast, both on the mainland and on the barrier islands that lie just offshore. A1A (mostly called Atlantic Avenue) is the main road on all the barrier islands, and it's here that you'll find the best beaches. The region defies any single description. In the far northeast are both the remote resort of Amelia Island, just south of the Georgia border, and Jacksonville, the only real high-rise city in northeast Florida. St. Augustine is the historic capital of this part of Florida. Farther south along the coast, the diversity continues among neighbors like Daytona Beach, where annual events geared toward spring-breakers, auto racers, and bikers create a party atmosphere; New Smyrna Beach, which offers quiet appeal; and Cocoa Beach, the ultimate boogie-board beach town. Inland are charming small towns, the sprawling Ocala National Forest, and bustling Gainesville, home of the University of Florida.

Great Itineraries

Even with 10 days, northeast Florida is too large to cover in depth, and even for a brief regional overview, you'd have to spend most of your time in the car. A better plan is to pick some spots that interest you and explore them more thoroughly.

Numbers in the text correspond to numbers in the margin and on the Northeast Florida and St. Augustine maps.

IF YOU HAVE 3 DAYS

Spend your first night in 🏨 **Jacksonville** ①, using it as a base to explore both the Jacksonville Museum of Contemporary Art and Amelia Island's Fort Clinch State Park, which contains one of America's best-preserved brick forts. Take I–95 south to **St. Augustine** ⑤–⑰ and see the restored **Spanish Quarter Museum** ⑧ before continuing down the coast. Enjoy Canaveral National Seashore, accessible from either 🏨 **New Smyrna Beach** ⑳ or 🏨 **Cocoa Beach** ㉑, and if the movie *Apollo 13* captured your attention, don't miss the Kennedy Space Center Visitor Complex.

IF YOU HAVE 5 DAYS

From 🏨 **Jacksonville** ① visit **Amelia Island** ④, including its historic district and Fort Clinch State Park; in town, see both the Jacksonville Museum of Contemporary Art and the Museum of Science and History. Going south on I–95, stop in 🏨 **St. Augustine** ⑤–⑰, where you can follow the Old City Walking Tour suggested by the **Visitor Information and Preview Center** ⑤ and stroll through the restored **Spanish Quar-**

ter Museum ⑧. Consider taking the slightly longer but more scenic Route A1A to ⊡ **Daytona Beach** ⑲, where you can visit the Museum of Arts and Sciences and the famous beaches. For your last night, stay in ⊡ **New Smyrna Beach** ⑳ or ⊡ **Cocoa Beach** ㉑, within reach of Canaveral National Seashore and Kennedy Space Center.

IF YOU HAVE 10 DAYS

As in the previous itineraries, start in ⊡ **Jacksonville** ① and visit the attractions mentioned above; by staying three nights, however, you can also see the Kingsley Plantation, Florida's oldest remaining plantation, and hike or picnic in Fort Clinch State Park on **Amelia Island** ④. Next, head to ⊡ **St. Augustine** ⑤–⑰. Three days here will enable you to conduct a more leisurely exploration of the extensive historic district and to take in the **Lightner Museum** ⑫, housed in one of Henry Flagler's fancy hotels. Another three-day stay, this time based at either ⊡ **Daytona Beach** ⑲, ⊡ **New Smyrna Beach** ⑳, or ⊡ **Cocoa Beach** ㉑, allows you to cover Daytona's Museum of Arts and Sciences, drive along the shoreline, spend some time at the beach, and see Canaveral National Seashore and the Kennedy Space Center Visitor Complex. Then head inland for a day in Ocala National Forest, a beautiful wilderness area.

When to Tour Northeast Florida

In December and January northeast Florida can get a bit chilly, but it still tends to fill up with Canadians escaping much colder temperatures. Auto-racing enthusiasts should be sure to visit Daytona in February, the height of the racing season. The ocean warms up by March, and college kids on spring break pack the beaches—but this is also the best month to see the azalea gardens in full bloom. Midsummer is breezy and hot but not as hot as in a northern city, as long as you stick to the beaches; inland, the summer heat and humidity can be stifling. If there's a shuttle launch during your visit, try to be near the Kennedy Space Center at the right time; it's an amazing sight to behold.

JACKSONVILLE TO AMELIA ISLAND

The northeasternmost corner of Florida is a land of tall pine trees, red earth reminiscent of neighboring Georgia, and coastal marshes. It can be 20 degrees colder than Miami in winter, and the "season" here (and the most expensive room rates) actually runs from April to September. Our discussion of the area starts in its hub—Jacksonville. From there we head to the coast, starting in the communities to the east, which serve as Jacksonville's beaches, and continuing north to Amelia Island and its old seaport town, Fernandina Beach.

Jacksonville

❶ *399 mi north of Miami, 120 mi south of Savannah, Georgia.*

One of Florida's oldest cities and, in terms of square miles (730), the largest U.S. city, Jacksonville makes for an underrated vacation spot. You'll find appealing downtown riverside areas, handsome residential neighborhoods, the region's only skyscrapers, and a thriving arts scene. Remnants of the Old South flavor the city, as does the sense of subtropical paradise for which Florida is famous.

Because Jacksonville was settled along both sides of the twisting St. Johns River, many attractions are on or near a riverbank, and the plentiful shoreline yields pretty vistas across the wide waterway. It helps to plan your trip carefully because both sides of the river, which is spanned by myriad bridges, have downtown areas and waterfront complexes of shops, restaurants, parks, and museums. Some attractions can be

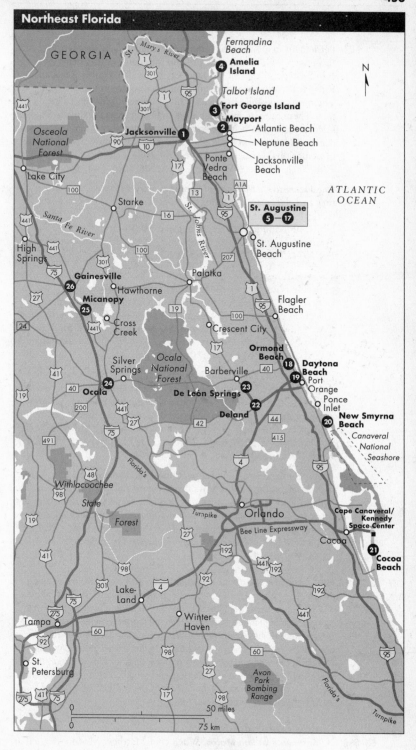

Northeast Florida

reached by water taxi, a handy alternative to driving back and forth across the bridges, but a car is generally necessary.

🐛 Permanent exhibits at the **Museum of Science and History** range from those on pre-Columbian history and the ecology and history of the St. Johns River to the Maple Leaf Civil War Collection, the hands-on Kidspace section, and a display on whales, dolphins, and manatees. The newest exhibit chronicles 12,000 years of northeast Florida history. There are also excellent, ever-changing special exhibits. Physical science shows are held weekends in the science theater. The Alexander Brest Planetarium features a popular 3-D laser show and many starry presentations throughout the year. ⊠ *1025 Museum Circle,* ☎ *904/ 396–7061.* ☞ *$6.* ⊙ *Weekdays 10–5, Sat. 10–6, Sun. 1–6.*

The **Jacksonville Museum of Contemporary Art** showcases contemporary and classic art, including the Koger collection of Asian porcelains, works by Pablo Picasso, and rare pre-Columbian artifacts. Special exhibits, film and lecture series, and workshops are also held. ⊠ *4160 Boulevard Center Dr.,* ☎ *904/398–8336.* ☞ *$3.* ⊙ *Tues.–Wed. and Fri. 10–4, Thurs. 10–9, weekends 1–5.*

The world-famous Wark Collection of early 18th-century Meissen porcelain is just one reason to see the **Cummer Gallery of Art.** Set amid leafy formal gardens, this former baron's estate includes 12 permanent collection galleries, displaying more than 2,000 items covering more than 4,000 years, and an interactive teaching gallery for kids and adults. ⊠ *829 Riverside Ave.,* ☎ *904/356–6857.* ☞ *$6, free Tues. 4– 9.* ⊙ *Tues. 10–9, Wed.–Sat. 10–5, Sun. noon–5.*

Fine collections of Boehm, Royal Copenhagen, Bing, and Grondahl porcelains are found at the **Alexander Brest Museum,** at Jacksonville University. Also on display are Steuben glass, cloisonné, pre-Columbian artifacts, and an extensive collection of ivories. The home of composer Frederick Delius, also on campus, has tours on request. ⊠ *2800 University Blvd. N,* ☎ *904/744–3950, ext. 3371.* ☞ *Free.* ⊙ *Weekdays 9–4:30, Sat. noon–5.*

🐛 A 10-year expansion and renovation of the **Jacksonville Zoo,** known for its outstanding collection of rare waterfowl, is still going on. The African Veldt is home to alligators, elephants, and white rhinos, among other species of African birds and mammals. Kids get a kick out of the petting zoo, and everyone goes ape over the newest exhibit, Great Apes of the World. ⊠ *8605 Zoo Rd., off Heckscher Dr. E,* ☎ *904/757–4462.* ☞ *$8.* ⊙ *Daily 9–5.*

OFF THE
BEATEN PATH   **FORT CAROLINE NATIONAL MEMORIAL –** Spread over 130 acres along the St. Johns River, 13 mi northeast of downtown Jacksonville via Route 113, this spot holds both historical and recreational interest. The original fort was built in the 1560s by French Huguenots, who were later slaughtered by the Spanish in the first major clash between European powers for control of what would become the United States. An oak-wooded pathway leads to a replica of the original fort—a great, sunny place to picnic (bring your own food and drink), stretch your legs, and explore a small museum. ⊠ *12713 Fort Caroline Rd.,* ☎ *904/641– 7155.* ☞ *Free.* ⊙ *Museum daily 9–5.*

Dining and Lodging

$$–$$$ ✕ **Matthew's at San Marco.** When chef Matthew Madure reigned at the Ritz-Carlton Amelia Island's dining room, he was the youngest ever to be in charge of a Ritz-Carlton signature restaurant. Now he's moved out on his own and into another smashing success. His small restau-

rant's spare decor (square edges, polished metal, blacks and whites) is a perfect foil for his dazzling cuisine—eclectic creations at their best. Try the sea bass fillet with tomato eggplant caviar, grilled bison with stewed Vidalia onions, or salmon escallop with foie gras and wild mushrooms, or be daring and order the five-course tasting menu, which changes nightly. ✉ *2107 Hendricks Ave.,* ☎ *904/396–9922. AE, DC, MC, V. Closed Sun. No lunch.*

$$–$$$ ✗ **Wilfried's 24 Miramar.** This stylish restaurant, with its long, narrow room minimally decorated in black and white, is hidden in a small shopping center on the south side of the river. The superb cuisine captures the essence of Californian, Asian, Latin, and Italian cooking, and it's difficult to choose among the inventive nightly specials. Intriguing starters include the spicy Thai crab cakes and crispy fried spinach. The hallmark dish is Beggar's Purse, a medley of lobster, scallops, shrimp, salmon, and mushrooms wrapped in phyllo pastry with a brandied lobster cream sauce. Chocolate soufflé is the renowned dessert here. ✉ *Miramar Shopping Center, 4446 Hendricks Ave.,* ☎ *904/ 448–2424. AE, MC, V. No lunch.*

$$–$$$ ✗ **Wine Cellar.** Thought by many to be the finest restaurant in Jack-
★ sonville, this elegant candlelighted spot specializes in classic Continental fare. Enjoy the house specialty—steak Diane—a fillet sautéed in butter, Madeira, shallots, mushrooms, and brandy. Or choose rack of lamb; grilled salmon with dill-mustard sauce; veal chop with morel sauce; or chicken topped with crabmeat, asparagus, and béarnaise sauce. Desserts include a bittersweet-chocolate mousse cake and a traditional cheesecake. ✉ *1314 Prudential Dr.,* ☎ *904/398–8989. Jacket required. AE, MC, V. Closed Sun. No lunch Sat.*

$–$$$ ✗ **River City Brewing Company.** Take one of the daily brewery tours at this popular south-bank brew pub overlooking the river; then sample the day's brew. Sandwiches and salads are featured at lunch, whereas dinner brings shrimp, fresh fish, grilled steaks, and seafood jambalaya. There's live music or a DJ Thursday–Saturday and jazz for Sunday brunch. ✉ *835 Museum Circle Dr., Southbank Riverwalk,* ☎ *904/398–2299. AE, MC, V.*

$ ✗ **Crawdaddy's.** Take it Cajun or cool. This riverfront fish shack, just off I–10 at I–95, is the place for seafood, jambalaya, and country chicken. Lunch is a sumptuous buffet, and there's a very popular Sunday brunch. Dig into the house specialty, catfish—all you can eat— then dance to a *fais-do-do* (Cajun dance) beat. ✉ *1643 Prudential Dr.,* ☎ *904/396–3546. AE, D, DC, MC, V.*

$$$ 🏨 **Jacksonville Omni Hotel.** This 16-story ultramodern facility is in the
★ heart of downtown. The splashy marble-floor lobby leads to the reception area, an upscale bar and lounge, and a restaurant with cozy banquettes and tables that look up to a soaring atrium. Sunday brunch is popular here. Extralarge rooms, many with spectacular river views, are stylishly decorated and include minibars. ✉ *245 Water St., 32202,* ☎ *904/355–6664,* 𝙁𝘼𝙓 *904/354–2970. 354 rooms. Restaurant, bar, pool, exercise room. AE, D, DC, MC, V.*

$$–$$$ 🏨 **Jacksonville Hilton.** Sitting right on the water, this handsome eight-
★ story, full-service hotel has a commanding presence. Its superb location on the south side of the St. Johns River puts it within easy walking distance of museums, restaurants, and the water taxi. Rooms are spacious, and many have outstanding river views and balconies. ✉ *1201 Riverplace Blvd., 32207,* ☎ *904/398–8800,* 𝙁𝘼𝙓 *904/398–5570. 290 rooms, 2 suites. 3 restaurants, bar, pool, spa, exercise room. AE, D, MC, V.*

$–$$ 🏨 **Comfort Suites Hotel.** In Baymeadows, near some currently "in" restaurants, clubs, and shops, this all-suites hotel is a real value. Units, decorated in breezy, radiant Florida hues, include refrigerators and sleep sofas. Master suites come with microwaves and VCRs. Rates include daily Continental breakfast and cocktails on weekdays. ⊠ *8333 Ellis Trail, 32256,* ☎ *904/739–1155,* FAX *904/731–0752. 128 suites. Pool, spa, jogging, coin laundry. AE, DC, MC, V.*

$–$$ ⊡ **House on Cherry St.** This early 20th-century treasure is furnished with pewter, Oriental rugs, antique canopy beds, and other remnants of a rich past. Fresh flowers in rooms add a nice touch, and Carol Anderson further welcomes guests to her riverside home with wine and hors d'oeuvres. A full breakfast is served. You can walk to the parks and gardens of the chic Avondale district. ⊠ *1844 Cherry St., 32205,* ☎ *904/384–1999. 4 rooms. Bicycles. MC, V.*

$–$$ ⊡ **Radisson Riverwalk Hotel.** This bustling five-story hotel, connected to the Riverwalk complex, has modern rooms with either a king-size or two double beds. It's within walking distance of four restaurants, a museum, and water taxis to Jacksonville Landing. Units overlooking the St. Johns River command the highest prices. ⊠ *1515 Prudential Dr., 32207,* ☎ *904/396–5100,* FAX *904/396–7154. 285 rooms, 19 suites. 3 restaurants, bar, no-smoking rooms, pool, 2 tennis courts. AE, DC, MC, V.*

$–$$ ⊡ **San Marco Point House.** In the style of an Old Florida cottage, this white and pale yellow house surrounded by tall oak trees provides both the homeyness of a B&B and a central location. Rooms are individually decorated—some wallpapered, some painted. The handsomest has a carved wooden bed and a peaceful view of the grassy yard. The inn is a two-minute drive from museums and a block from the St. Johns River. ⊠ *1709 River Rd., 32207,* ☎ *904/396–1448,* FAX *904/396–7760. 5 rooms. AE, MC, V.*

Nightlife and the Arts

THE ARTS

Broadway touring shows, top-name entertainers, and other major events are booked at the **Florida Theater Performing Arts Center** (⊠ 128 E. Forsyth St., ☎ 904/355–5661). The **Jacksonville Civic Auditorium** (⊠ 300 W. Water St., ☎ 904/630–0701) draws various types of popular entertainment; check local publications for schedules. The **Alhambra Dinner Theater** (⊠ 12000 Beach Blvd., ☎ 904/641–1212) serves up professional theater along with menus that change with each play. The oldest continuously operating community theater in the United States, **Theatre Jacksonville** (⊠ 2032 San Marco Blvd., ☎ 904/396–4425) features productions from Shakespeare to programs for children. The **Jacksonville Symphony Orchestra** (☎ 904/354–5479) presents a variety of concerts around town.

NIGHTLIFE

Cafe on the Square (⊠ 1974 San Marco Blvd., ☎ 904/399–4422) features live local blues, jazz, and rock bands Tuesday–Saturday. At **Club 5** (⊠ 1028 Park Ave., ☎ 904/355–1119), couples move to the sounds of alternative high-energy techno and disco music nightly. **River City Brewing Company** (⊠ 835 Museum Circle Dr., Southbank Riverwalk, ☎ 904/398–2299) showcases live local bands or DJs Thursday, Friday, and Saturday nights as well as jazz for Sunday brunch. At the **Roadhouse** (⊠ 797 Blanding Blvd., ☎ 904/264–0611), crowds dance to live alternative rock bands Thursday–Saturday.

Outdoor Activities and Sports

DOG RACING

Race seasons are split among three tracks. In town, the **Jacksonville Kennel Club** (⊠ 1440 N. McDuff Ave., ☎ 904/646–0001) runs races mid-April–November. The **Orange Park Kennel Club** (⊠ ½ mi south of I–295 on U.S. 17, ☎ 904/646–0001) has racing November–April. Dogs race at the **St. Johns Greyhound Park** (⊠ 7 mi south of I–95 on U.S. 1, ☎ 904/646–0001) March–April.

The region's blockbuster event is the **Gator Bowl** (☎ 904/396–1800), on New Year's Day. The NFL **Jacksonville Jaguars** (☎ 904/633–6000) play scheduled games all season.

Windsor Park Golf Club (⊠ 4747 Hodges Blvd., ☎ 904/223–4972) offers 18 holes of play with tree-lined fairways and natural marshlands.

Shopping

For a huge group of specialty shops and a number of restaurants, roam around the downtown **Jacksonville Landing** (⊠ 2 Independent Dr. at Main Street Bridge), on the north side of the river. The **Riverdale/Avondale Shopping Center** ⊠ 12 Riverside Ave.), in the heart of historic Avondale, is a quiet two-block area of one-of-a-kind art galleries, restaurants, and boutiques. Stop at the **San Marco Shopping Center** (⊠ 25 San Marco Blvd.) and wander through interesting stores and restaurants in 1920s Mediterranean Revival–style buildings.

Jacksonville Beaches

20 mi east of Jacksonville on U.S. 90 (Beach Blvd.).

Jacksonville's main beaches run along the barrier island that includes the popular, laid-back towns of Jacksonville Beach and Atlantic Beach and the area around Ponte Vedra Beach. The large number of private homes along Ponte Vedra's beaches makes access difficult, however.

Atlantic Beach is a favored surfing area. Around the popular Sea Turtle Inn you'll find catamaran rentals and instruction. Five areas have lifeguards on duty in the summer 10–6. **Neptune Beach,** south of Atlantic Beach, is more residential than its neighbor and offers easy access to quieter beaches. Surfers consider it one of the area's two best surfing sites, the other being Atlantic Beach. **Jacksonville Beach** is the liveliest of the long line of Jacksonville beaches. Young people flock here, and there are all sorts of games to play, beach concessions, rental shops, and a fishing pier.

Dining and Lodging

$$–$$$ ✗ **Gio's Cafe.** Dining areas on several levels make for a cozy atmosphere at this sophisticated Art Deco spot done in black and white. The cuisine is "Continental Italian with California flair," which means that a large selection of pasta creations share the menu with beef Wellington with a smoked lobster filling, veal and seafood dishes, and a roasted rack of lamb, prepared differently each night. The most popular dessert is the wild-berry fruit tart. ⊠ *900 Sawgrass Village, Ponte Vedra Beach,* ☎ *904/273–0101. AE, MC, V.*

$–$$ ✗ **Ragtime.** A New Orleans theme threads through everything from the Sunday jazz brunch to the beignets at this loud spot, popular with a sophisticated young bunch. If you aren't into creole and Cajun, have a simple po'boy sandwich or fish sizzled on the grill. Bouillabaisse, conch salad, and baked Brie are also good. ⊠ *207 Atlantic Blvd., Atlantic Beach,* ☎ *904/241–7877. AE, DC, MC, V.*

$ ✗ **Homestead.** A two-story log cabin built in 1934 is the setting for this down-home place, which has been around forever and is always busy. The specialty of the country-cooking restaurant is skillet-fried chicken with rice and gravy, but chicken and dumplings, deep-fried chicken gizzards, buttermilk biscuits, strawberry shortcake, and Sunday brunch also draw the locals. There are several dining rooms and a huge fireplace. ⊠ *1712 Beach Blvd., Jacksonville Beach,* ☎ *904/249–5240. AE, D, MC, V. No lunch.*

$$$$ 🏨 **Marriott at Sawgrass.** The grounds are beautifully manicured, but the main building and lobby areas feel more like a functional business hotel than a plush resort. Rooms are spacious and well appointed, with deep-color carpets and drapes, wood furniture, and roomy bathrooms. This is truly a full-service resort, and whether you've come to laze about or to spend your days busy with activities, you'll only need to leave the property to hit the beach. ⊠ *1000 TPC Blvd., Ponte Vedra Beach 32082,* ☎ *904/285–7777,* FAX *904/285–0906. 508 rooms, 21 suites. 3 restaurants, bar, 2 pools, wading pool, golf privileges, 36 holes of golf, putting green, 10 tennis courts, exercise room, horseback riding, boating, bicycles, children's programs. AE, D, DC, MC, V.*

$$$–$$$$ 🏨 **Ponte Vedra Lodge and Club.** At this small and elegant beachfront resort, white stucco and Spanish roof tiles yield a look that's Mediterranean villa grand luxe. Classy rooms with fancy window treatments and appealing artwork have cozy window seats and private balconies that overlook the Atlantic. Some have a whirlpool tub and gas fireplace. For more ocean views, try either of two restaurants, the bar, or the heated oceanfront pools, one of which is reserved for adults. Guests also have use of all the facilities—including four restaurants, two bars, 36 holes of golf, 15 tennis courts, a health club, and a full-service spa—at the lodge's much larger sister, the Ponte Vedra Inn & Club (☞ Outdoor Activities and Sports, *below*), which is 1½ mi up the road. ⊠ *607 Ponte Vedra Blvd., Ponte Vedra Beach 32080,* ☎ *904/273–9500 or 800/243–4304,* FAX *904/273–0210. 42 rooms, 24 suites. 3 restaurants, bar, 3 pools, golf privileges, health club, beach. AE, D, DC, MC, V.*

$$–$$$ 🏨 **Comfort Inn Oceanfront.** With the Atlantic as its front yard, this seven-story hotel offers ocean views from the private balconies of each of its soft pastel-color rooms. Kids of all ages have fun playing in four waterfalls that cascade into a giant free-form heated pool, and there are a rock grotto and spa. This is a great spot for families. ⊠ *1515 N. 1st St., Jacksonville Beach 32250,* ☎ *904/241–2311 or 800/654–8776,* FAX *904/249–3830. 165 rooms, 15 suites. Bar, deli, pool, spa, exercise room, beach, airport shuttle. AE, D, DC, MC, V.*

Nightlife

Ragtime Taproom Brewery (⊠ 207 Atlantic Blvd., Atlantic Beach, ☎ 904/241–7877) resonates with live local jazz and blues bands and progressive rock Thursday–Saturday.

Outdoor Activities and Sports

FISHING

One popular spot is the **Jacksonville Beach Fishing Pier,** which extends 1,200 ft into the Atlantic; the cost to fish is $3, 50¢ just to watch.

GOLF

Ponte Vedra Beach is home of the PGA Tour. **Ponte Vedra Inn & Club** (⊠ 200 Ponte Vedra Blvd., Ponte Vedra Beach, ☎ 904/285–1111 or 800/234–7842) offers 36 holes. **Ravines Inn & Golf Club** (⊠ 2932 Ravines Rd., Middleburg, ☎ 904/282–7888) has 18 holes. The 36-hole **Tournament Players Club at Sawgrass** (⊠ 110 TPC Blvd., Ponte Vedra Beach, ☎ 904/273–3235 or 800/457–4653) hosts the Tournament Players Championship in March.

TENNIS

Ponte Vedra Beach is the headquarters of the Association of Tennis Professionals (ATP). The **Marriott at Sawgrass** (☎ 904/285–7777) offers 19 courts. The **Ponte Vedra Inn & Club** (☎ 904/285–3856) has 15 Har-Tru courts.

Mayport

❷ *20 mi northeast of Jacksonville.*

Dating back more than 300 years, Mayport is one of the oldest fishing communities in the United States. Today it's home to several excellent and very casual seafood restaurants and a large commercial shrimp-boat fleet. It's also the navy's fourth-largest home port.

Kathryn Abbey Hanna Park is the area's showplace park. It offers beaches, showers, and snack bars that operate April–Labor Day.

En Route You can take your car on the fun **St. Johns River ferry** between Mayport and Fort George Island. ☎ *904/241–9969.* ✉ *$2.50 per car, pedestrians 50¢.* ⊘ *Daily 6:20 AM–10 PM every ½ hr.*

Fort George Island

❸ *25 mi northeast of Jacksonville.*

★ Built in 1792 by Zephaniah Kingsley, an eccentric slave trader, the **Kingsley Plantation** is the oldest remaining cotton plantation in the state. The ruins of 23 tabby (a cementlike mixture of sand and crushed shells) slave houses, a barn, and the modest Kingsley home are open to the public and reachable by ferry or bridge. ☎ *904/251–3537.* ✉ *Free.* ⊘ *Daily 9–5; ranger talks weekdays 1, weekends 1 and 3.*

At the **Talbot Island State Parks,** you'll find 17 mi of gorgeous beaches, sand dunes, and golden marshes that hum with birds and bugs. Come to picnic, fish, swim, snorkel, or camp. ✉ *12157 Heckscher Dr., Talbot Island,* ☎ *904/251–2320.* ✉ *$3.25 per vehicle with up to 8 people.* ⊘ *Daily 8–sunset.*

Amelia Island (Fernandina Beach)

❹ *35 mi northeast of Jacksonville.*

Although this island at the northeasternmost reach of Florida is a bit out of the way, it is worth the trip. Here you'll find 13 mi of beautiful beaches with enormous sand dunes along the island's eastern flank, a state park with a Civil War fort, sophisticated shops and restaurants, accommodations that range from bed-and-breakfasts to luxury resorts, and the quaint town of Fernandina Beach, on the northern end of the island, with its enchanting historic district. A century ago it sported thriving casinos and brothels, but those are gone, leaving Floridaís oldest continuously operating bar as the primary survivor of the town's wild days.

★ Stroll through the **Amelia Island Historic District,** containing more than 50 blocks of homes and other buildings listed on the National Register of Historic Places. Here 450 ornate structures built prior to 1927 offer some of the nation's finest examples of Queen Anne, Victorian, and Italianate mansions. Many date to the haven's glory days in the mid-19th century. Pick up a map for a self-guided tour at the chamber of commerce in the old railroad depot, once a stopping point on the first cross-state railroad.

Founded in 1859, **St. Peter's Episcopal Church** (✉ 801 Atlantic Ave., ☎ 904/261–4293) is a Gothic Revival structure with Tiffany glass-style memorials and an original, turn-of-the-century L. C. Harrison organ with magnificent hand-painted pipes. It once served as a school.

You'll probably recognize the **Amelia Island Lighthouse** (✉ 1 Lighthouse La., ☎ 904/261–3248) at first glance. This frequently photographed landmark, built in 1839, is one of the oldest structures on the island. It is still in operation and is visible 19 mi out to sea. The inside, however, is not open to the public.

★ One of the country's best-preserved and most complete brick forts can be found at **Fort Clinch State Park.** Fort Clinch was built to discourage further British intrusion after the War of 1812 and was occupied in 1863 by the Confederacy; a year later it was retaken by the North. During the Spanish-American War it was reactivated for a brief time but for the most part was not used. Today the 1,086-acre park offers camping, nature trails, carriage rides, swimming on a pristine beach, fishing in the surf or from a pier, picnicking, and numerous restored buildings to wander through, including furnished barracks, a kitchen, and a repair shop. Living-history reenactments showing life in the garrison at the time of the Civil War are periodically scheduled. Call for times. ⊠ *N. 14th St.,* ☎ *904/277–7274.* ⊠ *$3.25 per vehicle with up to 8 people.* ☉ *Daily 8–sunset.*

Amelia Island's eastern shore, which includes **Main Beach,** is one giant 13-mi stretch of white-sand beach edged with dunes, some 40 ft high. It's one of the few beaches in Florida where you are allowed to go horseback riding.

Dining and Lodging

$$$-$$$$ ★ ✕ **The Grill.** This award-winning signature restaurant of the Ritz-Carlton Amelia Island (☞ *below*) is quietly elegant and truly outstanding. Dine on seared bison tenderloin with grilled vegetables or salmon escallop with angel-hair pasta in tomato-basil oil. Those who choose the Adventurous Guest menu can sit back and relax while the chef creates a multicourse dinner especially for them. ⊠ *4750 Amelia Island Pkwy.,* ☎ *904/277–1100. Reservations essential. Jacket required. AE, DC, MC, V. No lunch.*

$$-$$$ ✕ **Beech Street Grill.** Hardwood floors, high ceilings, and marble fireplaces spread throughout many rooms create a pleasant environment in this lovingly restored 1889 sea captain's house. An extensive menu includes such house favorites as roasted lamb with mint and apple salsa, Parmesan-crusted red snapper with mustard-basil cream sauce, and crab-stuffed local shrimp with *tasso* (a Pacific Rim spice) ham gravy. A blackboard lists four or five fresh fish specials nightly. The outstanding wine list includes some coveted Californians. As this is an extremely popular restaurant, reservations are advised on weekends. ⊠ *801 Beech St.,* ☎ *904/277–3662. AE, MC, V. No lunch.*

$$-$$$ ★ ✕ **Down Under.** This casual place nestled at the edge of the A1A bridge has glorious views of the tranquil Intracoastal Waterway. Fresh local fish is the specialty here. Order baskets of fried shrimp or fried oysters; dine on stuffed tuna, shrimp scampi, or grilled tuna; or go for the seafood platter and a chance to taste it all. For landlubbers, chicken and steak are available. ⊠ *Rte. A1A at the Intracoastal Waterway,* ☎ *904/261–1001. AE, DC, MC, V. No lunch.*

$-$$ ★ ✕ **O'Kane's Irish Pub.** Stop here for authentic Irish fare: shepherd's pie, steak and Guinness pie, or fish-and-chips. Also on the menu are sandwiches, ribs, and pasta and an amazing soup that's served in a bowl of sourdough bread—you eat the whole thing! This is one of the few bars in the United States that still prepares Irish coffee the way they do in Ireland—with very cold, barely whipped heavy cream floating on top. ⊠ *318 Centre St.,* ☎ *904/261–1000. AE, MC, V.*

$$$$ ★ 🏨 **Ritz-Carlton Amelia Island.** Considered by many to be Florida's finest resort, this hotel woos guests with its stylish elegance, superb comfort, excellent service, and exquisite beach. All units in the eight-story building have balconies and ocean views. Suites and rooms are spacious and luxurious. Public areas are exquisitely maintained, grounds

are beautifully manicured, and fine cuisine can be had at a choice of restaurants, including the award-winning Grill. ⊠ *4750 Amelia Island Pkwy., 32034,* ☎ *904/277–1100. 449 rooms, 45 suites. 3 restaurants, 3 bars, indoor and outdoor pools, 18-hole golf course, 9 tennis courts, health club, beach, bicycles. AE, D, DC, MC, V.*

$$$–$$$$ 🏨 **Amelia Island Plantation.** This sprawling beachfront resort, one of the first to be "environmentally sensitive," encompasses ancient live-oak forests, marshes, lagoons, and some of the state's highest dunes. Some homes are occupied year-round, and a warm sense of community prevails. Accommodations range from home and condo rentals to a new full-service hotel: the Amelia Inn and Beach Club. Watch the sun rise over the Atlantic from large rooms done in pink and green. All have comfortable seating areas, balconies, and true ocean views. Much of the lobby is devoted to a popular piano bar, which is busy late into the evening. Though the resort is best known for golf and tennis, it's also a worthy destination for hiking and biking, as trails thread through the 1,300 acres. ⊠ *3000 First Coast Hwy., 32034,* ☎ *904/ 261–6161 or 800/874–6878,* FAX *904/277–5159. 250 rooms, 700 1- and 2-bedroom villas. 5 restaurants, 2 bars, 54 holes of golf, 23 tennis courts, health club, racquetball, beach, boating, fishing, bicycles, pro shops, children's programs. D, MC, V.*

$$–$$$ 🏨 **Elizabeth Pointe Lodge.** Built to resemble a Nantucket shingle-style house but blown up to the proportions of a lodge, this inn is set just behind the dunes. Oceanside units have great water views, albeit through disappointingly small windows. A chair-filled porch offers everyone a chance to rock in ocean breezes, and on cold nights guests can cluster around the living-room fireplace. Two adjacent cottages have suites. ⊠ *98 S. Fletcher Ave., Fernandina Beach, 32034,* ☎ *904/277– 4851. 25 rooms and suites. Beach. AE, MC, V.*

$$–$$$ 🏨 **Hoyt House Bed & Breakfast.** Follow a redbrick walkway up to this fine example of Queen Anne Victorian architecture, built in 1905. The house is wrapped by a wide veranda, where guests can relax in rockers. Shade trees keep the yard cool. Inside, inviting rooms show off antique and reproduction furniture and walls painted in rich hues. All rooms have private baths, and one has a whirlpool. In the late afternoon guests congregate in the parlor for complimentary wine and cheese. The house is in the historic district, just at the edge of downtown Fernandina Beach. ⊠ *804 Atlantic Ave., Fernandina Beach, 32034,* ☎ *904/277-4300 or 800/432–2085,* FAX *904/277–9626. 9 rooms. AE, MC, V.*

$$ 🏨 **Florida House Inn.** This rambling two-story clapboard inn, more than 100 years old, is definitely out of another era. Floors creak, and doorways are small. Rooms are decorated with four-poster beds, handmade quilts, and hooked rugs but have such modern amenities as king-size beds and whirlpool tubs. Some even have fireplaces. Guests relax in the cozy parlor and often dine in the popular restaurant, which serves heaping quantities at family-style breakfasts, lunches, and dinners. ⊠ *20 and 22 S. 3rd St., 32034,* ☎ *904/261–3300 or 800/258–3301,* FAX *904/277–3831. 15 rooms. Restaurant. AE, MC, V.*

$–$$$ 🏨 **Walford Inn.** A white picket fence frames the yard of this appealing inn a block from the heart of downtown Fernandina Beach. Oriental rugs lie on smooth hardwood floors. Spacious rooms contain stained-glass windows, fancy window treatments, and armoires and other antique and reproduction furnishings. Some have claw-foot tubs, others have whirlpools, and one has a working fireplace. A gourmet breakfast is served at a long mahogany table or outside on the porch. ⊠ *102 S. 7th St., 32034,* ☎ *904/277–6660 or 800/277–6660. 9 rooms. AE, MC, V.*

Outdoor Activities and Sports

GOLF

Designers Pete Dye, Bobby Weed, and Tom Fazio have created 54 challenging holes at the **Amelia Island Plantation** (✉ 3000 First Coast Hwy., ☎ 904/261–6161 or 800/874–6878). At the **Ritz-Carlton Amelia Island** (✉ 4750 Amelia Island Pkwy., ☎ 904/277–1100), live oaks, palm trees, and sand dunes frame 18 holes.

HORSEBACK RIDING

To gallop along the beach astride a horse, contact **Sea Horse Stables** (✉ 7500 First Coast Hwy., ☎ 904/261–4878).

TENNIS

Amelia Island Plantation (✉ 3000 First Coast Hwy., ☎ 904/277–5145 or 800/486–8366) sports 23 tennis courts and is the site of the nationally televised, top-rated Women's Tennis Association Championships in April and the Men's All-American Tennis Championship in September. The **Ritz-Carlton Amelia Island** (✉ 4750 Amelia Island Pkwy., ☎ 904/277–1100) features nine Har-Tru tennis courts.

Shopping

Within the Amelia Island Historic District are numerous shops, art galleries, and boutiques, many of which are clustered along cobblestoned **Centre Street**. The **Island Art Association Co-op Gallery** (✉ 205 Centre St., ☎ 904/261–7020) displays and sells paintings, prints, and other artwork by local artists.

ST. AUGUSTINE

35 mi south of Jacksonville.

Founded in 1565, St. Augustine claims to be the oldest U.S. city and has a wealth of historic buildings and attractions. Once you've visited the historic sites on the mainland, however, you haven't exhausted this city's charms; it also has 43 mi of beaches on two barrier islands to the east, both reachable by causeways. Several times a year St. Augustine holds historic reenactments, such as December's Grand Christmas Illumination, which marks the town's British occupation.

Exploring St. Augustine

The core of any visit is a tour of the historic district, a showcase for more than 60 historic sites and attractions, plus 144 blocks of historic houses listed on the National Register of Historic Places. You could probably spend several weeks exploring these treasures, but don't neglect other, generally newer, attractions found elsewhere in town. Pick the sights that interest you, as your time allows.

Numbers in the text correspond to numbers in the margin and on the St. Augustine map.

A Good Walk

A good place to start is the **Visitor Information and Preview Center** ⑤, where you can pick up maps, brochures, and information. It's on San Marco Avenue between Castillo Drive and Orange Street, right across from the big fort. From there cross Orange Street to reach the **City Gate** ⑥, the entrance to the city's popular restored area. Walk south on St. George Street to the **Oldest Wooden Schoolhouse** ⑦. Directly across from it is the **Spanish Quarter Museum** ⑧, a state-operated living-history village. Go out Fort Alley and cross San Marco Avenue to the impressive **Castillo de San Marcos National Monument** ⑨, a wonderful fort for exploring.

Now head west on Cuna Street and turn left on Cordova Street. Walk south three blocks to Valencia Street and turn right. At the end of the block you'll come to the splendid **Flagler Memorial Presbyterian Church** ⑩. Head one block south on Sevilla Street and turn left on King Street to find the **Museum of Historic St. Augustine Government House** ⑪ and two more of Henry Flagler's legacies: the **Lightner Museum** ⑫ and **Flagler College** ⑬. Continue two blocks east on King Street and turn right onto St. George Street to reach the **Ximenez-Fatio House** ⑭. For a taste of the turn of the century, head east on Artillery Lane to the **Oldest Store Museum** ⑮. Finally, head back north to the Bridge of Lions, the **Plaza de la Constitución** ⑯, and the **Basilica Cathedral of St. Augustine** ⑰.

TIMING

Though most sights keep the same hours (daytime only), a few are not open on Sunday, so it's best to visit Monday–Saturday. Besides, weekday mornings generally have the smallest crowds.

Sights to See

Anastasia State Recreation Area. Containing 1,700 protected acres of bird sanctuary, this Anastasia Island park draws families that like to hike, bike, camp, swim, and play on the beach. ⊠ *1340 Rte. A1A S,* ☎ *904/461–2033.* ⊡ *$3.25 per vehicle with up to 8 people.* ⊙ *Daily sunrise–sunset.*

⑰ **Basilica Cathedral of St. Augustine.** The cathedral holds the country's oldest written parish records, dating to 1594. Restored in the mid-1960s, the current structure (1797) had extensive changes after an 1887 fire. ⊠ *40 Cathedral Pl.,* ☎ *904/824–2806.* ⊡ *Donation welcome.* ⊙ *Weekdays 5:30 AM–5 PM, weekends 5:30 AM–7 PM.*

★ ⑨ **Castillo de San Marcos National Monument.** This massive structure looks every century of its 300 years. Park rangers provide an introductory narration, after which you're on your own to explore the moat, turrets, and 16-ft-thick walls. The fort was constructed of coquina, a soft limestone made of broken shells and coral. Built by the Spanish to protect St. Augustine from British raids (English pirates were handy with a torch), the fort was used as a prison during the Revolutionary and Civil wars. Garrison rooms depict the life of the era, and special cannon-firing demonstrations are held on weekends from Memorial Day to Labor Day. Children under 17 must be accompanied by an adult. ⊠ *1 Castillo Dr.,* ☎ *904/829–6506.* ⊡ *$4.* ⊙ *Daily 8:45–4:45.*

⑥ **City Gate.** The gate is a relic from the days when the Castillo's moat ran westward to the river and the Cubo Defense Line (defensive wall) protected against approaches from the north. ⊠ *St. George St.*

⑬ **Flagler College.** Originally one of two posh hotels Henry Flagler built in 1888, this building is a riveting structure replete with towers, turrets, and arcades decorated by Louis Comfort Tiffany. Now a small liberal arts college, the building is not open for tours, but you can look at the front courtyard. ⊠ *78 King St.,* ☎ *904/829–6481.*

⑩ **Flagler Memorial Presbyterian Church.** To look at a marvelous Venetian Renaissance structure, head to this church, built by Flagler in 1889. The dome towers more than 100 ft and is topped by a 20-ft Greek cross. ⊠ *Valencia and Sevilla Sts.* ⊙ *Weekdays 8:30–4:30.*

Fountain of Youth Archeological Park. Well north of St. Augustine's main sights is this tribute to explorer Ponce de León, marking the location of the legendary spring that flowed through folklore as the Fountain of Youth. In the complex is a springhouse, an explorer's globe, a planetarium, a Native American village, and exhibits about early Timucuan

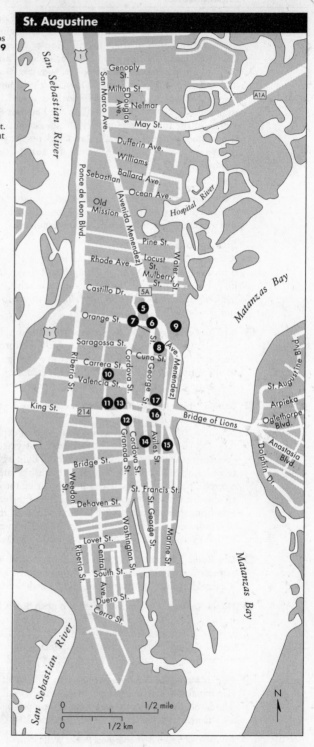

Indian inhabitants. ⊠ *155 Magnolia Ave.,* ☎ *904/829–3168.* ☒ *$4.75.* ☉ *Daily 9–5.*

★ ⑫ **Lightner Museum.** In his quest to turn Florida into an American Riviera, Henry Flagler built two fancy hotels in 1888—the Ponce de León, which became Flagler College (☞ *above*), and the Alcazar, which now houses this museum. The building showcases three floors of furnishings, costumes, and Victorian art glass plus a collection of ornate antique music boxes (demonstrations daily at 11 and 2). The Lightner Antiques Mall perches on three levels of what was the hotel's grandiose indoor pool. ⊠ *75 King St.,* ☎ *904/824–2874.* ☒ *$6.* ☉ *Museum daily 9–5.*

Mission of Nombre de Dios. This site, north of the historic district, commemorates where America's first Christian mass was celebrated. A 208-ft stainless-steel cross marks the spot where the mission's first cross was planted. ⊠ *San Marco Ave. and Old Mission Rd.,* ☎ *904/824–2809.* ☒ *Donation requested.* ☉ *Weekdays 8–5:30, weekends 9–5.*

⑪ **Museum of Historic St. Augustine Government House.** Featuring a collection of more than 300 artifacts from both archaeological digs and Spanish shipwrecks off the Florida coast, this museum reflects five centuries of history. ⊠ *48 King St.,* ☎ *904/825–5033.* ☒ *$3.* ☉ *Daily 10–5.*

Oldest House. Though the current building dates from the early 1700s, there has been a structure on this site since the early 1600s. Much of the city's history is seen in the building's changes and additions, from the coquina blocks used instead of wood soon after the town burned in 1702 to the house's enlargement during the British occupation. The house is a few blocks south of the Oldest Store Museum (☞ *below*). ⊠ *14 St. Francis St.,* ☎ *904/824–2872.* ☒ *$5.* ☉ *Daily 9–5.*

⑮ **Oldest Store Museum.** There are high-button shoes, lace-up corsets, patent drugs, and confectionery specialties at this re-creation of a turn-of-the-century general store. ⊠ *4 Artillery La.,* ☎ *904/829–9729.* ☒ *$5.* ☉ *Mon.–Sat. 9–5, Sun. noon–5.*

❼ **Oldest Wooden Schoolhouse.** Automated mannequins of a teacher and students relate the school's history. This tiny 18th-century building is built of cypress and cedar and thought to be one of the nation's oldest schoolhouses. Because it was the closest structure to the city gate, it served as a guardhouse and sentry shelter during the Seminole Wars. ⊠ *14 St. George St.,* ☎ *904/824–0192.* ☒ *$2.* ☉ *Daily 9–5.*

⑯ **Plaza de la Constitución.** The central area of the original settlement was laid out in 1598 by decree of King Philip II, and little has changed since. At its center is a monument to the Spanish constitution of 1812, while at the east end is a public market dating from Early American days. Just beyond is a statue of Juan Ponce de León, who "discovered" Florida in 1513. ⊠ *St. George St. and Cathedral Pl.*

St. Augustine Beach. This very popular strand is the closest beach to downtown. It's on the northern end of Anastasia Island, directly east of town. ⊠ *1200 Rte. A1A S,* ☎ *no phone.* ☒ *Free.*

❽ **Spanish Quarter Museum.** You can wander through the narrow streets at your own pace in this village comprising eight sites. Along your way you may see a blacksmith building his shop (a historic reconstruction) or artisans busy at candle dipping, spinning, weaving, and cabinetmaking. They are all making reproductions that will be used within the restored area. You'll find period artifacts and an orientation center in the **Triay**

House (⊠ 29 St. George St.), but buy your tickets at the Museum Store. ⊠ 33 St. George St., ☎ 904/825–6830. ⊠ $6. ☉ Daily 9–5.

Vilano Beach. The young gravitate to the public beaches at the southern tip of the barrier island just north of St. Augustine. ⊠ 3400 Coastal Hwy., ☎ no phone. ⊠ Free.

❺ Visitor Information and Preview Center. An entertaining film on the founding of St. Augustine, Dream of an Empire, is shown hourly 9–4. ⊠ 10 Castillo Dr., ☎ 904/825–1000. ⊠ $3. ☉ Daily 9–4.

OFF THE BEATEN PATH

WORLD GOLF HALL OF FAME – This stunning tribute to the game of golf is the centerpiece of World Golf Village, an extraordinary complex that includes golf courses, a golf academy, and a resort and convention center. The hall of fame features an IMAX theater as well as more than 70 separate exhibits that combine historical artifacts with the latest in interactive technology. ⊠ 21 World Golf Pl., ☎ 904/940–4200. ⊠ Hall of fame $9, IMAX film $6. ☉ Daily 10–6.

⑭ Ximenez-Fatio House. Originally built as a merchant's house and store in 1797, it became a tourist boardinghouse in the 1800s and is now restored as it was when it was an inn. ⊠ 20 Aviles St., ☎ 904/829–3575. ⊠ Donation welcome. ☉ Mon. and Thurs.–Sat. 11–4, Sun. 1–4.

Dining and Lodging

$$–$$$ ✕ **Old City House.** The dining room of a quaint bed-and-breakfast (☞
★   below) is the setting for this showcase of contemporary twists on traditional southwestern and Florida cuisine. Appetizers include alligator and smoked-sausage fritters, low-country fried grits, and chicken crepes. For entrées, try the grouper baked with horseradish and smoked bacon; the pork loin roulade filled with corn bread, fresh oysters, and apples; or the veal chop with a tomatillo and smoked jalapeño cream sauce. ⊠ 115 Cordova St., ☎ 904/826–0781. AE, MC, V. No lunch.

$$–$$$ ✕ **Raintree.** The oldest home in this part of the city, Raintree's building has been lovingly restored and is worth a visit even though the food is generally not outstanding. The buttery breads and pastries are baked on the premises. Try the rainbow trout, fillet of salmon, the vegetarian dishes, oven-roasted duck with raspberry sauce, or the Maine lobster special. The Raintree's madrigal-and-champagne dinners are especially fun. The wine list is impressive, and there's a selection of two dozen beers. Courtesy pickup is available from any lodging in the city. ⊠ 102 San Marco Ave., ☎ 904/824–7211. AE, DC, MC, V. No lunch.

$$ ✕ **La Parisienne.** Attentive and pleasantly lusty in its approach to hon-
★   est bistro cuisine, this tiny place in a white stucco building with a little flower-filled courtyard is a true find (which everyone has unfortunately now found). Weekend brunches are available, too. Try the roasted duck or chicken Provençale, but save room for the pastries at this excellent, very French restaurant. ⊠ 60 Hypolita St., ☎ 904/829–0055. Reservations essential. AE, MC, V. Closed Mon.

$–$$ ✕ **Columbia.** An heir to the original Columbia, founded in Tampa in 1905, this one serves time-honored Cuban and Spanish dishes: arroz con pollo, filet salteado (with a spicy sauce), and a fragrant paella. Sunday's Fiesta Brunch has everything from cheeses and cold meats to Belgian waffles. ⊠ 98 St. George St., ☎ 904/824–3341; 800/227–1905 in FL. AE, D, MC, V.

$–$$ ✕ **Florida Cracker Cafe.** Works by local artists adorn the walls of this
★   popular café in the heart of the historic district. Dine inside or outside on the shaded patio and enjoy fresh local seafood, pastas, salads, and hamburgers. Daily specials might include fried shrimp stuffed with crab

or seafood pasta salad. Key lime pie is the dessert of choice here. ⊠ *81 St. George St.,* ☎ *904/829–0397. AE, MC, V.*

$–$$ ✕ **Hooked on Harry's.** Though this casual eatery calls itself a seafood bar and grill, you might think you're on Bourbon Street when you step inside and get a whiff of the spicy cooking with a definite New Orleans flair. Red beans with rice and sausage, shrimp and crab étouffée, and jambalaya are house specialties, but the menu also includes po'boy burgers, fried oysters, blackened shrimp, and several spicy pastas. Tables are in several small rooms and are almost always full. ⊠ *46 Avenida Menendez,* ☎ *904/824–7765. AE, MC, V.*

$–$$ ✕ **King's Head British Pub.** Dark wood walls and a bar to belly up to lend an authentic touch to this English pub. Bangers and mash, fish-and-chips, steak and kidney pie, and other English pub fare are the order here as well as a superb selection of fine English beers on tap. ⊠ *6460 U.S. 1N,* ☎ *904/823–9787. AE, DC, MC, V.*

$ ✕ **Zaharias.** A short drive from downtown across the Bridge of Lions, this restaurant is big, busy, and buzzing with an air of open hospitality. Serve yourself from an enormous buffet instead of or in addition to ordering from the menu. Greek and Italian specialties include homemade pizza, a big gyro dinner served with a side of spaghetti, and shish kebabs, steaks, seafood, and sandwiches. ⊠ *3945 Rte. A1A S,* ☎ *904/ 471–4799. AE, MC, V. No lunch.*

$$$–$$$$ ▦ **Vistana Resort at World Golf Village.** Watch the action at the 17th
★ and 18th holes from many rooms at this golfer's haven. One- and two-bedroom units are in three six-story pink-and-green buildings that overlook a golf course and lakes in World Golf Village. Richly appointed rooms are painted deep shades of green or ochre and are decorated with framed prints and earth-tone fabrics. All units have a separate living room, a full kitchen, a washer and dryer, and a balcony. Nongolfers can spend their time relaxing by the pool or on the tennis courts. ⊠ *1 Front Nine Dr., 32092,* ☎ *904/940–2000 or 800/477–3340. 300 suites. 2 restaurants, 2 bars, pizzeria, 2 pools, 18-hole golf course, putting green, 10 tennis courts, health club. AE, D, DC, MC, V.*

$$–$$$ ▦ **Radisson Ponce de León Golf and Conference Resort.** Spread out over 350 acres, this resort and its lavish grounds are a spacious contrast to the narrow streets and crowds in the old city, and the location is a bit out of the way if you intend to spend a great deal of time sightseeing. There are plenty of other things to do, however. You can loll in the sun, seek the shade of century-old live oaks, or partake in many available sporting activities. Golf facilities include a regular course, a nine-hole pitch-and-putt course, and an 18-hole miniature putting course. Units range from standard rooms to oversize suites. ⊠ *4000 U.S. 1N, 32095,* ☎ *904/824–2821,* ℻ *904/824–8254. 200 rooms, 99 condos. Restaurant, bar, pool, 18-hole golf course, 6 tennis courts, croquet, horseshoes, jogging, shuffleboard, volleyball. AE, D, DC, MC, V.*

$$–$$$ ▦ **St. Francis Inn.** If the walls could whisper, this late-18th-century house would tell tales of slave uprisings, buried doubloons, and Confederate spies. The inn, a guest house since 1845, now offers rooms, suites, an apartment, and a five-room cottage. Furnishings are a mix of antiques and just plain old. It's in the historic district, and rates include Continental breakfast. ⊠ *279 St. George St., 32084,* ☎ *904/824–6068. 14 rooms, 2 suites. Pool, bicycles. MC, V.*

$$ ▦ **Carriage Way Bed and Breakfast.** A grandly restored Victorian
★ mansion, this B&B is within walking distance of the old town. Innkeepers Diane and Bill Johnson see to such welcoming touches as fresh flowers, home-baked breads, and evening cordials. A full breakfast is included in the rate. Special-occasion breakfasts, flowers, picnic lunches, romantic dinners, or a simple family supper can be arranged with ad-

vance notice. ⊠ *70 Cuna St., 32084,* ☎ *904/829–2467 or 800/908–9832. 9 rooms. Bicycles. D, MC, V.*

$$ 🏨 **Kenwood Inn.** For more than a century this stately Victorian inn
★ has welcomed wayfarers, and the Constant family continues the tradition. In the heart of the historic district, the inn is near restaurants and sightseeing. A Continental buffet breakfast of home-baked cakes and breads is included. ⊠ *38 Marine St., 32084,* ☎ *904/824–2116. 10 rooms, 4 suites. Pool. D, MC, V.*

$–$$$ 🏨 **Casablanca Inn on the Bay.** Centrally located just north of the Bridge of Lions and across the street from Matanzas Bay is where you'll find this restored 1914 stucco-and-stone house. Rooms vary in size and shape. Some have separate sitting rooms, some have views of the bay, and some have whirlpool tubs, but all are decorated with period and reproduction furniture. Breakfast is served at private tables in the sunny dining room or out on the patio. There's also a cozy parlor where you can sip a glass of complimentary sherry and curl up with a magazine or newspaper. Rates include a full breakfast. ⊠ *24 Avenida Menendez, 32084,* ☎ *904/829–0928,* ℻ *904/826–1892. 14 rooms, 4 suites. AE, D, DC, MC, V.*

$–$$$ 🏨 **Old City House Inn.** Although right downtown and close to everything, this charming inn is surrounded by brick walls and tall trees. The fully restored building is a fine example of Colonial Revival architecture. The light rooms, outfitted with eyelet bedspreads, are on the second floor, above the inn's restaurant, which is one of the best in the city. Each room has a private entrance, and a second-floor patio is reserved for guests. ⊠ *115 Cordova St., 32084,* ☎ *904/826–0113 or 800/653–4087,* ℻ *904/823–8960. 7 rooms. Restaurant. AE, MC, V.*

$–$$ 🏨 **Monterey Inn.** Location—right across from the Castillo de San Marcos National Monument and across the street from Matanzas Bay—is the draw of this modest two-story motel. It's within walking distance of many restaurants, museums, and shops. ⊠ *16 Avenida Menendez, 32084,* ☎ *904/824–4482,* ℻ *904/829–8854. 59 rooms. Coffee shop, pool. AE, D, DC, MC, V.*

Nightlife

Something is always happening at **Scarlett O'Hara's** (⊠ 70 Hypolita St., ☎ 904/824–6535). Some nights it's live blues, jazz, or reggae bands; on others it might be disco, Top 40, or karaoke; and many nights the early and late-night entertainment are completely different. **Trade Winds** (⊠ 124 Charlotte St., ☎ 904/829–9336) showcases live bands every night, from country and western to rock. Call for a schedule. Crowds head to **White Lion** (⊠ 20 Cuna St., ☎ 904/829–2388) for a variety of live music on Thursday, Friday, and Saturday.

Outdoor Activities and Sports

Fishing

Charter the *Sea Love II* (☎ 904/824–3328) or sign up to join a half- or full-day fishing trip.

Golf

The **Radisson Ponce de León Golf and Conference Resort** (⊠ 4000 U.S. 1N, ☎ 904/824–2821) offers 18 holes on a Donald Ross–designed championship course. You'll find 72 holes at the **Sheraton Palm Coast** (⊠ 300 Clubhouse Dr., Palm Coast, ☎ 904/445–3000). As part of its complex, **World Golf Village** (⊠ 21 World Golf Pl., ☎ 904/940–4000) has already opened an 18-hole layout named for and partially designed by Sam Snead and Gene Sarazen. A second course, the first designed collaboratively by Arnold Palmer and Jack Nicklaus, is scheduled for late 1999.

Tennis

The **Radisson Ponce de León Golf and Conference Resort** (✉ 4000 U.S. 1N, ☎ 904/824–2821) has six courts.

Water Sports

Surfboards and sailboards can be rented at the **Surf Station** (✉ 1002 Anastasia Blvd., ☎ 904/471–9463).

Side Trips

Marineland

🐚 *18 mi south of St. Augustine.*

One of the first aquarium attractions with shows ever built in the United States, Marineland is still a magic place. Dolphins grin, sea lions bark, and seals slither seductively to everyone's delight. The park has had financial problems and was closed temporarily, but it has reopened with limited hours. ✉ *Rte. A1A,* ☎ *904/460–1275.* 🎫 *$12.* ☉ *Wed.–Sun. 9:30–4:30.*

Ravine State Gardens

35 mi southwest of St. Augustine.

For a great picnic spot, make your way to one of the state's great azalea gardens, which began during the Depression as a WPA project. The ravines are atypical of flat Florida. They're steep and deep, threaded with brooks and rocky outcroppings, and floored with flatlands. Although any month is a good time to hike the shaded glens here, the azaleas are in full bloom in February and March. ✉ *Off Twig St. from U.S. 17S, Palatka,* ☎ *904/329–3721.* 🎫 *$3.25 per vehicle with up to 8 people.* ☉ *Daily 8–sunset.*

ALONG THE COAST

Daytona to New Smyrna Beach to Cocoa Beach

This section of coast covers only 75 mi yet comprises distinctly different areas, primarily because it includes three separate barrier islands. At the northern end are the small city of Daytona Beach and its neighbor to the north, Ormond Beach. Daytona is primarily known for auto racing and spring break, and its beach, which is at the southern end of the same barrier island that includes St. Augustine Beach, is fronted with a mixture of tall condos and apartments, hotels, and low-rise motels.

To the south is the small town of New Smyrna Beach. Its beach, which is lined with private houses, some empty land, and an occasional taller condominium, shares its own barrier island with Canaveral National Seashore and, farther south, the northern and inaccessible boundaries of the John F. Kennedy Space Center. As a result, the island is unusually unpopulated.

The towns of Cape Canaveral, Cocoa, and Cocoa Beach are still farther south and include the northern end of a third barrier island. Cocoa Beach is a laid-back beach town, but it gets crowded on weekends all year, as it's the closest beach to Orlando.

Ormond Beach

⑱ *60 mi south of St. Augustine.*

This town got its reputation as the birthplace of speed because early car enthusiasts such as Alexander Winton, R. E. Olds, and Barney Oldfield raced their autos on the sands here. The Birthplace of Speed Antique Car Show and Swap Meet is held every Thanksgiving, attracting enthusiasts from across the nation.

Ormond Beach borders the north side of Daytona Beach on both the mainland and the barrier island—nowadays you can't tell you've crossed from one to the other unless you notice the sign.

The scenic **Tomoka State Park** is a perfect location for fishing, camping, hiking, and boating. It is the site of a Timucuan Indian settlement discovered in 1605 by Spanish explorer Alvaro Mexia. Wooded campsites, bicycle and walking paths, and guided canoe tours on the Tomoka and Halifax rivers are the main attractions. ⊠ *2099 N. Beach St.,* ☎ *904/676–4050.* ⊑ *$3.25 per vehicle with up to 8 people; campsite $8 per day June–Dec., $16 per day Jan.–May; additional $2 for electric campsite.* ⊙ *Daily 8–sunset.*

Listed on the National Register of Historic Places, the **Casements,** the restored winter retreat of John D. Rockefeller, now serves as a cultural center and museum. Take a tour through the period Rockefeller Room, which displays some of the family's memorabilia. The estate and its formal gardens host an annual lineup of special events and exhibits; there is also a permanent exhibit of Hungarian folk art, musical instruments, and other utilitarian objects. ⊠ *25 Riverside Dr.,* ☎ *904/ 676–3216.* ⊑ *Donation welcome.* ⊙ *Mon.–Thurs. 9–9, Fri. 9–5, Sat. 9–noon.*

Take a walk through 4 acres of lush tropical gardens, past fish ponds and fountains, at the **Ormond Memorial Art Museum and Gardens.** Inside the museum are historical displays, a collection of symbolic religious paintings by Malcolm Fraser, and special exhibits by Florida artists. ⊠ *78 E. Granada Blvd.,* ☎ *904/676–3347.* ⊑ *Free.* ⊙ *Weekdays 10– 4, weekends noon–4.*

Dining and Lodging

$$–$$$ ✕ **La Crepe en Haut.** Outside stairs lead up to this quiet and elegant
★ classic French restaurant with several dining rooms and many window tables. Start with the onion soup, then try the fillet of beef with burgundy sauce or the roasted duck with berries, but leave room for a sweet fruit tart or a slice of creamy cheesecake from the dessert tray. The wine list includes many excellent French wines. ⊠ *142 E. Granada Blvd.,* ☎ *904/673–1999. AE, DC, MC, V. Closed Mon. No lunch Sat.*

$–$$ 🏨 **Mainsail Motel.** Although there is an attempt at a nautical motif, this three-story, U-shape building is rather plain looking. It is right on the beach, however. Rooms and suites are basic but comfortably furnished, rates are very reasonable, and management is caring. ⊠ *281 S. Atlantic Ave., 32176,* ☎ *904/677–2131,* 🖷 *904/676–0323. 48 rooms, 13 2-bedroom suites. Pool, wading pool, sauna, exercise room, beach. AE, D, DC, MC, V.*

Daytona Beach

⑲ *65 mi south of St. Augustine.*

Best known for the Daytona 500, Daytona has been the center of automobile racing since cars were first raced along the beach here in 1902. February is the biggest month for race enthusiasts, and there are weekly events at the International Speedway. During race weeks, bike weeks, the now notoriously popular spring breaks, and summer holidays, expect extremely heavy traffic along the strip of garishly painted motels, inexpensive restaurants, and tacky souvenir shops as well as on the beach itself, since driving on the sand is allowed. On the mainland, near the Inland Waterway, several blocks of Beach Street have been "street-scaped," and shops and restaurants open onto an inviting, broad brick sidewalk.

Daytona's newest attraction, **Adventure Landing** is a wet and dry park. On the water park side, kids of all ages float on a tube in the Lazy River, careen down 15 water slides, and get doused in the playhouse, where a 1,000-gallon bucket dumps water on them every eight minutes. If you don't want to get wet, you can still have fun. Race one- and two-seat go-carts on a ¼-mi, multilevel track. Play miniature golf on three different courses that thread through ominous caves and raging waterfalls. Or try your hand at any of 130 state-of-the-art video games and realistic simulators. ✉ *601 Earl St.,* ☎ *904/258–0071.* ▦ *Water park $19.95, miniature golf $6, go-carts $6 for single seat, $7.50 for double seat.* ⊙ *Daily 9–9.*

Racing enthusiasts make **Daytona USA** their first stop. The interactive motor-sports attraction lets visitors provide play-by-play commentary for a race, participate in a pit stop on a NASCAR Winston Cup stock car, computer-design their own race car, and talk to their favorite competitors through video. There's also an exhibit of the history of auto racing. Several cars are on display, including Dale Earnhardt's Number 3 Chevrolet Monte Carlo, which he drove to victory in the 1998 Daytona 500, and Sir Malcolm Campbell's fully restored Bluebird V, which reached 276 mph in the 1935 Daytona race, when races were still held on the beach. ✉ *1801 International Speedway Dr.,* ☎ *904/ 947–6800.* ▦ *$12.* ⊙ *Daily 9–6.*

One of only 12 photography museums in the country, the **Southeast Museum of Photography,** at Daytona Beach Community College, contains changing historical and contemporary exhibits. ✉ *1200 W. International Speedway Blvd.,* ☎ *904/254–4475.* ▦ *Donation welcome.* ⊙ *Tues. 10–3 and 5–7, Wed.–Fri. 10–4, weekends 1–4.*

The **Museum of Arts and Sciences** is one of the five largest museums in Florida. The humanities section includes displays of Chinese art and glass, silver, gold, and porcelain examples of decorative arts. The museum also has a large collection of pre-Castro Cuban art, Florida Native American items, pre-Columbian art, Indian and Persian miniature paintings, and an eye-popping complete skeleton of a giant sloth that is 13 ft long and 130,000 years old. ✉ *1040 Museum Blvd.,* ☎ *904/ 255–0285.* ▦ *$4.* ⊙ *Tues.–Fri. 10–4, weekends noon–5.*

Memorabilia from the early days of beach automobile racing are on display at the **Halifax Historical Society Museum,** as are historic photographs, Native American artifacts, a postcard exhibit, and a video that details city history. There's a shop for gifts and antiques, too. ✉ *252 S. Beach St.,* ☎ *904/255–6976.* ▦ *$3 Tues.–Fri., free Sat.* ⊙ *Tues.–Sat. 10–4.*

Daytona Beach, which bills itself as the "World's Most Famous Beach," permits you to drive your car right up to your beach site, spread out a blanket, and have all your belongings at hand; this is especially convenient for beachgoers who are elderly or have disabilities. However, heavy traffic during summer and holidays makes it dangerous for children, and families should be extra careful. The speed limit is 10 mph. To get your car on the beach, look for signs on Route A1A indicating beach access via beach ramps. Sand traps are not limited to the golf course, though—cars can get stuck.

PONCE INLET – At the southern tip of the barrier island that includes Daytona Beach is this sleepy town, where you'll find a small marina, a few bars, and informal restaurants specializing in very fresh fish. Boardwalks traverse delicate dunes and provide easy access to the beach, although recent storms have caused serious erosion. Marking this prime spot is the bright red, century-old **Ponce de León Lighthouse,** now a historic monument and museum. ⊠ *4931 S. Atlantic Ave.,* ☎ *904/761– 1821.* ☎ *$4.* ☉ *Daily 10–4.*

Dining and Lodging

$$–$$$$ ✕ **Gene's Steak House.** This family-operated restaurant, a bit west of town, has long upheld its reputation as *the* place for steaks. Completely rebuilt after a recent fire destroyed it, the steak house is still quiet and intimate, and the wine list is one of the state's most comprehensive. Though the menu does include seafood specialties, Gene's is basically a meat-and-potatoes paradise for beef eaters. ⊠ *4½ mi west of I–95/ I–4 interchange on U.S. 92,* ☎ *904/255–2059. AE, DC, MC, V. Closed Mon.*

$$ ✕ **Anna's Trattoria.** White table linens and flowers set the scene for
★ delightful Italian fare. Choose from two pages of delicious pasta items: spaghetti with Italian sausage and onions, angel-hair pasta with fresh chopped tomatoes and garlic, and spinach ravioli stuffed with spinach. There are also many veal and chicken dishes. ⊠ *304 Seabreeze Blvd.,* ☎ *904/239–9624. AE, MC, V. Closed Mon.*

$$ ✕ **Ristorante Rosario.** Chef Rosario Vinci has owned several successful restaurants in Florida, and Daytona is lucky that he chose this area for his latest venture. From the outside the building is not much to look at, but inside, candlelight creates an intimate atmosphere. The real draw, however, is the excellent northern Italian cuisine. Come here for tender veal marsala, *pollo pepperonata* (chicken breast sautéed in wine with roasted peppers and onions), or fresh local grouper poached in white wine. Pasta lovers can choose from a full page of selections, including tortellini *alla Rosario* and spaghetti *putanesca* (with sun-dried tomatoes, olives, capers, and anchovies). Save room for the sweet cannoli. ⊠ *5548 S. Ridgewood Ave., Port Orange,* ☎ *904/756–8800. MC, V. Closed Mon.*

$$ ✕ **St. Regis.** The creative menu here features such appetizers as shrimp cocktail and mushrooms stuffed with cheeses, followed by entrées like linguine with fresh vegetables, veal marsala, grilled filet mignon with a tangy mustard sauce, and breast of chicken with a berry salsa. Tables are in several intimate rooms and along the porch of this charmingly restored wooden house, built in the 1920s. ⊠ *509 Seabreeze Blvd.,* ☎ *904/252–8743. AE, MC, V. Closed Sun.*

$–$$ ✕ **Aunt Catfish's on the River.** This popular place on the southwest bank of the Intracoastal Waterway (off U.S. 1, just before you cross the Port Orange Causeway), just south of Daytona, is crowded day and night. Locals and visitors flock here for the great salad bar, the hot cinnamon rolls and hush puppies that come with any entrée, the southern-style chicken, and the freshly cooked seafood—fried shrimp, fried catfish, and crab cakes are specialties. ⊠ *4009 Halifax Dr., Port Orange,* ☎ *904/767–4768. AE, MC, V.*

$–$$ ✕ **McK's Tavern.** Crowds fill up the bar, the tables in the bar, and the cozy booths. The fare is simple but hearty—juicy burgers, spicy chili, homemade meat loaf and mashed potatoes, onion rings, and a long list of stuffed sandwiches. ⊠ *218 S. Beach St.,* ☎ *904/238–3321. AE, DC, MC, V.*

$$$–$$$$ ⊞ **Adam's Mark Resort.** Daytona's most luxurious high-rise hotel (15
★ stories) is set right on the beach, near the convention center and the
band shell. Every room has a great ocean view and is comfortably fur-
nished in pleasing pastels and blond oak. Guests can lounge around
the pool on the spacious deck or head to the beach. An elegant restau-
rant and a poolside bar are complemented by numerous other ameni-
ties. ⊠ *100 N. Atlantic Ave., 32118,* ☎ *904/254–8200 or 800/872–
9269,* FAX *904/253–0275. 420 rooms, 17 suites. 3 restaurants, bar, in-
door-outdoor pool, wading pool, beauty salon, health club, beach, play-
ground. AE, DC, MC, V.*

$$–$$$$ ⊞ **Daytona Beach Hilton.** Set right on the beach, this 11-story hotel is
a favorite with families. The pastel-color rooms are on the large side,
and most have balconies. Some have a kitchenette, patio, or terrace.
Convenient touches include a hair dryer, lighted makeup mirror, and
a bar with refrigerator. The rooftop restaurant affords awesome views
and is a popular stop for Sunday brunch. ⊠ *2637 S. Atlantic Ave., 32118,*
☎ *904/767–7350 or 800/525–7350,* FAX *904/760–3651. 214 rooms.
3 restaurants, 2 bars, pool, wading pool, hot tub, sauna, exercise
room, beach, video games, playground, coin laundry. AE, D, DC,
MC, V.*

$$–$$$ ⊞ **Perry's Ocean-Edge.** Long regarded as a family resort, Perry's is fa-
mous for its free homemade doughnuts and coffee—a breakfast ritual
served in the lush solarium. Units are in one two-story building and
two six-story buildings that face the beach. Three-quarters of the
rooms have kitchens, and most have great ocean views. Choose from
several pools, a wide beach, and a putting green. ⊠ *2209 S. Atlantic
Ave., 32118,* ☎ *904/255–0581 or 800/447–0002; 800/342–0102 in
FL;* FAX *904/258–7315. 108 rooms, 96 suites. Café, 1 indoor and 2 outdoor pools, putting green, shuffleboard, beach, video games. AE, D,
DC, MC, V.*

$$ ⊞ **Captain's Quarters Inn.** It may look like just another mid-rise hotel,
but the antique desk, Victorian love seat, and tropical greenery in the
lobby will change your mind. At this beachfront all-suite inn, freshly
baked goodies and coffee are served in the Galley, which overlooks the
ocean and resembles a family kitchen with a few extra tables and
chairs. Each guest suite features rich oak furnishings, a complete
kitchen, and a private balcony. Penthouse suites have fireplaces. ⊠ *3711
S. Atlantic Ave., Daytona Beach Shores 32127,* ☎ *904/767–3119,* FAX
904/760–7712. 25 suites. Pool, beach. AE, D, MC, V.

$$ ⊞ **Live Oak Inn.** This lovely B&B is in two restored homes next door
★ to each other, both listed on the National Register of Historic Places.
Each room is different, but all are beautifully furnished with antiques.
Some have long enclosed porches and look out over the marina or onto
gardens. Three have whirlpools. In the first floor of one house is a fine
restaurant and a small lounge and reception area. Downstairs in the
other is the breakfast room, and breakfast is included in the rate. ⊠
488 S. Beach St., 32114, ☎ *904/252–4667. 14 rooms. Restaurant, bar.
AE, MC, V.*

Nightlife and the Arts

THE ARTS

Broadway touring shows, symphony orchestras, international ballet companies, and popular entertainers appear at the **Ocean Center** (⊠ 101
N. Atlantic Ave., ☎ 904/254–4545; 800/858–6444 in FL). **Peabody
Auditorium** (⊠ 600 Auditorium Blvd., ☎ 904/255–1314) is used for
concerts and programs year-round. **Seaside Music Theater** (⊠ Box
2835, ☎ 904/252–3394) presents musicals in two venues January–March
and June–August.

NIGHTLIFE

Crowds flock to **Billy Bob's** (⊠ 2801 S. Ridgewood Ave., ☎ 904/756–0448) Tuesday–Saturday to dance to live country music. Popular **La Playa Penthouse Cocktail Lounge** (⊠ 2500 N. Atlantic Ave., ☎ 904/672–0990), on the top floor of the Best Western La Playa Resort, has a dance floor and live entertainment most nights. Acts range from contemporary musicians in their twenties to the original Platters, from the 1950s. If you're ready to twist, head to the **Memory Lane Rock and Roll Cafe** (⊠ 2424 N. Atlantic Ave., ☎ 904/673–5389), where DJs spin music from the '50s and '60s. **Razzles** (⊠ 640 N. Grandview St., ☎ 904/257–6236) is the hottest spot in Daytona. DJs play high-energy dance music from early evening to early morning.

Outdoor Activities and Sports

AUTO RACING

The massive **Daytona International Speedway,** on Daytona's major east–west artery, has year-round auto and motorcycle racing, including the Daytona 500 in February and the Pepsi 400 in July. ⊠ *U.S. 92,* ☎ *904/254–2700.* ⊙ *20-minute tours daily 9–5 except race days.*

DOG RACING

You can bet on the dogs every night but Sunday year-round at the **Daytona Beach Kennel Club** (⊠ U.S. 92 near International Speedway, ☎ 904/252–6484).

FISHING

Contact **Critter Fleet Marina** (⊠ 4950 S. Peninsula Dr., ☎ 904/767–7676) for full- or half-day deep-sea party trips.

GOLF

Indigo Lakes Golf Club (⊠ 312 Indigo Dr., ☎ 904/254–3607) offers 18 holes of golf. **Spruce Creek Golf & Country Club** (⊠ 1900 Country Club Dr., ☎ 904/756–6114) has an 18-hole course, a practice range, a driving range, and a pro shop.

WATER SPORTS

You can rent sailboards, surfboards, or boogie boards at the **Salty Dog** (⊠ 700 E. International Speedway Blvd., ☎ 904/258–0457).

Shopping

The **Volusia Mall** (⊠ 1700 W. International Speedway Blvd., ☎ 904/253–6783) has four anchor stores, including Burdines and Sears, plus many specialty shops. Daytona's **Flea Market** (⊠ I–4 at U.S. 92) is one of the South's largest.

New Smyrna Beach

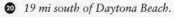 *19 mi south of Daytona Beach.*

This small town has a long dune-lined beach that abuts the Canaveral National Seashore. Behind the dunes sit beach houses, small motels, and an occasional high-rise (except at the extreme northern tip, none is higher than seven stories). Canal Street, on the mainland, and Flagler Avenue, home to many beachside shops and restaurants, have both been street-scaped and are now lined with wide brick sidewalks and stately palm trees. The town is also known for its internationally recognized artists' workshop.

Changing every two months, the gallery exhibits at the **Atlantic Center for the Arts** feature the works of internationally known artists. Mediums include sculpture, mixed media, video, drawings, prints, and paintings. Intensive three-week workshops are periodically run by visual, literary, and performing master artists such as Edward Albee, James

Dickey, and Beverly Pepper. ⊠ *1414 Art Center Ave.,* ☎ *904/427–6975.* ▣ *Free.* ☉ *Weekdays 9–5, Sun. 2–5.*

In a warehouse that has been converted into a stunning high-ceiling art gallery, **Arts on Douglas** features a new exhibit every month. All mediums are represented. Side galleries showcase the works of many Florida artists, including some remarkable metal sculptures by Doris Leeper. ⊠ *123 Douglas Ave.,* ☎ *904/428–1133.* ▣ *Free.* ☉ *Tues.–Sat. 10–5 and by appointment.*

Smyrna Dunes Park is on the northern tip of its barrier island. Here 1½ mi of boardwalks crisscross sand dunes and delicate dune vegetation as they lead to beaches and a fishing jetty. Botanical signs identify the flora, and there are picnic tables and an information center. ⊠ *N. Peninsula Ave.* ▣ *$3.* ☉ *Daily 7–sunset.*

New Smyrna Beach's public beach extends 7 mi from the northernmost part of the barrier island south to the Canaveral National Seashore. It is mostly hard-packed white sand, and from sunrise to sunset cars are allowed on certain parts (speed limit: 10 mph). The beach is lined with heaps of sandy dunes, but be warned: The dunes are endangered, and it's against the law to walk on or play in them or to pick the sea grass.

★ Miles of grassy, windswept dunes and a virtually empty beach await you at **Canaveral National Seashore,** a remarkable 57,000-acre park with 24 mi of undeveloped coastline. Stop at any of the six parking areas and follow the wooden walkways to the beach. Ranger-led weekly programs range from canoe trips to sea turtle talks. Call for a schedule. (For more information on sea turtles, check out the Close-Up in Chapter 4.) ⊠ *7611 S. Atlantic Ave.,* ☎ *904/428–3384.* ▣ *$5 per car.* ☉ *Daily 6–6.*

Dining and Lodging

$$–$$$ ★ ✕ **Skyline.** Watch private airplanes land and take off at the New Smyrna Beach airport as you dine on secretly seasoned Tony Barbera steaks, veal, shrimp, chicken, and fish. Both dining rooms are dimly lighted and elegant, and the lounge is a favorite spot for cocktails. A pianist plays music to dine by six nights a week, and there is a tiny dance floor. Prices are high for the area, but the fresh fish is excellent. ⊠ *2004 N. Dixie Fwy.,* ☎ *904/428–5325. AE, MC, V. No lunch.*

$–$$ ✕ **Chase's on the Beach.** Eat on a deck beneath the stars—gazing at either ocean or pool—or dine indoors. This place is popular day and night. Barefooted beachgoers wander up for beverages, hamburgers, and salads during the day (shoes required inside), whereas the evening crowd comes for fried shrimp, grouper sandwiches, and weekend entertainment. This is a great spot to see a night shuttle liftoff. ⊠ *3401 S. Atlantic Ave.,* ☎ *904/423–8787. AE, MC, V.*

$–$$ ★ ✕ **Victor's Backstreet Cuisine.** A blue neon sign lights the way to this tiny restaurant. Although the interior is humble—specials scrawled on a blackboard, tightly arranged wooden tables, and a small, open kitchen—the cuisine here is definitely bold. Spicy barbecue ribs, herb-seasoned tuna or chicken on a dense berry sauce, and sirloin with datil-pepper salsa are just some of the many choices. Specials could be filet mignon or ostrich prepared with a twist. You'll see Victor in the kitchen, working his culinary magic, and in the photos on the walls, accepting accolades. On weekends reservations are a must. ⊠ *103 S. Pine St.,* ☎ *904/426–5000. No credit cards. Closed Mon. No lunch.*

$ ★ ✕ **Toni and Joe's.** This longtime ultracasual favorite opens right onto the beach and has a large terrace perfect for people-watching. Head here (no shoes required) for the famous hoagies, long rolls of fresh bread stuffed with slices of steak, cheese, sweet peppers, and onions and heated until the cheese is perfectly melted. ✉ *309 Buenos Aires,* ☎ *904/427–6850. No credit cards.*

$ ✕ **Vincenzo's.** Vince and Annie run this casual spot with aplomb.
★ Vince is busy in the kitchen, cooking everything to order, and Annie's out front, greeting, seating, and charming the guests. The menu runs the gamut from subs to veal marsala, but the pizzas and pastas are the best around, from a dense and hearty lasagna to light angel-hair pasta with garlic and oil and florets of broccoli. The wine list is tiny but good, and the house wine, available by the glass or carafe, is a fine pinot grigio. ✉ *410 Flagler Ave.,* ☎ *904/423–4230. MC, V.*

$$–$$$ ⌂ **Holiday Inn Hotel Suites.** Families tend to like these comfortable suites, which sleep four, six, or eight people. Bedrooms are raised and set behind the living room, which opens out to a balcony and a spectacular view of the ocean. The furnishings are contemporary, and each unit has a full kitchen. ✉ *1401 S. Atlantic Ave., 32169,* ☎ *904/426–0020,* FAX *904/423–3977. 102 suites. Restaurant, bar, pool, beach. AE, MC, V.*

$$–$$$ ⌂ **Little River Inn Bed & Breakfast.** A formal driveway leads to this charming bed-and-breakfast in an Old Florida home built in 1883. The house, set on a slight rise, is surrounded by nearly 2 acres of oak trees and manicured green lawn and is across the road from the peaceful marshes of the Indian River. One guest room is on the first floor, three are on the second, and two are on the third. All have views of the river. Guests gather for breakfast in the sunny dining room, relax in a rocker on the wide terrace, or settle in a corner of the living room with a good book. Breakfast is included in the rate. ✉ *532 N. Riverside Dr., 32168,* ☎ *904/424–0100. 6 rooms. Bicycles. AE, MC, V.*

$–$$$ ⌂ **Riverview Hotel.** This former bridge tender's home, a landmark since
★ 1886, is set back from the Intracoastal Waterway at the edge of the North Causeway, which to this day has an operating drawbridge. Rooms open out to plant-filled verandas and balconies, and views look either through trees to the Intracoastal or onto the private courtyard and pretty pool. Each room is furnished differently with charming antique touches, such as an old washbasin, a quilt, or a rocking chair. A complimentary Continental breakfast is served in your room. The inn has an excellent gift shop and is near interesting art galleries and stores. ✉ *103 Flagler Ave., 32169,* ☎ *904/428–5858 or 800/945–7416,* FAX *904/423–8927. 19 rooms. Restaurant, pool, bicycles. AE, D, DC, MC, V.*

$–$$ ⌂ **Coastal Waters Inn.** Popular with families, this three-story, blue-and-white beachfront hotel has one- and two-bedroom suites with kitchens as well as standard rooms. Some units have excellent ocean views, and many have balconies or patios. Furnishings are spare but comfortable. The beach is literally steps away. ✉ *3509 S. Atlantic Ave., 32169,* ☎ *904/428–3800,* FAX *904/423–5002. 8 rooms, 32 suites. Pool, beach. AE, D, DC, MC, V.*

Nightlife

For remarkable jazz, stop by **Clancy's East Coast Grill** (✉ 1443 S. Dixie Fwy., ☎ 904/427–1090), where you can listen to the mellow sounds of well-known pianist Harold Blanchard most Saturday evenings.

Shopping

Flagler Avenue (North Causeway) is the major entranceway to the beach, and art galleries, gift shops, and surf shops line the street. Art lovers will want to stop at **Arts on Douglas** (✉ 123 Douglas St., ☎ 904/428–1133), displaying works by 50 artists plus a solo exhibit, which changes monthly.

Cocoa and Cocoa Beach

50 mi south of New Smyrna Beach.

The town of **Cocoa,** on the mainland, includes the quaint shopping area known as Olde Cocoa Village. Cocoa's neighbor on the barrier island ㉑ is **Cocoa Beach,** a popular year-round escape for folks who live in Central Florida. Motels and inexpensive restaurants line the beach, and Kennedy Space Center is just 10 minutes away.

North of Cocoa, **Playalinda Beach,** part of the **Canaveral National Seashore,** is the longest stretch of undeveloped coast on Florida's Atlantic seaboard. Hundreds of giant sea turtles come ashore here between May and August to lay their eggs, and the extreme northern area is favored by nude sun worshipers. There are no lifeguards, but park rangers patrol. Take Exit 80 from I–95 and follow Route 406 east across the Indian River, then Route 402 east for another 12 mi. ⊠ *Rte. 402, Titusville,* ☎ *407/267–1110.* ➡ *$5 per car.* ☉ *Daily 6–6.*

At the 140,000-acre **Merritt Island National Wildlife Refuge,** which adjoins the Canaveral National Seashore, you can see wildlife and rivers of grass up close. Wander along nature trails at this habitat for wintering migratory waterfowl, and take a self-guided, 7-mi driving tour along Black Point Wildlife Drive. On the Oak Hammock Foot Trail, you can learn about the plants of a hammock community. ⊠ *Rte. 402, across Titusville causeway,* ☎ *407/861–0667.* ➡ *Free.* ☉ *Daily sunrise–sunset.*

★ ℭ The **Kennedy Space Center Visitor Complex** is perhaps the best entertainment bargain in Florida. There are two narrated bus tours: One passes by some of NASA's office and assembly buildings, including current launch facilities and the space-shuttle launching and landing sites. The other goes to Cape Canaveral Air Force Station, where early launch pads and unmanned rockets that were later adapted for manned use illuminate the history of the early space program. Even more dramatic is the IMAX film *The Dream Is Alive,* shown hourly in the Galaxy Theater. Projected onto a 5½-story screen, this overwhelming 40-minute film, most of which was shot by the astronauts, takes you from astronaut training, through a thundering shuttle launch, and into the cabins where the astronauts live while in space. (Other exciting films capture footage from nine space-shuttle flights and focus on the earth from 200 mi up.) ⊠ *Rte. 405, Kennedy Space Center,* ☎ *407/452–2121 or 800/572–4636.* ➡ *Free, bus tours $8, IMAX film $6.* ☉ *Daily 9–sunset, last tour 2 hrs before dark; closed certain launch dates (call ahead).*

At the entrance to the Kennedy Space Center Visitor Complex, the **United States Astronaut Hall of Fame** focuses not only on the milestones of the space program but on the personal stories of the astronauts. Board a space shuttle replica to view videos of historic moments. ⊠ *6225 Vectorspace Blvd., off Rte. 405, Kennedy Space Center, Cocoa,* ☎ *407/ 269–6100.* ➡ *$13.95.* ☉ *Daily 9–5.*

The **Astronaut Memorial Planetarium and Observatory,** one of the largest public-access observatories in Florida, features a 24-inch telescope through which visitors can view objects in the solar system and deep space. The planetarium has two theaters that offer a choice of films. The Science Quest Hall houses an exhibit of scales calibrated to other planets. Weight watchers are thrilled to step on these. Travel 2½ mi east of I–95 Exit 75 on Route 520, and take Route 501 north for 1¾ mi. ⊠ *1519 Clearlake Rd., Cocoa,* ☎ *407/634–3732.* ➡ *Observatory and exhibit hall free, film $4.* ☉ *Open evenings but schedule changes monthly; call for current schedule.*

Don't overlook the hands-on discovery rooms and the Taylor Collection of Victorian memorabilia at the ☾ **Brevard Museum of History and Natural Science.** Its nature center has 22 acres of trails encompassing three distinct ecosystems—sand pine hills, lake lands, and marshlands. ⊠ *2201 Michigan Ave., Cocoa,* ☏ *407/632–1830.* ⚑ *$4.* ☾ *Mon.– Sat. 10–4, Sun.1–4.*

Cocoa Beach (⊠ Rte. A1A, ☏ 407/868–3274) has showers, playgrounds, changing areas, picnic areas with grills, snack shops, and plenty of well-maintained, inexpensive surf-side parking lots. Beach vendors offer a variety of necessities for sunning and swimming.

Exhibits of contemporary art; presentations of decorative arts, ethnographic works, photography, and experimental art forms; and hands-on activities for children are the draws at the ☾ **Brevard Museum of Art and Science.** ⊠ *1463 Highland Ave., Melbourne,* ☏ *407/242–0737.* ⚑ *$5.* ☾ *Tues.–Sat. 10–5, Sun. 1–5.*

Dining and Lodging

$$$ ✕ **Mango Tree Restaurant.** Dine in elegance at tables discretely spaced amid orchid gardens, with piano music playing in the background. House favorites include fresh grouper with shrimp and scallops glazed in hollandaise sauce and veal *française* à la Mango Tree (scallopini, very lightly breaded and glazed with a mushroom sauce). ⊠ *118 N. Atlantic Ave., Cocoa Beach,* ☏ *407/799–0513. AE, MC, V. Closed Mon. No lunch.*

$$ ✕ **Black Tulip.** Two cozy rooms create an intimate setting for elegant
★ cuisine in pleasant Cocoa Village. Starters include tortellini *Bolognese* (with ground veal, marinara sauce, and Parmesan), crab-stuffed mushrooms, and a delicious black-bean soup. Choose from such entrées as roast duckling with apples and cashews, steak au poivre, or linguine with chicken in a garlic and white wine sauce. Lunch selections are lighter and include sandwiches and salads. ⊠ *207 Brevard Ave., Cocoa,* ☏ *407/631–1133. AE, DC, MC, V.*

$$ ✕ **Cafe Margaux.** Choose indoor or outdoor seating at this small, romantic spot in restored Cocoa Village. The menu features an eclectic mix of classical French and Italian cuisine. Try the roast duck with berries or the fillet of beef with port wine sauce. ⊠ *220 Brevard Ave., Cocoa,* ☏ *407/639–8343. AE, DC, MC, V. Closed Tues.*

$ ✕ **Lone Cabbage Fish Camp.** The natural habitat of wildlife and local characters, this one-of-a-kind spot sits on the St. Johns River, 9 mi north of the Cocoa city limits and 4 mi west of I–95. Catfish, turtle, country ham, and alligator make the drive worthwhile. You can also fish from a dock here, buy bait, rent a canoe, or take an airboat ride (reservations essential). Check out the gator souvenirs behind the bar and the Swamp Monster, stuffed and mounted on the wall; it was "caught" by one of the owners, Charlie Jones. ⊠ *8199 Rte. 520, Cocoa,* ☏ *407/ 632–4199. No credit cards.*

$$–$$$ ⌷ **Cocoa Beach Hilton Oceanfront.** It's easy to pass by the Hilton, as its sign is sometimes hidden by the dense natural foliage that grows right out to the edge of Route A1A. Once you turn into the parking lot, however, it's impossible to miss. At seven stories, it's one of the tallest buildings in Cocoa Beach. Just a small strip of sand dunes separates this resort from a wide stretch of excellent beach. Most rooms have ocean views, but for true drama get a room on the east end directly facing the water. The floor-to-ceiling windows really show off the scenery. ⊠ *1550 N. Atlantic Ave., Cocoa Beach 32931,* ☏ *407/ 799–0003 or 800/526–2609,* ☎ *407/799–0344. 288 rooms, 9 suites. Restaurant, bar, pool, beach, video games, baby-sitting. AE, D, DC, MC, V.*

$$-$$$
★
🖬 **Inn at Cocoa Beach.** The finest accommodations in Cocoa Beach are in this charming oceanfront inn. Each spacious room is decorated differently, but all have some combination of reproduction 18th- and 19th-century armoires, four-poster beds, and comfortably upholstered chairs and sofas. There are several suites, some with whirlpool baths. All units have balconies or patios and views of the ocean. Included in the rate are an evening spread of wine and cheese and a sumptuous Continental breakfast with delicious homemade muffins and breads, served in the sunny breakfast room. ⊠ *4300 Ocean Beach Blvd., Cocoa Beach 32931,* ☎ *407/799–3460; 800/343–5307 outside FL;* FAX *407/784–8632. 46 rooms, 4 suites. Pool, beach. AE, D, MC, V.*

$-$$
🖬 **Wakulla Motel.** This popular motel is clean and comfortable and just two blocks from the beach. The bright rooms are decorated in tropical prints. Completely furnished five-room suites, designed to sleep six, are great for families; they comprise two bedrooms, a living room, dining room, and fully equipped kitchen. Outdoor grills are available. ⊠ *3550 N. Atlantic Ave., Cocoa Beach 32931,* ☎ *407/783–2230,* FAX *407/783–0980. 116 suites. 2 pools, shuffleboard, volleyball. AE, D, DC, MC, V.*

Outdoor Activities and Sports
Cape Marina (⊠ 800 Scallop Dr., Port Canaveral, ☎ 407/783–8410) has half- and full-day charter fishing trips.

Shopping
Ron Jon Surf Shop (⊠ 4151 N. Atlantic Ave., Cocoa Beach, ☎ 407/799–8840) is a local attraction in its own right—a castle that's purple, pink, and glittery as an amusement park, plunked right down in the middle of the beach community. This multilevel store is packed with swimwear and surfboards and is open 24 hours a day. It's worth a stop just to see what all those billboards are about.

In downtown Cocoa cobblestone walkways wind through **Olde Cocoa Village,** a cluster of restored turn-of-the-century buildings now occupied by restaurants and specialty shops purveying crafts, fine art, and clothing.

INLAND TOWNS

Inland you'll find peaceful little towns separated by miles and miles of two-lane roads running through acre upon acre of dense forest and flat pastureland and skirting one lake after another. Here you'll see cattle and not much else, but you'll also catch a glimpse of the few hills found in the state. Gentle and rolling, they're hardly worth noting to folks from true hill country, but they're significant enough in Florida for much of this area to be called the "hill and lake region."

Deland

㉒ *21 mi southwest of Daytona Beach.*

This quiet university town is home to Stetson University, established in 1886 by the eponymous hat magnate John Stetson. Other than the university, there isn't much to see, but several inviting state parks are nearby. As for other activities, there's great manatee watching during the winter as well as skydiving for both spectators and participants.

Soaring ceilings and neoclassical decor provide the backdrop at the **Duncan Gallery of Art,** on the Stetson University campus. The gallery hosts exhibits by southwestern and national artists and Stetson students. ⊠

Sampson Hall, Michigan and Amelia Aves., ☎ *904/734–4371.* ✉ *Donation welcome.* ☉ *Weekdays 10–4, weekends 1-4.*

One of the largest private collections of gems and minerals in the world can be found in the **Gillespie Museum of Minerals,** on the Stetson University campus. ✉ *Michigan and Amelia Aves.,* ☎ *904/822–7330.* ✉ *Donation welcome.* ☉ *Weekdays 9–noon and 1–4.*

February is the top month for sighting manatees, but they begin to head here in November, as soon as the water gets cold enough (below 68°F). **Blue Spring State Park,** once a river port where paddle wheelers stopped to take on cargoes of oranges, also contains a historic homestead that is open to the public. You can hike, camp, or picnic here. Your best bet for spotting a manatee is to walk along the boardwalk. ✉ *2100 W. French Ave., Orange City,* ☎ *904/775–3663.* ✉ *$4 per vehicle with up to 8 people.* ☉ *Daily 8–sunset.*

Dining and Lodging

$$ ✕ **Pondo's.** You lose about 50 years as you step into what was once a romantic hideaway for young pilots who trained in Deland during the war. The owner-chef specializes in whimsical veal dishes, but he also does fish, beef, and chicken. The old-fashioned bar will remind you of *Cheers,* and a pianist entertains Friday and Saturday. ✉ *1915 Old New York Ave.,* ☎ *904/734–1995. AE, MC, V.*

$–$$ ✕ **Dublin Station.** This large and dimly lighted bar and restaurant has dark wood walls, a wooden floor, and a thoroughly Irish streak. Nevertheless, in addition to lagers and ales, meat pies, and fish-and-chips, you can get chops, steaks, burgers, and salads. Seating is at a long bar, at tables in a lounge and dining room, in comfortable booths, or outside along the sidewalk. But whether it's day or night, the place is always busy. ✉ *105 W. Indiana Ave.,* ☎ *904/740–7720. AE, MC, V.*

$ ✕ **Original Holiday House.** This, the original of what has become a small chain of buffet restaurants, is enormously popular with senior citizens, families, and especially with college students (it's right across from the Stetson University campus). Patrons can choose from three categories: salads only, salads and vegetables only, or the full buffet. ✉ *704 N. Woodland Blvd.,* ☎ *904/734–6319. MC, V.*

$$–$$$ ▦ **Holiday Inn Deland.** Picture a little college town with a snazzy big-city hotel run by friendly, small-town folks with city savvy. An enormous painting by nationally known local artist Fred Messersmith dominates the plush lobby. Rooms are done in subdued colors and styles; prestige suites have housed the likes of Tom Cruise. Tennis and golf privileges at the Deland Country Club are offered. ✉ *350 E. International Speedway Blvd. (U.S. 92), 32724,* ☎ *904/738–5200 or 800/826–3233,* 𝖥𝖠𝖷 *904/734–7552. 138 rooms, 11 suites. Restaurant, bar, pool, golf privileges, nightclub. AE, D, MC, V.*

$–$$$ ▦ **University Inn.** For years this has been the choice of business travelers and visitors to Stetson University. Conveniently located on campus and next door to the popular Holiday House (☞ *above*) restaurant, this motel has clean, comfortable rooms and offers a Continental breakfast each morning. Some rooms have kitchenettes. ✉ *644 N. Woodland Blvd., 32720,* ☎ *904/734–5711 or 800/345–8991,* 𝖥𝖠𝖷 *904/734–5716. 60 rooms. Pool. AE, D, DC, MC, V.*

$–$$ ▦ **1888 House.** Spacious rooms, fireplaces, family heirlooms, and whirlpool baths make this a particularly enjoyable retreat. The building is of the distinctive Classic Revival style, with steep roofs and broad porches, excellent for rocking. Restaurants and historic sights are within easy walking distance. ✉ *124 N. Clara Ave., 32720,* ☎ *904/822–4647. 3 rooms. Bicycles. AE, MC, V.*

Outdoor Activities and Sports

BOATING

Pontoon boats, houseboats, and bass boats for the St. Johns River are available from **Hontoon Landing Marina** (⊠ 2317 River Ridge Rd., ☎ 904/734–2474).

FISHING

One of the most savvy guides to St. Johns River bass fishing is **Bob Stonewater** (☎ 904/736–7120). He'll tow his boat to meet clients at the launch best for the day's fishing. **Hontoon Landing Marina** (⊠ 2317 River Ridge Rd., ☎ 904/734–2474) rents bass boats and offers fishing guide service.

SKYDIVING

In addition to hosting competitions, Deland is home to tandem jumping. You are attached at the hip—literally—to an experienced instructor-diver, enabling even novices to take their maiden voyage after one day. For lessons contact **Skydive Deland** (⊠ 1600 Flightline Blvd., ☎ 904/738–3539), open daily 8–sunset.

De León Springs

㉓ *7 mi northwest of Deland, 26 mi southwest of Daytona Beach.*

This town (population 1,500) is a small spot on the map just outside the eastern edge of the Ocala National Forest.

Near the end of the last century, **De León Springs State Recreation Area** was promoted as a fountain of youth to winter tourists, but visitors are now content to swim, fish, and hike the nature trails. ⊠ *Off U.S. 17,* ☎ *904/985–4212.* ⊡ *$3.25 per vehicle with up to 8 people.* ☉ *Daily 8–sunset.*

Dining

$–$$ ✕ **Karlings Inn.** A sort of Bavarian Brigadoon, set beside a forgotten highway, this restaurant is decorated like a Black Forest inn. Karl Caeners oversees the preparation of the sauerbraten, red cabbage, and succulent roast duckling, as well as charcoal-grilled steaks, seafood, and fresh veal. The menu features Swiss, German, French, and Italian selections, and house specialties include blue crab cakes with spicy apricot sauce, seafood sausages (a blend of scallops, shrimp, and fish) served with a smoked chorizo and toasted garlic sauce, and roasted duck with Montmorency sauce. Ask to see the dessert tray. ⊠ *4640 N. U.S. 17,* ☎ *904/985–5535. MC, V. Closed Sun.–Mon. No lunch.*

Ocala National Forest

★ *Eastern entrance 40 mi west of Daytona Beach, northern entrance 52 mi south of Jacksonville.*

This delightful 366,000-acre wilderness with lakes, springs, rivers, hiking trails, campgrounds, and historic sites offers three major recreational areas. From east to west they are **Alexander Springs** (⊠ Off Rte. 40 via Rte. 445S), featuring a swimming lake and campground; **Salt Springs** (⊠ Off Rte. 40 via Rte. 19N), which has a natural saltwater spring where Atlantic blue crabs come to spawn each summer; and **Juniper Springs** (⊠ Off Rte. 40), with a picturesque stone waterwheel house, campground, natural-spring swimming pool, and hiking and canoe trails. ⊠ *Visitor center, 10863 E. Rte. 40, Silver Springs,* ☎ *352/625–7470.* ⊡ *Free.*

Lodging

$ 🛆 **Ocala National Forest.** Close to 30 campsites are sprinkled through-out the park and range from bare sites to those with electric hookups, showers, and bathrooms. Some have canoe runs nearby. Prices range from $5 to $13 per night. ☎ *352/625–7470 for campsite locations. No credit cards.*

Outdoor Activities and Sports

CANOEING

The 7-mi **Juniper Springs run** is a narrow, twisting, and winding canoe ride, which, though exhilarating, is not for the novice. You must ar-range with the canoe rental concession (✉ Rte. 40, ☎ 352/625–7470) for rehaul—getting picked up and brought back to where you started—but it's included in the rental price.

FISHING

Call **Captain Tom's** (✉ Rte. 40, Silver Springs, ☎ 352/546–4823) for charter fishing trips ranging from three hours to a full day.

HORSEBACK RIDING

The stable closest to Ocala that rents horses to the public, **Fiddler's Green Ranch** (✉ Demko Rd., Altoona, ☎ 800/947–2624) organizes trail rides into the national forest.

Ocala

🔳 *78 mi west of Daytona Beach, 123 mi southwest of Jacksonville.*

This is horse country. Here at the forest's western edge are dozens of horse farms with grassy paddocks and white wooden fences. Rolling hills and sweeping fields of bluegrass make the area feel more like Ken-tucky than Florida, which is entirely appropriate. The peaceful town is considered a center for Thoroughbred breeding and training, and Kentucky Derby winners have been raised in the region's training cen-ters. Sometimes the farms are even open to the public.

The **Appleton Museum of Art,** a three-building cultural complex, is a marble-and-granite tour de force with a serene esplanade and reflect-ing pool. The collection lives up to its surroundings, thanks to more than 6,000 pre-Columbian, Asian, African, and 19th-century objets d'art. ✉ *4333 E. Silver Springs Blvd.,* ☎ *352/236–7100.* 🔳 *$5.* ⊙ *Tues.– Sat. 10–4:30, Sun. 1–5.*

Garlit's Museum of Classic Cars houses one of the most unusual col-lections of cars and trucks in the world. More than 60 restored vehi-cles are on display, and an exhibit depicts the history of the automobile. ✉ *13700 S.W. 16th Ave.,* ☎ *352/245–8661.* 🔳 *$5.* ⊙ *Daily 9–5.*

OFF THE
BEATEN PATH   **SILVER SPRINGS** – The world's largest collection of artesian springs can be found outside Ocala at the western edge of the Ocala National For-est. The state's first tourist attraction, it was established in 1890 and is listed on the National Register of Historic Landmarks. Today the park presents wild-animal displays, glass-bottom boat tours in the Silver River, a jungle cruise on the Fort King Waterway, a Jeep safari through 35 acres of wilderness, an antique and classic car museum (☞ *above*), and walks through natural habitats. New exhibits include the Panther Prowl, which enables visitors to watch and photograph the endangered Florida panther, and the Big Gator Lagoon, a ½-acre swamp, featuring alliga-tors. A great place to cool off, **Silver Springs Wild Waters** has the park's giant wave pool and seven water-flume rides. Open late March–July, daily 10–5; August, daily 10–7; and September, weekends 10–5, it

costs $16.95. ⊠ *Rte. 40,* ☎ *352/236–2121.* ⊡ *$26.95.* ☉ *Daily 9–5:30.*

Dining and Lodging

$$–$$$ ✕ **Arthur's.** Don't pass up this elegant restaurant in the back of the lobby in the Ocala Silver Springs Hilton. Filet mignon with port sauce and chicken breast stuffed with spinach and sun-dried tomatoes are favorites, and the Sunday brunch is a must. ⊠ *3600 S.W. 36th Ave.,* ☎ *352/854–1400. AE, D, DC, MC, V.*

$$ ✕ **Petite Jardin.** In this cozy bistro, tables line the windows and walls, potted plants hang from the ceiling, and the menu is truly French. Start with scampi, escargots, or French onion soup. Then try the steak Diane flambé or duck Dijon. Dessert here is definitely worth the calories, but it's difficult to choose between the chocolate truffle mousse pie and the bananas Foster flambé. ⊠ *2209 E. Silver Springs Blvd.,* ☎ *352/351–4140. AE, MC, V. Closed Sun.*

$$–$$$ 🏨 **Seven Sisters Inn.** This showplace Queen Anne mansion is now an
★ award-winning B&B. Each room has been glowingly furnished with period antiques and has its own bath. Some have a fireplace, some a canopy bed. A wicker-furnished loft sleeps four. Rates include a gourmet breakfast and afternoon tea. ⊠ *820 S.E. Fort King St., 32671,* ☎ *352/867–1170. 8 rooms. AE, MC, V.*

$$ 🏨 **Ocala Silver Springs Hilton.** A winding, tree-lined boulevard leads to this nine-story pink tower, nestled in a forested patch of countryside just off I–75 and a bit removed from downtown. The marble-floor lobby, with a piano bar, greets you before you enter your spacious guest room, decorated in deeply colored, contemporary prints. ⊠ *3600 S.W. 36th Ave., 32674,* ☎ *352/854–1400,* FAX *352/854–4010. 178 rooms, 12 suites. Restaurant, bar, pub, pool, outdoor hot tub, 2 tennis courts. AE, D, DC, MC, V.*

Outdoor Activities and Sports

GOLF

Golden Ocala Golf Club (⊠ 7340 U.S. 27NW, ☎ 352/622–0172) has 18 holes.

JAI ALAI

The speediest of sports, jai alai is played year-round at **Ocala Jai Alai** (⊠ Rte. 318, Orange Lake, ☎ 352/591–2345).

Micanopy

㉕ *36 mi north of Ocala.*

Though this was the state's oldest inland town, site of both a Timucuan Indian settlement and a Spanish mission, there are few traces left from before white settlement, which began in 1821. Micanopy (pronounced micka-*no*-pee) does still draw those interested in the past, however. The beautiful little town, its streets lined with live oaks, is a mecca for antiques hunters. The main street has quite a few antiques shops, and in fall roughly 200 antiques dealers descend on the town for the annual Harvest Fall Festival.

A 20,000-acre wildlife preserve with ponds, lakes, trails, and a visitor
★ center with museum, **Paynes Prairie State Preserve** is a wintering area for many migratory birds and home to alligators and a wild herd of American bison. There was once a vast lake here, but a century ago it drained so abruptly that thousands of beached fish died in the mud. The remains of a ferry, stranded in the 1880s, can still be seen. Swimming, boating, picnicking, and camping are permitted. ⊠ *Off U.S. 441,*

1 mi north of Micanopy, ☎ *352/466–3397.* ▨ *$3.25 per vehicle with up to 8 people.* ☉ *Daily 8–sunset.*

OFF THE
BEATEN PATH

MARJORIE KINNAN RAWLINGS STATE HISTORIC SITE – Rawlings's readers will feel the writer's presence permeating this home, where the typewriter rusts on the ramshackle porch, the closet where she hid her booze during Prohibition yawns open, and clippings from her scrapbook reveal her legal battles and marital problems. Bring lunch and picnic in the shade of one of Rawlings's trees. Then visit her grave a few miles away at peaceful Island Grove. ▨ *Rte. 325,* ☎ *352/466–3672.* ▨ *Grounds free, tours $3.* ☉ *Daily 9–5; tours Oct.–July, hourly 10–11 and 1–4.*

Dining and Lodging

$–$$ ✕ **Wildflowers Cafe.** White tablecloths and well-spaced tables create a romantic atmosphere at this casual eatery. It's popular not just because it's about the only restaurant in the area open for dinner but also because of its cuisine: steaks, seafood, and Italian entrées like chicken marsala and spaghetti with meatballs as well as salads and sandwiches. ▨ *201 N. U.S. 441,* ☎ *352/466–4330. AE, MC, V. Closed Mon.*

$–$$$ ▣ **Herlong Mansion.** Spanish moss clings to the stately oak trees surrounding this beautifully restored, southern mansion, built in the early 1900s. The imposing Greek Revival–style B&B sports Corinthian columns and wide verandas perfect for relaxing in a rocker. Inside, rooms and suites are decorated with period furniture, Oriental rugs, and armoires. Some units have working fireplaces, leaded-glass windows, clawfoot tubs, or whirlpools. A full breakfast, which is included in the rate, is an event here and includes many courses and much innkeeper humor. ▨ *Cholokka Blvd., 32671,* ☎ *352/466-3322 or 800/437–5664. 7 rooms, 5 suites. AE, MC, V.*

Gainesville

㉖ *11 mi north of Micanopy on U.S. 441.*

This sprawling town is home to the University of Florida. Visitors are mostly Gator football fans and parents with kids enrolled at the university, so the styles and costs of accommodations are geared primarily to budget-minded travelers rather than luxury-seeking vacationers. In the surrounding area are several state parks and interesting gardens and geologic sites.

On the campus of the University of Florida, the ☺ **Florida Museum of Natural History** has several interesting replicas, including a Maya palace, a typical Timucuan household, and a full-size replica of a Florida cave. There are outstanding collections from throughout Florida's history, so spend at least half a day here. ▨ *34th St. at Hull Rd.,* ☎ *352/392–1721.* ▨ *Free.* ☉ *Mon.–Sat. 10–5, Sun. 1–5.*

About 10,000 years ago an underground cavern collapsed and created a geological treat. Today at **Devil's Millhopper State Geological Site,** you can see the botanical wonderland of exotic subtropical ferns and trees that has grown in the 500-ft-wide, 120-ft-deep sinkhole. You pass a dozen small waterfalls as you head down 232 steps to the bottom. ▨ *4732 Millhopper Rd., off U.S. 441,* ☎ *352/955–2008.* ▨ *$2 per vehicle, pedestrians $1.* ☉ *Daily 9–sunset.*

Dining and Lodging

$$–$$$ ✕ **Sovereign.** Crystal, candlelight, and a jazz pianist set a tone of re-
★ strained elegance in this 1878 carriage house—one of the area's fanciest restaurants. Veal specialties are notable, particularly the saltimbocca.

Duckling and rack of baby lamb are dependable choices, too. ⊠ *12 S.E. 2nd Ave.,* ☎ *352/378–6307. AE, D, DC, MC, V.*

$$ ✕ **Brasserie.** Dinner is a formal affair at this fine dining establishment. Waiters wear tuxedos, and tables wear fresh flowers. Dine on grilled satori bread, warm pistachio-crusted goat cheese, grilled swordfish with sun-dried-pimiento garlic oil, or a filet mignon with roasted Portobello mushrooms. Pause before you take a bite: The food arrangements here are true works of art! Though just a page, the wine list is very comprehensive. ⊠ *101 S.E. 2nd Ave.,* ☎ *352/375–6612. AE, D, DC, MC, V.*

$–$$ ✕ **Melting Pot.** Sit downstairs or upstairs in the cozy loft, and gather around the table. Eating is a group activity here. No matter what you order, you'll be doing the cooking. Dip slivers of fish or steak in sizzling hot oil, or cubes of crusty French bread in pots of melted cheese. Save room for dessert—more fondue, naturally—bits of fruit you dip into rich melted chocolate. ⊠ *418 E. University Ave.,* ☎ *352/372–5623. AE, MC, V. No lunch.*

$ ✕ **Market Street Pub.** This large British-style pub brews its own beer as well as serving up homemade sausage, fish-and-chips, salads, and hearty sandwiches. Dine indoors or outdoors at the sidewalk café. ⊠ *120 S.W. 1st Ave.,* ☎ *352/377–2927. AE, MC, V. No lunch weekends.*

$$–$$$ 🏨 **Residence Inn by Marriott.** One- and two-bedroom suites with a kitchen and fireplace make a cozy pied-à-terre. Cocktails, Continental breakfast, and a daily paper are part of the hospitality. The central location is convenient for the university or business traveler. ⊠ *4001 S.W. 13th St. (at U.S. 441 and Rte. 331), 32608,* ☎ *352/371–2101 or 800/331–3131,* 𝔽𝔸𝕏 *352/371–2101. 60 1-bedroom suites, 20 2-bedroom suites. Pool, exercise room, coin laundry. AE, D, DC, MC, V.*

Nightlife

DJ Chaps (⊠ 108 S. Main St., ☎ 352/377–1619) is Gainesville's only country-and-western dance club; it's always hopping. Gainesville's oldest bar, **Lillian's Music Store** (⊠ 112 S.E. 1st St., ☎ 352/372–1010) features rock and Top 40 music, live bands and karaoke. Call for schedules. Crowds gather weekends at **Richenbacher's** (⊠ 104 S. Main St., ☎ 352/375–5363) for blues, reggae, and hard rock sounds.

Outdoor Activities and Sports

AUTO RACING

Hot-rod auto racing goes on at the Gatornationals, championship competitions of the **National Hot Rod Association** (☎ 818/914–4761). They're held each year in late winter at the **Gainesville Raceway** (⊠ 1121 N. Rte. 225).

FOOTBALL

The games of the **University of Florida Gators** (☎ 352/375–4683) are extremely popular, and tickets are very hard to get.

NORTHEAST FLORIDA A TO Z

Arriving and Departing

By Bus

Greyhound Lines (☎ 800/231–2222) serves the region, with stations in Jacksonville (☎ 904/356–9976), St. Augustine (☎ 904/829–6401), Gainesville (☎ 352/376–5252), Daytona Beach (☎ 904/255–7076), and Deland (☎ 904/734–2747).

By Car

East–west traffic travels the northern part of the state on I–10, a cross-country highway stretching from Los Angeles to Jacksonville. Farther south, I–4 connects Florida's west and east coasts. Signs on I–4 designate it an east–west route, but actually the road rambles northeast from Tampa to Orlando, then heads north–northeast to Daytona. Two interstates head north–south on Florida's peninsula: I–95 on the east coast (from Miami to Houlton, Maine) and I–75 to the west.

By Plane

The main airport for the region is **Jacksonville International** (☎ 904/741–4902). It is served by **American** and **American Eagle** (☎ 800/433–7300), **Comair** (☎ 800/354–9822), **Continental** (☎ 800/525–0280), **Delta** (☎ 800/221–1212), **TWA** (☎ 800/221–2000), **United** (☎ 800/241–6522), and **US Airways** (☎ 800/428–4322). Vans from the Jacksonville airport to area hotels cost $16 per person. Taxi fare is about $20 to downtown, $40 to the beaches and Amelia Island. Among the limousine services, which must be booked in advance, is **Classic Limousine & Charters** (☎ 904/645–5466), which charges $28 for one to four people going downtown ($10 for each additional person) and $40 for one to four people going to the Jacksonville beaches or Amelia Island.

Daytona Beach International Airport (☎ 904/248–8069) is served by Delta. Taxi fare to beach hotels is about $10–$14; cab companies include **Yellow Cab** (☎ 904/252–5555), **Checker Cab** (☎ 904/258–6622), and **A&A Cab** (☎ 904/677–7777). **DOTS Transit Service** (☎ 904/257–5411) has scheduled service connecting the Daytona Beach airport to Orlando International Airport, the Sheraton Palm Coast area, Deland, Deland's Amtrak station, New Smyrna Beach, Sanford, and Deltona; fares are $26 one-way and $46 round-trip between the Daytona and Orlando airports, $20 one-way and $36 round-trip from the Orlando airport to Deland or Deltona.

Gainesville Regional Airport (☎ 352/373–0249) is served by **ASA–The Delta Connection** (☎ 800/282–3424), Comair, Delta, and US Airways. Taxi fare to the center of Gainesville is about $10; some hotels provide free airport pickup.

Although Orlando is not part of the area, visitors to northeastern Florida often choose to arrive at **Orlando International Airport** because of the huge number of convenient flights. Driving east on the Beeline Expressway brings you to Cocoa Beach in about an hour. You can reach Daytona, about a two-hour drive, by taking the Beeline Expressway to I–95 and driving north.

By Train

Amtrak (☎ 800/872–7245) schedules stops in Jacksonville, Deland, Waldo (near Gainesville), Ocala, and Palatka. The Auto Train carries cars between Sanford and Lorton, Virginia (just south of Washington, D.C.). Schedules vary depending on the season.

Getting Around

By Bus

Daytona Beach has an excellent bus network, **Votran** (☎ 904/756–7496), which serves the beach area, airport, shopping malls, and major arteries. Exact fare (75¢) is required.

By Car

Chief north–south routes are I–95, along the east coast, and I–75, which enters Florida south of Valdosta, Georgia, and joins the Sunshine Parkway toll road at Wildwood.

If you want to drive as close to the Atlantic as possible and are not in a hurry, stick with A1A. It runs along the barrier islands, changing its name several times along the way. Where there are no bridges between islands, cars must return to the mainland via causeways; some are low, with drawbridges that open for boat traffic on the inland waterway, and there can be unexpected delays. The Buccaneer Trail, which overlaps part of Route A1A, goes from St. Augustine north to Mayport (where a ferry is part of the state highway system), through marshlands and beaches, to the 300-year-old seaport town of Fernandina Beach, and then finally into Fort Clinch State Park.

Route 13 runs from Jacksonville to East Palatka along the east side of the St. Johns River through tiny hamlets. U.S. 17 travels the west side of the river, passing through Green Cove Springs and Palatka.

Route 19 runs north–south, and Route 40 runs east–west through the Ocala National Forest, giving a nonstop view of stately pines and bold wildlife. Short side roads lead to parks, springs, picnic areas, and campgrounds.

By Water Taxi

Connecting the banks of the St. Johns River, the **Bass Marine Water Taxi** (☎ 904/730–8685) runs from 11 to 10 daily (except during rainy or other bad weather) between several locations, including Riverwalk and Jacksonville Landing. The one-way trip takes about five minutes. Round-trip fare is $3; one-way fare is $1.50.

Contacts and Resources

Emergencies

Dial **911** for police or ambulance.

HOSPITALS

The following hospitals have 24-hour emergency rooms: **Alachua General** (⊠ 801 S.W. 2nd Ave., Gainesville, ☎ 352/372–4321), **Fish Memorial Hospital** (⊠ 401 Palmetto St., New Smyrna Beach, ☎ 904/424–5152), **Halifax Medical Center** (⊠ 303 N. Clyde Morris Blvd., Daytona, ☎ 904/254–4100), **Munroe Regional Medical Center** (⊠ 131 S.W. 15th St., Ocala, ☎ 352/351–7200), and **St. Luke's Hospital** (⊠ 4201 Belfort Rd., Jacksonville, ☎ 904/296–3700).

LATE-NIGHT PHARMACIES

Eckerd Drug (⊠ 4397 Roosevelt Blvd., Jacksonville, ☎ 904/389–0314) and **Walgreens** (⊠ 4150 N. Atlantic Ave., Cocoa, ☎ 407/799–9112; ⊠ 1500 Beville Rd., Daytona, ☎ 904/257–5773) stay open 24 hours.

Guided Tours

BOAT TOURS

La CRUISE (☎ 800/752–1778) has day and evening cruises from Mayport, with live bands, dancing, and gambling. In Jacksonville, **River Entertainment** (☎ 904/396–2333) has dinner and dancing cruises on five different boats; schedules vary with the season. **A Tiny Cruise Line** (☎ 904/226–2343) leaves from the Daytona Public Marina and explores the Intracoastal Waterway.

HISTORICAL TOURS

City tours of Jacksonville are offered by **Jacksonville Historical Society Tours** (☎ 904/396–6307) for groups and by arrangement.

Visitor Information

Most offices are open weekdays from between 8 and 9 to 5. **Amelia Island–Fernandina Beach Chamber of Commerce** (⊠ 102 Centre St., Amelia Island 32034, ☎ 904/261–3248). **Cocoa Beach Area Chamber**

of Commerce (✉ 400 Fortenberry Rd., Merritt Island 32952, ☎ 407/459–2200). **Destination Daytona!** (✉ 126 E. Orange Ave., Daytona 32120, ☎ 904/255–0415 or 800/854–1234). **Gainesville Visitors and Convention Bureau** (✉ 10 S.W. 2nd Ave., Suite 220, Gainesville 32608, ☎ 352/374–5231). **Jacksonville and Its Beaches Convention & Visitors Bureau** (✉ 6 E. Bay St., Suite 200, Jacksonville 32202, ☎ 904/798–9111). **Ocala–Marion County Chamber of Commerce** (✉ 110 E. Silver Springs Blvd., Ocala 32671, ☎ 352/629–8051). **St. Augustine Visitor Information Center** (✉ 10 Castillo Dr., St. Augustine 32084, ☎ 800/653–2489) is open daily 8:30–5:30.

11 THE FLORIDA FIFTY

GOLFING THROUGHOUT THE STATE

With more courses than any other state, Florida is a golfer's paradise. The warm climate makes for year-round play on hundreds of courses, from which we've chosen the 50 best from all corners of the state.

Updated by
Nancy Orr

HOW COULD GOLFERS FEEL UNDER PAR in the Sunshine State? One out of every 10 rounds of golf played in the United States is played here, and golfers visit Florida more than any other state, including Arizona, South Carolina, and California.

But there is plenty of green to go around. Florida has more golf courses than any other state, and it's always among the top five in the number of courses either newly opened or under construction each year—averaging 50. According to National Golf Foundation figures, the current count is 1,170 places at which to tee up.

Many of Florida's courses are private. Still, at last count roughly two-thirds were either public, "semiprivate," or private but offering limited access for nonmembers (for example, courses extending privileges to guests of nearby hotels). So if you're on your way to Florida to play golf, you'll have more than 700 places at which to test your skills.

A big part of the appeal of Florida golf is its year-round availability. Although a few courses might close for a day or two in fall to reseed greens and a few in northern Florida might delay morning tee times in winter when there's frost, it's still fair to say you can find a fairway here 365 days a year. That's why a large number of touring professionals—including Jack Nicklaus, Tiger Woods, and Mark O'Meara—have settled here.

What sort of play can you expect? It's no state secret that Florida is flat. With its highest elevation at 345 ft, it can't claim many naturally rolling courses. The world's leading golf-course designers, including Tom Fazio, Jack Nicklaus, and Ed Seay, have added the rolls and undulations that nature omitted. No designer, however, has been more notable in this regard than Pete Dye, pioneer of stadium-style courses, which are designed for large tournament audiences.

Deep rough is uncommon as a penalizing element in Florida play, short rough is especially prevalent during winter, and water and sand are common. Often lakes and canals have to be carved out to make fairways. Although Florida fairways are characteristically wide, greens tend to be heavily bunkered or protected by water. A diabolically popular invention of Florida course builders is the island green surrounded by water. Sand is also a natural part of the Florida environment, although a special fine-grain sand is sometimes imported; it isn't unusual to come across a hole in Florida with 10 or more traps, and several courses have more than 100 traps each. On the other hand, because the sandy soil drains well, the playing surface is more forgiving of iron shots than denser clay-rich soil. What this adds up to is a premium on accuracy when it comes to approach shots.

Wind also comes into play in Florida, particularly at courses near the state's 3,000 mi of coastline. Inland, it swirls and becomes unpredictable as it moves through tall pine and palm trees.

Finally, keep in mind that for most of the year, Florida greens are seeded with Bermuda grass. If you're familiar with putting on the bent-grass greens found in other parts of the country, you may find that the speed (on the slow side) and grain of Bermuda greens take getting used to.

The Florida Fifty

In a state with more than 1,100 courses, coming up with a mere 50 recommendations isn't easy. Even after discounting nine-hole courses, par-3 (sometimes called "executive") courses, courses that are private, and those with unusually restrictive policies for public play, hundreds of top-notch courses remain.

Detailing a sampling of what is available, from inexpensive municipal courses to luxurious resort courses, this chapter includes those repeatedly cited among Florida's best. This does not mean these are the only ones worth playing. Also, although just one course has been highlighted at each of the multicourse resorts covered (for example, Doral, Grand Cypress, PGA National), other courses at these resorts may also be among Florida's best. For that reason, the *total* number of holes at any resort is listed, not just the holes of the featured course.

Yardages listed are of the featured course and are intended as an indication of one course's length relative to others; yardages are calculated from the championship, or blue, tees. The championship length represents a course at its most difficult. Courses are typically between 400 and 800 yards shorter from the regular men's tees and between 1,000 and 1,500 yards shorter from the regular women's tees. With its large retirement population, Florida also has many facilities with seniors tees, usually in front of the regular men's tees and often designated as gold. A few designers—notably Jack Nicklaus—include five or more sets of tee boxes so as to make courses playable for everyone.

The United States Golf Association (USGA) ratings are also from the championship tees and indicate a course's relative difficulty; the rating is the average a scratch (0-handicap) golfer should expect to score. Any course with a rating of two or more strokes higher than par is considered especially demanding and generally suitable only for experienced golfers. If you're less experienced, look for courses with ratings below par.

Keep in mind that a golf course tends to be a work in progress; holes are often lengthened or shortened, greens are rebuilt, traps added, and so forth. The statistics and descriptions here were accurate at the time of publication, but courses may have undergone changes—even major overhauls—by the time you play them.

Because Florida courses tend to be flat, most are easy to walk, but unfortunately for people who enjoy walking, this is rarely an option anymore. Carts are usually mandatory, although a few courses allow late-afternoon players to walk, and some public courses allow you to stroll between holes. The official reason for requiring carts is that they speed up play, which is generally true. Operators concede, however, that cart rental means extra revenue. A note for anyone interested in walking (when and where it's permitted): In Florida, where the "golf community" is a pervasive concept, distances *between* holes can be substantial, a real estate ploy to allow more space for course-side homes and condos.

Greens fees are per-person regular-season rates, with mandatory cart fees (per person) included, where applicable. Greens fees, especially at resort courses, can be as much as 50% more during the high season—which generally runs from February to May—and substantially lower in slow summer months.

Many resorts offer golf packages, with greens fees included at a considerable discount. There are also companies specializing in golf packages.

Most courses (even some municipal ones) have dress codes. The standard requirement is a collared shirt and pants (often no jeans) or Bermuda-length shorts. Although many courses are less than militant

Florida Golf Courses

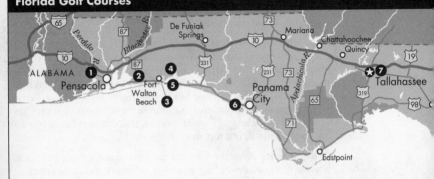

Gulf of Mexico

Panhandle
Bluewater Bay Resort, **4**
Kelly Plantation Golf Club, **3**
Killearn Country Club
& Inn, **7**
Marriott's Bay Point Resort, **6**
The Moors, **2**
Sandestin Beach Resort, **5**
Sportsman of Perdido, **1**

Northeast Florida
Amelia Island Plantation, **8**
Indigo Lakes Golf Club, **14**
Ponte Vedra Inn & Club, **11**
Ravines Inn & Golf
Club, **12**
Tournament Players Club
at Sawgrass, **10**
Windsor Park Golf Club, **9**
World Golf Village, **13**

Orlando Area
Bay Hill Golf Resort, **22**
Black Bear Golf Club, **15**
Falcon's Fire Golf Club, **20**
Grand Cypress Resort, **19**
Mission Inn Resort, **17**
Palisades Country Club, **18**
Southern Dunes Golf Club, **23**

Timacuan Golf & Country
Club, **16**
Walt Disney World Resort, **21**

Tampa Bay Area
Bloomingdale Golfers
Club, **27**
Buffalo Creek Golf Course, **28**
Legacy Golf Club at
Lakewood Ranch, **30**
Plantation Golf & Country
Club, **31**
Resort at Longboat Key
Club, **29**
Saddlebrook Resort
Tampa, **26**
Westin Innisbrook Resort, **25**
World Woods Golf Club, **24**

Southwest Florida
Cape Coral Golf & Tennis
Resort, **33**
Eastwood Golf Club, **32**
Lely Flamingo Island Club, **34**
Naples Beach Hotel & Golf
Club, **35**

Palm Beach
Binks Forest Golf Club, **40**
Boca Raton Resort
& Club, **43**
Breakers Hotel Golf Club, **39**

Emerald Dunes, **41**
Indian River Plantation
Marriott Beach Resort, **36**
PGA Golf Club at the
Reserve, **37**
PGA National Resort
& Spa, **38**
West Palm Beach Country
Club, **42**

Fort Lauderdale
Bonaventure Country
Club, **45**
Colony West Country
Club, **46**
Palm-Aire Country Club &
Resort, **44**

Miami
Crandon Park Golf Course, **50**
Don Shula's Hotel & Golf
Club, **49**
Doral Golf Resort
and Spa, **48**
Turnberry Isle Resort
& Club, **47**

GEORGIA

Amelia
Island

St. Mary's R.

8

9 Jacksonville

10

11

Osceola
National
Forest

Lake City

St. Johns River

12

13 St. Augustine

Santa Fe R.

Suwannee River

Gainesville

Ocala
National
Forest

14

Daytona Beach

Ocala

15

16

Titusville

NASA Kennedy
Space Center

Cape
Canaveral

17

18 **19**

Walt Disney
World

20 Orlando

Merritt Island

21

22

23

Winter
Haven

Melbourne

Florida's

Sebastian Inlet
Recreation Area

Tarpon Springs

24

25

26

Tampa

27

Clearwater

Tampa
Bay

St. Petersburg

28

Bradenton

29

30

Sarasota

Venice

31

Manatee R.

Peace R.

Kissimmee R.

Lake
Okeechobee

Vero Beach

Fort Pierce

36 Hutchinson
Island

37

38 West Palm
Beach

Singer
Island

40

39

41

Palm Beach

42

43 Boca Raton

44

45

46

Caloosahatchee R.

Cape
Coral

32 Fort Myers

Captiva Island

33

Sanibel Island

34 Naples

35

Big Cypress
National
Preserve

Fort Lauderdale

47 Miami Beach

48 Miami

49

50

Biscayne
Bay

Everglades
National
Park

Cape Sable

Florida Bay

Key Largo

Key
West

Florida Keys

ATLANTIC
OCEAN

Cedar Keys

in dress-code enforcement, come prepared to play by the rules. Additionally, soft-spike shoes are required on most—if not all—courses.

Prices quoted in the following chart refer to greens fees:

CATEGORY	COST
$$$$	over $100
$$$	$75–$100
$$	$50–$75
$	under $50

The Panhandle

Bluewater Bay Resort. Generally ranked by golf magazines among the top courses in northwest Florida, the Tom Fazio–designed layout features thick woods, water, and marshes on four nine-hole courses that combine to make six different 18-hole routes. ☒ *1950 Bluewater Blvd., Niceville 32578,* ☎ *850/897–3241 or 800/874–2128. Yardage: 6,817. Par: 72. USGA rating: 73.7. Total holes: 36.* ☒ *Greens fees $$. Cart optional after 1 in summer, 11:30 in winter. Restaurant, driving range, accommodations.*

Kelly Plantation Golf Club. A Fred Couples design, this masterpiece is on the Choctawhatchee Bay just ¼ mi from the Gulf of Mexico. Fairways meander through 200 acres of natural wetlands and along the bay. Generous landing areas and only one forced carry from the novice tees make it a playable course for all. Low handicappers will find the length, the gulf breeze, and the forced carries a test of strength and accuracy. ☒ *34851 Emerald Coast Pkwy., Destin 32541,* ☎ *850/659–7600. Yardage: 7,009. Par: 72. USGA rating: 74.2. Total holes: 18.* ☒ *Greens fees $$. Cart optional. Restaurant, driving range.*

Killearn Country Club & Inn. Home of the Tallahassee Open and the Centel Classic for the past 20 years, this course has a distinctive character courtesy of gently rolling fairways and clusters of large oak trees. ☒ *100 Tyron Circle, Tallahassee 32308,* ☎ *850/893–2144 or 800/476–4101. Yardage: 7,027. Par: 72. USGA rating: 71.8. Total holes: 27.* ☒ *Greens fees $. Cart optional. Special policies: must be an inn guest, member, or guest of member. Restaurant, driving range, accommodations.*

Marriott's Bay Point Resort. The Lagoon Legend course is a watery monster, with the beast coming into play on 16 holes. Completed in 1986, the course has one of the highest slope ratings in the nation and has consistently been ranked among the state's best. ☒ *100 Delwood Beach Rd., Panama City Beach 32411,* ☎ *850/235–6937 or 800/874–7105. Yardage: 6,921. Par: 72. USGA rating: 75.3. Total holes: 36.* ☒ *Greens fees $$. Cart mandatory. Special policies: tee times available 2 months in advance and lower greens fees for resort guests. Restaurant, driving range, accommodations.*

The Moors. Home of the PGA Seniors Emerald Coast Classic, this course has pot bunkers and native grasses bordering the broad fairways, creating a unique blend of Scottish- and Florida-style golf. ☒ *3220 Avalon Blvd., Milton 32583,* ☎ *850/995–4653 or 800/727–1010. Yardage: 6,828. Par: 70. USGA rating: 72.9. Total holes: 18.* ☒ *Greens fees $. Cart optional. Special policies: tee times available 3 days in advance. Restaurant, driving range, accommodations.*

Sandestin Beach Resort. The Links course requires play around and across canals on most of its holes. After little water on the first three holes, the fourth—a par-5 of 501 yards and ranked as one of Florida's toughest—is flanked by a lagoon and marsh. ☒ *9300 U.S. 98W, Destin 32541,* ☎ *850/267–8211 or 800/277–0800. Yardage: 6,710. Par: 72. USGA rating: 72.8. Total holes: 63.* ☒ *Greens fees $$. Cart op-*

tional. Special policies: tee-time preference and reduced greens fees for resort guests. Restaurants, driving range, accommodations.

Sportsman of Perdido. Accuracy is key here. On the par-5 11th, for example, water lines both sides of the fairway and the front of the green. ✉ *1 Doug Ford Dr., Pensacola 32507,* ☎ *850/492–1223. Yardage: 7,154. Par: 72. USGA rating: 73.8. Total holes: 18.* ⛳ *Greens fees $. Cart mandatory. Special policies: tee-time preference for resort guests and members. Restaurant, driving range, accommodations.*

Northeast Florida

Amelia Island Plantation. The Tom Fazio–designed Long Point Course is unusual for Florida: It features water on only three holes. Cedars, oaks, marshes, and ocean views make for unusually scenic play. ✉ *3000 First Coast Hwy., Amelia Island 32034,* ☎ *904/261–6161 or 800/874–6878. Yardage: 6,775. Par: 72. USGA rating: 73. Total holes: 54.* ⛳ *Greens fees $$$$. Cart mandatory. Restaurant, driving range, accommodations.*

Indigo Lakes Golf Club. Indigo Lakes is distinguished by its oversize greens, each averaging more than 9,000 square ft. ✉ *312 Indigo Dr., Daytona Beach 32114,* ☎ *904/254–3607. Yardage: 7,168. Par: 72. USGA rating: 73.5. Total holes: 18.* ⛳ *Greens fees $–$$. Cart mandatory. Special policies: tee times available a wk in advance. Restaurant, driving range.*

Ponte Vedra Inn & Club. Designed by Robert Trent Jones Sr., the Ocean Course features an island hole—the 147-yard ninth, said to have inspired Pete Dye's design of the 17th at the nearby TPC Stadium Course—and plays tough when the wind is up. ✉ *200 Ponte Vedra Blvd., Ponte Vedra Beach 32082,* ☎ *904/273–7710 or 800/234–7842. Yardage: 6,809. Par: 72. USGA rating: 72.2. Total holes: 36.* ⛳ *Greens fees $$$$. Cart mandatory. Special policies: must be an inn guest, member, or guest of member. Restaurant, driving range, accommodations.*

Ravines Inn & Golf Club. Mother Nature has provided a dramatic landscape and one not usually found in Florida. Forested rolling terrain and deep ravines are hallmarks of this Mark McCumber–designed course. Even seasoned players are challenged. ✉ *2932 Ravines Rd., Middleburg 32068,* ☎ *904/282–7888 or 800/728–4631. Yardage: 6,733. Par: 72. USGA rating: 72.4. Total holes: 18.* ⛳ *Greens fees $–$$. Cart mandatory. Restaurant, driving range, 18-hole putting course, accommodations.*

Tournament Players Club at Sawgrass. The Pete Dye–designed TPC Stadium Course—famed for its island 17th hole—vexes even the top pros who compete in the Tournament Players Championship. ✉ *110 TPC Blvd., Ponte Vedra Beach 32082,* ☎ *904/273–3235 or 800/457–4653. Yardage: 6,937. Par: 72. USGA rating: 73.3. Total holes: 36.* ⛳ *Greens fees $$$$. Cart optional. Special policies: must be a hotel guest, member, or guest of member. Restaurant, driving range, accommodations.*

Windsor Park Golf Club. Tree-lined fairways and natural marshlands come into play here. The 184-yard, par-3 16th is especially challenging—over water and with a green almost completely surrounded by bunkers. ✉ *4747 Hodges Blvd., Jacksonville 32224,* ☎ *904/223–4972. Yardage: 6,740. Par: 72. USGA rating: 71.9. Total holes: 18.* ⛳ *Greens fees $$. Cart optional after 3. Special policies: tee times available 5 days in advance. Restaurant, driving range.*

World Golf Village. Opened in summer 1998, the Slammer & the Squire course was named after Hall of Famers Sam Snead and Gene Sarazan, who assisted in the design. Having established a reputation for outstanding par-3s and uniquely designed greens, this course has been selected to host the Legends of Gold Golf Tournament. A second course, the first true collaboration between Arnold Palmer and Jack Nicklaus, is scheduled for completion by the end of 1999. ⊠ *21 World Golf Pl., St. Augustine 32092,* ☎ *904/940–6120. Yardage: 6,940. Par: 72. USGA rating: 73.8. Total holes: 18.* ⛳ *Greens fees: $$$$. Cart mandatory. Restaurant, driving range, accommodations.*

Orlando Area

Bay Hill Golf Resort. Updated by Arnold Palmer and Ed Seay in 1980, this has one of the hardest 18 holes you'll find anywhere. The openness and length may demand the use of every club in your bag, and the par-3s are superb. The 18th hole, often called the "Devil's Bathtub," is considered one of the toughest holes on the PGA Tour. ⊠ *9000 Bayhill Blvd., Orlando 32819,* ☎ *407/876–2429. Yardage: 7,207. Par: 72. USGA rating: 75.1. Total holes: 27.* ⛳ *Greens fees $$$$ (including lodging). Caddies available. Special policies: must be a resort guest, member, or guest of member. Restaurant, driving range, accommodations.*

Black Bear Golf Club. Dubbed a destination for those who eat, drink, and sleep golf, this Pete Dye course exemplifies his trademark unusual course design. Six sets of tees from 5,000 to 7,000 yards encourage all levels of play, but dramatic elevation changes, undulating greens, and sandy waste bunkers make it a bear. ⊠ *24505 Calusa Blvd., Eustis 32736,* ☎ *352/357–4732. Yardage: 7,002. Par: 72. USGA rating: 74.7. Total holes: 18.* ⛳ *Greens fees $–$$. Cart mandatory. Restaurant, driving range.*

Falcon's Fire Golf Club. This layout designed by respected golf architect Rees Jones features 131 strategically placed fairway bunkers that demand accuracy off the tee. Carts are equipped with global positioning systems (GPS) that display distance to green as well as other helpful stats and tips. ⊠ *3200 Seralago Blvd., Kissimmee 34746,* ☎ *407/239–5445. Yardage: 6,901. Par: 72. USGA rating: 72.5. Total holes: 18.* ⛳ *Greens fees $$$$. Cart mandatory. Special policies: tee times available a wk in advance. Restaurant, driving range.*

Grand Cypress Resort. The New Course is a Jack Nicklaus re-creation of the famed Old Course in St. Andrews, Scotland. Similarities include large undulating greens, bridges, and pot bunkers deep enough to have stairs for entry and exit. ⊠ *1 N. Jacaranda Dr., Orlando 32836,* ☎ *407/239–1909 or 800/297–7377. Yardage: 6,773. Par: 72. USGA rating: 72.2. Total holes: 45.* ⛳ *Greens fees $$$$. Cart optional. Special policies: must be a resort guest; tee times available 2 months in advance. Restaurant, driving range, accommodations.*

Mission Inn Resort. Originally built in 1926, the El Campéon course, which hosted the 1998 NCAA Division II national championship, is more characteristic of courses in the Carolinas and the Northeast. Tight and hilly fairways include an 85-ft tee-to-green elevation change. A recent renovation to the 11th hole added yardage and removed green-side bunkers. ⊠ *10400 Rte. 48, Howey-in-the-Hills 34737,* ☎ *352/324–3885 or 800/874–9053. Yardage: 6,860. Par: 72. USGA rating: 73.6. Total holes: 36.* ⛳ *Greens fees $$–$$$. Cart mandatory. Special policies: tee times available a wk in advance. Restaurant, driving range, accommodations.*

Palisades Country Club. Overlooking Lake Minneola, this Joe Lee–designed course is known for its roller-coaster-like fairways and generous landing areas. ⊠ *16510 Palisades Blvd., Clermont 34711,* ☎ *352/394–0085. Yardage: 7,004. Par: 72. USGA rating: 73.8. Total holes: 18.* ⛳ *Greens fees $$. Cart mandatory. Special policies: tee times available a wk in advance. Restaurant, driving range.*

Southern Dunes Golf Club. This is the perfect course for low handicappers. Designed by Steve Smyers and opened in 1993, it is exceptionally long, with elevation changes of more than 100 ft in places. Expansive fairways are flanked by more than 180 bunkers—some planted in scrub. ✉ *2888 Southern Dunes Blvd., Haines City 33844,* ☎ *941/421–4653 or 800/632–6400. Yardage: 7,227. Par: 72. USGA rating: 74.7. Total holes: 18.* ⛳ *Greens fees $$–$$$. Cart mandatory. Special policies: tee times available 14 days in advance, earlier with $5 per per-person surcharge. Restaurant, driving range, accommodations.*

Timacuan Golf & Country Club. This two-part course was designed by Ron Garl: Part I, the front nine, is open, with lots of sand; Part II, the back nine, is heavily wooded. ✉ *550 Timacuan Blvd., Lake Mary 32746,* ☎ *407/321–0010. Yardage: 6,915. Par: 71. USGA rating: 73.2. Total holes: 18.* ⛳ *Greens fees $$–$$$. Cart mandatory. Special policies: tee times available 5 days in advance. Restaurant, driving range.*

Walt Disney World Resort. Where else would you find a sand trap shaped like the head of a well-known mouse? There are five championship courses here—all on the PGA Tour. *Golf Digest*'s pick as Florida's seventh-best layout, the Osprey Ridge course, designed by Tom Fazio, incorporates elevated tees and greens and rolling fairways with a relaxing tour into forested, undeveloped acreage. ✉ *Bonnet Creek Golf Club, Lake Buena Vista 32830,* ☎ *407/939–4653. Yardage: 7,101. Par: 72. USGA rating: 73.9. Total holes: 99.* ⛳ *Greens fees $$$$. Cart mandatory. Special policies: tee times available 60 days in advance for resort guests, 30 days in advance for the public. Restaurant, driving range, accommodations.*

Tampa Bay Area

Bloomingdale Golfers Club. Surrounded by an 80-acre wetlands area, these 18 holes offer majestic scenery comprising 200-year-old oaks and stands of pines. A close encounter with the abundant wildlife is always a possibility, and there are, reportedly, more than 60 bird species (including a bald eagle) in residence. For golfers, however, birdies and eagles are hard to come by. ✉ *4113 Great Golfers Pl., Valrico 33594,* ☎ *813/685–4105. Yardage: 7,165. Par: 72. USGA rating: 74.4. Total holes: 18.* ⛳ *Greens fees $$. Cart mandatory. Restaurant, driving range.*

Buffalo Creek Golf Course. This Manatee County–owned course resembling a Scottish links and designed by Lakeland, Florida–based golf architect Ron Garl is in as good condition as most private clubs. It's challenging but playable, with few water-lined fairways or traps in front of the greens. ✉ *8100 Erie Rd., Palmetto 34221,* ☎ *941/776–2611. Yardage: 7,005. Par: 72. USGA rating: 73.1. Total holes: 18.* ⛳ *Greens fees $. Cart optional. Special policies: tee times available 2 days in advance. Restaurant, driving range.*

Legacy Golf Club at Lakewood Ranch. Designed by Arnold Palmer, this course takes advantage of its natural environment. Fairways wind through natural preserves, elevated tee boxes are offered on each hole, and mighty oaks and streams protect the beautifully manicured greens. ✉ *8255 Legacy Golf Club, Bradenton 34202,* ☎ *941/907–7067. Yardage: 7,067. Par: 72. USGA rating: 73.7. Total holes: 18.* ⛳ *Greens fees $$. Cart mandatory. Special policies: tee times available a wk in advance. Restaurant, driving range.*

Plantation Golf & Country Club. The long Bobcat course has rolling fairways and large greens. Because there's water on 16 holes and greens aren't visible from the tees on 12 holes, shot placement and club selection are critical. The club plays host to the annual LPGA qualifying school. ✉ *500 Rockley Blvd., Venice 34293,* ☎ *941/493–2000. Yardage: 6,514. Par: 72. USGA rating: 71.2. Total holes: 36.* ⛳ *Greens*

*fees $. Cart mandatory. Special policies: reserved for members Nov.–
Apr.; tee times available 2 days in advance. Restaurant, driving range,
accommodations.*

Resort at Longboat Key Club. Water, water everywhere: Amid canals
and lagoons, the Islandside Course brings water into play on all but
one hole, and play can be especially tough when the wind comes off
Sarasota Bay or the Gulf of Mexico. ✉ *301 Gulf of Mexico Dr., Longboat Key 34228,* ☎ *941/383–8821. Yardage: 6,792. Par: 72. USGA
rating: 73.8. Total holes: 45.* ⚐ *Greens fees $$$$. Cart mandatory.
Special policies: must be a resort guest or member; tee times available
3 days in advance. Restaurant, driving range, accommodations.*

Saddlebrook Resort Tampa. The Saddlebrook course, designed by
Arnold Palmer, is relatively short, but the premium is on accuracy, with
lots of water to avoid. Large undulating greens make four-putting a
constant concern. ✉ *5700 Saddlebrook Way, Wesley Chapel 33543,*
☎ *813/973–1111 or 800/729–8383. Yardage: 6,564. Par: 70. USGA
rating: 72. Total holes: 36.* ⚐ *Greens fees $$$–$$$$. Cart mandatory.
Special policies: tee times available 2 months in advance for resort guests.
Restaurant, driving range, accommodations.*

Westin Innisbrook Resort. Innisbrook's Copperhead course, generally
ranked among Florida's toughest, is likened to those found in the Car-
olinas. Its undulating terrain and long dog-leg par-4s test both strength
and accuracy. ✉ *U.S. 19, Tarpon Springs 34684,* ☎ *727/942–2000.
Yardage: 7,087. Par: 71. USGA rating: 74.4. Total holes: 72.* ⚐ *Greens
fees $$$$. Cart mandatory. Special policies: must be a resort guest or
a member of a U.S. or Canadian golf club. Restaurant, driving range,
accommodations.*

World Woods Golf Club. Opened in 1993, this club has been recognized
as one of the country's finest golf facilities. The Rolling Oaks Course,
designed by Tom Fazio, is a challenge thanks to rolling hills and large,
multitiered greens. Well-manicured fairways, lined with live oaks, dog-
woods, and azaleas, are reminiscent of Augusta National, home of the
Masters. ✉ *17590 Ponce de León Blvd., Brooksville 34614,* ☎ *352/
796–5500. Yardage: 6,982. Par: 72. USGA rating: 73.5. Total holes:
48.* ⚐ *Greens fees $$. Cart optional. Special policies: tee times available a month in advance. Restaurant, 22-acre practice area with 4-sided
driving range, 2-acre putting course.*

Southwest Florida

Cape Coral Golf & Tennis Resort. Although this short and not too difficult course is playable for all skill levels, its 100 bunkers make it especially good for those who consider themselves experts in sand play.
✉ *4003 Palm Tree Blvd., Cape Coral 33904,* ☎ *941/542–7879 or 800/
648–1475. Yardage: 6,707. Par: 72. USGA rating: 72.0. Total holes:
27.* ⚐ *Greens fees $$. Cart mandatory. Special policies: tee times
available 3 days in advance. Restaurant, driving range, accommoda-
tions.*

Eastwood Golf Club. Included on many lists of America's best public
courses, Eastwood demands accuracy, with tight fairways, water, and
well-bunkered greens. ✉ *4600 Bruce Herd La., Fort Myers 33905,* ☎
*941/275–4848. Yardage: 6,772. Par: 72. USGA rating: 73.3. Total holes:
18.* ⚐ *Greens fees $$. Cart optional after 1 in summer, 2 in spring,
and 3 in winter. Driving range, snack bar.*

Lely Flamingo Island Club. The Robert Trent Jones course, completed
in 1991, was the first of three built at this resort-in-the-making. Multilevel greens are guarded by a fleet of greedy bunkers, but the wide,
rolling fairways generally keep errant drives in play. ✉ *8004 Lely Resort Blvd., Naples 34113,* ☎ *941/793–2223 or 800/388–4653. Yardage:*

7,171. Par: 72. USGA rating: 75.0. Total holes: 54. ⊠ Greens fees $$$$.
Cart mandatory. Special policies: tee times available 3 days in advance. Restaurant, driving range.

Naples Beach Hotel & Golf Club. Originally built in 1930, this is one
of Florida's oldest courses. It's short and flat, but strategic bunkering,
narrow fairways, and smaller greens can make for challenging play. A
$1 million renovation in 1998 included redesigns of holes 9, 10, and
11, as well as improved drainage and irrigation. ⊠ 851 Gulfshore Blvd.
N, Naples 34102, ☎ 941/261–2222 or 800/237–7600. Yardage: 6,488.
Par: 72. USGA rating: 71.2. Total holes: 18. ⊠ Greens fees $$$$. Cart
mandatory. Special policies: tee times available 3 days in advance; preferred tee times for resort guests. Restaurant, driving range, accommodations.

Palm Beach

Binks Forest Golf Club. Designed by Johnny Miller and opened in
1990, this true Carolina-style course has tree-lined fairways and rolling
hills and is both challenging and picturesque. Miller has called it
"Florida's version of Pinehurst." ⊠ 400 Binks Forest Dr., Wellington
33414, ☎ 561/795–0595. Yardage: 7,065. Par: 72. USGA rating: 75.
Total holes: 18. ⊠ Greens fees $$$. Cart mandatory in season. Special policies: tee times available 5 days in advance. Restaurant, driving range.

Boca Raton Resort & Club. The Resort Course, extensively redesigned
by Gene Bates in 1997, challenges all skill levels thanks to water hazards on 16 holes, 6- to 30-ft elevation changes, and cascading water
on three holes. A new instructional area, home to the Nicklaus/Flick
Golf Instructional Programs, opened in 1998. ⊠ 501 E. Camino Real,
Boca Raton 33432, ☎ 561/447–3076 or 800/327–0101. Yardage:
6,253. Par: 71. USGA rating: 69.3. Total holes: 36. ⊠ Greens fees $$$$.
Cart mandatory. Special policies: must be a resort guest, member, or
guest of member; tee times available 5 days in advance. Restaurant,
driving range, accommodations.

Breakers Hotel Golf Club. Although the Ocean Course is Florida's oldest, the Kenny Green redesign on the back nine of the West Course probably makes it the more challenging of the two. The signature hole, the
par-4 ninth, requires a carry over water twice and is considered the
second most difficult hole in South Florida. ⊠ 1 S. County Rd., Palm
Beach 33480, ☎ 561/655–6611 or 800/833–3141. Yardage: 6,893. Par:
71. USGA rating: 72.0. Total holes: 36. ⊠ Greens fees $$$$. Cart
mandatory. Special policies: must be a hotel guest or member; free shuttle bus to West Course, 11 mi off-site. Restaurant, driving range, accommodations.

Emerald Dunes. This Tom Fazio–designed course, ranked as one of the
top 10 public courses in the United States by The Golfer, was created
for both professional and novice players. Each hole has five tees. The
SuperDune, a man-made mountain rising more than 50 ft, comes into
play on three tees and three greens, and most of the course and the 60
acres of lakes can be seen from its peak. ⊠ 2100 Emerald Dunes Dr.,
West Palm Beach 33411, ☎ 561/684–4653 or 888/650–4653. Yardage:
7,006. Par: 72. USGA rating: 73.8. Total holes: 18. ⊠ Greens fees $$$$.
Cart optional. Special policies: tee times available 30 days in advance.
Restaurant, driving range.

Indian River Plantation Marriott Beach Resort. This par-61 course is
classic Florida—flat with lots of palms and bunkers and made tricky
by ocean breezes. ⊠ 555 N.E. Ocean Blvd., Hutchinson Island, Stuart 34996, ☎ 561/225–3700. Yardage: 4,048. Par: 61. USGA rating:
59.9. Total holes: 18. ⊠ Greens fees $. Cart mandatory. Special poli-

cies: must be a resort guest or member; tee times available a month in advance for resort guests. Restaurant, driving range, accommodations.

PGA Golf Club at the Reserve. The first club owned and operated by the PGA of America, this public facility is as much for the hacker as for the pro. The Tom Fazio–designed South Course is typical Florida golf, with sprawling palm tree–lined fairways and greens surrounded by massive bunkers, some of which trail off into lakes. Dedicated to preserving the environment, the club has been awarded Audubon International's Signature Status and is home to more than 250 bird species as well as other animals. (A third, Pete Dye–designed, course is scheduled for early 2000.) ⊠ *1916 Perfect Dr., Port St. Lucie 34986,* ☎ *407/467–1300 or 800/800–4653. Yardage: 7,087. Par: 72. USGA rating: 74.5. Total holes: 54.* ⛳ *Greens fees $$. Cart mandatory. Special policies: tee times available 4 days in advance, 30 days in advance with surcharge. Restaurant, driving range, accommodations.*

PGA National Resort & Spa. Home of the PGA of America, this is the site of the annual Seniors Championship and has hosted the 1987 PGA Championship, the 1983 Ryder Cup, and the 1982 Grand Slam of Golf. The Champion Course, redesigned by Jack Nicklaus, demands length and accuracy, with water on 17 holes and more than 100 traps. ⊠ *1000 Ave. of the Champions, Palm Beach Gardens 33418,* ☎ *561/627–1800. Yardage: 6,777. Par: 72. USGA rating: 73.7. Total holes: 90.* ⛳ *Greens fees $$$$. Cart mandatory. Special policies: must be a resort guest, member, or golf pro; higher greens fees for Champion Course. Restaurant, driving range, accommodations.*

West Palm Beach Country Club. Wide fairways leading to large greens with tiered surfaces surrounded by deep bunkers are the hallmark of this course. Even without a water hazard, the traps combined with the deep bunkers require a lofted recovery. ⊠ *7001 Parker Ave., West Palm Beach 33405,* ☎ *561/582–2019. Yardage: 6,800. Par: 72. USGA rating: 71.0 Total holes: 18.* ⛳ *Greens fees $. Cart optional after 1. Special policies: tee times available a day in advance. Restaurant, driving range.*

Fort Lauderdale

Bonaventure Country Club. Designed by Joe Lee, the East Course is considered one of Florida's top 10, with plenty of trees, water, and bunkers lining the fairways. The highlight hole is the par-3 third, where the green fronts a waterfall. ⊠ *200 Bonaventure Blvd., Fort Lauderdale 33326,* ☎ *954/389–2100. Yardage: 7,011. Par: 72. USGA rating: 74.2. Total holes: 36.* ⛳ *Greens fees $$$. Cart mandatory. Special policies: tee times available 3 days in advance. Restaurant, driving range, accommodations.*

Colony West Country Club. Water is the biggest hazard on the Championship Course; you'll run into it on 14 holes. The par-4 12th through a cypress forest can be problematic if accuracy is lacking. ⊠ *6800 N.W. 88th Ave., Tamarac 33321,* ☎ *954/726–8430. Yardage: 7,271. Par: 71. USGA rating: 73.7. Total holes: 36.* ⛳ *Greens fees $$. Cart mandatory. Special policies: tee times available 3 days in advance. Restaurant.*

Palm-Aire Country Club & Resort. Formerly the Oaks Golf & Racquet Club, this resort completed a $3 million restoration of the Oaks Course, renaming it the Mighty Oaks. The Tom Fazio layout puts a premium on driving, with tree-lined fairways and a combination of large and small well-trapped greens. ⊠ *3701 Oaks Clubhouse Dr., Pompano Beach 33069,* ☎ *954/978–1737 or 877/725–6247. Yardage: 6,747. Par: 72. USGA rating: 72. Total holes: 94 (including a 22-hole executive course).*

☎ *Greens fees $$$$. Cart mandatory. Special policies: tee times available 4 days in advance. Restaurant, driving range, accommodations.*

Miami

Crandon Park Golf Course. Regularly rated highly among U.S. public courses, this one—formerly the Links at Key Biscayne—is surrounded by mangrove swamps and inhabited by many bird species and alligators. It's the site of the Royal Caribbean Classic on the PGA Seniors Tour. ✉ *6700 Crandon Blvd., Key Biscayne 33149,* ☎ *305/361–9129. Yardage: 7,107. Par: 72. USGA rating: 75.1. Total holes: 18.* ☎ *Greens fees $$–$$$. Cart optional after 2. Special policies: tee times available 5 days in advance. Restaurant, driving range.*

Don Shula's Hotel & Golf Club. Large greens and elevated tees—unusual in South Florida—are features of the championship course. For golfers who can't get enough, there's also a par-3 course that's lighted at night. ✉ *7601 Miami Lakes Dr., Miami Lakes 33014,* ☎ *305/820–8106. Yardage: 7,055. Par: 72. USGA rating: 72.3. Total holes: 36.* ☎ *Greens fees $–$$$. Cart mandatory. Special policies: tee times available a week in advance for members, 3 days in advance for nonmembers. Restaurant, driving range, accommodations.*

Doral Golf Resort and Spa. The 18th hole on the renovated Blue Course, nicknamed the "Blue Monster" and venue for the Doral-Ryder Open, rates among the hardest finishing holes on the PGA Tour. Veteran pro Ray Floyd reportedly called it the toughest par-4 in the world. (The Greg Norman–redesigned White Course is slated to re-open in early 2000 as the Great White.) ✉ *4400 N.W. 87th Ave., Miami 33178,* ☎ *305/592–2000 or 800/713–6725. Yardage: 7,125. Par: 72. USGA rating: 74.5. Total holes: 99.* ☎ *Greens fees $$$$. Cart mandatory. Special policies: tee time preference for hotel guests; higher greens fees for Blue Course. Restaurant, driving range, accommodations.*

Turnberry Isle Resort & Club. The Robert Trent Jones South Course, which has hosted the PGA Seniors Championship, mixes old and new: a double green, similar to those at the Old Course at St. Andrews, Scotland, and a modern island green, on the 545-yard, par-5 18th. ✉ *19999 W. Country Club Dr., Aventura 33180,* ☎ *305/932–6200 or 800/327–7028. Yardage: 7,003. Par: 72. USGA rating: 73.7. Total holes: 36.* ☎ *Greens fees $$$$. Cart mandatory. Special policies: must be a hotel guest or member; tee times available 2 days in advance. Restaurant, driving range, accommodations.*

12 BACKGROUND AND ESSENTIALS

Portrait of Florida

Books and Audio

Smart Travel Tips A to Z

FLORIDA, MY FLORIDA

Howdy, Kids. Looks like you'll be coming to Florida. Personally, I couldn't think of a better place to visit (except that I live here already). And why not? The folks at the tourist board say that Florida is sun-sational! And they're right. Without Florida there would be no space program, no Disney empire, no tropical Deco, no pink lawn flamingos. And you know the way Florida sticks down into the Caribbean? If Florida wasn't the United States' East Coast counterweight, our nation would just flip right over into the Pacific Ocean—and that's a geological fact.

Florida is *different*. It has almost as many millionaires as migrant workers and an equal number of rednecks and rocket scientists. It houses muck farms and million-dollar condos, and its churches welcome straitlaced Baptists and pious practitioners of Santeria, a mixture of Haitian voodoo, African tribal religions, and Christianity. Florida is where you can spend your vacation clapping happily as a robot bear sings Patsy Cline or screaming in terror as a real live alligator devours a senior citizen's toy poodle. This state may not be schizophrenic, but it does display multiple personalities.

Are you familiar with the saying attributed to Harvey Korman or somebody else that America is the melting pot of the world? Well, Florida is the melting pot of America. In 1990 a U.S. Census Bureau report revealed that less than a third of Florida's population are natives and only 13% were born in other states south of the Mason-Dixon line. You'll notice this when you visit, because Florida is the only state in the Deep South where you'll see the Union and Confederacy living side by side. Ironically, down here northerners live in the south and

southerners live in the north. No one knows why this is; it just is.

If you're wondering if you'll receive a warm welcome, don't worry. The land of sunshine accommodates just about everybody. In 1950 this was the 20th most populous state; now we're number four. During the Mariel Boatlift of 1980, 125,000 Cuban defectors showed up, and we didn't even call out the National Guard—we only did that when a similar number of New Yorkers arrived for the opening of the new Miami Bloomingdale's.

This influx of outsiders is nothing new. In 1513 Ponce de León decided to land in Florida to avoid the traffic around Newark. That did it. By 1565 Ponce's foothold became the oldest permanent settlement in what would become the United States. Check your history books, and you'll see this was a half century before the English arrived in Jamestown and the Pilgrims knocked on Plymouth Rock. It seemed everybody wanted to be in Florida. While the French, English, and Spanish spent 250 years battling for possession of the territory, Caribbean pirates sailing the Gulf Stream were making withdrawals from the explorers' ships and using Florida's hidden bays and swamps as safe-deposit boxes. Eventually, the pirates and foreign pioneers cleared out, and in 1821 the United States paid Spain $5 million for 59,000 square mi of marshes, mosquitoes, and alligators.

Later, Virginians and Carolinians began moving south to create panhandle communities like Quincy, Madison, and Monticello. Then in the late 1880s Henry M. Flagler started building a hotel and railroad empire that started in St. Augustine, arrived in Miami by 1896, and reached the end of the line in Key

West in 1912. Thanks to Flagler's promotional and engineering abilities, northern tourists started heading south and have been arriving ever since.

Although it rarely makes the evening news anymore, people are still battling over Florida. Retirees, dropouts, drug runners, natives, multinational companies, and foreign tourists all want to claim Florida for their own. So what's all the fuss about?

The answer, my friend, is blowing in the warm Atlantic winds that comfort us in the middle of January, in the primeval pleasures of paddling a canoe down the Wekiva River, in the 3,000-plus varieties of indigenous plants and flowers that color our landscape, and in the fire, smoke, and thunder of the space shuttle as it blazes into the clear blue sky above the Indian River. You'll find it in more than 400 species of birds, ranging from cardinals, ospreys, and bald eagles to wading egrets, herons, and pink flamingos. It is felt in the 220 days of sunshine we savor each a year and the approximately 1 inch of snow a century that we don't.

These are the types of things you may not know about the Shoeshine State. That is why my editors looked at my birth certificate and tan lines to confirm that I was a native and then asked me to share with you the many-splendored things that make up this paradoxical paradise. Even with my 35 years of memories and hundreds of thousands of miles spent trekking, biking, motorcycling, and stumbling across my favorite subtropical peninsula, this is a difficult task. Relating all that Florida represents is an impossibility because the typical Floridian could be grunting for worms in Sopchoppy, rounding up cattle in Kissimmee, or posing for the cover of a European fashion magazine in Miami.

And it's not only Americans who come to Florida. Hit Palm Beach during polo season, and you'll find that even Prince Charles is an occasional Floridian. If you stay a while (and you simply *must*), you'll find yourself eavesdropping on conversations spoken in a Berlitz blitz of mother tongues: Haitian, Chinese, Serbo-Croatian, Portuguese, Yiddish, Italian, Greek, Spanish, Jamaican, Russian, French, Esperanto . . . E Pluribus Unum, y'all. Only California (a relatively insignificant state somewhere out west) challenges Florida in terms of its social, cultural, and environmental diversity. You may have heard its residents claim that in one day they can breakfast on the beach, lunch in the desert, and enjoy dinner in the mountains. So? With a full tank of gas and a fast car (my cousin Chick's got a cherry '74 Pacer), Floridians can leave Pensacola in the western panhandle, drive beside the crystal blue gulf on U.S. 98, head north to Tallahassee to tell the governor not to stay the execution, cruise over to St. Augustine for a carriage ride, and drop down to Daytona Beach to hoist a brew with some bikers.

Then it's lunchtime.

Afterward, they'd head to Disney for a quick twirl in a teacup, scoot over to Cape Kennedy to bid adieu to the crew of the space shuttle (there's a French astronaut on board), race over to Tampa's Ybor City to snag a stogie, fill up the tank, and head south to dine at one of Miami's oceanfront cafés before meeting Jimmy Buffett in Key West to slam a pitcher of margaritas.

There's a whole lotta shakin' goin' on, that's for sure, but there is one thing missing from Florida: Old Florida. October 1, 1971, was the day that Disney drove old Dixie down. Over the last quarter century a new state has emerged, reflecting a not-so-perfect union. It is one of sprawling theme parks that provide a big bang for the buck. It is a place where part-time tourists become full-time residents, and corridors of condos, generic housing developments, strip malls, and highways are built to appease them. The changing nature of Key West is a prime example. A generation ago this was a laid-back island paradise filled with eclectic lodgings and quixotic characters. Then it was popularized in song and literature and through word of mouth until the buzz reached executive boardrooms. Today the island's individuality is endangered by a homogenized mass of Hôtels Banal and rich refugees who are turning the once casual hideaway into the places they left behind.

Keep in mind this is the opinion of someone who knew Florida B.D. (Before Disney). When Disney opened, I was a perceptive nine-year-old who had filed away the singular offerings of this endangered lifestyle. The essence of Florida was in the air as my mom and I drove past thick groves of plump oranges and savored the sweet smell of the delicate blossoms. At night the air was perfumed with Central Florida's omnipresent gardenias, night-blooming jasmine, honeysuckle, and pine. Back then Orlando was so quiet that at night I could hear the lonesome train whistles from 6 mi away.

For entertainment I swam in a creek called Snake Run and took field trips to orange juice factories. Our family would visit roadside attractions where we could SEE! Walking Catfish! And SEE! Big Sam, the World's Largest Bull! We'd travel to places like Bok Tower, in Lake Wales, and tranquil Tarpon Springs, the "sponge capital of America." (It's not your fault you were unaware that America had a sponge capital; you didn't own this book yet.)

As a friend, let me give you a tip: When you come to Florida, keep this book with you wherever you go—even in the bath. It will help you find traces of Old Florida in small towns like Micanopy and Mount Dora. You'll find it at Florida's old faithful attractions: Weeki Wachee, Cypress Gardens, Silver Springs, and Monkey Jungle. You'll experience it at Florida's wealth of botanical gardens and at rare winters-only resorts.

I miss the old place, Ma, I really do. Yet despite its changing ways, my state could still whip your state with one hand tied behind its back. Our strength is in our diversity. In South Florida you may find redneck Crackers eating swamp cabbage and gator tail in one eatery, while across the street the nouveau riche are digging into a Key West pink shrimp curry over subgum noodle pancake. Our menus may be unusual, but we require such nourishment to participate in a wide world of sports.

Floridians leap from planes at 15,000 ft and plunge into blue waters to explore real reefs and artificial ones built upon the hulls of sunken 727s. We motorcycle, ski, sail, paddle, soar, float, climb, cruise, race, run, trek, and, on rare occasions, spelunk. And if you don't like physical activity, what the hell? When you're through sipping margaritas from a coconut shell, sit in the stands and watch pro teams in Miami, Orlando, St. Pete, Tampa, Sunrise, and Jacksonville beat up on visiting players in football, baseball, roller hockey, arena football, ice hockey, and basketball.

Many of our activities are in the great outdoors. We love nature, and we treasure our manatees, sea turtles, and bald eagles. Although it's true that developers and engineers have drained, dredged, and destroyed a million-plus acres of Everglades and other environmentally sensitive land, we're trying to fix things up real nice for your arrival. Stiff fines are handed out to anyone who plucks the sea oats that hold the sandy shoreline in place, and we've set aside hundreds of thousands of acres for wildlife refuges, nature preserves, and state and national parks. Florida, I'll have you know, was the first state to establish a national forest and national bird sanctuary.

Measures such as these have led to fringe benefits. This environmental Valhalla cannot help but foster artistic pursuits. JFK wrote *Profiles in Courage* in Palm Beach, Ernest Hemingway spent 12 years in Key West getting drunk and writing books, and the *National Enquirer* is based in Lantana. Ray Charles attended the Florida School of the Deaf and Blind, in St. Augustine; the Beatles made their second *Ed Sullivan Show* appearance from Miami; and the Rolling Stones wrote "(I Can't Get No) Satisfaction" at (but not as a reflection on) a Clearwater hotel. Artist Robert Rauschenburg lives on Captiva and. . . oh, you get the idea.

Right now you're probably saying, "Gee, Florida sure sounds great, but what about my personal safety? Does the welcome center really issue flak jackets?" Fair enough. After several high-profile tourist killings in the early 1990s, Florida has taken preventive measures to provide you with protection. Police are stationed at major rest stops, rental cars no longer display rental tags, Miami has designated routes for tourists to follow, and tourist-oriented police safeguard visitors. Much of your safety is up to you, though. Protect yourself by using common sense and asking locals what parts of town to avoid. Now, I don't

share this with just anyone, but you should feel safer knowing that it was *in Florida* that G-men gunned down that scofflaw Ma Barker and her boy Fred. You can bet your bottom dollar our cops would do the same thing today if gangsters tried to hurt someone as nice as you.

If this book doesn't convince you that Florida is the most perfect state in the union, when you get here, ask for me. I'll fill up the DeSoto with some high-test ethyl, put the top down, and we'll take off to see some of Florida's 4,300 square mi of wonderful waterways, where we can swim with manatees or snorkel, scuba, or paddle to our heart's content. I'll take you to a happening diner in Orlando and a great bookstore in St. Pete. If there's time, we'll go tubing down the Ichetucknee and then hook up with some of my hepcat friends down in Coconut Grove.

Now stop reading and get down here.

–Gary McKechnie

WHAT TO READ
BEFORE YOU GO

If you plan to spend time at the beach, bring along some good books about Florida to get you in the mood. Or, if you'll be doing a lot of driving, pick up some audiotapes (some of these titles are available on cassette).

Suspense novels that are rich in details about Florida include Pulitzer Prize–winner Edna Buchanan's *Miami, It's Murder* and *Contents Under Pressure*; Les Standiford's *Done Deal*, about violence in the Miami construction business; former prosecuting attorney Barbara Parker's *Suspicion of Innocence*; Clifford Irving's *Final Argument*; Elmore Leonard's *La Brava*; John D. MacDonald's *The Empty Copper Sea*; Joan Higgins's *A Little Death Music*; and Charles Willeford's *Miami Blues*. James W. Hall features Florida in many of his big sellers, such as *Mean High Tide*, the chilling *Bones of Coral*, and *Hard Aground*.

Marjorie Kinnan Rawlings's classic *The Yearling* poignantly portrays life in the brush country, and her *Cross Creek* re-creates the memorable people she knew there. Peter Matthiessen's *Killing Mister Watson* re-creates turn-of-the-century lower southwest Florida.

Look for *Princess of the Everglades*, a novel about the 1926 hurricane, by Charles Mink, and *Snow White and Rose Red* and *Jack and the Beanstalk*, Ed McBain's novels about a gulf city attorney. Miami's Carl Hiaasen has turned out lots of Florida-based books, including *Double Whammy* and *Lucky You*.

Other recommended titles include Roxanne Pulitzer's *Facade*, set against a backdrop of Palm Beach; Pat Booth's *Miami*; Sam Harrison's *Bones of Blue Coral* and *Birdsong Ascending*; T. D. Allman's *Miami*; Joan Didion's *Miami*; David Rieff's *Going to Miami*; Alice Hoffman's *Turtle Moon*; *Scavenger Reef* and *Florida Straits*, by Laurence Shames; *To Have and Have Not*, by Ernest Hemingway; *The Day of the Dolphin*, by Robert Merle; and *Their Eyes Were Watching God*, by Zora Neale Hurston.

Among recommended nonfiction books are *The Commodore's Story*, by Ralph Munroe and Vincent Gilpin, a luminous reminiscence about the golden years (pre-railroad) of Coconut Grove; *Key West Writers and Their Homes*, by Lynn Kaufelt; *The Everglades: River of Grass*, by Marjory S. Douglas; *The Other Florida*, by Gloria Jahoda; and *Florida's Sandy Beaches*, University Press of Florida. Mark Derr's *Some Kind of Paradise* is an excellent review of the state's environmental follies; John Rothchild's *Up for Grabs*, equally good, is about Florida's commercial lunacy. Good anthologies include *The Florida Reader: Visions of Paradise* (Maurice O'Sullivan and Jack Lane, editors), *The Rivers of Florida* (Del and Marty Marth, editors), and *Subtropical Speculations: An Anthology of Florida Science Fiction* (Richard Mathews and Rick Wilber, editors).

A good companion to this guide, Fodor's *Compass American Guides: Florida* has handsome photos and historical, cultural, and topical essays.

Books that are also available on audiotape include Peter Dexter's *The Paperboy*, as well as several by Carl Hiaasen: *Native Tongue*, *Skin Tight*, *Stormy Weather*, *Strip Tease*, and *The Tourist Season*, his immensely funny declaration of war against the state's environment-despoiling hordes.

ESSENTIAL INFORMATION

AIR TRAVEL

BOOKING YOUR FLIGHT

When you book **look for nonstop flights** and **remember that "direct" flights stop at least once.** Try to avoid connecting flights, which require a change of plane.

CARRIERS

➤ MAJOR AIRLINES: **American** (☎ 800/523–3223). **Continental** (☎ 800/525–0280). **Delta** (☎ 800/221–1212). **Midway** (☎ 800/446–4392). **Northwest** (☎ 800/225–2525). **Southwest** (☎ 800/435–9792). **TWA** (☎ 800/221–2000). **United** (☎ 800/241–6522). **US Airways** (☎ 800/428–4322).

➤ REGIONAL AIRLINES: **AirTran** (☎ 800/247–8726) to Fort Lauderdale, Fort Myers, Jacksonville, Orlando, Tampa, and West Palm Beach.

Midwest Express (☎ 800/452–2022) to Fort Lauderdale, Fort Myers, Orlando, and Tampa.

➤ FROM THE U.K.: **American** (☎ 0345/789–789). **British Airways** (☎ 0345/222–111). **Continental** (☎ 0800/776–464) via Newark. **Delta** (☎ 0800/414–767). **Northwest** (☎ 0990/561–000) via Detroit or Minneapolis. **TWA** (☎ 0800/222–222) via St. Louis. **United** (☎ 0800/888–555). **Virgin Atlantic** (☎ 01293/747–747).

CHECK-IN & BOARDING

Assuming that not everyone with a ticket will show up, airlines routinely overbook planes. When that happens, airlines ask for volunteers to give up their seats. In return these volunteers usually get a certificate for a free flight and are rebooked on the next flight out. If there are not enough volunteers, the airline must choose who will be denied boarding. The first to get bumped are passengers who checked in late and those flying on discounted tickets, so **get to the gate and check in as early as possible,** especially during peak periods. Heightened security at Miami International Airport has meant that it's suggested you check in 90 minutes before departure for a domestic flight, two hours for an international flight.

Always **bring a government-issued photo ID to the airport.** You may be asked to show it before you are allowed to check in.

CUTTING COSTS

The least-expensive airfares to Florida must usually be purchased in advance and are non-refundable. It's smart to **call a number of airlines, and when you are quoted a good price, book it on the spot**—the same fare may not be available the next day. Always **check different routings** and look into using different airports. Travel agents, especially low-fare specialists (☞ Discounts & Deals, *below*), are helpful.

Consolidators are another good source. They buy tickets for scheduled international flights at reduced rates from the airlines, then sell them at prices that beat the best fare available directly from the airlines, usually without restrictions. Sometimes you can even get your money back if you need to return the ticket. Carefully read the fine print detailing penalties for changes and cancellations, and **confirm your consolidator reservation with the airline.**

When you **fly as a courier** you trade your checked-luggage space for a ticket deeply subsidized by a courier service. There are restrictions on when you can book and how long you can stay.

➤ CONSOLIDATORS: **Cheap Tickets** (☎ 800/377–1000). **Up & Away Travel** (☎ 212/889–2345). **Discount Airline**

Ticket Service (☎ 800/576–1600). Unitravel (☎ 800/325–2222). **World Travel Network** (☎ 800/409–6753).

➤ CHEAP RATES FROM THE U.K.: Flight Express Travel (77 New Bond St., London W1Y 9DB, ☎ 0171/409–3311). **Trailfinders** (42–50 Earls Court Rd., London W8 6FT, ☎ 0171/937–5400). **Travel Cuts** (295A Regent St., London W1R 7YA, ☎ 0171/637–3161).

ENJOYING THE FLIGHT

For more legroom **request an emergency-aisle seat.** Don't sit in the row in front of the emergency aisle or in front of a bulkhead, where seats may not recline. If you have dietary concerns, **ask for special meals when booking.** These can be vegetarian, low-cholesterol, or kosher, for example. On long flights, try to maintain a normal routine, to help fight jetlag. At night **get some sleep.** By day **eat lightly, drink water** (not alcohol), and **move around the cabin** to stretch your legs.

FLYING TIMES

Flying times to Florida vary based on the city you're flying to, but typical times are 3 hours from New York, 4 hours from Chicago, and 5–5½ hours from Los Angeles.

HOW TO COMPLAIN

If your baggage goes astray or your flight goes awry, complain right away. Most carriers require that you **file a claim immediately.**

➤ AIRLINE COMPLAINTS: U.S. Department of Transportation **Aviation Consumer Protection Division** (✉ C-75, Room 4107, Washington, DC 20590, ☎ 202/366–2220). **Federal Aviation Administration Consumer Hotline** (☎ 800/322–7873).

AIRPORTS

Because Florida is dotted with both major and regional airports, you can usually pick one quite close to your destination and often choose from a couple of nearby options. If you're destined for the north side of Miami-Dade County (metro Miami), **consider flying into Fort Lauderdale–Hollywood International**; it's much easier to use than Miami International.

➤ AIRPORT INFORMATION: **Daytona Beach International** (☎ 904/248–8069). **Fort Lauderdale–Hollywood International** (☎ 954/359–1200). **Jacksonville International** (☎ 904/741–4902). **Miami International** (☎ 305/876–7000). **Orlando International** (☎ 561/825–2001). **Palm Beach International** (☎ 561/471–7420). **Tampa International** (☎ 727/870–8700).

BIKE TRAVEL

BIKES IN FLIGHT

Most airlines accommodate bikes as luggage, provided they are dismantled and boxed. For bike boxes, often free at bike shops, you'll pay about $5 (at least $100 for bike bags) from airlines. International travelers can sometimes substitute a bike for a piece of checked luggage at no charge; otherwise, the cost is about $100. Domestic and Canadian airlines charge $25–$50.

BUS TRAVEL

FARES & SCHEDULES

Greyhound passes through practically every major city in Florida. For schedules and fares, **contact your local Greyhound Information Center.**

➤ BUS INFORMATION: **Greyhound** (☎ 800/231–2222).

CAMERAS & PHOTOGRAPHY

➤ PHOTO HELP: **Kodak Information Center** (☎ 800/242–2424). *Kodak Guide to Shooting Great Travel Pictures,* available in bookstores or from Fodor's Travel Publications (☎ 800/533–6478; $16.50 plus $4 shipping).

EQUIPMENT PRECAUTIONS

Always **keep your film and tape out of the sun or a parked car on a hot day.** Carry an extra supply of batteries, and **be prepared to turn on your camera or camcorder** to prove to security personnel that the device is real. Always **ask for hand inspection of film,** which becomes clouded after successive exposures to airport X-ray machines, and **keep videotapes away from metal detectors.**

CAR RENTAL

On-season rates in Miami begin at $36 a day and $170 a week for an economy car with air-conditioning, an automatic transmission, and unlimited mileage. Rates in Orlando begin at $35 a day and $149 a week. Rates in Fort Lauderdale begin at $36 a day and $159 a week. Rates in Tampa begin at $33 a day and $147 a week. This does not include tax on car rentals, which is 6%. Bear in mind that rates fluctuate tremendously—both above and below these quoted figures—depending on demand and the season. Rental cars are more expensive (and harder to find) during peak holidays and in season.

It used to be that major rental agencies were located at the airport whereas cheaper firms weren't. Now however, all over Florida, even the majors might be off airport property. It varies firm to firm and airport to airport. Speedy check-in and frequent shuttle buses make off-airport rentals almost as convenient as on-site service. However, it's wise to allow a little extra time for bus travel between the rental agency and the airport.

CUTTING COSTS

To get the best deal **book through a travel agent who will shop around.** Also **price local car-rental companies,** although the service and maintenance may not be as good as those of a major player. Remember to ask about required deposits, cancellation penalties, and drop-off charges if you're planning to pick up the car in one city and leave it in another. If you're traveling during a holiday period, also make sure that a confirmed reservation guarantees you a car.

Do **look into wholesalers,** companies that do not own fleets but rent in bulk from those that do and often offer better rates than traditional car-rental operations.

➤ MAJOR AGENCIES: **Alamo** (☎ 800/327–9633; 0181/759–6200 in the U.K.). **Avis** (☎ 800/331–1212; 800/879–2847 in Canada; 02/9353–9000 in Australia; 09/525–1982 in New Zealand). **Budget** (☎ 800/527–0700; 0144/227–6266 in the U.K.). **Dollar** (☎ 800/800–4000; 0181/897–0811

in the U.K., where it is known as Eurodollar; 02/9223–1444 in Australia). **Hertz** (☎ 800/654–3131; 800/263–0600 in Canada; 0181/897–2072 in the U.K.; 02/9669–2444 in Australia; 03/358–6777 in New Zealand). **National InterRent** (☎ 800/227–7368; 0345/222525 in the U.K., where it is known as Europcar InterRent).

➤ LOCAL AGENCIES: **Apex Rent A Car** (☎ 954/782–3400) in Fort Lauderdale. **Florida Auto Rental** (☎ 954/764–1008 or 800/327–3791) in Fort Lauderdale. **InterAmerican Car Rental** (☎ 305/871–3030) in Fort Lauderdale, Miami Beach, Orlando, and Tampa. **Preferred Rent-A-Car** (☎ 727/287–1872 or 800/526–5499) in Tampa–St. Petersburg. **Snappy Car Rental** (☎ 407/859–8808) in Orlando. **Tropical Rent-a-Car** ☎ 305/294–8136) in Key West. **Ugly Duckling Rent-A-Car** (☎ 407/240–7368 or 800/843–3825) in Orlando.

➤ WHOLESALERS: **Auto Europe** (☎ 207/842–2000 or 800/223–5555, FAX 800/235–6321).

INSURANCE

When driving a rented car you are generally responsible for any damage to or loss of the vehicle as well as for any property damage or personal injury that you may cause. Before you rent see what coverage your personal auto-insurance policy and credit cards already provide.

For about $15 to $20 per day, rental companies sell protection, known as a collision- or loss-damage waiver (CDW or LDW), that eliminates your liability for damage to the car.

In most states you don't need a CDW if you have personal auto insurance or other liability insurance. However, **make sure you have enough coverage to pay for the car.** If you do not have auto insurance or an umbrella policy that covers damage to third parties, purchasing liability insurance and a CDW or LDW is highly recommended.

REQUIREMENTS & RESTRICTIONS

In Florida you must be 21 to rent a car, and rates may be higher if you're under 25. You'll pay extra for child seats (about $3 per day), which are compulsory for children under five, and for additional drivers (about $2 per day). Non-U.S. residents will need a reservation voucher, a passport, a driver's license, and a travel policy that covers each driver, in order to pick up a car.

SURCHARGES

Before you pick up a car in one city and leave it in another **ask about drop-off charges or one-way service fees,** which can be substantial. Note, too, that some rental agencies charge extra if you return the car before the time specified in your contract. To avoid a hefty refueling fee **fill the tank just before you turn in the car,** but be aware that gas stations near the rental outlet may overcharge.

CAR TRAVEL

Three major interstates lead to Florida. I–95 begins in Maine, runs south through the Mid-Atlantic states, and enters Florida just north of Jacksonville. It continues south past Daytona Beach, the Space Coast, Vero Beach, Palm Beach, and Fort Lauderdale, eventually ending in Miami.

I–75 begins in Michigan at the Canadian border and runs south through Ohio, Kentucky, Tennessee, and Georgia, then moves south through the center of the state before veering west into Tampa. It follows the west coast south to Naples, then crosses the state through the northern section of the Everglades, and ends in Fort Lauderdale.

California and all the most southern states are connected to Florida by I–10, which moves east from Los Angeles through Arizona, New Mexico, Texas, Louisiana, Mississippi, and Alabama; it enters Florida at Pensacola and runs straight across the northern part of the state, ending in Jacksonville.

ROAD CONDITIONS

Florida has its share of traffic problems. Downtown areas of such major cities as Miami, Orlando, and Tampa can be extremely congested during rush hours, usually 7 to 9 AM and 4 to 6 PM on weekdays. When you drive

the interstate system in Florida, try to **plan your trip so that you are not entering, leaving, or passing through a large city during rush hour,** when traffic can slow to 10 mph for 10 mi or more. In addition, snowbirds usually rent in Florida for a month at a time, which means they all arrive on the first of the month and leave on the 31st. Believe it or not, from November to March, when the end and beginning of a month occur on a weekend, north–south routes like I–75 and I–95 almost come to a standstill during daylight hours. It's best to avoid traveling on these days if possible.

RULES OF THE ROAD

Speed limits are 55 mph on state highways, 30 mph within city limits and residential areas, and 55–70 mph on interstates and Florida's Turnpike. Be alert for signs announcing exceptions.

SAFETY

Before setting off on any drive, **make sure you know where you're going** and carry a map. At the car-rental agency or at your hotel **ask if there are any areas that you should avoid.** Always **keep your doors locked,** and ask questions only at toll booths, gas stations, or other obviously safe locations. Also, **don't stop if your car is bumped from behind** or if you're asked for directions. One hesitates to foster rude behavior, but at least for now the roads are too risky to stop any place you're not familiar with (other than as traffic laws require). If you'll be renting a car, **ask the car-rental agency for a cellular phone.** Alamo, Avis, and Hertz are among the companies with in-car phones.

CHILDREN IN FLORIDA

If you are renting a car don't forget to **arrange for a car seat** when you reserve.

FLYING

If your children are two or older **ask about children's airfares.** As a general rule, infants under two not occupying a seat fly at greatly reduced fares or even for free.

Experts agree that it's a good idea to use safety seats aloft for children weighing less than 40 pounds. Airlines set their own policies: U.S. carriers usually require that the child be ticketed, even if he or she is young enough to ride free, since the seats must be strapped into regular seats. Do **check your airline's policy about using safety seats during takeoff and landing.** And since safety seats are not allowed just everywhere in the plane, get your seat assignments early.

When reserving, **request children's meals or a freestanding bassinet** if you need them. But note that bulkhead seats, where you must sit to use the bassinet may lack an overhead bin or storage space on the floor.

LODGING

Florida may have the highest concentration of hotels with organized children's programs in the United States. Activities range from simple fun and recreation to shell-hunting on Marco Island at Marriott's Marco Island Resort and learning about the Keys' environment from marine-science counselors at Cheeca Lodge. Sometimes kids' programs are complimentary; sometimes there's a charge. Not all accept children in diapers, and some offer programs when their central reservations services say they don't. Some programs are only offered during peak seasons or restrict hours in less-busy times. It always pays to **confirm details with the hotel in advance.** And **reserve space as soon as possible**; programs are often full by the morning or evening you need them.

Most hotels in Florida allow children under a certain age to stay in their parents' room at no extra charge, but others charge for them as extra adults; be sure to **find out the cutoff age for children's discounts.**

➤ FORT LAUDERDALE: **Marriott's Harbor Beach Resort's Beachside Buddies** (3030 Holiday Dr., Fort Lauderdale, FL 33316, ☎ 954/525–4000 or 800/228–9290), ages 5–12.

➤ THE KEYS: **Cheeca Lodge's Camp Cheeca** (MM 82, OS, Box 527, Islamorada, FL 33036, ☎ 800/327–2888), ages 6–12. **Westin Beach Resort's Westin Kids Club** (MM 96.9, BS, 97000 Overseas Hwy., Key Largo, FL 33037, ☎ 305/852–5553 or 800/325–3535), ages 5–12.

➤ MIAMI AREA: **Sonesta Beach Resort's Just Us Kids** (350 Ocean Dr., Key Biscayne, FL 33149, ☎ 800/766–3782), ages 5–13.

➤ NORTHEAST FLORIDA: **Amelia Island Plantation's Kid's Camp Amelia** (3000 First Coast Hwy., Amelia Island, FL 32034, ☎ 904/261–6161), ages 3–10.

➤ ORLANDO AREA: **Delta Orlando Resort's Wally's Club Kids Creative Center** (5715 Major Blvd., Orlando, FL 32819, ☎ 800/877–1133), ages 4–12. **Holiday Inn Hotel & Suites Main Gate East** (5678 W. Irlo Bronson Memorial Hwy., Kissimmee, FL 32741, ☎ 407/396–4488 or 800/465–4329), ages 4–12. **Holiday Inn SunSpree Resort Lake Buena Vista's Camp Holiday** (13351 Rte. 535, Orlando, FL 32821, ☎ 800/366–6299), ages 2–12. **Hyatt Regency Grand Cypress Resort's Camp Gator** (1 Grand Cypress Blvd., Orlando, FL 32819, ☎ 407/239–1234 or 800/228–9000), ages 5–12. **Renaissance Orlando Resort's Shamu's Playhouse** (6677 Sea Harbor Dr., Orlando, FL 32821, ☎ 407/351–5555 or 800/468–3571), ages 4–12.

➤ PALM BEACH AND THE TREASURE COAST: **Club Med's Sandpiper** (Port St. Lucie [mailing address: 40 W. 57th St., New York, NY 10019], ☎ 800/258–2633), Baby Club ages 4–24 months, Mini Club ages 2–11. **Indian River Plantation Marriott Beach Resort's Pineapple Bunch Children's Camp** (555 N.E. Ocean Blvd., Hutchinson Island, Stuart, FL 34996, ☎ 561/225–3700), ages 4–12, plus a teen program.

➤ SOUTHWEST FLORIDA: **Marriott's Marco Island Resort's Kids Klub** (400 S. Collier Blvd., Marco Island, FL 33937, ☎ 800/228–9290), ages 5–12. **Radisson Suite Beach Resort's Radisson Rascals** (600 S. Collier Blvd., Marco Island, FL 33937, ☎ 800/333–3333), ages 5–12. **Sanibel Harbour Resort & Spa's Kids Klub** (17260 Harbour Pointe Dr., Fort Myers, FL 33908, ☎ 800/767–7777), ages 5–12. **South Seas Plantation's Explorer Kids' Club** (5400 Plantation

Rd., Captiva Island, FL 33924, ☎ 800/227–8482), ages 3–11, plus activities for teens.

SIGHTS & ATTRACTIONS

Places that are especially good for children are indicated by a rubber duckie icon in the margin.

CONSUMER PROTECTION

Whenever shopping or buying travel services in Florida, **pay with a major credit card** so you can cancel payment or get reimbursed if there's a problem. If you're doing business with a particular company for the first time, **contact your local Better Business Bureau and the attorney general's offices** in your state and the company's home state, as well. Have any complaints been filed? Finally, if you're buying a package or tour, always **consider travel insurance** that includes default coverage (☞ Insurance, *below*).

➤ LOCAL BBBs: **Council of Better Business Bureaus** (✉ 4200 Wilson Blvd., Suite 800, Arlington, VA 22203, ☎ 703/276–0100, FAX 703/525–8277).

CUSTOMS & DUTIES

When shopping, **keep receipts** for all purchases. Upon reentering the country, **be ready to show customs officials what you've bought.** If you feel a duty is incorrect or object to the way your clearance was handled, note the inspector's badge number and ask to see a supervisor. If the problem isn't resolved, write to the appropriate authorities, beginning with the port director at your point of entry.

IN AUSTRALIA

Australia residents who are 18 or older may bring home A$400 worth of souvenirs and gifts (including jewelry), 250 cigarettes or 250 grams of tobacco, and 1,125 ml of alcohol (including wine, beer, and spirits). Residents under 18 may bring back A$200 worth of goods. Prohibited items include meat products. Seeds, plants, and fruits need to be declared upon arrival.

➤ INFORMATION: **Australian Customs Service** (Regional Director, ✉ Box 8, Sydney, NSW 2001, ☎ 02/9213–2000, FAX 02/9213–4000).

IN CANADA

Canadian residents who have been out of Canada for at least 7 days may bring home C$500 worth of goods duty-free. If you've been away less than 7 days but more than 48 hours, the duty-free allowance drops to C$200; if your trip lasts 24–48 hours, the allowance is C$50. You may not pool allowances with family members. Goods claimed under the C$500 exemption may follow you by mail; those claimed under the lesser exemptions must accompany you. Alcohol and tobacco products may be included in the 7-day and 48-hour exemptions but not in the 24-hour exemption. If you meet the age requirements of the province or territory through which you reenter Canada, you may bring in, duty-free, 1.14 liters (40 imperial ounces) of wine or liquor *or* 24 12-ounce cans or bottles of beer or ale. If you are 16 or older you may bring in, duty-free, 200 cigarettes and 50 cigars. Check ahead of time with Revenue Canada or the Department of Agriculture for policies regarding meat products, seeds, plants, and fruits.

You may send an unlimited number of gifts worth up to C$60 each duty-free to Canada. Label the package UNSOLICITED GIFT—VALUE UNDER $60. Alcohol and tobacco are excluded.

➤ INFORMATION: **Revenue Canada** (✉ 2265 St. Laurent Blvd. S, Ottawa, Ontario K1G 4K3, ☎ 613/993–0534; 800/461–9999 in Canada).

IN NEW ZEALAND

Homeward-bound residents 17 or older may bring back $700 worth of souvenirs and gifts. Your duty-free allowance also includes 4.5 liters of wine or beer; one 1,125-ml bottle of spirits; and either 200 cigarettes, 250 grams of tobacco, 50 cigars, or a combination of the three up to 250 grams. Prohibited items include meat products, seeds, plants, and fruits.

➤ INFORMATION: **New Zealand Customs** (Custom House, ✉ 50 Anzac Ave., Box 29, Auckland, New

Zealand, ☎ 09/359–6655, FAX 09/359–6732).

IN THE U.K.

From countries outside the EU, including the United States, you may bring home, duty-free, 200 cigarettes or 50 cigars; 1 liter of spirits or 2 liters of fortified or sparkling wine or liqueurs; 2 liters of still table wine; 60 milliliters of perfume; 250 milliliters of toilet water; plus £136 worth of other goods, including gifts and souvenirs. If returning from outside the EU, prohibited items include meat products, seeds, plants, and fruits.

➤ INFORMATION: **HM Customs and Excise** (✉ Dorset House, Stamford St., Bromley Kent BR1 1XX, ☎ 0171/202–4227).

IN THE U.S.

Non-U.S. residents ages 21 and older may import into the United States 200 cigarettes or 50 cigars or 2 kilograms of tobacco, 1 liter of alcohol, and gifts worth $100. Meat products, seeds, plants, and fruits are prohibited.

➤ INFORMATION: **U.S. Customs Service** (inquiries, ✉ 1300 Pennsylvania Ave. NW, Washington, DC 20229, ☎ 202/927–6724; complaints, ✉ Office of Regulations and Rulings, 1300 Pennsylvania Ave. NW, Washington, DC 20229; registration of equipment, ✉ Resource Management, 1300 Pennsylvania Ave. NW, Washington, DC 20229, ☎ 202/927–0540).

DINING

The restaurants we list are the cream of the crop in each price category.

CATEGORY	COST*
$$$$	over $50
$$$	$35–$50
$$	$20–$35
$	under $20

*per person for a three-course meal, excluding drinks, service, and 6% sales tax (more in some counties)

One cautionary word: Raw oysters have been identified as a problem for people with chronic illness of the liver, stomach, or blood, or who have immune disorders. Since 1993, all Florida restaurants serving raw oysters are required to post a notice in plain view of all patrons warning of the risks associated with consuming them.

RESERVATIONS & DRESS

Reservations are always a good idea: we mention them only when they're essential or are not accepted. Book as far ahead as you can, and reconfirm as soon as you arrive. We mention dress only when men are required to wear a jacket or a jacket and tie.

DISABILITIES & ACCESSIBILITY

➤ COMPLAINTS: **Disability Rights Section** (✉ U.S. Department of Justice, Civil Rights Division, Box 66738, Washington, DC 20035-6738, ☎ 202/514–0301; 800/514–0301; 202/514–0301 TTY; 800/514–0301 TTY, FAX 202/307–1198) for general complaints. **Aviation Consumer Protection Division** (☞ Air Travel, *above*) for airline-related problems. **Civil Rights Office** (✉ U.S. Department of Transportation, Departmental Office of Civil Rights, S-30, 400 7th St. SW, Room 10215, Washington, DC 20590, ☎ 202/366–4648, FAX 202/366–9371) for problems with surface transportation.

LODGING

When discussing accessibility with an operator or reservations agent **ask hard questions.** Are there any stairs, inside *or* out? Are there grab bars next to the toilet *and* in the shower/tub? How wide is the doorway to the room? To the bathroom? For the most extensive facilities meeting the latest legal specifications **opt for newer accommodations.**

TRAVEL AGENCIES

In the United States, although the Americans with Disabilities Act requires that travel firms serve the needs of all travelers, some agencies specialize in working with people with disabilities.

➤ TRAVELERS WITH MOBILITY PROBLEMS: **Access Adventures** (✉ 206 Chestnut Ridge Rd., Rochester, NY 14624, ☎ 716/889–9096), run by a former physical-rehabilitation counselor. **Accessible Vans of the Rockies, Activity and Travel Agency** (✉ 2040 W. Hamilton Pl., Sheridan, CO 80110, ☎ 303/806–5047 or 888/

837–0065, FAX 303/781–2329). **Care-Vacations** (✉ 5-5110 50th Ave., Leduc, Alberta T9E 6V4, ☎ 780/986–6404 or 780/986–8332) has group tours and is especially helpful with cruise vacations. **Flying Wheels Travel** (✉ 143 W. Bridge St., Box 382, Owatonna, MN 55060, ☎ 507/451–5005 or 800/535–6790, FAX 507/451–1685). **Hinsdale Travel Service** (✉ 201 E. Ogden Ave., Suite 100, Hinsdale, IL 60521, ☎ 630/325–1335).

➤ TRAVELERS WITH DEVELOPMENTAL DISABILITIES: **New Directions** (✉ 5276 Hollister Ave., Suite 207, Santa Barbara, CA 93111, ☎ 805/967–2841 or 888/967–2841, FAX 805/964–7344). **Sprout** (✉ 893 Amsterdam Ave., New York, NY 10025, ☎ 212/222–9575 or 888/222–9575, FAX 212/222–9768).

DISCOUNTS & DEALS

Be a smart shopper and **compare all your options** before making decisions. A plane ticket bought with a promotional coupon from travel clubs, coupon books, and direct-mail offers may not be cheaper than the least expensive fare from a discount ticket agency. And always keep in mind that what you get is just as important as what you save.

DISCOUNT RESERVATIONS

To save money **look into discount-reservations services** with toll-free numbers, which use their buying power to get a better price on hotels, airline tickets, even car rentals. When booking a room, always **call the hotel's local toll-free number** (if one is available) rather than the central reservations number—you'll often get a better price. Always ask about special packages or corporate rates.

➤ AIRLINE TICKETS: ☎ **800/FLY–4–LESS**. ☎ **800/FLY–ASAP**.

➤ HOTEL ROOMS: **Accommodations Express** (☎ 800/444–7666). **Central Reservation Service (CRS)** (☎ 800/548–3311). **Hotel Reservations Network** (☎ 800/964–6835). **Players Express Vacations** (☎ 800/458–6161). **Room Finders USA** (☎ 800/473–7829). **RMC Travel** (☎ 800/245–5738). **Steigenberger Reservation Service** (☎ 800/223–5652).

PACKAGE DEALS

Don't confuse packages and guided tours. When you buy a package, you travel on your own, just as though you had planned the trip yourself. Fly/drive packages, which combine airfare and car rental, are often a good deal.

ECOTOURISM

Florida's varied environment is one of its chief draws; it's also very fragile. If you're out in nature, follow the basic rules of environmental responsibility: Take nothing but pictures; leave nothing but footprints. Most important, **be extremely careful around the tenuous dunes.** Picking the sea grasses that hold the dunes in place can carry stiff fines, as can walking or playing or digging in the dunes. So stay on the beach, gaze at the beautiful dunes, but don't go on them. An afternoon of roughhousing can completely destroy a dune. Ecotours (listed under Guided Tours in each chapter's A to Z section) operate throughout the state and can help you see some of what makes Florida so distinct, usually in a way that makes the least impact possible.

GAY & LESBIAN TRAVEL

Destinations within Florida that have a reputation for being especially gay and lesbian friendly include South Beach and Key West.

➤ GAY- AND LESBIAN-FRIENDLY TRAVEL AGENCIES: **Different Roads Travel** (✉ 8383 Wilshire Blvd., Suite 902, Beverly Hills, CA 90211, ☎ 323/651–5557 or 800/429–8747, FAX 323/651–3678). **Kennedy Travel** (✉ 314 Jericho Turnpike, Floral Park, NY 11001, ☎ 516/352–4888 or 800/237–7433, FAX 516/354–8849). **Now Voyager** (✉ 4406 18th St., San Francisco, CA 94114, ☎ 415/626–1169 or 800/255–6951, FAX 415/626–8626). **Yellowbrick Road** (✉ 1500 W. Balmoral Ave., Chicago, IL 60640, ☎ 773/561–1800 or 800/642–2488, FAX 773/561–4497). **Skylink Travel and Tour** (✉ 1006 Mendocino Ave., Santa Rosa, CA 95401, ☎ 707/546–9888 or 800/225–5759, FAX 707/546–9891), serving lesbian travelers.

HEALTH

BEACH AND SUN SAFETY

If you are unaccustomed to strong subtropical sun, you run a risk of sunburn and heat prostration, even in winter. So **hit the beach or play tennis, golf, or another outdoor sport before 10 or after 3.** If you must be out at midday, **limit strenuous exercise, drink plenty of liquids, and wear a hat.** If you begin to feel faint, get out of the sun immediately and sip water slowly. Even on overcast days, ultraviolet rays shine through the haze, so **use a sunscreen with an SPF of at least 15,** and have children wear a waterproof SPF 30 or better.

While you're frolicking on the beach, **steer clear of what looks like blue bubbles on the sand.** These are Portuguese man-of-wars, and their tentacles can cause an allergic reaction. Also be careful of other large jellyfish, some of which can sting.

Before swimming, **make sure there's no undertow.** (Since you can't necessarily see if there is one, check with a lifeguard.) Rip currents, caused when the tide rushes out through a narrow break in a sandbar, can overpower even the strongest swimmer. If you're caught in one, resist the urge to swim straight back to shore—you'll never make it. Instead, stay calm, swim parallel to the shore until you are outside the current's pull, and then work your way in. And always **exercise extra caution when the surf is up.**

If you walk across a grassy area on the way to the beach, you'll probably encounter sand spurs. They are quite tiny, light brown, and remarkably prickly. You'll feel them before you see them; if you get stuck with one, just pull it out.

DIVERS' ALERT

Do not fly within 24 hours of scuba diving.

HOLIDAYS

Major national holidays include New Year's Day (Jan. 1); Martin Luther King, Jr., Day (3rd Mon. in Jan.); President's Day (3rd Mon. in Feb.); Memorial Day (last Mon. in May); Independence Day (July 4); Labor Day (1st Mon. in Sept.); Thanksgiving Day (4th Thurs. in Nov.); Christmas Eve and Christmas Day (Dec. 24 and 25); and New Year's Eve (Dec. 31).

INSURANCE

The most useful travel insurance plan is a comprehensive policy that includes coverage for trip cancellation and interruption, default, trip delay, and medical expenses (with a waiver for preexisting conditions).

Without insurance you will lose all or most of your money if you cancel your trip, regardless of the reason. Default insurance covers you if your tour operator, airline, or cruise line goes out of business. Trip-delay covers expenses that arise because of bad weather or mechanical delays. Study the fine print when comparing policies.

British and Australian citizens need extra medical coverage when traveling overseas.

Always **buy travel policies directly from the insurance company**; if you buy it from a cruise line, airline, or tour operator that goes out of business you probably will not be covered for the agency or operator's default, a major risk. Before you make any purchase **review your existing health and home-owner's policies** to find what they cover away from home.

► TRAVEL INSURERS: In the U.S., **Access America** (⊠ 6600 W. Broad St., Richmond, VA 23230, ☎ 804/285–3300 or 800/284–8300), **Travel Guard International** (⊠ 1145 Clark St., Stevens Point, WI 54481, ☎ 715/345–0505 or 800/826–1300). In Canada, **Voyager Insurance** (⊠ 44 Peel Center Dr., Brampton, Ontario L6T 4M8, ☎ 905/791–8700; 800/668–4342 in Canada).

► INSURANCE INFORMATION: In the U.K., the **Association of British Insurers** (⊠ 51–55 Gresham St., London EC2V 7HQ, ☎ 0171/600–3333, FAX 0171/696–8999). In Australia, the **Insurance Council of Australia** (☎ 03/9614–1077, FAX 03/9614–7924).

LODGING

Florida has every conceivable type of lodging—from tree houses to penthouses, mansions for hire to hostels. Even with occupancy rates inching above 70%, there are almost always rooms available, except maybe at Christmas and other holidays. Affordable lodgings can be found in even the most glittery resort towns, typically motel rooms that may cost as little as $50–$60 a night; they may not be in the best part of town, mind you, but they won't be in the worst, either (perhaps along busy highways where you'll need the roar of the air-conditioning to drown out the traffic). Since beachfront properties tend to be more expensive, **look for properties a little off the beach.** Still, many beachfront properties are surprisingly affordable, too, as in places like St. Pete Beach, on the west coast, and Cocoa Beach, on the east coast.

Children are welcome generally everywhere in Florida. Pets are another matter, so **inquire ahead of time if you're bringing an animal with you.**

In the busy seasons—over Christmas and from late January through Easter in the southern half of the state, during the summer along the Panhandle and around Jacksonville, and all over Florida during holiday weekends in summer—always **reserve ahead for the top properties.** Fall is the slowest season: Rates are low and availability is high. St. Augustine stays busy all summer because of its historic flavor. Key West is jam-packed for Fantasy Fest at Halloween. If you're not booking through a travel agent, call the visitors bureau or the chamber of commerce in the area where you're going to check whether any special event is scheduled for when you plan to arrive. If demand isn't especially high for the time you have in mind, you can often **save by showing up at a lodging in mid- to late afternoon**—desk clerks are typically willing to negotiate with travelers in order to fill those rooms late in the day. In addition, **check with chambers of commerce for discount coupons for selected properties.**

The lodgings we list are the cream of the crop in each price category. We always list the facilities that are available—but we don't specify whether they cost extra: When pricing accommodations, always ask what's included and what costs extra.

CATEGORY	COST*
$$$$	over $220
$$$	$140–$220
$$	$80–$140
$	under $80

All prices are for a standard double room, excluding 6% sales tax (more in some counties) and 1%–4% tourist tax.

APARTMENT & VILLA RENTALS

If you want a home base that's roomy enough for a family and comes with cooking facilities **consider a furnished rental.** These can save you money, especially if you're traveling with a group. Home-exchange directories sometimes list rentals as well as exchanges.

➤ INTERNATIONAL AGENTS: **Europa-Let/Tropical Inn-Let** (✉ 92 N. Main St., Ashland, OR 97520, ☎ 541/482–5806 or 800/462–4486, FAX 541/482–0660). **Hometours International** (✉ Box 11503, Knoxville, TN 37939, ☎ 423/690–8484 or 800/367–4668). **Interhome** (✉ 1990 N.E. 163rd St., Suite 110, Miami Beach, FL 33162, ☎ 305/940–2299 or 800/882–6864, FAX 305/940–2911). **Rent-a-Home International** (✉ 7200 34th Ave. NW, Seattle, WA 98117, ☎ 206/789–9377, FAX 206/789–9379). **Vacation Home Rentals Worldwide** (✉ 235 Kensington Ave., Norwood, NJ 07648, ☎ 201/767–9393 or 800/633–3284, FAX 201/767–5510). **Hideaways International** (✉ 767 Islington St., Portsmouth, NH 03801, ☎ 603/430–4433 or 800/843–4433, FAX 603/430–4444; membership $99).

B&BS

Small inns and guest houses are increasingly numerous in Florida, but they vary tremendously, ranging from economical places that are plain but serve a good home-style breakfast to elegantly furnished Victorian houses with four-course gourmet morning meals and rates to match. Many offer a homelike setting. In fact, many are in private homes with owners who treat you almost like family, while others are more businesslike. It's a good idea to **make specific inquiries of B&Bs you're interested in.**

➤ HISTORIC INN ASSOCIATION: **Inn Route, Inc.** (Box 6187, Palm Harbor, FL 34684, ☎ ℻ 281/499–1374 or 800/524–1880).

➤ RESERVATION SERVICES: **Bed & Breakfast Co., Tropical Florida** (Box 262, Miami, FL 33243, ☎ ℻ 305/661–3270). **Bed & Breakfast Scenic Florida** (Box 3385, Tallahassee, FL 32315-3385, ☎ 850/386–8196). **RSVP Florida & St. Augustine** (Box 3603, St. Augustine, FL 32085, ☎ 904/471–0600). **Suncoast Accommodations of Florida** (8690 Gulf Blvd., St. Pete Beach, FL 33706, ☎ 727/360–1753).

CAMPING

For information on camping facilities, **contact the national and state parks and forests you plan to visit and the Florida Department of Environmental Protection** (☞ Parks & Preserves, *below*).

To find a commercial campground, **pick up a copy of the free annual "Florida Camping Directory,"** which lists 220 campgrounds, with 66,000 sites. It's available at Florida welcome centers, from the Florida Tourism Industry Marketing Corporation (☞ Visitor Information, *below*), and from the Florida Association of RV Parks & Campgrounds.

➤ CAMPING ASSOCIATION: **Florida Association of RV Parks & Campgrounds** (1340 Vickers Dr., Tallahassee, FL 32303-3041, ☎ 850/562–7151, ℻ 850/562–7179).

CONDOS

➤ CONDO GUIDE: *The Condo Lux Vacationer's Guide to Condominium Rentals in the Southeast* (Vintage Books/Random House, New York; $9.95), by Jill Little.

HOME EXCHANGES

If you would like to exchange your home for someone else's **join a home-exchange organization,** which will send you its updated listings of available exchanges for a year and will

include your own listing in at least one of them. It's up to you to make specific arrangements.

➤ EXCHANGE CLUBS: **HomeLink International** (✉ Box 650, Key West, FL 33041, ☎ 305/294–7766 or 800/638–3841, ℻ 305/294–1448; $88 per year). **Intervac U.S.** (✉ Box 590504, San Francisco, CA 94159, ☎ 800/756–4663, ℻ 415/435–7440; $83 per year).

HOSTELS

No matter what your age you can **save on lodging costs by staying at hostels.** In some 5,000 locations in more than 70 countries around the world, Hostelling International (HI), the umbrella group for a number of national youth-hostel associations, offers single-sex, dorm-style beds and, at many hostels, couples rooms and family accommodations. Membership in any HI national hostel association, open to travelers of all ages, allows you to stay in HI-affiliated hostels at member rates (one-year membership is about $25 for adults; hostels run about $10–$25 per night). Members also have priority if the hostel is full; they're eligible for discounts around the world, even on rail and bus travel in some countries.

➤ ORGANIZATIONS: **Hostelling International—American Youth Hostels** (✉ 733 15th St. NW, Suite 840, Washington, DC 20005, ☎ 202/783–6161, ℻ 202/783–6171). **Hostelling International—Canada** (✉ 400–205 Catherine St., Ottawa, Ontario K2P 1C3, ☎ 613/237–7884, ℻ 613/237–7868). **Youth Hostel Association of England and Wales** (✉ Trevelyan House, 8 St. Stephen's Hill, St. Albans, Hertfordshire AL1 2DY, ☎ 01727/855215 or 01727/845047, ℻ 01727/844126). **Australian Youth Hostel Association** (✉ 10 Mallett St., Camperdown, NSW 2050, ☎ 02/9565–1699, ℻ 02/9565–1325). **Youth Hostels Association of New Zealand** (✉ Box 436, Christchurch, New Zealand, ☎ 03/379–9970, ℻ 03/365–4476). Membership in the U.S. $25, in Canada C$26.75, in the U.K. £9.30, in Australia $44, in New Zealand $24.

HOTELS

Wherever you look in Florida, it seems, you'll find lots of plain, inexpensive motels and luxurious resorts, independents alongside national chains, and an ever-growing number of modern properties as well as quite a few timeless classics. In fact, since Florida has been a favored travel destination for some time, vintage hotels are everywhere, both grand edifices like the Breakers in Palm Beach, the Boca Raton Resort & Club in Boca Raton, the Biltmore in Coral Gables, and the Casa Marina in Key West as well as smaller, historic places, like the Governors Inn in Tallahassee and the New World Inn in Pensacola.

All hotels listed have private bath unless otherwise noted.

➤ HOTEL AND MOTEL ASSOCIATION: **Florida Hotel & Motel Association** (200 W. College Ave., Box 1529, Tallahassee, FL 32301-1529, ☎ 850/224-2888).

➤ RESERVATION SERVICES: **Accommodations Express** (☎ 800/663-7666, FAX 609/525-0111). **Florida Hotel Network** (521 Lincoln Rd., Miami Beach, FL 33139, ☎ 800/538-3616, FAX 305/538-3616). **Florida Sunbreak** (169 Lincoln Rd., Miami Beach, FL 33139, ☎ 305/532-1516, FAX 305/781-1312).

➤ TOLL-FREE NUMBERS: **Adam's Mark** (☎ 800/444-2326). **Baymont Inns** (☎ 800/428-3438). **Best Western** (☎ 800/528-1234). **Choice** (☎ 800/221-2222). **Clarion** (☎ 800/252-7466). **Colony** (☎ 800/777-1700). **Comfort** (☎ 800/228-5150). **Days Inn** (☎ 800/325-2525). **Doubletree and Red Lion Hotels** (☎ 800/222-8733). **Embassy Suites** (☎ 800/362-2779). **Fairfield Inn** (☎ 800/228-2800). **Forte** (☎ 800/225-5843). **Four Seasons** (☎ 800/332-3442). **Hilton** (☎ 800/445-8667). **Holiday Inn** (☎ 800/465-4329). **Howard Johnson** (☎ 800/654-4656). **Hyatt Hotels & Resorts** (☎ 800/233-1234). **Inter-Continental** (☎ 800/327-0200). **La Quinta** (☎ 800/531-5900). **Marriott** (☎ 800/228-9290). **Le Meridien** (☎ 800/543-4300). **Nikko Hotels International** (☎ 800/645-5687). **Omni** (☎ 800/843-6664). **Quality Inn** (☎ 800/228-5151). **Radisson** (☎ 800/333-3333). **Ramada** (☎ 800/228-2828). **Renaissance Hotels & Resorts** (☎ 800/468-3571). **Ritz-Carlton** (☎ 800/241-3333). **Sheraton** (☎ 800/325-3535). **Sleep Inn** (☎ 800/221-2222). **Westin Hotels & Resorts** (☎ 800/228-3000). **Wyndham Hotels & Resorts** (☎ 800/822-4200).

VACATION OWNERSHIP RESORTS

Vacation ownership resorts sell hotel rooms, condominium apartments, and villas in weekly, monthly, or quarterly increments. The weekly arrangement is most popular; it's often referred to as "interval ownership" or "time sharing." Of more than 3,000 vacation ownership resorts around the world, some 500 are in Florida, with the heaviest concentration in the Walt Disney World/Orlando area. Non-owners can rent at many of these resorts by contacting the individual property or a real-estate broker in the area.

MAIL & SHIPPING

The fastest way to receive mail, assuming that you know where you will be staying, is to have it sent to that address. However, if you don't know exactly where you'll be, you can have mail sent to you care of General Delivery in the town where you'll be staying, remembering the zip code. Then you simply pick up your mail at that post office. This method works best in small towns, where prompt retrieval is more assured. Allow anywhere from a few days to a week or much longer for delivery of mail from overseas, depending on the origin.

MONEY MATTERS

Prices throughout this guide are given for adults. Substantially reduced fees are almost always available for children, students, and senior citizens. For information on taxes, *see* Taxes, *below.*

ATMS

Automatic Teller Machines (ATMs) are ubiquitous in Florida. In addition to banks, you will find them at grocery store chains like Publix and Food

Lion and in shopping malls big and small.

CREDIT CARDS

Should you use a credit card? A credit card allows you to delay payment and gives you certain rights as a consumer (☞ Consumer Protection, *above*). Throughout this guide, the following abbreviations are used: AE, American Express; D, Discover; DC, Diner's Club; MC, Master Card; and V, Visa.

NATIONAL PARKS

Look into discount passes to save money on park entrance fees. The Golden Eagle Pass ($50) gets you and your companions free admission to all parks for one year. (Camping and parking are extra). Both the Golden Age Passport ($10), for those 62 and older, and the Golden Access Passport (free), for travelers with disabilities, entitle holders to free entry to all national parks, plus 50% off fees for the use of many park facilities and services. You must show proof of age and of U.S. citizenship or permanent residency (such as a U.S. passport, driver's license, or birth certificate) and, if requesting Golden Access, proof of disability. All three passes are available at all national park entrances where entrance fees are charged. Golden Eagle and Golden Access passes are also available by mail.

➤ PASSES BY MAIL: **National Park Service** (✉ National Capitol Area Office, 1100 Ohio Dr. SW, Washington, DC 20242, ☎ 202/208–4747).

STATE PARKS

Florida's Department of Environmental Protection (DEP) is responsible for hundreds of historic buildings, landmarks, nature preserves, and parks. When requesting a free *Florida State Park Guide,* mention which parts of the state you plan to visit. For information on camping facilities at the state parks, ask for the free "Florida State Parks, Fees and Facilities" and "Florida State Parks Camping Reservation Procedures" brochures. Responding to cutbacks in its budget, the DEP established Friends of Florida State Parks, a citizen support organization open to all.

➤ STATE PARKS INFORMATION: **Florida Department of Environmental Protection** (Marjory Stoneman Douglas Bldg., MS 535, 3900 Commonwealth Blvd., Tallahassee, FL 32399-3000, ☎ 850/488–2850, FAX 850/488–3947); **Friends of Florida State Parks** (☎ 850/488–8243).

PRIVATE PRESERVES

➤ FLORIDA SANCTUARY INFORMATION: **National Audubon Society** (Sanctuary Director, Miles Wildlife Sanctuary, R.R. 1, Box 294, W. Cornwall Rd., Sharon, CT 06069, ☎ 203/364–0048). **Nature Conservancy** (222 S. Westmonte Dr., Suite 300, Altamonte Springs, FL 32714, ☎ 407/682–3554; offices at 250 Tequesta Dr., Suite 301, Tequesta, FL 33469, ☎ 561/744–6668; 201 Front St., Suite 222, Key West, FL 33040, ☎ 305/296–3880; 225 E. Stuart Ave., Lake Wales, FL 33853, ☎ 941/678–1551; 625 N. Adams St., Tallahassee, FL 32301, ☎ 850/222–2473; Comeau Bldg., 319 Clematis St., Suite 611, West Palm Beach, FL 33401, ☎ 561/833–4226).

OUTDOORS & SPORTS

Recreational opportunities abound throughout Florida. The Governor's Council on Physical Fitness and Sports puts on the Sunshine State Games each July in a different part of the state.

➤ GENERAL INFORMATION: **Florida Department of Environmental Protection** (Office of Greenways, MS 585, 3900 Commonwealth Blvd., Tallahassee, FL 32399-3000, ☎ 850/487–4784) for information on bicycling, canoeing, kayaking, and hiking trails.

➤ MARINE CHARTS: **Tealls, Inc.** (111 Saguaro La., Marathon, FL 33050, ☎ 305/743–3942, FAX 305/743–3942; $7.95 set, $3.60 each individual chart).

BIKING

Biking is a popular Florida sport. Rails to Trails, a nationwide group that turns unused railroad rights-of-way into bicycle and walking paths, has made great inroads in Florida, particularly around the Tampa–St. Pete area. In addition, just about every town in Florida has its own set of bike paths and a bike rental outfit.

For bike information, **check with Florida's Department of Transportation (DOT),** which publishes free bicycle trail guides, dispenses free touring information packets, and provides names of bike coordinators around the state.

➤ BICYCLE INFORMATION: **DOT state bicycle-pedestrian coordinator** (605 E. Suwannee St., MS 82, Tallahassee, FL 32399-0450, ☎ 850/488–1234).

CANOEING & KAYAKING

You can canoe or kayak along 1,550 mi of trails encompassing creeks, rivers, and springs. Both the DEP (☞ General Information, *above*) and outfitter associations provide information on trails and their conditions, events, and contacts for trips and equipment rental.

➤ OUTFITTERS AND OUTFITTING ASSOCIATIONS: **Canoe Outpost System** (2816 N.W. Rte. 661, Arcadia, FL 33821, ☎ 941/494–1215), comprising five outfitters. **Florida Professional Paddlesports Association** (Box 1764, Arcadia, FL 34265, ☎ no phone).

FISHING

In Atlantic and gulf waters, fishing seasons and other regulations vary by location and species. You will need to **buy one license for freshwater fishing and another license for saltwater fishing.** Nonresident fees for a saltwater license are $30. Nonresidents can purchase freshwater licenses good for seven days ($15) or for one year ($30). Typically, you'll pay a $1.50 surcharge at most any marina, bait shop, Kmart, Wal-Mart, or other license vendor.

➤ FISHING INFORMATION: **Florida Game and Fresh Water Fish Commission** (620 S. Meridian St., Tallahassee, FL 32399-1600, ☎ 850/488–1960) for the free *Florida Fishing Handbook* with license vendors, regional fishing guides, and educational bulletins.

HORSEBACK RIDING

Horseback riding is a popular sport outside of Florida's metropolitan areas. There are trails around the state and even beaches on which you can ride.

➤ HORSEBACK RIDING INFORMATION: Horse & Pony (6229 Virginia La., Seffner, FL 33584, ☎ 813/621–2510).

JOGGING, RUNNING, & WALKING

Many towns have walking and running trails, and most of Florida's beaches stretch on for miles, testing the limits of even the most stalwart runners and walkers. Local running clubs all over the state sponsor weekly public events.

➤ CLUBS & EVENTS: **Miami Runners Club** (7920 S.W. 40th St., Miami, FL 33155, ☎ 305/227–1500, FAX 305/220–2450) for South Florida events.

PARI-MUTUEL SPORTS

Jai-alai frontons and greyhound-racing tracks are in most major Florida cities. Patrons can bet on the teams or dogs or on televised horse races.

➤ SCHEDULES: Department of Business & Professional Regulations **Division of Pari-Mutuel Wagering** (8405 N.W. 53rd St., Suite C-250, Miami, FL 33166, ☎ 305/470–5675, FAX 305/470–5686).

TENNIS

Tennis is extremely popular in Florida, and virtually every town has well-maintained public courts. In addition, many tennis tournaments are held in the state.

➤ TOURNAMENT AND EVENT SCHEDULES: **United States Tennis Association Florida Section** (1280 S.W. 36th Ave., Suite 305, Pompano Beach, FL 33069, ☎ 954/968–3434, FAX 954/968–3986; yearbook $11).

WILDERNESS & RECREATION AREAS

Florida is studded with trails, rivers, and parks that are ideal for hiking, bird-watching, canoeing, bicycling, and horseback riding.

➤ PUBLICATIONS: **"Florida Trails: A Guide to Florida's Natural Habitats,"** available from Florida Tourism Industry Marketing Corporation (☞ Visitor Information, *below*), for bicycling, canoeing, horseback riding, and walking trails; camping; snorkeling and scuba diving; and Florida ecosystems. **Florida Wildlife Viewing Guide**, available from Falcon Press (Box 1718, Helena, MT 59624, ☎ 800/582–2665); $7.95 plus $3 shipping, by Susan Cerulean and Ann Morrow, for marked wildlife-watching sites. **"Recreation Guide to District Lands,"** available from St. Johns River Water Management District (Box 1429, Palatka, FL 32178-1429); free for marine, wetland, and upland recreational areas.

PACKING

The northern part of the state is much cooler in winter than the southern part, and you'll want to take a heavy sweater if you plan on traveling there in the colder months. Even in the summer ocean breezes can be cool, so always **take a sweater or jacket** just in case.

The Miami area and the Tampa–St. Petersburg area are warm year-round and often extremely humid in summer months. Be prepared for sudden summer storms, but keep in mind that plastic raincoats are uncomfortable in the high humidity.

Dress is casual throughout the state, with sundresses, jeans, or walking shorts appropriate during the day; **bring comfortable walking shoes or sneakers** for theme parks. A few restaurants request that men wear jackets and ties, but most do not. Be prepared for air-conditioning working in overdrive.

You can generally swim year-round in peninsular Florida from about New Smyrna Beach south on the Atlantic coast and from Tarpon Springs south on the Gulf Coast. Be sure to **take a sun hat and sunscreen** because the sun can be fierce, even in winter and even if it is chilly or overcast.

In your carry-on luggage **bring an extra pair of eyeglasses or contact lenses** and **enough of any medication you take** to last the entire trip. You may also want your doctor to write a spare prescription using the drug's generic name, since brand names may vary from country to country. In luggage to be checked, **never pack prescription drugs or valuables.** To avoid customs delays, carry medications in their original packaging. And don't forget to copy down and carry addresses of offices that handle refunds of lost traveler's checks.

CHECKING LUGGAGE

How many carry-on bags you can bring with you is up to the airline. Most allow two, but not always, so make sure that everything you carry aboard will fit under your seat, and get to the gate early. Note that if you have a seat at the back of the plane, you'll probably board first, while the overhead bins are still empty.

If you are flying internationally, note that baggage allowances may be determined not by piece but by weight—generally 88 pounds (40 kilograms) in first class, 66 pounds (30 kilograms) in business class, and 44 pounds (20 kilograms) in economy.

Airline liability for baggage is limited to $1,250 per person on flights within the United States. On international flights it amounts to $9.07 per pound or $20 per kilogram for checked baggage (roughly $640 per 70-pound bag) and $400 per passenger for unchecked baggage. You can buy additional coverage at check-in for about $10 per $1,000 of coverage, but it excludes a rather extensive list of items, shown on your airline ticket.

Before departure **itemize your bags' contents** and their worth, and label the bags with your name, address, and phone number. (If you use your home address, cover it so that potential thieves can't see it readily.) Inside each bag **pack a copy of your itinerary.** At check-in **make sure that each bag is correctly tagged** with the destination airport's three-letter code. If your bags arrive damaged or fail to arrive at all, file a written report with the airline before leaving the airport.

PASSPORTS & VISAS

➤ U.K. CITIZENS: **U.S. Embassy Visa Information Line** (☎ 01891/200–290; calls cost 49p per minute, 39p per minute cheap rate) for U.S. visa information. **U.S. Embassy Visa Branch** (⊠ 5 Upper Grosvenor Sq., London W1A 1AE) for U.S. visa information; send a self-addressed, stamped envelope. Write the U.S. **Consulate General** (⊠ Queen's

House, Queen St., Belfast BTI 6EO) if you live in Northern Ireland. Write the **Office of Australia Affairs** (✉ 59th fl., MLC Centre, 19-29 Martin Pl., Sydney NSW 2000) if you live in Australia. Write the **Office of New Zealand Affairs** (✉ 29 Fitzherbert Terr., Thorndon, Wellington) if you live in New Zealand.

PASSPORT OFFICES

The best time to apply for a passport or to renew is during the fall and winter. Before any trip, check your passport's expiration date, and, if necessary, renew it as soon as possible.

➤ AUSTRALIAN CITIZENS: **Australian Passport Office** (☎ 131–232).

➤ NEW ZEALAND CITIZENS: **New Zealand Passport Office** (☎ 04/494–0700 for information on how to apply; 04/474–8000 or 0800/225–050 in New Zealand for information on applications already submitted).

➤ U.K. CITIZENS: **London Passport Office** (☎ 0990/210–410) for fees and documentation requirements and to request an emergency passport.

SENIOR-CITIZEN TRAVEL

Since Florida has a significant retired population, senior-citizen discounts are ubiquitous. To qualify for age-related discounts **mention your senior-citizen status up front** when booking hotel reservations (not when checking out) and before you're seated in restaurants (not when paying the bill). When renting a car ask about promotional car-rental discounts, which can be cheaper than senior-citizen rates.

➤ EDUCATIONAL PROGRAMS: **Elderhostel** (✉ 75 Federal St., 3rd fl., Boston, MA 02110, ☎ 877/426–8056, 🖷 877/426–2166).

STUDENTS IN FLORIDA

Students flock to the beaches of Florida during spring break, but there are also special tours for students year round.

➤ STUDENT I.D.S & SERVICES: **Council on International Educational Exchange** (CIEE, ✉ 205 E. 42nd St., 14th fl., New York, NY 10017, ☎ 212/822–2600 or 888/268–6245, 🖷 212/822–2699) for mail orders only,

in the U.S. **Travel Cuts** (✉ 187 College St., Toronto, Ontario M5T 1P7, ☎ 416/979–2406 or 800/667–2887) in Canada.

TAXES

SALES TAX

Florida's sales tax is currently 6%, but local sales and tourist taxes can raise that number considerably, especially for certain items, such as lodging. Miami hoteliers, for example, collect roughly 12.5% for city and resort taxes. It's best to **ask about additional costs up front,** to avoid a rude awakening.

TIME

Except for the western portion of the Panhandle, which is in the Central Time Zone, most of Florida is in the Eastern Time Zone.

TIPPING

Whether they carry bags, open doors, deliver food, or clean rooms, hospitality employees work to receive a portion of your travel budget. In deciding how much to give, **base your tip on what the service is and how well it's performed.**

In transit, tip an airport valet $1–$3 per bag, a taxi driver 15%–20% of the fare.

For hotel staff, recommended amounts are $1–$3 per bag for a bellhop, $1–$2 per night per guest for chambermaids, $5–$10 for special concierge service, $1–$3 for a doorman who hails a cab or parks a car, 15% of the greens fee for a caddy, 15%–20% of the bill for a massage, and 15% of a room service bill.

In a restaurant, give 15%–20% of your bill before tax to the server, 5%–10% to the maître d', 15% to a bartender, and 15% of the wine bill for a wine steward who makes a special effort in selecting and serving wine.

TOURS & PACKAGES

On a prepackaged tour or independent vacation everything is prearranged so you'll spend less time planning—and often get it all at a good price.

BOOKING WITH AN AGENT

Travel agents are excellent resources. But it's a good idea to collect brochures from several agencies because some agents' suggestions may be influenced by relationships with tour and package firms that reward them for volume sales. If you have a special interest **find an agent with expertise in that area**; ASTA (☞ Travel Agencies, *below*) has a database of specialists worldwide.

Make sure your travel agent knows the accommodations and other services of the place they're recommending. Ask about the hotel's location, room size, beds, and whether it has a pool, room service, or programs for children, if you care about these. Has your agent been there in person or sent others whom you can contact?

Do some homework on your own, too: Local tourism boards can provide information about lesser-known and small-niche operators, some of which may sell only direct.

BUYER BEWARE

Each year consumers are stranded or lose their money when tour operators—even large ones with excellent reputations—go out of business. So **check out the operator.** Ask several travel agents about its reputation, and try to **book with a company that has a consumer-protection program.** (Look for information in the company's brochure). In the United States, members of the National Tour Association and United States Tour Operators Association are required to set aside funds to cover your payments and travel arrangements in case the company defaults. It's also a good idea to choose a company that participates in the American Society of Travel Agent's Tour Operator Program (TOP); ASTA will act as mediator in any disputes between you and your tour operator.

Remember that the more your package or tour includes the better you can predict the ultimate cost of your vacation. Make sure you know exactly what is covered, and **beware of hidden costs.** Are taxes, tips, and transfers included? Entertainment and excursions? These can add up.

➤ TOUR-OPERATOR RECOMMENDATIONS: **American Society of Travel Agents** (☞ Travel Agencies, *below*). **National Tour Association** (NTA, ✉ 546 E. Main St., Lexington, KY 40508, ☎ 606/226–4444 or 800/682–8886). **United States Tour Operators Association** (USTOA, ✉ 342 Madison Ave., Suite 1522, New York, NY 10173, ☎ 212/599–6599 or 800/468–7862, FAX 212/599–6744).

TRAIN TRAVEL

Amtrak provides north–south service on two routes to the major cities of Jacksonville, Orlando, Tampa, West Palm Beach, Fort Lauderdale, and Miami and east–west service through Jacksonville, Tallahassee, and Pensacola, with many stops in between on all routes.

➤ TRAIN INFORMATION: **Amtrak** (☎ 800/872–7245).

TRAVEL AGENCIES

A good travel agent puts your needs first. Look for an agency that has been in business at least five years, emphasizes customer service, and has someone on staff who specializes in your destination. In addition **make sure the agency belongs to a professional trade organization.** The American Society of Travel Agents (ASTA), with 27,000 agents in some 170 countries, is the largest and most influential in the field. Operating under the motto "Integrity in Travel," it maintains and enforces a strict code of ethics and will step in to help mediate any agent-client disputes if necessary. ASTA also maintains a website that includes a directory of agents. (Note that if a travel agency is also acting as your tour operator, *see* Buyer Beware *in* Tours & Packages, *above*).

➤ LOCAL AGENT REFERRALS: **American Society of Travel Agents** (ASTA, ☎ 800/965–2782 24-hr hot line, FAX 703/684–8319). **Association of Canadian Travel Agents** (✉ 1729 Bank St., Suite 201, Ottawa, Ontario K1V 7Z5, ☎ 613/521–0474, FAX 613/521–0805). **Association of British Travel Agents** (✉ 55–57 Newman St., London W1P 4AH, ☎ 0171/637–2444, FAX 0171/637–0713). **Australian Federation of Travel Agents** (✉ Level 3, 309 Pitt St., Sydney 2000, ☎ 02/

9264–3299, FAX 02/9264–1085).
**Travel Agents' Association of New
Zealand** (⊠ Box 1888, Wellington
10033, ☎ 04/499–0104, FAX 04/499–
0786).

VISITOR INFORMATION

For general information about
Florida's attractions, contact the
office below; welcome centers are
located on I–10, I–75, I–95, and U.S.
231 (near Graceville) and in the lobby
of the New Capitol in Tallahassee.
For regional tourist bureaus and
chambers of commerce see individual
chapters.

➤ STATE: **Florida Tourism Industry
Marketing Corporation** (Box 1100,
661 E. Jefferson St., Suite 300, Tallahassee, FL 32302, ☎ 850/487–1462,
FAX 850/224–2938).

➤ IN THE U.K.: **ABC Florida** (Box 35,
Abingdon, Oxon. OX14 4TB, ☎
0891/600–555, 50p per minute; send
£2 for vacation pack).

WEB SITES

The state of Florida is very visitor-
oriented and has created a terrific
web site—www.flausa.com—with
superb links to help you find out all
you want to know. It's a wonderful
place to learn about everything from
fancy resorts to camping trips to car
routes to beach towns.

WHEN TO GO

Florida is a state for all seasons,
although most visitors prefer October–April, particularly in South
Florida.

Winter remains the height of the
tourist season, when South Florida is
crowded with "snowbirds" fleeing
cold weather in the North. (It did
snow in Miami once in the 1970s, but
since then the average snowfall has
been exactly 00.00 inches.) Hotels,
bars, discos, restaurants, shops, and
attractions are all crowded. Hollywood and Broadway celebrities
appear in sophisticated supper clubs,
and other performing artists hold the
stage at ballets, operas, concerts, and
theaters. From mid-December
through January 2, Walt Disney
World's Magic Kingdom is lavishly
decorated, and there are daily parades
and other extravaganzas, as well as
overwhelming crowds. In the Jacksonville and Panhandle area, winter is
off-season—an excellent bargain.

For the college crowd, spring vacation is still the time to congregate in
Florida, especially in Panama City
Beach and the Daytona Beach area;
Fort Lauderdale, where city officials
have refashioned the beachfront more
as a family resort, no longer indulges
young revelers, so it's much less
popular with college students than it
once was.

Summer in Florida, as smart budget-
minded visitors have discovered, is
often hot and very humid, but along
the coast, ocean breezes make the
season quite bearable and many
hotels lower their prices considerably.
In the Panhandle and Central Florida,
summer is peak season. Theme park
lines shrink only after children return
to school in September. Large numbers of international visitors keep
year-round visitation high at theme
parks.

For senior citizens, fall is the time for
discounts for many attractions and
hotels in Orlando and along the
Pinellas Suncoast in the Tampa Bay
area.

CLIMATE

What follows are average daily maximum and minimum temperatures for
major cities in Florida.

KEY WEST (THE KEYS)

Jan.	76F	24C	May	85F	29C	Sept.	90F	32C
	65	18		74	23		77	25
Feb.	76F	24C	June	88F	31C	Oct.	83F	28C
	67	19		77	25		76	24
Mar.	79F	26C	July	90F	32C	Nov.	79F	26C
	68	20		79	26		70	21
Apr.	81F	27C	Aug.	90F	32C	Dec.	76F	24C
	72	22		79	26		67	19

MIAMI

Jan.	74F	23C	May	83F	28C	Sept.	86F	30C
	63	17		72	22		76	24
Feb.	76F	24C	June	85F	29C	Oct.	83F	28C
	63	17		76	24		72	22
Mar.	77F	25C	July	88F	31C	Nov.	79F	26C
	65	18		76	24		67	19
Apr.	79F	26C	Aug.	88F	31C	Dec.	76F	26C
	68	20		77	25		63	17

ORLANDO

Jan.	70F	21C	May	88F	31C	Sept.	88F	31C
	49	9		67	19		74	23
Feb.	72F	22C	June	90F	32C	Oct.	83F	28C
	54	12		72	22		67	19
Mar.	76F	24C	July	90F	32C	Nov.	76F	24C
	56	13		74	23		58	14
Apr.	81F	27C	Aug.	90F	32C	Dec.	70F	21C
	63	17		74	23		52	11

➤ FORECASTS: **Weather Channel Connection** (☎ 900/932–8437), 95¢ per minute from a Touch-Tone phone.

FESTIVALS AND SEASONAL EVENTS

➤ DEC.: **Monthlong Victorian Seaside Christmas** takes place oceanside on Amelia Island (☎ 904/277–0717). **Christmas in St. Augustine** is a three-week festival with caroling, tours of turn-of-the-century churches and cottages, and musical performances (☎ 904/829–5681). **Walt Disney World's Very Merry Christmas Parade in the Magic Kingdom** celebrates the season at the Magic Kingdom (☎ 407/931–7369). **Winterfest Boat Parade** is on the Intracoastal Waterway, Fort Lauderdale (☎ 954/767–0686). At the end of the month, **Coconut Grove King Mango Strut** is a parody of the Orange Bowl Parade (☎ 305/445–1865).

➤ JAN.: Early in the month, **Polo Season** opens at the Palm Beach Polo and Country Club (☎ 561/793–1440). **Outback Bowl Blast** is a street festival with live music in Tampa's Ybor City (☎ 813/874–2695). On January 6, **Greek Epiphany Day** includes religious celebrations, parades, music, dancing, and feasting at the St. Nicholas Greek Orthodox Cathedral in Tarpon Springs (☎ 813/937–6109). Mid-month, **Art Deco Weekend** spotlights Miami Beach's historic district with an Art Deco street fair, a 1930s-style Moon Over Miami Ball, and live entertainment (☎ 305/672–2014). **Martin Luther King Jr. Festivals** are celebrated throughout the state—including Orlando (☎ 407/246–2221). **Taste of the Grove Food and Music Festival** is a popular fund-raiser put on in Coconut Grove's Peacock Park by area restaurants (☎ 305/444–7270). In late January, **Miami Rivers Blues Festival** takes place on the south bank of the river next to Tobacco Road (☎ 305/374–1198).

➤ FEB.: The **Edison Festival of Lights,** in various locations around Fort Myers, celebrates Thomas A. Edison's long winter residence in the city (☎ 941/334–2999). The **Florida Strawberry Festival,** in Plant City, has for more than six decades celebrated the town's winter harvest with two weeks of country-music stars, rides, exhibits, and strawberry delicacies (☎ 813/752–9194). The juried **Naples National Art Festival,** at Cambier Park, features works by more than 200 artists from throughout the country (☎ 941/262–6517). The **Gasparilla Festival** celebrates the legendary pirate's invasion of Tampa with street parades, an art festival, and music (☎ 800/448–2672). **International Carillon Festival** takes place at the Bok Tower Gardens, Lake Wales (☎ 941/676–1408). **Olustee Battle Festival,** in Lake City, is the second-largest Civil War reenactment in the nation after the one in Gettysburg (☎ 904/752–3610 or 904/758–1312). **Speed Weeks** is a three-week celebration of auto racing that culminates in the famous Daytona 500, at the Daytona International Speedway in Daytona Beach (☎ 904/254–2700 or 800/854–1234).

The **Coconut Grove Art Festival,** mid-month, is the state's largest (☎ 305/447–0401). The **Florida Citrus Festival and Polk County Fair,** in Winter Haven, showcases the citrus harvest with displays and entertainment (☎ 941/967–3175). The **Florida Manatee Festival,** in Crystal River, focuses on both the river and the endangered manatee (☎ 352/795–3149). The **Florida State Fair,** in Tampa, includes carnival rides and 4-H competitions (☎ 813/621–7821). The **Miami Film Festival,** sponsored by the Film Society of America, is 10 days of international, domestic, and local films (☎ 305/377–3456). The **Labelle Swamp Cabbage Festival,** the last full weekend in February, is a salute to the state tree, the cabbage palm (☎ 941/675–0125).

➤ FEB.–MAR.: The **Winter Equestrian Festival,** at the Palm Beach Polo and Country Club in West Palm Beach, includes more than 1,000 horses and three grand-prix equestrian events (☎ 561/798–7000).

➤ MAR.: The **Sanibel Shell Fair,** which runs for four days starting the first Thursday of the month, is the largest event of the year on Sanibel Island (☎ 941/472–2155). The **Azalea Festival** is a beauty pageant, arts-and-crafts show, and parade held in downtown Palatka and Riverfront Park (☎ 904/328–1503). **Bike Week,** one of Daytona's biggest annual events, draws 400,000 riders from across the U.S. for 10 days of races, plus parades and even coleslaw wrestling (☎ 904/255–0981). **Winter Park Sidewalk Arts Festival** is one of the Southeast's most prestigious outdoor fine arts festivals and features internationally known artists (☎ 407/672–6390). The **Sarasota Jazz Festival** is a showcase for well-known musicians from around the world (☎ 941/336–1552).

➤ MID-MAR. AND EARLY JULY: The **Arcadia All-Florida Championship Rodeo** is professional rodeo at its best (☎ 941/494–2014 or 800/749–7633).

➤ LATE MAR.–LATE APR.: **Springtime Tallahassee** is a major cultural, sporting, and culinary event in the capital (☎ 850/224–5012).

The **Blessing of the Fleet** is held by the bay in St. Augustine on Palm Sunday (☎ 904/829–1711). **Sandestin Wine Tasting** includes wine tastings, wine seminars, and live music (☎ 850/267–8092).

➤ APR.: The **Delray Affair,** in early April, is the biggest event in the area and features arts, crafts, and food (☎ 561/279–1880). The **Cedar Key Sidewalk Arts Festival** is celebrated in one of the state's most historic towns mid-month (☎ 352/543–5600).

➤ LATE APR.–EARLY MAY: The **Conch Republic Celebration** honors the founding fathers of the Conch Republic, "the small island nation of Key West" (☎ 305/296–0123). The **Sun 'n' Fun Festival,** in Clearwater, includes a bathtub regatta, golf tournament, and nighttime parade (☎ 727/462–6531).

➤ MAY: The **Shell Air & Sea Show** draws more than 2 million to the Fort Lauderdale beachfront for performances by big names in aviation, such as the navy's Blue Angels and the air force's Thunderbirds (☎ 954/467–3555). In mid-May, the **Arabian Nights Festival,** in Opa-locka, is a mix of contemporary and fantasy-inspired entertainment (☎ 305/758–4166). **Tropicool Fest** draws thousands to more than 30 concerts as well as arts and sports events for two weeks all around Naples (☎ 941/262–6141).

➤ JUNE: The **Miami-Bahamas Goombay Festival,** in Miami's Coconut Grove, celebrates the city's Bahamian heritage the first weekend of the month (☎ 305/443–7928 or 305/372–9966). The **Billy Bowlegs Festival,** in Fort Walton Beach, is a week of entertaining activities in memory of a pirate who ruled the area in the late 1700s (☎ 800/322–3319). **International Mangrove Fest,** in Naples, is an ecotourism event that combines musical concerts, kids' activities, sand-sculpting contests, canoe tours through mangroves, and a program of activities by the Nature Conservancy (☎ 941/594–6038).

➤ JUNE–JULY: **Beethoven by the Beach,** in Fort Lauderdale, features Beethoven's symphonies, chamber pieces, and piano concertos performed by the Florida Philharmonic (☎ 954/561–2997).

➤ AUG.: The **Annual Wausau Possum Funday & Parade** is held in Possum Palace, Wausau, early in the month (☎ 904/638–7888).

➤ SEPT.: **Caryville Worm Fiddling Day,** on Labor Day, is the biggest day of the year in Caryville (☎ 904/548–5116). The **Anniversary of the Founding of St. Augustine** is held on the grounds of the Mission of Nombre de Dios (☎ 904/825–1010).

➤ OCT.: The **Destin Seafood Festival** gives you two days to sample smoked amberjack, fried mullet, and shark kebabs (☎ 800/322–3319). The **Fort Lauderdale International Boat Show,** the world's largest show based on exhibit size, displays boats of every size, price, and description at the Bahia Mar marina and four other venues (☎ 954/764–7642). The **Jacksonville Jazz Festival** is three days of jazz performances, arts and crafts, and food, plus the Great American Jazz Piano Competition (☎ 904/353–7770). The **Fort Lauderdale International Film Festival** showcases independent cinema from around the world (☎ 954/563–0500). **Biketoberfest** is highlighted by championship racing at the Daytona International Speedway, the Main Street Rally, concerts, and swap meets that last four days (☎ 904/854–1234). **Boggy Bayou Mullet Festival** is a three-day hoedown in mid-October in celebration of the "Twin Cities," Valparaiso and Niceville, and the famed scavenger fish, the mullet (☎ 904/678–1615). The **Cedar Key Seafood Festival** is held on Main Street in Cedar Key (☎ 352/543–5600). The **Fall RiverFest Arts Festival** takes place downtown along the St. Johns River in Palatka (☎ 904/328–8998). **Fantasy Fest,** in Key West, is a no-holds-barred Halloween costume party, parade, and town fair (☎ 305/296–1817).

➤ NOV.: The **Florida Seafood Festival** is Apalachicola's celebration of its famous oyster harvest, with oyster-shucking-and-consumption contests and parades (☎ 904/653–9419). The **Miami Book Fair International,** the largest book fair in the United States, is held on the Wolfson campus of Miami-Dade Community College (☎ 305/237–3032).

➤ EARLY NOV.–LATE FEB.: The **Orange Bowl and Junior Orange Bowl Festival,** in the Miami area, are best known for the King Orange Jamboree Parade and the Orange Bowl Football Classic but also include more than 20 youth-oriented events (☎ 305/371–3351).

INDEX

NOTES

L@@king
© FOR A
great place to go?

We know just the place. In fact, it attracts more than 125,000 visitors a day, making it one of the world's most popular travel destinations. It's previewtravel.com, the Web's comprehensive resource for travelers. It gives you access to over 500 airlines, 25,000 hotels, rental cars, cruises, vacation packages and support from travel experts 24 hours a day. Plus great information from Fodor's travel guides and travelers just like you. All of which makes previewtravel.com quite a find.

Preview Travel has everything you need to plan & book your next trip.

air, car & hotel reservations

vacation packages & cruises

destination planning & travel tips

24-hour customer service

© 1999 Preview Travel, Inc. Visitors estimated from Media Metrix 3/99 Key Measures Web Report.
CST #2022036-40

previewtravel.com

preview travel

aol keyword: previewtravel
www.previewtravel.com

FODOR'S FLORIDA 2000

EDITOR: Andrea E. Lehman

Editorial Contributors: Pamela Acheson, Marianne Camas, Catherine Fredman, Kendall Hamersly, Herb Hiller, Ann Hughes, Alan Macher, Diane Marshall, Gary McKechnie, Valerie Meyer, Peter Oliver, Nancy Orr, Helayne Schiff, Rowland Stiteler, Geoffrey Tomb

Editorial Production: Tom Holton

Maps: David Lindroth, *cartographer*; Steven Amsterdam, *map editor*

Design: Fabrizio La Rocca, *creative director*; Guido Caroti, *art director*; Jolie Novak, *photo editor*

Production/Manufacturing: Robert B. Shields

COPYRIGHT

Copyright © 1999 by Fodor's Travel Publications, Inc.

Fodor's is a registered trademark of Fodor's Travel Publications, Inc. All rights reserved under International and Pan-American Copyright Conventions. Published in the United States by Fodor's Travel Publications, Inc., a subsidiary of Random House, Inc., New York, and simultaneously in Canada by Random House of Canada Limited, Toronto. Distributed by Random House, Inc., New York.

No maps, illustrations, or other portions of this book may be reproduced in any form without written permission from the publisher.

ISBN 0–679–00316–9

ISSN 0193–9556

SPECIAL SALES

Fodor's Travel Publications are available at special discounts for bulk purchases for sales promotions or premiums. Special editions, including personalized covers, excerpts of existing guides, and corporate imprints, can be created in large quantities for special needs. For more information, contact your local bookseller or write to Special Markets, Fodor's Travel Publications, 201 East 50th Street, New York, NY 10022. Inquiries from Canada should be directed to your local Canadian bookseller or sent to Random House of Canada, Ltd., Marketing Department, 2775 Matheson Boulevard East, Mississauga, Ontario L4W 4P7. Inquiries from the United Kingdom should be sent to Fodor's Travel Publications, 20 Vauxhall Bridge Road, London SW1V 2SA, England.

PRINTED IN THE UNITED STATES OF AMERICA
10 9 8 7 6 5 4 3 2 1

IMPORTANT TIP

Although all prices, opening times, and other details in this book are based on information supplied to us at press time, changes occur all the time in the travel world, and Fodor's cannot accept responsibility for facts that become outdated or for inadvertent errors or omissions. So **always confirm information when it matters,** especially if you're making a detour to visit a specific place.

PHOTOGRAPHY

Len Kaufman, cover (Everglades National Park).

Biscayne National Park: Steven Frink, p. 8A.

©Busch Entertainment Corporation, p. 19D, 30A.

Dania Jai-Alai, p. 11D.

Daytona International Speedway, p. 25D.

Delano Hotel, p. 30J.

©Disney Enterprises, Inc., p. 16B. *The Florida Aquarium,* p. 30B.

Greater Fort Lauderdale Convention and Visitors Bureau, p. 10A, 10B, 11C, 11E.

Gumbo Limbo Nature Center, p. 12A.

Dave G. Houser, p. 20A.

The Image Bank: Derek Berwin, p. 16A. *Bob Brooks,* p. 13E. *James M. Carmichael,* p. 21F. *Luis Castañeda,* p. 7E, 8B, 24A. *Angelo Cavalli,* p. 6C, 7F, 15D, 18A, 25F. *Gary Crallé,* p. 12C, 13D, 17D. *Joe Devenney,* p. 20B. *Grant V. Faint,* p. 6B, 32. *Robert Holland,* p. 9D. *Jeff Hunter,* p. 15E. *Walter Iooss, Jr.,* p. 14A. *Patti McConville,* p. 24B. *Michael Melford,* p. 1, 14B, 19C. *Eric Meola,* p. 23D. *Marvin E. Newman,* p. 9C. *Guido Alberto Rossi,* p. 30I. *Nicolas Russell,* p. 7D. *Pete Turner,* p. 20C. *Jürgen Vogt,* 19E, 24C.

Lee Island Coast Visitor & Convention Bureau, p. 2 bottom center.

Norman's Restaurant, p. 30G.

Okaloosa TDC/CVB/Film Commission, p. 22B.

Smallwood's Store: John Gillan, p. 9E.

Tampa/Hillsborough Convention and Visitors Association, Inc., p. 30H.

Universal Studios Escape, p. 17C, 17E.

Visit Florida Tourism, p. 2 top left, 2 top right, 2 bottom left, 2 bottom right, 3 top left, 3 top right, 3 bottom left, 3 bottom right, 4-5, 6A, 12B, 13F, 14C, 15 top, 18B, 20D, 21E, 22A, 23C, 23E, 25E, 26A, 27, 28B, 28C, 29D, 30C, 30D, 30E, 30F.

ABOUT OUR WRITERS

EVERY Y2K TRIP is a significant trip. So if there was ever a time you needed excellent travel information, it's now. Acutely aware of that fact, we've pulled out all stops in preparing *Fodor's Florida*. To help you zero in on what to see in Florida, we've gathered some great color photos of the key sights in every area. To show you how to put it all together, we've created great itineraries and neighborhood walks. And to direct you to the places that are truly worth your time and money in this important year, we've rallied the team of endearing picky know-it-alls we're pleased to call our writers. Having seen all corners of Florida, they're real experts. If you knew them, you'd poll them for tips yourself.

On her way to the Caribbean, former New York publishing exec **Pamela Acheson** stopped in the Sunshine State and fell in love, after discovering that there's much more to it than theme parks. She likes nothing better than to drive around to neat little towns, undiscovered beaches, and other less-traveled places as she writes about her new home.

Starting behind an old manual typewriter at his hometown newspaper, **Alan Macher** has written everything from human-interest stories to speeches. He makes his home in Boca Raton, where he can play tennis and bike along Route A1A year-round.

Intrepid traveler and intrepid shopper **Diane Marshall** was formerly editor and publisher of the newsletter "The Savvy Shopper: The Traveler's Guide to Shop-ping Around the World." From her home in the Keys, she has written for numerous travel guides, newspapers, magazines, and on-line services.

Florida native and Elvis fan **Gary McKechnie** has written humor and travel articles for newspapers and magazines nationwide and has produced award-winning training films and resort videos.

Formerly with *Southern Living* magazine, travel writer **Nancy Orr** has the delightful southern drawl that proves she's at home in northern Florida.

Having recently relocated to the Tampa Bay area, **Rowland Stiteler,** who previously served as editor and dining critic of *Orlando* and *Central Florida* magazines, enjoys exploring his new backyard. Stiteler, a journalist for 25 years, won top honors for best feature story in the 1994 Florida Magazine Association awards competition.

Don't Forget to Write

We love feedback—positive and negative—and follow up on all suggestions. So contact the Florida editor at editors@fodors.com or c/o Fodor's, 201 East 50th Street, New York, New York 10022. Have a wonderful trip!

Karen Cure

Karen Cure
Editorial Director